Explorations in
CORE MATH

Geometry

HOUGHTON MIFFLIN HARCOURT

Contents

▶ **Chapter 1 Foundations for Geometry**

	Chapter Overview	1
CC.9-12.G.CO.1	1-1 Understanding Points, Lines, and Planes	5
CC.9-12.G.CO.12	1-2 Measuring and Constructing Segments	9
CC.9-12.G.CO.12	1-3 Measuring and Constructing Angles	15
CC.9-12.G.CO.9	1-4 Pairs of Angles	21
CC.9-12.A.CED.4	1-5 Using Formulas in Geometry	27
CC.9-12.G.GPE.4	1-6 Midpoint and Distance in the Coordinate Plane	31
CC.9-12.G.CO.5	1-7 Transformations in the Coordinate Plane	37
	Performance Tasks	45
	Assessment Readiness	47

▶ **Chapter 2 Geometric Reasoning**

	Chapter Overview	49
PREP FOR CC.9-12.G.CO.9	2-1 Using Inductive Reasoning to Make Conjectures	53
CC.MP.3	2-2 Conditional Statements	57
CC.MP.3	2-3 Using Deductive Reasoning to Verify Conjectures	61
CC.MP.3	2-4 Biconditional Statements and Definitions	67
PREP FOR CC.9-12.G.CO.9	2-5 Algebraic Proof	71
CC.9-12.G.CO.9	2-6 Geometric Proof	75
CC.9-12.G.CO.9	2-7 Flowchart and Paragraph Proofs	79
	Performance Tasks	83
	Assessment Readiness	85

▶ Chapter 3 Parallel and Perpendicular Lines

Chapter Overview			**87**
PREP FOR **CC.9-12.G.CO.9**	**3-1**	Lines and Angles	91
CC.9-12.G.CO.9	**3-2**	Angles Formed by Parallel Lines and Transversals	95
CC.9-12.G.CO.12	**3-3**	Proving Lines Parallel	103
CC.9-12.G.CO.12	**3-4**	Perpendicular Lines	107
CC.9-12.G.GPE.6	**3-5**	Slopes of Lines	113
CC.9-12.G.GPE.5	**3-6**	Lines in the Coordinate Plane	117
		Performance Tasks	123
		Assessment Readiness	125

▶ Chapter 4 Triangle Congruence

Chapter Overview			**127**
CC.9-12.G.CO.5	**4-1**	Congruence and Transformations	131
CC.9-12.G.GPE. 7	**4-2**	Classifying Triangles	137
CC.9-12.G.CO.10	**4-3**	Angle Relationships in Triangles	141
CC.9-12.G.CO.7	**4-4**	Congruent Triangles	147
CC.9-12.G.CO.8	**4-5**	Triangle Congruence: SSS and SAS	153
CC.9-12.G.SRT.5	**4-6**	Triangle Congruence: ASA, AAS, and HL	161
CC.9-12.G.GPE.5	**4-7**	Triangle Congruence: CPCTC	167
CC.9-12.G.GPE.4	**4-8**	Introduction to Coordinate Proof	173
CC.9-12.G.CO.10	**4-9**	Isosceles and Equilateral Triangles	179
		Performance Tasks	185
		Assessment Readiness	187

▶ Chapter 5 Properties and Attributes of Triangles

Chapter Overview			**189**
CC.9-12.G.GPE.2	**5-1**	Perpendicular and Angle Bisectors	193
CC.9-12.G.C.3	**5-2**	Bisectors of Triangles	199
CC.9-12.G.GPE.4	**5-3**	Medians and Altitudes of Triangles	205
CC.9-12.G.GPE.4	**5-4**	The Triangle Midsegment Theorem	211
CC.9-12.G.CO.10	**5-5**	Indirect Proof and Inequalities in One Triangle	215
CC.9-12.G.CO.10	**5-6**	Inequalities in Two Triangles	219
CC.9-12.G.SRT.8	**5-7**	The Pythagorean Theorem	223
CC.9-12.G.SRT.8	**5-8**	Applying Special Right Triangles	227
		Performance Tasks	233
		Assessment Readiness	235

Chapter 6 Polygons and Quadrilaterals

Chapter Overview. **237**

CC.9-12.G.CO.13	**6-1**	Properties and Attributes of Regular Polygons	241
CC.9-12.G.CO.11	**6-2**	Properties of Parallelograms.	245
CC.9-12.G.SRT.5	**6-3**	Conditions for Parallelograms.	253
CC.9-12.G.CO.11	**6-4**	Properties of Special Parallelograms.	257
CC.9-12.G.GPE.4	**6-5**	Conditions for Special Parallelograms	263
CC.9-12.G.CO.9	**6-6**	Properties of Kites and Trapezoids	269
		Performance Tasks	273
		Assessment Readiness	275

Chapter 7 Similarity

Chapter Overview. **277**

PREP FOR CC.9-12.G.SRT.2	**7-1**	Ratios in Similar Polygons.	281
CC.9-12.G.SRT.2	**7-2**	Similarity and Transformations	287
CC.9-12.G.SRT.3	**7-3**	Triangle Similarity AA, SSS, SAS	297
CC.9-12.G.SRT.4	**7-4**	Applying Properties of Similar Triangles	303
CC.9-12.G.SRT.5	**7-5**	Using Proportional Relationships.	307
CC.9-12.G.CO.2	**7-6**	Dilations and Similarity in the Coordinate Plane	313
		Performance Tasks	317
		Assessment Readiness.	319

Chapter 8 Right Triangles and Trigonometry

Chapter Overview. **321**

CC.9-12.G.SRT.4	**8-1**	Similarity in Right Triangles.	325
CC.9-12.G.SRT.6	**8-2**	Trigonometric Ratios	329
CC.9-12.G.SRT.8	**8-3**	Solving Right Triangles.	339
CC.9-12.G.SRT.8	**8-4**	Angles of Elevation and Depression	343
CC.9-12.G.SRT.10(+)	**8-5**	Law of Sines and Law of Cosines.	347
CC.9-12.G.SRT.11(+)	**8-6**	Vectors	357
		Performance Tasks	361
		Assessment Readiness	363

© Houghton Mifflin Harcourt Publishing Company

Chapter 9   Extending Transformational Geometry

Chapter Overview **365**

CC.9-12.G.CO.5   **9-1**   Reflections 369

CC.9-12.G.CO.4   **9-2**   Translations 377

CC.9-12.G.CO.2   **9-3**   Rotations 383

CC.9-12.G.CO.5   **9-4**   Compositions of Transformations 391

CC.9-12.G.CO.3   **9-5**   Symmetry 395

CC.9-12.G.CO.5   **9-6**   Tessellations 401

CC.9-12.G.CO.2   **9-7**   Dilations 405

Performance Tasks 409

Assessment Readiness 411

Chapter 10   Extending Perimeter, Circumference, and Area

Chapter Overview **413**

CC.9-12.G.SRT.9(+)   **10-1**   Developing Formulas for Triangles and Quadrilaterals 417

CC.9-12.G.GMD.1   **10-2**   Developing Formulas for Circles and Regular Polygons . . . 421

CC.9-12.G.MG.3   **10-3**   Composite Figures 427

CC.9-12.G.GPE.7   **10-4**   Perimeter and Area in the Coordinate Plane 431

CC.9-12.G.CO.2   **10-5**   Effects of Changing Dimensions Proportionally 437

CC.9-12.S.CP.1   **10-6**   Geometric Probability 441

Performance Tasks 447

Assessment Readiness 449

Chapter 11   Spatial Reasoning

Chapter Overview **451**

CC.9-12.G.GMD.4   **11-1**   Solid Geometry 455

CC.9-12.G.MG.2   **11-2**   Volume of Prisms and Cylinders 461

CC.9-12.G.GMD.1   **11-3**   Volume of Pyramids and Cones 469

CC.9-12.G.GMD.3   **11-4**   Spheres 481

Performance Tasks 487

Assessment Readiness 489

▶ Chapter 12   Circles

Chapter Overview **491**

CC.9-12.G.C.2   **12-1**   Lines That Intersect Circles. 495

CC.9-12.G.C.2   **12-2**   Arcs and Chords 499

CC.9-12.G.C.5   **12-3**   Sector Area and Arc Length 503

CC.9-12.G.C.2   **12-4**   Inscribed Angles 513

CC.9-12.G.C.4(+)   **12-5**   Angle Relationships in Circles 519

CC.9-12.G.C.2   **12-6**   Segment Relationships in Circles. 523

CC.9-12.A.REI.7   **12-7**   Circles in the Coordinate Plane 527

        Performance Tasks 537

        Assessment Readiness 539

▶ Chapter 13   Probability

Chapter Overview **541**

CC.9-12.S.CP.9(+)   **13-1**   Permutations and Combinations. 545

CC.9-12.S.MD.6(+)   **13-2**   Theoretical and Experimental Probability 553

CC.9-12.S.CP.4   **13-3**   Independent and Dependent Events 559

CC.9-12.S.CP.3   **13-4**   Two-Way Tables 567

CC.9-12.S.CP.7   **13-5**   Compound Events 573

        Performance Tasks 579

        Assessment Readiness 581

Correlation of *Explorations in Core Math*
to the Common Core State Standards **C1**

Learning the Standards for Mathematical Practice

The Common Core State Standards include eight Standards for Mathematical Practice. Here's how *Explorations in Core Math Geometry* helps you learn those standards as you master the Standards for Mathematical Content.

1 Make sense of problems and persevere in solving them.

In *Explorations in Core Math Geometry*, you will work through Explores and Examples that present a solution pathway for you to follow. You will be asked questions along the way so that you gain an understanding of the solution process, and then you will apply what you've learned in the Practice for the lesson.

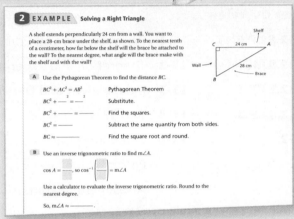

2 EXAMPLE Solving a Right Triangle

A shelf extends perpendicularly 24 cm from a wall. You want to place a 28-cm brace under the shelf, as shown. To the nearest tenth of a centimeter, how far below the shelf will the brace be attached to the wall? To the nearest degree, what angle will the brace make with the shelf and with the wall?

A Use the Pythagorean Theorem to find the distance BC.

$BC^2 + AC^2 = AB^2$ Pythagorean Theorem

$BC^2 + \underline{\quad}^2 = \underline{\quad}^2$ Substitute.

$BC^2 + \underline{\quad} = \underline{\quad}$ Find the squares.

$BC^2 = \underline{\quad}$ Subtract the same quantity from both sides.

$BC \approx \underline{\quad}$ Find the square root and round.

B Use an inverse trigonometric ratio to find $m\angle A$.

$\cos A = \underline{\quad}$, so $\cos^{-1} \underline{\quad} = m\angle A$

Use a calculator to evaluate the inverse trigonometric ratio. Round to the nearest degree.

So, $m\angle A \approx \underline{\quad}$.

2 Reason abstractly and quantitatively.

When you solve a real-world problem in *Explorations in Core Math Geometry*, you will learn to represent the situation symbolically by translating the problem into a mathematical expression or equation. You will use these mathematical models to solve the problem and then state your answer in terms of the problem context. You will reflect on the solution process in order to check your answer for reasonableness and to draw conclusions.

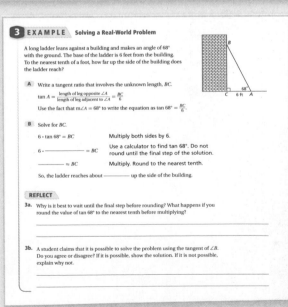

3 EXAMPLE Solving a Real-World Problem

A long ladder leans against a building and makes an angle of 68° with the ground. The base of the ladder is 6 feet from the building. To the nearest tenth of a foot, how far up the side of the building does the ladder reach?

A Write a tangent ratio that involves the unknown length, BC.

$\tan A = \frac{\text{length of leg opposite } \angle A}{\text{length of leg adjacent to } \angle A} = \frac{BC}{6}$

Use the fact that $m\angle A = 68°$ to write the equation as $\tan 68° = \frac{BC}{6}$.

B Solve for BC.

$6 \cdot \tan 68° = BC$ Multiply both sides by 6.

$6 \cdot \underline{\quad} = BC$ Use a calculator to find $\tan 68°$. Do not round until the final step of the solution.

$\underline{\quad} \approx BC$ Multiply. Round to the nearest tenth.

So, the ladder reaches about $\underline{\quad}$ up the side of the building.

REFLECT

3a. Why is it best to wait until the final step before rounding? What happens if you round the value of $\tan 68°$ to the nearest tenth before multiplying?

3b. A student claims that it is possible to solve the problem using the tangent of $\angle B$. Do you agree or disagree? If it is possible, show the solution. If it is not possible, explain why not.

③ Construct viable arguments and critique the reasoning of others.

Throughout *Explorations in Core Math Geometry*, you will be asked to make conjectures, construct a mathematical argument, explain your reasoning, and justify your conclusions. Reflect questions offer opportunities for cooperative learning and class discussion. You will have additional opportunities to critique reasoning in Error Analysis problems.

> **REFLECT**
>
> **2a.** Given that $\triangle PQR \cong \triangle STU$, $PQ = 2.7$ ft, and $PR = 3.4$ ft, is it possible to determine the length of $\overline{TU}$? If so, find the length. If not, explain why not.
>
> _____
>
> _____
>
> **2b.** A student claims that any two congruent triangles must have the same perimeter. Do you agree or disagree? Why?
>
> _____
>
> _____

> **3.** **Error Analysis** A student who is 72 inches tall wants to find the height of a flagpole. He measures the length of the flagpole's shadow and the length of his own shadow at the same time of day, as shown in his sketch below. Explain the error in the student's work.
>
> The triangles are similar by the AA Similarity Criterion, so corresponding sides are proportional.
> $\frac{x}{72} = \frac{48}{128}$
> $x = 72 \cdot \frac{48}{128}$, so $x = 27$ in.
>
>
>
> 72 in.   48 in.   128 in. x
>
> _____
>
> _____

④ Model with mathematics.

Explorations in Core Math Geometry presents problems in a variety of contexts such as science, business, and everyday life. You will use models such as equations, tables, diagrams, and graphs to represent the information in the problem and to solve the problem. Then you will interpret your results in context.

> **④ EXAMPLE**   Solving a Real-World Problem
>
> Police want to set up a camera to identify drivers who run the red light at point C on Mason Street. The camera must be mounted on a fence that intersects Mason Street at a 40° angle, as shown, and the camera should ideally be 120 feet from point C. What points along the fence, if any, are suitable locations for the camera?
>
> Mason Street   170 ft C A 40°   Fence
>
> **A** Because the side opposite $\angle A$ is shorter than $\overline{AC}$, it may be possible to form two triangles. Use the Law of Sines to find possible values for $m\angle B$.
>
> $\frac{\sin A}{a} = \frac{\sin B}{b}$ Law of Sines
>
> $\frac{\sin 40°}{120} = \frac{\sin B}{170}$ Substitute.
>
> $\frac{170 \sin 40°}{120} = \sin B$ Solve for $\sin B$.
>
> _____ $\approx \sin B$ Use a calculator. Round to 4 decimal places.
>
> Mason Street   170 ft C 120 ft A 40° B B Fence
>
> There is an acute angle and an obtuse angle that have this value as their sine. To find the acute angle, use a calculator and round to the nearest tenth.
>
> $\sin^{-1}($_____$) \approx$ _____
>
> To find the obtuse angle, note that $\angle 1$ and $\angle 2$ have the same sine, $\frac{y}{\sqrt{x^2+y^2}}$, and notice that these angles are supplementary. Thus, the obtuse angle is supplementary to the acute angle you found above.
>
> $(-x, y)$ $\sqrt{x^2+y^2}$ $\sqrt{x^2+y^2}$ (x, y) y y 2   1
>
> So, $m\angle B \approx$ _____ or _____.

> **REFLECT**
>
> **4a.** How you can check your answers?
>
> _____
>
> **4b.** Suppose the camera needs to be *at most* 120 feet from point C. In this case, where should the camera be mounted along the fence?
>
> _____
>
> _____
>
> **4c.** What is the minimum distance at which the camera can be located from point C if it is to be mounted on the fence? Explain your answer.
>
> _____
>
> _____

5 Use appropriate tools strategically.

You will use a variety of tools in *Explorations in Core Math Geometry*, including manipulatives, paper and pencil, and technology. You might use manipulatives to develop concepts, paper and pencil to practice skills, and technology (such as graphing calculators, spreadsheets, or geometry software) to investigate more complicated mathematical ideas.

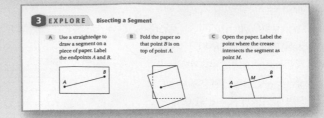

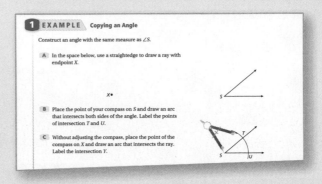

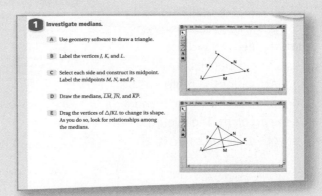

6 Attend to precision.

Precision refers not only to the correctness of arithmetic calculations, algebraic manipulations, and geometric reasoning but also to the proper use of mathematical language, symbols, and units to communicate mathematical ideas. Throughout *Explorations in Core Math Geometry* you will demonstrate your skills in these areas when you are asked to calculate, describe, show, explain, prove, and predict.

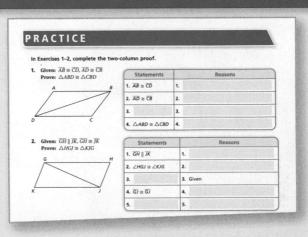

⑦ Look for and make use of structure.

In *Explorations in Core Math Geometry*, you will look for patterns or regularity in mathematical structures such as expressions, equations, geometric figures, and graphs. Becoming familiar with underlying structures will help you build your understanding of more complicated mathematical ideas.

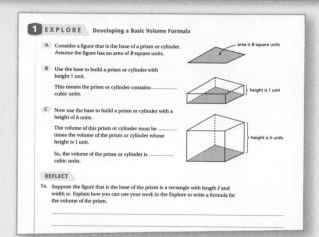

1 EXPLORE Developing a Basic Volume Formula

A Consider a figure that is the base of a prism or cylinder. Assume the figure has an area of B square units.

area is B square units

B Use the base to build a prism or cylinder with height 1 unit.

This means the prism or cylinder contains _____ cubic units.

height is 1 unit

C Now use the base to build a prism or cylinder with a height of h units.

The volume of this prism or cylinder must be _____ times the volume of the prism or cylinder whose height is 1 unit.

So, the volume of the prism or cylinder is _____ cubic units.

height is h units

REFLECT

1a. Suppose the figure that is the base of the prism is a rectangle with length ℓ and width w. Explain how you can use your work in the Explore to write a formula for the volume of the prism.

⑧ Look for and express regularity in repeated reasoning.

In *Explorations in Core Math Geometry*, you will have the opportunity to explore and reflect on mathematical processes in order to come up with general methods for performing calculations and solving problems.

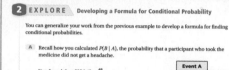

2 EXPLORE Developing a Formula for Conditional Probability

You can generalize your work from the previous example to develop a formula for finding conditional probabilities.

A Recall how you calculated $P(B\,|\,A)$, the probability that a participant who took the medicine did not get a headache.

You found that $P(B\,|\,A) = \frac{48}{60}$.

Use the table shown here to help you write this quotient in terms of events A and B.

$P(B\,|\,A) =$ _____

		Event A		
		Took Medicine	No Medicine	TOTAL
Event B	Headache	12	15	27
	No Headache	$48 = n(A \cap B)$	25	$73 = n(B)$
	TOTAL	$60 = n(A)$	40	100

B Now divide the numerator and denominator of the quotient by $n(S)$, the number of outcomes in the sample space. This converts the counts to probabilities.

$P(B\,|\,A) = \dfrac{\underline{\quad}/n(S)}{\underline{\quad}/n(S)} =$ _____

REFLECT

2a. Write a formula for $P(A\,|\,B)$ in terms of $n(A \cap B)$ and $n(B)$.

2b. Write a formula for $P(A\,|\,B)$ in terms of $P(A \cap B)$ and $P(B)$.

Foundations for Geometry

Chapter Focus

This unit introduces the building blocks of geometry. You will learn how definitions of essential geometric terms, such as *line segment* and *angle*, are built from more basic terms. You will also learn to use a variety of tools and techniques to construct geometric figures. Finally, you will begin to transform geometric figures in the coordinate plane and use coordinates to determine midpoints and lengths of edges.

Chapter at a Glance

COMMON CORE

Lesson		Standards for Mathematical Content
1-1	Understanding Points, Lines, and Planes	CC.9-12.G.CO.1
1-2	Measuring and Constructing Segments	CC.9-12.G.CO.12
1-3	Measuring and Constructing Angles	CC.9-12.G.CO.12
1-4	Pairs of Angles	CC.9-12.A.CED.1, CC.9-12.G.CO.1, CC.9-12.G.CO.9
1-5	Using Formulas in Geometry	CC.9-12.A.CED.4
1-6	Midpoint and Distance in the Coordinate Plane	CC.9-12.G.GPE.4, CC.9-12.G.GPE.6
1-7	Transformations in the Coordinate Plane	CC.9-12.G.CO.2, CC.9-12.G.CO.5, Prep for CC.9-12.G.CO.6
	Performance Tasks	
	Assessment Readiness	

CHAPTER 1

Unpacking the Standards

Understanding the standards and the vocabulary terms in the standards will help you know exactly what you are expected to learn in this chapter.

COMMON CORE CC.9-12.G.CO.1

Know precise definitions of angle, … and line segment, based on the undefined notions of point, line, …

Key Vocabulary

angle *(ángulo)* A figure formed by two rays with a common endpoint.
segment of a line *(segmento de una línea)* A part of a line consisting of two endpoints and all points between them.

What It Means For You — Lessons 1-1, 1-4

Geometry begins with a few basic concepts and definitions, and builds them into a way to answer all sorts of questions about shapes and measures.

EXAMPLE
Figures are identified by letters, sometimes in multiple ways.

Points: A, B, C
Line: k or $\overleftrightarrow{BC}$ or $\overleftrightarrow{CB}$
Segments: $\overline{AB}$ or $\overline{BA}$, $\overline{BC}$ or $\overline{CB}$
Rays: $\overrightarrow{BC}$, $\overrightarrow{BA}$
Angle: $\triangle ABC$ or $\triangle CBA$

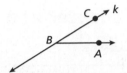

CHAPTER 1

COMMON CORE CC.9-12.G.CO.5

Given a geometric figure and a rotation, reflection, or translation, draw the transformed figure using, e.g., graph paper, tracing paper, or geometry software. Specify a sequence of transformations that will carry a given figure onto another.

Key Vocabulary

transformation *(transformación)* A change in the position, size, or shape of a figure or graph.
rotation *(rotación)* A transformation about a point P, also known as the center of rotation, such that each point and its image are the same distance from P. All of the angles with vertex P formed by a point and its image are congruent.
reflection *(reflexión)* A transformation across a line, called the line of reflection, such that the line of reflection is the perpendicular bisector of each segment joining each point and its image.
translation *(traslación)* A transformation that shifts or slides every point of a figure or graph the same distance in the same direction.

What It Means For You — Lesson 1-7

You can change a shape's position and orientation in the plane without changing the actual shape or its size using translations, rotations, and reflections.

EXAMPLE
Reflecting the figures on the left half of the quilt across the vertical line will carry them onto the figures on the right half.

COMMON CORE **CC.9-12.G.CO.12**

Make formal geometric constructions with a variety of tools and methods (compass and straightedge, string, reflective devices, paper folding, dynamic geometric software, etc.).

Key Vocabulary

construction (construcción) A method of creating a figure that is considered to be mathematically precise. Figures may be constructed by using a compass and straightedge, geometry software, or paper folding.

What It Means For You **Lessons 1-2, 1-3**

Construction methods give you precise ways to create or copy geometric figures without having to measure and/or estimate.

EXAMPLE

How can you divide $\overline{XY}$ in half without measuring?

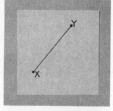

Fold the paper in half so that the points X and Y line up exactly.

Unfold the paper and mark the point M where the fold meets the segment. You have found the midpoint of $\overline{XY}$!

COMMON CORE **CC.9-12.G.GPE.4**

Use coordinates to prove simple geometric theorems algebraically.

Key Vocabulary

coordinate (coordenada) A number used to identify the location of a point. On a number line, one coordinate is used. On a coordinate plane, two coordinates are used, called the x-coordinate and the y-coordinate. In space, three coordinates are used, called the x-coordinate, the y-coordinate, and the z-coordinate.

What It Means For You **Lesson 1-6**

You can prove some properties of geometric figures by using coordinates and algebra. These proofs sometimes involve the Distance Formula or the Midpoint Formula.

EXAMPLE

The midpoint of $\overline{AB}$, point M, has coordinates $M\left(\frac{0+x}{2}, \frac{0+y}{2}\right)$.

Area $\triangle AMC = \frac{1}{2}(x)\left(\frac{y}{2}\right) = \frac{xy}{4}$.

Area $\triangle ABC = \frac{1}{2}(x)(y) = \frac{xy}{2}$.

The area of triangle AMC is half the area of triangle ABC.

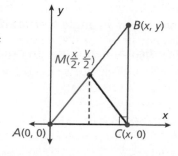

CHAPTER 1

Key Vocabulary

adjacent angles *(ángulos adyacentes)* Two angles in the same plane with a common vertex and a common side, but no common interior points.

angle *(ángulo)* A figure formed by two rays with a common endpoint.

angle bisector *(bisectriz de un ángulo)* A ray that divides an angle into two congruent angles.

bisect *(trazar una bisectriz)* To divide into two congruent parts.

circle *(círculo)* The set of points in a plane that are a fixed distance from a given point called the center of the circle.

complementary angles *(ángulos complementarios)* Two angles whose measures have a sum of 90°.

congruent angles *(ángulos congruentes)* Angles that have the same measure.

distance between two points *(distancia entre dos puntos)* The absolute value of the difference of the coordinates of the points.

endpoint *(extremo)* A point at an end of a segment or the starting point of a ray.

line *(línea)* An undefined term in geometry, a line is a straight path that has no thickness and extends forever.

midpoint *(punto medio)* The point that divides a segment into two congruent segments.

ray *(rayo)* A part of a line that starts at an endpoint and extends forever in one direction.

rigid motion *(movimiento rígido)* A transformation that does not change the size or shape of a figure.

segment of a line *(segmento de una línea)* A part of a line consisting of two endpoints and all points between them.

side of an angle *(lado de un ángulo)* One of the two rays that form an angle.

supplementary angles *(ángulos suplementarios)* Two angles whose measures have a sum of 180°.

transformation *(transformación)* A change in the position, size, or shape of a figure or graph.

vertex of an angle *(vértice de un ángulo)* The common endpoint of the sides of the angle.

vertical angles *(ángulos opuestos por el vértice)* The nonadjacent angles formed by two intersecting lines.

Understanding Points, Lines, and Planes
Going Deeper

Essential question: *How do you use undefined terms as the basic elements of geometry?*

In geometry, the terms *point, line,* and *plane* are undefined terms. Although these terms do not have formal definitions, the table shows how mathematicians use these words.

Term	Geometric Figure	Ways to Reference the Figure
A **point** is a specific location. It has no dimension and is represented by a dot.	• P	Point *P*
A **line** is a connected straight path. It has no thickness and it continues forever in both directions.	*A* *B* → ℓ	Line ℓ, line *AB*, line *BA*, $\overleftrightarrow{AB}$, or $\overleftrightarrow{BA}$
A **plane** is a flat surface that has no thickness and extends forever.	•J •L K• M	A script capital letter, or three points on the plane that do not all lie on a line. plane M, or plane *JKL*

As shown in the following table, other terms can be defined using the above terms as building blocks.

Term	Geometric Figure	Ways to Reference the Figure
A **line segment** (or *segment*) is a portion of a line consisting of two points and all points between them.	*C* *D*	Line segment *CD*, line segment *DC*, $\overline{CD}$, or $\overline{DC}$
A **ray** is a portion of a line that starts at a point and continues forever in one direction.	*G* *H* →	Ray *GH* or $\overrightarrow{GH}$

An **endpoint** is a point at either end of a line segment or the starting point of a ray. In the above examples, *C* and *D* are the endpoints of $\overline{CD}$, and point *G* is the endpoint of $\overrightarrow{GH}$.

CC.9–12.G.CO.1

1 EXAMPLE Naming Geometric Figures

Use the figure at the right in Parts A and B.

A One name for the line shown in the figure is $\overleftrightarrow{PQ}$.

Other names for $\overleftrightarrow{PQ}$ are _____

B $\overline{PQ}$ is a line segment because it is a portion of a line consisting of two points and all the points between them.

Other names for $\overline{PQ}$ are _____

1a. Why does the order in which you name the points when you name a ray matter? Use points *P* and *Q* in your answer.

_____

_____

PRACTICE

Use the figure to name each of the following.

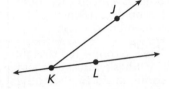

1. a line _____

2. two line segments _____

3. three rays _____

Imagine four different points, *A*, *B*, *C*, and *D*, all lie on a line in that order.

4. Name two rays contained in the line that have no points in common.

_____

5. Name two rays contained in the line that have exactly one point in common.

_____

6. Name two rays contained in the line that have more than one point in common. Describe the points that the rays have in common.

_____

The figure at the right shows plane F containing points *U*, *V*, *W*, and *X*.

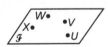

7. What are some ways to name plane F using the points?

_____

8. What are the names of some lines that are contained in the plane?

_____

9. Suppose point *Z* is placed somewhere along $\overleftrightarrow{VW}$. Why is "plane *VZW*" not used as another name for plane F?

_____

_____

_____

Additional Practice

Use the figure for Exercises 1–7.

1. Name a plane. _____

2. Name a segment. _____

3. Name a line. _____

4. Name three collinear points.

   _____

5. Name three noncollinear points.

   _____

6. Name the intersection of a line and a segment not on the line. _____

7. Name a pair of opposite rays. _____

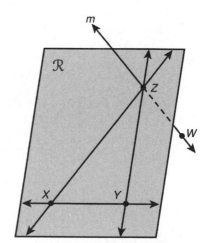

Use the figure for Exercises 8–11.

8. Name the points that determine plane R.

   _____

9. Name the point at which line *m* intersects

   plane R. _____

10. Name two lines in plane R that intersect line *m*.

    _____

11. Name a line in plane R that does not intersect

    line *m*. _____

Draw your answers in the space provided.

Michelle Kwan won a bronze medal in figure skating at the 2002 Salt Lake City Winter Olympic Games.

12. Michelle skates straight ahead from point *L* and stops at point *M*. Draw her path.

13. Michelle skates straight ahead from point *L* and continues through point *M*. Name a figure that represents her path. Draw her path.

14. Michelle and her friend Alexei start back to back at point *L* and skate in opposite directions. Michelle skates through point *M*, and Alexei skates through point *K*. Draw their paths.

Problem Solving

Use the map of part of San Antonio for Exercises 1 and 2.

1. Name a point that appears to be collinear with $\overline{EF}$. Which streets intersect at this point?

   _____

   _____

2. Explain why point A is NOT collinear with $\overline{BE}$.

   _____

   _____

3. Suppose $\overline{UV}$ represents the pencil that you are using to do your homework and plane P represents the paper that you are writing on. Describe the relationship between $\overline{UV}$ and plane P.

   _____

   _____

4. Two cyclists start at the same point, but travel along two straight streets in different directions. If they continue, how many times will their paths cross again? Explain.

   _____

   _____

Choose the best answer.

5. In a building, planes W, X, and Y represent each of the three floors; planes Q and R represent the front and back of the building; planes S and T represent the sides. Which is a true statement?

   A Planes W and Y intersect in a line.

   B Planes Q and X intersect in a line.

   C Planes W, X, and T intersect in a point.

   D Planes Q, R, and S intersect in a point.

6. Suppose point G represents a duck flying over a lake, points H and J represent two ducks swimming on the lake, and plane L represents the lake. Which is a true statement?

   F There are two lines through G and J.

   G The line containing G and H lies in plane L.

   H G, H, and J are noncoplanar.

   J There is exactly one plane containing points G, H, and J.

Use the figure for Exercise 7.

7. A frame holding two pictures sits on a table. Which is NOT a true statement?

   A $\overline{PN}$ and $\overline{NM}$ lie in plane T.

   B $\overline{PN}$ and $\overline{NM}$ intersect in a point.

   C $\overleftrightarrow{LM}$ and N intersect in a line.

   D P and $\overline{NM}$ are coplanar.

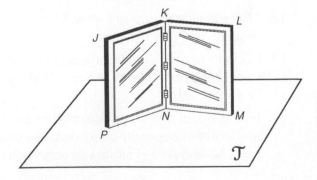

Measuring and Constructing Segments

Going Deeper

Essential question: *What tools and methods can you use to copy a segment, bisect a segment, and construct a circle?*

The **distance along a line** is undefined until a unit distance, such as 1 inch or 1 centimeter, is chosen. By placing a ruler alongside the line, you can associate a number from the ruler with each of two points on the line and then take the absolute value of the difference of the numbers to find the distance between the points. This distance is the **length** of the segment determined by the points.

In the figure, the length of $\overline{RS}$, written RS, is the distance between R and S. $RS = |4 - 1| = |3| = 3$ cm.

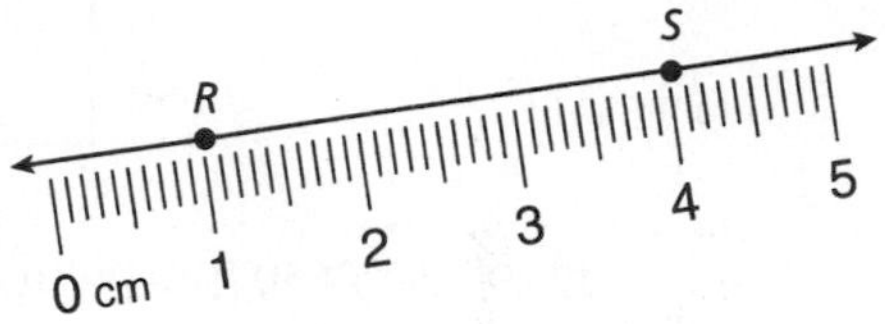

A *construction* is a geometric drawing that uses only a compass and a straightedge. You can construct a line segment whose length is equal to that of a given segment by using only these tools.

CC.9–12.G.CO.12

1 EXAMPLE Copying a Segment

Construct a segment with the same length as $\overline{AB}$.

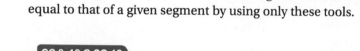

A In the space below, draw a line segment that is longer than $\overline{AB}$. Choose an endpoint of the segment and label it C.

B Set the opening of your compass to the distance AB, as shown.

C Place the point of the compass on C. Make a small arc that intersects your line segment. Label the point D where the arc intersects the segment. $\overline{CD}$ is the required line segment.

REFLECT

1a. Why does this construction result in a line segment with the same length as $\overline{AB}$?

_____

_____

1b. What must you assume about the compass for this construction to work?

_____

_____

The **midpoint** of a line segment is the point that divides the segment into two segments that have the same length. The midpoint is said to **bisect** the segment. In the figure, the tick marks show that $PM = MQ$. Therefore, M is the midpoint of $\overline{PQ}$ and M bisects $\overline{PQ}$.

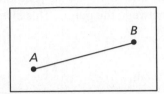

CC.9–12.G.CO.12

2 EXPLORE   Bisecting a Segment

A Use a straightedge to draw a segment on a piece of paper. Label the endpoints A and B.

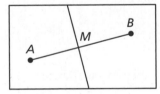

B Fold the paper so that point B is on top of point A.

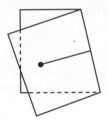

C Open the paper. Label the point where the crease intersects the segment as point M.

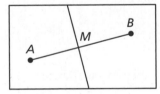

REFLECT

2a. How can you use a ruler to check the construction?

_____

2b. Fold your paper along the segment. What happens to the crease that bisects the segment? What can you say about the four angles formed at point M?

_____

_____

2c. Explain how you could use paper folding to divide a line segment into four segments of equal length.

_____

_____

A **circle** is the set of all points in a plane that are a fixed distance from a point called the **center** of the circle. A **radius** is a line segment whose endpoints are the center of the circle and any point on the circle. The length of such a segment is also called the radius.

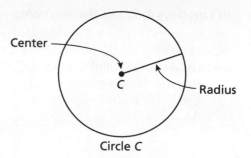

Center

Radius

C

Circle C

CC.9–12.G.CO.12

3 EXAMPLE   **Constructing a Circle**

Construct a circle with radius *AB*.

A •————————• B

A   In the space at right, draw a point and label it *C*. This will be the center of the circle.

B   Set the opening of your compass to the distance *AB*.

C   Place the point of the compass on *C* and draw a circle.

REFLECT

3a. How could you use a piece of string, a thumbtack, and a pencil to construct a circle with radius *AB*?

_____

_____

_____

PRACTICE

Use the figure to construct each figure in the space provided.

1. a segment with the same length as $\overline{KJ}$

2. a circle with radius *KL*

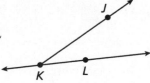

J

K   L

3. Is it possible to construct the midpoint of a ray? Why or why not?

_____

_____

In Exercises 4–7, use the segments shown.

A •———————• B
C •————————————————• D

4. Use a compass and straightedge to construct a segment whose length is $AB + CD$.

5. Use a compass and straightedge to construct a segment whose length is $CD - AB$.

6. Use a compass and straightedge to construct a triangle that has two sides of length AB and one side of length CD.

7. Use a compass and straightedge to construct a triangle that has two sides of length CD and one side of length AB.

Additional Practice

For Exercises 1–4, use the segment shown below. Draw your answers in the space provided.

1. Use a compass and straightedge to construct $\overline{XY}$ with the same length as $\overline{UV}$.

2. Use a compass and straightedge to construct a segment whose length is 2 · *UV*.

3. Use a compass and straightedge to construct a triangle with sides of length *UV*.

4. Copy $\overline{UV}$. Then bisect $\overline{UV}$ and label the midpoint *M*. Construct a circle with center *M* and radius *MU*. Construct a second circle with center *V* and radius *MU*.

Problem Solving

For Exercises 1–3, use the circle shown.

1. Copy the circle.

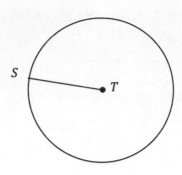

2. Explain how you can use your construction from Exercise 1 to construct two half circles with radius *ST*. Then construct the two half circles.

   _____

   _____

   _____

3. Construct a segment *MN* that is the same length as $\overline{ST}$. Then construct a triangle that has exactly two sides with length *MN*. How does the length of the third side compare with 2 • *MN*?

Choose the best answer.

4. Julia drew $\overline{PQ}$ on a piece of paper. She folded the paper so that point *P* was on top of point *Q*, forming a crease through $\overline{PQ}$. She labeled the intersection of this crease and $\overline{PQ}$ point *S*. If *PQ* = 2.4 centimeters, then what is the length of $\overline{QS}$?

   A 0.6 cm   C 2.4 cm

   B 1.2 cm   D 4.8 cm

5. Points *J*, *K*, and *L* lie on the same line, and point *K* is between *J* and *L*. Todd constructs $\overline{SV}$ with the same length as $\overline{JL}$. Then he draws point *T* on $\overline{SV}$ so that $\overline{ST}$ is the same length as $\overline{JK}$. Which statement is *not* true?

   F *JK* = *ST*

   G *ST* = *SV* − *TV*

   H *SV* = *JK* + *KL*

   J *TV* = *ST* + *KL*

Measuring and Constructing Angles
Going Deeper

Essential question: *What tools and methods can you use to copy an angle and bisect an angle?*

Video Tutor

An **angle** is a figure formed by two rays with the same endpoint. The common endpoint is the **vertex** of the angle. The rays are the **sides** of the angle.

Angles may be measured in degrees (°). There are 360° in a circle, so an angle that measures 1° is $\frac{1}{360}$ of a circle. You write m$\angle A$ for the measure of $\angle A$.

Angles may be classified by their measures.

Acute Angle	Right Angle	Obtuse Angle	Straight Angle
$0° < m\angle A < 90°$	$m\angle A = 90°$	$90° < m\angle A < 180°$	$m\angle A = 180°$

CC.9–12.G.CO.12

1 EXAMPLE Copying an Angle

Construct an angle with the same measure as $\angle S$.

A In the space below, use a straightedge to draw a ray with endpoint X.

$X \bullet$

S

B Place the point of your compass on S and draw an arc that intersects both sides of the angle. Label the points of intersection T and U.

C Without adjusting the compass, place the point of the compass on X and draw an arc that intersects the ray. Label the intersection Y.

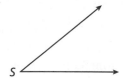

D Place the point of the compass on U and open it to the distance TU.

E Without adjusting the compass, place the point of the compass on Y and draw an arc. Label the intersection with the first arc Z.

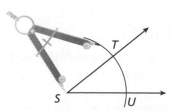

F Use a straightedge to draw $\overrightarrow{XZ}$.

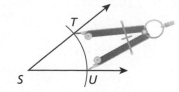

1a. How can you use a protractor to check your construction?

_____

1b. If you draw ∠X so that its sides appear to be longer than the sides shown for ∠S, can the two angles have the same measure? Explain.

_____

_____

An **angle bisector** is a ray that divides an angle into two angles that both have the same measure. In the figure, $\overrightarrow{BD}$ bisects ∠ABC, so m∠ABD = m∠DBC. The arcs in the figure show equal angle measures.

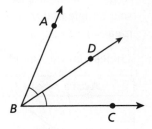

The following example shows how you can use a compass and straightedge to bisect an angle.

CC.9–12.G.CO.12

2 E X A M P L E **Constructing the Bisector of an Angle**

Construct the bisector of ∠M. Work directly on the angle at right.

A Place the point of your compass on point M. Draw an arc that intersects both sides of the angle. Label the points of intersection P and Q.

B Place the point of the compass on P and draw an arc in the interior of the angle.

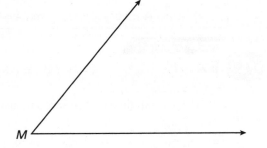

C Without adjusting the compass, place the point of the compass on Q and draw an arc that intersects the arc from Step B. Label the intersection of the arcs R.

D Use a straightedge to draw $\overrightarrow{MR}$.

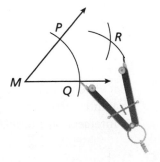

2a. Explain how you could use paper folding to construct the bisector of an angle.

_____

_____

Construct an angle with the same measure as the given angle.

1.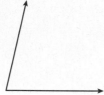

2.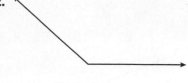

3.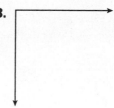

Construct the bisector of the angle.

4.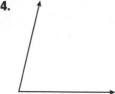

5.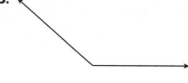

6.

7. Explain how you can use a compass and straightedge to construct an angle that has twice the measure of ∠A. Then do the construction in the space provided.

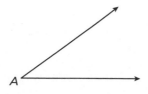

_____

_____

_____

8. Explain how you can use a compass and straightedge to construct an angle that has $\frac{1}{4}$ the measure of $\angle B$. Then do the construction in the space provided.

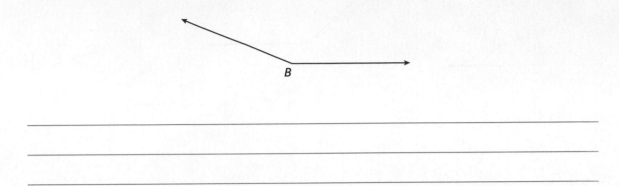

_____

_____

_____

Additional Practice

For Exercises 1 and 2, use the figure shown.

1. Use a compass and straightedge to construct angle bisector $\overrightarrow{DG}$. Given that m∠EDF = 90°, find m∠EDG.

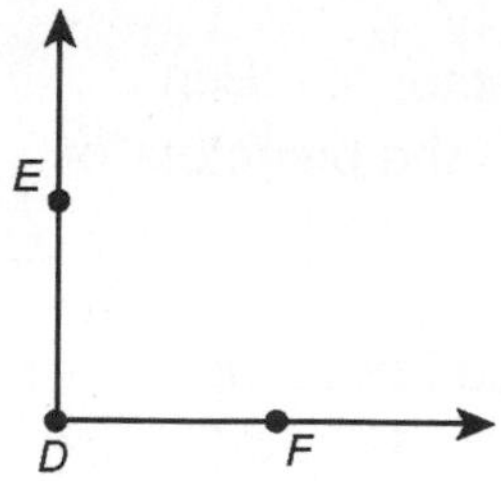

   m∠EDG = _____

2. Use your construction of ∠EDG from Exercise 1. Construct ∠XYZ with the same measure as ∠EDG.

3. Use a straightedge to draw an acute angle. Use a compass and straightedge to copy the angle. Then bisect the copy of the angle.

4. Use a straightedge to draw an obtuse angle. Use a compass and straightedge to copy the angle. Then bisect the copy of the angle.

Problem Solving

For Exercises 1–2, use the figure shown.

1. Construct the bisector of ∠B in △ ABC. Construct the bisectors of ∠A and ∠C.

2. What do you notice about the bisectors?

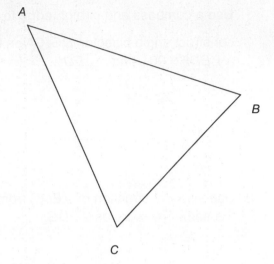

_____

_____

_____

3. Construct an angle whose measure is four times as great as m∠K, shown below.

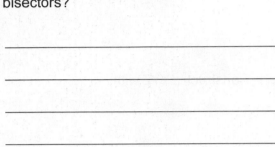

Choose the best answer.

4. Mark drew ∠PQR with measure 168°. He constructed the angle bisector $\overrightarrow{QX}$. Then he bisected ∠PQX by constructing $\overrightarrow{PY}$. What is m∠PQY?

   A 21°   B 42°   C 84°   D 168°

5. Paula bisected ∠XYZ, forming angles ∠XYW and ∠WYZ. Given that ∠XYZ is an obtuse angle, which statement cannot be true?

   F m∠WYZ is less than 90°.

   G m∠WYZ = m∠XYW

   H m∠WYZ is greater than 90°.

   J m∠XYZ = 2 • m∠XYW

Pairs of Angles
Going Deeper

Essential question: *How can you use angle pairs to solve problems?*

Recall that two rays with a common endpoint form an angle. The two rays form the sides of the angle, and the common endpoint marks the vertex. You can name an angle several ways: by its vertex, by a point on each ray and the vertex, or by a number.

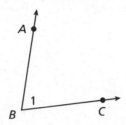

Angle names: ∠ABC, ∠CBA, ∠B, ∠1

It is useful to work with pairs of angles and to understand how pairs of angles relate to each other. **Congruent angles** are angles that have the same measure.

CC.9–12.G.CO.1

1 EXPLORE   Measuring Angles

A Using a ruler, draw a pair of intersecting lines. Label each angle from 1 to 4.

B Use a protractor to help you complete the chart.

Angle	Measure of Angle
m∠1	
m∠2	
m∠3	
m∠4	
m∠1 + m∠2	
m∠2 + m∠3	
m∠3 + m∠4	
m∠4 + m∠1	

REFLECT

1a. Conjecture Share your results with other students. Make a conjecture about pairs of angles that are opposite of each other. Make a conjecture about pairs of angles that are next to each other.

_____

_____

Vertical angles are the opposite angles formed by two intersecting lines. Vertical angles are congruent because the angles have the same measure. **Adjacent angles** are pairs of angles that share a vertex and one side but do not overlap.

Complementary angles are two angles whose measures have a sum of 90°. **Supplementary angles** are two angles whose measures have a sum of 180°. You have discovered in Explore 1 that adjacent angles formed by two intersecting lines are supplementary.

CC.9–12.G.CO.9

2 EXAMPLE   Identifying Angles and Angle Pairs

Use the diagram below.

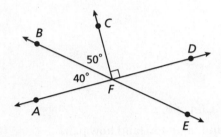

A   Name a pair of adjacent angles. _____

B   Name a pair of vertical angles. _____

C   Name a pair of complementary angles. _____

D   Name an angle that is supplementary to ∠CFE. _____

E   Name an angle that is supplementary to ∠BFD. _____

F   Name an angle that is supplementary to ∠CFD. _____

G   Name a pair of non-adjacent angles that are complementary. _____

REFLECT

2a. What is the measure of ∠DFE? Explain how you found the measure.

_____

_____

2b. Are ∠CFB and ∠DFE vertical angles? Why or why not?

_____

_____

2c. Are ∠BFD and ∠AFE vertical angles? Why or why not?

_____

_____

3 EXAMPLE   Finding Angle Measures

Find the measure of each angle.

A ∠*BDC*

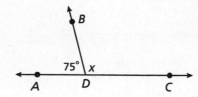

∠*BDC* and _____ are _____ angles.

The sum of their measures is _____.

Write an equation to help you find the measure of ∠*BDC*.

$75 + x =$ _____

In the box, solve the equation for *x*.

m∠*BDC* = [　　　] .

B ∠*EHF*

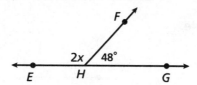

∠*EHF* and _____ are _____ angles.

The sum of their measures is _____.

In the box, write and solve an equation
to help you find m∠*EHF*.

m∠*EHF* = [　　　] .

REFLECT

3a. A friend claims that two acute angles are complementary and their measures
are $2x°$ and $(30 - 5x)°$. If your friend is right, what equation must be true?

_____

_____

3b. Solve the equation you found and interpret the answer. Evaluate your friend's claim.

_____

_____

_____

PRACTICE

Use the figure for Exercises 1–5.

1. m∠QUP + m∠PUT = _____

2. Name a pair of supplementary angles.

   _____

3. Name a pair of vertical angles.

   _____

4. Name a pair of adjacent angles.

   _____

5. What is the measure of ∠QUN? Explain your answer.

   _____

   _____

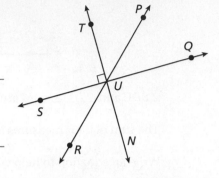

Solve for the indicated angle measure or variable.

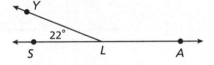

6. m ∠YLA = _____

7. x = _____

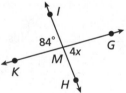

8. The railroad tracks meet the road as shown.
   The town will allow a parking lot at angle J
   if the measure of angle J is greater than 38°.
   Can a parking lot be built at angle J?
   Why or why not?

   _____

   _____

   _____

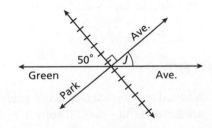

9. **Error Analysis** A student states that when the sum of two angle measures equals
   180°, the two angles are complementary. Explain why the student is incorrect.

   _____

   _____

Additional Practice

1. ∠PQR and ∠SQR form a linear pair. Find the sum of their measures. _____

2. Name the ray that ∠PQR and ∠SQR share. _____

Use the figures for Exercises 3 and 4.

3. supplement of ∠Z _____

4. complement of ∠Y _____

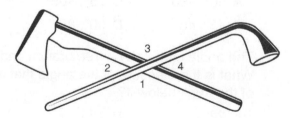

5. An angle measures 12 degrees less than three times its supplement. Find the

measure of the angle. _____

6. An angle is its own complement. Find the measure of a supplement to this angle.

_____

7. ∠DEF and ∠FEG are complementary. m∠DEF = (3x − 4)°, and m∠FEG = (5x + 6)°.

Find the measures of both angles. _____

8. ∠DEF and ∠FEG are supplementary. m∠DEF = (9x + 1)°, and m∠FEG = (8x + 9)°.

Find the measures of both angles. _____

Use the figure for Exercises 9 and 10.

In 2004, several nickels were minted to commemorate the Louisiana
Purchase and Lewis and Clark's expedition into the American West. One
nickel shows a pipe and a hatchet crossed to symbolize peace between the
American government and Native American tribes.

9. Name a pair of vertical angles.

_____

_____

10. Name a linear pair of angles.

_____

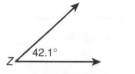

11. ∠ABC and ∠CBD form a linear pair and have
    equal measures. Tell if ∠ABC is acute, right,
    or obtuse.

12. ∠KLM and ∠MLN are complementary. $\overrightarrow{LM}$
    bisects ∠KLN. Find the measures of ∠KLM
    and ∠MLN.

Problem Solving

Use the drawing of part of the Eiffel Tower for Exercises 1–5.

1. Name a pair of angles that appear to be complementary.

   _____

2. Name a pair of supplementary angles.

   _____

3. If m∠CSW = 45°, what is m∠JST? How do you know?

   _____

   _____

4. If m∠FKB = 135°, what is m∠BKL? How do you know?

   _____

   _____

5. Name three angles whose measures sum to 180°.

   _____

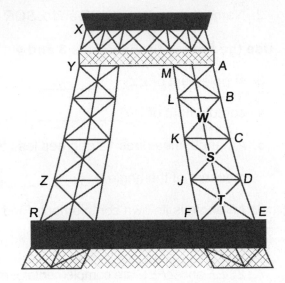

Choose the best answer.

6. A landscaper uses paving stones for a walkway. Which are possible angle measures for a° and b° so that the stones do not have space between them?

   A 50°, 100°   C 75°, 105°

   B 45°, 45°   D 90°, 80°

7. The angle formed by a tree branch and the part of the trunk above it is 68°. What is the measure of the angle that is formed by the branch and the part of the trunk below it?

   F 22°   H 158°

   G 112°   J 180°

8. ∠R and ∠S are complementary. If m∠R = (7 + 3x)° and m∠S = (2x + 13)°, which is a true statement?

   A ∠R is acute.   C ∠R and ∠S are right angles.

   B ∠R is obtuse.   D m∠S > m∠R

Using Formulas in Geometry
Extension: Rewriting Formulas

Essential question: *How can you express formulas in different ways?*

If you solve a formula for an unknown variable, you can substitute the known quantities into the rewritten formula to find the unknown value directly.

Video Tutor

CC.9–12.A.CED.4

1 EXAMPLE   **Solving Formulas for Specified Variables**

A triangle with area 24 square inches has a base of 3 inches. What is its height?

A   The area A of a triangle with base b and height h is given by the formula $A = \frac{1}{2}bh$. Solve the formula for h. Explain your steps.

$A = \frac{1}{2}bh$ .... Write the original formula.

$2A = bh$ .... Multiply each side by _____.

$\frac{2A}{b} = h$ .... Divide each side by _____.

B   Use the rewritten formula to solve the problem.

$h = \frac{2A}{b}$ .... Write the rewritten formula.

$h = \dfrac{2\left(\right)}{}$ .... Substitute given values.

$h = $ .... Evaluate.

REFLECT

1a. Suppose a problem gives you the area and the height of a triangle and asks for the base. What might you do?

_____

_____

_____

1b. Show how to use the original formula to solve the problem in the example without rewriting the formula.

_____

2 EXAMPLE   Rewriting Formulas to Solve Problems

Four congruent rectangles are arranged around a central rectangle as shown.
Write an expression for the perimeter P of the figure. Then solve for x.

Distance around left rectangle: 5   + x +   5

Distance around upper rectangle: x +   5   +   ▢

Distance around right rectangle: 5   +   ▢   +   ▢

Distance around lower rectangle: ▢   +   ▢   +   ▢

$P =$ ▢$x +$ ▢$(5) = 6x + 30$

$P -$ ▢ $= 6x$

$\dfrac{▢}{▢} = x$

REFLECT

2a. Write a problem that can be solved using the diagram and formula for x above.

_____

_____

PRACTICE

1. Simple interest is calculated with the formula $I = Prt$, where P is principal, r is the annual interest rate, and t is years. Solve the formula for t. Then find how long it will take a deposit of \$500 to earn \$100 with an annual interest rate of 5%.

_____

2. The diagram at the right shows a plan for a garden border using four semicircles each with radius r. Write a formula for the total length T of the curved border. Then solve for r.

_____

3. **Error Analysis** The average a of two numbers x_1 and x_2 is one half their sum, or $a = \frac{1}{2}(x_1 + x_2)$. When Pat solved for x_1, she incorrectly wrote $x_1 = 2a + x_2$. What mistake did Pat make? What is the correct formula?

_____

Additional Practice

The perimeter of a rectangle is given by the formula $A = 2\ell + 2w$, where ℓ is the length of the rectangle and w is the width of the rectangle. Use this formula for Exercises 1 and 2.

1. Solve the formula for w, the width of the rectangle. Show your work.

_____

_____

2. The perimeter of a rectangle is 24.5 feet, and its length is 6.25 feet. Use your formula from Exercise 1 to find the width of the rectangle.

_____

For Exercises 3–5, write and solve a formula to find each value. Use 3.14 for π.

3. The circumference of a circle is 18.84 inches. Find the diameter of the circle.

_____

4. The circumference of a circle is 28.26 inches. Find the radius of the circle.

_____

5. The area of a circle is 113.04 cm². Find the radius of the circle.

_____

Use the figure for Exercises 6 and 7.

Lucas has a 39-foot-long rope. He uses all the rope to outline this T-shape in his backyard. All the angles in the figure are right angles.

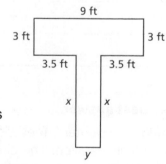

6. Write a formula for the perimeter of the T-shape in terms of x and y. Solve the formula for x.

_____

7. Find the value of y and use that value in your formula from Exercise 6 to find x.

_____

Problem Solving

Use the diagram of a hockey field for Exercises 1–4.

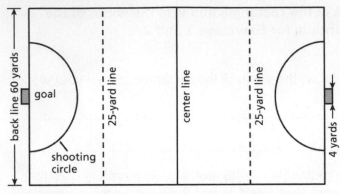

1. The area of the field is 6000 square yards. Write and solve a formula to find the width of the field.

   _____

   _____

   _____

2. Write and solve a formula to find the perimeter of the field.

   _____

   _____

   _____

3. The area enclosed by one shooting circle is 401.92 square yards. Write and solve a formula to find the radius of the shooting circle. Use 3.14 for π.

   _____

   _____

   _____

4. Write and solve a formula to find the area of the field excluding the two shooting circles.

   _____

   _____

   _____

Choose the best answer.

5. A rectangular counter 3 feet wide and 5 feet long has a circle cut out of it in order to have a sink installed. The circle has a diameter of 18 inches. What is the approximate area of the remaining countertop surface? Use 3.14 for π.

   A 13.2 ft^2 C 18.9 ft^2

   B 15.0 ft^2 D 29.5 ft^2

6. The base of a triangular garden measures 5.5 feet. It takes 33 pounds of mulch to cover the garden. If 4 pounds of mulch are needed to cover a square foot, what is the height of the garden?

   F 1.5 ft   H 4 ft

   G 3 ft   J 6.6 ft

Midpoint and Distance in the Coordinate Plane
Going Deeper

Essential question: *How can you find midpoints of segments and distances in the coordinate plane?*

Video Tutor

CC.9–12.G.GPE.6

1 **E X P L O R E** **Finding Midpoints of Line Segments**

Follow the steps below for each of the given line segments.

A Use a ruler to measure the length of the line segment to the nearest millimeter.

B Find half the length of the segment. Measure this distance from one endpoint to locate the midpoint of the segment. Plot a point at the midpoint.

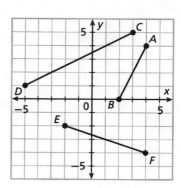

C Record the coordinates of the segment's endpoints and the coordinates of the segment's midpoint in the table below.

D In each row of the table, compare the *x*-coordinates of the endpoints to the *x*-coordinate of the midpoint. Then compare the *y*-coordinates of the endpoints to the *y*-coordinate of the midpoint. Look for patterns.

Endpoint	Endpoint Coordinates	Endpoint	Endpoint Coordinates	Midpoint Coordinates
A		B		
C		D		
E		F		

REFLECT

1a. Make a conjecture: If you know the coordinates of the endpoints of a line segment, how can you find the coordinates of the midpoint?

_____

_____

1b. What are the coordinates of the midpoint of a line segment with endpoints at the origin and at the point (*a*, *b*)?

_____

The patterns you observed can be generalized to give a formula for the coordinates of the midpoint of any line segment in the coordinate plane.

> ### The Midpoint Formula
>
> The midpoint M of $\overline{AB}$ with endpoints $A(x_1, y_1)$ and $B(x_2, y_2)$ is given by $M\left(\dfrac{x_1 + x_2}{2}, \dfrac{y_1 + y_2}{2}\right)$.

CC.9–12.G.GPE.4

2 EXAMPLE   Using the Midpoint Formula

$\overline{PQ}$ has endpoints $P(-4, 1)$ and $Q(2, -3)$. Prove that the midpoint M of $\overline{PQ}$ lies in Quadrant III.

A Use the given endpoints to identify x_1, x_2, y_1, and y_2.

$x_1 = -4$, $x_2 = 2$, $y_1 =$ _____ , $y_2 =$ _____

B By the midpoint formula, the x-coordinate of M is $\dfrac{x_1 + x_2}{2} = \dfrac{-4 + 2}{2} = \dfrac{-2}{2} = -1$.

The y-coordinate of M is $\dfrac{y_1 + y_2}{2} = \dfrac{\boxed{} + \boxed{}}{2} = \dfrac{\boxed{}}{2} = \boxed{}$.

M lies in Quadrant III because _____

REFLECT

2a. What must be true about PM and QM? Show that this is the case.

_____

_____

PREP FOR CC.9–12.G.GPE.4

3 EXPLORE   Finding a Distance in the Coordinate Plane

You can use the Pythagorean Theorem to help you find the distance between the points $A(2, 5)$ and $B(-4, -3)$.

A Plot the points A and B in the coordinate plane at right.

B Draw $\overline{AB}$.

C Draw a vertical line through point A and a horizontal line through point B to create a right triangle. Label the intersection of the vertical line and the horizontal line as point C.

D Each small grid square is 1 unit by 1 unit. Use this fact to find the lengths AC and BC.

$AC =$ _____ $BC =$ _____

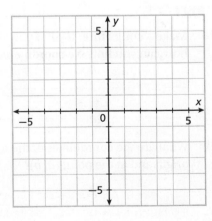

E By the Pythagorean Theorem, $AB^2 = AC^2 + BC^2$.
Complete the following using the lengths from Step D.

$$AB^2 = \boxed{}^2 + \boxed{}^2$$

F Simplify the right side of the equation. Then solve for AB.

$$AB^2 = \underline{\hspace{2cm}}, AB = \underline{\hspace{2cm}}$$

3a. Explain how you solved for AB in Step F.

_____

3b. Can you use the above method to find the distance between any two points in the coordinate plane? Explain.

_____

_____

The process of using the Pythagorean Theorem can be generalized to give a formula for finding the distance between two points in the coordinate plane.

The Distance Formula

The distance between two points (x_1, y_1) and (x_2, y_2) in the coordinate plane is

$$\sqrt{(x_2 - x_1)^2 + (y_2 - y_1)^2}.$$

CC.9–12.G.GPE.4

4 EXAMPLE Using the Distance Formula

Prove that $\overline{CD}$ is longer than $\overline{AB}$.

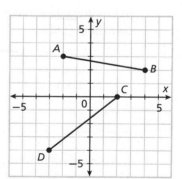

A Write the coordinates of A, B, C, and D.

$A(-2, 3)$, B _____, C _____, D _____

B Use the distance formula to find AB and CD.

$$AB = \sqrt{[4 - (-2)]^2 + (2 - 3)^2} = \sqrt{6^2 + (-1)^2} = \sqrt{36 + 1} = \sqrt{37}$$

$$CD = \sqrt{\left(\boxed{} - \boxed{}\right)^2 + \left(\boxed{} - \boxed{}\right)^2} = \sqrt{\left(\boxed{}\right)^2 + \left(\boxed{}\right)^2} = \sqrt{\boxed{}}$$

So, $\overline{CD}$ is longer than $\overline{AB}$ because _____

4a. When you use the distance formula, does the order in which you subtract the x-coordinates and the y-coordinates matter? Explain.

_____

1. Find the coordinates of the midpoint of
   $\overline{AB}$ with endpoints $A(-10, 3)$ and $B(2, -2)$. _____

2. $\overline{RS}$ has endpoints $R(3, 5)$ and $S(-3, -1)$. Prove that the midpoint M of $\overline{RS}$ lies
   on the y-axis.

   _____

   _____

3. $\overline{CD}$ has endpoints $C(1, 4)$ and $D(5, 0)$. $\overline{EF}$ has endpoints $E(4, 5)$ and $F(2, -1)$.
   Prove that the segments have the same midpoint.

   _____

   _____

Use the figure for Exercises 4–6.

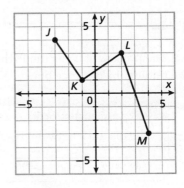

4. Find the distance between J and L. _____

5. Find the length of $\overline{LM}$. _____

6. Prove that $JK = KL$.

   _____

   _____

7. $\overline{GH}$ has endpoint $G(2, 7)$ and midpoint $M(5, 1)$. Write two equations you can use
   to find the coordinates of the endpoint H. Then solve the equations and write the
   coordinates of H.

   _____

   _____

   _____

8. A segment $\overline{AB}$ has endpoints $A(x_1, y_1)$ and $B(x_2, y_2)$. The segment is reflected
   across the x-axis. Find the coordinates of the reflected segment. Then show the
   length of the reflected segment is the same as the length of the original segment.
   Explain your reasoning.

   _____

   _____

   _____

   _____

Additional Practice

Find the coordinates of the midpoint of each segment.

1. $\overline{TU}$ with endpoints $T(5, -1)$ and $U(1, -5)$

   $(3, -3)$

2. $\overline{VW}$ with endpoints $V(-2, -6)$ and $W(x + 2, y + 3)$ $(0, -3)$

   $(-1, -3/2)$

3. Y is the midpoint of $\overline{XZ}$. X has coordinates $(2, 4)$, and Y has coordinates $(-1, 1)$. Find the coordinates of Z.

   $(-6, -4)$

Use the figure for Exercises 4–7.

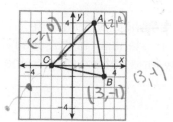

4. Find AB. _____ $\sqrt{26}$

5. Find BC. _____ $\sqrt{26}$

6. Find CA. _____ $\sqrt{20}$

7. Name a pair of congruent segments. _____ AB, BC

   Same length or letters

Find the distances.

8. Use the Distance Formula to find the distance, to the nearest tenth, between $K(-7, -4)$ and $L(-2, 0)$.

   $\sqrt{29}$

9. Use the Pythagorean Theorem to find the distance, to the nearest tenth, between $F(9, 5)$ and $G(-2, 2)$.

   $\sqrt{130}$

Use the figure for Exercises 10 and 11.

Snooker is a kind of pool or billiards played on a 6-foot-by-12-foot table. The side pockets are halfway down the rails (long sides).

10. Find the distance, to the nearest tenth of a foot, diagonally across the table from corner pocket to corner pocket.

    $\sqrt{180}$

11. Find the distance, to the nearest tenth of an inch, diagonally across the table from corner pocket to side pocket.

    $\sqrt{72}$

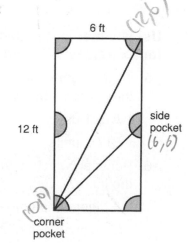

6 ft $(12, 6)$

12 ft

side pocket
$(6, 6)$

$(0, 0)$

corner pocket

Problem Solving

For Exercises 1 and 2, use the diagram of a tennis court.

1. A singles tennis court is a rectangle 27 feet wide and 78 feet long. Suppose a player at corner *A* hits the ball to her opponent in the diagonally opposite corner *B*. Approximately how far does the ball travel, to the nearest tenth of a foot?

   82.5

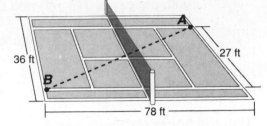

2. A doubles tennis court is a rectangle 36 feet wide and 78 feet long. If two players are standing in diagonally opposite corners, about how far apart are they, to the nearest tenth of a foot?

   85.9

A map of an amusement park is shown on a coordinate plane, where each square of the grid represents 1 square meter. The water ride is at (–17, 12), the roller coaster is at (26, –8), and the Ferris wheel is at (2, 20). Find each distance to the nearest tenth of a meter.

3. What is the distance between the water ride and the roller coaster?

   47.4

4. A caricature artist is at the midpoint between the roller coaster and the Ferris wheel. What is the distance from the artist to the Ferris wheel?

   18.4

Use the map of the Sacramento Zoo on a coordinate plane for Exercises 5–7. Choose the best answer.

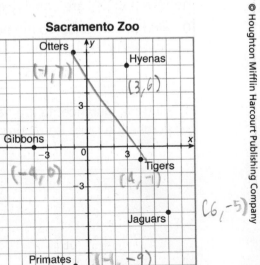

5. To the nearest tenth of a unit, how far is it from the tigers to the hyenas?

   A 5.1 units   C 9.9 units

   (B) 7.1 units   D 50.0 units

6. Between which of these exhibits is the distance the least?

   F tigers and primates

   G hyenas and gibbons

   (H) otters and gibbons

   J tigers and otters

7. Suppose you walk straight from the jaguars to the tigers and then to the otters. What is the total distance to the nearest tenth of a unit?

   A 11.4 units   (C) 13.9 units

   B 13.0 units   D 14.2 units

Transformations in the Coordinate Plane
Extension: Properties of Rigid Motions

Essential question: *How do you identify transformations that are rigid motions?*

CC.9–12.G.CO.2

1 ENGAGE   Introducing Transformations

A **transformation** is a function that changes the position, shape, and/or size of a figure. The inputs for the function are points in the plane; the outputs are other points in the plane. A figure that is used as the input of a transformation is the **pre-image**. The output is the **image**.

For example, the transformation T moves point A to point A'. Point A is the pre-image, and A' is the image. You can use function notation to write $T(A) = A'$. Note that a transformation is sometimes called a *mapping*. Transformation T maps point A to point A'.

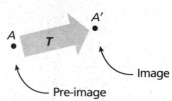

Coordinate notation is one way to write a rule for a transformation on a coordinate plane. The notation uses an arrow to show how the transformation changes the coordinates of a general point, (x, y).

For example, the notation $(x, y) \rightarrow (x + 2, y - 3)$ means that the transformation adds 2 to the x-coordinate of a point and subtracts 3 from its y-coordinate. Thus, this transformation maps the point $(6, 5)$ to the point $(8, 2)$.

REFLECT

1a. Explain how to identify the pre-image and image in $T(E) = F$.

_____

1b. Consider the transformation given by the rule $(x, y) \rightarrow (x + 1, y + 1)$. What is the domain of this function? What is the range? Describe the transformation.

_____

_____

_____

1c. Transformation T maps points in the coordinate plane by moving them vertically up or down onto the x-axis. (Points on the x-axis are unchanged by the transformation.) Explain how to use coordinate notation to write a rule for transformation T.

_____

_____

2 **EXPLORE** Classifying Transformations

Investigate the effects of various transformations on the given right triangle.

- Use coordinate notation to help you find the image of each vertex of the triangle.
- Plot the images of the vertices.
- Connect the images of the vertices to draw the image of the triangle.

A $(x, y) \rightarrow (x - 4, y + 3)$ **B** $(x, y) \rightarrow (-x, y)$ **C** $(x, y) \rightarrow (-y, x)$

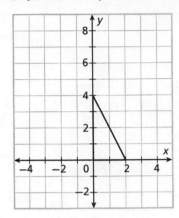 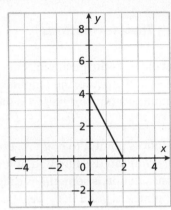 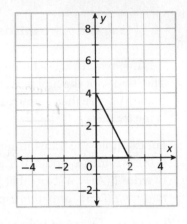

D $(x, y) \rightarrow (2x, 2y)$ **E** $(x, y) \rightarrow (2x, y)$ **F** $(x, y) \rightarrow (x, \frac{1}{2}y)$

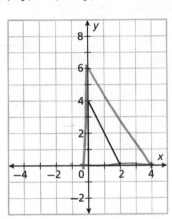 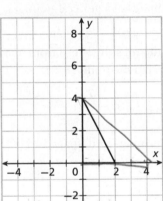 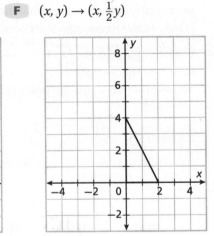

REFLECT

2a. A transformation *preserves distance* if the distance between any two points of the pre-image equals the distance between the corresponding points of the image. Which of the above transformations preserve distance?

_____

2b. A transformation *preserves angle measure* if the measure of any angle of the pre-image equals the measure of the corresponding angle of the image. Which of the above transformations preserve angle measure?

_____

A **rigid motion** (or *isometry*) is a transformation that changes the position of a figure without changing the size or shape of the figure.

PREP FOR CC.9–12.G.CO.6

3 EXAMPLE Identifying Rigid Motions

The figures show the pre-image ($\triangle ABC$) and image ($\triangle A'B'C'$) under a transformation. Determine whether the transformation appears to be a rigid motion. Explain.

A

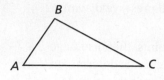 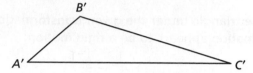

The transformation does not change the size or shape of the figure

Therefore, _This is a rigid motion_

B

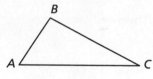

The transformation changes the shape of the figure.

Therefore, _not RM_

C

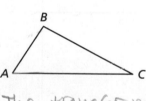 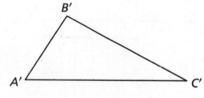

The transformation changes the size of the figure, therefore not RM

REFLECT

3a. How could you use tracing paper or a transparency to help you identify rigid motions?

_____

_____

_____

_____

3b. Which of the transformations on the previous page appear to be rigid motions?

ABC

Rigid motions have some important properties. These are summarized below.

Properties of Rigid Motions (Isometries)

- Rigid motions preserve distance.
- Rigid motions preserve angle measure.
- Rigid motions preserve betweenness.
- Rigid motions preserve collinearity.

Reflections, rotations, and translations are all rigid motions. So, they all preserve distance, angle measure, betweenness, and collinearity.

The above properties ensure that if a figure is determined by certain points, then its image after a rigid motion is also determined by those points. For example, $\triangle ABC$ is determined by its vertices, points A, B, and C. The image of $\triangle ABC$ after a rigid motion is the triangle determined by A', B', and C'.

PRACTICE

Draw the image of the triangle under the given transformation. Then tell whether the transformation appears to be a rigid motion.

1. $(x, y) \rightarrow (x + 3, y)$

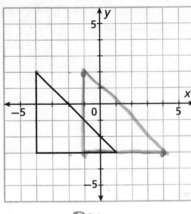

_____RM_____

2. $(x, y) \rightarrow (3x, 3y)$

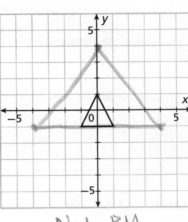

_____Not RM_____

3. $(x, y) \rightarrow (x, -y)$

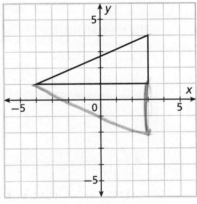

_____RM_____

4. $(x, y) \rightarrow (-x, -y)$

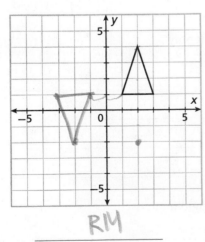

_____RM_____

5. $(x, y) \rightarrow (x, 3y)$

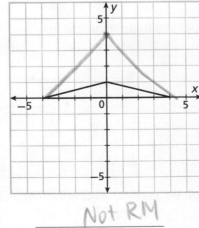

_____Not RM_____

6. $(x, y) \rightarrow (x - 4, y - 4)$

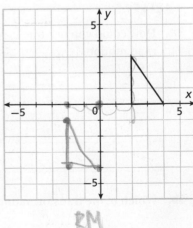

_____RM_____

The figures show the pre-image (*ABCD*) and image (*A′B′C′D′*) under a transformation. Determine whether the transformation appears to be a rigid motion. Explain.

7.

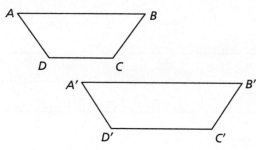

The transformation changes
the size so it is not a RM

8.

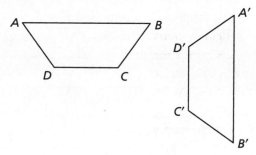

RM

9.

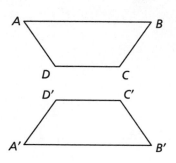

RM

10.

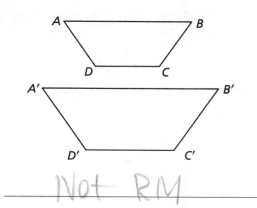

Not RM

In Exercises 11–14, consider a transformation *T* that maps △*XYZ* to △*X′Y′Z′*.

11. What is the image of $\overline{XY}$? _____

12. What is *T*(*Z*)? _____

13. What is the pre-image of ∠*Y′*? _____

14. Can you conclude that *XY* = *X′Y′*? Why or why not?

_____

15. Point *M* is the midpoint of $\overline{AB}$. After a rigid motion, can you conclude that *M′* is the midpoint of $\overline{A′B′}$? Why or why not?

_____

_____

16. Error Analysis A student claims that all of the transformations in Exercises 1—6 preserve angle measure. However, the student made an error. Which of the exercises shows a transformation that *does not* preserve angle measure? Use a protractor to estimate the measures of the angles in the pre-image triangle and image triangle to justify your answer.

_____

_____

_____

_____

Additional Practice

Use the figure for Exercises 1–3.

The figure in the plane at right shows the preimage in the transformation $ABCD \rightarrow A'B'C'D'$. Match the number of the image (below) with the name of the correct transformation.

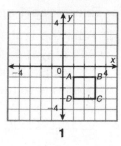

1

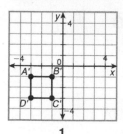 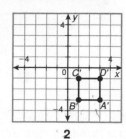 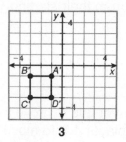

1   2   3

1. rotation ___3___   2. translation ___|___   3. reflection ___2___

4. A figure has vertices at $D(-2, 1)$, $E(-3, 3)$, and $F(0, 3)$. After a transformation, the image of the figure has vertices at $D'(-1, -2)$, $E'(-3, -3)$, and $F'(-3, 0)$. Draw the preimage and the image. Then identify the transformation.

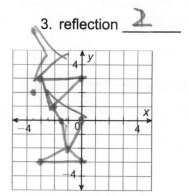

_____It flipped over x axis, $\frac{1}{y}$_____

5. A figure has vertices at $G(0, 0)$, $H(-1, -2)$, $I(-1.5, 0)$, and $J(-2.5, 2)$. Find the coordinates for the image of $GHIJ$ after the translation $(x, y) \rightarrow (x - 2.5, y + 4)$.

Use the figure for Exercise 6.

6. A parking garage attendant will make the most money when the maximum number of cars fits in the parking garage. To fit one more car in, the attendant moves a car from position 1 to position 2. Write a rule for this translation.

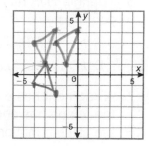

_____$(x, y) \rightarrow (x - 7, y + 5)$_____

7. A figure has vertices at $X(-1, 1)$, $Y(-2, 3)$, and $Z(0, 4)$. Draw the image of XYZ after the translation $(x, y) \rightarrow (x - 2, y)$ and a 180° rotation around X.

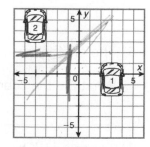

Problem Solving

Use the diagram of the starting positions of five basketball players for Exercises 1 and 2.

1. After the first step of a play, player 3 is at (−1.5, 0) and player 4 is at (1, 0.5). Write a rule to describe the translations of players 3 and 4 from their starting positions to their new positions.

   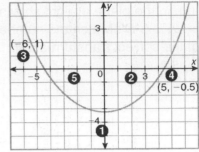

   _____

   _____

2. For the second step of the play, player 3 is to move to a position described by the rule $(x, y) \rightarrow (x - 4, y - 2)$ and player 4 is to move to a position described by the rule $(x, y) \rightarrow (x + 3, y - 2)$. What are the positions of these two players after this step of the play?

   _____

Use the diagram for Exercises 3–5.

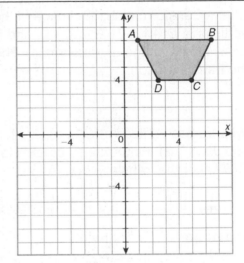

3. Find the coordinates of the image of *ABCD* after it is moved 6 units left and 2 units up.

   _____

4. The original image is moved so that its new coordinates are $A'(-1, 7)$, $B'(-6\frac{1}{2}, 7)$, $C'(-5, 4)$, and $D'(-2\frac{1}{2}, 4)$. Identify the transformation.

   _____

5. The original image is translated so that the coordinates of B' are $(11\frac{1}{2}, 17)$.

   What are the coordinates of the other three vertices of the image after this translation?

   _____

6. Triangle *HJK* has vertices $H(0, -9)$, $J(-1, -5)$, and $K(7, 8)$. What are the coordinates of the vertices after the translation $(x, y) \rightarrow (x - 1, y - 3)$?

   A $H'(-1, 12)$, $J'(-2, 8)$, $K'(6, -5)$ C $H'(-1, -12)$, $J'(-2, -8)$, $K'(6, 5)$

   B $H'(1, -12)$, $J'(2, -8)$, $K'(-6, 5)$ D $H'(1, 12)$, $J'(2, 8)$, $K'(-6, -5)$

7. A segment has endpoints at $S(2, 3)$ and $T(-2, 8)$. After a transformation, the image has endpoints at $S'(2, 3)$ and $T'(6, 8)$. Which best describes the transformation?

   F reflection across the *y*-axis   H rotation about the origin

   G translation $(x, y) \rightarrow (x + 8, y)$ J rotation about the point (2, 3)

Performance Tasks

COMMON CORE

CC.9-12.A.SSE.1
CC.9-12.G.CO.1
CC.9-12.G.CO.5

⭐ **1.** A square table is set with four identical place settings, one on each side of the table. Each setting consists of a plate and spoon, with the spoon always to the right of the plate. If you start with one setting, what transformation describes the location of each of the other three? Express your answer in terms of degrees, lines of reflection, or directions from the original place setting.

⭐ **2.** Without using the word "square," how would you explain how to draw one to a classmate on the telephone?

⭐⭐ **3.** The east-west streets and north-south avenues of a certain city are numbered consecutively from south to north and east to west. All blocks are squares with the same side lengths. Mandy is standing on the corner of 56th Street and 12th Avenue. Mark is standing on the corner of 32nd Street and 18th Avenue. Mark calls Mandy and asks her to meet him at a spot halfway between their current locations.

a. Use the Midpoint Formula to find out where Mark wants to meet. Show your work.

b. Mandy says that Mark walks faster than she does, so he should have to walk farther. Assume that Mark walks 1.25 times as fast as Mandy. If Mandy's distance walked in a given time period is d, what is the distance Mark can walk in the same time period?

c. Use your results in part **b** to write and solve an equation to find the distances Mark and Mandy should each walk.

continued

4. Tanya is using the tile design shown at right to tile her bathroom floor. Each tile has the pattern on only one side.

a. Tanya wants to make a pattern by creating 2-by-2 squares using the tile. Draw an example of a 2-by-2 square she could create and explain what transformations she could use to make the square.

b. Tanya wants to make the 2-by-2 square shown at right. What transformation would she need to use to make it? Why is this not physically possible?

Name _____ **Class** _____ **Date** _____

MULTIPLE CHOICE

1. Which term has the following definition?

   It is a portion of a line consisting of two points and all points between them.

   A. angle **C.** line segment

   B. endpoint **D.** ray

2. Each figure shows the pre-image ($\triangle JKL$) and image ($\triangle J'K'L'$) under a transformation. Which transformation appears to be a rigid motion?

   F.
   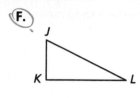

   G.
   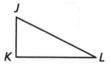

   H.
   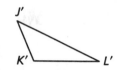

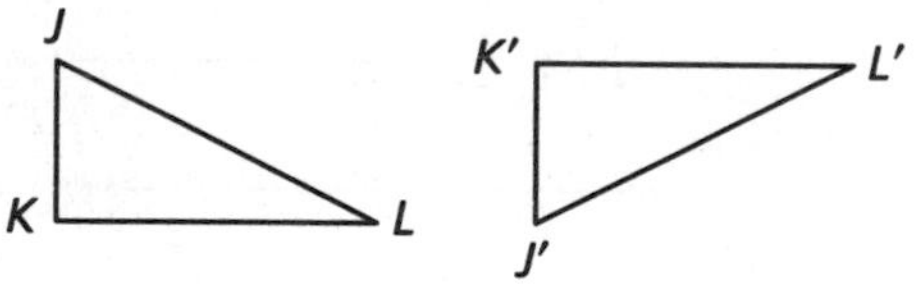

   J.
   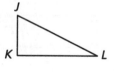

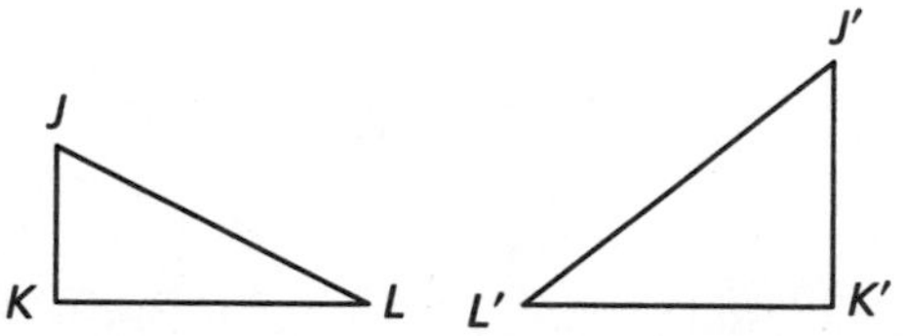

3. Lisa wants to use a compass and straightedge to copy $\overline{XY}$. She uses the straightedge to draw a line segment, and she labels one endpoint Q. What should she do next?

   A. Open the compass to distance XY.

   B. Open the compass to distance XQ.

   C. Use a ruler to measure $\overline{XY}$.

   D. Use the straightedge to draw $\overline{XQ}$.

4. You want to prove that $\overline{AB}$ is longer than $\overline{CD}$. To do so, you use the distance formula to find the lengths of the segments. Which of the following are the correct lengths?

   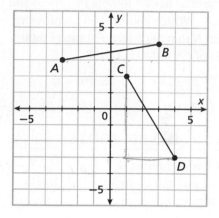

   F. $AB = 7, CD = 8$

   G. $AB = \sqrt{37}, CD = \sqrt{34}$

   H. $AB = \sqrt{49}, CD = \sqrt{64}$

   J. $AB = 37, CD = 34$

5. Kendrick is using a compass and straightedge to copy $\angle Q$. The figure shows the portion of the construction that he has already completed. Where should Kendrick place the point of the compass to do the next step of the construction?

   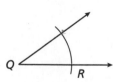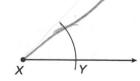

   A. point Q

   B. point R

   C. point X

   D. point Y

6. Which of the following is the correct phrase to complete the definition of an angle?

An angle is a figure formed by two rays _____.

   F. that intersect

   G. with one point in common

   H. that do not overlap

   J. with the same endpoint

7. A segment has endpoints $P(-6,-5)$ and $Q(6, 1)$. Which coordinates identify the point N that partitions $\overline{PQ}$ such that the ratio of PN to NQ is 1 to 3?

   A. $(-3, -3.5)$ **C.** $(0, -2)$

   B. $(-2, -3)$ **D.** $(3, -0.5)$

CONSTRUCTED RESPONSE

8. $\overline{GH}$ has endpoints $G(1, 3)$ and $H(-5, -1)$. Prove that the midpoint of $\overline{GH}$ lies in Quadrant II.

_____

_____

_____

_____

_____

_____

9. Perform the following transformations on the given right triangle and describe the effects.

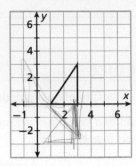

a. Plot the image of the triangle after the transformation $(x, y) \rightarrow (2x, 2y)$.

b. Plot the image of the triangle after the transformation $(x, y) \rightarrow (x, -y)$.

c. Explain why each transformation does or does not appear to be a rigid motion.

_____

_____

_____

_____

_____

_____

_____

_____

$$\frac{X_1 + X_2}{2} = X_{midpoint}$$

$$(-2, 1)$$

Geometric Reasoning

Chapter Focus

This unit introduces some of the building blocks of formal reasoning, such as conditional statements. You will make conjectures using inductive reasoning and either disprove them by finding a counterexample or prove them using deductive reasoning. Finally, you will begin to write algebraic and geometric proofs including proofs that justify key relationships among lines and angles.

Chapter at a Glance

COMMON CORE

Lesson		Standards for Mathematical Content
2-1	Using Inductive Reasoning to Make Conjectures	Prep for CC.9-12.G.CO.9
2-2	Conditional Statements	CC.MP.3
2-3	Using Deductive Reasoning to Verify Conjectures	CC.MP.3
2-4	Biconditional Statements and Definitions	CC.MP.3
2-5	Algebraic Proof	Prep for CC.9-12.G.CO.9
2-6	Geometric Proof	CC.9-12.G.CO.9
2-7	Flowchart and Paragraph Proofs	CC.9-12.G.CO.9
	Performance Tasks	
	Assessment Readiness	

CHAPTER 2

Unpacking the Standards

Understanding the standards and the vocabulary terms in the standards will help you know exactly what you are expected to learn in this chapter.

COMMON CORE **CC.MP.3**

Construct viable arguments and critique the reasoning of others. Mathematically proficient students understand and use stated assumptions, definitions, and previously established results in constructing arguments. They make conjectures and build a logical progression of statements to explore the truth of their conjectures. They are able to analyze situations by breaking them into cases, and can recognize and use counterexamples. They justify their conclusions, communicate them to others, and respond to the arguments of others. They reason inductively about data, making plausible arguments that take into account the context from which the data arose. …

Key Vocabulary

definition *(definición)* A statement that describes a mathematical object and can be written as a true biconditional statement.

conjecture *(conjetura)* A statement that is believed to be true.

counterexample *(contraejemplo)* An example that proves that a conjecture or statement is false.

inductive reasoning *(razonamiento inductivo)* The process of reasoning that a rule or statement is true because specific cases are true.

What It Means For You
Lessons 2-1, 2-2, 2-3, 2-4

Mathematics is a language of logic, with precise definitions and rules. Building your math skills and your logical reasoning skills work together hand-in-hand.

EXAMPLE   Precise definitions
Precise definitions are important in math and in everyday life. For example, how does someone define a bird?

Jen's Conjecture
"If an animal is a vertebrate with wings, then it is a bird."

Your Counterexample
"Bats are vertebrates with wings, but they aren't birds."

Tim's Conjecture
"If an animal has a beak and lays hard-shelled eggs, then it is a bird."

Your Counterexample
"Tortoises have beaks, and some of them lay hard-shelled eggs."

Your Definition
A bird is a warm-blooded, winged, feathered vertebrate that lays eggs.

Is this true of all birds? Does it include any animal that is not a bird? If the answers are "yes" and "no," then it is a good definition.

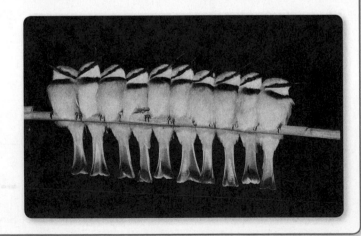

COMMON CORE **CC.9-12.A.REI.1**

Explain each step in solving a simple equation as following from the equality of numbers asserted at the previous step, starting from the assumption that the original equation has a solution. Construct a viable argument to justify a solution method.

Key Vocabulary
equation *(ecuación)* A mathematical statement that two expressions are equivalent.

What It Means For You — Lesson 2-5

You use properties of equality to justify, or prove, that each step is valid when you solve equations. This type of reasoning prepares you to write geometric proofs.

EXAMPLE
A family took out a loan to buy a new car that cost $22,000. The down payment was $4,000. The loan was interest free for a period of 5 years. The equation $5(12)p + 4,000 = 22,000$ represents this situation, where p is the monthly loan payment.

$5(12)p + 4,000 = 22,000$	*Given*
$60p + 4,000 = 22,000$	*Simplify.*
$60p = 18,000$	*Subtraction Property of Equality*
$p = 300$	*Division Property of Equality*

COMMON CORE **CC.9-12.G.CO.9**

Prove theorems about lines and angles.

Key Vocabulary
proof *(demostración)* An argument that uses logic to show that a conclusion is true.
theorem *(teorema)* A statement that has been proven.
line *(línea)* An undefined term in geometry, a line is a straight path that has no thickness and extends forever.
angle *(ángulo)* A figure formed by two rays with a common endpoint.

What It Means For You — Lessons 2-6, 2-7

With just a few definitions, properties, and postulates, you can begin to prove simple theorems about line segments, linear pairs, right angles, vertical angles, and complementary or supplementary angles.

EXAMPLE
Given: ∠1 and ∠3 are vertical angles.

Prove: ∠1 ≅ ∠3

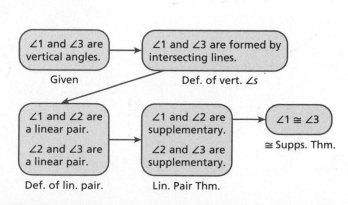

Key Vocabulary

angle *(ángulo)* A figure formed by two rays with a common endpoint.

biconditional statement *(enunciado bicondicional)* A statement that can be written in the form "*p* if and only if *q*."

conditional statement *(enunciado condicional)* A statement that can be written in the form "if *p*, then *q*," where *p* is the hypothesis and *q* is the conclusion.

conjecture *(conjetura)* A statement that is believed to be true.

counterexample *(contraejemplo)* An example that proves that a conjecture or statement is false.

deductive reasoning *(razonamiento deductivo)* The process of using logic to draw conclusions.

definition *(definición)* A statement that describes a mathematical object and can be written as a true biconditional statement.

equation *(ecuación)* A mathematical statement that two expressions are equivalent.

inductive reasoning *(razonamiento inductivo)* The process of reasoning that a rule or statement is true because specific cases are true.

linear pair *(par lineal)* A pair of adjacent angles whose noncommon sides are opposite rays.

opposite rays *(rayos opuestos)* Two rays that have a common endpoint and form a line.

postulate *(postulado)* A statement that is accepted as true without proof. Also called an axiom.

proof *(demostración)* An argument that uses logic to show that a conclusion is true.

supplementary angles *(ángulos suplementarios)* Two angles whose measures have a sum of 180°.

theorem *(teorema)* A statement that has been proven.

vertical angles *(ángulos opuestos por el vértice)* The nonadjacent angles formed by two intersecting lines.

2-1

Using Inductive Reasoning to Make Conjectures
Going Deeper

Essential question: *How can you use examples to support or disprove a conjecture?*

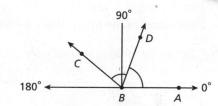

Video Tutor

PREP FOR CC.9–12.G.CO.9

1 EXPLORE **Making Conjectures about Bisectors of Obtuse Angles**

A Draw several obtuse angles. Recall that an obtuse angle is an angle whose measure is between 90° and 180°. One such angle, ∠ABC, is shown in the diagram. Ray $\overrightarrow{BD}$ shows the angle bisector of ∠ABC.

B Using a protractor, measure each angle. Record each measure for each drawing.

C Construct the angle bisector of each angle you drew. Record the measures of the two angles determined by the bisectors on your drawings.

D Fill in the table to record your work. Angle 1 is an example for you.

Angle	1	2	3	4	5	6
Measure	140°					
Measures of Angles Formed by Bisector	70°					
	70°					

REFLECT

1a. Based on your table, make a conjecture about the classification of the angles formed when you bisect an obtuse angle.

_____

_____

1b. Write a range of angle measures for each of the two angles formed by the angle bisector in each of your diagrams. Justify your range.

_____

_____

_____

2 EXPLORE Making Conjectures about Double Angles of Acute Angles

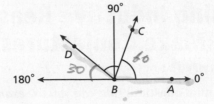

A Draw several acute angles. Recall that an acute angle measures between 0° and 90°. One such angle, ∠*ABC*, is shown in the diagram. Be sure to draw 30° and 60° angles as examples.

B Using a protractor, measure each angle. Record each measure on each angle drawing.

C Using angle construction, draw an adjacent angle for each original angle. In the diagram above, ∠*CBD* is the congruent adjacent angle. Record the measures of the original angles and the double angles on your drawings.

D Fill in the table to record your work. Angle 1 is an example for you.

Angle	1	2	3	4	5	6
Measure	70°					
Double Angle Measure	140°					

REFLECT

2a. Comment on the following conjecture: When an acute angle is copied so that the new angle is adjacent to the original angle, the resulting double angle is always obtuse.

False, could be an acute or right angle

2b. How many angles must you test in order to determine that the conjecture above is not always true?

at least 2

2c. For what angle measure will an angle along with its adjacent copy form neither an acute nor an obtuse angle? Explain.

When it's 45°

Additional Practice

In each figure, all possible diagonals are drawn from a single vertex. Use the figures in Exercises 1 and 2.

A   B   C   D

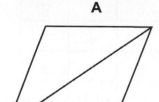 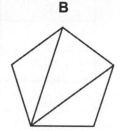 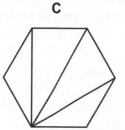 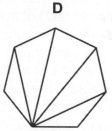

1. Fill in the table.

Figure	A	B	C	D
Number of sides	4	5	6	7
Number of triangles formed	2	3	4	5

2. Use inductive reasoning to make a conjecture about the number of triangles formed when all possible diagonals are drawn from one vertex of a polygon with *n* sides.

     the is 2 triangle less than the number of sides

Complete each conjecture.

3. The square of any negative number is ___positive___.

4. The number of segments determined by *n* points is _____.

Show that each conjecture is false by finding a counterexample.

5. For any integer n, $n^3 > 0$.

     False $-1^3 < 0$

6. Each angle in a right triangle has a different measure.

      False

7. For many years in the United States, each bank printed its own currency. The variety of different bills led to widespread counterfeiting. By the time of the Civil War, a significant fraction of the currency in circulation was counterfeit. If one Civil War soldier had 48 bills, 16 of which were counterfeit, and another soldier had 39 bills, 13 of which were counterfeit, make a conjecture about what fraction of bills were counterfeit at the time of the Civil War.

     $\frac{1}{3}$ is counterfeit

Problem Solving

1. Residents of an apartment complex were given use of plots of land in a community garden. Some of the plots were shaped like triangles. The lengths (in feet) of the three sides *a*, *b*, and *c* of some of the triangular plots are shown in the table. For each triangular plot, compare the sum of the lengths of any two sides to the length of the third side. Then use inductive reasoning to make a conjecture comparing the sum of the lengths of any two sides of a triangle to the length of the third side.

Triangle	a	b	c
D	6	8	10
E	9	6	5
F	5	7	5
G	10	15	9

Every one of the sum of any + 2 sides is bigger than the 3rd side.

The times for the first eight matches of the Santa Barbara Open women's volleyball tournament are shown. Show that each conjecture is false by finding a counterexample.

Match	1	2	3	4	5	6	7	8
Time	0:31	0:56	0:51	0:18	0:50	0:34	1:03	0:36

2. Every one of the first eight matches lasted less than 1 hour.

In match 7, it was 1:03

3. These matches were all longer than a half hour.

In match 4, it was 18 min

For each of the tiles shown, all of the angles have the same measure. Use a protractor to find the measure of the angles for each tile. Select the best answer.

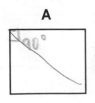 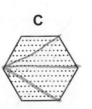

A   B   C

4. Which expressions could you use in the given order to complete the following statement: Figure ▢ has ▢ sides and the sum of the angle measures is ▢ × 180°.

   A B; 5; 3
   B A; 4; 4
   C C; 6; 3
   D A; 4; 3

   360
   75
   x°

5. Which is a reasonable conjecture?

   F The sum of the angle measures of a polygon with *n* sides is $(4n)°$.

   G The sum of the angle measures of a polygon with *n* sides is $n(360°)$.

   H The sum of the angle measures of a polygon with *n* sides is $(n - 2)(180°)$.

   J The sum of the angle measures of a polygon with *n* sides is $(n - 2)(360°)$.

Conditional Statements
Extension: Inference Using Venn Diagrams

Essential question: *How can you use a Venn diagram to interpret conditional statements?*

A conditional statement is one that has the form *If p, then q*, denoted $p \rightarrow q$. The notation $\sim p$ is used to denote "not *p*." You can use Venn diagrams to study conditionals.

Video Tutor

CC.MP.3

1 EXPLORE   **Using Venn Diagrams to Analyze Conditional Statements**

Shade the region in the Venn diagram that represents each statement. Part A is already filled in as an example.

All dogs are animals. If **an object is a dog**, then **it is an animal**.
                 p   *q*

A   *p*

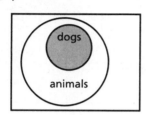

B   *q*

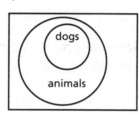

C $\sim p$

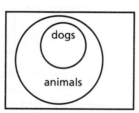

D $\sim q$

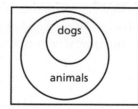

REFLECT

1a. If you know $p \rightarrow q$ and you also know *q* is true, then can you conclude that *p* is true or that *p* is false? Explain how the Venn diagram supports your answer.

can't conclude cause could be another animal

1b. If you know $p \rightarrow q$ and you also know *p* is false, then can you conclude that *q* is true or that *q* is false? Explain how the Venn diagram supports your answer.

can't conclude cause could be dog or not

1c. If you know $p \rightarrow q$ and you know $\sim q$, then what can you conclude?

It can't be a dog

Four Venn diagrams related to $q \rightarrow p$ are shown. Shade the region that represents each statement.

1. q

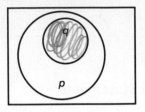

2. p

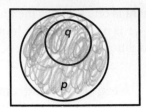

3. $\sim q$

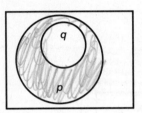

4. $\sim p$

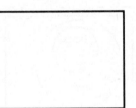

5. If you know $q \rightarrow p$, what other symbolic statement can you make? Explain.

_____

_____

6. In the box, draw a Venn diagram that conveys $p \rightarrow q$ and $q \rightarrow p$. Describe it. If both a conditional and its converse are true, what can you say about the inverse and contrapositive?

_____

_____

7. In the box, draw a Venn diagram that conveys $p \rightarrow q$ and $q \rightarrow r$. Describe it. Write at least two symbolic statements that you can infer using the diagram.

_____

_____

Additional Practice

Identify the hypothesis and conclusion of each conditional.

1. If you can see the stars, then it is night.

   Hypothesis: _If you see_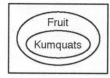

   Conclusion: _____

2. A pencil writes well if it is sharp.

   Hypothesis:_____

   Conclusion:_____

Write a conditional statement from each of the following.

3. Three noncollinear points determine a plane.

   If you have 3 NC points, then it is a plane

4. _____

   Fruit
   Kumquats

   If it a kumquat, it is a fruit

Determine if each conditional is true. If false, give a counterexample.

5. If two points are noncollinear, then a right triangle contains one obtuse angle.

   False

6. If a liquid is water, then it is composed of hydrogen and oxygen.

   true

7. If a living thing is green, then it is a plant.

   False

8. "If G is at 4, then GH is 3." Write the converse, inverse, and contrapositive of this statement. Find the truth value of each.

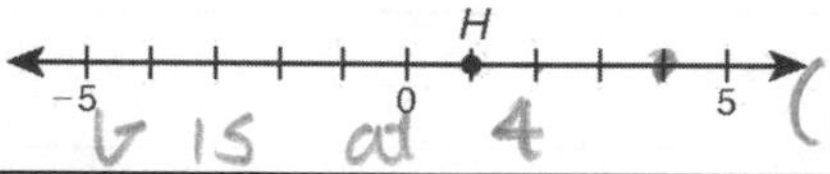

   Converse: _if GH is 3, then G is at 4_ 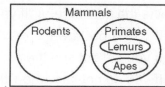 _(False)_

   Inverse: _____

   Contrapositive: _____

This chart shows a small part of the *Mammalia* class of animals, the mammals. Write a conditional to describe the relationship between each given pair.

Mammals
Rodents   Primates
          Lemurs
          Apes

9. primates and mammals _a primate is a mammal_

10. lemurs and rodents _they are both mammal_

11. rodents and apes _they are both mamals_

12. apes and mammals _an ape is an animal_

Problem Solving

1. Write the converse, inverse, and contrapositive of the conditional statement. Find the truth value of each.

   If it is April, then there are 30 days in the month.

   _____

   _____

   _____

2. Write a conditional statement from the diagram. Then write the converse, inverse, and contrapositive. Find the truth value of each.

   _____

   _____

   _____

   _____

   _____

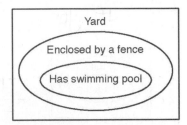

Use the table and the statements listed. Write each conditional and find its truth value.

p: 1777   *q*: 30 stars   *r*: after 1818   *s*: less than 50 stars

U.S. Flag	
Year	Number of Stars
1777	13
1818	20
1848	30
1959	50

3. $p \rightarrow q$_____

   _____

4. $r \rightarrow s$ _____

5. $q \rightarrow s$_____

Choose the best answer.

6. What is the converse of "If you saw the movie, then you know how it ends"?

   A If you know how the movie ends, then you saw the movie.

   B If you did not see the movie, then you do not know how it ends.

   C If you do not know how the movie ends, then you did not see the movie.

   D If you do not know how the movie ends, then you saw the movie.

7. What is the inverse of "If you received a text message, then you have a cell phone"?

   F If you have a cell phone, then you received a text message.

   G If you do not have a cell phone, then you did not receive a text message.

   H If you did not receive a text message, then you do not have a cell phone.

   J If you received a text message, then you do not have a cell phone.

Using Deductive Reasoning to Verify Conjectures
Going Deeper

Essential question: *How can you connect statements to visualize a chain of reasoning?*

Deductive reasoning connects true statements to form a valid conclusion. This process can be represented visually by using arrows to show how one true statement follows from a previous true statement. Such a diagram shows the sequence used to link given statements to a final conclusion.

Video Tutor

CC.MP.3

1 EXAMPLE Showing Logical Reasoning

Draw arrows to show the logical reasoning used to prove the statement. Some arrows are already drawn to help you.

A **Given:** m, and the conditional statements in the boxes

Prove: c

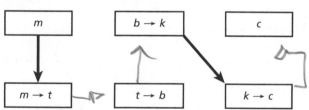

B **Given:** c, d, and the conditional statements in the boxes

Prove: z

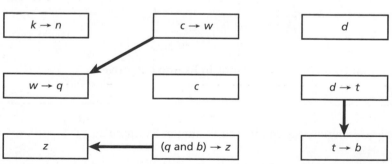

REFLECT

1a. Write a symbolic statement that the chain of reasoning in each part proves.

Part A:_____   Part B:_____

1b. In a chain of reasoning, what do you call the statements that have arrows only pointing *away* from them? What do you call the statements that have arrows only pointing *toward* them?

_____

© Houghton Mifflin Harcourt Publishing Company

1c. Are there any statements in Part B that are not used in the chain of reasoning? Explain.

_____

1d. In the space below, arrange the statements from Part B and draw arrows connecting them in a way that makes the order of the reasoning clearer.

2 EXAMPLE Completing a Chain of Logical Reasoning

Draw arrows to show the logical reasoning used to prove the statement. Provide any missing information.

Given: k, and the conditional statements in the boxes

Prove: b

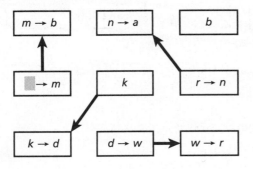

REFLECT

2a. Write a symbolic statement that your chain of reasoning in Example 2 proves.

_____

2b. Is there more than one way to complete the chain of reasoning in Example 2? Explain.

_____

_____

2c. In Example 2, suppose the box with the missing information is completely blank. Is there more than one way to complete the chain of reasoning? Explain.

_____

_____

Draw arrows to show the logical reasoning used to prove the statement.

1. Given: *z*, and statements in boxes

   Prove: *c*

| c | a → p | z → m |

| p → c | m → a | z |

2. Given: *j*, and statements in boxes

   Prove: *x*

| b → k | w → b | j → w |

| k → x | j | x |

3. Given: *t*, *y*, and statements in boxes

   Prove: *q*

| q | y | t → d |

| y → k | n → s | t |

| (s and k) → q | d → n |

4. Given: *h*, *m*, and statements in boxes

   Prove: *r*

| r | (p and z) → r |

| m → p | b → z | h |

| m | g → w | h → b |

Draw arrows to show the logical reasoning used to prove the statement. Provide any missing information.

5. Given: *b*, and statements in boxes

   Prove: *e*

| j → n | n → f | e |

| s → j | b → r | ▨ → x |

| r → s | b | x → e |

6. Given: *g*, and statements in boxes

   Prove: *a*

| e → t | k → d | t → ▨ |

| g | c → e | n → a |

| g → c | a | m → z |

7. Write a symbolic statement for each conditional statement. Then represent the chain of reasoning using symbolic statements linked by arrows.

Band members must stay after school on Wednesday.

If the marching band performs at halftime, then the band practices on Wednesday.

If the band practices on Wednesday, then band members must stay after school on Wednesday.

If there is a football game on Friday, then the marching band performs at halftime.

There is a football game on Friday.

Additional Practice

Draw arrows to show the logical reasoning used to prove the statement.

1. **Given:** y, and statements in boxes.
   Prove: a

$y \rightarrow t$	a	$p \rightarrow a$

$t \rightarrow z$	y	$z \rightarrow p$

2. **Given:** m, and statements in boxes.
   Prove: j

m	$n \rightarrow j$	$k \rightarrow n$

$z \rightarrow k$	$m \rightarrow z$	j

3. **Given:** h, q, and statements in boxes.
   Prove: f

$r \rightarrow u$	$h \rightarrow n$	h

$u \rightarrow j$	$(n \text{ and } x) \rightarrow f$	f

$q \rightarrow r$	$j \rightarrow x$	q

4. **Given:** b, y, and statements in boxes.
   Prove: j

j	$z \rightarrow k$	$(x \text{ and } n) \rightarrow j$

$t \rightarrow z$	y	$k \rightarrow n$

$y \rightarrow t$	b	$b \rightarrow x$

Draw arrows to show the logical reasoning used to prove the statement. Provide any missing information.

5. **Given:** a, and statements in boxes.
   Prove: w

$u \rightarrow q$	q	$c \rightarrow i$

w	$ \rightarrow c$	$i \rightarrow k$

$e \rightarrow u$	$k \rightarrow w$	$a \rightarrow e$

6. **Given:** a, and statements in boxes.
   Prove: z

$s \rightarrow k$	$(x \text{ and } k) \rightarrow z$	$v \rightarrow s$

z	x	$a \rightarrow $

$g \rightarrow x$	a	g

Problem Solving

Write a symbolic statement for each conditional statement. Then represent the chain of reasoning using symbolic statements linked by arrows.

1. Paloma can drive her parents' car.   _____

   Paloma passes her road test.   _____

   Paloma is covered by her parents' motor vehicle insurance.   _____

   If Paloma passes her road test, then she will get her driver's
   license.   _____

   If Paloma has a driver's license and is covered by insurance, then
   she can drive her parents car.   _____

Given *t* and *z*, and the conditional statements in the boxes shown, Jeremy drew arrows to complete the chain of reasoning. Select the best answer.

2. Which statement can you *not* assume to be true from the chain of reasoning?

   A $t \to w$

   B $t \to n$

   C $z \to y$

   D $(n \text{ and } y) \to w$

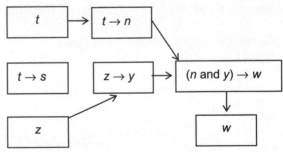

3. Which symbolic statement did Jeremy prove?

   F $t \to n \to w$

   G $z \to (y \text{ and } w)$

   H $(t \text{ and } z) \to w$

   J $(n \text{ and } y) \to w$

4. Which statement is *not* necessary in the chain of reasoning?

   A $t \to n$

   B $t \to s$

   C z

   D $z \to y$

Biconditional Statements and Definitions
Going Deeper

Essential question: *How can you analyze the truth of a biconditional statement?*

You have seen *If p, then q* and the notation $p \rightarrow q$. The notation **iff** is shorthand for *if and only if* and means a pair of statements.

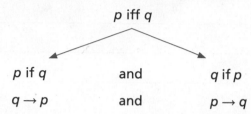

p iff q

p if q   and   q if p

q → p   and   p → q

The conjunction of these two statements is a biconditional statement. It is true only if both parts are true. It is false if either part is false.

CC.MP.3
1 EXAMPLE   Analyzing Biconditionals and Definitions

A student defined *square* this way:

A polygon is a square if and only if it has four right angles.

A Write the biconditional as a pair of conditional statements.

If a polygon _____is a square_____, then the polygon has four right angles.

If a polygon _____has 4 right angles_____, then the polygon is a square.

B Analyze each part and tell whether it is true or false. If false, give a counterexample. Explain your thinking.

square → four right angles

_____True_____

four right angles → square

_____False, could be a rectangle_____

C Tell whether the student's definition of square is a good one. Explain.

_____It was not good_____

1a. Why is it necessary to prove only one of the two parts of a biconditional is false to conclude that the biconditional is false?

_____

_____

1b. Revise the student's definition of a square so that it is a good one.

_____

_____

_____

PRACTICE

1. A student defined a scalene triangle as follows: A triangle is scalene if and only if it is a right triangle. Is the biconditional true or false? Justify your claim.

_____

_____

_____

2. A student defined a rectangle as a parallelogram with opposite sides the same length. Describe what is wrong with this definition. Then write a correct definition of a rectangle.

_____

_____

_____

3. An acute triangle is a triangle whose angles are acute. Find the error in the following statement.

A triangle is acute if and only if it has one or more acute angles.

_____

_____

_____

_____

Additional Practice

Write the conditional statement and converse within each biconditional.

1. The tea kettle is whistling if and only if the water is boiling.

   Conditional: _If the tea kettle is whistling, then the water is boiling_

   Converse: _____

2. A biconditional is true if and only if the conditional and converse are both true.

   Conditional: _If the biconditional is true, then the conditional and converse are both true_

   Converse: _____

For each conditional, write the converse and a biconditional statement.

3. Conditional: If n is an odd number, then $n - 1$ is divisible by 2.

   Converse: _____

   Biconditional: _If $n - 1$ is divisible by 2, then n is an odd number_

4. Conditional: An angle is obtuse when it measures between 90° and 180°.

   Converse: _____

   Biconditional: _If an angle measures between 90° and 180°, it is an obtuse angle._

Determine whether a true biconditional can be written from each conditional statement. If not, give a counterexample.

5. If the lamp is unplugged, then the bulb does not shine.

   counter ex.
   The lamp can be plugged and the power could be off

6. The date can be the 29th if and only if it is not February.

   It can be written.

Write each definition as a biconditional.

7. A cube is a three-dimensional solid with six square faces.

   If it is a three-dimensional solid with 6 square faces, then it is a cube

8. Tanya claims that the definition of *doofus* is "her younger brother."

   If the definition is her younger brother, then the word is doofus.

Problem Solving

Use the table for Exercises 1–4. Determine if a true biconditional statement can be written from each conditional. If so, then write a biconditional. If not, then explain why not.

Mountain Bike Races	Characteristics
Cross-country	A massed-start race. Riders must carry their own tools to make repairs.
Downhill	Riders start at intervals. The rider with the lowest time wins.
Freeride	Courses contain cliffs, drops, and ramps. Scoring depends on the style and the time.
Marathon	A massed-start race that covers more than 250 kilometers.

1. If a mountain bike race is mass-started, then it is a cross-country race.

_____

_____

_____

2. If a mountain bike race is downhill, then time is a factor in who wins.

_____

_____

_____

3. If a mountain bike race covers more than 250 kilometers, then it is a marathon race.

_____

_____

_____

4. If a race course contains cliffs, drops, and ramps, then it is not a marathon race.

_____

_____

_____

Choose the best answer.

5. The cat is the only species that can hold its tail vertically while it walks.

   A The converse of this statement is false.

   B The biconditional of this statement is false.

   C The biconditional of this statement is true.

   D This statement cannot be written as a biconditional.

6. Which conditional statement can be used to write a true biconditional?

   F If you travel 2 miles in 4 minutes, then distance is a function of time.

   G If the distance depends on the time, then distance is a function of time.

   H If y increases as x increases, then y is a function of x.

   J If y is not a function of x, then y does not increase as x increases.

Algebraic Proof
Going Deeper

Essential question: *What kinds of justifications can you use in writing algebraic and geometric proofs?*

PREP FOR CC.9–12.G.CO.9

1 ENGAGE   Introducing Proofs

In mathematics, a **proof** is a logical argument that uses a sequence of statements to prove a conjecture. Once the conjecture is proved, it is called a **theorem**.

Each statement in a proof must follow logically from what has come before and must have a reason to support it. The reason may be a piece of given information, a definition, a previously proven theorem, or a mathematical property.

The table states some properties of equality that you have seen in earlier courses. You have used these properties to solve algebraic equations and you will often use these properties as reasons in a proof.

Properties of Equality	
Addition Property of Equality	If $a = b$, then $a + c = b + c$.
Subtraction Property of Equality	If $a = b$, then $a - c = b - c$.
Multiplication Property of Equality	If $a = b$, then $ac = bc$.
Division Property of Equality	If $a = b$ and $c \neq 0$, then $\frac{a}{c} = \frac{b}{c}$.
Reflexive Property of Equality	$a = a$
Symmetric Property of Equality	If $a = b$, then $b = a$.
Transitive Property of Equality	If $a = b$ and $b = c$, then $a = c$.
Substitution Property of Equality	If $a = b$, then b can be substituted for a in any expression.

REFLECT

1a. Given the equation $3 = x - 2$, you quickly write the solution as $x = 5$. Which property or properties of equality are you using? Explain.

_____ APOE _____

_____

1b. Give an example of an equation that you can solve using the Division Property of Equality. Explain how you would use this property to solve the equation.

_____ $4x = 16 \;\to\; x = 4$ _____

_____

A **postulate** (or *axiom*) is a statement that is accepted as true without proof. Like undefined terms, postulates are basic building blocks of geometry. The following postulate states that the lengths of segments "add up" in a natural way.

Segment Addition Postulate

If B is between A and C, then
$AB + BC = AC$.

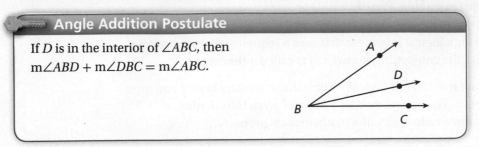

The Angle Addition Postulate is similar to the Segment Addition Postulate.

Angle Addition Postulate

If D is in the interior of $\angle ABC$, then
$m\angle ABD + m\angle DBC = m\angle ABC$.

Properties of equality and postulates can be used as reasons in proofs. Note how the proof shown below in Exercise 1 is arranged in a two-column format so that it is easy to see the logical sequence of the statements and their corresponding reasons.

PRACTICE

1. If A, B, C, and D are collinear, as shown in the figure, with $AC = BD$, then $AB = CD$. Complete the proof by writing the missing statements or reasons.

   Given: $AC = BD$
   Prove: $AB = CD$

Statements	Reasons
1. $AC = BD$, AB	1. Given
2. $AC = AB + BC$; $BD = BC + CD$	2. SAP
3. $AB - BC = CD - BC$	3. Substitution Property of Equality
4. $AB = CD$	4. SPAE

2. In the figure, X is the midpoint of $\overline{WY}$, and Y is the midpoint of $\overline{XZ}$. Explain how to prove $WX = YZ$.

_____

_____

Additional Practice

Solve each equation. Show all your steps and write a justification for each step.

1. $\frac{1}{5}(a + 10) = -3$

2. $t + 6.5 = 3t - 1.3$

3. The formula for the perimeter P of a rectangle with length ℓ and width w is $P = 2(\ell + w)$. Find the length of the rectangle shown here if the perimeter is $9\frac{1}{2}$ feet.

   Solve the equation for ℓ and justify each step.

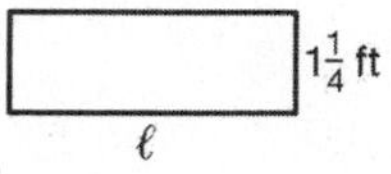

$1\frac{1}{4}$ ft

ℓ

Write a justification for each step.

4.

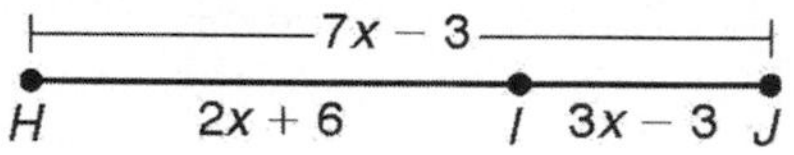

$\begin{array}{c} \vdash\quad 7x - 3 \quad\dashv \\ H \quad 2x + 6 \quad I \quad 3x - 3 \quad J \end{array}$

$HJ = HI + IJ$ _____

$7x - 3 = (2x + 6) + (3x - 3)$ _____

$7x - 3 = 5x + 3$ _____

$7x = 5x + 6$ _____

$2x = 6$ _____

$x = 3$ _____

Identify the property that justifies each statement.

5. $m = n$, so $n = m$.

6. $\angle ABC \cong \angle ABC$

_____

7. $\overline{KL} \cong \overline{LK}$

_____

8. $p = q$ and $q = -1$, so $p = -1$.

_____

Problem Solving

1. Because of a recent computer glitch, an airline mistakenly sold tickets for round-trip flights at a discounted price. The equation $n(p + t) = 3298.75$ relates the number of discounted tickets sold n, the price of each ticket p, and the tax per ticket t. What was the discounted price of each ticket if 1015 tickets were sold and the tax per ticket was $1.39? Solve the equation for p. Justify each step.

2. The equation $C = 7.25s + 15.95a$ describes the total cost of admission C to the aquarium. How many student tickets were sold if the total cost for the entire class and 6 adults was $298.70? Solve the equation for s. Justify each step.

> s = number of student tickets
>
> a = number of adult tickets
>
> C = total cost of admission

Refer to the figure. Choose the best answer.

3. Which could be used to find the value of x?

    A Segment Addition Postulate

    B Angle Addition Postulate

    C Transitive Property of Congruence

    D Definition of supplementary angles

4. What is $m\angle SQR$?

    F 28°   H 61°

    G 29°   J 62°

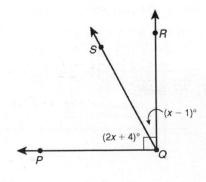

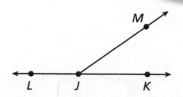

2-6

Geometric Proof
Going Deeper

Essential question: *How can you organize the deductive reasoning of a geometric proof?*

You will use the Angle Addition Postulate and the following definitions to prove an important theorem about angles.

Opposite rays are two rays that have a common endpoint and form a straight line. A **linear pair** of angles is a pair of adjacent angles whose noncommon sides are opposite rays.

In the figure, $\overrightarrow{JK}$ and $\overrightarrow{JL}$ are opposite rays; $\angle MJK$ and $\angle MJL$ are a linear pair of angles.

Recall that two angles are *complementary* if the sum of their measures is 90°. Two angles are *supplementary* if the sum of their measures is 180°. The following theorem ties together some of the preceding ideas.

CC.9–12.G.CO.9

1 PROOF   **Linear Pair Theorem**

If two angles form a linear pair, then they are supplementary.

Given: $\angle MJK$ and $\angle MJL$ are a linear pair of angles.
Prove: $\angle MJK$ and $\angle MJL$ are supplementary.

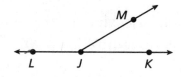

A   Develop a plan for the proof.

Since it is given that $\angle MJK$ and $\angle MJL$ are a linear pair of angles, $\overrightarrow{JL}$ and $\overrightarrow{JK}$ are opposite rays. They form a straight angle. Explain why $m\angle MJK + m\angle MJL$ must equal 180°.

_____

B   Complete the proof by writing the missing reasons. Choose from the following reasons.

Angle Addition Postulate	Definition of opposite rays
Substitution Property of Equality	Given

Statements	Reasons
1. $\angle MJK$ and $\angle MJL$ are a linear pair.	1. Given
2. $\overrightarrow{JL}$ and $\overrightarrow{JK}$ are opposite rays.	2. Definition of linear pair
3. $\overrightarrow{JL}$ and $\overrightarrow{JK}$ form a straight line.	3. DOOR
4. $m\angle LJK = 180°$	4. Definition of straight angle
5. $m\angle MJK + m\angle MJL = m\angle LJK$	5. AAP
6. $m\angle MJK + m\angle MJL = 180°$	6. SPOE
7. $\angle MJK$ and $\angle MJL$ are supplementary.	7. Definition of supplementary angles

© Houghton Mifflin Harcourt Publishing Company

1a. Is it possible to prove the theorem by measuring $\angle MJK$ and $\angle MJL$ in the figure and showing that the sum of the angle measures is 180°? Explain.

Yes because it would add up to 180

1b. The proof shows that if two angles form a linear pair, then they are supplementary. Is this statement true in the other direction? That is, if two angles are supplementary, must they be a linear pair? Why or why not?

Yes if it adds up to 180°, it is a straight line

PRACTICE

1. You can use the Linear Pair Theorem to prove a result about vertical angles. Complete the proof by writing the missing statements or reasons.

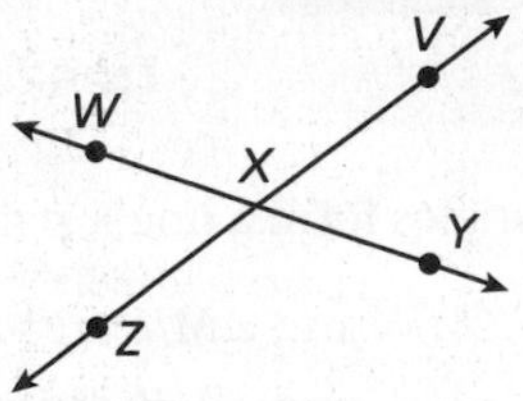

Given: $\angle VXW$ and $\angle ZXY$ are vertical angles, as shown.

Prove: $m\angle VXW = m\angle ZXY$

Statements	Reasons
1. $\angle VXW$ and $\angle ZXY$ are vertical angles.	1. *Given*
2. $\angle VXW$ and $\angle ZXY$ are formed by intersecting lines.	2. Definition of vertical angles
3. $\angle VXW$ and $\angle WXZ$ are a linear pair. $\angle WXZ$ and $\angle ZXY$ are a linear pair.	3. Definition of linear pair
4. $\angle VXW$ and $\angle WXZ$ are supplementary.	4. *DOSA*
5. $m\angle VXW + m\angle WXZ = 180°$	5. *Substitusion*
6.	6. Linear Pair Theorem
7. *$\angle WXY = \angle ZXV$*	7. Definition of supplementary angles
8. $m\angle VXW + m\angle WXZ = m\angle WXZ + m\angle ZXY$	8. Transitive Property of Equality
9. $m\angle VXW = m\angle ZXY$	9. *Subtraction*

Additional Practice

Write a justification for each step.

Given: $AB = EF$, B is the midpoint of $\overline{AC}$,
and E is the midpoint of $\overline{DF}$.

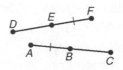

1. B is the midpoint of $\overline{AC}$,
   and E is the midpoint of $\overline{DF}$. _____

2. $\overline{AB} \cong \overline{BC}$, and $\overline{DE} \cong \overline{EF}$. _____

3. $AB = BC$, and $DE = EF$. _____

4. $AB + BC = AC$, and $DE + EF = DF$. _____

5. $2AB = AC$, and $2EF = DF$. _____

6. $AB = EF$ _____

7. $2AB = 2EF$ _____

8. $AC = DF$ _____

9. $\overline{AC} \cong \overline{DF}$ _____

Fill in the blanks to complete the two-column proof.

10. **Given:** $\angle HKJ$ is a straight angle.
    $\overline{KI}$ bisects $\angle HKJ$.
    Prove: $\angle IKJ$ is a right angle.

Proof:

Statements	Reasons
1. a._____	1. Given
2. $m\angle HKJ = 180°$	2. b._____
3. c._____	3. Given
4. $\angle IKJ \cong \angle IKH$	4. Def. of $\angle$ bisector
5. $m\angle IKJ = m\angle IKH$	5. Def. of $\cong$ $\angle$s
6. d._____	6. $\angle$ Add. Post.
7. $2m\angle IKJ = 180°$	7. e. Subst. (Steps _____)
8. $m\angle IKJ = 90°$	8. Div. Prop. of $=$
9. $\angle IKJ$ is a right angle.	9. f._____

Problem Solving

1. Refer to the diagram of the stained-glass window and use the given plan to write a two-column proof.

   Given: ∠1 and ∠3 are supplementary.
   ∠2 and ∠4 are supplementary.
   ∠3 ≅ ∠4

   Prove: ∠1 ≅ ∠2

   Plan: Use the definition of supplementary angles to write the given information in terms of angle measures. Then use the Substitution Property of Equality and the Subtraction Property of Equality to conclude that ∠1 ≅ ∠2.

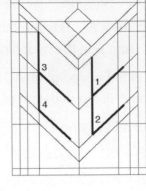

The position of a sprinter at the starting blocks is shown in the diagram. Which statement can be proved using the given information? Choose the best answer.

2. **Given:** ∠1 and ∠4 are right angles.

   A ∠3 ≅ ∠5   C m∠1 + m∠4 = 90°

   B ∠1 ≅ ∠4   D m∠3 + m∠5 = 180°

3. **Given:** ∠2 and ∠3 are supplementary.
   ∠2 and ∠5 are supplementary.

   F ∠3 ≅ ∠5   H ∠3 and ∠5 are complementary.

   G ∠2 ≅ ∠5   J ∠1 and ∠2 are supplementary.

Flowchart and Paragraph Proofs
Going Deeper

Essential question: *What are some formats you can use to organize geometric proofs?*

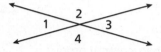

Video Tutor

CC.9–12.G.CO.9

1 PROOF **Vertical Angles Theorem**

If two angles are vertical angles, then they have equal measures.

Given: ∠1 and ∠3 are vertical angles.
Prove: m∠1 = m∠3

A Develop a plan for the proof.

Since ∠1 and ∠2 are a linear pair, and ∠2 and ∠3 are a linear pair, these pairs of angles are supplementary. This means m∠1 + m∠2 = 180° and m∠2 + m∠3 = 180°. By substitution, m∠1 + m∠2 = m∠2 + m∠3. What is the final step in the plan?

_____

B Complete a flowchart proof of the Vertical Angles Theorem by supplying the missing statements and reasons.

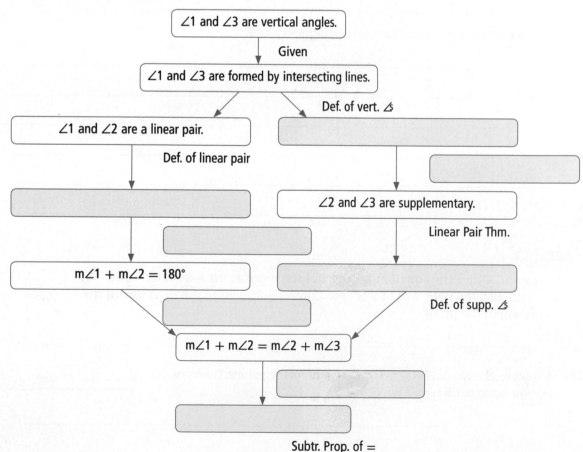

REFLECT

1a. Explain how to find m∠1, m∠2, and m∠3 in the figure.

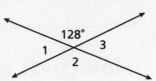

_____

_____

CC.9–12.G.CO.9

2 PROOF   Common Segments Theorem

If *A*, *B*, *C*, and *D* are collinear, as shown in the figure, with $AB = CD$, then $AC = BD$.

Given: $AB = CD$
Prove: $AC = BD$

A   Complete the two-column proof.

Statements	Reasons
1. $AB = CD$	1.
2. $BC = BC$	2.
3. $AB + BC = BC + CD$	3.
4. $AB + BC = AC;\ BC + CD = BD$	4.
5. $AC = BD$	5.

B   Use the two-column proof to write a paragraph proof.

_____

_____

_____

_____

_____

_____

REFLECT

2a. A student writes the equation in Step 3 of the proof as $AB + BC = CD + BC$. Explain why the right side of this equation is equivalent to the right side of the equation in the proof.

_____

2b. A student claims that $PR = QS$ by the Common Segments Theorem. Do you agree or disagree? Why?

_____

_____

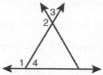

Additional Practice

1. Use the given two-column proof to write a flowchart proof.

    Given: $\angle 4 \cong \angle 3$

    Prove: $m\angle 1 = m\angle 2$

Statements	Reasons
1. $\angle 1$ and $\angle 4$ are supplementary, $\angle 2$ and $\angle 3$ are supplementary.	1. Linear Pair Thm.
2. $\angle 4 \cong \angle 3$	2. Given
3. $\angle 1 \cong \angle 2$	3. $\cong$ Supps. Thm.
4. $m\angle 1 = m\angle 2$	4. Def. of $\cong$ $\angle$s

2. Use the given two-column proof to write a paragraph proof.

    Given: $AB = CD$, $BC = DE$

    Prove: C is the midpoint of $\overline{AE}$.

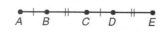

Statements	Reasons
1. $AB = CD$, $BC = DE$	1. Given .
2. $AB + BC = CD + DE$	2. Add. Prop. of $=$
3. $AB + BC = AC$, $CD + DE = CE$	3. Seg. Add. Post.
4. $AC = CE$	4. Subst.
5. $\overline{AC} \cong \overline{CE}$	5. Def. of $\cong$ segs.
6. C is the midpoint of $\overline{AE}$.	6. Def. of mdpt.

_____

_____

_____

_____

_____

Problem Solving

The diagram shows the second-floor glass railing at a mall.

1. Use the given two-column proof to write a flowchart proof.

   Given: ∠2 and ∠3 are supplementary.

   Prove: ∠1 and ∠3 are supplementary.

   Two-Column Proof:

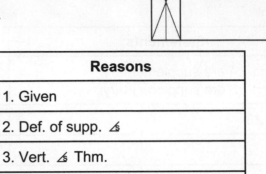

Statements	Reasons
1. ∠2 and ∠3 are supplementary.	1. Given
2. m∠2 + m∠3 = 180°	2. Def. of supp. ∡
3. ∠2 ≅ ∠1	3. Vert. ∡ Thm.
4. m∠2 = m∠1	4. Def. of ≅ ∡
5. m∠1 + m∠3 = 180°	5. Subst.
6. ∠1 and ∠3 are supplementary.	6. Def. of supp. ∡

Choose the best answer.

2. Which would NOT be included in a paragraph proof of the two-column proof above?

   A Since ∠2 and ∠3 are supplementary, m∠2 = m∠3.

   B ∠2 ≅ ∠1 by the Vertical Angles Theorem.

   C Using substitution, m∠1 + m∠3 = 180°.

   D m∠2 = m∠1 by the definition of congruent angles.

Performance Tasks

⭐ **1.** In the figure, $\overleftrightarrow{PQ}$ bisects $\angle RST$. Part of the proof that $\angle RSP \cong \angle TSP$ is provided below. Write the correct statement for each reason.

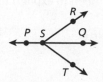

1. Given

2. Definition of angle bisector

3. Linear pairs are supplementary.

4. Linear pairs are supplementary.

5. Supplements of congruent angles are congruent.

⭐ **2.** In the figure, $\angle AKD \cong \angle B$ and $\angle BKC \cong \angle D$. The statements for proving that $\angle B \cong \angle D$ are provided. Write the correct reason for each statement.

1. $\angle AKD \cong \angle B$

2. $\angle BKC \cong \angle D$

3. $\angle AKD \cong \angle BKC$

4. $\angle B \cong \angle D$

3. Given: $\overleftrightarrow{MN}$ and $\overleftrightarrow{GH}$ intersect at R and are not perpendicular.
Prove: One pair of vertical angles is obtuse and the other pair is acute.

a. Draw and label a diagram that represents the given information.

b. Explain why each linear pair has one acute angle and one obtuse angle.

c. What do you still need to explain to complete the proof?

4. Given: $\overleftrightarrow{HC}$ bisects $\angle BHD$, m$\angle CHD = x°$.
Prove: m$\angle AHB = (180 - 2x)°$

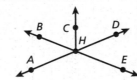

Name _____ Class _____ Date _____

MULTIPLE CHOICE

1. Show that the conjecture is false by finding a counterexample.

   Conjecture: If $a > b$, then $\frac{a}{b} > 0$.

   A. $a = 11, b = -3$

   B. $a = 11, b = 3$

   C. $a = 3, b = 11$

   D. $a = -11, b = 3$

2. There is a myth that a duck's quack does not echo. A group of scientists observed a duck in a special room, and they found that the quack does echo. Therefore, the myth is false.

   Is the conclusion a result of inductive or deductive reasoning?

   F. Since the conclusion is based on a pattern of observation, it is a result of inductive reasoning.

   G. Since the conclusion is based on a pattern of observation, it is a result of deductive reasoning.

   H. Since the conclusion is based on logical reasoning from scientific research, it is a result of inductive reasoning.

   J. Since the conclusion is based on logical reasoning from scientific research, it is a result of deductive reasoning.

3. Let x be an integer from 1 to 6. Make a table of values for the rule $x^2 - 16x + 64$. Make a conjecture about the type of number generated by the rule. Continue your table. What value of x generates a counterexample?

   A. The pattern appears to be a decreasing set of perfect squares.

   $x = 9$ generates a counterexample.

   B. The pattern appears to be a decreasing set of prime numbers.

   $x = 8$ generates a counterexample.

   C. The pattern appears to be a decreasing set of perfect squares.

   $x = 7$ generates a counterexample.

   D. The pattern appears to be an increasing set of perfect squares.

   $x = 8$ generates a counterexample.

4. What are the missing reasons that justify the solution of the equation $4x - 6 = 34$?

$4x - 6 = 34$	Given equation
$\underline{+6 \quad +6}$	[1]
$4x = 40$	Simplify.
$\frac{4x}{4} = \frac{40}{4}$	[2]
$x = 10$	Simplify.

   F. [1] Substitution Property of Equality; [2] Division Property of Equality

   G. [1] Addition Property of Equality; [2] Division Property of Equality

   H. [1] Division Property of Equality; [2] Subtraction Property of Equality

   J. [1] Addition Property of Equality; [2] Reflexive Property of Equality

5. Steps 2 and 3 can be justified with the same reason. What is that reason?

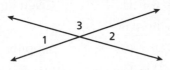

Statements	Reasons
1. $EG = FH$	1. Given
2. $EG = EF + FG$	2. ?
3. $FH = FG + GH$	3. ?
4. $EF + FG = FG + GH$	4. Substitution Prop. of =
5. $EG = FH$	5. Substitution Prop. of =

  A. Substitution Property of Equality

  B. Addition Property of Equality

  C. Segment Addition Postulate

  D. Angle Addition Postulate

6. Alberto is proving that vertical angles have the same measure. He begins as shown below. Which reason should he use for Step 3?

Given: $\angle 1$ and $\angle 2$ are vertical angles.
Prove: $m\angle 1 = m\angle 2$

Statements	Reasons
1. $\angle 1$ and $\angle 2$ are vertical angles.	1. Given
2. $\angle 1$ and $\angle 3$ are a linear pair.	2. Definition of linear pair
3. $\angle 1$ and $\angle 3$ are supplementary.	3. ?

  F. Definition of supplementary angles

  G. Definition of vertical angles

  H. Vertical Angles Theorem

  J. Linear Pair Theorem

CONSTRUCTED RESPONSE

7. A gardener has 54 feet of fencing for a garden. To find the width of the rectangular garden, the gardener uses the formula $P = 2l + 2w$, where P is the perimeter, l is the length, and w is the width of the rectangle. The gardener wants to fence a garden that is 15 feet long. How wide is the garden? Solve the equation for w, and justify each step.

_____

_____

_____

_____

_____

_____

_____

_____

8 Find the value of x and justify each step, given that $m\angle JKL = 100°$.

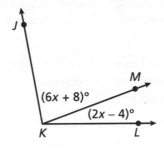

_____

_____

_____

_____

_____

_____

_____

Parallel and Perpendicular Lines

Chapter Focus

In this unit, you will explore the angles that are formed when lines intersect in a plane and how those angles are related when two parallel lines are intersected by another line. You will also study slopes of lines in the coordinate plane in order to determine whether they are parallel or perpendicular. Finally, you will write the equation of a line that is parallel or perpendicular to a given line and passes through a given point.

COMMON
CORE

Chapter at a Glance

Lesson		Standards for Mathematical Content
3-1	Lines and Angles	Prep for CC.9-12.G.CO.9
3-2	Angles Formed by Parallel Lines and Transversals	CC.9-12.G.CO.9
3-3	Proving Lines Parallel	CC.9-12.G.CO.12
3-4	Perpendicular Lines	CC.9-12.G.CO.9, CC.9-12.G.CO.12
3-5	Slopes of Lines	CC.9-12.G.GPE.6
3-6	Lines in the Coordinate Plane	CC.9-12.G.GPE.5
	Performance Tasks	
	Assessment Readiness	

CHAPTER 3

Unpacking the Standards

Understanding the standards and the vocabulary terms in the standards will help you know exactly what you are expected to learn in this chapter.

COMMON CORE CC.9-12.G.CO.1

Know precise definitions of … perpendicular line, parallel line, …

Key Vocabulary

perpendicular lines *(líneas perpendiculars)* Lines that intersect at 90° angles.

parallel lines *(líneas paralelas)* Lines in the same plane that do not intersect.

What It Means For You   Lessons 3-3, 3-4

Parallel and perpendicular lines form the building blocks not only of the real world, but also of the mathematical study of lines and angles.

EXAMPLE

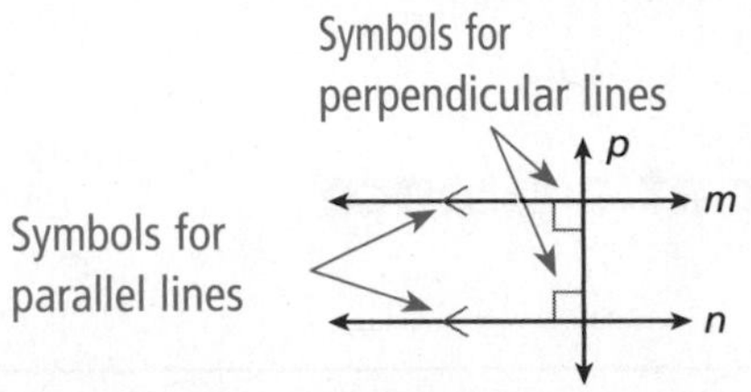

Symbols for perpendicular lines

Symbols for parallel lines

Line m is parallel to line n: $m \parallel n$

Line m is perpendicular to line p: $m \perp p$

Line n is perpendicular to line p: $n \perp p$

COMMON CORE CC.9-12.G.CO.9

Prove theorems about lines and angles.

Key Vocabulary

proof *(demostración)* An argument that uses logic to show that a conclusion is true.

theorem *(teorema)* A statement that has been proven.

line *(línea)* An undefined term in geometry, a line is a straight path that has no thickness and extends forever.

angle *(ángulo)* A figure formed by two rays with a common endpoint.

What It Means For You   Lessons 3-2, 3-3, 3-4

A line crossing a pair of parallel lines forms pairs of angles that are either congruent or supplementary. You can use simple proofs to show these relationships.

EXAMPLE

In the diagram, line p is parallel to line q.

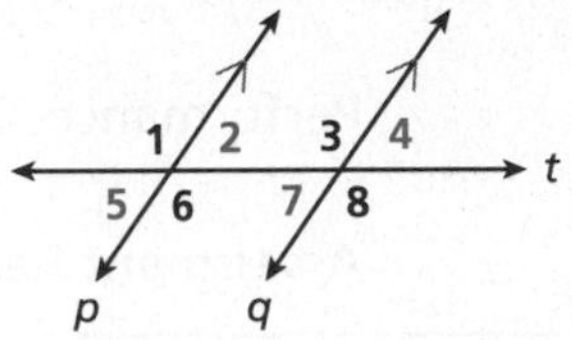

You can show that:

(1) Any pair of black numbered angles is a pair of congruent angles.

(2) Any pair of blue numbered angles is a pair of congruent angles.

(3) Any pair of one black and one blue numbered angle is a pair of supplementary angles.

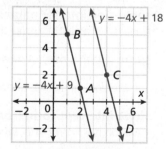

COMMON CORE CC.9-12.G.MG.1

Use geometric shapes, their measures, and their properties to describe objects…

What It Means For You Lessons 3-1, 3-3

Once you have established a few geometric principles, you can use them to recognize real-world relationships among objects.

EXAMPLE

A sandbar runs parallel to the shoreline.

Water is pushed up near the shore by the wind and waves.

Some of the water breaks back out through the sandbar toward open water, flowing perpendicularly to the sandbar.

Because the rip current is perpendicular to the sandbar, it is also perpendicular to the shoreline.

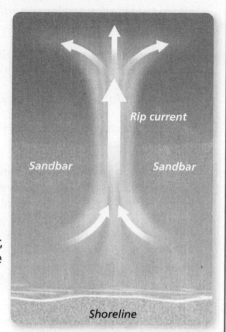

Rip current

Sandbar Sandbar

Shoreline

COMMON CORE CC.9-12.G.GPE.5

Prove the slope criteria for parallel and perpendicular lines and use them to solve geometric problems (e.g., find the equation of a line parallel or perpendicular to a given line that passes through a given point).

Key Vocabulary

slope (*pendiente*) A measure of the steepness of a line. If (x_1, y_1) and (x_2, y_2) are any two points on the line, the slope of the line, known as m, is represented by the equation $m = \dfrac{y_2 - y_1}{x_2 - x_1}$.

What It Means For You Lesson 3-6

Parallel lines have the same slope. Perpendicular lines have slopes whose product is −1. You can use these facts to conclude that lines are parallel or perpendicular, or to identify slopes of lines.

EXAMPLE

The slope of $\overleftrightarrow{AB}$ is −4.

The slope of $\overleftrightarrow{CD}$ is −4.

The slopes are the same.

So, $\overleftrightarrow{AB} \parallel \overleftrightarrow{CD}$.

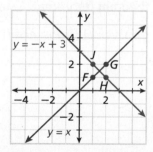

The slope of $\overleftrightarrow{FG}$ is 1.

The slope of $\overleftrightarrow{JH}$ is −1.

The product of the slopes is −1.

So, $\overleftrightarrow{FG} \perp \overleftrightarrow{JH}$.

Key Vocabulary

alternate exterior angles *(ángulos alternos externos)* For two lines intersected by a transversal, a pair of angles that lie on opposite sides of the transversal and outside the other two lines.

alternate interior angles *(ángulos alternos internos)* For two lines intersected by a transversal, a pair of nonadjacent angles that lie on opposite sides of the transversal and between the other two lines.

angle *(ángulo)* A figure formed by two rays with a common endpoint.

converse *(recíproco)* The statement formed by exchanging the hypothesis and conclusion of a conditional statement.

corresponding angles of lines intersected by a transversal *(ángulos correspondientes de líneas cortadas por una transversal)* For two lines intersected by a transversal, a pair of angles that lie on the same side of the transversal and on the same sides of the other two lines.

line *(línea)* An undefined term in geometry, a line is a straight path that has no thickness and extends forever.

perpendicular bisector of a segment *(mediatriz de un segmento)* A line perpendicular to a segment at the segment's midpoint.

perpendicular lines *(líneas perpendiculars)* Lines that intersect at 90° angles.

parallel lines *(líneas paralelas)* Lines in the same plane that do not intersect.

point-slope form *(forma de punto y pendiente)* $y - y_1 = m(x - x_1)$, where m is the slope and (x_1, y_1) is a point on the line.

proof *(demostración)* An argument that uses logic to show that a conclusion is true.

reflection *(reflexión)* A transformation across a line, called the line of reflection, such that the line of reflection is the perpendicular bisector of each segment joining each point and its image.

same-side interior angles *(ángulos internos del mismo lado)* For two lines intersected by a transversal, a pair of angles that lie on the same side of the transversal and between the two lines.

slope *(pendiente)* A measure of the steepness of a line. If (x_1, y_1) and (x_2, y_2) are any two points on the line, the slope of the line, known as m, is represented by the equation $m = \dfrac{y_2 - y_1}{x_2 - x_1}$.

slope-intercept form *(forma de pendiente-intersección)* The slope-intercept form of a linear equation is $y = mx + b$, where m is the slope and b is the y-intercept.

theorem *(teorema)* A statement that has been proven.

transversal *(transversal)* A line that intersects two coplanar lines at two different points.

CHAPTER 3

Lines and Angles
Going Deeper

Essential question: *How many distinct angle measures are formed when three lines in a plane intersect in different ways?*

A **transversal** is a line that intersects two coplanar lines at two different points. In the diagram at the right, three coplanar lines determine a triangle. There are three points of intersection and six pairs of angle measures. In the Explore below, you will see that the six angles need not all have distinct measures.

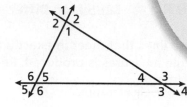

Video Tutor

PREP FOR **CC.9–12.G.CO.9**

1 EXPLORE   Sketching Different Triangle Possibilities

Sketch three intersecting lines that form a triangle so that the given number of distinct angle measures is produced. Record the angle measures.

A only five angle measures

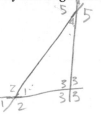

_____

B only four angle measures

_____

C only three angle measures

_____

D only two angle measures

_____

REFLECT

1a. Which lines in your diagrams are transversals? Explain.

_____

1b. How many distinct angle measures are formed at each intersection? Explain.

_____

© Houghton Mifflin Harcourt Publishing Company

1c. If three lines are drawn in a plane, must they always intersect at three points? If not, describe other ways the lines might intersect.

_____

_____

PREP FOR CC.9–12.G.CO.9

2 EXPLORE   Sketching Different Intersection Possibilities

Sketch three lines that meet in exactly two points so that the given number of distinct angle measures is produced. Record the angle measure(s).

A only two angle measures

B only one angle measure

_____   _____

REFLECT

2a. Which lines in your diagrams are transversals? Explain.

_____

_____

2b. Compare your sketches with the work of other students. Are the angle measures you found the same or different from those of others? Explain.

_____

_____

_____

_____

2c. Draw three coplanar lines that intersect in exactly one point. How many distinct angle measures can be formed? Draw examples for all possible cases.

_____

Additional Practice

For Exercises 1–3, refer to the figure from the lesson, shown at the right.

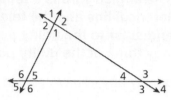

1. What is true of the measures of any two angles labeled with the same number? Explain how you know.

   _____

   _____

2. What is the sum of the measures of the angles labeled 5 and 6? Explain how you know.

   _____

   _____

3. Identify any other angle pairs in the figure for which the sum of the angle measures is the same as for the pair in Exercise 2.

   _____

For Exercises 4–7, refer to the figure, in which *x* and *y* are parallel lines.

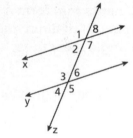

4. Identify a transversal. _____

5. Identify all pairs of vertical angles. _____

6. Suppose you know that m∠2 = m∠4 = 50°. Find the measure of each numbered angle.

   _____

7. Given that m∠2 = m∠4, what do you know about ∠2 and ∠3? Explain your reasoning.

   _____

   _____

   _____

© Houghton Mifflin Harcourt Publishing Company

Problem Solving

For Exercises 1 and 2, refer to the figure, which shows a utility pole with an electrical line and a telephone line. The angled wire is a tension wire. Assume that the electrical line and the telephone line are perpendicular to the utility pole. (For these exercises, you may think of the utility pole as a line.)

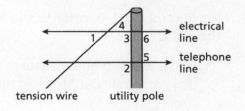

1. Identify any transversals in the figure. Explain your reasoning.

_____

_____

2. Identify any congruent angles. Explain your reasoning.

_____

_____

_____

For Exercises 3–5, refer to the figure, which shows four intersecting segments that form a quadrilateral with eight pairs of angle measures. Sketch four intersecting segments that form a quadrilateral so that the given number of distinct angle measures is produced. Record the angle measures.

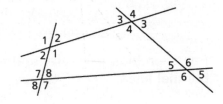

3. only one angle measure

4. only three angle measures

_____   _____

5. Each of the segments in the figure shown above is contained in a line. How many of those lines are transversals? Explain your reasoning.

_____

_____

Angles Formed by Parallel Lines and Transversals
Going Deeper

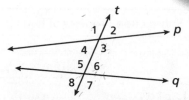

Video Tutor

Essential question: *How can you prove and use theorems about angles formed by transversals that intersect parallel lines?*

CC.9–12.G.CO.9

1 ENGAGE **Introducing Transversals**

Recall that a *transversal* is a line that intersects two coplanar lines at two different points. In the figure, line *t* is a transversal. The table summarizes the names of angle pairs formed by a transversal.

Angle Pair	Example
Corresponding angles lie on the same side of the transversal and on the same sides of the intersected lines.	∠1 and ∠5
Same-side interior angles lie on the same side of the transversal and between the intersected lines.	∠3 and ∠6
Alternate interior angles are nonadjacent angles that lie on opposite sides of the transversal between the intersected lines.	∠3 and ∠5
Alternate exterior angles are angles that lie on opposite sides of the transversal outside the intersected lines.	∠2 and ∠8

The following postulate is the starting point for proving theorems about parallel lines that are intersected by a transversal.

Same-Side Interior Angles Postulate

If two parallel lines are cut by a transversal, then the pairs of same-side interior angles are supplementary.

Given $p \parallel q$, ∠4 and ∠5 are supplementary.
Given $p \parallel q$, ∠3 and ∠6 are supplementary.

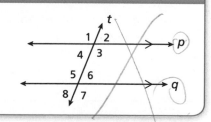

REFLECT

1a. Explain how you can find m∠3 in the postulate diagram if $p \parallel q$ and m∠6 = 61°.

_____

_____

1b. In the postulate diagram, suppose $p \parallel q$ and line *t* is perpendicular to line *p*. Can you conclude that line *t* is perpendicular to line *q*? Explain.

_____

_____

2 PROOF Alternate Interior Angles Theorem

If two parallel lines are cut by a transversal, then the
pairs of alternate interior angles have the same measure.

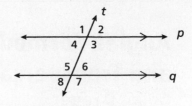

Given: $p \parallel q$
Prove: $m\angle 3 = m\angle 5$

Complete the proof by writing the missing reasons. Choose from the following reasons.
You may use a reason more than once.

| Same-Side Interior Angles Postulate | Given | Definition of supplementary angles |

| Subtraction Property of Equality | Substitution Property of Equality | Linear Pair Theorem |

Statements	Reasons
1. $p \parallel q$	1.
2. $\angle 3$ and $\angle 6$ are supplementary.	2.
3. $m\angle 3 + m\angle 6 = 180°$	3.
4. $\angle 5$ and $\angle 6$ are a linear pair.	4.
5. $\angle 5$ and $\angle 6$ are supplementary.	5.
6. $m\angle 5 + m\angle 6 = 180°$	6.
7. $m\angle 3 + m\angle 6 = m\angle 5 + m\angle 6$	7.
8. $m\angle 3 = m\angle 5$	8.

REFLECT

2a. Suppose $m\angle 4 = 57°$ in the above figure. Describe two different ways to
determine $m\angle 6$.

_____

_____

2b. In the above figure, explain why $\angle 1$, $\angle 3$, $\angle 5$, and $\angle 7$ all have the same measure.

_____

_____

_____

2c. In the above figure, is it possible for all eight angles to have the same measure?
If so, what is that measure?

_____

_____

3 PROOF   **Corresponding Angles Theorem**

If two parallel lines are cut by a transversal, then the
pairs of corresponding angles have the same measure.

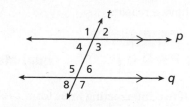

Given: $p \parallel q$
Prove: $m\angle 1 = m\angle 5$

Complete the proof by writing the missing reasons.

Statements		Reasons
1. $p \parallel q$	1.	
2. $m\angle 3 = m\angle 5$	2.	
3. $m\angle 1 = m\angle 3$	3.	
4. $m\angle 1 = m\angle 5$	4.	

REFLECT

3a. Explain how you can you prove the Corresponding Angles Theorem using the
Same-Side Interior Angles Postulate and a linear pair of angles.

_____

_____

_____

Many postulates and theorems are written in the form "If p, then q." The **converse** of
such a statement has the form "If q, then p." The converse of a postulate or theorem may
or may not be true. The converse of the Same-Side Interior Angles Postulate is accepted
as true, and this makes it possible to prove that the converses of the previous theorems
are true.

Converse of the Same-Side Interior Angles Postulate

If two lines are cut by a transversal so that a pair of same-side interior
angles are supplementary, then the lines are parallel.

Converse of the Alternate Interior Angles Theorem

If two lines are cut by a transversal so that a pair of alternate interior
angles have the same measure, then the lines are parallel.

Converse of the Corresponding Angles Theorem

If two lines are cut by a transversal so that a pair of corresponding
angles have the same measure, then the lines are parallel.

A *paragraph proof* is another way of presenting a mathematical argument. As in a two-column proof, the argument must flow logically and every statement should have a reason.

CC.9–12.G.CO.9

4 PROOF   **Equal-Measure Linear Pair Theorem**

If two intersecting lines form a linear pair of angles with equal measures, then the lines are perpendicular.

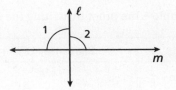

Given: $m\angle 1 = m\angle 2$
Prove: $\ell \perp m$

Complete the following paragraph proof.

It is given that $\angle 1$ and $\angle 2$ form a linear pair. Therefore, $\angle 1$ and $\angle 2$ are supplementary

by the _____. By the definition of supplementary angles,

$m\angle 1 + m\angle 2 = 180°$. It is also given that $m\angle 1 = m\angle 2$. So, $m\angle 1 + m\angle 1 = 180°$ by the

_____. Simplifying gives $2m\angle 1 = 180°$ and $m\angle 1 = 90°$

by the Division Property of Equality. Therefore, $\angle 1$ is a right angle and $\ell \perp m$ by the

_____.

REFLECT

4a. State the converse of the Equal-Measure Linear Pair Theorem shown above. Is the converse true?

_____

_____

PRACTICE

In Exercises 1–2, complete each proof by writing the missing statements or reasons.

1. If two parallel lines are cut by a transversal, then the pairs of alternate exterior angles have the same measure.

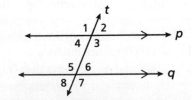

Given: $p \parallel q$
Prove: $m\angle 1 = m\angle 7$

Statements	Reasons
1. $p \parallel q$	**1.**
2. $m\angle 1 = m\angle 5$	**2.**
3. $m\angle 5 = m\angle 7$	**3.**
4. $m\angle 1 = m\angle 7$	**4.**

2. Prove the Converse of the Alternate Interior Angles Theorem.

Given: m∠3 = m∠5
Prove: p ∥ q

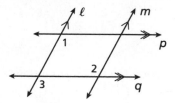

Statements	Reasons
1. m∠3 = m∠5	**1.**
2. ∠5 and ∠6 are a linear pair.	**2.** Definition of linear pair
3.	**3.** Linear Pair Theorem
4. m∠5 + m∠6 = 180°	**4.**
5. m∠3 + m∠6 = 180°	**5.**
6. ∠3 and ∠6 are supplementary.	**6.**
7. p ∥ q	**7.**

3. Complete the paragraph proof.

Given: ℓ ∥ m and p ∥ q
Prove: m∠1 = m∠2

It is given that p ∥ q, so m∠1 = m∠3 by the _____.

It is also given that ℓ ∥ m, so m∠3 = m∠2 by the _____.

Therefore, m∠1 = m∠2 by the _____.

4. The figure shows a given line m, a given point P, and the construction of a line ℓ that is parallel to line m. Explain why line ℓ is parallel to line m.

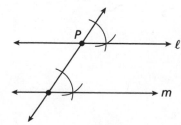

_____

_____

_____

_____

5. Can you use the information in the figure to conclude that $p \parallel q$? Why or why not?

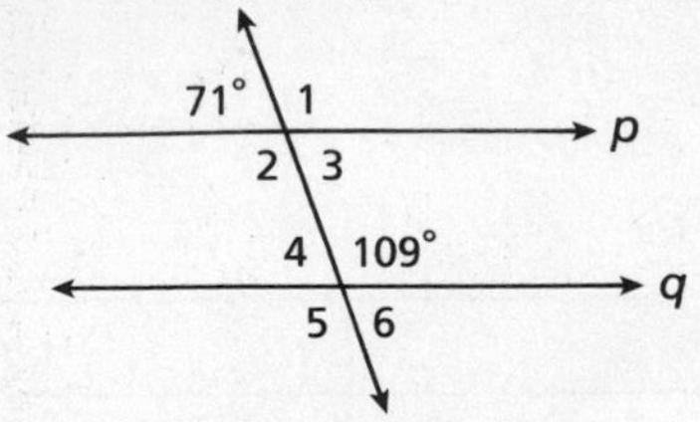

71° 1
2 3
4 109°
5 6

p

q

_____

_____

_____

_____

© Houghton Mifflin Harcourt Publishing Company

Additional Practice

Find each angle measure.

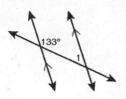

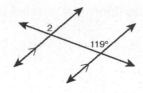

1. m∠1 _____

2. m∠2 _____

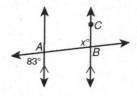

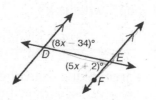

3. m∠ABC _____

4. m∠DEF _____

Complete the two-column proof to show that same-side exterior angles are supplementary.

5. **Given:** $p \parallel q$

   Prove: $m\angle 1 + m\angle 3 = 180°$

   Proof:

Statements	Reasons
1. $p \parallel q$	1. Given
2. a. _____	2. Lin. Pair Thm.
3. ∠1 ≅ ∠2	3. b. _____
4. c. _____	4. Def. of ≅ ⦞
5. d. _____	5. e. _____

6. Ocean waves move in parallel lines toward the shore. The figure shows Sandy Beaches windsurfing across several waves. For this exercise, think of Sandy's wake as a line. $m\angle 1 = (2x + 2y)°$ and $m\angle 2 = (2x + y)°$. Find x and y.

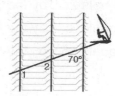

   $x =$ _____

   $y =$ _____

Problem Solving

Find each value. Name the postulate or theorem that you used to find the values.

1. In the diagram of movie theater seats, the incline of the floor, *f*, is parallel to the seats, *s*.

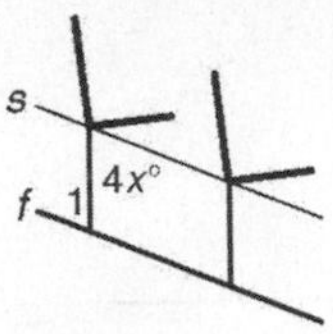

   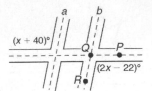

   If m∠1 = 68°, what is *x*?

   _____

2. In the diagram, roads *a* and *b* are parallel.

   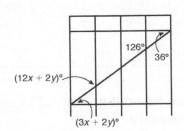

   What is the measure of ∠PQR?

   _____

3. In the diagram of the gate, the horizontal bars are parallel and the vertical bars are parallel. Find *x* and *y*.

   _____

   _____

   _____

   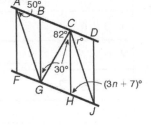

Use the diagram of a staircase railing for Exercises 4 and 5. $\overline{AG} \parallel \overline{CJ}$ **and** $\overline{AD} \parallel \overline{FJ}$. **Choose the best answer.**

4. Which is a true statement about the measure of ∠DCJ?

   A It equals 30°, by the Alternate Interior Angles Theorem.

   B It equals 30°, by the Corresponding Angles Postulate.

   C It equals 50°, by the Alternate Interior Angles Theorem.

   D It equals 50°, by the Corresponding Angles Postulate.

5. Which is a true statement about the value of *n*?

   F It equals 25°, by the Alternate Interior Angles Theorem.

   G It equals 25°, by the Same-Side Interior Angles Theorem.

   H It equals 35°, by the Alternate Interior Angles Theorem.

   J It equals 35°, by the Same-Side Interior Angles Theorem.

Proving Lines Parallel
Connection: Constructing Parallel Lines

Essential question: *How can you construct a line parallel to another line that passes through a given point?*

Video Tutor

Parallel lines lie in the same plane and do not intersect. In the figure, line ℓ is parallel to line m and you write $\ell \parallel m$. The arrows on the lines also indicate that the lines are parallel.

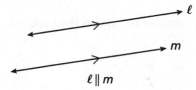

$\ell \parallel m$

CC.9–12.G.CO.12

1 EXAMPLE **Constructing Parallel Lines**

Construct a line parallel to line m that passes through point P. Work directly on the figure below.

A Choose points Q and R on line m.

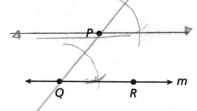

B Use a straightedge to draw $\overleftrightarrow{PQ}$.

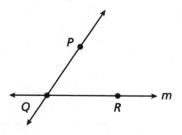

C Copy $\angle PQR$ at point P, as shown. Label line ℓ. Line ℓ is the required line.

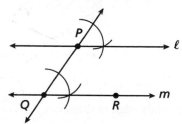

REFLECT

1a. Why does it make sense to copy $\angle PQR$ to get a line parallel to line m?

_____

_____

1b. Is it possible to construct a line parallel to a given line m that passes through a point P that is *on* line m? Why or why not?

_____

_____

1c. Write an if-then statement that justifies the method used in the construction of parallel lines.

_____

_____

PRACTICE

Construct a line parallel to line _m_ that passes through point _P_.

1.

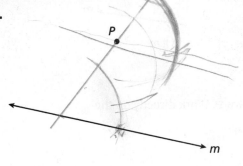

2.

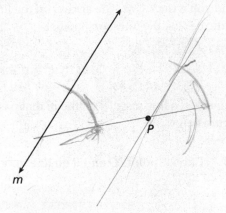

3. You can use what you know about constructing parallel lines to divide a given line segment into three equal parts. Follow the directions and work directly on $\overline{AB}$ in the space below.

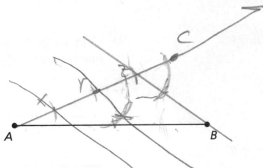

a. Use a straightedge to draw a ray $\overrightarrow{AC}$ as shown.

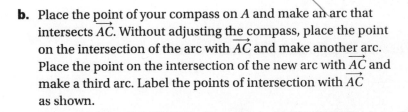

b. Place the point of your compass on _A_ and make an arc that intersects $\overrightarrow{AC}$. Without adjusting the compass, place the point on the intersection of the arc with $\overrightarrow{AC}$ and make another arc. Place the point on the intersection of the new arc with $\overrightarrow{AC}$ and make a third arc. Label the points of intersection with $\overrightarrow{AC}$ as shown.

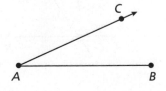

c. Use the straightedge to draw $\overleftrightarrow{ZB}$. Then construct lines parallel to $\overline{ZB}$ that pass through _X_ and _Y_. These lines divide $\overline{AB}$ into three equal parts.

d. Use a ruler to check that you have divided $\overline{AB}$ into three equal parts.

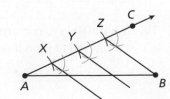

Additional Practice

Construct a line parallel to line *r* that passes through point *P*.

1.

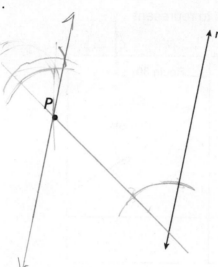

2.

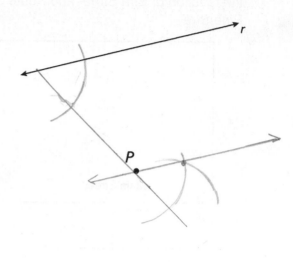

3. Use the parallel line construction to divide $\overrightarrow{CD}$ into four congruent parts.

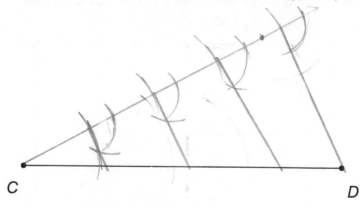

4. Construct a line parallel to $\overline{AB}$ through a point that is a distance *XY* away from $\overline{AB}$ as measured along line *m*.

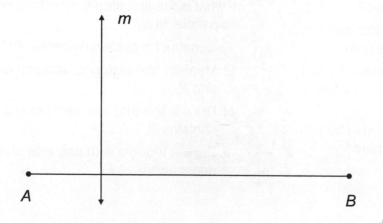

Problem Solving

1. A cartographer is creating a map of the city center, as shown below. Pine Street is parallel to Main Street and passes through the intersection of Elm Street and Route 30. Construct a line to represent Pine Street.

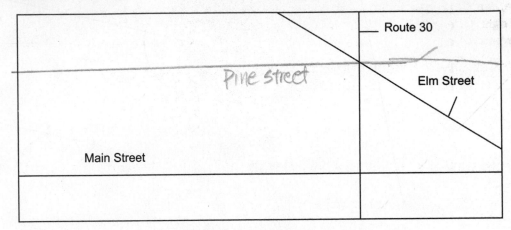

2. A graphic designer is drawing a logo, as shown below. In the logo, $AB = BC = DE = EF$. Construct another line so that the logo is divided into four rectangles that all have the same area.

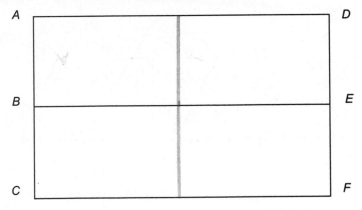

Select the best answer.

3. Which of the following facts do you use when constructing parallel lines?

   A A transversal that intersects two parallel lines is parallel to both.

   B Corresponding angles formed by two parallel lines and a transversal are congruent.

   C Corresponding angles formed by two parallel lines are supplementary.

   D All right angles are congruent.

4. When given a line m and a point P not on m, what is the first step in constructing a line parallel to m?

   F Construct a circle with center P.

   G Measure the distance between m and P.

   H Draw a line that intersects m and contains P.

   J Draw a triangle with one side on m and a vertex at P.

Perpendicular Lines
Going Deeper

Essential question: *How can you construct perpendicular lines and prove theorems about perpendicular bisectors?*

Perpendicular lines are lines that intersect at right angles. In the figure, line ℓ is perpendicular to line m and you write $\ell \perp m$. The right angle mark in the figure indicates that the lines are perpendicular.

The **perpendicular bisector** of a line segment is a line perpendicular to the segment at the segment's midpoint.

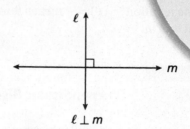

3-4

Video Tutor

$\ell \perp m$

CC.9–12.G.CO.12

1 EXAMPLE Constructing a Perpendicular Bisector

Construct the perpendicular bisector of $\overline{AB}$. Work directly on the figure below.

A Place the point of your compass at A. Using a compass setting that is greater than half the length of $\overline{AB}$, draw an arc.

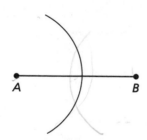

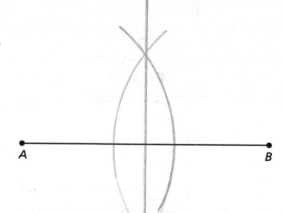

B Without adjusting the compass, place the point of the compass at B and draw an arc intersecting the first arc at C and D.

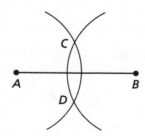

C Use a straightedge to draw $\overleftrightarrow{CD}$. $\overleftrightarrow{CD}$ is the perpendicular bisector of $\overline{AB}$.

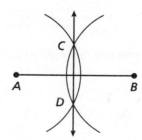

REFLECT

1a. How can you use a ruler and protractor to check the construction?

_____

_____

You can use reflections and their properties to prove a theorem about perpendicular bisectors. Refer to the diagram in the Proof below as you read this definition of reflection.

A **reflection** across line m maps a point A to its image B as follows.

- Line m is the perpendicular bisector of $\overline{AB}$ if and only if A is not on line m.

- The image of P is P if and only if P is on line m.

The notation $r_m(A) = B$ means that the image of point A after a reflection across line m is point B. The notation $r_m(P) = P$ means that the image of point P is point P, which implies that P is on line m.

2 PROOF   Perpendicular Bisector Theorem

If a point is on the perpendicular bisector of a segment, then it is equidistant from the endpoints of the segment.

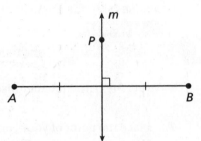

Given: P is on the perpendicular bisector m of $\overline{AB}$.

Prove: $PA = PB$

Complete the following proof.

Consider the reflection across line m. Then $r_m(P) = P$ because

_____

Also, $r_m(A) = B$ by the definition of reflection.

Therefore, $PA = PB$ because _____

REFLECT

2a. Suppose you use a compass and straightedge to construct the perpendicular bisector of a segment, $\overline{AB}$. If you choose a point P on the perpendicular bisector, how can you use your compass to check that P is equidistant from A and B?

_____

_____

_____

2b. What conclusion can you make about $\triangle KLJ$ in the figure? Explain.

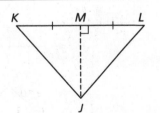

_____

_____

2c. Describe the point on the perpendicular bisector of a segment that is closest to the endpoints of the segment.

_____

_____

The converse of the Perpendicular Bisector Theorem is also true. In order to prove the converse, you will use the Pythagorean Theorem.

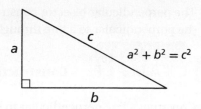

Recall that the Pythagorean Theorem states that in a right triangle with legs of length a and b and hypotenuse of length c, $a^2 + b^2 = c^2$.

CC.9–12.G.CO.9

3 PROOF   Converse of the Perpendicular Bisector Theorem

If a point is equidistant from the endpoints of a segment, then it lies on the perpendicular bisector of the segment.

Given: $PA = PB$

Prove: P is on the perpendicular bisector m of $\overline{AB}$.

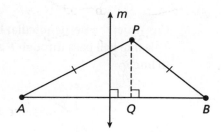

A Use the method of *indirect proof*. Assume the *opposite* of what you want to prove and show this leads to a contradiction.

Assume that point P is *not* on the perpendicular bisector m of $\overline{AB}$. Then when you draw a perpendicular from P to the line containing A and B, the perpendicular intersects this line at a point Q, which is not the midpoint of $\overline{AB}$.

B Complete the following to show that this assumption leads to a contradiction.

$\overline{PQ}$ forms two right triangles, $\triangle AQP$ and $\triangle BQP$.

$AQ^2 + QP^2 = PA^2$ and $BQ^2 + QP^2 = PB^2$ by _____

Subtract these equations:

$$\begin{array}{r} AQ^2 + QP^2 = PA^2 \\ BQ^2 + QP^2 = PB^2 \\ \hline AQ^2 - BQ^2 = PA^2 - PB^2 \end{array}$$

However, $PA^2 - PB^2 = 0$ because _____

Therefore, $AQ^2 - BQ^2 = 0$. This means $AQ^2 = BQ^2$ and $AQ = BQ$. This contradicts the fact that Q is not the midpoint of $\overline{AB}$. Thus, the initial assumption must be incorrect, and P must lie on the perpendicular bisector of $\overline{AB}$.

REFLECT

3a. In the proof, once you know $AQ^2 = BQ^2$, why can you conclude $AQ = BQ$?

_____

3b. Explain how the converse of the Perpendicular Bisector Theorem justifies the compass-and-straightedge construction of the perpendicular bisector of a segment.

_____

_____

_____

_____

The perpendicular bisector construction can be used as part of the method for drawing the perpendicular to a line through a given point not on the line.

CC.9–12.G.CO.12

4 EXAMPLE Constructing a Perpendicular to a Line

Construct a line perpendicular to line *m* that passes through point *P*. Work directly on the figure at right.

A Place the point of your compass at *P*. Draw an arc that intersects line *m* at two points, *A* and *B*.

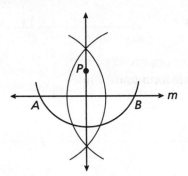

B Construct the perpendicular bisector of $\overline{AB}$. This line will pass through *P* and be perpendicular to line *m*.

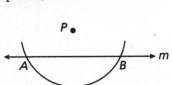

REFLECT

4a. Does the construction still work if point *P* is on line *m*? Why or why not?

_____

_____

PRACTICE

1. Construct the perpendicular bisector of the segment shown below.

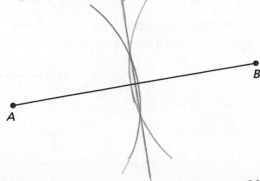

2. Construct a line perpendicular to line *m* that passes through point *P*.

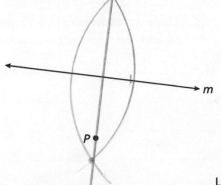

Additional Practice

1. Construct a line perpendicular to line *r*.

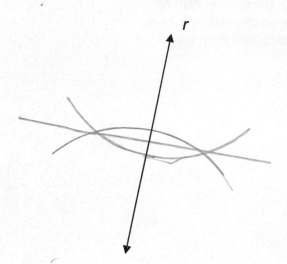

2. Construct the perpendicular bisector of $\overline{CD}$.

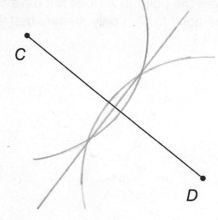

3. Construct a line perpendicular to *m* through *P*. Then, using your two perpendicular lines, construct a right triangle that has *P* as a vertex and a hypotenuse with length *XY*.

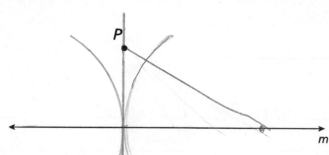

Use the diagram to find the given quantity.

4.

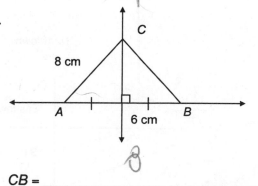

CB = _____

5.

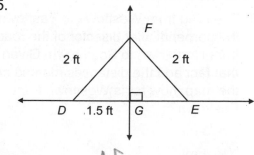

GE = _____

Problem Solving

1. Use geometric constructions to find a single point that is equidistant from *A* and *B*, and also equidistant from *C* and *D*. (*Note*: The distance from the point to *A* does not have to be the same as the distance from the point to *C*. It only matters that the point is equidistant from each pair.)

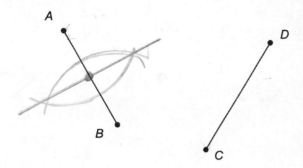

2. If the two segments from Exercise 1 were arranged so that they were both part of the same line, as shown below, could you still find a point that is equidistant from A and B, and also equidistant from C and D? Explain why or why not.

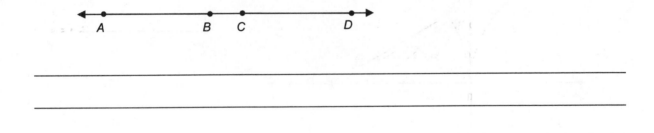

_____

_____

_____

Select the best answer.

3. The road from Westtown to Easttown is the perpendicular bisector of the road from Northtown to Southtown. Given that fact and the distances marked on the map, how far is Westtown from Easttown?

   A 3 mi

   B 4 mi

   C 5 mi

   D 6 mi

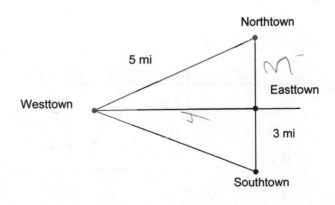

Slopes of Lines
Extension: Using Slope to Partition Segments

Essential question: *How do you find the point on a directed line segment that partitions the segment in a given ratio?*

Recall that the *slope* of a straight line in a coordinate plane is the ratio of the *rise* to the *run*.

In the figure, the slope of $\overline{AB}$ is $\frac{rise}{run} = \frac{4}{8} = \frac{1}{2}$.

In the next several lessons, you will see how to use slope to solve geometry problems and to prove geometry theorems.

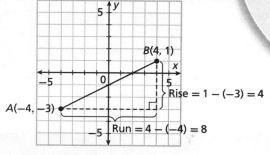

B(4, 1)

Rise = 1 − (−3) = 4

A(−4, −3)

Run = 4 − (−4) = 8

The following example also uses the idea of a *directed line segment*. This means the line segment has a direction associated with it, usually specified by moving from one endpoint to the other.

CC.9–12.G.GPE.6

1 EXAMPLE Partitioning a Segment

Find the coordinates of the point *P* that lies along the directed line segment from *A*(3, 4) to *B*(6, 10) and partitions the segment in the ratio 3 to 2.

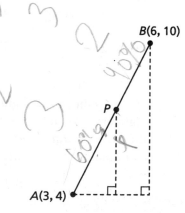

A Convert the ratio to a percent.

Point *P* is $\frac{3}{3+2} = \frac{3}{5}$ of the distance from *A* to *B*.

This is ___60___ % of the distance from *A* to *B*.

B Find the rise and run for $\overline{AB}$.

Rise = 10 − 4 = 6   Run = ___3___

C The slope of $\overline{AP}$ must be the same as the slope of $\overline{AB}$.

So, to find the coordinates of *P*, add ___60___ % of the run to the *x*-coordinate of

A and add ___40___ % of the rise to the *y*-coordinate of *A*.

x-coordinate of *P* = 3 + 0.6 · 3 = ___4.8___

y-coordinate of *P* = 4 + 0.6 · 6 = ___6.4___

So, the coordinates of *P* are ___(4.8, 6.4)___.

1a. Explain how you can check that the slope of $\overline{AP}$ equals the slope of $\overline{AB}$.

_____

_____

1b. Explain how you can use the distance formula to check that P partitions $\overline{AB}$ in the ratio 3 to 2.

_____

_____

_____

PRACTICE

1. Find the coordinates of the point P that lies along the directed segment from $C(-3, -2)$ to $D(6, 1)$ and partitions the segment in the ratio 2 to 1.

(3, 0)

_____

2. Find the coordinates of the point P that lies along the directed segment from $R(-3, -4)$ to $S(5, 0)$ and partitions the segment in the ratio 2 to 3.

(1.8, 2.4)

_____

3. Find the coordinates of the point P that lies along the directed segment from $J(-2, 5)$ to $K(2, -3)$ and partitions the segment in the ratio 4 to 1.

_____

4. Find the coordinates of the point P that lies along the directed segment from $M(5, -2)$ to $N(-5, 3)$ and partitions the segment in the ratio 1 to 3.

_____

5. The map shows a straight highway between two towns. Highway planners want to build two new rest stops between the towns so that the two rest stops divide the highway into three equal parts. Find the coordinates of the points at which the rest stops should be built.

$(-1, -\frac{1}{3}), (1, 1\frac{1}{3})$

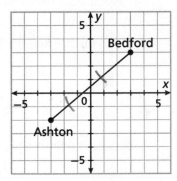

6. $\overleftrightarrow{RS}$ passes through $R(-3, 1)$ and $S(4, 3)$. Find a point P on $\overleftrightarrow{RS}$ such that the ratio of RP to SP is 5 to 4. Is there more than one possibility? Explain.

_____

_____

3-5

Additional Practice

Use the slope formula to determine the slope of each line.

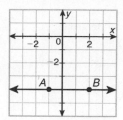

1. $\overleftrightarrow{AB}$ _____ 0 _____

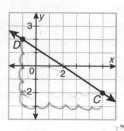

2. $\overleftrightarrow{CD}$ _____ -2/3 _____

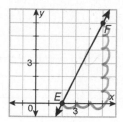

3. $\overleftrightarrow{EF}$ _____ 2 _____

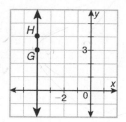

4. $\overleftrightarrow{GH}$ ___ undefined ___

5. Find the coordinates of the point P that lies along the directed line segment from A(3, 1) to B(6, 7) and partitions the segment in the ratio 2 to 1.

(5,5)

6. Find the coordinates of the point P that lies along the directed line segment from C(−3, −2) to D(5, 2) and partitions the segment in the ratio 1 to 4.

(4.6, −1.2)

7. Find the coordinates of the point P that lies along the directed line segment from E(−5, 5) to F(−2, −2) and partitions the segment in the ratio 1 to 1.5.   2, 3

(−3.8, 7.8)

8. Find the coordinates of the point P that lies along the directed line segment from G(1, 1) to H(8, 1) and partitions the segment in the ratio 1 to 3.

(2.75, 0)

Problem Solving

1. The map shows a highway between Acton and Beauville and its intersection with Highway 10. A power station needs to be built along the highway between Acton and Beauville. The station must to be located so that the ratio of its distance to Acton to its distance to Beauville is 2 to 3, but the builders also want to locate it south of Highway 10. Can this be achieved? Explain why or why not.

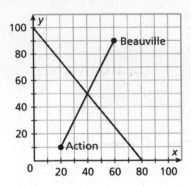

2. The segment represented by endpoints $C(1, 1)$ and $D(7, 3)$ is *not* directed. What two points would partition the segment such that the ratio of the lengths is 1 to 2?

Select the best answer.

3. Which point partitions the directed segment from $A(-3, -2)$ to $B(5, -1)$ in a ratio of 2 to 3?

   A $\left(1\frac{1}{5}, -1\frac{2}{5}\right)$

   B $\left(\frac{1}{5}, -1\frac{3}{5}\right)$

   C $\left(2\frac{1}{3}, -1\frac{2}{3}\right)$

   D $\left(-\frac{1}{3}, -1\frac{1}{3}\right)$

4. The directed line segment from $C(-2, -1)$ to $D(4, 2)$ is partitioned by $P(2, 1)$. What is the ratio of CP to DP?

   F 1:1   H 1:2

   G 2:1   J 2:3

5. A directed line segment from $E(-3, 3.6)$ to $F(5.3, 3.6)$ is partitioned by point P in the ratio 2:7. What is the y-coordinate of P?

   A 0.3

   B 1.15

   C 1.35

   D 3.6

Lines in the Coordinate Plane
Going Deeper

Essential question: *How can you use slope to write equations of lines that are parallel or perpendicular?*

Video Tutor

Recall that a linear function can be expressed as a linear equation. You can write a linear equation in different forms depending upon the information you are given and the problem you are trying to solve.

Slope-Intercept Form

The equation of a line with slope m and y-intercept b is $y = mx + b$.

Point-Slope Form

The equation of a line with slope m that passes through the point (x_1, y_1) is $y - y_1 = m(x - x_1)$.

CC.9–12.G.GPE.5

1 EXAMPLE   Writing Equations of Parallel Lines

Write the equation of each line in slope-intercept form.

A The line parallel to $y = -2x + 3$ that passes through $(1, -4)$

The given line is in slope-intercept form and its slope is _____.

The required line has slope _____ because parallel lines have the same slope.

$y - y_1 = m(x - x_1)$ Use point-slope form.

$y - \underline{\hspace{1cm}} = \underline{\hspace{1cm}}(x - \underline{\hspace{1cm}})$ Substitute for m, x_1, and y_1.

$y + \underline{\hspace{1cm}} = \underline{\hspace{3cm}}$ Simplify each side of the equation.

$y = \underline{\hspace{3cm}}$ Write the equation in slope-intercept form.

B The line that passes through $(2, 3)$ and is parallel to the line through $(1, -2)$ and $(7, 1)$

The slope of the line through $(1, -2)$ and $(7, 1)$ is

$m = \dfrac{y_2 - y_1}{x_2 - x_1} = \dfrac{\boxed{} - \boxed{}}{\boxed{} - \boxed{}} = \dfrac{\boxed{}}{\boxed{}} = \underline{\hspace{0.6cm}}.$

So, the required line has slope _____.

$y - y_1 = m(x - x_1)$ Use point-slope form.

$y - \underline{\hspace{1cm}} = \underline{\hspace{1cm}}(x - \underline{\hspace{1cm}})$ Substitute for m, x_1, and y_1.

$y = \underline{\hspace{3cm}}$ Simplify and write slope-intercept form.

© Houghton Mifflin Harcourt Publishing Company

1a. In Part A, how can you check that you wrote the correct equation?

_____

_____

1b. In Part A, once you know the slope of the required line, how can you finish solving the problem using the slope-intercept form of a linear equation?

_____

_____

CC.9–12.G.GPE.5

2 EXAMPLE **Writing Equations of Perpendicular Lines**

Write the equation of the line perpendicular to $y = 3x - 8$ that passes through (3, 1). Write the equation in slope-intercept form.

A First find the slope of the required line.

The given line is in slope-intercept form and its slope is _____.

Let the required line have slope m. Since the lines are perpendicular, the product of their slopes is −1.

So, _____ $\cdot m = -1$, and therefore, $m =$ _____.

B Now use point-slope form to find the equation of the required line.

$$y - y_1 = m(x - x_1)$$ Use point-slope form.

$y -$ _____ $=$ _____ $(x -$ _____ $)$ Substitute for m, x_1, and y_1.

$y -$ _____ $=$ _____   Distributive Property

$y =$ _____   Write the equation in slope-intercept form.

REFLECT

2a. How do you find the slope of the given line?

_____

_____

2b. How can you use graphing to check your answer?

_____

_____

2c. Confirm your answer by graphing on the grid below.

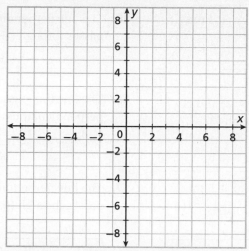

PRACTICE

Write the equation of each line in slope-intercept form.

1. The line with slope 3 that passes through $(0, 6)$

$$6y = 3x + 6$$

2. The line with slope -4 that passes through $(0, -5)$

$$y = -4x - 5$$

3. The line with slope -1 that passes through $(3, 5)$

$$y = -x + 8$$

4. The line with slope 5 that passes through $(2, -5)$

$$y = 5x - 15$$

5. The line parallel to $y = 5x + 1$ that passes through $(3, 8)$

$$y = 5x - 7$$

6. The line parallel to $y = -3x - 2$ that passes through $(-2, 7)$

$$y = -3x + 1$$

7. The line that passes through $(-1, 0)$ and is parallel to the line through $(0, 1)$ and $(2, -3)$

$$y = -2x - 2$$

8. The line that passes through $(3, 5)$ and is parallel to the line through $(3, 3)$ and $(-3, -1)$

$$y = 2/3 x + 3$$

9. The line parallel to $x - 3y = -12$ that passes through $(-3, 4)$

$$y = 1/3 x + 5$$

10. The line parallel to $3x + y = 8$ that passes through $(0, -4)$

$$y = -3x - 4$$

11. Use the slope-intercept form of a linear equation to prove that if two lines are parallel then they have the same slope. (*Hint:* Use an indirect proof. Assume the lines have different slopes, m_1 and m_2. Write the equations of the lines and show that there must be a point of intersection.)

For example, $y = x + 1$ and $y = -x + 1$ are not parrallel because they intersect at point $(0, 1)$.

Write the equation of each line in slope-intercept form.

12. The line perpendicular to $y = \frac{1}{2}x + 1$ that passes through (1, 4)

$y = -2x + 6$

13. The line perpendicular to $y = -x + 2$ that passes through (−1, −7)

$y = x \cancel{\phi} - 6$

14. The line that passes through (1, 2) and is perpendicular to the line through (3, −2) and (−3, 0)

$y = -3x + 5$

15. The line that passes through (−2, 3) and is perpendicular to the line through (0, 1) and (−3, −1)

$y = 3/2x + 6$

16. The line perpendicular to $2y = x + 5$ that passes through (2, 1)

$y = 2x - 3$

17. The line perpendicular to $3x + y = 8$ that passes through (0, −2)

$y = \cancel{1/1} 1/3x - 2$

18. **Error Analysis** A student was asked to find the equation of the line perpendicular to $y - 2x = 1$ that passes through the point (4, 3). The student's work is shown at right. Explain the error and give the correct equation.

the slope should be $-1/2$

$y = -\frac{1}{2}x + 1$

> The given line has slope −2, so the required line has slope $\frac{1}{2}$.
>
> $y - y_1 = m(x - x_1)$ *Use point-slope form.*
>
> $y - 3 = \frac{1}{2}(x - 4)$ *Substitute for m, x_1, y_1.*
>
> $y - 3 = \frac{1}{2}x - 2$ *Distributive Property*
>
> $y = \frac{1}{2}x + 1$ *Add 3 to both sides.*

19. Are the lines given by the equations $-4x + y = 5$ and $-x + 4y = 12$ parallel, perpendicular, or neither? Why?

parrallel because they have the same slope

20. Consider the points $A(-7, 10)$, $B(12, 7)$, $C(10, -24)$, and $D(-8, -3)$. Which two lines determined by these points are perpendicular? Explain.

AC and BD because their slopes are ~~opposite~~ the inverse of each other.

$AB = \frac{3}{-19}$ $BC = \frac{31}{2}$

$AC = \frac{34}{-17} = -2$ $BD = \frac{10}{20} = \frac{1}{2}$

$AD = \frac{13}{1}$

Additional Practice

Write the equation of each line in the given form.

1. the horizontal line through (3, 7) in point-slope form

   _____

2. the line with slope $-\dfrac{8}{5}$ through (1, –5) in point-slope form

   _____

3. the line through $\left(-\dfrac{1}{2}, -\dfrac{7}{2}\right)$ and (2, 14) in slope-intercept form

   _____

4. the line with x-intercept –2 and y-intercept –1 in slope-intercept form

   _____

Graph each line.

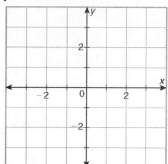

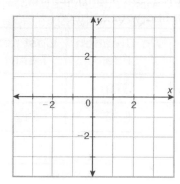

5. $y + 3 = \dfrac{3}{4}(x + 1)$

6. $y = -\dfrac{4}{3}x + 2$

Determine whether the lines are parallel, intersect, or coincide.

7. $x - 5y = 0, \ y + 1 = \dfrac{1}{5}(x + 5)$ _____

8. $2y + 2 = x, \ \dfrac{1}{2}x = -1 + y$ _____

9. $y = 4(x - 3), \ \dfrac{3}{4} + 4y = -\dfrac{1}{4}x$ _____

An *aquifer* is an underground storehouse of water. The water is in tiny crevices and pockets in the rock or sand, but because aquifers underlay large areas of land, the amount of water in an aquifer can be vast. Wells and springs draw water from aquifers.

10. Two relatively small aquifers are the Rush Springs (RS) aquifer and the Arbuckle-Simpson (AS) aquifer, both in Oklahoma. Suppose that starting on a certain day in 1985, 52 million gallons of water per day were taken from the RS aquifer, and 8 million gallons of water per day were taken from the AS aquifer. If the RS aquifer began with 4500 million gallons of water and the AS aquifer began with 3000 million gallons of water and no rain fell, write a slope-intercept equation for each aquifer and find how many days passed until both aquifers held the same amount of water. (Round to the nearest day.)

_____

Problem Solving

Use the following information for Exercises 1 and 2. Josh can order 1 color ink cartridge and 2 black ink cartridges for his printer for $78. He can also order 1 color ink cartridge and 1 black ink cartridge for $53.

1. Let *x* equal the cost of a color ink cartridge and *y* equal the cost of a black ink cartridge. Write a system of equations to represent this situation.

   _____

2. What is the cost of each cartridge?

   _____

3. Ms. Williams is planning to buy T-shirts for the cheerleading camp that she is running. Both companies' total costs would be the same after buying how many T-shirts? Use a graph to find your solution.

	Art Creation Fee	Cost per T-shirt
Company A	$70	$10
Company B	$50	$12

   _____

   _____

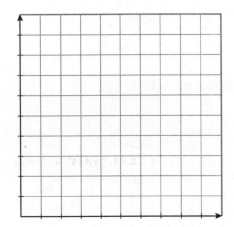

Choose the best answer.

4. Two floats begin a parade at different times, but travel at the same speeds. Which is a true statement about the lines that represent the distance traveled by each float at a given time?

   A The lines intersect.

   B The lines are parallel.

   C The lines are the same.

   D The lines have a negative slope.

5. A piano teacher charges $20 for each half hour lesson, plus an initial fee of $50. Another teacher charges $40 per hour, plus a fee of $50. Which is a true statement about the lines that represent the total cost by each piano teacher?

   F The lines intersect.

   G The lines are parallel.

   H The lines are the same.

   J The lines have a negative slope.

6. Serina is trying to decide between two similar packages for starting her own Web site. Which is a true statement?

   A Both packages cost $235.50 for 5 months.

   B Both packages cost $295 for 10 months.

   C Both packages cost $355 for 15 months.

   D The packages will never have the same cost.

	Design and Setup	Monthly Fee to Host
Package A	$150.00	$14.50
Package B	$175.00	$12.00

Performance Tasks

COMMON
CORE

CC.9-12.G.CO.1
CC.9-12.G.CO.9
CC.9-12.G.GPE.5
CC.9-12.G.MG.1

★ **1.** A spoke on a bicycle wheel rotates as the bicycle moves forward. After what fraction of a full rotation is the spoke perpendicular to the line containing the original position of the spoke? How many degrees is this? Name two times that this happens.

★ **2.** Cables called *guy wires* are often used to stabilize a vertical structure, such as a tall antenna. In the figure at the right, $\overline{AG}$ represents an antenna, and $\overline{AB}$ and $\overline{AC}$ represent the guy wires. The antenna is perpendicular to the ground, represented by $\overline{BC}$. Is the length of $\overline{AG}$ less than or greater than 6 ft? Can you tell if $\overline{AB}$ is less than or greater than 6 ft? In both cases, explain how you know.

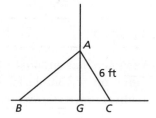

★ **3.** Nancy is tiling her kitchen floor with striped square tiles. She puts
★ her first tile down so that the stripes are approximately parallel to the wall of the kitchen, as shown.

   a. Nancy wants to make sure that the stripes are exactly parallel to the wall. She has a protractor, but no other useful tools. How can she confirm that the stripes are where she wants them to be?

continued

b. Nancy uses the protractor and finds that the stripes aren't quite parallel to the wall. What angle measures could she have found that tell her this? Given your measurements, which way should she turn the tile to fix the situation, clockwise or counterclockwise?

★ **4.** A segment has endpoints (a, b) and (c, d). The segment is translated so that its image is 6 units up and 3 units left of the preimage. Are the two segments parallel, perpendicular, or neither? Prove your answer.

Name _____ Class _____ Date _____

MULTIPLE CHOICE

1. Keiko is writing the proof shown below. Which reason should she use for Step 2?

Given: $\ell \parallel m$
Prove: $m\angle 4 = m\angle 6$

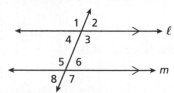

Statements	Reasons
1. $\ell \parallel m$	1. Given
2. $\angle 4$ and $\angle 5$ are supplementary.	2. ?

   A. Definition of supplementary angles

   B. Same-Side Interior Angles Postulate

   C. Linear Pair Theorem

   D. Vertical Angles Theorem

2. Which compass-and-straightedge construction do you use when you construct a line parallel to a given line through a point not on the line?

   F. copying an angle

   G. copying a segment

   H. bisecting an angle

   J. bisecting a segment

3. What is the equation of the line through the point (3, 3) that is perpendicular to the line $y = -\frac{1}{2}x + 2$?

   A. $y = 2x - 3$ **C.** $y = -\frac{1}{2}x + \frac{9}{2}$

   B. $y = -2x - 9$ **D.** $y = 2x + 3$

4. Which of the following points along the directed segment from M to N partitions the segment in the ratio 3 to 1?

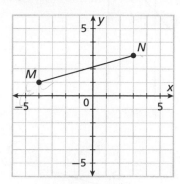

   F. $(-2.5, 6.25)$ **H.** $(-2.25, 1.5)$

   G. $(1.25, 2.5)$ **J.** $(5.25, 1.5)$

5. Which equation represents a line that is not parallel to the others?

   A. $2x + y = 3$ **C.** $-2x - y = -1$

   B. $2x - y = -5$ **D.** $-2x - y = 4$

6. What is the equation of the line parallel to line m that passes through point P?

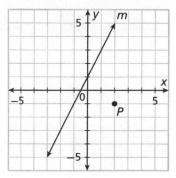

   F. $y = -2x + 3$ **H.** $y = -\frac{1}{2}x$

   G. $y = 2x - 5$ **J.** $y = \frac{1}{2}x - 2$

7. Which lines can be proven parallel given the following diagram?

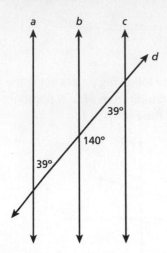

A. $a \parallel b$ **C.** $b \parallel c$

B. $a \parallel c$ **D.** $b \parallel d$

CONSTRUCTED RESPONSE

8. Find the equation of the line through the point (1, 5) that is parallel to the line that passes through (2, 1) and (0, −5).

_____

9. Write an equation in slope-intercept form of the line that is perpendicular to the line with equation $y = 2x + 1$ and that passes through point $P(6, 0)$. Explain your reasoning.

_____
_____
_____
_____
_____
_____
_____
_____

10. Work directly on the figure below to construct a line parallel to $\overleftrightarrow{AB}$ that passes through point P.

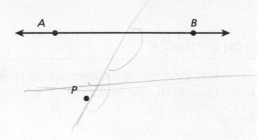

11. Work directly on the figure below to construct the perpendicular bisector of $\overline{JK}$.

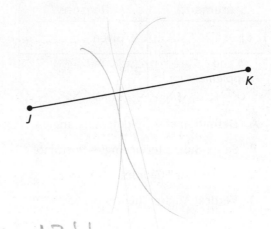

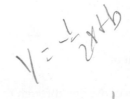

$0 = 12 + 1$

$y = -\frac{1}{2}x + 6$

$y = -\frac{1}{2}x + b$

$y = -\frac{1}{2}x + 3$

Triangle Congruence

Chapter Focus

You have already learned that rigid motions preserve the size and shape of a figure. In this unit, you will learn that two figures are congruent (have the same size and shape) if and only if one figure can be mapped to the other by a sequence of rigid motions. You will also learn that there are some shortcuts for showing that triangles are congruent. Once you know these shortcuts, which are called congruence criteria, you will use them to prove facts about triangles. Along the way, you will also learn to write coordinate proofs.

Chapter at a Glance

COMMON CORE

Lesson		Standards for Mathematical Content
4-1	Congruence and Transformations	CC.9-12.G.CO.5, CC.9-12.G.CO.6
4-2	Classifying Triangles	CC.9-12.G.GPE.4, CC.9-12.G.GPE 7
4-3	Angle Relationships in Triangles	CC.9-12.G.CO.10
4-4	Congruent Triangles	CC.9-12.G.CO.7
4-5	Triangle Congruence: SSS and SAS	CC.9-12.G.CO.8, CC.9-12.G.CO.9, CC.9-12.G.SRT.5
4-6	Triangle Congruence: ASA, AAS, and HL	CC.9-12.G.CO.8, CC.9-12.G.CO.10, CC.9-12.G.SRT.5
4-7	Triangle Congruence: CPCTC	CC.9-12.G.GPE.5
4-8	Introduction to Coordinate Proof	CC.9-12.G.GPE.4
4-9	Isosceles and Equilateral Triangles	CC.9-12.G.CO.10
	Performance Tasks	
	Assessment Readiness	

CHAPTER 4

© Houghton Mifflin Harcourt Publishing Company

Unpacking the Standards

Understanding the standards and the vocabulary terms in the standards will help you know exactly what you are expected to learn in this chapter.

COMMON CORE **CC.9-12.G.CO.6**

Use geometric descriptions of rigid motions to transform figures and to predict the effect of a given rigid motion on a given figure; …

Key Vocabulary
transformation *(transformación)* A change in the position, size, or shape of a figure or graph.
rigid motion *(movimiento rígido)* A transformation that does not change the size or shape of a figure.

What It Means For You — Lesson 4-1

In geometry, when you reposition a figure but don't change its size or shape in the process, you have performed what is called a *rigid motion*.

EXAMPLE
You can create the pattern on the grid by a series of rigid motions—in this case reflections and rotations—of one of the blue crescent shapes.

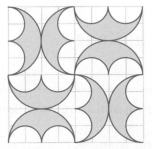

COMMON CORE **CC.9-12.G.SRT.5**

Use congruence … criteria for triangles to solve problems and to prove relationships in geometric figures.

Key Vocabulary
congruent *(congruente)* Having the same size and shape, denoted by ≅.
triangle *(triángulo)* A three-sided polygon.

What It Means For You — Lessons 4-5, 4-6

When two triangles are *congruent*, it means that matching sides have the same measure and matching angles have the same measure. You can use this fact to help you solve problems.

EXAMPLE
You can use congruent triangles to find the distance across a canyon by measuring distances on only one side of the canyon.

Walk from *D* perpendicular to $\overline{BD}$ until you are in line with *C* and *A*. Call this point *E*. The distance *DE* is the same as the distance *AB* across the canyon.

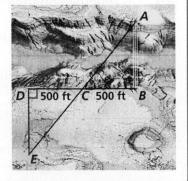

COMMON CORE CC.9-12.G.CO.10

Prove theorems about triangles.

Key Vocabulary

proof *(demostración)* An argument that uses logic to show that a conclusion is true.

theorem *(teorema)* A statement that has been proven.

There are theorems about angle measures involved with triangles, about sides and angles in special types of triangles, and about side and angle relationships that identify when triangles are congruent. Proving these theorems makes them available for solving new problems.

EXAMPLE Exterior Angle Theorem

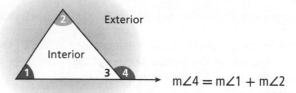

$m\angle 4 = m\angle 1 + m\angle 2$

EXAMPLE Isosceles Triangle Theorem

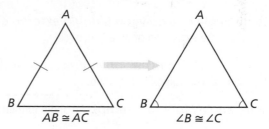

$\overline{AB} \cong \overline{AC}$ $\angle B \cong \angle C$

CHAPTER 4

COMMON CORE CC.9-12.G.GPE.4

Use coordinates to prove simple geometric theorems algebraically.

Key Vocabulary

coordinate *(coordenada)* A number used to identify the location of a point. On a number line, one coordinate is used. On a coordinate plane, two coordinates are used, called the *x*-coordinate and the *y*-coordinate. In space, three coordinates are used, called the *x*-coordinate, the *y*-coordinate, and the *z*-coordinate.

Positioning geometric diagrams on a coordinate grid makes algebraic tools such as the Midpoint and Distance Formulas available to you to prove geometric relationships.

EXAMPLE

You can use coordinates and the Distance Formula to prove that $\overline{AB}$, which joins the midpoints of $\overline{PR}$ and $\overline{QR}$, is half as long as $\overline{PQ}$.

$$AB = \sqrt{(4-0)^2 + (0-3)^2}$$
$$= \sqrt{16 + 9}$$
$$= 5$$
$$PQ = \sqrt{(8-0)^2 + (0-6)^2}$$
$$= \sqrt{64 + 36}$$
$$= 10$$

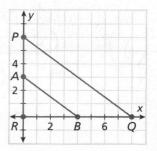

Key Vocabulary

acute triangle *(triángulo acutángulo)* A triangle with three acute angles.

base of an isosceles triangle *(base de un triángulo isosceles)* The side opposite the vertex angle.

base angle of an isosceles triangle *(ángulo base de un triángulo isosceles)* One of the two angles that have the base of the triangle as a side.

congruent *(congruente)* Having the same size and shape, denoted by $\cong$.

coordinate *(coordenada)* A number used to identify the location of a point. On a number line, one coordinate is used. On a coordinate plane, two coordinates are used, called the x-coordinate and the y-coordinate. In space, three coordinates are used, called the x-coordinate, the y-coordinate, and the z-coordinate.

corollary *(corolario)* A theorem whose proof follows directly from another theorem.

equilateral triangle *(triángulo equilátero)* A triangle with three congruent sides.

exterior angle of a polygon *(ángulo externo de un polígono)* An angle formed by one side of a polygon and the extension of an adjacent side.

indirect proof *(demostración indirecta)* A proof in which the statement to be proved is assumed to be false and a contradiction is shown.

interior angle *(ángulo interno)* An angle formed by two sides of a polygon with a common vertex.

isosceles triangle *(triángulo isosceles)* A triangle with at least two congruent sides.

leg of an isosceles triangle *(cateto de un triángulo isosceles)* One of the two congruent sides of the isosceles triangle.

obtuse triangle *(triángulo obtusángulo)* A triangle with one obtuse angle.

remote interior angle *(ángulo interno remoto)* An interior angle of a polygon that is not adjacent to the exterior angle.

right triangle *(triángulo rectángulo)* A triangle with one right angle.

rigid motion *(movimiento rígido)* A transformation that does not change the size or shape of a figure.

scalene triangle *(triángulo escaleno)* A triangle with no congruent sides.

transformation *(transformación)* A change in the position, size, or shape of a figure or graph.

triangle *(triángulo)* A three-sided polygon.

vertex angle of an isosceles triangle *(ángulo del vértice de un triángulo isosceles)* The angle formed by the legs of an isosceles triangle.

CHAPTER 4

Congruence and Transformations
Going Deeper

Essential question: *How can you use transformations to determine whether figures are congruent?*

Video Tutor

Two figures are *congruent* if they have the same size and shape. A more formal mathematical definition of congruence depends on the notion of rigid motions.

Two plane figures are **congruent** if and only if one can be obtained from the other by rigid motions (that is, by a sequence of reflections, translations, and/or rotations.)

CC.9–12.G.CO.6

1 E X A M P L E **Determining If Figures are Congruent**

Use the definition of congruence in terms of rigid motions to determine whether the two figures are congruent and explain your answer.

A △*ABC* and △*DEF* have different sizes.

Since rigid motions preserve distance, there is no sequence of rigid motions that will map △*ABC* to △*DEF*.

Therefore, ___it is not a rigid motion___

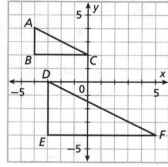

B You can map *JKLM* to *PQRS* by the translation that has the following coordinate notation:

_____

A translation is a rigid motion.

Therefore, ___It is congruent___

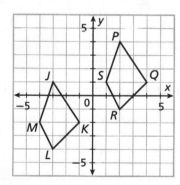

REFLECT

1a. Why does the fact that △*ABC* and △*DEF* have different sizes lead to the conclusion that there is no sequence of rigid motions that maps △*ABC* to △*DEF*?

_____

_____

The definition of congruence tells you that when two figures are known to be congruent, there must be some sequence of rigid motions that maps one to the other. You will investigate this idea in the next example.

CC.9–12.G.CO.5

2 EXAMPLE   Finding a Sequence of Rigid Motions

For each pair of congruent figures, find a sequence of rigid motions that maps one figure to the other.

A   You can map △ABC to △RST by a reflection followed by a translation. Provide the coordinate notation for each.

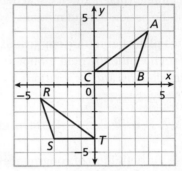

Reflection: _____ over the y axis _____

Followed by...

Translation: _____ y − 5 _____

B   You can map △DFG to △HJK by a rotation followed by a translation. Provide the coordinate notation for each.

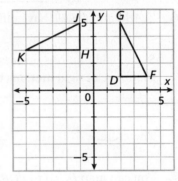

Rotation: _____ point D 90° counter clockwise _____

Followed by...

Translation: _____ x + 2 , y + 2 _____

REFLECT

2a. Explain how you could use tracing paper to help you find a sequence of rigid motions that maps one figure to another congruent figure.

_____

_____

2b. Given two congruent figures, is there a *unique* sequence of rigid motions that maps one figure to the other? Use one or more of the above examples to explain your answer.

_____

_____

3 EXPLORE   Investigating Congruent Segments and Angles

A Use a straightedge to trace $\overline{AB}$ on a piece of tracing paper. Then slide, flip, and/or turn the tracing paper to determine if there is a sequence of rigid motions that maps $\overline{AB}$ to one of the other line segments.

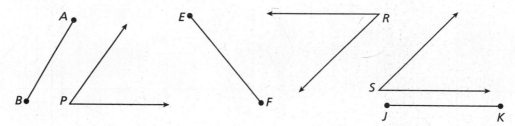

B Repeat the process with the other line segments and the angles in order to determine which pairs of line segments and which pairs of angles, if any, are congruent.

Congruent line segments: _____

Congruent angles: _____

C Use a ruler to measure the congruent line segments. Use a protractor to measure the congruent angles.

REFLECT

3a. Make a conjecture about congruent line segments.

_____

3b. Make a conjecture about congruent angles.

_____

The symbol of congruence is ≅. You read the statement $\overline{UV} \cong \overline{XY}$ as "Line segment UV is congruent to line segment XY."

Congruent line segments have the same length, so $\overline{UV} \cong \overline{XY}$ implies $UV = XY$ and vice versa. Congruent angles have the same measure, so $\angle C \cong \angle D$ implies $m\angle C = m\angle D$ and vice versa. Because of this, there are properties of congruence that resemble the properties of equality, and you can use these properties as reasons in proofs.

Properties of Congruence	
Reflexive Property of Congruence	$\overline{AB} \cong \overline{AB}$
Symmetric Property of Congruence	If $\overline{AB} \cong \overline{CD}$, then $\overline{CD} \cong \overline{AB}$.
Transitive Property of Congruence	If $\overline{AB} \cong \overline{CD}$ and $\overline{CD} \cong \overline{EF}$, then $\overline{AB} \cong \overline{EF}$.

Use the definition of congruence in terms of rigid motions to determine whether the two figures are congruent and explain your answer.

1.

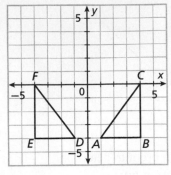

2.

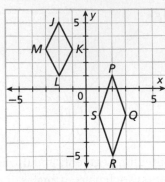

3.

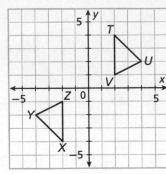

_____

_____

_____

For each pair of congruent figures, find a sequence of rigid motions that maps one figure to the other. Give coordinate notation for the transformations you use.

4.

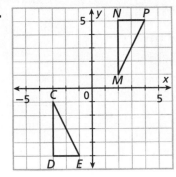

5.

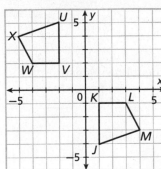

6.

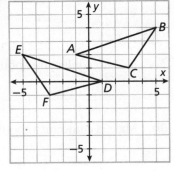

_____

_____

_____

_____

7. $\triangle ABC \cong \triangle DEF$ and $\triangle DEF \cong \triangle GHJ$. Can you conclude $\triangle ABC \cong \triangle GHJ$? Explain.

_____

_____

4-1

Additional Practice

Apply the transformation *M* to the polygon with the given vertices.
Identify and describe the transformation.

1. *M*: (*x*, *y*) → (*x* − 2, *y* + 3)

   A(−1, −3), *B*(2, −1), *C*(2, −4)

   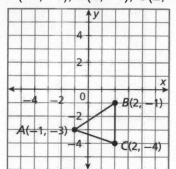

2. *M*: (*x*, *y*) → (−*x*, *y*)

   P(−1, 2), *Q*(−2, −3), *R*(1, −2)

   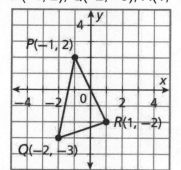

3. *M*: (*x*, *y*) → (*y*, −*x*)

   G(−4, 3), *H*(−2, 3), *J*(−2, −1), *K*(−4, −1)

   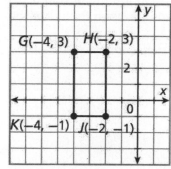

4. *M*: (*x*, *y*) → (2*x*, 2*y*)

   E(−2, 2), *F*(1, 1), *G*(2, 2)

   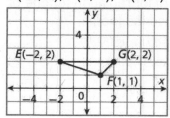

Determine whether the polygons with the given vertices are congruent.

5. *A*(−4, 4), *B*(−2, 4), *C*(−2, 2), *D*(−3, 1),

   E(−4, 2); *P*(2, 6), *Q*(4, 6), *R*(4, 4),

   S(3, 3), *T*(2, 4)

   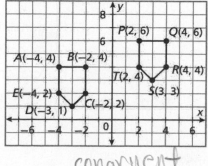

   congruent

6. *P*(4, 4), *Q*(−4, 2), *R*(−2, 6);

   J(2, 2), *K*(−2, 1), *L*(−1, 3)

   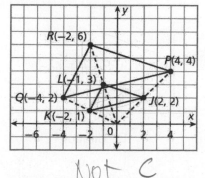

   Not C

1. Irena is designing a quilt. She made this diagram to follow when making her quilt. What transformation(s) are used on the triangles to create the pattern in the quilt design?

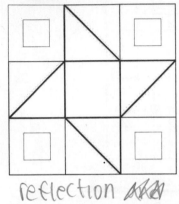

reflection ✗✗✗

2. An architect used this design for a stained glass window. What frieze transformation(s) is used to create the pattern in the window?

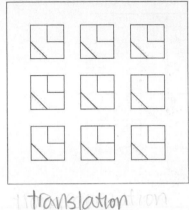

translation

3. A graphic artist incorporated the universal symbol for radiation for one of his designs. Describe the transformation(s) he used.

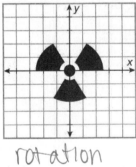

rotation

4. Richard developed a tessellating shape for floor tile. Describe the series of transformations he used to create the design.

translation

Choose the best answer.

5. A team flag is made using a fabric with the design shown. What transformation is used?

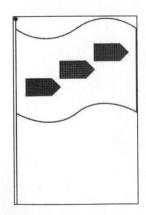

(A) translation
B reflection
C rotation
D dilation _(changing sizes)_

6. An art student used transformations in all her art. What transformation did she use for her design shown?

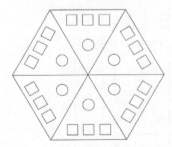

F translation
G reflection
(H) rotation
J dilation

4-2

Classifying Triangles
Connection: Coordinate Methods

Essential question: *How can you classify triangles in the coordinate plane?*

Recall that triangles can be classified by their side lengths. A *scalene* triangle has no congruent sides, an *isosceles* triangle has at least two congruent sides, and an *equilateral* triangle has three congruent sides.

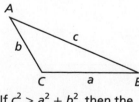
Video Tutor

CC.9–12.G.GPE.4

1 EXAMPLE   Classifying Triangles by Side Lengths

A triangle in the coordinate plane has vertices $P(4, 0)$, $Q(-3, 3)$, and $R(4, 6)$. Classify the triangle by its sides. Then write an expression for the perimeter of the triangle.

A   Find the side lengths of the triangle using the distance formula.

$$PQ = \sqrt{(x_2 - x_1)^2 + (y_2 - y_1)^2} = \sqrt{(-)^2 + (-)^2} = $$

$$QR = \sqrt{(x_2 - x_1)^2 + (y_2 - y_1)^2} = \sqrt{(-)^2 + (-)^2} = $$

$$RP = \sqrt{(x_2 - x_1)^2 + (y_2 - y_1)^2} = \sqrt{(-)^2 + (-)^2} = $$

B   Use the side lengths to classify the triangle.

$\triangle PQR$ is _____ because _____

C   Use the side lengths to write an expression for the perimeter of the triangle.

Perimeter $= PQ + QR + RP = $

REFLECT

1a. Explain how you know that $\triangle PQR$ is not equilateral.

_____

1b. The points $T(0, 0)$, $U(a, b)$, and $V(b, a)$ form a triangle. Explain why the triangle can be classified as isosceles.

_____

_____

You can use the side lengths of a triangle to classify a triangle as *obtuse*, *acute*, or *right* as shown below. Test the longest side c to classify the largest angle C.

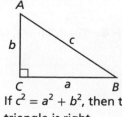

If $c^2 > a^2 + b^2$, then the triangle is obtuse.

If $c^2 = a^2 + b^2$, then the triangle is right.

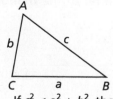

If $c^2 < a^2 + b^2$, then the triangle is acute.

© Houghton Mifflin Harcourt Publishing Company

2 EXAMPLE Classifying Triangles by Angles Using Side Lengths

A triangle in the coordinate plane has vertices $J(-1, 0)$, $K(2, 4)$, and $M(7, 1)$. Classify the triangle by its angles. Then write an expression for the perimeter of the triangle.

A Find the side lengths of the triangle using the distance formula.

$JK = $ _____

$KM = $ _____

$MJ = $ _____

B Use the side lengths to classify the triangle. The largest angle is opposite the longest side length.

$c^2 = a^2 + b^2$ Compare c^2 to $a^2 + b^2$.

[____] $\overset{?}{=}$ [____] $+$ [____]   Substitute the longest side length for c.

[____] $\overset{?}{=}$ [____] $+$ [____]   Simplify.

[____] $>$ [____]   Add and compare.

Since $c^2 > a^2 + b^2$, the angle opposite the longest side is _____ and the triangle is _____.

C Write an expression for the perimeter: Perimeter $= 5 + $ [____] $+$ [____]

REFLECT

2a. Explain why the points $A(0, 0)$, $B(k, k)$, and $C(2k, 0)$ are vertices of a right triangle.

_____

_____

PRACTICE

A triangle has the given vertices. Classify the triangle by its sides. Then write an expression for the perimeter of the triangle.

1. $L(-2, -2)$, $M(1, 3)$, $N(3, 0)$

_____

2. $F(1, -1)$, $G(3, 5)$, $H(5, -1)$

_____

A triangle has the given vertices. Classify the triangle by its sides. Then write an expression for the perimeter of the triangle.

3. $D(5, 5)$, $E(-1, 1)$, $F(-1, 5)$

_____

4. $X(-3, 1)$, $Y(4, 6)$, $Z(2, 2)$

_____

4-2

Additional Practice

Classify each triangle by its angle measures.
(*Note:* Some triangles may belong to
more than one class.)

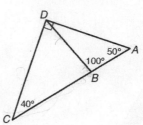

1. △ABD

    obtuse, scalene

2. △ADC

    right, scalene

3. △BCD

    acute, scalene

Classify each triangle by its side lengths.
(*Note:* Some triangles may belong to more than one class.)

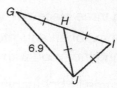

4. △GIJ

    scalene

    obtuse, ~~isoceles~~

5. △HIJ

    acute, equaladeral

6. △GHJ

    acute, isosceles

Find the side lengths of each triangle.

7.

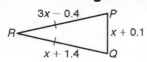

    _2.3, 2.3, 1_

8.

$5n = \frac{15}{4}$

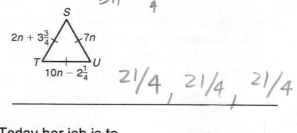

    _21/4, 21/4, 21/4_

9. Min works in the kitchen of a catering company. Today her job is to cut whole pita bread into small triangles. Min uses a cutting machine, so every pita triangle comes out the same. The figure shows an example. Min has been told to cut 3 pita triangles for every guest. There will be 250 guests. If the pita bread she uses comes in squares with 20-centimeter sides and she doesn't waste any bread, how many squares of whole pita bread will Min have to cut up?

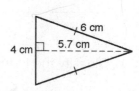

    50 squares

10. Follow these instructions and use a protractor to draw a triangle with sides of 3 cm, 4 cm, and 5 cm. First draw a 5-cm segment. Set your compass to 3 cm and make an arc from one end of the 5-cm segment. Now set your compass to 4 cm and make an arc from the other end of the 5-cm segment. Mark the point where the arcs intersect. Connect this point to the ends of the 5-cm segment. Classify the triangle by sides and by angles. Use the Pythagorean Theorem to check your answer.

    obtuse   scalene triangle

Problem Solving

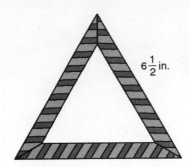

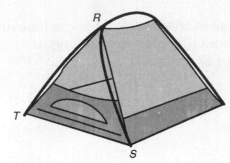

1. Aisha makes triangular picture frames by gluing three pieces of wood together in the shape of an equilateral triangle and covering the wood with ribbon. Each side of a frame is $6\frac{1}{2}$ inches long. How many frames can she cover with 2 yards of ribbon?

_____

2. A tent's entrance is in the shape of an isosceles triangle in which $\overline{RT} \cong \overline{RS}$. The length of $\overline{TS}$ is 1.2 times the length of a side. The perimeter of the entrance is 14 feet. Find each side length.

_____

Use the figure and the following information for Exercises 3 and 4.

The distance "as the crow flies" between Santa Fe and Phoenix is 609 kilometers. This is 245 kilometers less than twice the distance between Santa Fe and El Paso. Phoenix is 48 kilometers closer to El Paso than it is to Santa Fe.

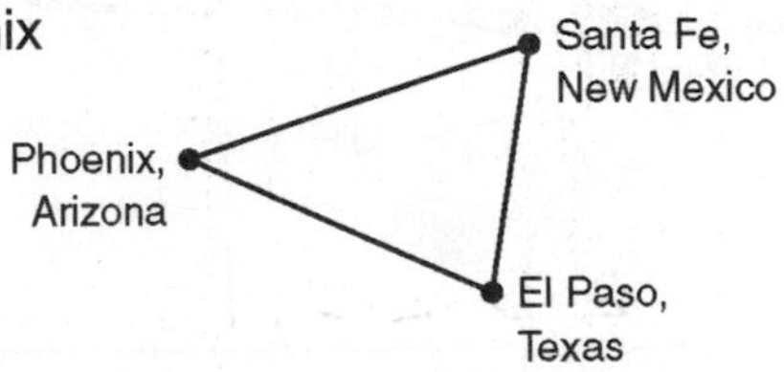

3. What is the distance between each pair of cities?

_____

_____

4. Classify the triangle that connects the cities by its side lengths. _____

Choose the best answer.

A *gable*, as shown in the diagram, is the triangular portion of a wall between a sloping roof.

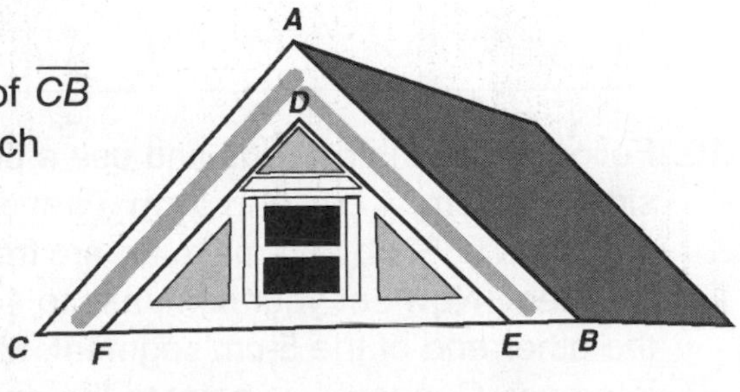

5. Triangle *ABC* is an isosceles triangle. The length of $\overline{CB}$ is 12 feet 4 inches and the congruent sides are each $\frac{3}{4}$ this length. What is the perimeter of $\triangle ABC$?

   A 31 ft 4 in.   C 21 ft 7 in.

   B 30 ft 10 in.   D 18 ft 6 in.

6. In $\triangle DEF$, $\overline{DE}$ and $\overline{DF}$ are each 6 feet 3 inches long. This length is 0.75 times the length of $\overline{FE}$. What is the perimeter of $\triangle DEF$?

   F 12 ft 4 in.   H 17 ft 2 in.

   G 14 ft 7 in.   J 20 ft 10 in.

Angle Relationships in Triangles
Focus on Reasoning

Essential question: *What are some theorems about angle measures in triangles?*

COMMON CORE

CC.9-12.G.CO.10

1 **Investigate the angle measures of a triangle.**

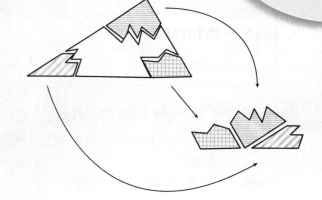

A Use a straightedge to draw a large triangle on a sheet of paper.

B Cut out the triangle.

C Tear off the angles of the triangle.

D Place the angles together so their sides are adjacent and their vertices meet at a point. Take note of how the angles come together.

E Repeat the process by drawing different triangles. Be sure you try an acute triangle, a right triangle, and an obtuse triangle. In each case, note how the angles come together.

REFLECT

1a. Compare your work with that of other students. What always seems to be true about the three angles of a triangle when they are placed together?

_____

1b. Make a conjecture: What can you say about the sum of the angle measures in a triangle?

_____

1c. An equiangular triangle has three congruent angles. What do you think is true about the angles of an equiangular triangle? Why?

_____

1d. In a right triangle, what is the relationship of the measures of the two acute angles?

_____

The relationship you investigated above is known as the Triangle Sum Theorem.

The sum of the angle measures in
a triangle is 180°.

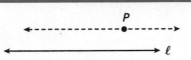

$$m\angle A + m\angle B + m\angle C = 180°$$

The proof of the Triangle Sum Theorem depends upon a postulate known as the
Parallel Postulate.

The Parallel Postulate

Through a point P not on a
line ℓ, there is exactly one line
parallel to ℓ.

2 **Prove the Triangle Sum Theorem.**

The sum of the angle measures in a triangle is 180°.

Given: $\triangle ABC$

Prove: $m\angle 1 + m\angle 2 + m\angle 3 = 180°$

(ause its logic

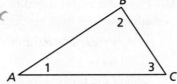

A Understand the plan for the proof.

Draw a line through B that is parallel to $\overline{AC}$. This creates
three angles that form a straight angle, so the sum of their
measures is 180°. Use the fact that alternate interior angles
have the same measure to conclude that the sum of the
measures of the angles in a triangle is 180°.

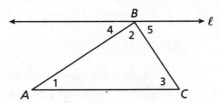

B Complete the proof.

Statements	Reasons
1. Draw ℓ through point B parallel to $\overline{AC}$.	1.
2. $m\angle 4 = m\angle 1$ and $m\angle 5 = m\angle 3$	2.
3. $m\angle 4 + m\angle 2 + m\angle 5 = 180°$	3. Angle Addition Postulate and definition of straight angle
4.	4.

REFLECT

2a. Give an indirect proof to show why it is not possible for a triangle to have
two right angles.

_____

_____

_____

A **corollary** to a theorem is a statement that can be proved easily by using the theorem. A useful corollary to the Triangle Sum Theorem involves exterior angles of a triangle.

When you extend the sides of a polygon, the original angles may be called **interior angles** and the angles that form linear pairs with the interior angles are the **exterior angles**.

Each exterior angle of a triangle has two remote interior angles. A **remote interior angle** is an interior angle that is not adjacent to the exterior angle.

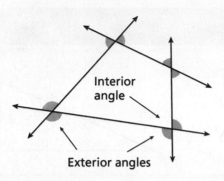

Interior angle

Exterior angles

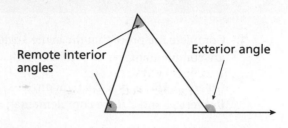

Remote interior angles

Exterior angle

3 **Prove the Exterior Angle Theorem.**

The measure of an exterior angle of a triangle is equal to the sum of the measures of its remote interior angles.

Given: $\triangle ABC$
Prove: $m\angle 4 = m\angle 1 + m\angle 2$

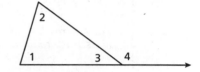

Complete the proof.

Statements	Reasons
1. $\angle 3$ and $\angle 4$ are supplementary.	**1.**
2. $m\angle 3 + m\angle 4 = 180°$	**2.**
3.	**3.** Triangle Sum Theorem
4. $m\angle 3 + m\angle 4 = m\angle 1 + m\angle 2 + m\angle 3$	**4.**
5. $m\angle 4 = m\angle 1 + m\angle 2$	**5.**

REFLECT

3a. Explain how you could verify the Exterior Angle Theorem using a method similar to that of the Explore.

_____

_____

Another important corollary of the Triangle Sum Theorem is the Quadrilateral Sum Theorem. You will prove the theorem as an exercise.

> ### Quadrilateral Sum Theorem
>
> The sum of the angle measures in a quadrilateral is 360°.

PRACTICE

1. Complete the proof that the acute angles of a right triangle are complementary.

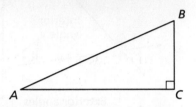

Given: △ABC with ∠C a right angle
Prove: ∠A and ∠B are complementary.

Statements	Reasons
1. ∠C is a right angle.	**1.**
2. m∠C = 90°	**2.**
3. m∠A + m∠B + m∠C = 180°	**3.**
4.	**4.** Substitution Property of Equality
5.	**5.** Subtraction Property of Equality
6. ∠A and ∠B are complementary.	**6.**

2. Write a paragraph proof of the Quadrilateral Sum Theorem.

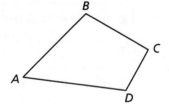

Given: Quadrilateral ABCD
Prove: m∠A + m∠B + m∠C + m∠D = 360°
(*Hint:* Draw diagonal $\overline{AC}$ and number the angles formed.)

_____

_____

_____

_____

3. If two angles of one triangle are congruent to two angles of another triangle, must the third angles of the triangles also be congruent? Why or why not?

_____

_____

_____

_____

Additional Practice

(handwritten: 78.9 / 101.1)

1. An area in central North Carolina is known as the Research Triangle because of the relatively large number of high-tech companies and research universities located there. Duke University, the University of North Carolina at Chapel Hill, and North Carolina State University are all within this area. The Research Triangle is roughly bounded by the cities of Chapel Hill, Durham, and Raleigh. From Chapel Hill, the angle between Durham and Raleigh measures 54.8°. From Raleigh, the angle between Chapel Hill and Durham measures 24.1°. Find the angle between Chapel Hill and Raleigh from Durham.

Diagram: Durham, N (north arrow); 10.7 mi; Chapel Hill; 54.8; 21.4 mi; 24.1; 25.7 mi; Raleigh

(handwritten answer: 101.1°)

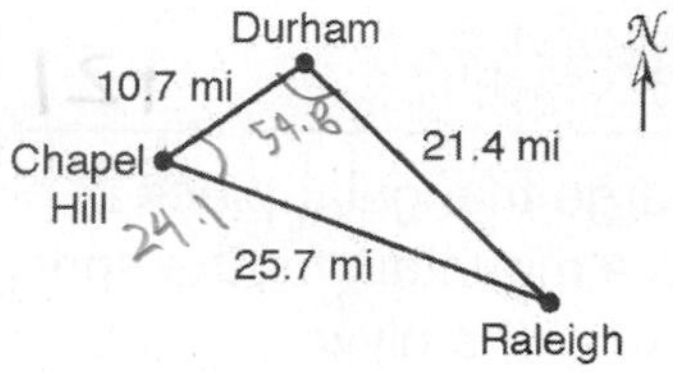

2. The acute angles of right triangle *ABC* are congruent. Find their measures. *(handwritten: 60°)*

The measure of one of the acute angles in a right triangle is given. Find the measure of the other acute angle.

3. 44.9° *(handwritten: 45.1° / 134.9)*

4. $(90 - z)°$ *(handwritten: z)*
(handwritten: $180 = (90 + 90 - z) + t$ 156)

5. 0.3° *(handwritten: 89.7°)*

Find each angle measure.

(labels: D, C 120°, 60, A, B)

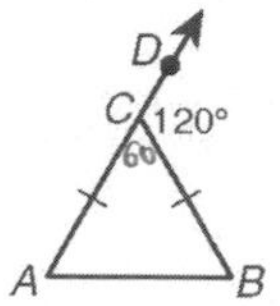

(handwritten: 90°, 90)

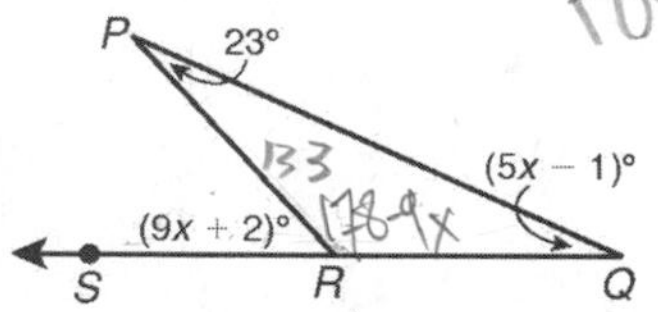

(P, 23°; 133; (5x − 1)°; (9x + 2)°; 178 − 9x; S, R, Q)
(handwritten: 180 (9x + 2) / 178 − 9x / 178 − 9x = / x =)

6. m∠B *(handwritten: 60°, 60°, 60°)*

7. m∠PRS *(handwritten: 133° 47°)*

8. In △LMN, the measure of an exterior angle at *N* measures 99°.
$m\angle L = \frac{1}{3}x°$ and $m\angle M = \frac{2}{3}x°$. Find m∠L, m∠M, and m∠LNM.
(handwritten: m∠L = 27   m∠NM = 180 / m∠M = 54)

9. m∠E and m∠G *(handwritten: m∠E = 20 44 / m∠G = 44)*

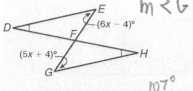
(E, D, F, (6x − 4)°, (5x + 4)°, G, H)
(handwritten: 107° 107° / (5 × 2))

10. m∠T and m∠V *(handwritten: m∠T = 108 / m∠V = 108)*

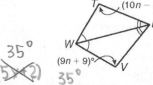
(T, (10n − 2)°, U, W, (9n + 9)°, V)
(handwritten: 35° / 35°)

11. In △ABC and △DEF, m∠A = m∠D and m∠B = m∠E. Find m∠F if an exterior angle at *A* measures 107°, m∠B = (5x + 2)°, and m∠C = (5x + 5)°. *(handwritten: 38° / 38°)*

12. The angle measures of a triangle are in the ratio 3 : 4 : 3. Find the angle measures of the triangle. *(handwritten: 54°, 72°, 54°)*
(handwritten: 60 80 60 / 36 48 56 / 30 40 30 / 51 68 51 / 54 72 54)

© Houghton Mifflin Harcourt Publishing Company

Problem Solving

1. The locations of three food stands on a fair's midway are shown. What is the measure of the angle labeled $x°$?

   121

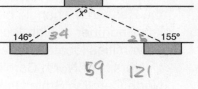

146° 34   155°
59 121

2. A large triangular piece of plywood is to be painted to look like a mountain for the spring musical. The angles at the base of the plywood measure 76° and 45°. What is the measure of the top angle that represents the mountain peak?

   $121 + 59 = 59$

   59

Use the figure of the banner for Exercises 3 and 4.

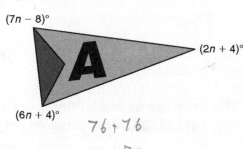

$(7n - 8)°$

$(2n + 4)°$

$(6n + 4)°$

3. What is the value of n? $7n - 8 = 6n + 4$
   $n = 12$

   12

4. What is the measure of each angle in the banner?

   72, 72, 38

   $76 + 76 = 152$

Use the figure of the athlete pole vaulting for Exercises 5 and 6.

$23 + 90 = 113$
$+ 67$

$67 + 113$

$c°$ $b°$ $58°$
$a°$ $x°$

5. What is $x°$, the measure of the angle that the pole makes when it first touches the ground?

   32

6. At takeoff, $a° = 23°$. What is $c°$, the measure of the angle the pole makes with the athlete's body?

   113°

The figure shows a path through a garden. Choose the best answer.

L M 30°

95

Q 55° 55°   82° N
P

7. What is the measure of $\angle QLP$?

   A 20°   C 110°
   Ⓑ 70°   D 125°

8. What is the measure of $\angle LPM$?

   F 85°   Ⓗ 95°
   G 90°   J 125°

9. What is the measure of $\angle PMN$?

   A 98°   C 60°
   Ⓑ 68°   D 55°

Congruent Triangles
Connection: Using Rigid Motions

Essential question: *How can you use properties of rigid motions to draw conclusions about corresponding sides and corresponding angles in congruent triangles?*

When you know that two triangles are congruent, you can make conclusions about the sides and angles of the triangles.

Video Tutor

CC.9–12.G.CO.7

1 EXAMPLE Finding an Unknown Dimension

$\triangle ABC \cong \triangle DEF$. Find DE and m$\angle B$. Explain your reasoning.

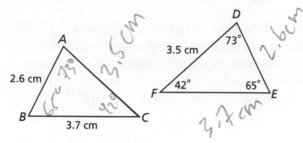

A Complete the following to find DE.

Because $\triangle ABC \cong \triangle DEF$, there is a sequence of rigid motions that maps $\triangle ABC$ to $\triangle DEF$.

This same sequence of rigid motions maps $\overline{AB}$ to _____.

This means $\overline{AB} \cong$ _____.

Congruent segments have the same length, so $AB =$ _____.

$AB =$ _____, so $DE =$ _____.

B To find m$\angle B$, use similar reasoning to show that $\angle B \cong$ _____.

So, m$\angle B =$ _____.

REFLECT

1a. If you know $\triangle ABC \cong \triangle DEF$, what six congruence statements about segments and angles can you write? Why?

_____

_____

_____

When two triangles are congruent, the **corresponding parts** are the sides and angles that are images of each other. You write a congruence statement for two figures by matching the corresponding parts. In other words, the statement $\triangle ABC \cong \triangle DEF$ contains the information that $\overline{AB}$ corresponds to $\overline{DE}$ (and $\overline{AB} \cong \overline{DE}$), $\angle A$ corresponds to $\angle D$ (and $\angle A \cong \angle D$), and so on.

The following theorem is often abbreviated CPCTC. The proof of the theorem is similar to the argument presented in the previous example.

Corresponding Parts of Congruent Triangles are Congruent Theorem (CPCTC)

If two triangles are congruent, then corresponding sides are congruent and corresponding angles are congruent.

The converse of CPCTC is also true. That is, if you are given two triangles and you know that the six pairs of corresponding sides and corresponding angles are congruent, then you can conclude that the triangles are congruent. In the next lesson, you will see that you need only three pairs of congruent corresponding parts in order to conclude that the triangles are congruent, provided they are chosen in the right way.

CC.9–12.G.CO.7

2 EXAMPLE Using CPCTC

$\triangle RGK \cong \triangle MQB$. Write six congruence statements about corresponding parts.

A Identify corresponding sides.

Corresponding sides

Corresponding sides are named using pairs of letters in the same position on either side of the congruence statement.

$\overline{RG} \cong \overline{MQ}$; $\overline{GK} \cong$ _____ ; _____ $\cong$ _____

B Identify corresponding angles.

Corresponding angles

Corresponding angles are named using letters in the same position on either side of the congruence statement.

$\angle R \cong \angle M$; $\angle G \cong$ _____ ; _____ $\cong$ _____

2a. Given that $\triangle PQR \cong \triangle STU$, $PQ = 2.7$ ft, and $PR = 3.4$ ft, is it possible to determine the length of $\overline{TU}$? If so, find the length. If not, explain why not.

_____

_____

2b. A student claims that any two congruent triangles must have the same perimeter. Do you agree or disagree? Why?

_____

_____

PRACTICE

1. $\triangle ABC \cong \triangle DEF$. Find AB and m$\angle E$.

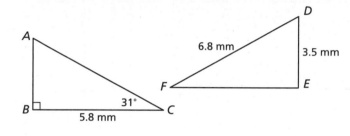

2. $\triangle MNP \cong \triangle QRS$. Find NP and m$\angle P$.

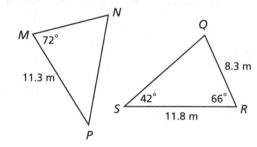

_____   _____

3. $\triangle JKL \cong \triangle LMJ$. Find JK and m$\angle JLM$.

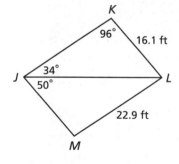

4. $\triangle ABC \cong \triangle DEF$. Find DF and m$\angle EDC$.

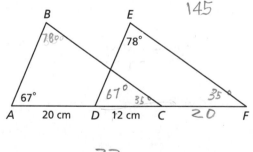

145

32

_____   _____

For each given congruence statement, write six congruence statements about corresponding parts.

5. $\triangle JWT \cong \triangle GKH$

6. $\triangle PQL \cong \triangle KYU$

7. $\triangle HTJ \cong \triangle NRZ$

_____   _____   _____

_____   _____   _____

_____   _____   _____

8. The figure shows a portion of the truss of a bridge. $\triangle ABG \cong \triangle BCH \cong \triangle HGB$.

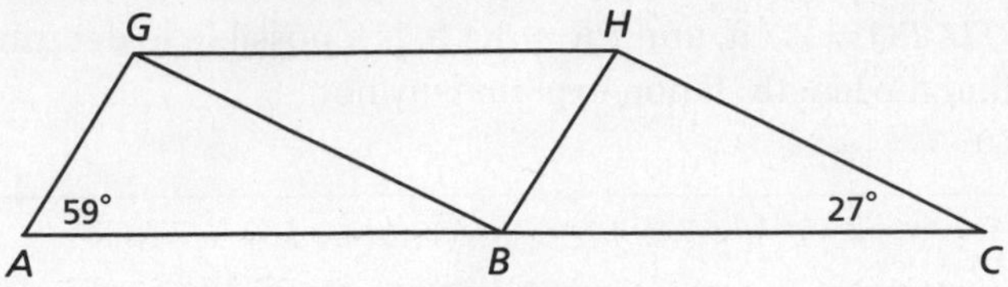

a. Is it possible to determine m∠*GBH*? If so, how? If not, why not?

_____

_____

_____

b. A student claims that *B* is the midpoint of $\overline{AC}$. Do you agree? Explain.

_____

_____

_____

© Houghton Mifflin Harcourt Publishing Company

Additional Practice

In baseball, home plate is a pentagon. Pentagon *ABCDE* is a diagram of a regulation home plate. The baseball rules are very specific about the exact dimensions of this pentagon so that every home plate is congruent to every other home plate. If pentagon *PQRST* is another home plate, identify each congruent corresponding part.

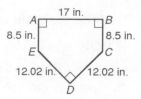

1. ∠*S* ≅ _____

2. ∠*B* ≅ _____

3. $\overline{EA}$ ≅ _____

4. ∠*E* ≅ _____

5. $\overline{PQ}$ ≅ _____

6. $\overline{TS}$ ≅ _____

Given: △*DEF* ≅ △*LMN*. Find each value.

7. m∠*L* = _____

8. *EF* = _____

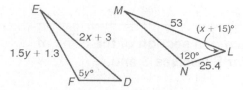

9. Write a two-column proof.

Given: ∠*U* ≅ ∠*UWV* ≅ ∠*ZXY* ≅ ∠*Z*,
$\overline{UV}$ ≅ $\overline{WV}$, $\overline{XY}$ ≅ $\overline{ZY}$, $\overline{UX}$ ≅ ∠*WZ*

Prove: △*UVW* ≅ △*XYZ*

Proof:

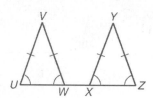

10. **Given:** △*CDE* ≅ △*HIJ*, *DE* = 9*x*, and *IJ* = 7*x* + 3. Find *x* and *DE*.

_____

11. **Given:** △*CDE* ≅ △*HIJ*, m∠*D* = (5*y* + 1)°, and m∠*I* = (6*y* − 25)°.
    Find *y* and m∠*D*.

_____

Problem Solving

Use the diagram of the fence for Exercises 1 and 2.

$\triangle RQW \cong \triangle TVW$

1. If m$\angle RWQ = 36°$ and m$\angle TWV = (2x + 5)°$, what is the value of x?

_____

2. If $RW = (3y - 1)$ feet and $TW = (y + 5)$ feet, what is the length of $\overline{RW}$?

_____

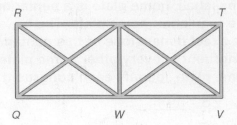

Use the diagram of a section of the Bank of China Tower for Exercises 3 and 4.

$\triangle JKL \cong \triangle LHJ$

3. What is the value of x?

_____

4. Find m$\angle JHL$.

_____

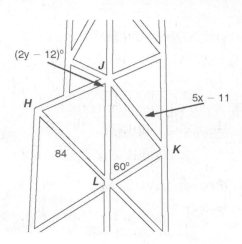

Choose the best answer.

5. Chairs with triangular seats were popular in the Middle Ages. Suppose a chair has a seat that is an isosceles triangle and the congruent sides measure $1\frac{1}{2}$ feet. A second chair has a triangular seat with a perimeter of $5\frac{1}{10}$ feet, and it is congruent to the first seat. What is a side length of the second seat?

   A $1\frac{4}{5}$ ft   C 3 ft

   B $2\frac{1}{10}$ ft   D $3\frac{3}{5}$ ft

Use the diagram for Exercises 6 and 7.

6. C is the midpoint of $\overline{EB}$ and $\overline{AD}$. What additional information would allow you to prove $\triangle ABC \cong \triangle DEC$ by the definition of congruent triangles?

   F $\overline{EB} \cong \overline{AD}$ H $\angle ECD \cong \angle ACB$

   G $\overline{DE} \cong \overline{AB}$ J $\angle A \cong \angle D$, $\angle B \cong \angle E$

7. If $\triangle ABC \cong \triangle DEC$, $ED = 4y + 2$, and $AB = 6y - 4$, what is the length of $\overline{AB}$?

   A 3   C 14

   B 12   D 18

Triangle Congruence: SSS and SAS
Going Deeper

Essential question: *How can you establish the SSS and SAS triangle congruence criteria using properties of rigid motions?*

Video Tutor

You have seen that when two triangles are congruent, the corresponding sides and corresponding angles are congruent. Conversely, if all six pairs of corresponding sides and corresponding angles of two triangles are congruent, then the triangles are congruent.

The proofs of the SSS and SAS congruence criteria that follow serve as proof of this converse. In each case, the proof demonstrates a "shortcut," in which only three pairs of congruent corresponding parts are needed in order to conclude that the triangles are congruent.

CC.9–12.G.CO.8

1 PROOF **SSS Congruence Criterion**

If three sides of one triangle are congruent to three sides of another triangle, then the triangles are congruent.

Given: $\overline{AB} \cong \overline{DE}$, $\overline{BC} \cong \overline{EF}$, and $\overline{AC} \cong \overline{DF}$.

Prove: $\triangle ABC \cong \triangle DEF$

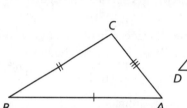

To prove the triangles are congruent, you will find a sequence of rigid motions that maps $\triangle ABC$ to $\triangle DEF$. Complete the following steps of the proof.

A Since $\overline{AB} \cong \overline{DE}$, there is a sequence of rigid motions that maps $\overline{AB}$ to _____.

Apply this sequence of rigid motions to $\triangle ABC$ to get $\triangle A'B'C'$, which shares a side with $\triangle DEF$.

If C' lies on the same side of $\overline{DE}$ as F, reflect $\triangle A'B'C'$ across $\overline{DE}$. This results in the figure at right.

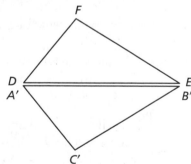

B $\overline{A'C'} \cong \overline{AC}$ because _____.

It is also given that $\overline{AC} \cong \overline{DF}$.

Therefore, $\overline{A'C'} \cong \overline{DF}$ because of the _____ Property of Congruence.

By a similar argument, $\overline{B'C'} \cong$ _____.

C Because $\overline{A'C'} \cong \overline{DF}$, D lies on the perpendicular bisector of $\overline{FC'}$, by the Converse of the Perpendicular Bisector Theorem. Similarly, because $\overline{B'C'} \cong \overline{EF}$, E lies on the perpendicular bisector of $\overline{FC'}$. So, $\overline{DE}$ is the perpendicular bisector of $\overline{FC'}$.

By the definition of reflection, the reflection across $\overline{DE}$ maps C' to _____.

The proof shows that there is a sequence of rigid motions that maps $\triangle ABC$ to $\triangle DEF$. Therefore, $\triangle ABC \cong \triangle DEF$.

1a. The proof uses the fact that congruence is transitive. That is, if you know figure $A \cong$ figure B, and figure $B \cong$ figure C, you can conclude that figure $A \cong$ figure C. Why is this true?

_____

_____

_____

You can use reflections and their properties to prove theorems about angle bisectors. These theorems will be very useful in proofs later on.

The first proof is an indirect proof (or a *proof by contradiction*). To write such a proof, you assume that what you are trying to prove is false and you show that this assumption leads to a contradiction.

CC.9–12.G.CO.9

2 PROOF   **Angle Bisection Theorem**

If a line bisects an angle, then each side of the angle is the image of the other under a reflection across the line.

Given: Line m is the bisector of $\angle ABC$.

Prove: The image of $\overrightarrow{BA}$ under a reflection across line m is $\overrightarrow{BC}$.

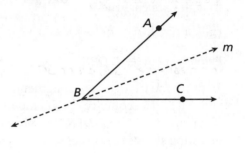

A Assume what you are trying to prove is false.

Assume that the image of $\overrightarrow{BA}$ under a reflection across line m is *not* $\overrightarrow{BC}$. In that case, let the reflection image of $\overrightarrow{BA}$ be $\overrightarrow{BA'}$, which is not the same ray as $\overrightarrow{BC}$.

B Complete the following to show that this assumption leads to a contradiction.

Let D be a point on line m in the interior of $\angle ABC$. Then $\angle DBC$ and $\angle DBA'$ must have different measures.

However, $m\angle DBA = m\angle DBC$ since line m is

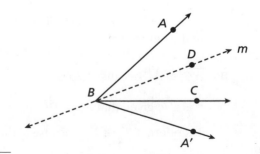

_____

That means $\angle DBA$ and $\angle DBA'$ must have different measures.

This is a contradiction because reflections preserve _____

Therefore, the initial assumption must be incorrect, and the image of $\overrightarrow{BA}$ under a reflection across line m is $\overrightarrow{BC}$.

2a. Explain how you can use paper folding to explain why the Angle Bisection Theorem makes sense.

_____

_____

CC.9–12.G.CO.9

3 **PROOF**   **Reflected Points on an Angle Theorem**

If two points of an angle are located the same distance from the vertex but on different sides of the angle, then the points are images of each other under a reflection across the line that bisects the angle.

Given: Line m is the bisector of $\angle ABC$ and $BA = BC$.

Prove: $r_m(A) = C$ and $r_m(C) = A$.

Complete the following proof.

It is given that line m is the bisector of $\angle ABC$. Therefore, when $\overrightarrow{BA}$ is reflected across line m, its image is $\overrightarrow{BC}$.

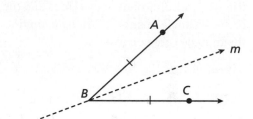

This is justified by _____

This means that $r_m(A)$ lies on $\overrightarrow{BC}$. Let $r_m(A) = A'$.

Since point B is on the line of reflection, $r_m(B) = B$, and since reflections preserve distance, $BA = BA'$.

However, it is given that $BA = BC$. By the Substitution Property of Equality, you can conclude that

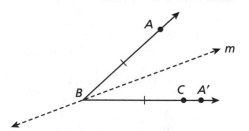

_____

Thus, A' and C are two points on $\overrightarrow{BC}$ that are the same distance from point B. This means $A' = C$, so $r_m(A) = C$.

A similar argument shows that $r_m(C) = A$.

3a. Using the above argument as a model, write out a similar argument that shows that $r_m(C) = A$.

_____

_____

_____

_____

_____

_____

3b. In the figure on the previous page, suppose you reflect point *A* across line *m*. Then you reflect the image of point *A* across line *m*. What is the final location of the point? Why?

_____

_____

_____

4 PROOF   SAS Congruence Criterion

If two sides and the included angle of one triangle are congruent to two sides and the included angle of another triangle, then the triangles are congruent.

Given: $\overline{AB} \cong \overline{DE}$, $\angle B \cong \angle E$, and $\overline{BC} \cong \overline{EF}$.

Prove: $\triangle ABC \cong \triangle DEF$

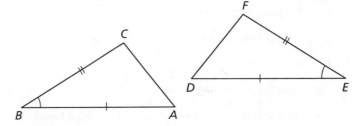

To prove the triangles are congruent, you will find a sequence of rigid motions that maps $\triangle ABC$ to $\triangle DEF$. Complete the following steps of the proof.

A The first step is the same as the first step in the proof of the SSS Congruence Criterion. In particular, the fact that $\overline{AB} \cong \overline{DE}$ means there is a sequence of rigid motions that results in the figure at right.

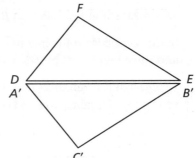

B Rigid motions preserve distance, so $\overline{B'C'} \cong \overline{BC}$. Also, it is given that $\overline{BC} \cong \overline{EF}$.

So, _____ because congruence is transitive.

It is given that $\angle DEF \cong \angle B$. Also, $\angle B \cong$ _____ because rigid motions preserve angle measure.

Therefore, $\angle DEF \cong$ _____ because congruence is transitive. You can use this to conclude that $\overline{DE}$ is the bisector of $\angle FEC'$.

C Now consider the reflection across $\overline{DE}$.

Under this reflection, the image of C' is _____ by the Reflected Points on an Angle Theorem.

The proof shows that there is a sequence of rigid motions that maps $\triangle ABC$ to $\triangle DEF$. Therefore, $\triangle ABC \cong \triangle DEF$.

4a. Explain how the Reflected Points on an Angle Theorem lets you conclude that the image of C' under a reflection across $\overline{DE}$ is F.

_____

_____

 CC.9–12.G.SRT.5

5 EXAMPLE Using the SSS Congruence Criterion

Complete the proof.

Given: M is the midpoint of $\overline{RT}$; $\overline{SR} \cong \overline{ST}$

Prove: $\triangle RSM \cong \triangle TSM$

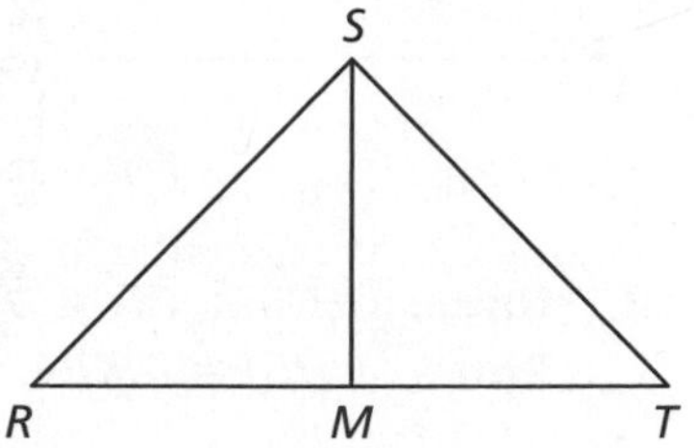

A Use a colored pen or pencil to mark the figure using the given information.

B Write a statement in each cell to complete the proof. The reason for each statement is provided.

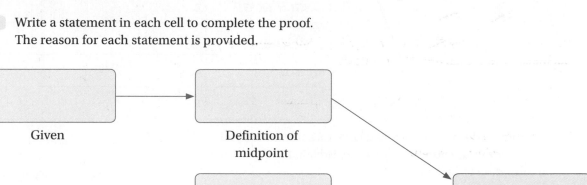

Given

Definition of midpoint

Reflexive Property of Congruence

SSS Congruence Criterion

Given

5a. What piece of additional given information in the above example would allow you to use the SAS Congruence Criterion to prove that $\triangle RSM \cong \triangle TSM$?

_____

_____

5b. Suppose the given information had been that M is the midpoint of $\overline{RT}$ and $\angle R \cong \angle T$. Would it have been possible to prove $\triangle RSM \cong \triangle TSM$? Explain.

_____

_____

PRACTICE

Complete the two-column proof.

1. **Given:** $\overline{AB} \cong \overline{CD}$, $\overline{AD} \cong \overline{CB}$
Prove: $\triangle ABD \cong \triangle CBD$

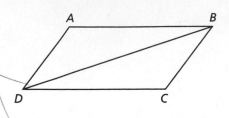

Statements	Reasons
1. $\overline{AB} \cong \overline{CD}$	1.
2. $\overline{AD} \cong \overline{CB}$	2.
3.	3.
4. $\triangle ABD \cong \triangle CBD$	4.

2. **Given:** $\overline{GH} \parallel \overline{JK}$, $\overline{GH} \cong \overline{JK}$
Prove: $\triangle HGJ \cong \triangle KJG$

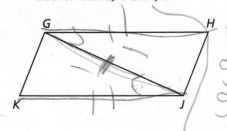

Statements	Reasons
1. $\overline{GH} \parallel \overline{JK}$	1. Given
2. $\angle HGJ \cong \angle KJG$	2. Def of alternate angles
3. GH ≅ JK	3. Given
4. $\overline{GJ} \cong \overline{GJ}$	4. Reflexive Property
5. →	5. SAS

3. To find the distance *JK* across a large rock formation, you locate points as shown in the figure. Explain how to use this information to find *JK*.

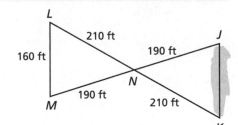

_____

_____

4. To find the distance *RS* across a lake, you locate points as shown in the figure. Can you use this information to find *RS*? Explain.

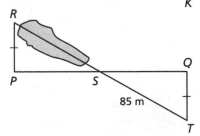

_____

_____

5. $\triangle DEF \cong \triangle GHJ$, $DF = 3x + 2$, $GJ = 6x - 13$, and $HJ = 5x$. Find *HJ*.

_____

6. In the figure, $\overleftrightarrow{MC}$ is the perpendicular bisector of $\overline{AB}$. Is it possible to prove that $\triangle AMC \cong \triangle BMC$? Why or why not?

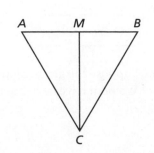

_____

_____

_____

Additional Practice

Write whether SSS or SAS, if either, can be used to prove the triangles congruent. If no triangles can be proved congruent, write *neither*.

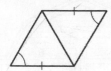

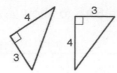

1. _____neither_____

2. _____SAS_____

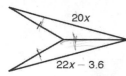

3. ~~SAS~~ neither

4. _____SSS_____

Find the value of *x* so that the triangles are congruent.

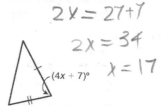

$2x = 27 + 7$
$2x = 34$
$x = 17$

$2x = -3.6$
$x = 1\frac{3}{5}$

5. *x* = _____1.8_____

6. *x* = _____17_____

The Hatfield and McCoy families are feuding over some land. Neither family will be satisfied unless the two triangular fields are exactly the same size. You know that *C* is the midpoint of each of the intersecting segments. Write a two-column proof that will settle the dispute.

7. **Given:** *C* is the midpoint of $\overline{AD}$ and $\overline{BE}$.

   Prove: $\triangle ABC \cong \triangle DEC$

   Proof:

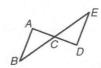

Problem Solving

Use the diagram for Exercises 1 and 2.

A shed door appears to be divided into congruent right triangles.

1. Suppose $\overline{AB} \cong \overline{CD}$. Use SAS to show $\triangle ABD \cong \triangle DCA$.

   ASS

   _____

   _____

   _____

   _____

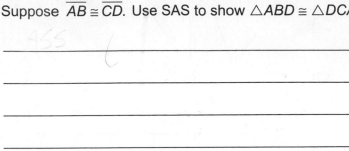

2. J is the midpoint of AB and $\overline{AK} \cong \overline{BK}$. Use SSS to explain why $\triangle AKJ \cong \triangle BKJ$.

   _____

   _____

   _____

3. A *balalaika* is a Russian stringed instrument. Show that the triangular parts of the two balalaikas are congruent for $x = 6$.

   SAS   boi

   _____

   _____

   _____

   _____

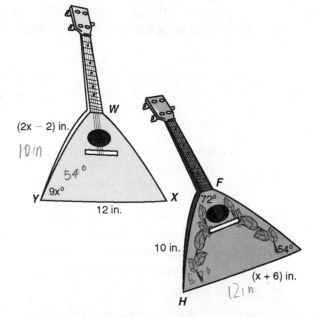

(2x − 2) in.

10 in

54°

9x°

12 in.

W

Y

X

F

72°

10 in.

54°

(x + 6) in.

12 in

H

A quilt pattern of a dog is shown. Choose the best answer.

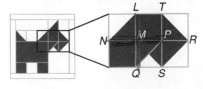

4. $ML = MP = MN = MQ = 1$ inch. Which statement is correct?

   A $\triangle LMN \cong \triangle QMP$ by SAS.

   (B) $\triangle LMN \cong \triangle QMP$ by SSS.

   C $\triangle LMN \cong \triangle MQP$ by SAS.

   D $\triangle LMN \cong \triangle MQP$ by SSS.

5. P is the midpoint of $\overline{TS}$ and $TR = SR = 1.4$ inches. What can you conclude about $\triangle TRP$ and $\triangle SRP$?

   F $\triangle TRP \cong \triangle SRP$ by SAS.

   (G) $\triangle TRP \cong \triangle SRP$ by SSS.

   H $\triangle TRP \cong \triangle SPR$ by SAS.

   J $\triangle TRP \cong \triangle SPR$ by SSS.

Triangle Congruence: ASA, AAS, and HL
Going Deeper

Essential question: *How can you establish and use the ASA and AAS triangle congruence criteria?*

Video Tutor

CC.9–12.G.CO.8

1 PROOF   **ASA Congruence Criterion**

If two angles and the included side of one triangle are congruent to two angles and the included side of another triangle, then the triangles are congruent.

Given: $\overline{AB} \cong \overline{DE}$, $\angle A \cong \angle D$, and $\angle B \cong \angle E$.

Prove: $\triangle ABC \cong \triangle DEF$

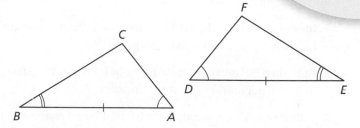

To prove the triangles are congruent, you will find a sequence of rigid motions that maps $\triangle ABC$ to $\triangle DEF$. Complete the following steps of the proof.

A The first step is the same as the first step in the proof of the SSS Congruence Criterion. In particular the fact that $\overline{AB} \cong \overline{DE}$, means there is a sequence of rigid motions that results in the figure at right.

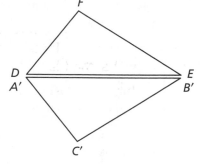

B As in the previous proofs, you can use the fact that rigid motions preserve angle measure and transitivity of congruence to show the following:

$\angle C'A'B' \cong$ _____ and $\angle C'B'A' \cong$ _____.

This means $\overline{DE}$ bisects both $\angle FDC'$ and _____.

By the Angle Bisection Theorem, under a reflection across $\overleftrightarrow{DE}$, $\overrightarrow{A'C'}$ maps to $\overrightarrow{DF}$, and $\overrightarrow{B'C'}$ maps to $\overrightarrow{EF}$. Since the image of C' lies on both $\overrightarrow{DF}$ and $\overrightarrow{EF}$, the image of C' must be F.

The proof shows that there is a sequence of rigid motions that maps $\triangle ABC$ to $\triangle DEF$. Therefore, $\triangle ABC \cong \triangle DEF$.

REFLECT

1a. Explain how knowing that the image of C' lies on both $\overrightarrow{DF}$ and $\overrightarrow{EF}$ allows you to conclude that the image of C' is F.

Once you have shown that two triangles are congruent, you can use the fact that corresponding parts of congruent triangles are congruent (CPCTC) to draw conclusions about side lengths and angle measures.

CC.9–12.G.SRT.5

2 EXAMPLE Using the ASA Congruence Criterion

Solve the following problem.

You want to find the distance across a river. In order to find the distance *AB*, you locate points as described below. Explain how to use this information and the figure to find *AB*.

1. Identify a landmark, such as a tree, at *A*. Place a marker (*B*) directly across the river from *A*.

2. At *B*, turn 90° away from *A* and walk 1000 feet in a straight line. Place a marker (*C*) at this location.

3. Continue walking another 1000 feet. Place a marker (*D*) at this location.

4. Turn 90° away from the river and walk until the marker *C* aligns with *A*. Place a marker (*E*) at this location. Measure $\overline{DE}$.

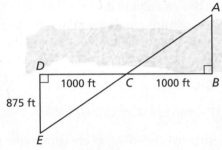

A Show $\triangle ABC \cong \triangle EDC$.

• Based on the information marked in the figure, which pairs of sides or pairs of angles do you know to be congruent?

_____

• What additional pair of sides or pair of angles do you know to be congruent? Why?

_____

• How can you conclude that $\triangle ABC \cong \triangle EDC$?

_____

B Use corresponding parts of congruent triangles.

• Which side of $\triangle EDC$ corresponds to $\overline{AB}$? _____

• What is the length of $\overline{AB}$? Why?

_____

REFLECT

2a. Suppose you had walked 500 feet from *B* to *C* and then walked another 500 feet from *C* to *D*. Would that have changed the distance *ED*? Explain.

_____

_____

You have already used three triangle congruence criteria: SSS, SAS, and ASA. There is another criterion that is useful in proofs, the AAS Congruence Criterion.

🔑 AAS Congruence Criterion

If two angles and a non-included side of one triangle are congruent to two angles and the corresponding non-included side of another triangle, then the triangles are congruent.

CC.9–12.G.CO.10

3 PROOF   **ASA Congruence Criterion**

Given: $\angle B \cong \angle E$, $\angle C \cong \angle F$, $\overline{AC} \cong \overline{DF}$

Prove: $\triangle ABC \cong \triangle DEF$

To prove the triangles are congruent, you can use the Triangle Sum Theorem and reasoning about the angles of the triangles to show that $\angle A \cong \angle D$. Then you can show the triangles are congruent by using ASA.

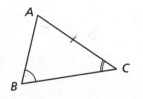 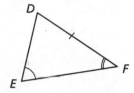

Complete the proof by filling in the missing statements and reasons.

Statements	Reasons
1. $\angle B \cong \angle E$, $\angle C \cong \angle F$	1. Given
2. $m\angle A + m\angle B + m\angle C = 180°$	2. Triangle Sum Theorem
3. $m\angle A = 180° - m\angle B - m\angle C$	3. ~~Sum of triangles = 180°~~
4. $m\angle D + m\angle E + m\angle F = 180°$	4. Sum of triangles = 180°
5.	5. Subtraction Property of Equality
6. $m\angle B = m\angle E$, $m\angle C = m\angle F$	6. Definition of congruent angles
7. $m\angle D = 180° - m\angle B - m\angle C$	7.
8. $m\angle A = m\angle D$	8. Transitive Property of Equality
9. $\angle A \cong \angle D$	9.
10. $\overline{AC} \cong \overline{DF}$	10. Given
11.	11. ASA Congruence Criterion

REFLECT

3a. Which prior steps of the proof are used in step 8?

_____

3b. Which prior steps of the proof are used in the last step? Explain.

_____

_____

1. Complete the proof.

   Given: $\overline{GE}$ bisects $\angle DGF$ and $\angle DEF$.

   Prove: $\triangle GDE \cong \triangle GFE$

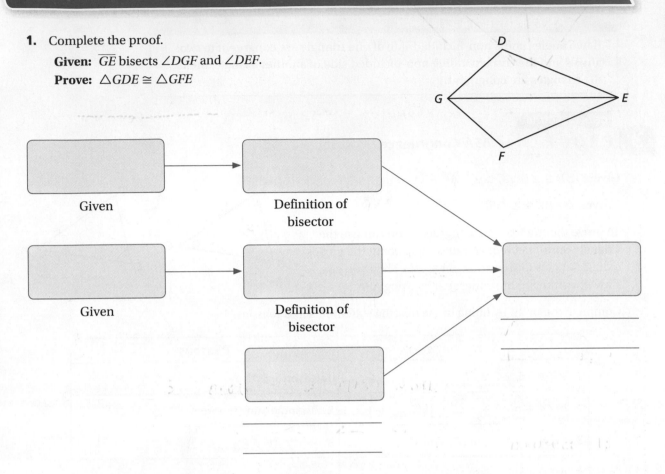

Given	Definition of bisector

Given	Definition of bisector

2. **a.** Write a two-column proof in the table provided at right. You may not need to use all the rows of the table for your proof.

   Given: $\angle QMP \cong \angle PNQ$, $\angle MPQ \cong \angle NQP$

   Prove: $\triangle MQP \cong \triangle NPQ$

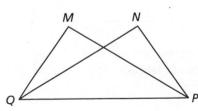

Statements	Reasons
1.	1.
2.	2.
3.	3.
4.	4.
5.	5.
6.	6.

   b. What additional congruence statements can you write using CPCTC?

Additional Practice

Students in Mrs. Marquez's class are watching a film on the uses of geometry in architecture. The film projector casts the image on a flat screen as shown in the figure. The dotted line is the bisector of $\angle ABC$. Tell whether you can use each congruence theorem to prove that $\triangle ABD \cong \triangle CBD$. If not, tell what else you need to know.

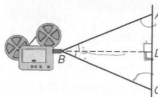

1. Hypotenuse-Leg

    Need to know Hypotenuse

2. Angle-Side-Angle

    Could prove

3. Angle-Angle-Side

    Need to know angle C and A

Write which postulate, if any, can be used to prove the pair of triangles congruent.

4. _neither_   5. _A SAS ASA_

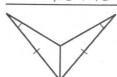

6. _neither_   7. _AHS_

Write a paragraph proof.

8. **Given:** $\angle PQU \cong \angle TSU$,
      $\angle QUR$ and $\angle SUR$ are right angles.
   Prove: $\triangle RUQ \cong \triangle RUS$

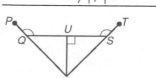

Problem Solving

Use the following information for Exercises 1 and 2.

Melanie is at hole 6 on a miniature golf course. She walks <u>east 7.5 meters to hole 7</u>. She then faces south, turns 67° west, and walks to hole 8. From hole 8, she faces north, turns 35° west, and walks to hole 6.

1. Draw the section of the golf course described. Label the measures of the angles in the triangle.

2. Is there enough information given to determine the location of holes 6, 7, and 8? Explain.

_____ NO _____

3. A section of the front of an English Tudor home is shown in the diagram. If you know that $\overline{KN} \cong \overline{LN}$ and $\overline{JN} \cong \overline{MN}$, can you use HL to conclude that $\triangle JKN \cong \triangle MLN$? Explain.

_____

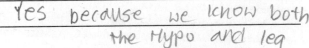
Yes because we know both
the Hypo and leg

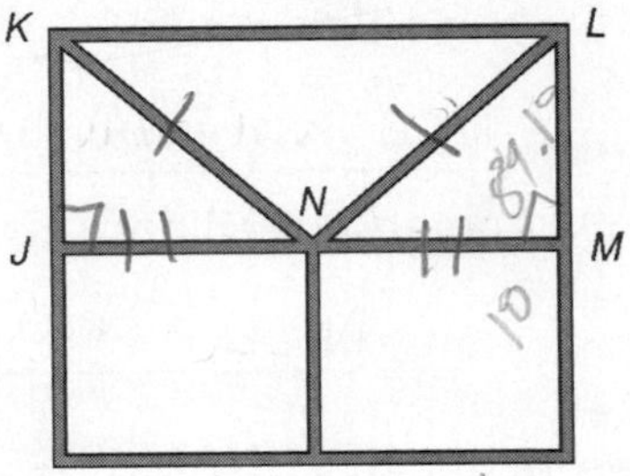

Use the diagram of a kite for Exercises 4 and 5.

$\overline{AE}$ is the angle bisector of $\angle DAF$ and $\angle DEF$.

God proved it

100 %

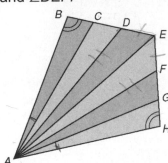

4. What can you conclude about $\triangle DEA$ and $\triangle FEA$?

   A $\triangle DEA \cong \triangle FEA$ by HL.

   B $\triangle DEA \cong \triangle FEA$ by AAA.

   C $\triangle DEA \cong \triangle FEA$ by ASA.

   D $\triangle DEA \cong \triangle FEA$ by SAS.

5. Based on the diagram, what can you conclude about $\triangle BCA$ and $\triangle HGA$?

   F $\triangle BCA \cong \triangle HGA$ by HL.

   G $\triangle BCA \cong \triangle HGA$ by AAS.

   H $\triangle BCA \cong \triangle HGA$ by ASA.

   J It cannot be shown using the given information that $\triangle BCA \cong \triangle HGA$.

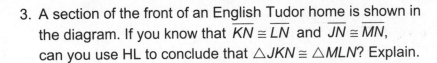

Triangle Congruence: CPCTC
Connection: Proving Slope Criteria

Essential question: *How can CPCTC be used in proving slope criteria for parallel and perpendicular lines?*

Slope is useful for determining whether two lines are parallel.

Video Tutor

> ### Slope Criterion for Parallel Lines
>
> Two non-vertical lines are parallel if and only if they have the same slope.

Because the theorem is stated as a biconditional (*if and only if*), the proof has two parts, one for each "direction" of the theorem.

CC.9–12.G.GPE.5

1 PROOF   **Parallel Lines Have the Same Slope**

Given: Non-vertical lines m and n, $m \parallel n$

Prove: Line m and line n have the same slope.

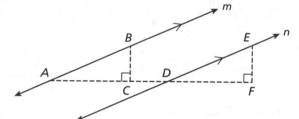

A   Let A and B be two points on line m. Draw a horizontal line through A and a vertical line through B to create the "slope triangle," $\triangle ABC$.

Extend $\overline{AC}$ to intersect line n at point D and then extend it to point F so that $AC = DF$. Draw a vertical line through F intersecting line n at point E.

B   Since $m \parallel n$, $\angle BAC \cong \angle EDF$ by _____.

$\triangle BAC \cong \triangle EDF$ by _____.

So, $\overline{BC} \cong \overline{EF}$ by _____.

This means $BC = EF$, so $\frac{BC}{AC} = \frac{EF}{DF}$ by _____.

This shows that the slope of m equals the slope of n by the definition of slope.

REFLECT

1a. Does the above proof work if the lines are horizontal? If not, does the theorem still hold? Explain.

_____

_____

1b. How can you estimate the slope of lines m and n in the above figure?

_____

2 PROOF   **Lines with the Same Slope Are Parallel**

Given: Line *m* and line *n* have the same slope.

Prove: *m* ∥ *n*

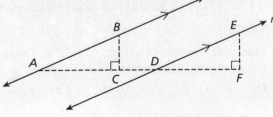

A Let *A* and *B* be two points on line *m*. Draw a horizontal line through *A* and a vertical line through *B* to create the "slope triangle," △*ABC*.

Extend $\overline{AC}$ to intersect line *n* at point *D* and then extend it to point *F* so that *DF* = *AC*. Draw a vertical line through *F* intersecting line *n* at point *E*.

B Since line *m* and line *n* have the same slope, $\frac{BC}{AC} = \underline{\quad}$.

But *DF* = *AC*, so by substitution, $\frac{BC}{AC} = \underline{\quad}$.

Multiplying both sides by *AC* shows that *BC* = _____.

C Now △*BAC* ≅ △*EDF* by _____.

So, ∠*BAC* ≅ ∠*EDF* by _____.

This shows *m* ∥ *n* by _____.

REFLECT

2a. In the proof above, what are the names of the corresponding angles in the two triangles that are used to show that the triangles are congruent? How do you know they are congruent?

_____

_____

_____

2b. In the proof above, what are the names of the corresponding angles in the two triangles that are used to show that line *m* and line *n* are parallel? What transversal is involved in the reasoning?

_____

_____

Slope is useful for determining whether two lines are perpendicular.

> ### Slope Criterion for Perpendicular Lines
>
> Two non-vertical lines are perpendicular if and only if the product of their slopes is -1.

Like the Slope Criterion for Parallel Lines, the theorem is stated as a biconditional. Therefore, the proof has two parts, one for each "direction" of the theorem.

CC.9–12.G.GPE.5

3 PROOF   **Perpendicular Lines Have Slopes Whose Product Is -1**

Given: Non-vertical lines m and n, $m \perp n$

Prove: The product of the slope of line m and the slope of line n is -1.

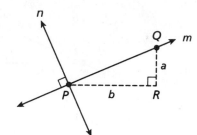

A   Assume the lines intersect at point P, and assume the slope of line m is positive. (You can write a similar proof in the case that the slope of line m is negative.)

Let Q be a point on line m, and draw the "slope triangle," $\triangle PQR$, as shown.

The slope of line m is _____, where a and b are both positive.

B   Rotate $\triangle PQR$ 90° around point P. This gives $\triangle PQ'R'$, as shown.

$\triangle PQ'R'$ is a slope triangle for line n.

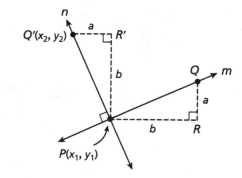

Let the coordinates of P be (x_1, y_1) and let the coordinates of Q' be (x_2, y_2).

Then the slope of line n is $\dfrac{y_2 - y_1}{x_2 - x_1} = \dfrac{b}{\boxed{}} = -\dfrac{\boxed{}}{\boxed{}}$.

C   Find the product of the slope of line m and the slope of line n.

The product of the slopes is _____ · _____ = _____.

So, the product of the slope of line m and the slope of line n is _____.

REFLECT

3a.   When you calculate the slope of line n, why is $x_2 - x_1$ negative?

_____

3b.   Does the theorem apply when one of the lines is horizontal? Explain.

_____

4 PROOF   **Lines with Slopes Whose Product Is −1 Are Perpendicular**

Given: The product of the slope of line m and the slope of line n is −1.

Prove: $m \perp n$

A   Let line m have positive slope $\frac{a}{b}$, where a and b are both positive.

Let line n have slope z. It is given that $z \cdot \frac{a}{b} = -1$.

Solving for z shows that the slope of line n is _____.

B   Assume the lines intersect at point P. Set up slope triangles for lines m and n as shown.

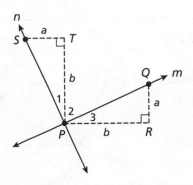

Then $\overline{ST} \cong$ _____ and $\overline{PT} \cong$ _____.

Also, $\angle T \cong \angle R$ because _____.

So, $\triangle STP \cong \triangle QRP$ by _____.

C   Now $\angle 1 \cong \angle 3$ by _____.

$\overline{PT}$ is a vertical line segment and $\overline{PR}$ is a horizontal line segment, so $\angle TPR$

is a right angle. This means $\angle 2$ and $\angle 3$ are _____.

By substitution, $\angle 2$ and $\angle 1$ are _____.

But $m\angle 1 + m\angle 2 = m\angle SPQ$ by the Angle Addition Postulate.

So, $m\angle SPQ =$ _____ and line m is perpendicular to line n.

REFLECT

4a. The proof begins by assuming that line m has a positive slope. If the product of the slopes of two lines is −1, how do you know that one of the lines must have a positive slope?

_____

_____

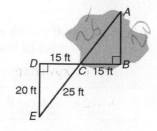

4-7

Additional Practice

1. Heike Dreschler set the Woman's World Junior Record for the long jump in 1983. She jumped about 23.4 feet. The diagram shows two triangles and a pond. Explain whether Heike could have jumped the pond along path *BA* or along path *CA*.

_____

_____

_____

_____

_____

Write a flowchart proof.

2. **Given:** ∠L ≅ ∠J, $\overline{KJ} \parallel \overline{LM}$

   Prove: ∠LKM ≅ ∠JMK

Write a two-column proof.

3. **Given:** *FGHI* is a rectangle.

   Prove: The diagonals of a rectangle have equal lengths.

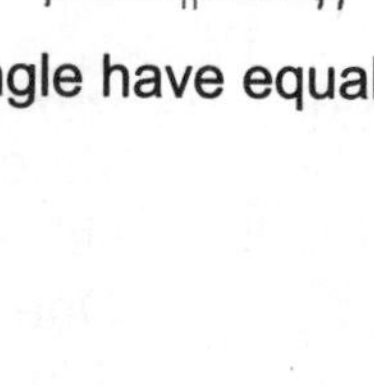

Problem Solving

1. Two triangular plates are congruent. The area of one of the plates is 60 square inches. What is the area of the other plate? Explain.

   60 square inches because congruent means same in both shape and size and angle measures.

2. An archaeologist draws the triangles to find the distance XY across a ravine. What is XY? Explain.

   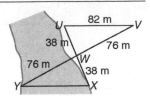

   82 m because NVW and XWXY are congruent due to the SSS

3. A city planner sets up the triangles to find the distance RS across a river. Describe the steps that she can use to find RS.

   N
   40 ft
   P   65 ft   Q   65 ft   R
                                           40 ft
                                           S

   _____

   _____

   _____

   _____

   _____

Choose the best answer.

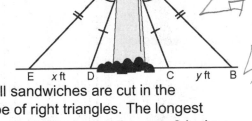

4. A lighthouse and the range of its shining light are shown. What can you conclude?

   A $x = y$ by CPCTC   C $\angle AED \cong \angle ADE$ by CPCTC

   B $x = 2y$ D $\angle AED \cong \angle ACB$

   A
   E   x ft   D   C   y ft   B

5. A rectangular piece of cloth 15 centimeters long is cut along a diagonal to form two triangles. One of the triangles has a side length of 9 centimeters. Which is a true statement?

   F The second triangle has an angle measure of 15° by CPCTC.

   G The second triangle has a side length of 9 centimeters by CPCTC.

   H You cannot make a conclusion about the side length of the second triangle.

   J The triangles are not congruent.

6. Small sandwiches are cut in the shape of right triangles. The longest sides of all the sandwiches are 3 inches. One sandwich has a side length of 2 inches. Which is a true statement?

   A All the sandwiches have a side length of 2 inches by CPCTC.

   B All the sandwiches are isosceles triangles with side lengths of 2 inches.

   C None of the other sandwiches have side lengths of 2 inches.

   D You cannot make a conclusion using CPCTC.

Introduction to Coordinate Proof
Going Deeper

Essential question: *How do you write a coordinate proof?*

You have already seen a wide range of purely geometric proofs. These
proofs used postulates and theorems to build logical arguments.
Now you will learn how to write coordinate proofs. These proofs also
use logic, but they apply ideas from algebra to help demonstrate
geometric relationships.

Video Tutor

$$z = \sqrt{(y^2 - y')^2 + (x^2 - x')^2}$$

CC.9–12.G.GPE.4

1 EXAMPLE   **Proving or Disproving a Statement**

Prove or disprove that the triangle with vertices $A(4, 2)$, $B(-1, 4)$, and $C(2, -3)$
is an isosceles triangle.

A   Plot the vertices and draw the triangle.

B   Use the distance formula to find the length of each
    side of $\triangle ABC$.

$$AB = \sqrt{(-1-4)^2 + (4-2)^2} = \sqrt{(-5)^2 + 2^2} = \sqrt{29}$$

$$BC = \underline{\sqrt{-7^2 + 9} \;=\; \sqrt{58} = 7.07}$$

$$AC = \underline{\sqrt{25 + 4} \;=\; \sqrt{29}}$$

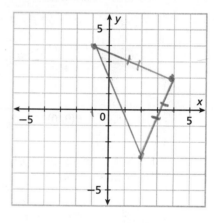

C   Draw a conclusion based on your results. State whether or not the triangle is
    isosceles and why.

_____

REFLECT

1a. What other conclusion(s) can you make about the sides or angles of $\triangle ABC$?
Explain.

_____

_____

1b. Suppose you map $\triangle ABC$ to $\triangle A'B'C'$ by the translation $(x, y) \rightarrow (x - 3, y - 2)$.
Is $\triangle A'B'C'$ an isosceles triangle? Why or why not?

_____

_____

You can write a coordinate proof to prove general facts about geometric figures. The first step in such a proof is using variables to assign general coordinates to a figure using only what is known about the figure.

CC.9–12.G.GPE.4

2 EXAMPLE Writing a Coordinate Proof

Prove that in a right triangle, the midpoint of the hypotenuse is equidistant from all three vertices.

A Assign coordinates to the figure.

Let the triangle be $\triangle ABC$. Since the triangle is a right triangle, assume $\angle B$ is a right angle. Place $\angle B$ at the origin and place the legs along the positive x- and y-axes.

Since the proof involves a midpoint, use multiples of 2 in assigning coordinates to A and C, as shown.

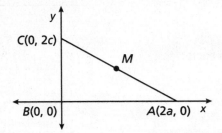

B Let M be the midpoint of the hypotenuse, $\overline{AC}$. Use the midpoint formula to find the coordinates of M.

$$M\left(\frac{\boxed{} + \boxed{}}{2}, \frac{\boxed{} + \boxed{}}{2}\right) = M\left(\boxed{}, \boxed{}\right)$$

C Use the distance formula to find MA, MB, and MC.

$$MA = \sqrt{\left(\boxed{} - \boxed{}\right)^2 + \left(\boxed{} - \boxed{}\right)^2} = \sqrt{\boxed{}^2 + \boxed{}^2}$$

$$MB = \sqrt{\left(\boxed{} - \boxed{}\right)^2 + \left(\boxed{} - \boxed{}\right)^2} = \sqrt{\boxed{}^2 + \boxed{}^2}$$

$$MB = \sqrt{\left(\boxed{} - \boxed{}\right)^2 + \left(\boxed{} - \boxed{}\right)^2} = \sqrt{\boxed{}^2 + \boxed{}^2}$$

So, the midpoint of the hypotenuse is equidistant from all three vertices because

_____

_____

REFLECT

2a. Explain why it is more convenient to assign the coordinates as $A(2a, 0)$ and $C(0, 2c)$ rather than $A(a, 0)$ and $C(0, c)$.

_____

_____

2b. Can you write the proof by assigning the coordinates as $A(2n, 0)$ and $C(0, 2n)$?

_____

_____

_____

PRACTICE

1. Prove or disprove that the triangle with vertices $R(-2, -2)$, $S(1, 4)$, and $T(4, -5)$ is an equilateral triangle.

_____

_____

_____

_____

_____

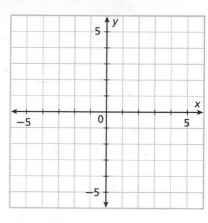

2. Refer to the triangle you drew in Exercise 1 to prove or disprove that the triangle with vertices $R(-2, -2)$, $S(1, 4)$, and $T(4, -5)$ is a right triangle.

_____

_____

_____

3. $\triangle ABC$ has vertices $A(-4, 1)$, $B(-3, 4)$, and $C(-1, 1)$. $\triangle DEF$ has vertices $D(2, -3)$, $E(5, -2)$, and $F(2, 0)$. Prove or disprove that the triangles are congruent.

_____

_____

_____

_____

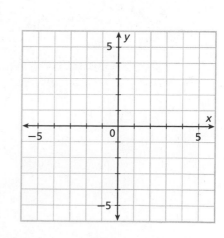

4. Write a coordinate proof to prove that the diagonals of a rectangle are congruent. Use the space at right to show how to assign coordinates. Then write the proof below.

_____

_____

_____

_____

5. Error Analysis A student proves that every right triangle is isosceles by assigning coordinates as shown at right and by using the distance formula to show that $PQ = a$ and $RQ = a$. Explain the error in the student's proof.

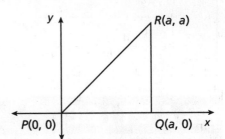

_____

_____

_____

_____

Additional Practice

Position an isosceles triangle with sides of 8 units, 5 units, and 5 units in the coordinate plane. Label the coordinates of each vertex. (*Hint:* Use the Pythagorean Theorem.)

1. Center the long side on the *x*-axis at the origin.

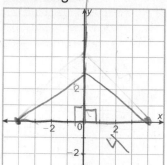

2. Place the long side on the *y*-axis centered at the origin.

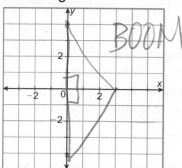

Write a coordinate proof.

3. **Given:** Rectangle *ABCD* has vertices *A*(0, 4), *B*(6, 4), *C*(6, 0), and *D*(0, 0). *E* is the midpoint of $\overline{DC}$. *F* is the midpoint of $\overline{DA}$.

   Prove: The area of rectangle *DEGF* is one-fourth the area of rectangle *ABCD*.

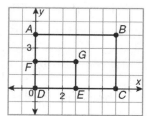

Problem Solving

Round to the nearest tenth for Exercises 1 and 2.

1. A fountain is at the center of a square courtyard. If one grid unit represents one yard, what is the distance from the fountain at (0, 0) to each corner of the courtyard? **4.2**

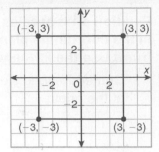

2. Noah started at his home at $A(0, 0)$, walked with his dog to the park at $B(4, 2)$, walked to his friend's house at $C(8, 0)$, then walked home. If one grid unit represents 20 meters, what is the distance that Noah and his dog walked? **178**

8.9

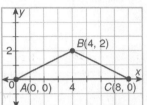

Use the following information for Exercises 3 and 4.

Rachel started her cycling trip at $G(0, 7)$. Malik started his trip at $J(0, 0)$. Their paths crossed at $H(4, 2)$.

3. Draw their routes in the coordinate plane.

4. If one grid unit represents $\frac{1}{2}$ mile, who had ridden farther when their paths crossed? Explain.

Rachel because her distance was farther away from point H.

Choose the best answer.

5. Two airplanes depart from an airport at $A(9, 11)$. The first airplane travels to a location at $N(-250, 80)$, and the second airplane travels to a location at $P(105, -400)$. Each unit represents 1 mile. What is the distance, to the nearest mile, between the two airplanes?

$480^2 + 355^2$

   A 335.3 mi

   B 477.9 mi

   C 490.3 mi

   (D) 597.0 mi

6. A corner garden has vertices at $Q(0, 0)$, $R(0, 2d)$, and $S(2c, 0)$. A brick walkway runs from point Q to the midpoint M of $\overline{RS}$. What is QM?

   F (c, d)

   G $c^2 + d^2$

   H $\sqrt{c + d}$

   (J) $\sqrt{c^2 + d^2}$

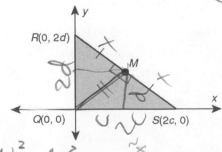

$M = 4d^2 + 4c^2$

$QM = 16d^2 + 16c^2$

Isosceles and Equilateral Triangles
Focus on Reasoning

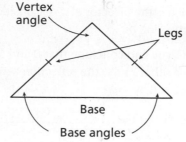

COMMON
CORE

CC.9-12.G.CO.10

Essential question: *What special relationships exist among the sides and angles of isosceles triangles?*

Recall that an *isosceles* triangle is a triangle with at least two congruent sides. The congruent sides are called the **legs** of the triangle. The angle formed by the legs is the **vertex angle**. The side of the triangle opposite the vertex angle is the **base**. The angles that have the base as a side are the **base angles**.

1 **Investigate isosceles triangles.**

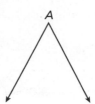 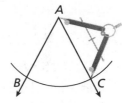

A Work on a separate sheet of paper. Use a straightedge to draw an angle. Label it ∠A.

B Place the point of your compass on the vertex of the angle and draw an arc that intersects the sides of the angle at B and C.

C Use the straightedge to draw $\overline{BC}$.

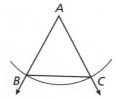

D Use a protractor to measure ∠B and ∠C. Record the measures in the table under the column for Triangle 1.

E Repeat the process two more times, drawing different angles and using different compass settings. In each case, note m∠B and m∠C in the table.

	Triangle 1	**Triangle 2**	**Triangle 3**
m∠B			
m∠C			

REFLECT

1a. How do you know the triangles you constructed were isosceles triangles?

_____

_____

1b. Compare your work with that of other students. Then make a conjecture about isosceles triangles.

_____

2 Prove the Isosceles Triangle Theorem.

The base angles of an isosceles triangle are congruent.

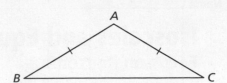

Given: $\overline{AB} \cong \overline{AC}$
Prove: $\angle B \cong \angle C$

Complete the proof.

Draw line m, which is the bisector of $\angle A$. Consider the reflection across line m.

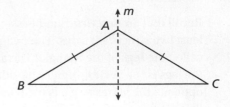

Because $AB = AC$, you can conclude that B and C are images of each other under the reflection across line m. This is justified by

_____

So, $\angle B$ and $\angle C$ are images of each other and therefore $\angle B \cong \angle C$, because

_____

REFLECT

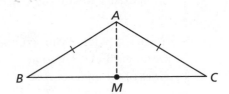

2a. A different proof of the Isosceles Triangle Theorem is based on letting point M be the midpoint of $\overline{BC}$ and drawing $\overline{AM}$. Explain the steps of this proof.

_____

_____

_____

3 Prove the Converse of the Isosceles Triangle Theorem.

If two angles of a triangle are congruent, then the sides opposite them are congruent.

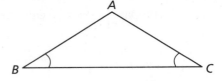

Given: $\angle B \cong \angle C$
Prove: $\overline{AB} \cong \overline{AC}$

Complete the proof.

Draw line m, which is the bisector of $\angle A$. Let point X be the point where line m intersects $\overline{BC}$.

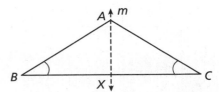

Then, by the definition of angle bisector,

_____

Also, $\overline{AX} \cong \overline{AX}$ by the Reflexive Property of Congruence. Therefore, $\triangle BAX \cong \triangle CAX$ by the AAS Congruence Criterion.

So, $\overline{AB} \cong \overline{AC}$ by _____

3a. An equiangular triangle has three congruent angles. An equilateral triangle has three congruent sides. Use the figure to help you explain why an equiangular triangle must also be an equilateral triangle.

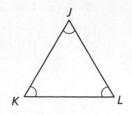

_____

_____

_____

PRACTICE

Find the measure of the indicated angle.

1. m∠B

$180 - 48 = 132$

$132 \div 2 = 66$

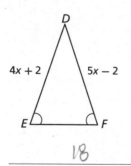

$\underline{\quad 66° \quad}$

2. m∠J

$180 - 118 = 62$

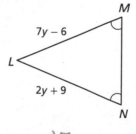

$\underline{\quad 31° \quad}$

3. m∠R

$\begin{array}{c} 134 \\ 46 \end{array}$

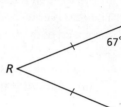

$\underline{\quad 46° \quad}$

Find the length of the indicated side.

4. $\overline{DF}$

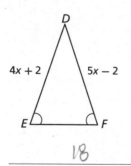

$4x + 2 \qquad 5x - 2$

$\underline{\quad 18 \quad}$

$-x = -4$

5. $\overline{LM}$

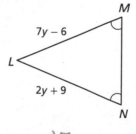

$7y - 6$

$2y + 9$

$\underline{\quad 15 \quad}$

$5y = 15$

$y = 3$

6. $\overline{RS}$

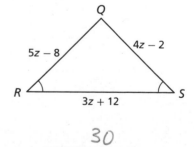

$5z - 8 \qquad 4z - 2$

$3z + 12$

$\underline{\quad 30 \quad}$

$z = 6$

7. Error Analysis Two students are asked to find the angle measures of △XYZ, given that △XYZ is isosceles. Their work is shown below. Is either answer incorrect? Explain.

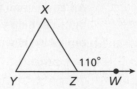

Lee's Answer	Skyler's Answer
m∠Z = 70°. Since an isosceles triangle has two congruent angles, m∠X = m∠Y = 55°.	m∠Z = 70°. Since base angles are congruent, m∠Y = 70° also. This leaves 40° for m∠X.

_____

_____

8. A boat travels at a constant speed parallel to a coastline that is approximately a straight line. An observer on the coast at point *P* uses radar to find the distance to the boat when the boat makes an angle of 35° with the coastline. Then, 5 seconds later, the observer finds the distance to the boat when it makes an angle of 70° with the coastline. The observer wants to know if it is possible to calculate the speed of the boat.

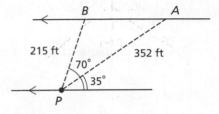

a. Is it possible to determine the distance the boat traveled, *AB*? If so, find the distance and explain your method. If not, explain why not.

_____

_____

_____

b. Is it possible to determine the speed of the boat? If so, find the speed and explain your method. If not, explain why not.

_____

_____

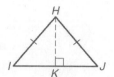

4-9

Additional Practice

An altitude of a triangle is a perpendicular segment from a vertex
to the line containing the opposite side. Write a paragraph proof
that the altitude to the base of an isosceles triangle bisects the base.

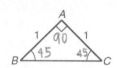

1. **Given:** $\overline{HI} \cong \overline{HJ}, \overline{HK} \perp \overline{IJ}$

   Prove: $\overline{HK}$ bisects $\overline{IJ}$.

2. An *obelisk* is a tall, thin, four-sided monument that tapers to a pyramidal top.
   The most well-known obelisk to Americans is the Washington Monument on
   the National Mall in Washington, D.C. Each face of the pyramidal top of the
   Washington Monument is an isosceles triangle. The height of each triangle is
   55.5 feet, and the base of each triangle measures 34.4 feet. Find the length,
   to the nearest tenth of a foot, of one of the two equal legs of the triangle. _____

Find each value.

3. $m\angle X = $ __45°__

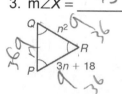

$n^2 = 3n + 18$

$n^2 - 3n - 18 = 0$

$(n - 6)(n + 3)$

$n = 6, -3$

4. $BC = $ __√2__

180 − 28 = 152

152 ÷ 2 = 76

5. $PQ = $ __6, −3__

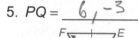

$30t + 20 = 60$

$30t = 80$

$t = $

6. $m\angle K = $ __76°__

18n = 180

n = 10

7. $t = $ __8/3__

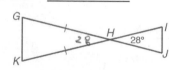

8. $n = $ __10__

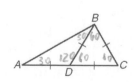

9. $m\angle A = $ __30°__

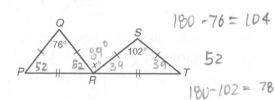

180 − 76 = 104

52

180 − 102 = 78

91 + 89

10. $x = $ __89°__

Problem Solving

$2n = -16$
$n = +8$

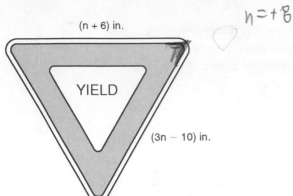

(n + 6) in.

YIELD

(3n − 10) in.

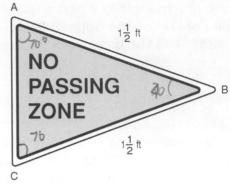

A

$1\frac{1}{2}$ ft

NO PASSING ZONE

40

B

76

$1\frac{1}{2}$ ft

C

70°

1. A "Yield" sign is an equiangular triangle. What are the lengths of the sides?

   14 in

2. The measure of ∠C is 70°. What is the measure of ∠B?

   40°

3. Samantha is swimming along $\overrightarrow{HF}$. When she is at point H, she sees a necklace straight ahead of her but on the bottom of the pool at point J. Then she swims 11 more feet to point G. Use the diagram to find GJ, the distance Samantha is from the necklace. Explain.

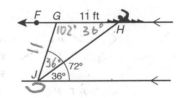

F G   11 ft
102° 36° H
36° 72°
J 36°

   11ft   cause   it   isoseclor

   Isosceles

Choose the best answer.

4. A billiards triangle is equiangular. What is the perimeter?

   A $5\frac{1}{8}$ in.   C $11\frac{1}{4}$ in.

   B $10\frac{1}{4}$ in.   D $33\frac{3}{4}$ in.

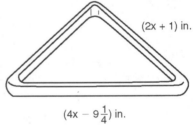

(2x + 1) in.

(4x − 9$\frac{1}{4}$) in.

5. A triangular shaped trellis has angles R, S, and T that measure 73°, 73°, and 34°, respectively. If $ST = 4y + 6$ and $TR = 7y − 21$, what is the value of y?

   F 5   H 11
   G 9   J 15

6. Two triangular tiles each have two sides measuring 4 inches. Which is a true statement?

   A Their corresponding angles are congruent.   C The triangles may be congruent.

   B The triangles are congruent.   D The triangles cannot be congruent.

7. What is the value of x in the figure?

   F 42°   H 96°
   G 90°   J 106°

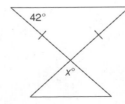

42°

x°

© Houghton Mifflin Harcourt Publishing Company

Performance Tasks

COMMON
CORE

CC.9-12.G.CO.10
CC.9-12.G.SRT.5
CC.9-12.G.GPE.4

⭐ **1.** The Pep Club wants to duplicate the school pennant. The pennant is in the shape of a triangle. Two of the sides have the same measure of 22 inches. Does the club need to make any other measurements to create the duplicate? If so, what does the club need to measure? Explain your answer.

> 22 ⟋△ 22   You have to measure the base.

⭐ **2.** Two angles of a triangular tabletop measure 35° and 50°. The shortest side of the table measures 30 inches. Two angles of a second triangular tabletop measure 50° and 95°. The shortest side of this tabletop also measures 30 inches. Are the two tabletops congruent? Justify your answer.

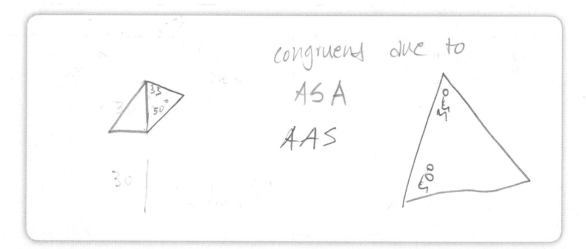

> congruent due to
> ASA
> AAS

⭐ **3.**
⭐ In the diagram, $\overline{AC}$ bisects $\overline{BD}$ at K and $\overline{BD}$ bisects $\overline{AC}$ at K.

    a. What must you know in order to prove that $\overline{AB} \parallel \overline{DC}$?

    b. Write a plan to prove the criteria you gave in part **a**.

    c. Prove $\overline{AB} \parallel \overline{DC}$.

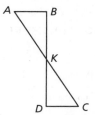

continued

4. The vertices of a triangle are $X(2, 2)$, $Y(5, 6)$, and $Z(8, 2)$.

a. Prove that point Y lies on the perpendicular bisector of $\overline{XZ}$.

b. After a transformation, the images of points X and Z are $X'(-2, -2)$ and. $Z'(-2, -8)$. The transformation preserves distance and angle. Name two possibilities for the coordinates of point Y'.

c. Choose either of the possibilities for the location of point Y' you named in part **b**. Use it to prove that $\triangle XYZ \cong \triangle X'Y'Z'$.

Name _____ Class _____ Date _____

MULTIPLE CHOICE

1. *J* is the midpoint of $\overline{GH}$. $\overline{GK}$ is parallel to $\overline{LH}$. Which congruence criterion can be used to prove $\triangle GJK \cong \triangle HJL$?

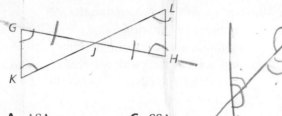

A. ASA

B. SAS

C. SSA

D. SSS

2. Jessica wants to prove that an equilateral triangle has three congruent angles. She begins as shown below. Which reason should she use for Step 2?

Given: $\overline{AB} \cong \overline{AC} \cong \overline{BC}$

Prove: $\angle A \cong \angle B \cong \angle C$

Statements	Reasons
1. $\overline{AB} \cong \overline{AC}$	**1.** Given
2. $\angle B \cong \angle C$	**2.** ?
3.	**3.**

F. Triangle Sum Theorem

G. ASA Congruence Criterion

H. Isosceles Triangle Theorem

J. CPCTC

3. $\overline{PN} \cong \overline{QN}$, and $\overline{MN}$ bisects $\angle PNQ$. Which congruence criterion can be used to prove $\triangle MPN \cong \triangle MQN$?

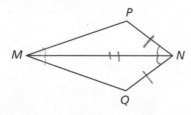

A. ASA

B. SAS

C. SSA

D. SSS

4. Which sequence of transformations maps $\triangle RST$ to $\triangle UVW$?

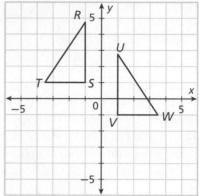

F. reflection across the *x*-axis followed by a 180° rotation around the origin

G. reflection across the *y*-axis followed by the translation $(x, y) \rightarrow (x, y - 2)$

H. translation $(x, y) \rightarrow (x - 2, y)$ followed by a reflection across the *y*-axis

J. rotation of 180° around the origin followed by a reflection across the *x*-axis

5. Tyrell's teacher asks him to prove or disprove that the triangle with vertices $A(1, 1)$, $B(2, 5)$, and $C(6, 4)$ is an isosceles triangle. Which of the following should he do?

A. Disprove the statement by using the distance formula to show that $\overline{AB}$, $\overline{BC}$, and $\overline{AC}$ all have different lengths.

B. Prove the statement by using the distance formula to show that $AB = BC$.

C. Prove the statement by using the distance formula to show that $AB = AC$.

D. Prove the statement by using the distance formula to show that $BC = AC$.

6. What is the perimeter, in linear units, of a triangle with vertices $(0, 3)$, $(4, 5)$, and $(4, 0)$?

F. 10

G. $\sqrt{70}$

H. $10 + \sqrt{20}$

J. $5 + \sqrt{6} + \sqrt{7}$

CONSTRUCTED RESPONSE

7. To find the distance AB across a pond, you locate points as follows.

Starting at A and walking along a straight path, you walk 28 feet and put a marker at C. Then you walk 28 feet farther and put a marker at D.

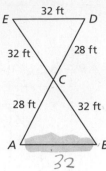

Starting at B, you walk to C, measuring the distance you walked (32 feet). Then you walk 32 feet farther and put a marker at E. Finally, you measure the distance from D to E, as shown. Explain how to use this information to find AB.

It shows that the triangles are congruent using SSS so AB is equal to ED

8. Determine whether the figures shown below are congruent. Explain your answer using rigid motions.

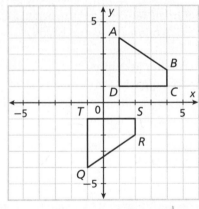

Yes because it only reflected and translated, not changed shape or size.

9. Given that $\triangle JKL \cong \triangle MNP$, use the definition of congruence in terms of rigid motions to explain why $\overline{KL}$ must be congruent to $\overline{NP}$.

by CPCTC is has to be congruent

10. You are writing a proof that the SSS Congruence Criterion follows from the definition of congruence in terms of rigid motions. You start with two triangles, $\triangle ABC$ and $\triangle DEF$, such that $\overline{AB} \cong \overline{DE}$, $\overline{BC} \cong \overline{EF}$, and $\overline{AC} \cong \overline{DF}$.

You use the fact that $\overline{AB} \cong \overline{DE}$ to conclude that there is a sequence of rigid motions that maps $\overline{AB}$ onto $\overline{DE}$. Applying this sequence of rigid motions to $\triangle ABC$ leads to this figure.

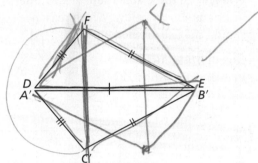

Why is $\overline{DE}$ the perpendicular bisector of $\overline{FC'}$?

Properties and Attributes of Triangles

Chapter Focus

In this unit, you will examine the relationships between lines that bisect the angles and sides of a triangle and circles inscribed in or circumscribed about the triangles. You will also examine how the midsegment of a triangle divides the sides proportionally. Finally, you will learn how to compare side lengths in triangles using triangle inequalities and to find unknown side lengths in right triangles by using the Pythagorean Theorem or special right triangles.

Chapter at a Glance

COMMON CORE

Lesson		Standards for Mathematical Content
5-1	Perpendicular and Angle Bisectors	CC.9-12.G.GPE.2
5-2	Bisectors of Triangles	CC.9-12.G.C.3
5-3	Medians and Altitudes of Triangles	CC.9-12.G.CO.10, CC.9-12.G.GPE.4
5-4	The Triangle Midsegment Theorem	CC.9-12.G.CO.10, CC.9-12.G.GPE.4
5-5	Indirect Proof and Inequalities in One Triangle	CC.9-12.G.CO.10
5-6	Inequalities in Two Triangles	CC.9-12.G.CO.10
5-7	The Pythagorean Theorem	CC.9-12.G.SRT.8
5-8	Applying Special Right Triangles	CC.9-12.G.SRT.6, CC.9-12.G.SRT.8
	Performance Tasks	
	Assessment Readiness	

CHAPTER 5

Unpacking the Standards

Understanding the standards and the vocabulary terms in the standards will help you know exactly what you are expected to learn in this chapter.

(COMMON CORE) CC.9-12.G.G.C.3

Construct the inscribed and circumscribed circles of a triangle, ...

Key Vocabulary

construction *(construcción)* A method of creating a figure that is considered to be mathematically precise. Figures may be constructed by using a compass and straightedge, geometry software, or paper folding.

inscribed circle *(círculo inscrito)* A circle in which each side of the polygon is tangent to the circle.

circumscribed circle *(círculo circunscrito)* Every vertex of the polygon lies on the circle.

What It Means For You — Lesson 5-3

Inscribed and circumscribed circles of triangles relate to special points, angles, and segments associated with triangles. *Inscribe* means to write inside, and *circumscribe* means to write around—think circumference.

EXAMPLE   **Inscribed Circle**
The circle is inscribed in the triangular pennant. It touches each side at one point.

EXAMPLE   **Circumscribed Circle**
The circle is circumscribed around the triangle. It passes through each vertex. Its center is the intersection point of the perpendicular bisectors of the sides.

(COMMON CORE) CC.9-12.G.CO.9

Prove theorems about lines and angles.

Key Vocabulary

proof *(demostración)* An argument that uses logic to show that a conclusion is true.

theorem *(teorema)* A statement that has been proven.

line *(línea)* An undefined term in geometry, a line is a straight path that has no thickness and extends forever.

angle *(ángulo)* A figure formed by two rays with a common endpoint.

What It Means For You — Lessons 5-1, 5-2, 5-3, 5-4

Many segments associated with triangles, such as those that bisect angles or sides, are perpendiculars, connect midpoints, and so on, have special properties that you can prove.

EXAMPLE

Medians $\overline{AY}$, $\overline{CX}$, and $\overline{BZ}$ meet in a single point P.

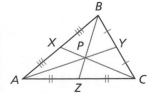

Midsegment $\overline{DE}$ is parallel to side $\overline{AC}$.

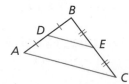

© Houghton Mifflin Harcourt Publishing Company; Photo credit: ...otoDisc/Getty Images

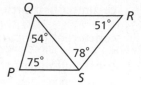

COMMON CORE **CC.9-12.G.CO.10**

Prove theorems about triangles.

Key Vocabulary

proof *(demostración)* An argument that uses logic to show that a conclusion is true.

theorem *(teorema)* A statement that has been proven.

triangle *(triángulo)* A three-sided polygon.

What It Means For You   Lessons 5-3, 5-4, 5-5, 5-6

You can prove theorems about the relationships among side lengths and angle measures within a single triangle and between two or more triangles.

EXAMPLE   Relationships within a triangle

Because m∠*PSQ* = 51° by the Triangle Sum Theorem, it is the smallest angle in △*PSQ*. So, the opposite side, $\overline{PQ}$, is the shortest side of △*PSQ*.

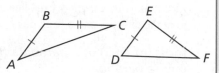

EXAMPLE   Relationships between triangles

By the Hinge Theorem, if *m∠B* > *m∠E* in the two triangles shown with congruent sides as marked, then *AC* > *DF*.

COMMON CORE **CC.9-12.G.SRT.8**

Use ... the Pythagorean Theorem to solve right triangles in applied problems.

Key Vocabulary

Pythagorean Theorem *(Teorema de Pitágoras)* If a right triangle has legs of lengths *a* and *b* and a hypotenuse of length *c*, then $a^2 + b^2 = c^2$.

right triangle *(triángulo rectángulo)* A triangle with one right angle.

What It Means For You   Lessons 5-7, 5-8

You can use the relationship between the side lengths of a right triangle to solve real-world problems.

EXAMPLE

The diagram shows the recommended position for placing a ladder. Given the length *L* of the ladder, you can use the Pythagorean Theorem to find *x*, the distance from the base of the wall to place the foot of the ladder.

$$L^2 = x^2 + (4x)^2$$

$$L^2 = 17x^2$$

$$\frac{L^2}{17} = x^2$$

$$\frac{L}{\sqrt{17}} = x$$

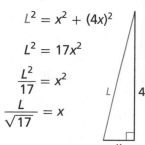

Key Vocabulary

centroid of a triangle *(centroide de un triángulo)* The point of concurrency of the three medians of a triangle. Also known as the *center of gravity*.

circumscribed circle *(círculo circunscrito)* Every vertex of the polygon lies on the circle.

concurrent *(concurrente)* Three or more lines that intersect at one point.

construction *(construcción)* A method of creating a figure that is considered to be mathematically precise. Figures may be constructed by using a compass and straightedge, geometry software, or paper folding.

directrix *(directriz)* A fixed line used to define a *parabola*. Every point on the parabola is equidistant from the directrix and a fixed point called the *focus*.

focus (pl. foci) of a parabola *(foco de una parábola)* A fixed point *F* used with a *directrix* to define a *parabola*.

incenter of a triangle *(incentro de un triángulo)* The point of concurrency of the three angle bisectors of a triangle.

inscribed circle *(círculo inscrito)* A circle in which each side of the polygon is tangent to the circle.

median of a triangle *(mediana de un triángulo)* A segment whose endpoints are a vertex of the triangle and the midpoint of the opposite side.

midsegment of a triangle *(segmento medio de un triángulo)* A segment that joins the midpoints of two sides of the triangle.

parabola *(parábola)* The shape of the graph of a quadratic function. Also, the set of points equidistant from a point *F*, called the *focus*, and a line *d*, called the *directrix*.

point of concurrency *(punto de concurrencia)* A point where three or more lines coincide.

Pythagorean Theorem *(Teorema de Pitágoras)* If a right triangle has legs of lengths *a* and *b* and a hypotenuse of length *c*, then $a^2 + b^2 = c^2$.

right triangle *(triángulo rectángulo)* A triangle with one right angle.

CHAPTER 5

Perpendicular and Angle Bisectors
Extension: Perpendicular Bisectors and Parabolas

Essential question: *How do you write the equation of a parabola given its focus and directrix?*

The distance from a point to a line is the length of the perpendicular segment from the point to the line. In the figure, the distance from point *A* to line ℓ is *AB*.

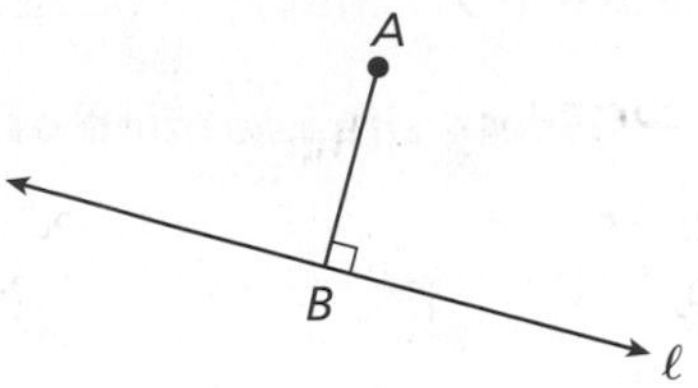

You will use the idea of the distance from a point to a line below.

PREP FOR **CC.9–12.G.GPE.2**

1 EXPLORE   Creating a Parabola

Follow these instructions to plot a point. You will report the approximate coordinates of the point to your teacher, who will create a graph consisting of all points from everyone in the class. Be sure to work as accurately as possible.

A   Choose a point on line ℓ. Plot a point *Q* at this location.

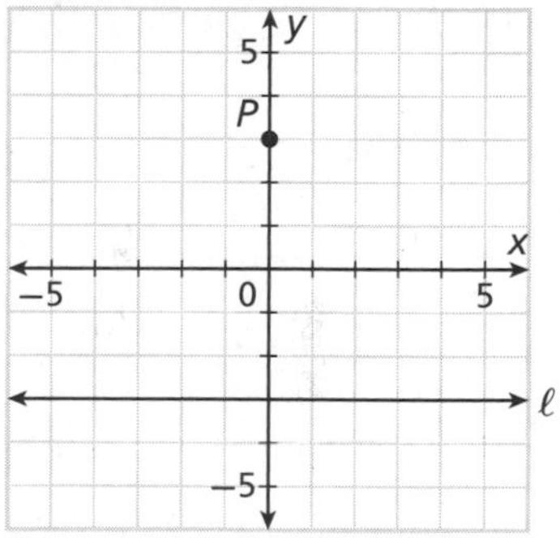

B   Using a straightedge, draw a perpendicular to ℓ that passes through point *Q*. Label this line *m*.

C   Use the straightedge to draw $\overline{PQ}$. Then use a compass and straightedge to construct the perpendicular bisector of $\overline{PQ}$.

D   Plot a point *X* where the perpendicular bisector intersects line *m*.

E   Write the approximate coordinates of point *X* and report the coordinates to your teacher.

_____

REFLECT

1a. Use the figure to help you explain why the point *X* that you plotted is equidistant from point *P* and line ℓ.

_____

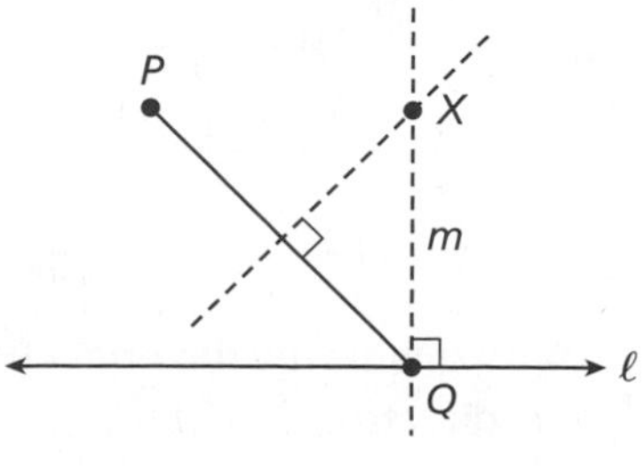

1b. What do you notice about the set of points your teacher plotted?

_____

© Houghton Mifflin Harcourt Publishing Company

A **parabola** is the set of all points P in a plane that are equidistant from a given point, called the **focus**, and a given line, called the **directrix**.

To derive the general equation of a parabola, you can use the above definition, the distance formula, and the idea that the distance from a point to a line is the length of the perpendicular segment from the point to the line.

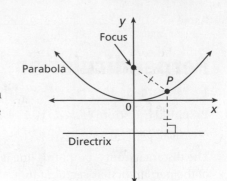

CC.9–12.G.GPE.2

2 **EXPLORE**   **Deriving the Equation of a Parabola**

A   Let the focus of the parabola be $F(0, p)$ and let the directrix be the line $y = -p$. Let P be a point on the parabola with coordinates (x, y).

B   Let Q be the point of intersection of the perpendicular from P and the directrix. Then the coordinates of Q are $(x, -p)$.

C   By the definition of a parabola, $FP = QP$.

By the distance formula,
$$FP = \sqrt{(x - 0)^2 + (y - p)^2} = \sqrt{x^2 + (y - p)^2}$$
and $QP = \sqrt{(x - x)^2 + (y - (-p))^2} = \sqrt{0 + (y + p)^2} = |y + p|$.

_____ = _____		Set FP equal to QP.
_____ = _____		Square both sides.
_____ = _____		Expand the squared terms.
_____ = _____		Subtract y^2 and p^2 from both sides.
_____ = _____		Add $2py$ to both sides.
_____ = _____		Solve for y.

REFLECT

2a. Explain how the value of p determines whether the parabola opens up or down.

_____

_____

_____

_____

2b. Explain why the origin $(0, 0)$ is always a point on a parabola with focus $F(0, p)$ and directrix $y = -p$.

_____

_____

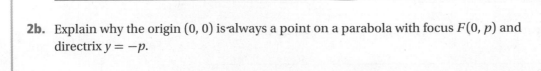

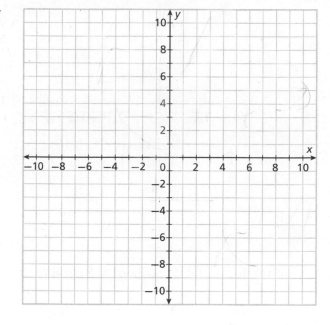

3 **EXAMPLE** **Writing the Equation of a Parabola**

Write the equation of the parabola with focus $(0, -4)$ and directrix $y = 4$.
Then graph the parabola.

A The focus of the parabola is $(0, p)$, so $p =$ _____ .

The general equation of a parabola is $y = \frac{1}{4p} x^2$.

So, the equation of this parabola is _____ .

B To graph the parabola, complete the table of values. Then plot points and draw the curve.

x	y
−8	
−4	
0	
4	
8	

REFLECT

3a. The *vertex* of a parabola is the midpoint of the perpendicular segment from the focus to the directrix. What is the vertex of the parabola you graphed?

_____

3b. Does your graph lie above or below the *x*-axis? Why does this make sense based on the parabola's equation?

_____

_____

3c. Describe any symmetry your graph has. Why does this make sense based on the parabola's equation?

_____

_____

_____

Write the equation of the parabola with the given focus and directrix. Then graph the parabola.

1. focus: $(0, 2)$; directrix: $y = -2$

2. focus: $(0, -5)$; directrix: $y = 5$

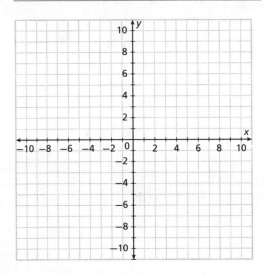

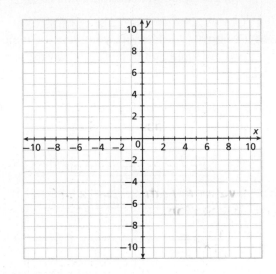

Find the focus and directrix of the parabola with the given equation.

3. $y = -\frac{1}{24}x^2$

4. $y = 2x^2$

5. Complete the table by writing the equation of each parabola. Then use a calculator to graph the equations in the same window to help you make a conjecture: What happens to the graph of a parabola as the focus and directrix move apart?

Focus	(0, 1)	(0, 2)	(0, 3)	(0, 4)
Directrix	$y = -1$	$y = -2$	$y = -3$	$y = -4$
Equation				

6. Find the length of the line segment that is parallel to the directrix of a parabola, that passes through the focus, and that has endpoints on the parabola.

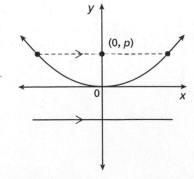

Additional Practice

Write the equation of the parabola with the given focus and directrix.

1. focus: (0, 10), directrix: $y = -10$

2. focus(0, −6), directrix: $y = 6$

3. focus (0, −13), directrix: $y = 13$

4. focus (0, 1.5), directrix: $y = -1.5$

5. focus (0, −3), directrix: $y = 3$

6. focus (0, −5.5), directrix: $y = 5.5$

Find the value of p, the focus, and the directrix of the parabola with the given equation.

7. $y = -\dfrac{1}{12}x^2$

8. $y = \dfrac{1}{32}x^2$

9. $y = -\dfrac{1}{36}x^2$

10. $y = \dfrac{1}{8}x^2$

11. $y = \dfrac{1}{48}x^2$

12. $y = -\dfrac{1}{10}x^2$

13. Find the value of p, the focus, and the directrix of
the parabola with equation $y = -\dfrac{1}{28}x^2$. Then
graph the parabola.

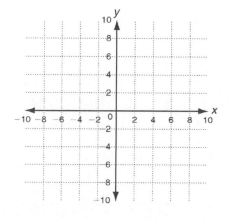

Problem Solving

A model of a parabolic mirror has a cross section that can be modeled by the equation $y = \dfrac{1}{96}x^2$.

1. You want to graph the equation of the cross section of the model.

   a. What are the coordinates of the vertex of the parabola?

   _____

   b. Find the distance, p, from the vertex to both the focus and the directrix of the parabola.

   _____

   c. Find the coordinates of the focus.

   _____

   d. Write the equation of the directrix.

   _____

   e. Sketch a graph of the cross section of the model including the focus and the directrix.

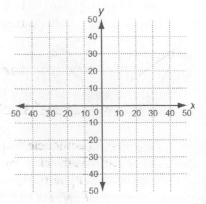

2. You want to construct a model of a different parabolic mirror. For this model, you want the focus to be (0, 18) and the directrix to be $y = -18$. Write the equation of the new parabola.

   _____

Choose the letter for the best answer.

3. Melissa wrote the equation of a parabola with focus (0, –5) and directrix $y = 5$. Which equation should Melissa have written?

   A $y = -\dfrac{1}{20}x^2$ C $y = -\dfrac{1}{5}x^2$

   B $y = \dfrac{1}{20}x^2$ D $y = \dfrac{1}{5}x^2$

4. A solar trough used to collect solar energy has a reflective surface. The surface has a cross section that is a parabola with equation $y = \dfrac{1}{24}x^2$. What is the focus of the parabola?

   F (0, –6)

   G (–6, 0)

   H (6, 0)

   J (0, 6)

Bisectors of Triangles
Going Deeper

Essential question: *How do you construct the circle that circumscribes a triangle, and how do you inscribe a circle in a triangle?*

A circle is said to **circumscribe** a polygon if the circle passes through all of the polygon's vertices. In the figure, circle *C* circumscribes △*XYZ* and this circle is called the **circumcircle** of △*XYZ*.

In order to construct the circumcircle of a triangle, you need to find the center of the circle. This point is called the **circumcenter** of the triangle. The following example will guide you through the reasoning process to do this.

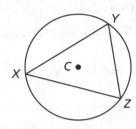

Video Tutor

CC.9–12.G.C.3

1 EXAMPLE **Constructing a Circumscribed Circle**

Work directly on the figure to construct the circumcircle of △*PQR*.

A The circumcircle will pass through *P*, *Q*, and *R*. So, the center of the circle must be equidistant from all three points. In particular, the center must be equidistant from *P* and *R*. What is the set of points equidistant from *P* and *R*?

_____

Use a compass and straightedge to construct this set of points.

B Similarly, the center must be equidistant from *Q* and *R*. What is the set of points equidistant from *Q* and *R*?

_____

Use a compass and straightedge to construct this set of points.

C The center must lie at the intersection of the two sets of points you constructed. Label this point *C*.

D Place the point of your compass at *C* and open it to the distance *CP*. Then draw the circumcircle.

REFLECT

1a. Suppose you started by constructing the set of points equidistant from *P* and *Q*, and then you constructed the set of points equidistant from *Q* and *R*. Would you have found the same center point? Check by doing this construction.

_____

A circle is **inscribed** in a polygon if each side of the polygon is tangent to the circle. In the figure, circle *C* is inscribed in quadrilateral *WXYZ* and this circle is called the **incircle** of the quadrilateral.

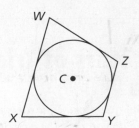

In order to construct the incircle of a triangle, you need to find the center of the circle. This point is called the **incenter** of the triangle. The following example will guide you through the reasoning process for constructing an inscribed circle in a triangle.

CC.9–12.G.C.3

2 EXAMPLE   Constructing an Inscribed Circle

Work directly on the figure to inscribe a circle in △*PQR*.

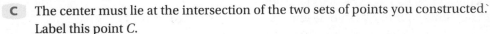

A   The center of the inscribed circle must be equidistant from the sides of △*PQR*. In particular, the center must be equidistant from $\overline{PQ}$ and $\overline{PR}$. What is the set of points equidistant from $\overline{PQ}$ and $\overline{PR}$?

_____

Use a compass and straightedge to construct this set of points.

B   Similarly, the center must be equidistant from $\overline{PR}$ and $\overline{QR}$. What is the set of points equidistant from $\overline{PR}$ and $\overline{QR}$?

_____

Use a compass and straightedge to construct this set of points.

C   The center must lie at the intersection of the two sets of points you constructed. Label this point *C*.

D   Place the point of your compass at *C* and open the compass until the pencil just touches a side of △*PQR*. Then draw the inscribed circle.

REFLECT

2a.   Suppose you started by constructing the set of points equidistant from $\overline{PR}$ and $\overline{QR}$, and then constructed the set of points equidistant from $\overline{QR}$ and $\overline{QP}$. Would you have found the same center point? Check by doing this construction.

_____

2b.   Is it possible for the incenter of a triangle to fall outside the triangle? If so, give an example and describe the triangle.

_____

_____

Construct the circumcircle of each triangle.

1.

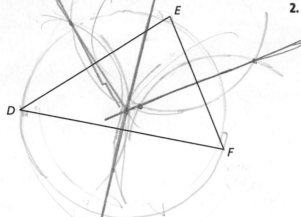

2.

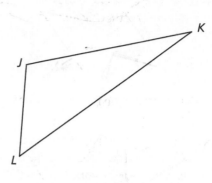

3.

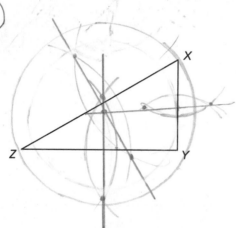

4.

5. Explain how to use a compass and straightedge to locate the center of a circle. (*Hint:* Start by plotting three points on the circle.)

_____

_____

_____

6. Use a compass and straightedge to locate the circumcenter of an acute triangle, a right triangle, and an obtuse triangle. Considering these constructions and the other constructions from this lesson, what can you say about the location of a triangle's circumcenter?

_____

_____

_____

Construct the inscribed circle for each triangle.

7.

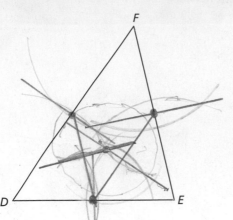

8.

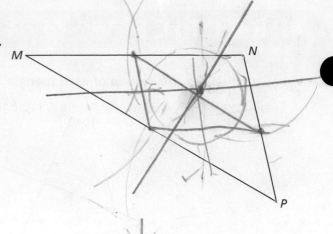

9.

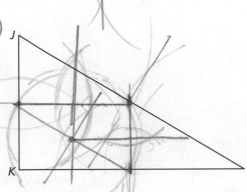

10.

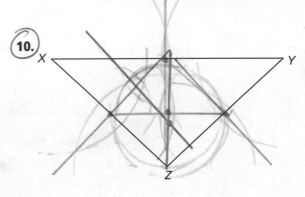

11. Explain how you can use paper folding to find the incenter of a triangle.

_____

_____

_____

12. Is it possible for the incenter and the circumcenter of a triangle to be the same point? If so, describe a triangle for which this is true. If not, explain why not.

_____

_____

_____

Additional Practice

Construct the circumcircle of each triangle.

1.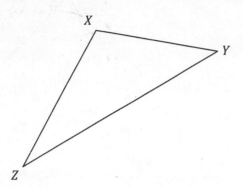

2.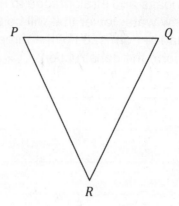

Construct the incircle of each triangle.

3.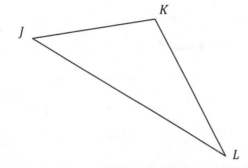

4.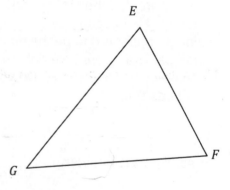

Complete using one of these words: *incenter, circumcenter.*

5. To locate the _____ of a triangle, you can construct the perpendicular bisector of each side of the triangle.

6. To locate the _____ of a triangle, you can construct the angle bisector of each angle of the triangle.

7. A car's logo is the triangle shown. Raleigh has to use this logo as the center of the steering wheel. Explain how Raleigh can do this. Sketch his design on the figure.

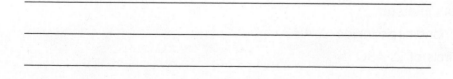

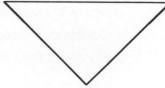

Problem Solving

1. The diagram shows the locations of three cities, labeled *X*, *Y*, and *Z*. Explain how to use a compass and straightedge to mark a location for a new water tower that will be the same distance from each of the three cities. Then perform the construction.

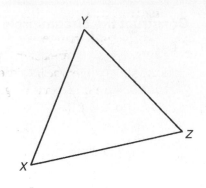

_____

_____

_____

_____

2. Paulo drew a right triangle by using a corner of a piece of paper to draw the right angle. Then he constructed the circumcircle of his right triangle. He noticed that the longest side of the triangle appeared to be the diameter of the triangle. Draw your own right triangle. Then construct its circumcircle. Do you get the same result as Paulo?

_____

Choose the best answer.

3. An architect draws △ *JKL* to represent a triangular sitting area in a mall. The architect then constructs the angle bisectors of the angles of the triangle and finds that the bisectors intersect at a point 5 centimeters from $\overline{JK}$. On the architect's drawing, what is the distance of this point from $\overline{KL}$?

   A 2.5 cm   B 5 cm   C 7.5 cm   D 10 cm

4. A new gym is to be located the same distance from three schools. You have a compass and straightedge and a map with points *A*, *B*, and *C* representing the three schools. How can you locate the new gym?

   F Construct the perpendicular bisectors of the sides of △ *ABC* and find the point where the perpendicular bisectors intersect.

   G Construct the bisectors of the angles of △ *ABC* and find the point where the bisectors intersect.

   H Construct an inscribed circle inside △ *ABC*.

   J Construct the incircle of △ *ABC*.

Medians and Altitudes of Triangles
Focus on Reasoning

Essential question: *What can you conclude about the medians of a triangle?*

A **median** of a triangle is a line segment whose
endpoints are a vertex of the triangle and the
midpoint of the opposite side. Every triangle
has three medians. In the figure, $\overline{LM}$ is
a median of $\triangle JKL$.

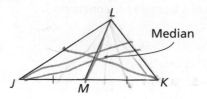

Median

COMMON
CORE

CC.9-12.G.CO.10,
CC.9-12.G.GPE.4

1 **Investigate medians.**

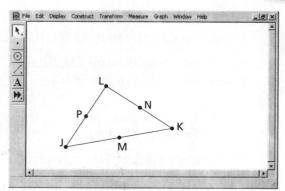

A Use geometry software to draw a triangle.

B Label the vertices *J*, *K*, and *L*.

C Select each side and construct its midpoint.
Label the midpoints *M*, *N*, and *P*.

D Draw the medians, $\overline{LM}$, $\overline{JN}$, and $\overline{KP}$.

E Drag the vertices of $\triangle JKL$ to change its shape.
As you do so, look for relationships among
the medians.

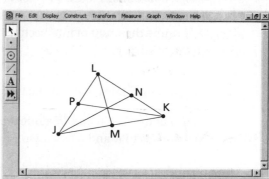

REFLECT

1a. Compare your observations with those of other students. Then make a conjecture.
What can you say about the medians of a triangle?

_____

_____

1b. Paul draws $\triangle ABC$ and the medians from vertices *A* and *B*. He finds that the medians
intersect at a point and he labels this point *X*. Paul claims that point *X* lies outside
$\triangle ABC$. Do you think this is possible? Explain.

_____

_____

Three or more lines are said to be **concurrent** when they intersect at a point. The point is called the **point of concurrency**. You have seen that the medians of a triangle are concurrent. The point of concurrency of the medians of a triangle is called the **centroid** of the triangle.

Concurrency of Medians Theorem

The medians of a triangle are concurrent.

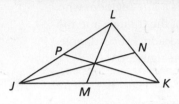

2 **Prove the Concurrency of Medians Theorem.**

Given: $\triangle JKL$ with medians $\overline{LM}$, $\overline{JN}$, and $\overline{KP}$.
Prove: The medians intersect at a point.

Complete the coordinate proof.

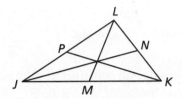

A Understand the plan for the proof.

Assign coordinates to the vertices of the triangle and find the coordinates of the midpoint of each side. Write an equation for the line containing each median. Determine the point of intersection of two of the lines. Show that this point lies on the third line.

B Assign coordinates to the vertices of the triangle.

Place J at the origin and $\overline{JK}$ along the x-axis. Assign coordinates to K and L as shown.

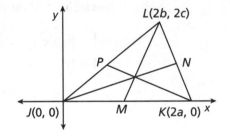

C Find the coordinates of the midpoint of each side. Use the midpoint formula.

$$M\left(\frac{\boxed{}+\boxed{}}{2}, \frac{\boxed{}+\boxed{}}{2}\right) = M\left(\boxed{}, \boxed{}\right)$$

$$N\left(\frac{\boxed{}+\boxed{}}{2}, \frac{\boxed{}+\boxed{}}{2}\right) = N\left(\boxed{}, \boxed{}\right)$$

$$P\left(\frac{\boxed{}+\boxed{}}{2}, \frac{\boxed{}+\boxed{}}{2}\right) = P\left(\boxed{}, \boxed{}\right)$$

D Write the equation for the line containing $\overline{JN}$. To do so, use the *point-slope form* of the equation of a line: If a line has slope m and passes through (x_0, y_0), then the line's equation is $y - y_0 = m(x - x_0)$.

Slope of $\overline{JN} = \dfrac{c - 0}{a + b - 0} = \dfrac{c}{a + b}$

To write the equation of $\overleftrightarrow{JN}$, use the fact that the line passes through $(0, 0)$.

Equation of $\overleftrightarrow{JN}$: $y - 0 = \dfrac{c}{a + b}(x - 0)$ or $y = \dfrac{c}{a + b}x$

E Write the equations for the lines containing $\overline{LM}$ and $\overline{PK}$.

Slope of $\overline{LM} = \dfrac{\boxed{} - \boxed{}}{\boxed{} - \boxed{}} = \underline{}$

Equation of $\overleftrightarrow{LM}$: $y - \boxed{} = \underline{}\ (x - \boxed{})$ or $y = \underline{}\ (x - \boxed{})$

Slope of $\overline{PK} = \dfrac{\boxed{} - \boxed{}}{\boxed{} - \boxed{}} = \underline{}$

Equation of $\overleftrightarrow{PK}$: $y - \boxed{} = \underline{}\ (x - \boxed{})$ or $y = \underline{}\ (x - \boxed{})$

F Find the point of intersection of $\overleftrightarrow{JN}$ and $\overleftrightarrow{LM}$. To do so, set the right side of the equation for $\overleftrightarrow{JN}$ equal to the right side of the equation for $\overleftrightarrow{LM}$. Then solve for x, to find the x-coordinate of the point of intersection.

$\dfrac{c}{a + b}x = \dfrac{2c}{2b - a}(x - a)$	Write the equation for x.
$cx(2b - a) = 2c(x - a)(a + b)$	Multiply both sides by $(a + b)(2b - a)$.
$2bcx - acx = (2cx - 2ac)(a + b)$	Multiply.
_____	Multiply on right side of equation.
_____	Subtract $2bcx$ from both sides.
_____	Subtract $2acx$ from both sides.
_____	Factor out ac; divide both sides by ac.
_____	Divide both sides by -3.

To find the y-coordinate of the point of intersection, substitute this value of x into the equation for $\overleftrightarrow{JN}$ and solve for y.

$y = \dfrac{c}{a + b}x = \dfrac{c}{a + b} \cdot \underline{} = \underline{}$

The coordinates of the point of intersection of $\overleftrightarrow{JN}$ and $\overleftrightarrow{LM}$ are _____.

G Now show that the point you found in Step F lies on $\overleftrightarrow{PK}$. To do so, substitute the x-coordinate of the point into the equation for $\overleftrightarrow{PK}$. Then simplify to show that the corresponding y-value is the same as the y-coordinate you calculated in Step F.

$y = \frac{c}{b - 2a}(x - 2a)$ Write the equation for $\overleftrightarrow{PK}$.

_____   Substitute the x-coordinate of the point.

_____   Subtract inside the parentheses.

_____   Factor the numerator inside the parentheses.

_____   Divide to remove common factors.

_____   Simplify.

Because this y-value is the same as the y-coordinate of the point of intersection from Step F, the point also lies on $\overleftrightarrow{PK}$. This shows that the medians are concurrent.

REFLECT

2a. Explain how you can find the coordinates of the centroid of a triangle with vertices $R(0, 0)$, $S(6, 0)$, and $T(3, 9)$.

_____

_____

_____

2b. A student proves the Concurrency of Medians Theorem by first assigning coordinates to the vertices of $\triangle JKL$ as $J(0, 0)$, $K(2a, 0)$, and $L(2a, 2c)$. The students says that this choice of coordinates makes the algebra in the proof a bit easier. Do you agree with the student's choice of coordinates? Explain.

_____

_____

2c. A student claims that the averages of the x-coordinates and of the y-coordinates of the vertices of a triangle are the x- and y-coordinates of the centroid. Does the coordinate proof of the Concurrency of Medians Theorem support the claim? Explain.

_____

_____

_____

Name _____ Class _____ Date _____

Additional Practice

Use the figure for Exercises 1–4. $GB = 12\frac{2}{3}$ and $CD = 10$.

Find each length.

1. FG _____ $6\frac{1}{3}$ _____

2. BF _____ 19 _____

3. GD _____ $3\frac{1}{3}$ _____

4. CG _____ $6\frac{2}{3}$ _____

(handwritten work): $12\frac{2}{3} = \frac{2}{3}$, $2x = 38$, $x = 19$, $\frac{38}{3} \cdot x \cdot \frac{3}{}$, $\frac{x}{10} = \frac{1}{3}$

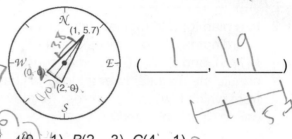

5. A triangular compass needle will turn most easily if it is attached to the compass face through its centroid. Find the coordinates of the centroid.

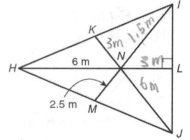

N (1, 5.7)
W (0, 0) E
(2, 0)
S

$(\underline{1}, \underline{1.9})$

Find the orthocenter of the triangle with the given vertices.

6. $X(-5, 4)$, $Y(2, -3)$, $Z(1, 4)$

$(\underline{-2}, \underline{-\frac{1}{3}})$

7. $A(0, -1)$, $B(2, -3)$, $C(4, -1)$

$(\underline{2}, \underline{-\frac{1}{3}})$

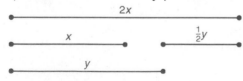

Use the figure for Exercises 8 and 9. $\overline{HL}, \overline{IM},$ and $\overline{JK}$ are medians of $\triangle HIJ$.

8. Find the area of the triangle. _____

9. If the perimeter of the triangle is 49 meters, then find the length of $\overline{MH}$. (*Hint:* What kind of a triangle is it?)

_____

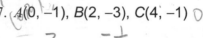

I
K 3m 1.5m
H ——— 6 m ——— N 3m L
2.5 m M 6m
J

10. Two medians of a triangle were cut apart at the centroid to make the four segments shown below. Use what you know about the Centroid Theorem to reconstruct the original triangle from the four segments shown. Measure the side lengths of your triangle to check that you constructed medians. (*Note:* There are many possible answers.)

$2x$
_____•

x
_____• $\frac{1}{2}y$ _____•

y
_____•

(handwritten): 2, -3 2, -1   -1 -3 2

Problem Solving

1. The diagram shows the coordinates of the vertices of a triangular patio umbrella. The umbrella will rest on a pole that will support it. Where should the pole be attached so that the umbrella is balanced?

   <u>(4, 4.5)</u>

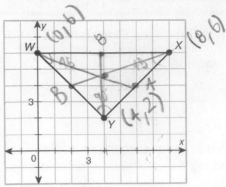

2. In a plan for a triangular wind chime, the coordinates of the vertices are $J(10, 2)$, $K(7, 6)$, and $L(12, 10)$. At what coordinates should the manufacturer attach the chain from which it will hang in order for the chime to be balanced?

   <u>$(9\frac{2}{3}, 6)$</u>

3. Triangle PQR has vertices at $P(-3, 5)$, $Q(-1, 7)$, and $R(3, 1)$. Find the coordinates of the orthocenter and the centroid.

   _____

Choose the best answer.

4. A triangle has coordinates at $A(0, 6)$, $B(8, 6)$, and $C(5, 0)$. $\overline{CD}$ is a median of the triangle, and $\overline{CE}$ is an altitude of the triangle. Which is a true statement?

   A The coordinates of D and E are the same.

   B The distance between D and E is 1 unit.

   C The distance between D and E is 2 units.

   D D is on the triangle, and E is outside the triangle.

5. Lines j and k contain medians of $\triangle DEF$. Find y and z.

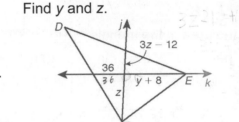

   F $y = 16$; $z = 4$ H $y = 64$; $z = 4.8$

   G $y = 32$; $z = 4$ **J** $y = 108$; $z = 8$

6. An inflatable triangular raft is towed behind a boat. The raft is an equilateral triangle. To maintain balance, the seat is at the centroid B of the triangle. What is AB, the distance from the seat to the tow rope? Round to the nearest tenth.

   A 18.7 in.

   B 37.4 in.

   C 43.1 in.

   D 56.0 in.

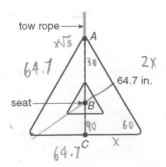

The Triangle Midsegment Theorem
Focus on Reasoning

Essential question: *What must be true about the segment that connects the midpoints of two sides of a triangle?*

A **midsegment** of a triangle is a line segment that connects the midpoints of two sides of the triangle.

COMMON CORE

CC.9-12.G.CO.10,
CC.9-12.G.GPE.4

1 **Investigate midsegments.**

  A   Use geometry software to draw a triangle.

  B   Label the vertices *A*, *B*, and *C*.

  C   Select $\overline{AB}$ and construct its midpoint. Select $\overline{AC}$ and construct its midpoint. Label the midpoints *D* and *E*.

  D   Draw the midsegment, $\overline{DE}$.

  E   Measure the lengths of $\overline{DE}$ and $\overline{BC}$.

  F   Measure $\angle ADE$ and $\angle ABC$.

  G   Drag the vertices of $\triangle ABC$ to change its shape. As you do so, look for relationships in the measurements.

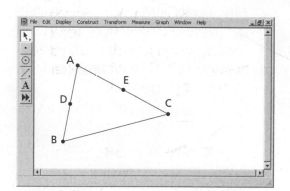

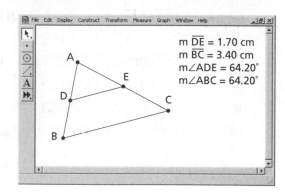

REFLECT

1a. How is the length of $\overline{DE}$ related to the length of $\overline{BC}$?

_____

1b. How is m$\angle ADE$ related to m$\angle ABC$? What does this tell you about $\overline{DE}$ and $\overline{BC}$? Explain.

_____

1c. Compare your results with those of other students. Then state a conjecture about a midsegment of a triangle.

_____

_____

2 **Prove the Midsegment Theorem.**

A midsegment of a triangle is parallel to the third side
of the triangle and is half as long as the third side.

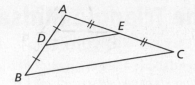

Given: $\overline{DE}$ is a midsegment of $\triangle ABC$.
Prove: $\overline{DE} \parallel \overline{BC}$ and $DE = \frac{1}{2} BC$.

A Use a coordinate proof. Place $\triangle ABC$ on a
coordinate plane so that one vertex is at the origin
and one side lies on the x-axis, as shown. For
convenience, assign vertex C the coordinates
$(2p, 0)$ and assign vertex A the coordinates $(2q, 2r)$.

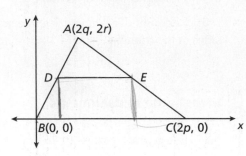

B Use the midpoint formula to find the coordinates of
D and E. Complete the calculations.

$$D\left(\frac{2q + 0}{2}, \frac{2r + 0}{2}\right) = D(q, r)$$

$$E\left(\frac{\boxed{} + \boxed{}}{2}, \frac{\boxed{} + \boxed{}}{2}\right) = E\left(\boxed{}, \boxed{}\right)$$

C To prove that $\overline{DE} \parallel \overline{BC}$, first find the slopes of $\overline{DE}$ and $\overline{BC}$.

Slope of $\overline{DE} = \dfrac{\boxed{} - \boxed{}}{\boxed{} - \boxed{}} = \boxed{}$

Slope of $\overline{BC} = \dfrac{\boxed{} - \boxed{}}{\boxed{} - \boxed{}} = \boxed{}$

What conclusion can you make based on the slopes? Why?

_____

D Show how to use the distance formula to prove that $DE = \frac{1}{2} BC$.

_____

_____

REFLECT

2a. Explain why it is more convenient to assign the coordinates as $C(2p, 0)$ and
$A(2q, 2r)$ rather than $C(p, 0)$ and $A(q, r)$.

_____

2b. Explain how the perimeter of $\triangle JKL$ compares to that of $\triangle MNP$.

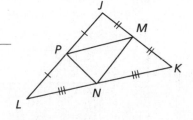

Additional Practice

Use the figure for Exercises 1–6. Find each measure.

1. *HI* _____

2. *DF* _____

3. *GE* _____

4. m∠*HIF* _____

5. m∠*HGD* _____

6. m∠*D* _____

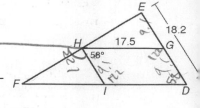

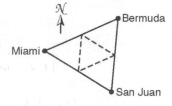

The Bermuda Triangle is a region in the Atlantic Ocean off the southeast coast of the United States. The triangle is bounded by Miami, Florida; San Juan, Puerto Rico; and Bermuda. In the figure, the dotted lines are midsegments.

Dist. (mi)	
Miami to San Juan	1038
Miami to Bermuda	1042
Bermuda to San Juan	965

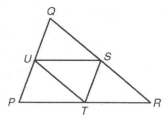

7. Use the distances in the chart to find the perimeter of the Bermuda Triangle.

_____

8. Find the perimeter of the midsegment triangle within the Bermuda Triangle.

_____

9. How does the perimeter of the midsegment triangle compare to the perimeter of the Bermuda Triangle?

_____

Write a two-column proof that the perimeter of a midsegment triangle is half the perimeter of the triangle.

10. **Given:** $\overline{US}$, $\overline{ST}$, and $\overline{TU}$ are midsegments of △*PQR*.

 Prove: The perimeter of $\triangle STU = \frac{1}{2}(PQ + QR + RP)$.

Problem Solving

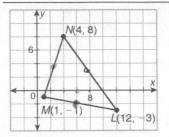

1. The vertices of △JKL are J(–9, 2), K(10, 1), and L(5, 6). $\overline{CD}$ is the midsegment parallel to $\overline{JK}$. What is the length of $\overline{CD}$? Round to the nearest tenth.

   9.5

2. In △QRS, QR = 2x + 5, RS = 3x – 1, and SQ = 5x. What is the perimeter of the midsegment triangle of △QRS?

3. Is XY a midsegment of △LMN if its endpoints are X(8, 2.5) and Y(6.5, –2)? Explain.

   yes because it's the middle points

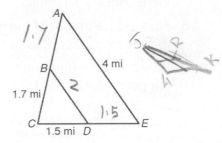

4. The diagram at right shows horseback riding trails. Point B is the halfway point along path $\overline{AC}$. Point D is the halfway point along path $\overline{CE}$. The paths along $\overline{BD}$ and $\overline{AE}$ are parallel. If riders travel from A to B to D to E, and then back to A, how far do they travel?

   9.2 mi

Choose the best answer.

5. Right triangle FGH has midsegments of length 10 centimeters, 24 centimeters, and 26 centimeters. What is the area of △FGH?

   A 60 cm²

   C 240 cm²

   B 120 cm²

   D 480 cm²

6. In triangle HJK, m∠H = 110°, m∠J = 30°, and m∠K = 40°. If R is the midpoint of $\overline{JK}$, and S is the midpoint of $\overline{HK}$, what is m∠JRS?

   F 150°   H 110°

   G 140°   J 30°

Use the diagram for Exercises 7 and 8.

On the balance beam, V is the midpoint of $\overline{AB}$, and W is the midpoint of $\overline{YB}$.

7. The length of $\overline{VW}$ is $1\frac{7}{8}$ feet. What is AY?

   A $\frac{7}{8}$ ft   C $3\frac{3}{4}$ ft

   B $\frac{15}{16}$ ft   D $7\frac{1}{2}$ ft

8. The measure of ∠AYW is 50°. What is the measure of ∠VWB?

   F 45°   H 90°

   G 50°   J 130°

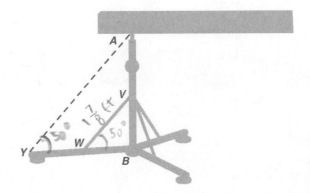

5-5

Indirect Proof and Inequalities in One Triangle
Going Deeper

Essential question: *How can you use inequalities related to triangle side lengths and angle measures in proofs?*

Two important facts about triangles are stated below.

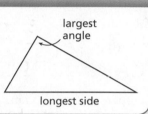

Video Tutor

Angle-Side Relationships in Triangles

- If two sides of a triangle are not congruent, then the larger angle is opposite the longer side.

- If two angles of a triangle are not congruent, then the longer side is opposite the larger angle.

largest angle

longest side

CC.9–12.G.CO.10

1 EXAMPLE Proving Side Relationships

Supply reasons to complete the proof that *KL < MN*.

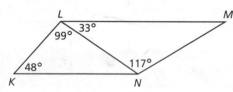

m∠*LNK* + 48° + 99° = 180°,
m∠*LMN* + 33° + 117° = 180°

_____

m∠*LNK* = 33° and m∠*LMN* = 30°

_____

In △*KLN*, 33° < 48° implies *KL* < *LN*.

_____

In △*LMN*, 30° < 33° implies *LN* < *MN*.

_____

KL < *MN*

Transitive Property of Inequality

REFLECT

1a. Can the Transitive Property of Inequality be used to compare *KN* and *LM*? Explain.

_____

_____

1b. Can the Transitive Property of Inequality be used to compare *KL* and *LM*? Explain.

_____

_____

© Houghton Mifflin Harcourt Publishing Company

CC.9–12.G.CO.10

2 EXAMPLE   Proving Angle Relationships

Supply reasons to complete the proof that m∠*BCA* < m∠*BAD*.

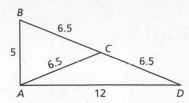

Since ⬚ < ⬚ , m∠*BCA* < m∠*ABC*.   _____

Since 12 < 13, ⬚⬚⬚⬚⬚ .   The larger angle is opposite the longer side.

m∠*BCA* < m∠*BAD*   _____

REFLECT

2a. Compare m∠*BCA* and m∠*BAC*. Explain how the comparison allows you to
conclude m∠*BCA* < m∠*BAD* in another way.

_____

_____

_____

PRACTICE

1. Given the information in the diagram, prove that *PQ* < *PS*.

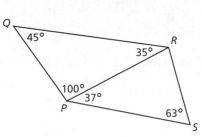

_____

_____

_____

_____

2. Given the information in the diagram, prove that m∠*DEA* < m∠*ABC*.

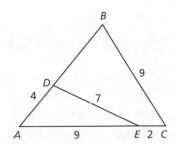

_____

_____

_____

_____

Additional Practice

Write an indirect proof that the angle measures of a triangle cannot add to more than 180°.

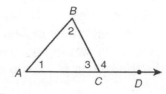

1. State the assumption that starts the indirect proof.

   _____

2. Use the Exterior Angle Theorem and the Linear Pair Theorem to write the indirect proof.

3. Write the angles of $\triangle DEF$ in order from smallest to largest.

   _____

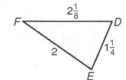

4. Write the sides of $\triangle GHI$ in order from shortest to longest.

   _____

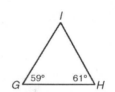

Tell whether a triangle can have sides with the given lengths. If not, explain why not.

5. 8, 8, 16 _____
6. 0.5, 0.7, 0.3 _____
7. $10\frac{1}{2}$, 4, 14 _____

8. $3x + 2$, x^2, $2x$ when $x = 4$ _____
9. $3x + 2$, x^2, $2x$ when $x = 6$ _____

The lengths of two sides of a triangle are given. Find the range of possible lengths for the third side.

10. 8.2 m, 3.5 m

11. 298 ft, 177 ft

12. $3\frac{1}{2}$ mi, 4 mi

   _____   _____   _____

13. The annual Cheese Rolling happens in May at Gloucestershire, England. As the name suggests, large, 7–9 pound wheels of cheese are rolled down a steep hill, and people chase after them. The first person to the bottom wins cheese. Renaldo wants to go to the Cheese Rolling. He plans to leave from Atlanta and fly into London (4281 miles). On the return, he will fly back from London to New York City (3470 miles) to visit his aunt. Then Renaldo heads back to Atlanta. Atlanta, New York City, and London do not lie on the same line. Find the range of the total distance Renaldo could travel on his trip.

   _____

© Houghton Mifflin Harcourt Publishing Company

Problem Solving

1. A charter plane travels from Barrow, Alaska, to Fairbanks. From Fairbanks, it flies to Nome, and then back to its starting point in Barrow. Which of the three legs of the trip is the longest?

_____

2. Three cell phone towers are shown at the right. The measure of ∠M is 10° less than the measure of ∠K. The measure of ∠L is 1° greater than the measure of ∠K. Which two towers are closest together?

_____

Use the figure for Exercises 3 and 4.

In disc golf, a player tries to throw a disc into a metal basket target. Four disc golf targets on a course are shown at right.

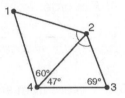

3. Which two targets are closest together?

4. Which two targets are farthest apart?

_____   _____

Choose the best answer.

5. The distance from Jacksonville to Tampa is 171 miles. The distance from Tampa to Miami is 206 miles. Use the Triangle Inequality Theorem to find the range for the distance from Jacksonville to Miami.
   A $0 \text{ mi} < d < 35 \text{ mi}$
   B $0 \text{ mi} < d < 377 \text{ mi}$
   C $35 \text{ mi} < d < 377 \text{ mi}$
   D $-35 \text{ mi} < d < 377 \text{ mi}$

6. In Jessica's room, the distance from the door D to the closet C is 4 feet. The distance from the closet to the window W is 6 feet. The distance from the window to the door is 8 feet. On a floor plan of her room, $\triangle CDW$ is drawn. Order the angles from least to greatest measure.
   F ∠C, ∠D, ∠W   H ∠W, ∠C, ∠D
   G ∠D, ∠C, ∠W   J ∠W, ∠D, ∠C

7. Walking paths at a park are shown. Which route represents the greatest distance?

   A A to B to D C C to B to D
   B A to D to B D C to D to B

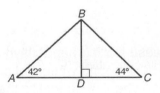

Inequalities in Two Triangles
Going Deeper

Essential question: *When two sides of a triangle have fixed lengths and the angle included by them changes, how does the third side length change?*

Video Tutor

CC.9–12.G.CO.10

1 E X P L O R E   **Comparing Triangles with Two Congruent Sides**

A   Using a protractor, draw an angle. Along each side, measure a distance *a* of your choice. Then join the three points obtained to form a triangle like the one below, △XYZ. Draw several such triangles, using various angle measures, such as 30°, 60°, 90°, 120°, and 150°, but keeping the distance *a* the same.

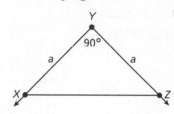

B   In each triangle you construct, measure the length of the third side, *XZ*. Label the lengths on your diagrams.

C   Record your results in the table.

Angle measure					
Distance *a*					
Length of third side					

REFLECT

1a. Classify the triangles you drew.

_____

_____

1b. In general terms, how does changing the included angle affect the length of the third side? Conversely, as the length of the third side increases, how is the angle opposite the third side affected?

_____

_____

1c. What is the range of possible values for the third side?

_____

_____

2 **EXPLORE** **Comparing Triangles with Different Side Lengths**

A Repeat the steps of the previous Explore, but use two different distances, *a* and *b*, of your choice. Draw several triangles, using various angle measures, such as 30°, 60°, 90°, 120°, and 150°, but keeping the distances *a* and *b* the same each time.

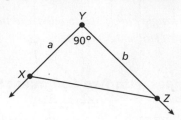

B In each triangle you construct, measure the length of the third side, *XZ*. Label the lengths on your diagrams.

C Record your results in the table.

Angle measure					
Distance *a*					
Distance *b*					
Length of third side					

REFLECT

2a. Classify the triangles you drew.

_____

_____

2b. How do your results compare with Explore 1?

_____

_____

2c. What is the range of possible values for the third side? Explain.

_____

_____

2d. If side lengths *a* and *b* are different, is it possible to adjust the angle between them to make an isosceles triangle? Under what conditions is this possible?

_____

_____

5-6

Additional Practice

100%

Compare the given measures.

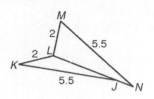

1. m∠K and m∠M

   m∠K < m∠M

2. AB and DE

   DE ⧸ AB

3. QR and ST

   QR > ST

Find the range of values for x.

4.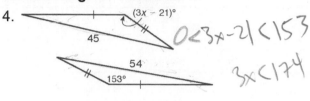

   (3x − 21)°
   45
   54
   153°

   0 < 3x−21 < 153
   3x < 174

   7 < x < 58

6.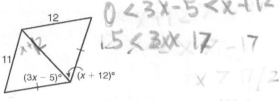

   12
   x+2
   11
   (3x − 5)° (x + 12)°

   0 < 3x−5 < x+12 5
   15 < 3xx 17 _ 17
   x 7 17/2

   3x−5+ x+ 5/3 < x < 17/2

5.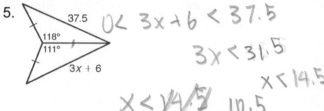

   37.5
   118°
   111°
   3x + 6

   0 < 3x+6 < 37.5
   3x < 31.5
   x < 14.5 10.5

   2 < x < 10.5

7.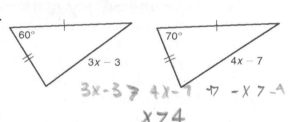

   60°
   3x − 3
   70°
   4x − 7

   3x−3 > 4x−7 −7 − x 7 −4
   x 7 4

8. You have used a compass to copy and bisect segments and angles and to draw arcs and circles. A compass has a drawing leg, a pivot leg, and a hinge at the angle between the legs. Explain why and how the measure of the angle at the hinge changes if you draw two circles with different diameters.

_____

_____

_____

_____

_____

_____

_____

Problem Solving

1. The angle that a person makes as he or she is sitting changes with the task. The diagram shows the position of a student at his desk. In which position is the angle measure *a*° at which he is sitting the greatest? The least? Explain.

45 in.

a°

relaxed

32 in.

a°

writing

36 in.

a°

typing

_____

_____

_____

_____

2. Two cyclists start from the same location and travel in opposite directions for 2 miles each. Then the first cyclist turns right 90° and continues for another mile. At the same time, the second cyclist turns 45° left and continues for another mile. At this point, which cyclist is closer to the original starting point?

_____

_____

3. A compass is used to draw a circle. Then the compass is opened wider and another circle is drawn. Explain how this illustrates the Hinge Theorem.

_____

_____

_____

_____

Choose the best answer.

4. Two sides of each triangle in the circle are formed from the radii of the circle. Compare *EF* and *FG*.

   A *EF = FG*

   B *EF < FG*

   C *EF > FG*

   D Not enough information is given.

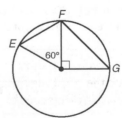

5. Compare m∠*Y* and m∠*M*.

   F m∠*Y* = m∠*M*

   G m∠*Y* > m∠*M*

   H m∠*Y* < m∠*M*

   J Not enough information is given.

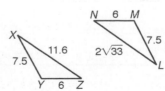

5-7

The Pythagorean Theorem
Going Deeper

Essential question: *How can you apply the Pythagorean Theorem?*

Video Tutor

CC.9–12.G.SRT.8

1 EXAMPLE **Using the Pythagorean Theorem with Lengths**

A shelf extends perpendicularly 24 cm from a wall. You want to place a 28-cm brace under the shelf, as shown. To the nearest tenth of a centimeter, how far below the shelf will the brace be attached to the wall?

Use the Pythagorean Theorem to find the distance *BC*.

$BC^2 + AC^2 = AB^2$ Pythagorean Theorem

$BC^2 + \underline{}^2 = \underline{}^2$ Substitute.

$BC^2 + \underline{} = \underline{}$ Find the squares.

$BC^2 = \underline{}$ Subtract the same quantity from both sides.

$BC \approx \underline{}$ Find the square root and round.

So, the brace should be attached to the wall about _____ below the shelf.

REFLECT

1a. Suppose you know that m∠*CAB* ≈ 31°. What is m∠*CBA*? Explain.

_____

_____

CC.9–12.G.SRT.8

2 EXAMPLE **Using the Pythagorean Theorem with Velocities**

You paddle a canoe due north across a river at a rate of 3 mi/h. The river has a 1 mi/h current that flows due east. What is your canoe's actual speed?

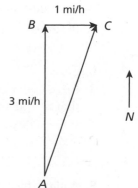

A Model the situation with arrows whose lengths represent speeds. The arrow that represents the paddling speed is three times the length of the arrow that represents the river speed.

B Use the Pythagorean Theorem to find *AC*.

$AC^2 = \underline{}^2 + \underline{}^2$ Pythagorean Theorem

$AC^2 = \underline{}$ Square the terms and add.

$AC \approx \underline{}$ Take the square root of both sides. Round to the nearest tenth.

So, the actual speed of the canoe is about _____.

2a. Why does it make sense that the canoe's actual speed is greater than both the speed at which you paddle and the speed of the current?

_____

_____

PRACTICE

Use the Pythagorean Theorem to find the missing side length. Round to the nearest tenth.

1.
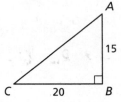

_____

2.
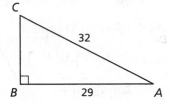

_____

3.
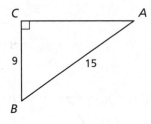

_____

4.
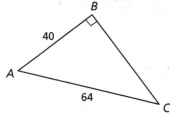

_____

5.
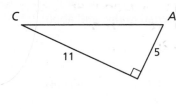

_____

6.
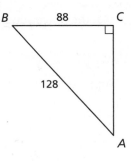

_____

7. A ladder leans against a wall and reaches a point 15 feet up the wall. The base of the ladder is 3.9 feet from the wall. To the nearest tenth of a foot, what is the length of the ladder?

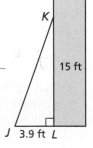

_____

8. A 7.2-meter guy wire goes from the top of a utility pole to a point on the ground that is 3 meters from the base of the pole. To the nearest tenth of a meter, how tall is the utility pole?

_____

9. A plane flies due north at 500 mi/h. There is a crosswind blowing due east at 60 mi/h. What is the plane's actual speed to the nearest tenth?

_____

Additional Practice

Find the value of *x*. Give your answer in simplest radical form.

1.
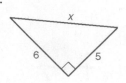

$36+25=61$ $\sqrt{61}$

2.
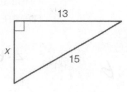

$\sqrt{56}$

3.
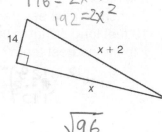

$196+x^2 = x^2+4$
$196 = 2x^2 + 4$
$192 = 2x^2$

$\sqrt{96}$

4. The aspect ratio of a TV screen is the ratio of the width to the height of the image. A regular TV has an aspect ratio of 4 : 3. Find the height and width of a 42-inch TV screen to the nearest tenth of an inch. (The measure given is the length of the diagonal across the screen.)

$4x + 3x = 42$ $H = 18$ in $W = 24$ in

5. A "wide-screen" TV has an aspect ratio of 16 : 9. Find the length of a diagonal on a wide-screen TV screen that has the same height as the screen in Exercise 4.

_____

Find the missing side lengths. Give your answer in simplest radical form. Tell whether the side lengths form a Pythagorean Triple.

$9 + 81 = 90$

6.

$36 + x^2 = 42.25$
$x =$

2.5

7.
$400 + 225$
$= x^2$

25

8.
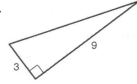

≈ 9.5

Tell whether the measures can be the side lengths of a triangle. If so, classify the triangle as acute, obtuse, or right.

9. 15, 18, 20 $225+$
   obtuse

10. 7, 8, 11
    obtuse

11. 6, 7, $3\sqrt{13}$
    No

12. Kitty has a triangle with sides that measure 16, 8, and 13. She does some calculations and finds that $256 + 64 > 169$. Kitty concludes that the triangle is obtuse. Evaluate Kitty's conclusion and Kitty's reasoning.

Her conclusion is ~~wrong~~ right because it should be $256 > 169 + 64$ but her reasoning was wrong.

Problem Solving

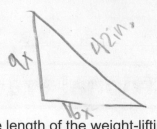

1. It is recommended that for a height of 20 inches, a wheelchair ramp be 19 feet long. What is the value of x to the nearest tenth?

$19^2 = \left(\dfrac{28}{12}\right)^2 + x^2$

$361 =$

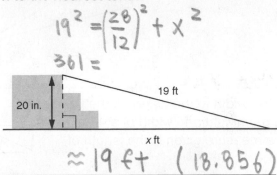

20 in.   19 ft

x ft

$\approx 19\,ft \quad (18.856)$

2. Find x, the length of the weight-lifting incline bench. Round to the nearest tenth.

$2.6^2 +$

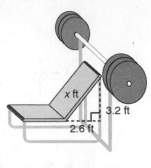

x ft   3.2 ft

2.6 ft

$4.1\,ft$

3. A ladder 15 feet from the base of a building reaches a window that is 35 feet high. What is the length of the ladder to the nearest foot?

35

15

$38\,ft$

4. In a wide-screen television, the ratio of width to height is 16 : 9. What are the width and height of a television that has a diagonal measure of 42 inches? Round to the nearest tenth.

1600

$W = 36.6$

$H = 20.6$

Choose the best answer.

5. The distance from Austin to San Antonio is about 74 miles, and the distance from San Antonio to Victoria is about 102 miles. Find the approximate distance from Austin to Victoria.

  A 28 mi   C 126 mi

  B 70 mi   D 176 mi

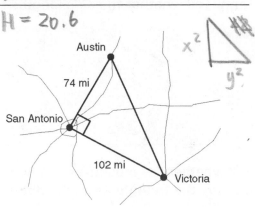

Austin

74 mi

San Antonio

102 mi

Victoria

x^2

y^2

1764

6. What is the approximate perimeter of $\triangle DEC$ if rectangle $ABCD$ has a length of 4.6 centimeters?

  F 5.1 cm

  G 6.5 cm

  H 9.8 cm

  J 11.1 cm

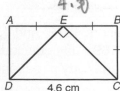

4.5

A   E   B

D   4.6 cm   C

$x^2 + x^2 = 4.6^2$

$2x^2 = 21.16$

$x^2 = 10.58$

$x = 3.25$

$\begin{array}{r} 6.50 \\ +4.6 \\ \hline 11.1 \end{array}$

7. The legs of a right triangle measure $3x$ and 15. If the hypotenuse measures $3x + 3$, what is the value of x?

  A 12   C 36

  B 16   D 221

$3x + 15 = 3x + 3$

$9x^2 + 225 = 9x^2 + 18x + 9$

$18x = 216 \quad x = 12$

8. A cube has edge lengths of 6 inches. What is the approximate length of a diagonal d of the cube?

  F 6 in.   H 10.4 in.

  G 8.4 in.   J 12 in.

6

Applying Special Right Triangles
Going Deeper

Essential question: *What can you say about the side lengths associated with special right triangles?*

There are two special right triangles that arise frequently in problem-solving situations. It is useful to know the relationships among the side lengths of these triangles.

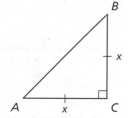

Video Tutor

CC.9–12.G.SRT.6

1 EXPLORE   **Investigating an Isosceles Right Triangle**

A   The figure shows an isosceles right triangle. What is the measure of each base angle of the triangle? Why?

_____

_____

B   Let the legs of the right triangle have length x. You can use the Pythagorean Theorem to find the length of the hypotenuse in terms of x.

$AB^2 = x^2 + x^2$ Pythagorean Theorem

$AB^2 = $ _____   Combine like terms.

$AB = $ _____   Find the square root of both sides and simplify.

REFLECT

1a. A student claims that if you know one side length of an isosceles right triangle, then you know all the side lengths. Do you agree or disagree? Explain.

_____

_____

_____

1b. Explain how to find y in the right triangle at right.

_____

_____

_____

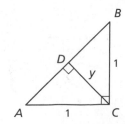

2 EXPLORE Investigating Another Special Right Triangle

A In the figure, △ABD is an equilateral triangle and $\overline{BC}$ is a perpendicular from B to $\overline{AD}$. Explain how to find the angle measures in △ABC.

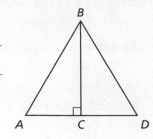

_____

_____

B Explain why △ACB ≅ △DCB.

_____

_____

_____

_____

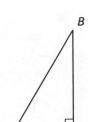

C Let the length of $\overline{AC}$ be x. What is the length of $\overline{AB}$? Why?

_____

_____

D In the space below, show how to use the Pythagorean Theorem to find the length of $\overline{BC}$.

_____

_____

_____

_____

REFLECT

2a. What is the ratio of the side lengths in a right triangle with acute angles that measure 30° and 60°?

_____

2b. Error Analysis A student drew a right triangle with a 60° angle and a hypotenuse of length 10. Then he labeled the other side lengths as shown. Explain how you can tell just by glancing at the side lengths that the student made an error. Then explain the error.

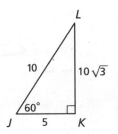

_____

_____

The right triangles you investigated are sometimes called 45°-45°-90° and 30°-60°-90° right triangles. The side-length relationships that you discovered can be used to find lengths in any such triangles.

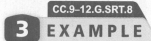

3 **E X A M P L E** **Solving Special Right Triangles**

A Refer to the diagram of the 45°-45°-90° triangle. Fill in the calculations that help you find the missing side lengths. Give answers in simplest radical form.

$AC = \boxed{}$

$BC = AC \cdot \boxed{} = \boxed{}$

$AB = AC \cdot \boxed{} = \boxed{}$

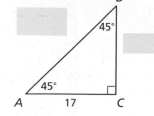

B Refer to the diagram of the 30°-60°-90° triangle. Fill in the calculations that help you find the missing side lengths. Give answers in simplest radical form.

$DE = \boxed{}$

$DF = DE \div \boxed{} = \boxed{}$

$EF = DF \cdot \boxed{} = \boxed{}$

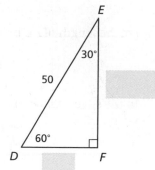

C Add the side lengths you calculated to the diagrams.

REFLECT

3a. Suppose you are given the length of the hypotenuse of a 45°-45°-90° triangle. How can you calculate the length of a leg?

_____

3b. Suppose you are given the length of the longer leg of a 30°-60°-90° triangle. How can you calculate the length of the shorter leg?

_____

3c. When finding a leg length in a 45°-45°-90° triangle, one student gave the answer $\frac{30}{\sqrt{2}}$ and another gave the answer $15\sqrt{2}$. Show the answers are equivalent.

_____

_____

SOHCAHTOA

PRACTICE

Find the value of x. Give your answer in simplest radical form.

1.
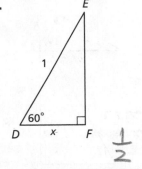

$3\sqrt{2}$

2.
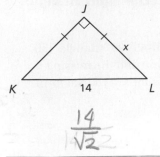

$\frac{14}{\sqrt{2}}$

3.
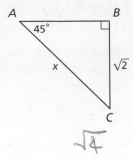

$\sqrt{4}$

4.
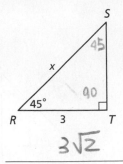

$\frac{1}{2}$

5.
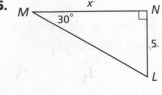

$5\sqrt{3}$

6.
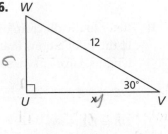

$6\sqrt{3}$

7.
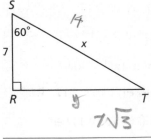

$7\sqrt{3}$

8.
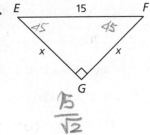

$\frac{15}{\sqrt{2}}$

9.
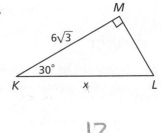

12

10. Error Analysis Two students were asked to find the value of x in the figure at right. Which student's work is correct? Explain the other student's error.

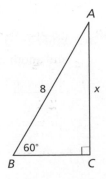

| **Roberto's Work** |
| In a 30°-60°-90° triangle, the hypotenuse is twice as long as the shorter leg, so $BC = 4$. The ratio of the lengths of the legs is $1:\sqrt{3}$, so $x = 4\sqrt{3}$. |

| **Aaron's Work** |
| In a 30°-60°-90° triangle, the side lengths are in a ratio of $1:\sqrt{3}:2$, so x must be $\sqrt{3}$ times the length of $\overline{AB}$. Therefore, $x = 8\sqrt{3}$. |

Additional Practice

Find the value of *x* in each figure. Give your answer in simplest radical form.

1.

$8\sqrt{16}$
_____

2.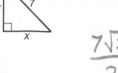

$\dfrac{7\sqrt{2}}{2}$
_____

3.

2
_____

Find the values of *x* and *y*. Give your answers in simplest radical form.

4.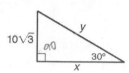

$x = \underline{30}$ $y = \underline{20\sqrt{3}}$

5.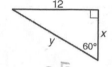

$x = \underline{\dfrac{12\sqrt{3}}{3}}$ $y = \underline{\dfrac{24\sqrt{3}}{3}}$

6.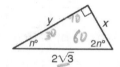

$x = \underline{\dfrac{2\sqrt{3}}{2}}$ $y = \underline{12}$

Lucia is an archaeologist trekking through the jungle of the Yucatan Peninsula. She stumbles upon a stone structure covered with creeper vines and ferns. She immediately begins taking measurements of her discovery. (*Hint:* Drawing some figures may help.)

7. Around the perimeter of the building, Lucia finds small alcoves at regular intervals carved into the stone. The alcoves are triangular in shape with a horizontal base and two sloped equal-length sides that meet at a right angle. Each of the sloped sides measures $14\frac{1}{4}$ inches. Lucia has also found several stone tablets inscribed with characters. The stone tablets measure $22\frac{1}{8}$ inches long. Lucia hypothesizes that the alcoves once held the stone tablets. Tell whether Lucia's hypothesis may be correct. Explain your answer.

It is not correct cause the length width is smaller than $22\frac{1}{8}$.

8. Lucia also finds several statues around the building. The statues measure $9\frac{7}{16}$ inches tall. She wonders whether the statues might have been placed in the alcoves. Tell whether this is possible. Explain your answer.

Yes because both the length carid width is over $9\frac{7}{16}$.

Problem Solving

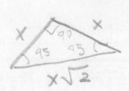

For Exercises 1–6, give your answers in simplest radical form.

1. In bowling, the pins are arranged in a pattern based on equilateral triangles. What is the distance between pins 1 and 5?

   $12\sqrt{3} = \approx 15.6$

2. To secure an outdoor canopy, a 64-inch cord is extended from the top of a vertical pole to the ground. If the cord makes a 60° angle with the ground, how tall is the pole?

   ≈ 55.4 in

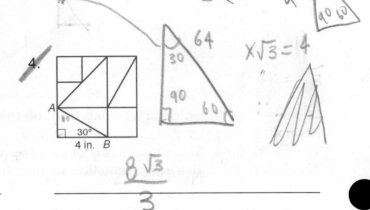

Find the length of $\overline{AB}$ in each quilt pattern.

3.

   B
   3 in.
   A 3 in. C

   ≈ 4.24 in

4.

   A
   30°
   4 in. B

   $\dfrac{8\sqrt{3}}{3}$

Choose the best answer.

5. An equilateral triangle has an altitude of 21 inches. What is the side length of the triangle?

   $x = 14\sqrt{3}$

6. A shelf is an isosceles right triangle, and the longest side is 38 centimeters. What is the length of each of the other two sides?

   $19\sqrt{2}$

Use the figure for Exercises 7 and 8.

Assume △JKL is in the first quadrant, with m∠K = 90°.

7. Suppose that $\overline{JK}$ is a leg of △JKL, a 45°-45°-90° triangle. What are possible coordinates of point L?

   A (6, 4.5)   C (6, 2)
   B (7, 2)   D (8, 7)

8. Suppose △JKL is a 30°-60°-90° triangle and $\overline{JK}$ is the side opposite the 60° angle. What are the approximate coordinates of point L?

   F (4.9, 2)   H (8.7, 2)
   G (4.5, 2)   J (7.1, 2)

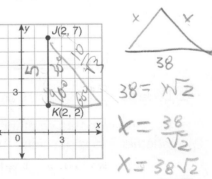

$38 = x\sqrt{2}$

$x = \dfrac{38}{\sqrt{2}}$

$x = \dfrac{38\sqrt{2}}{2}$

$x = 19\sqrt{2}$

CHAPTER 5

Performance Tasks

COMMON
CORE

CC.9-12.G.CO.9
CC.9-12.G.CO.10
CC.9-12.G.SRT.4
CC.9-12.G.C.3
CC.9-12.G.MG.3

⭐ **1.** A *gore* is a triangular piece of material often used to make a skirt flare out. A tailor is inserting an isosceles gore in each of two skirts designed from the same pattern. Each skirt is 27 inches from the waist to the hem. The vertex angle of the gore inserted in one skirt is 26 degrees. The tailor wants the other skirt to have less of a flare. What will be different about the gore in the second skirt? Use the Hinge Theorem to explain.

⭐ **2.** An auditorium is in the shape of an equilateral triangle. The stage extends from one vertex of the triangle to the midsegment, and the seating area extends from the midsegment to the rear wall. The rear wall measures 112 feet. What is the perimeter of the seating area?

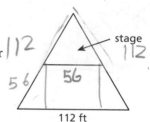

112   stage
112
56   56
112 ft

280 ft

⭐⭐ **3.** Gus is making a bookshelf in the shape of an isosceles triangle. The sides will be cherry wood and each of the four shelves, including the bottom shelf at the base, will be birch. The shelves will be evenly spaced vertically, and the base will be 48 inches long.

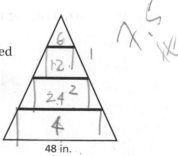

6
12   1
24   2
4
48 in.

a. What will be the length of each of the shelves?

b. How many feet of birch does Gus need?   100 in

c. Gus expects to lose $\frac{1}{4}$ inch of wood with each cut he makes. He can purchase 6-foot planks of birch. How many planks does he need? Explain.

2 planks

continued

d. After Gus makes all the necessary cuts, what is the total length of the piece(s) of birch he will have left over?

★★★ **4.** Three people are repairing a fence around a rectangular field. They need to share tools, so they want to leave the tools they are not using in a place equidistant from the places they are repairing. Person *A* is working 700 feet north of the southwest corner. Person *B* is working 1200 feet east and 1000 feet north of the southwest corner. Person *C* is working 1500 feet east of the southwest corner. Find the point that is equidistant from all three points. Round to the nearest foot, and describe the point with distances relative to the southwest corner. Show your work.

Name _____ Class _____ Date _____

MULTIPLE CHOICE

1. What is an equation of the parabola with focus $F(0, -6)$ and directrix $y = 6$?

A. $y = \frac{1}{24}x^2$ **C.** $x = -\frac{1}{24}y^2$

B. $x = \frac{1}{24}y^2$ **D.** $y = -\frac{1}{24}x^2$

2. Write an equation in standard form for the parabola whose graph is shown.

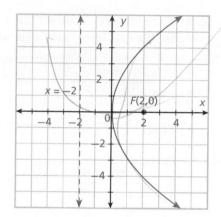

F. $y = -\frac{1}{8}x^2$ **H.** $x = \frac{1}{8}y^2$

G. $y = \frac{1}{8}x^2$ **J.** $x = -\frac{1}{8}y^2$

3. Jessica is using a compass and straightedge to construct the inscribed circle for $\triangle PQR$. Which of the following should be her first step?

A. Construct the bisector of $\angle Q$.

B. Construct the perpendicular bisector of $\overline{QR}$.

C. Construct the perpendicular from P to $\overline{QR}$.

D. Construct the midpoint of $\overline{PR}$.

4. What can you conclude about $m\angle ABC$ and $m\angle CBD$ and why?

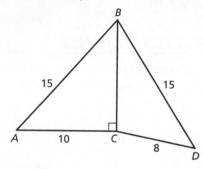

F. $m\angle ABC > m\angle CBD$
(Hinge Theorem)

G. $m\angle ABC > m\angle CBD$
(Triangle Inequality theorem)

H. $m\angle ABC < m\angle CBD$
(Converse of the Hinge Theorem)

J. $m\angle ABC < m\angle CBD$
(Converse of the Pythagorean Theorem)

5. The lengths of the two legs of a right triangle are 2 inches and 4 inches. What is the length of the hypotenuse in simplest radical form?

A. $\sqrt{6}$ inches

B. $2\sqrt{3}$ inches

C. $2\sqrt{5}$ inches

D. $\sqrt{20}$ inches

6. A square courtyard has a straight walkway from one corner to the opposite corner. If each wall of the courtyard is 20 feet long, what is the length of the walkway?

F. 10 feet

G. 20 feet

H. $20\sqrt{2}$ feet

J. $20\sqrt{3}$ feet

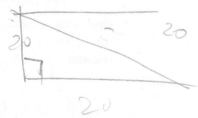

7. The sides of an equilateral triangle are 40 inches long. What is the height of the triangle?

A. 20 feet

B. 80 feet

C. $20\sqrt{3}$ feet

D. $40\sqrt{3}$ feet

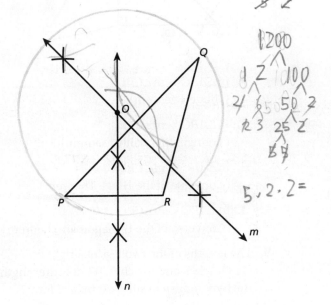

CONSTRUCTED RESPONSE

8. The diagram below shows the first several steps of a construction.

a. What is line m in relation to the triangle?

perpendicular bisector of QP

b. What is line n in relation to the triangle?

bisects PR

c. Draw a circle centered at O that passes through point P. Identify the circle in relation to $\triangle PQR$.

circle 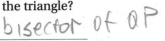 circumscribed triangle

9. In an indirect proof, you begin by assuming that the conclusion is false. Then you show that this assumption leads to a contradiction.

Suppose that you want to prove that obtuse $\triangle RST$ does not have a right angle.

a. What is the given information?

_____

b. What are you trying to conclude?

_____

c. If you assume that the conclusion is false, what must be true instead?

_____

d. Let $\angle R$ be a right angle. Assume $\angle S$ is a right or obtuse angle. Justify each statement.

Statements
1. $m\angle R = 90°$, $m\angle S \geq 90°$
2. $m\angle R + m\angle S + m\angle T = 180°$
3. $\quad 90° + m\angle S + m\angle T = 180°$
4. $\qquad\qquad m\angle S = 90° - m\angle T$
5. $\qquad\qquad 90° \leq 90° - m\angle T$
6. $\qquad\qquad m\angle T \leq 0°$

_____

_____

_____

_____

_____

_____

e. What is the contradicion?

_____

_____

_____

_____

Polygons and Quadrilaterals

Chapter Focus

At the beginning of this unit, you will inscribe polygons in circles. Then you will focus your study of polygons on parallelograms and other special quadrilaterals. Your knowledge of triangle congruence criteria will be useful in proving properties of parallelograms. You will also develop criteria that can be used to show that a quadrilateral is a parallelogram and you will investigate special parallelograms, including rectangles and rhombuses.

Chapter at a Glance

COMMON CORE

Lesson		Standards for Mathematical Content
6-1	Properties and Attributes of Regular Polygons	CC.9-12.G.CO.13
6-2	Properties of Parallelograms	CC.9-12.G.CO.11, CC.9-12.G.SRT.5
6-3	Conditions for Parallelograms	CC.9-12.G.CO.11, CC.9-12.G.SRT.5
6-4	Properties of Special Parallelograms	CC.9-12.G.CO.11, CC.9-12.G.SRT.5
6-5	Conditions for Special Parallelograms	CC.9-12.G.GPE.4
6-6	Properties of Kites and Trapezoids	CC.9-12.G.CO.9
	Performance Tasks	
	Assessment Readiness	

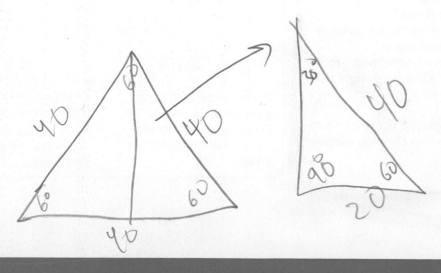

Unpacking the Standards

Understanding the standards and the vocabulary terms in the standards will help you know exactly what you are expected to learn in this chapter.

COMMON CORE CC.9-12.G.CO.13

Construct an equilateral triangle, a square, and a regular hexagon inscribed in a circle.

Key Vocabulary

equilateral triangle *(triángulo equilátero)* A triangle with three congruent sides.

square *(cuadrado)* A quadrilateral with four congruent sides and four right angles.

regular polygon *(polígono regular)* A polygon that is both equilateral and equiangular.

hexagon *(hexágono)* A six-sided polygon.

circle *(círculo)* The set of points in a plane that are a fixed distance from a given point called the center of the circle.

What It Means for You
Lesson 6-1

Using a compass and straightedge, or by paper folding, you can construct geometric figures precisely without having to measure by applying geometric definitions and theorems.

EXAMPLE
In a regular hexagon, each triangle formed by two radii and an edge is equilateral. This means you can inscribe a regular hexagon in a circle by marking the radius *AP* six times around the circle.

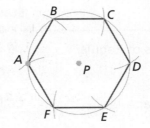

COMMON CORE CC.9-12.G.CO.9

Prove theorems about lines and angles.

Key Vocabulary

proof *(demostración)* An argument that uses logic to show that a conclusion is true.

theorem *(teorema)* A statement that has been proven.

line *(línea)* An undefined term in geometry, a line is a straight path that has no thickness and extends forever.

angle *(ángulo)* A figure formed by two rays with a common endpoint.

What It Means for You
Lessons 6-2, 6-3, 6-4, 6-5, 6-6

You can use simple theorems about angles, segments, and so on to prove theorems about the angles, sides, and diagonals in various polygons, including special quadrilaterals.

EXAMPLE

Pentagon

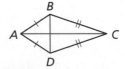

The sum of the interior angle measures of the pentagon is the sum of the interior angle measures of 3 triangles: 3(180°) = 540°.

A kite has exactly two pairs of congruent consecutive sides.

From this definition, you can prove that the diagonals of a kite are perpendicular.

COMMON CORE **CC.9-12.G.CO.11**

Prove theorems about parallelograms.

Key Vocabulary
parallelogram *(paralelogramo)*
A quadrilateral with two pairs of parallel sides.

What It Means for You Lessons 6-2, 6-3, 6-4, 6-5

Parallelograms, including rectangles and squares, are everywhere around you. You can prove the many special relationships about their sides and angles that make them so important.

EXAMPLE

 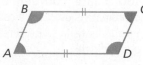

$\overline{AB} \parallel \overline{CD}, \overline{BC} \parallel \overline{DA}$

$\overline{AB} \cong \overline{CD} \quad \angle A \cong \angle C$
$\overline{BC} \cong \overline{DA} \quad \angle B \cong \angle D$

COMMON CORE **CC.9-12.G.GPE.4**

Use coordinates to prove simple geometric theorems algebraically.

Key Vocabulary
coordinate *(coordenada)* A number used to identify the location of a point. On a number line, one coordinate is used. On a coordinate plane, two coordinates are used, called the *x*-coordinate and the *y*-coordinate. In space, three coordinates are used, called the *x*-coordinate, the *y*-coordinate, and the *z*-coordinate.

What It Means for You Lesson 6-5

Coordinates can help you prove theorems about special quadrilaterals because the parallel and/or congruent segments, right angles, and so on, make them easy to represent on a coordinate grid.

EXAMPLE
A rhombus is a quadrilateral with four congruent sides.

To prove that quadrilateral *ABCD* is a rhombus, use the Distance Formula to show that:

$AB = BC = CD = AD = 5$

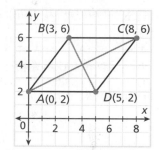

COMMON CORE **CC.9-12.G.GPE.5**

Prove the slope criteria for parallel and perpendicular lines and use them to solve geometric problems …

Key Vocabulary
slope *(pendiente)* A measure of the steepness of a line. If (x_1, y_1) and (x_2, y_2) are any two points on the line, the slope of the line, known as *m*, is represented by the equation $m = \dfrac{y_2 - y_1}{x_2 - x_1}$.
parallel lines *(líneas paralelas)* Lines in the same plane that do not intersect.
perpendicular lines *(líneas perpendiculares)* Lines that intersect at 90° angles.

What It Means for You Lesson 6-5

Because the special quadrilaterals involve parallel or perpendicular sides and/or diagonals, the slopes of these segments are important for establishing these relationships.

EXAMPLE
A second way to prove that quadrilateral *ABCD* from the previous standard is a rhombus:

Use the slope formula to show that:

slope $\overline{AB}$ = slope $\overline{CD}$

slope $\overline{AD}$ = slope $\overline{BC}$

slope $\overline{AC} \times$ slope $\overline{BD} = -1$

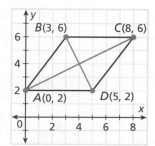

CHAPTER 6

Key Vocabulary

circle *(círculo)* The set of points in a plane that are a fixed distance from a given point called the center of the circle.

coordinate *(coordenada)* A number used to identify the location of a point. On a number line, one coordinate is used. On a coordinate plane, two coordinates are used, called the *x*-coordinate and the *y*-coordinate. In space, three coordinates are used, called the *x*-coordinate, the *y*-coordinate, and the *z*-coordinate.

diagonal of a polygon *(diagonal de un polígono)* A segment connecting two nonconsecutive vertices of a polygon.

equilateral triangle *(triángulo equilátero)* A triangle with three congruent sides.

hexagon *(hexágono)* A six-sided polygon.

isosceles trapezoid *(trapecio isósceles)* A trapezoid in which the legs are congruent.

perpendicular lines *(líneas perpendiculars)* Lines that intersect at 90° angles.

parallel lines *(líneas paralelas)* Lines in the same plane that do not intersect.

parallelogram *(paralelogramo)* A quadrilateral with two pairs of parallel sides.

rectangle *(rectángulo)* A quadrilateral with four right angles.

regular polygon *(polígono regular)* A polygon that is both equilateral and equiangular.

rhombus *(rombo)* A quadrilateral with four congruent sides.

slope *(pendiente)* A measure of the steepness of a line. If (x_1, y_1) and (x_2, y_2) are any two points on the line, the slope of the line, known as m, is represented by the equation $m = \dfrac{y_2 - y_1}{x_2 - x_1}$.

square *(cuadrado)* A quadrilateral with four congruent sides and four right angles.

trapezoid *(trapecio)* A quadrilateral with exactly one pair of parallel sides.

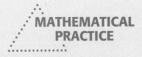

MATHEMATICAL PRACTICE

The Common Core Standards for Mathematical Practice describe varieties of expertise that mathematics educators at all levels should seek to develop in their students. Opportunities to develop these practices are integrated throughout this program.

1. **Make sense of problems and persevere in solving them.**
2. **Reason abstractly and quantitatively.**
3. **Construct viable arguments and critique the reasoning of others.**
4. **Model with mathematics.**
5. **Use appropriate tools strategically.**
6. **Attend to precision.**
7. **Look for and make use of structure.**
8. **Look for and express regularity in repeated reasoning**

Properties and Attributes of Regular Polygons

Connection: Inscribing Regular Polygons

Essential question: *How do you inscribe a regular polygon in a circle?*

A polygon is said to be **inscribed** in a circle if all of the polygon's vertices lie on the circle. In the figure, $\triangle XYZ$ is inscribed in circle C. You can also say that circle C circumscribes $\triangle XYZ$.

In this lesson, you will use a compass and straightedge to inscribe regular polygons in a circle.

Video Tutor

CC.9–12.G.CO.13

1 EXPLORE   Inscribing a Regular Hexagon

Use the space at right to inscribe a regular hexagon in a circle.

A Use your compass to draw a circle O. Label a point A on the circle.

B Without adjusting the compass, place the point of the compass at A and draw an arc that intersects the circle. Label the point of intersection B.

C Without adjusting the compass, place the point of the compass at B and draw an arc that intersects the circle. Label the point of intersection C.

D Continue in this way until you have located six points, A, B, C, D, E, and F. Then use your straightedge to draw $\overline{AB}$, $\overline{BC}$, $\overline{CD}$, $\overline{DE}$, $\overline{EF}$, and $\overline{FA}$.

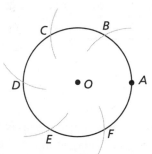

REFLECT

1a. Explain why *ABCDEF* must be a regular hexagon. (*Hint:* Consider the triangles that are formed when you draw the diameters $\overline{AD}$, $\overline{BE}$, and $\overline{CF}$.)

_____

_____

_____

1b. How can you modify this construction to construct an inscribed equilateral triangle?

_____

2 EXPLORE **Inscribing a Square**

Use the space at right to inscribe a square in a circle.

A Use your compass to draw a circle O.

B Use your straightedge to draw a diameter $\overline{AB}$.

C Use the compass and straightedge to construct the perpendicular bisector of $\overline{AB}$.

D Label the points where the perpendicular bisector intersects the circle as C and D.

E Use the straightedge to draw $\overline{AD}$, $\overline{DB}$, $\overline{BC}$, and $\overline{CA}$.

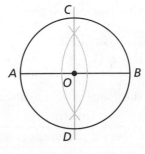

REFLECT

2a. Explain why $ADBC$ must have four congruent sides.

_____

_____

_____

_____

2b. Explain why all of the angles of $ADBC$ must be right angles.

_____

_____

_____

2c. How can you use the above construction as the starting point for inscribing a regular octagon in a circle?

_____

_____

_____

Additional Practice

In Exercises 1–4, you will inscribe a square in a circle. Use the space at the right to complete your sketch.

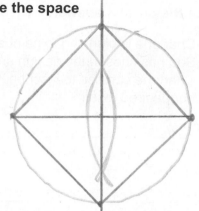

1. Use the method of Explore 2 of the lesson to draw circle *O* and diameter $\overline{AB}$, and to construct $\overline{CD}$, the perpendicular bisector of $\overline{AB}$.

2. Construct the bisector of ∠*AOC*. Label the point where the bisector intersects the circle *W*.

3. Construct the bisectors of ∠*COB*, ∠*BOD*, and ∠*AOD*, in that order. Label the points where the bisectors intersect the circle *X*, *Y*, and *Z* (in that order).

4. Use your straightedge to draw *WXYZ*. Explain how you know that *WXYZ* is a square.

_____

_____

_____

A dodecahedron is a twelve-sided polygon. In Exercises 5–8, you will inscribe a regular dodecahedron in a circle.

5. Use the method of Explore 1 from the lesson to draw a circle *O* and label point *A*. Draw the first arc and label the point of intersection *C*. Draw the remaining indicated arcs, but do not label the points.

6. Use your straightedge to draw $\overline{OA}$ and $\overline{OC}$, construct the bisector of ∠*COA*. Label the point where the bisector intersects the circle *B*..

7. Place the point of your compass at point *B* and open the compass until the pencil just touches point *C*. Without adjusting the compass, place the point of the compass at *C* and draw an arc that intersects the circle. Label the point of intersection *D*. Continue in this way until you have located 12 points lettered *A* through *L*.

8. Use your straightedge to draw *ABCDEFGHIJKL*. Explain how you know that *ABCDEFGHIJKL* is a regular dodecahedron.

_____

_____

_____

Problem Solving

Write the correct answer.

1. Charlene is planning to paint a circular mirror to look like stained glass. She has chosen the design shown. Explain two different methods Charlene can use to inscribe regular polygons in the circle and produce her desired result.

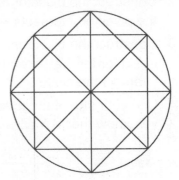

_____

_____

_____

_____

_____

_____

_____

_____

Harry is designing an advertising logo. He originally sketched a pattern for a dodecagon (a twelve-sided figure) inscribed in a circle, as shown. He is considering using a different inscribed polygon instead. Choose the best answer.

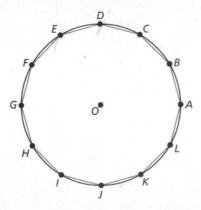

2. For which inscribed polygon can Harry *not* use the existing pattern without performing any additional construction?

   A equilateral triangle

   B square

   C regular hexagon

   D regular octagon

3. Harry decides to inscribe a regular 24-sided polygon in the circle. Instead of starting over from scratch, he decides to use his existing pattern. He erases the sides of the dodecagon but leaves the labeled points. What would be a good next step?

   F Draw segments connecting every two consecutive points (for instance, A and C, and C and E).

   G Construct the bisector of $\angle AOB$.

   H Construct the bisector of $\angle LOB$.

   J Construct the perpendicular bisector of $\overline{GA}$.

Properties of Parallelograms
Focus on Reasoning

Essential question: *What can you conclude about the sides, angles, and diagonals of a parallelogram?*

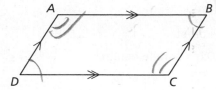

COMMON CORE

CC.9-12.G.CO.11, CC.9-12.G.SRT.5

Recall that a *parallelogram* is a quadrilateral that has two pairs of parallel sides. You use the symbol ▱ to name a parallelogram. For example, the figure shows ▱*ABCD*.

1 **Investigate parallelograms.**

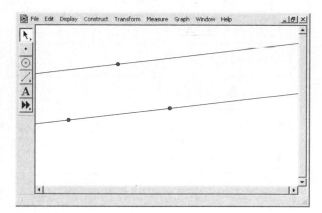

A Use the straightedge tool of your geometry software to draw a straight line. Then plot a point that is not on the line. Select the point and line, go to the Construct menu, and construct a line through the point that is parallel to the line. This will give you a pair of parallel lines, as shown.

B Repeat Step A to construct a second pair of parallel lines that intersect those from Step A.

C The intersections of the parallel lines create a parallelogram. Plot points at these intersections. Label the points *A*, *B*, *C*, and *D*.

D Use the Measure menu to measure each angle of the parallelogram.

E Use the Measure menu to measure the length of each side of the parallelogram. (You can do this by measuring the distance between consecutive vertices.)

F Drag the points and lines in your construction to change the shape of the parallelogram. As you do so, look for relationships in the measurements.

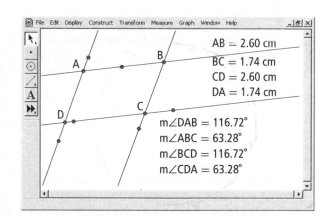

REFLECT

1a. Make a conjecture about the sides and angles of a parallelogram.

_____

_____

You may have discovered the following theorem about parallelograms.

> ### Theorem
>
> If a quadrilateral is a parallelogram, then opposite sides are congruent.

2 **Prove that opposite sides of a parallelogram are congruent.**

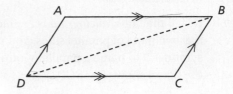

Complete the proof.

Given: *ABCD* is a parallelogram.

Prove: $\overline{AB} \cong \overline{CD}$ and $\overline{AD} \cong \overline{BC}$

Statements	Reasons
1. *ABCD* is a parallelogram.	1.
2. Draw $\overline{DB}$.	2. Through any two points there exists exactly one line.
3. $\overline{AB} \parallel \overline{DC}$; $\overline{AD} \parallel \overline{BC}$	3.
4. $\angle ADB \cong \angle CBD$; $\angle ABD \cong \angle CDB$	4.
5. $\overline{DB} \cong \overline{DB}$	5.
6.	6. ASA Congruence Criterion
7. $AB \cong CD$; $AD \cong BC$	7.

> **REFLECT**

2a. Explain how you can use the rotational symmetry of a parallelogram to give an argument that supports the above theorem.

_____

_____

_____

2b. One side of a parallelogram is twice as long as another side. The perimeter of the parallelogram is 24 inches. Is it possible to find all the side lengths of the parallelogram? If so, find the lengths. If not, explain why not.

_____

_____

Essential question: *What can you conclude about the diagonals of a parallelogram?*

A segment that connects any two nonconsecutive vertices of a polygon is a **diagonal**. A parallelogram has two diagonals. In the figure, $\overline{AC}$ and $\overline{BD}$ are diagonals of $\square ABCD$.

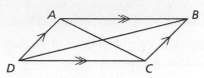

3 Investigate diagonals of parallelograms.

A Use geometry software to construct a parallelogram. (See Lesson 4-2 for detailed instructions.) Label the vertices of the parallelogram *A, B, C,* and *D.*

B Use the segment tool to construct the diagonals, $\overline{AC}$ and $\overline{BD}$.

C Plot a point at the intersection of the diagonals. Label this point *E.*

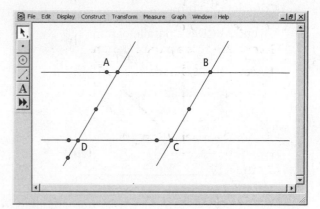

D Use the Measure menu to measure the length of $\overline{AE}$, $\overline{BE}$, $\overline{CE}$, and $\overline{DE}$. (You can do this by measuring the distance between the relevant endpoints.)

E Drag the points and lines in your construction to change the shape of the parallelogram. As you do so, look for relationships in the measurements.

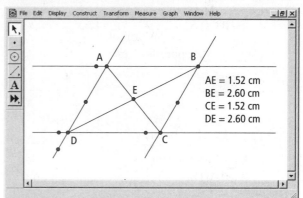

AE = 1.52 cm
BE = 2.60 cm
CE = 1.52 cm
DE = 2.60 cm

REFLECT

3a. Make a conjecture about the diagonals of a parallelogram.

_____

3b. A student claims that the perimeter of $\triangle AEB$ is always equal to the perimeter of $\triangle CED$. Without doing any further measurements in your construction, explain whether or not you agree with the student's statement.

_____

_____

You may have discovered the following theorem about parallelograms.

Theorem

If a quadrilateral is a parallelogram, then the diagonals bisect each other.

4 **Prove diagonals of a parallelogram bisect each other.**

Complete the proof.

Given: ABCD is a parallelogram.

Prove: $\overline{AE} \cong \overline{CE}$ and $\overline{BE} \cong \overline{DE}$.

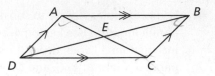

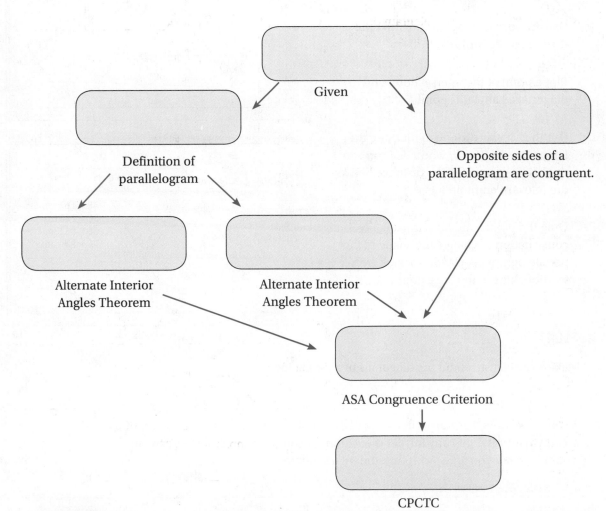

Given

Definition of
parallelogram

Opposite sides of a
parallelogram are congruent.

Alternate Interior
Angles Theorem

Alternate Interior
Angles Theorem

ASA Congruence Criterion

CPCTC

REFLECT

4a. Explain how you can prove the theorem using a different congruence criterion.

_____

_____

_____

The angles of a parallelogram also have an important property. It is stated in the following theorem, which you will prove as an exercise.

Theorem

If a quadrilateral is a parallelogram, then opposite angles are congruent.

PRACTICE

1. Prove the above theorem about opposite angles of a parallelogram.

Given: *ABCD* is a parallelogram.
Prove: $\angle A \cong \angle C$ and $\angle B \cong \angle D$

(*Hint:* You only need to prove that $\angle A \cong \angle C$. A similar argument can be used to prove that $\angle B \cong \angle D$. Also, you may or may not need to use all the rows of the table in your proof.)

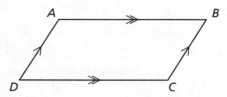

Statements	Reasons
1.	1.
2.	2.
3.	3.
4.	4.
5.	5.
6.	6.
7.	7.

2. Explain why consecutive angles of a parallelogram are supplementary.

_____

_____

_____

3. In the figure, *JKLM* is a parallelogram. Find the measure of each of the numbered angles.

_____

_____

4. A city planner is designing a park in the shape of a parallelogram. As shown in the figure, there will be two straight paths through which visitors may enter the park. The paths are bisectors of consecutive angles of the parallelogram, and the paths intersect at point *P*.

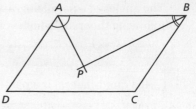

a. Work directly on the parallelograms below and use a compass and straightedge to construct the bisectors of ∠*A* and ∠*B*. Then use a protractor to measure ∠*APB* in each case.

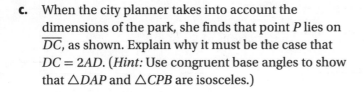

Make a conjecture about ∠*APB*.

_____

b. Write a paragraph proof to show that your conjecture is always true. (*Hint:* Suppose m∠*BAP* = *x*°, m∠*ABP* = *y*°, and m∠*APB* = *z*°. What do you know about *x* + *y* + *z*? What do you know about 2*x* + 2*y*?)

_____

_____

_____

_____

c. When the city planner takes into account the dimensions of the park, she finds that point *P* lies on $\overline{DC}$, as shown. Explain why it must be the case that *DC* = 2*AD*. (*Hint:* Use congruent base angles to show that △*DAP* and △*CPB* are isosceles.)

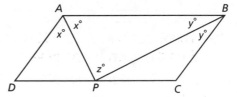

_____

_____

_____

_____

_____

© Houghton Mifflin Harcourt Publishing Company

360 − 114 = 246

114 + 1

Name_____ Class_____ Date_____

Additional Practice

A gurney is a wheeled cot or stretcher used in hospitals. Many gurneys are made so that the base will fold up for easy storage in an ambulance. When partially folded, the base forms a parallelogram. In ▱ *STUV*, *VU* = 91 centimeters, *UW* = 108.8 centimeters, and m∠*TSV* = 57°. Find each measure.

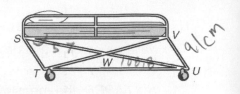

1. *SW*

108.8

2. *TS*

91

3. *US*

217.6

4. m∠*SVU*

123°

5. m∠*STU*

123°

6. m∠*TUV*

57°

JKLM is a parallelogram. Find each measure.

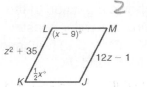

$2(x-9) + (\frac{1}{2}x) = 360$

$= 360$

7. m∠*L*

117°

8. m∠*K*

63°

9. *MJ*

71

VWXY is a parallelogram. Find each measure.

10. *VX*

42/2 = 21

11. *XZ*

10.5

12. *ZW*

15

13. *WY*

30

14. Three vertices of ▱ *ABCD* are *B*(−3, 3), *C*(2, 7), and *D*(5, 1). Find the coordinates of vertex *A*.

_____

Write a two-column proof.

15. **Given:** *DEFG* is a parallelogram.

   Prove: m∠*DHG* = m∠*EDH* + m∠*FGH*

Problem Solving

opposite side (same)
opposite angles (same)
diagnols bisted each other ✓

Use the diagram for Exercises 1 and 2.

The wall frames on the staircase wall form parallelograms *ABCD* and *EFGH*.

A = 3B

1. In □ *ABCD*, the measure of ∠*A* is three times the measure of ∠*B*. What are the measures of ∠*C* and ∠*D*?

   C = 3D
   _____

2. In □ *EFGH*, *FH* = 5x inches, *EG* = (2x + 4) inches, and *JG* = 8 inches. What is the length of *JH*?

   2x + 4 = 16
   = 2x = 12
   x = 6

   15 inches
   _____

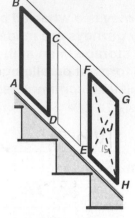

3. The diagram shows a section of the support structure of a roller coaster. In □ *JKLM*, *JK* = (3z − 0.9) feet, and *LM* = (z + 2.7) feet. Find *JK*.

   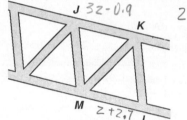
   J 3z − 0.9
   K
   M z + 2.7 L

   2z = 3.6
   z = 1.8

   3.9 ft
   _____

4. In □ *TUVW*, part of a ceramic tile pattern, m∠*TUV* = (8x + 1)° and m∠*UVW* = (12x + 19)°. Find m∠*TUV*.

   8x + 1 = 12x + 19   − 4x = 18

   x = − 4.5

   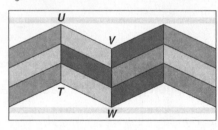

   37°
   _____

Choose the best answer.

5. What is the measure of ∠*Z* in parallelogram *WXYZ*?

   A 18°

   Ⓑ 74°

   C 106°

   D 108°

   n = 18   *36*

   18
   15 360 − 36 = 2 148
   90 + 16 = 106

   (5n + 16)°
   (6n − 2)°

   z | 2²   *74*

6. The perimeter of □ *CDEF* is 54 centimeters. Find the length of $\overline{FC}$ if $\overline{DE}$ is 5 centimeters longer than $\overline{EF}$.

   F 11 cm

   G 14 cm

   Ⓗ 16 cm

   J 44 cm

   4x + 10 = 54
   4x = 64
   x = 16

7. In □ *PQRS*, *QT* = 7x, *TS* = 2x + 2.5, *RT* = 2y, and *TP* = y + 3. Find the perimeter of △*PTS*.

   A 6   C 12

   B 9.5   Ⓓ 17.3

   y = 3   TS = 3.5
   x = 0.5   PT = 6

Conditions for Parallelograms
Going Deeper

Essential question: *What criteria can you use to prove that a quadrilateral is a parallelogram?*

The converses of the theorems you developed in the last two lessons are all true. These provide several criteria that can be used to prove that a quadrilateral is a parallelogram.

Video Tutor

> ### Opposite Sides Criterion for a Parallelogram
> If both pairs of opposite sides of a quadrilateral are congruent, then the quadrilateral is a parallelogram.

CC.9–12.G.SRT.5

1 PROOF **Opposite Sides Criterion for a Parallelogram**

Complete the proof.

Given: $\overline{AB} \cong \overline{DC}$ and $\overline{AD} \cong \overline{BC}$

Prove: *ABCD* is a parallelogram.

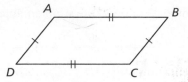

Statements	Reasons
1. Draw $\overline{DB}$.	**1.** Through any two points there exists exactly one line.
2. $\overline{DB} \cong \overline{DB}$	**2.**
3. $\overline{AB} \cong \overline{DC}$; $\overline{AD} \cong \overline{BC}$	**3.**
4.	**4.** SSS Congruence Criterion
5. $\angle ABD \cong \angle CDB$; $\angle ADB \cong \angle CBD$	**5.**
6. $\overline{AB} \parallel \overline{DC}$; $\overline{AD} \parallel \overline{BC}$	**6.**
7. *ABCD* is a parallelogram.	**7.**

> **REFLECT**

1a. A quadrilateral has two sides that are 3 cm long and two sides that are 5 cm long. A student states that the quadrilateral must be a parallelogram. Do you agree? Why or why not?

_____

_____

CC.9–12.G.CO.11

2 PROOF   Opposite Angles Criterion for a Parallelogram

Complete the paragraph proof.

Given: $\angle A \cong \angle C$ and $\angle B \cong \angle D$.

Prove: $ABCD$ is a parallelogram.

$m\angle A + m\angle B + m\angle C + m\angle D = 360°$ by _____.

From the given information, $m\angle A = m\angle C$ and $m\angle B = m\angle D$. By substitution,

$m\angle A + m\angle D + m\angle A + m\angle D = 360°$ or $2m\angle A + 2m\angle D = 360°$. Dividing both

sides by 2 gives _____.

Therefore, $\angle A$ and $\angle D$ are supplementary and so $\overline{AB} \parallel \overline{DC}$ by

_____. A similar

argument shows that $\overline{AD} \parallel \overline{BC}$, so $ABCD$ is a parallelogram by definition.

REFLECT

2a. What property or theorem justifies dividing both sides of the equation by 2 in the above proof?

_____

_____

PRACTICE

1. Write a paragraph proof for the following.

> ## Bisecting Diagonals Criterion for a Parallelogram
>
> If the diagonals of a quadrilateral bisect each other, then the quadrilateral is a parallelogram.
>
>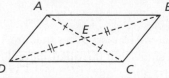

_____

_____

_____

_____

Name _____ Class _____ Date _____

6-3

Additional Practice

For Exercises 1 and 2, determine whether the figure is a parallelogram for the given values of the variables. Explain your answers.

1. $x = 9$ and $y = 11$

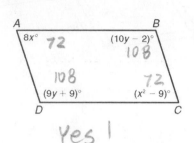

Yes!

2. $a = 4.3$ and $b = 13$

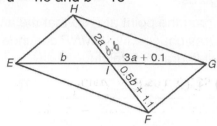

No because HI and HF are not the same distance.

Determine whether each quadrilateral must be a parallelogram. Justify your answers.

3.
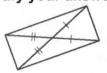

No

4.
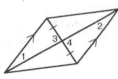

Yes

5.

No

Use the given method to determine whether the quadrilateral with the given vertices is a parallelogram.

6. Find the slopes of all four sides: $J(-4, -1)$, $K(-7, -4)$, $L(2, -10)$, $M(5, -7)$

JK = 1   JL = -3/2   JM = -2/3   Yes

KL = -2/3   KM = -1/4   LM = #1

Distance formula

7. Find the lengths of all four sides: $P(2, 2)$, $Q(1, -3)$, $R(-4, 2)$, $S(-3, 7)$

Not Parallelogram

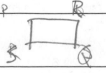

8. Find the slopes and lengths of one pair of opposite sides:

$T\left(\frac{3}{2}, -2\right), U\left(\frac{3}{2}, 4\right), V\left(-\frac{1}{2}, 0\right), W\left(-\frac{1}{2}, -6\right)$

TU L - 65   VW = 6   length - Parallelogram

5 - 0   -1   0

Chapter 6   255   Lesson 3

Problem Solving

Use the diagram for Exercises 1 and 2.

A *pantograph* is a drawing instrument used to magnify figures.

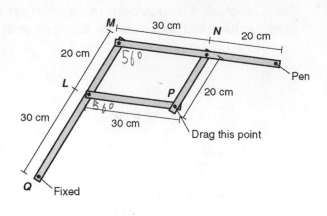

1. If you drag the point at *P* so that the angle measures change, will *LMNP* continue to be a parallelogram? Explain.

   No because angles M and P will no longer be congruent.

2. If you drag the point at *P* so that m∠*LMN* = 56°, what will be the measure of ∠*QLP*?

   56°

3. In the state flag of Maryland, m∠*G* = 60° and m∠*H* = 120°. Name one more condition that would allow you to conclude that *EFGH* is a parallelogram.

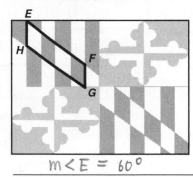

   m∠E = 60°

4. The graphs of $y = 2x$, $y = 2x - 5$, and $y = -x$ in the coordinate plane contain three sides of a quadrilateral. Give an equation of a line whose graph contains a segment that can complete the quadrilateral to form a parallelogram. Explain.

   $y = -x + 1$

Choose the best answer.

5. For which value of *n* is *QRST* a parallelogram?

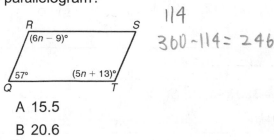

   114
   360 − 114 = 246

   A 15.5

   B 20.6

   Ⓒ 22

   D 25

6. Under what conditions must *ABCD* be a parallelogram?

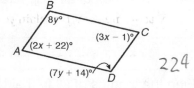

   224

   136

   F *x* = 23

   G *y* = 14

   Ⓗ *x* = 23 and *y* = 14

   J *x* = 14 and *y* = 23

Properties of Special Parallelograms
Focus on Reasoning

Essential question: *What are the properties of rectangles and rhombuses?*

A **rectangle** is a quadrilateral with four right angles. The figure shows rectangle *ABCD*.

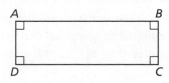

COMMON CORE

CC.9-12.G.CO.11,
CC.9-12.G.SRT.5

1 **Investigate properties of rectangles.**

A Use a tile or pattern block and the following method to draw three different rectangles on a separate sheet of paper.

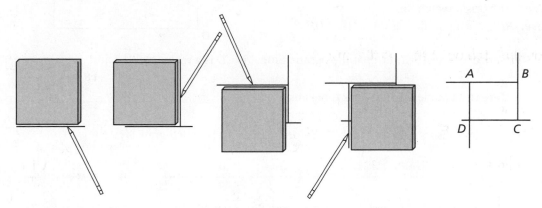

B Use a ruler to measure the sides and the diagonals of each rectangle. Keep track of the measurements and compare your results to those of other students.

REFLECT

1a. Why does the above method produce a rectangle? What must you assume about the tile?

_____

_____

_____

1b. Do you think every rectangle is a parallelogram? Make a conjecture based upon your measurements and explain your thinking.

_____

_____

1c. Make a conjecture about the diagonals of a rectangle.

_____

You may have discovered the following theorem about rectangles.

Rectangle Theorem

A rectangle is a parallelogram with congruent diagonals.

In order to prove the above theorem, it is convenient to use a theorem that states that all right angles are congruent. The proof of this theorem is straightforward: If $\angle X$ and $\angle Y$ are right angles, then $m\angle X = 90°$ and $m\angle Y = 90°$ so $m\angle X = m\angle Y$ and $\angle X \cong \angle Y$.

2 Prove the Rectangle Theorem.

Complete the proof.

Given: *ABCD* is a rectangle.
Prove: *ABCD* is a parallelogram; $\overline{AC} \cong \overline{BD}$.

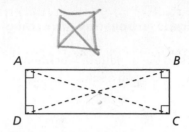

A First prove that *ABCD* is a parallelogram. Since *ABCD* is a rectangle, $\angle A$ and

$\angle C$ are right angles. So, $\angle A \cong \angle C$ because _____.

By similar reasoning, $\angle B \cong \angle D$. Therefore, *ABCD* is a parallelogram by

_____.

B Now prove that the diagonals are congruent. Since *ABCD* is a parallelogram,

$\overline{AD} \cong \overline{BC}$ because _____.

Also, $\overline{DC} \cong \overline{DC}$ by the reflexive property of congruence. By the definition

of a rectangle, $\angle D$ and $\angle C$ are right angles, and so $\angle D \cong \angle C$ because

all right angles are congruent.

Therefore, $\triangle ADC \cong \triangle BCD$ by _____

and $\overline{AC} \cong \overline{BD}$ by _____.

REFLECT

2a. Error Analysis A student says you can also prove the diagonals are congruent by using the SSS Congruence Criterion to show that $\triangle ADC \cong \triangle BCD$. Do you agree? Explain.

_____

_____

A **rhombus** is a quadrilateral with four congruent sides. The figure shows rhombus *JKLM*.

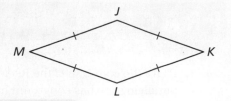

The following is a summary of some properties of rhombuses. You will prove these properties below and in the exercises.

> **Properties of Rhombuses**
>
> If a quadrilateral is a rhombus, then
> • the quadrilateral is a parallelogram.
> • the diagonals are perpendicular.
> • each diagonal bisects a pair of opposite angles.

The proof of the first property is straightforward. If a quadrilateral is a rhombus, then opposite sides are congruent. Therefore, the quadrilateral is also a parallelogram by the Opposite Sides Criterion for a Parallelogram.

3 **Prove diagonals of a rhombus are perpendicular.**

Complete the proof.

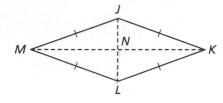

Given: *JKLM* is a rhombus.
Prove: $\overline{JL} \perp \overline{MK}$

Since *JKLM* is a rhombus, $\overline{JM} \cong \overline{JK}$. Because *JKLM* is also a parallelogram,

$\overline{MN} \cong \overline{KN}$ because _____.

By the Reflexive Property of Congruence, $\overline{JN} \cong \overline{JN}$, so _____

by the SSS Congruence Criterion. So, $\angle JNM \cong \angle JNK$ by _____.

By the Linear Pair Theorem, $\angle JNM$ and $\angle JNK$ are _____.

This means m$\angle JNM$ + m$\angle JNK$ = 180°.

Since the angles are congruent, m$\angle JNM$ = _____

so m$\angle JNK$ + m$\angle JNK$ = 180° or 2m$\angle JNK$ = 180°. Therefore, m$\angle JNK$ = 90°

and $\overline{JL} \perp \overline{MK}$.

REFLECT

3a. What can you say about the image of *J* after a reflection across $\overline{MK}$? Why?

_____

1. Prove the converse of the Rectangle Theorem. That is, if a parallelogram has congruent diagonals, then the parallelogram is a rectangle.

   Given: $ABCD$ is a parallelogram; $\overline{AC} \cong \overline{BD}$.
   Prove: $ABCD$ is a rectangle.

   _____

   _____

   _____

   _____

   _____

   _____

2. Prove that if a quadrilateral is a rhombus, then each diagonal bisects a pair of opposite angles.

   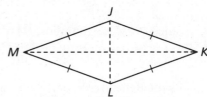

   Given: $JKLM$ is a rhombus.
   Prove: $\overline{MK}$ bisects $\angle JML$ and $\angle JKL$;
           $\overline{JL}$ bisects $\angle MJK$ and $\angle MLK$.

   _____

   _____

   _____

   _____

3. A *square* is a quadrilateral with four right angles and four congruent sides. In the space at right, draw a Venn diagram to show how squares, rectangles, rhombuses, and parallelograms are related to each other.

Additional Practice

Tell whether each figure must be a rectangle, rhombus, or square based on the information given. Use the most specific name possible.

1.

rectangle

2.

square

3.

rhombus

A modern artist's sculpture has rectangular faces. The face shown here is 9 feet long and 4 feet wide. Find each measure in simplest radical form. (*Hint:* Use the Pythagorean Theorem.)

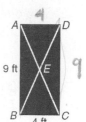

4. $DC =$ _9_

5. $AD =$ _4_

6. $DB =$ _$\sqrt{97}$_

7. $AE =$ _$\sqrt{97}/2$_

make right triangle

***VWXY* is a rhombus. Find each measure.**

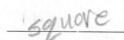
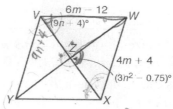

8. $XY =$ _36_

9. $m\angle YVW =$ _~~109~~ 107°_

10. $m\angle VYX =$ _~~71~~ 73°_

11. $m\angle XYZ =$ _~~42.31~~ 53.5°_

$2m = 16$
$m = 8$

$3n^2 - 0.75 = 90$

36

$3n^2 = 90.75$

12. The vertices of <u>square</u> *JKLM* are $J(-2, 4)$, $K(-3, -1)$, $L(2, -2)$, and $M(3, 3)$. Find each of the following to show that the diagonals of square *JKLM* are congruent perpendicular bisectors of each other.

$JL =$ _7.2_ $6/-4$

$KM =$ _7.2_

slope of $\overline{JL} =$ _-3/2_

slope of $\overline{KM} =$ _-3/2_

Find middle   midpoint of $\overline{JL} = ($ _0_ , _1_ $)$

midpoint of $\overline{KM} = ($ _0_ , _1_ $)$

Write a paragraph proof.

13. **Given:** *ABCD* is a rectangle.
    Prove: $\angle EDC \cong \angle ECD$

$(-3, -1)$ $(3, 3)$

$36 + 16 = 52$

Problem Solving

Use the diagram for Exercises 1 and 2.

The soccer goalposts determine rectangle *ABCD*.

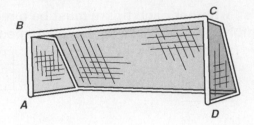

1. The distance between goalposts, *BC*, is three times the distance from the top of the goalpost to the ground. If the perimeter of *ABCD* is $21\frac{1}{3}$ yards, what is the length of $\overline{BC}$?

   _____

2. The distance from *B* to *D* is approximately $(x + 10)$ feet, and the distance from *A* to *C* is approximately $(2x - 5.3)$ feet. What is the approximate distance from *A* to *C*?

   _____

3. *MNPQ* is a rhombus. The measure of ∠*MRQ* is $(13t - 1)°$, and the measure of ∠*PQR* is $(7t + 4)°$. What is the measure of ∠*PQM*?

   _____

4. The *scissor lift* forms rhombus *PQRS* with $PQ = (7b - 5)$ meters and $QR = (2b - 0.5)$ meters. If *S* is the midpoint of $\overline{RT}$, what is the length of $\overline{RT}$?

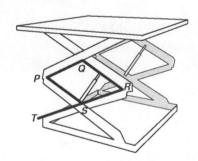

5. The diagram shows the lid of a rectangular case that holds 80 CDs. What are the dimensions of the case?

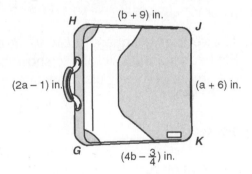

   _____

Choose the best answer.

6. What is the measure of ∠1 in the rectangle?

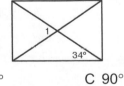

   A 34° C 90°

   B 68° D 146°

7. A square graphed on the coordinate plane has a diagonal with endpoints *E*(2, 3) and *F*(0, −3). What are the coordinates of the endpoints of the other diagonal?

   F (4, −1) and (−2, 1)

   G (4, 0) and (−2, 1)

   H (4, −1) and (−3, 1)

   J (3, −1) and (−2, 1)

6-5

Conditions for Special Parallelograms
Connection: Using Coordinate Methods

Essential question: *How can you use slope in coordinate proofs?*

You have already used the distance formula and the midpoint formula in coordinate proofs. As you will see, slope is useful in coordinate proofs whenever you need to show that lines are parallel or perpendicular.

Video Tutor

CC.9–12.G.GPE.4

1 EXAMPLE Proving a Quadrilateral Is a Parallelogram

Prove or disprove that the quadrilateral determined by the points $A(4, 4)$, $B(3, 1)$, $C(-2, -1)$, and $D(-1, 2)$ is a parallelogram.

A Plot the points on the coordinate plane at right.

Then draw quadrilateral $ABCD$.

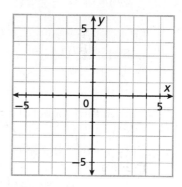

B To determine whether $ABCD$ is a parallelogram, find the slope of each side of the quadrilateral.

Slope of $\overline{AB} = \dfrac{y_2 - y_1}{x_2 - x_1} = \dfrac{1 - 4}{3 - 4} = \dfrac{-3}{-1} = 3$

Slope of $\overline{BC} = \dfrac{y_2 - y_1}{x_2 - x_1} = \dfrac{\boxed{} - \boxed{}}{\boxed{} - \boxed{}} = \dfrac{\boxed{}}{\boxed{}} = \boxed{}$

Slope of $\overline{CD} = \dfrac{y_2 - y_1}{x_2 - x_1} = \dfrac{\boxed{} - \boxed{}}{\boxed{} - \boxed{}} = \dfrac{\boxed{}}{\boxed{}} = \boxed{}$

Slope of $\overline{DA} = \dfrac{y_2 - y_1}{x_2 - x_1} = \dfrac{\boxed{} - \boxed{}}{\boxed{} - \boxed{}} = \dfrac{\boxed{}}{\boxed{}} = \boxed{}$

C Compare slopes. The slopes of opposite sides are _____.

This means opposite sides are _____.

So,_____.

REFLECT

1a. Is there a way to write a proof that does not use slope? Explain.

_____

_____

2 EXAMPLE Proving a Quadrilateral Is a Rectangle

Prove or disprove that the quadrilateral determined by the points $Q(2, -3)$, $R(-4, 0)$, $S(-2, 4)$, and $T(4, 1)$ is a rectangle.

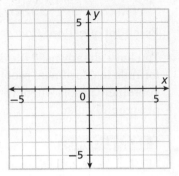

A Plot the points on the coordinate plane at right.

Then draw quadrilateral $QRST$.

B To determine whether $QRST$ is a rectangle, find the slope of each side of the quadrilateral.

Slope of $\overline{QR} = \dfrac{y_2 - y_1}{x_2 - x_1} = \dfrac{0 - (-3)}{-4 - 2} = \dfrac{3}{-6} = -\dfrac{1}{2}$

Slope of $\overline{RS} = \dfrac{y_2 - y_1}{x_2 - x_1} = \dfrac{\boxed{} - \boxed{}}{\boxed{} - \boxed{}} = \dfrac{\boxed{}}{\boxed{}} = \boxed{}$

Slope of $\overline{ST} = \dfrac{y_2 - y_1}{x_2 - x_1} = \dfrac{\boxed{} - \boxed{}}{\boxed{} - \boxed{}} = \dfrac{\boxed{}}{\boxed{}} = \boxed{}$

Slope of $\overline{TQ} = \dfrac{y_2 - y_1}{x_2 - x_1} = \dfrac{\boxed{} - \boxed{}}{\boxed{} - \boxed{}} = \dfrac{\boxed{}}{\boxed{}} = \boxed{}$

C Find the product of the slopes of adjacent sides.

(slope of $\overline{QR}$)(slope of $\overline{RS}$) = _____ · _____ = _____

(slope of $\overline{RS}$)(slope of $\overline{ST}$) = _____ · _____ = _____

(slope of $\overline{ST}$)(slope of $\overline{TQ}$) = _____ · _____ = _____

(slope of $\overline{TQ}$)(slope of $\overline{QR}$) = _____ · _____ = _____

You can conclude that adjacent sides are _____.

So, _____.

REFLECT

2a. What would you expect to find if you used the distance formula to calculate SQ and RT? Explain.

_____

_____

2b. Explain how to prove that $QRST$ is not a square.

_____

_____

1. Prove or disprove that the quadrilateral determined by the points $J(-3, 1)$, $K(3, 3)$, $L(2, -1)$, and $M(-4, -3)$ is a parallelogram.

_____

_____

_____

2. Prove or disprove that the quadrilateral determined by the points $A(-2, 3)$, $B(5, 3)$, $C(3, -1)$, and $D(-3, -1)$ is a parallelogram.

_____

_____

_____

3. Prove or disprove that the quadrilateral determined by the points $Q(-3, 4)$, $R(5, 2)$, $S(4, -1)$, and $T(-4, 1)$ is a rectangle.

_____

_____

_____

4. Prove or disprove that the quadrilateral determined by the points $W(1, 5)$, $X(4, 4)$, $Y(2, -2)$, and $Z(-1, -1)$ is a rectangle.

_____

_____

_____

5. Prove or disprove that the quadrilateral determined by the points $D(-2, 3)$, $E(3, 4)$, $F(0, -2)$, and $G(-4, -1)$ has exactly two parallel sides.

_____

_____

_____

6. Consider points $L(3, -4)$, $M(1, -2)$, and $N(5, 2)$.

   a. Find the coordinates of point P so that the quadrilateral determined by points L, M, N, and P is a parallelogram. Is there more than one possibility? Explain.

   _____

   _____

   b. Are any of the parallelograms a rectangle? Why?

   _____

   _____

7. You are using a coordinate plane to create a quadrilateral. You start by drawing $\overline{MN}$, as shown.

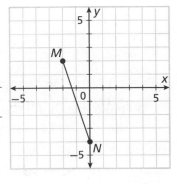

   a. You decide to translate $\overline{MN}$ by the translation $(x, y) \rightarrow (x + 3, y + 2)$. What type of quadrilateral is $MM'N'N$? Why?

   _____

   _____

   b. Do you get the same type of quadrilateral for any translation of $\overline{MN}$ that results in a quadrilateral $MM'N'N$? Explain. (*Hint:* Find the coordinates of M' and N' under a general translation, $(x, y) \rightarrow (x + a, y + b)$. Then consider the slopes of the sides of quadrilateral $MM'N'N$.)

   _____

   _____

   _____

   _____

   _____

   c. You decide you want $MM'N'N$ to be a rectangle. What translations can you use? (*Hint:* What must be true about a and b?)

   _____

8. Rhombus $OPQR$ has vertices $O(0, 0)$, $P(a, b)$, $Q(a + b, a + b)$, and $R(b, a)$. Prove the diagonals of the rhombus are perpendicular.

   _____

   _____

   _____

Additional Practice

1. On the National Mall in Washington, D.C., a reflecting pool lies between the Lincoln Memorial and the World War II Memorial. The pool has two 2300-foot-long sides and two 150-foot-long sides. Tell what additional information you need to know in order to determine whether the reflecting pool is a rectangle. (*Hint:* Remember that you have to show it is a parallelogram first.)

First, you have to know if the opposite angles are congruent
(parallelogram) and then you have to know if all the angles
are right angles. (rectangle)

Use the figure for Exercises 2–5. Determine whether each conclusion is valid. If not, tell what additional information is needed to make it valid.

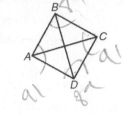

2. **Given:** $\overline{AC}$ and $\overline{BD}$ bisect each other. $\overline{AC} \cong \overline{BD}$

   Conclusion: *ABCD* is a square.

   if angles are right angles

3. **Given:** $\overline{AC} \perp \overline{BD}, \overline{AB} \cong \overline{BC}$

   Conclusion: *ABCD* is a rhombus.

   Valid

4. **Given:** $\overline{AB} \cong \overline{DC}, \overline{AD} \cong \overline{BC}$, $m\angle ADB = m\angle ABD = 45°$

   Conclusion: *ABCD* is a square.

   Valid

5. **Given:** $\overline{AB} \parallel \overline{DC}, \overline{AD} \cong \overline{BC}, \overline{AC} \cong \overline{BD}$

   Conclusion: *ABCD* is a rectangle.

   right angles

Find the lengths and slopes of the diagonals to determine whether a parallelogram with the given vertices is a rectangle, rhombus, or square. Give all names that apply.

6. *E*(–2, –4), *F*(0, –1), *G*(–3, 1), *H*(–5, –2)   _ALL_

   distance *EG* = _5.1_   *FH* = _5.1_

   slope of $\overline{EG}$ = _–5_   slope of $\overline{FH}$ = _–1/5_

7. *P*(–1, 3), *Q*(–2, 5), *R*(0, 4), *S*(1, 2)   _Rhombus_

   PR = _$\sqrt{2}$_   *QS* = _$\sqrt{18}$_

   slope of $\overline{PR}$ = _1_   slope of $\overline{QS}$ = _–1_

Problem Solving

(handwritten at top: quad → paralel → rectangle)

1. An amusement park has a rectangular observation deck with walkways above the bungee jumping and sky jumping. The distance from the center of the deck to points *E*, *F*, *G*, and *H* is 15 meters. Explain why *EFGH* must be a rectangle.

   (handwritten answer: Because FH and GE are the same length (30 m))

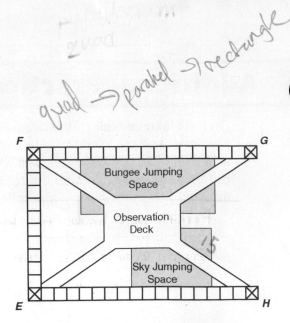

2. In the mosaic, $\overline{AB} \parallel \overline{CD}$ and $\overline{BC} \parallel \overline{DA}$. If *AB* = 4 inches and *BC* = 4 inches, can you conclude that *ABCD* is a square? Explain.

   (handwritten: para - rhombus)

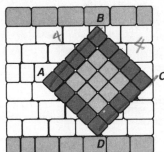

   (handwritten answer: No because you don't know if it's right angles)

3. If $\overline{TV} \cong \overline{US}$, explain why the basketball backboard must be a rectangle.

   (handwritten: para -)

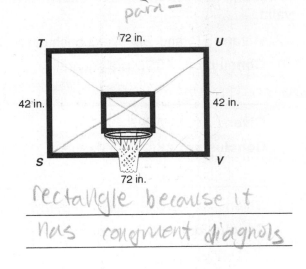

   (handwritten answer: rectangle because it has congruent diagnols)

Choose the best answer.

4. The vertices of a parallelogram are *N*(0, −4), *P*(6, −1), *Q*(4, 3), and *R*(−2, 0). Classify the parallelogram as specifically as possible.

   A rectangle only
   B square
   C rhombus only
   D quadrilateral

   (handwritten: 4w+5=90, 4w=85)

5. Choose the best description for the quadrilateral.

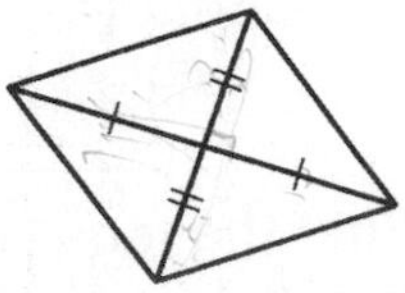

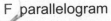

   F parallelogram
   G parallelogram and rectangle
   H parallelogram and rhombus
   J parallelogram and square

6. In parallelogram *KLMN*, m∠*L* = (4*w* + 5)°. Choose the value of *w* that makes *KLMN* a rectangle.

   A 90
   B 85
   C 43.75
   D 21.25

7. The coordinates of three vertices of quadrilateral *ABCD* are *A*(3, −1), *B*(10, 0), and *C*(5, 5). For which coordinates of *D* will the quadrilateral be a rhombus?

   F (−1, 4)   H (−1, 3)
   G (−2, 4)   J (−2, 3)

Chapter 6   268   Lesson 5

© Houghton Mifflin Harcourt Publishing Company

Properties of Kites and Trapezoids
Going Deeper

Essential Question: *How can auxiliary segments be used in proofs?*

Proof of a theorem may require the use of an auxiliary segment or line added to a geometric diagram to help you.

> ### Theorem
>
> If a trapezoid has one pair of congruent base angles, then the trapezoid is isosceles.
>
> If $\angle A \cong \angle D$, then $\overline{AB} \cong \overline{DC}$.
>
>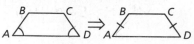

CC.9–12.G.CO.9

1 PROOF   **Reasoning from Congruent Angles to Congruent Sides**

Complete the proof.

Given: *ABCD* is a trapezoid with $\overline{BC} \parallel \overline{AD}$, $\angle A \cong \angle D$, as shown in the diagram.

Prove: *ABCD* is an isosceles trapezoid.

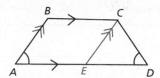

Statements	Reasons
1. $\overline{BC} \parallel \overline{AD}$	1.
2. Draw $\overline{CE} \parallel \overline{AB}$ intersecting $\overline{AD}$ at *E*.	2. Parallel Postulate
3. *ABCE* is a parallelogram.	3. Definition of parallelogram
4. $\overline{AB} \cong \overline{CE}$	4. If a quadrilateral is a parallelogram, then _____.
5. $\angle A \cong \angle CED$	5. Corresponding Angles Postulate
6.	6. Given
7. $\angle D \cong \angle CED$	7. Substitution *(Steps 5, 6)*
8.	8. Converse of Isosceles Triangle Theorem
9. $\overline{AB} \cong \overline{CD}$	9. _____ *(Steps 4, 8)*
10. *ABCD* is an isosceles trapezoid.	10.

REFLECT

1a. What are the parallel lines and transversal involved in Step 5 of the proof?

_____

1b. Can you prove the theorem on the previous page if you are given $\angle B \cong \angle C$ instead of $\angle A \cong \angle D$? Explain a possible approach.

_____

_____

_____

The converse of the theorem on the preceding page is also true.

CC.9–12.G.CO.9

2 PROOF   **Reasoning from Congruent Sides to Congruent Angles**

Complete the proof.

Given: *ABCD* is an isosceles trapezoid with $\overline{BC} \parallel \overline{AD}$, $\overline{AB} \cong \overline{CD}$, as shown in the diagram.

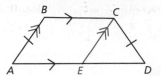

Prove: $\angle A \cong \angle D$

Statements	Reasons
1. $\overline{BC} \parallel \overline{AD}$	1. Given
2. Draw $\overline{CE} \parallel \overline{AB}$ intersecting $\overline{AD}$ at *E*.	2.
3. $\angle A \cong \angle CED$	3. Corresponding Angles Postulate
4. *ABCE* is a parallelogram.	4. Definition of parallelogram
5. $\overline{AB} \cong \overline{CE}$	5. If a quadrilateral is a parallelogram, then its opposite sides are congruent.
6.	6.
7. $\overline{CD} \cong \overline{CE}$	7. Substitution *(Steps 5, 6)*
8. $\angle CED \cong \angle D$	8.
9. $\angle A \cong \angle D$	9. Transitive Prop. of Congruence *(Steps 3, 8)*

REFLECT

2a. Given that $\angle A \cong \angle D$ as proved above, how can you prove that $\angle B \cong \angle C$ in the isosceles trapezoid?

_____

_____

_____

Additional Practice

The midsegment of a trapezoid is the segment whose endpoints are the midpoints of the legs. According to the Trapezoid Midsegment Theorem, (1) the midsegment of a trapezoid is parallel to each base, and (2) its length is one half the sum of the lengths of the bases.

1. Complete this proof of Part 1 of the theorem.

   Given: *ABCD* is a trapezoid with $\overline{BC} \parallel \overline{AD}$,

   M is the midpoint of $\overline{AB}$, *N* is the midpoint of $\overline{CD}$.

   Prove: $\overline{MN} \parallel \overline{AD}$, $\overline{MN} \parallel \overline{BC}$

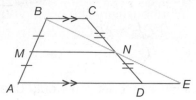

1. $\overline{BC} \parallel \overline{AD}$	1. Given
2. Draw $\overleftrightarrow{BN}$ intersecting $\overleftrightarrow{AD}$ in point *E*.	2. Through any two points there is exactly one line; if two lines intersect, they intersect in exactly one point.
3. ∠*BCD* ≅ ∠*CDE*	3.
4. ∠*BNC* ≅ ∠*END*	4. Vertical Angles
5. *N* is the midpoint of $\overline{CD}$.	5. Given
6. $\overline{NC} \cong \overline{ND}$	6. Definition of midpoint
7. △ *BNC* ≅ △ *END*	7.
8. $\overline{BN} \cong \overline{NE}$	8. CPCTC
9.	9. Definition of midpoint
10. $\overline{MN} \parallel \overline{AD}$	10. Triangle Midsegment Theorem
11. ∠*ABC* and ∠*BAD* are supplementary; ∠*NMA* and ∠*BAD* are supplementary.	11. Same-side interior angles
12. ∠*ABC* ≅ ∠*NMA*	12.
13. $\overline{MN} \parallel \overline{BC}$	13. Converse of Corresponding Angles

2. Describe how you could use the Triangle Midsegment Theorem to

   prove Part 2 of the theorem, that is, $MN = \frac{1}{2}(AD + BC)$?

   _____

   _____

Problem Solving

A kite is a quadrilateral with exactly two pairs of congruent consecutive sides. Anil is making a kite for a kite-flying contest. For Exercises 1–3, use the kite pattern that he drew.

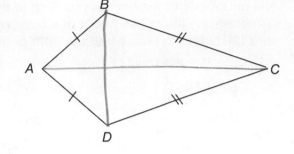

1. What auxiliary line could you use to prove that
   △ ABC ≅ △ ADC?

   $\overline{AC}$

2. Describe how you would use the auxiliary line in your answer to Exercise 1 to complete the proof that △ ABC ≅ △ ADC.

   SSS

3. The diagonals of a kite are perpendicular. Describe how you could prove that in kite ABCD, $\overline{AC}$ ⊥ $\overline{BD}$.

   Bees can't fly

Choose the best answer.

4. Trapezoid PQRS has base angles that measure $(9r + 21)°$ and $(15r - 21)°$. Find the value of r so that PQRS is isosceles. H

   A 3 $-6r = -42$
   B 5 $r = 7$
   C 7
   D 14

5. In kite KLMN, find the measure of ∠M.

   F 100.5°
   G 101°
   H 122°
   J 130°

   $79 + 101$

6. In the design, eight isosceles trapezoids surround a regular octagon. What is the measure of ∠B in trapezoid ABCD?

   A 35°
   B 45°
   C 55°
   D 65°

   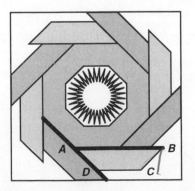

Performance Tasks

★ **1.** An architect is drawing a floor plan for a garage on a coordinate plane. The architect has located three corners of the garage at $A(0, 0)$, $B(4, 6)$, and $C(7, 4)$. If the garage must be in the shape of a rectangle, what are the coordinates of point D? Justify your answer.

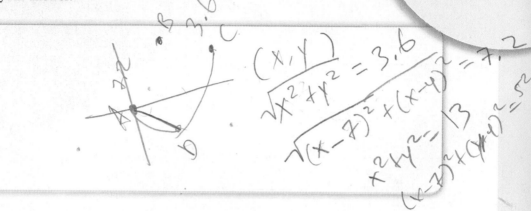

★ **2.** An ironing board manufacturer designs a folding ironing board with two legs. Each leg runs diagonally under the board from one end of the board to the floor, crossing over the other leg in the middle. Both legs are the same length. The designer connects the endpoints of the legs to form a quadrilateral. Which specific quadrilaterals could be formed? Explain your answer.

★★ **3.** The endpoints of one diagonal of quadrilateral $WXYZ$ are $W(7, 12)$ and $Y(12, 2)$. The endpoints of the other diagonal are $X(12, 12)$ and $Z(4, 8)$.

  a. Are the diagonals congruent? How do you know?

  b. Are the diagonals perpendicular? Explain.

  c. Do the diagonals bisect each other? Explain.

  d. What is the most descriptive name for quadrilateral $WXYZ$?

continued

 4. The four vertices of a quadrilateral are given as $A(11, 7)$, $B(13, 4)$, $C(0, -7)$ and $D(x, y)$. Choose values for x and y such that $ABCD$ is a trapezoid, and then prove that your figure is a trapezoid.

Name _____ **Class** _____ **Date** _____

MULTIPLE CHOICE

1. Rosa is using the figure below to prove that the diagonals of a parallelogram bisect each other. She starts by stating that $\overline{LM} \cong \overline{PN}$ since opposite sides of a parallelogram are congruent. What should she show next in order to prove that $\triangle LQM \cong \triangle NQP$?

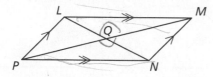

A. $\overline{LP} \cong \overline{MN}$

B. $\overline{LN} \cong \overline{MP}$

C. $\angle QLP \cong \angle QNM$ and $\angle QPL \cong \angle QMN$

D. $\angle MLQ \cong \angle PNQ$ and $\angle LMQ \cong \angle NPQ$

2. Ming is proving that opposite sides of a parallelogram are congruent. He begins as shown. Which reason should he use for Step 3?

Given: PQRS is a parallelogram.
Prove: $\overline{PQ} \cong \overline{RS}$; $\overline{PS} \cong \overline{QR}$

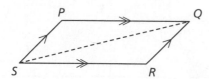

Statements	Reasons
1. PQRS is a parallelogram	1. Given
2. Draw $\overline{SQ}$.	2. Through 2 pts. there is exactly one line.
3. $\overline{PQ} \parallel \overline{RS}$; $\overline{PS} \parallel \overline{QR}$	3. ?

F. Definition of parallelogram

G. Alternate Interior Angles Theorem

H. Reflexive Property of Congruence

J. CPCTC

3. DEFG is a rhombus. You want to prove the property that a diagonal of a rhombus bisects a pair of opposite angles. To prove that $\overrightarrow{DF}$ bisects $\angle GDE$, you first show that $\triangle GDF \cong \triangle EDF$ using the definition of rhombus, the Reflexive Property of Congruence, and the SSS Congruence Criterion. What other reasons are needed to complete the proof?

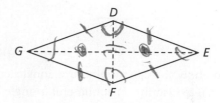

A. Isosceles Triangle Theorem; SAS Congruence Criterion

B. Definition of perpendicular; Triangle Sum Theorem

C. If a quadrilateral is a parallelogram, then opposite angles are congruent; definition of angle bisector

D. Congruent Parts of Congruent Triangles are Congruent; definition of angle bisector

4. Which property of rectangles is not true for all parallelograms?

F. opposite sides are parallel

G. opposite sides are congruent

H. diagonals are congruent

J. diagonals bisect each other

CONSTRUCTED RESPONSE

5. Use a compass and straightedge to construct a regular hexagon that is inscribed in circle O.

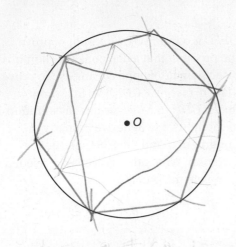

6. Explain how you can modify your construction in Item 5 to inscribe an equilateral triangle in circle O.

_____

_____

_____

7. Prove or disprove that the quadrilateral determined by the points $A(-3, 1)$, $B(3, 3)$, $C(4, -1)$, and $D(-2, -3)$ is a rectangle.

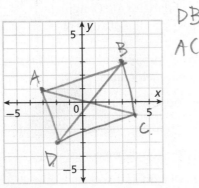

$DB = \frac{6}{5}$

$AC =$

disprove, DB is not ~~PDC~~ congrument to AC

_____

_____

_____

8. Prove the following. You may not need all the rows of the table in your proof.

Given: *ABCD* is a rectangle. $\overline{AE} \cong \overline{FB}$
Prove: $\triangle DAF \cong \triangle CBE$

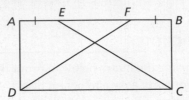

Statements	Reasons
1.	1.
2.	2.
3.	3.
4.	4.
5.	5.
6.	6.
7.	7.
8.	8.

Similarity

Chapter Focus

Informally speaking, two figures are similar if they have the same shape, but not necessarily the same size. In this unit, you will put this idea into mathematical terms. To do so, you will first study a new transformation, the dilation. As you did with congruence, you will develop criteria that can be used to show that two triangles are similar. Then you will apply similarity to a wide range of real-world problems and mathematical theorems.

Chapter at a Glance

COMMON
CORE

Lesson		Standards for Mathematical Content
7-1	Ratios in Similar Polygons	Prep for CC.9-12.G.SRT.1b, Prep for CC.9-12.G.SRT.2
7-2	Similarity and Transformations	CC.9-12.G.CO.2, CC.9-12.G.SRT.1, CC.9-12.G.SRT.2, CC.9-12.G.C.1
7-3	Triangle Similarity AA, SSS, SAS	CC.9-12.G.SRT.2, CC.9-12.G.SRT.3
7-4	Applying Properties of Similar Triangles	CC.9-12.G.SRT.4, CC.9-12.G.SRT.5
7-5	Using Proportional Relationships	CC.9-12.G.SRT.5, CC.9-12.G.MG.3
7-6	Dilations and Similarity in the Coordinate Plane	CC.9-12.G.CO.2
	Performance Tasks	
	Assessment Readiness	

CHAPTER 7

© Houghton Mifflin Harcourt Publishing Company

Unpacking the Standards

Understanding the standards and the vocabulary terms in the standards will help you know exactly what you are expected to learn in this chapter.

COMMON CORE **CC.9-12.G.SRT.2**

Given two figures, ... decide if they are similar; explain using similarity transformations the meaning of similarity for triangles as the equality of all corresponding pairs of angles and the proportionality of all corresponding pairs of sides.

Key Vocabulary

similar polygons *(polígonos semejantes)* Two polygons whose corresponding angles are congruent and whose corresponding side lengths are proportional.

similarity transformation *(transformación de semejanza)* A transformation that produces similar figures.

triangle *(triángulo)* A three-sided polygon.

corresponding angles of polygons *(ángulos correspondientes de los polígonos)* Angles in the same position in two different polygons that have the same number of angles.

corresponding sides of polygons *(lados correspondientes de los polígonos)* Sides in the same position in two different polygons that have the same number of sides.

What It Means For You
Lessons 7-1, 7-2, 7-3

Two figures are similar if they have the same shape but not necessarily the same size. When two figures are similar, you can dilate one of them and then slide, flip, and/or rotate it so that it coincides with the other. As a result, corresponding angles of similar figures are congruent and corresponding side lengths are proportional.

EXAMPLE **Similar figures**

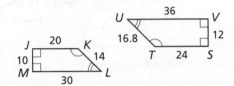

The figures are similar because you can multiply all the side lengths of the smaller figure by 1.2, rotate it 180°, and slide it so that it coincides with the larger figure.

NON-EXAMPLE **Non-similar figures**

The rectangles are not similar. There is no combination of dilations, slides, flips, and/or rotations that will cause the two figures to coincide.

CC.9-12.G.SRT.5

Use ... similarity criteria for triangles to solve problems and to prove relationships in geometric figures.

What It Means For You — Lessons 7-4, 7-5

Postulates and theorems can be used as shortcuts to prove that two triangles are similar. For example, the Angle-Angle (AA) Similarity Postulate states that if two angles of a triangle are congruent to two angles of another triangle, then the triangles are similar. This means that if you know the angle measures of two triangles, you can quickly check whether the triangles are similar.

EXAMPLE **AA similarity**

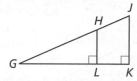

Angles *L* and *K* are right angles, so they are congruent. Triangles *GHL* and *GJK* both contain angle *G*. Therefore, triangles *GHL* and *GJK* are similar by AA similarity.

CC.9-12.G.MG.1

Use geometric shapes, their measures, and their properties to describe objects ...

What It Means For You — Lesson 7-5

Geometric relationships apply to objects in the real world. For example, you can use properties of triangle similarity to find the heights of objects that are difficult or impossible to measure directly.

EXAMPLE **Indirect measurement**

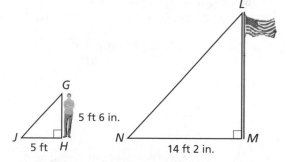

5 ft 6 in.

5 ft

14 ft 2 in.

You can use properties of similar triangles to find the height of this flagpole.

CHAPTER 7

Key Vocabulary

center of a circle *(centro de un círculo)* The point inside a circle that is the same distance from every point on the circle.

center of dilation *(centro de dilatación)* The intersection of the lines that connect each point of the image with the corresponding point of the preimage.

circle *(círculo)* The set of points in a plane that are a fixed distance from a given point called the center of the circle.

dilation *(dilatación)* A transformation in which the lines connecting every point P with its image P' all intersect at a point C known as the center of dilation, and $\frac{CP'}{CP}$ is the same for every point P other than C; a transformation that changes the size of a figure but not its shape.

radius of a circle *(radio de un círculo)* A segment whose endpoints are the center of a circle and a point on the circle; the distance from the center of a circle to any point on the circle.

scale factor *(factor de escala)* The multiplier used on each dimension to change one figure into a similar figure.

similarity ratio *(razón de semejanza)* The ratio of linear measurements in the preimage to corresponding measurements in the image in a pair of similar figures.

similar polygons *(polígonos semejantes)* Two polygons whose corresponding angles are congruent and whose corresponding side lengths are proportional.

similarity transformation *(transformación de semejanza)* A transformation that produces similar figures.

triangle *(triángulo)* A three-sided polygon.

corresponding angles of polygons *(ángulos correspondientes de los polígonos)* Angles in the same position in two different polygons that have the same number of angles.

corresponding sides of polygons *(lados correspondientes de los polígonos)* Sides in the same position in two different polygons that have the same number of sides.

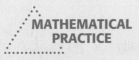

MATHEMATICAL PRACTICE

The Common Core Standards for Mathematical Practice describe varieties of expertise that mathematics educators at all levels should seek to develop in their students. Opportunities to develop these practices are integrated throughout this program.

1. Make sense of problems and persevere in solving them.
2. Reason abstractly and quantitatively.
3. Construct viable arguments and critique the reasoning of others.
4. Model with mathematics.
5. Use appropriate tools strategically.
6. Attend to precision.
7. Look for and make use of structure.
8. Look for and express regularity in repeated reasoning

Ratios in Similar Polygons
Going Deeper

Essential question: *How can you use ratios of corresponding side lengths to solve problems involving similar polygons?*

Two polygons are **similar polygons** if and only if their corresponding angles are congruent and their corresponding side lengths are proportional. The *similarity ratio* of two similar figures is the ratio of any side length in the first figure to the corresponding side length in the second figure. To prove that two figures with corresponding angles congruent are similar, show that corresponding side lengths are proportional.

PREP FOR **CC.9–12.G.SRT.2**

1 EXAMPLE Determining Polygon Similarity

Corresponding angles in each pair are congruent. Use ratios of corresponding side lengths to tell whether the figures are similar. If so, name the similarity ratio.

A rectangle *ABCD* to rectangle *WXYZ*

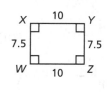

Determine the ratios of corresponding lengths and corresponding widths.

$$\frac{BC}{XY} = \frac{16}{10} = \frac{8}{5} = 1.6$$

$$\frac{AB}{WX} = \frac{12}{7.5} = 1.6$$

The polygons ___*are*___ similar. The similarity ratio is $\frac{8}{5}$, or 8 to 5.

B parallelogram *KLMN* to parallelogram *PQRS*

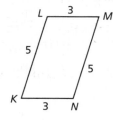

Determine the ratios of the lengths of corresponding opposite sides.

$$\frac{KL}{PQ} = \frac{5}{6.25} = .8$$

$$\frac{KN}{PS} = \frac{3}{4} = .75$$

The polygons ___*aren't*___ similar, because $0.8 \neq 0.75$. There is no similarity ratio.

REFLECT

1a. If you measure the angles in two figures and find that corresponding angles are not congruent, what conclusion can you draw about the figures? How is this a shortcut in determining if figures are similar?

_____

_____

1b. Describe how to find the *similarity ratio* of two similar figures when you are given lengths of corresponding sides.

_____

_____

PREP FOR **CC.9–12.G.SRT.1b**

2 **EXPLORE**   **Finding Unknown Lengths in Similar Polygons**

The trapezoids below are similar.

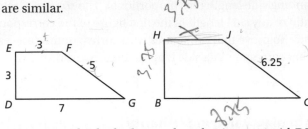

A What ratio can you use to multiply the known length 5 in trapezoid *DEFG* to get the known length 6.25 in trapezoid *BHJC*?

The known length of a side of trapezoid *BHJC* will be the _____ of a fraction

and the corresponding side length of trapezoid *DEFG* will be the _____ of that fraction.

$\dfrac{JC}{FG} = \dfrac{6.25}{5} = 1.25$ The required ratio is _____.

B Use this ratio as a multiplier to find the unknown side lengths in trapezoid *BHJC*.

$\dfrac{HJ}{EF} = \boxed{}$ → $HJ = \boxed{} \times EF$ → $HJ = \boxed{}$

$\dfrac{BH}{DE} = \boxed{}$ → $BH = \boxed{} \times DE$ → $BH = \boxed{}$

$\dfrac{BC}{DG} = \boxed{}$ → $BC = \boxed{} \times DG$ → $BC = \boxed{}$

REFLECT

2a. The ratio you used in the Explore can be called the *scale factor* of the first figure to the second figure. Complete the following: To find the scale factor of two

similar figures, use the ratio of a side length in the _____ figure to the

corresponding side length in the _____ figure.

2b. How is a scale factor used to find unknown side lengths in the second figure?

_____

_____

2c. Suppose figure A is similar to figure B. How is the similarity ratio of A to B related to the scale factor of A to B?

_____

Corresponding angles in each pair are congruent. Use ratios of corresponding sides to tell whether the figures are similar. If so, identify the similarity ratio.

1. triangle *XYZ* to triangle *ABC*

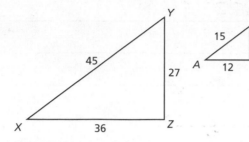

_____

_____

_____

_____

2. trapezoid *JHLK* to trapezoid *DGFE*

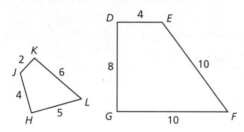

_____

_____

_____

_____

3. polygon *MNBCE* to polygon *RSTUV*

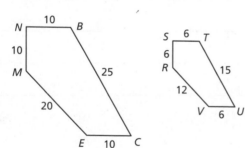

_____

_____

_____

_____

4. The angles in rhombus A are congruent to the corresponding angles in rhombus B. The sides of rhombus A are 7 units long. The sides of rhombus B are 9 units long. Explain why the rhombuses are similar.

_____

_____

The figures in each pair are similar. Find the lengths of the sides in the second figure. Show your work.

5. quadrilateral *ABCD*   quadrilateral *PQRS*

$\frac{10}{14} = \frac{6}{x}$

$10 = 84$

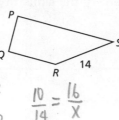

$\frac{10}{14} = \frac{8}{x}$ $10x = 112$

$x = 11.2$ $\frac{10}{14} = \frac{16}{x}$

$10x =$

$\overline{QR} = 11.2$

$\overline{PQ} = 8.4$

$\overline{PS} = 22.4$

6. polygon *BCHZRT*   polygon *ANGYPJ*

$3/2 =$

$\frac{3}{2} = \frac{x}{3}$

$2x = 9 \rightarrow x = 4.5$ $\frac{3}{2} \neq \frac{x}{1}$ $2x = 3$

$\overline{AN} = 3/2\,x$ $\overline{PJ} = 3/2\,x$

$\overline{NG} = 4.5x$

$\overline{GY} = 3x$

$\overline{PY} = 3/2\,x$

7. $\triangle AED \sim \triangle ABC$. In the diagram below, consider $\triangle AED$ to be the first triangle and $\triangle ABC$ to be the second triangle.

$\frac{21}{7} = \frac{x}{5}$

$7x = 105$

$x = 15$

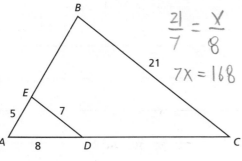

$\frac{21}{7} = \frac{x}{8}$

$7x = 168$

$\overline{EB} = 15$

$\overline{DC} = 24$

8. Polygons *WXYZ* and *DEFG* are similar and $k > 0$. Identify the similarity ratio of *WXYZ* to *DEFG* and the scale factor. Explain.

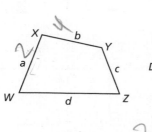

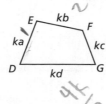

Similarity Ratio = k

$\frac{ka}{a} = \frac{kb}{b}$

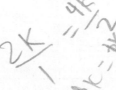

Additional Practice

Identify the pairs of congruent corresponding angles and the corresponding sides.

1.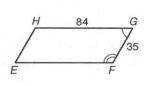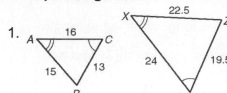

2.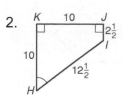

_____   _____

_____   _____

_____   _____

Determine whether the polygons are similar. If so, write the similarity ratio and a similarity statement. If not, explain why not.

3. parallelograms *EFGH* and *TUVW*

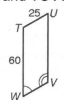

4. △*CDE* and △*LMN*

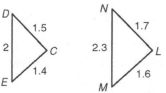

_____   _____

_____   _____

Tell whether the polygons must be similar based on the information given in the figures.

5.

all sides congruent = right angles

6.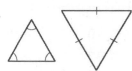

all 3x

7.

2 pairs of congruent sides

8.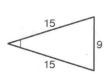

3 sides, 3 angles

= equalaterial

Problem Solving

1. *EFGH ~ JKLM*. What is the value of *x*?

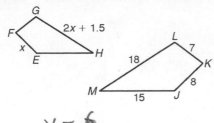

$$x = 6$$

2. The ratio of a model scale die cast motorcycle is 1 : 18. The model is $5\frac{1}{4}$ inches long. What is the length of the actual motorcycle in feet and inches?

   94.5 inches
   7.875 ft

3. A diagram of a new competition swimming pool is shown. If the width of the pool is 25 meters, find the length of the actual pool.

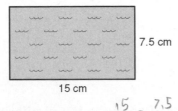

7.5 cm

15 cm

$$\frac{15}{25} = \frac{7.5}{x}$$

12.5 meters

4. Rectangle A has side lengths 16.4 centimeters and 10.8 centimeters. Rectangle B has side lengths 10.25 centimeters and 6.75 centimeters. Determine whether the rectangles are similar. If so, write the similarity ratio.

   Not similar

Choose the best answer.

5. A pet store has various sizes of guinea pig cages. A diagram of the top view of one of the cages is shown. What are possible dimensions of this cage?

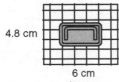

4.8 cm

6 cm

   A 28 in. by 24 in.   C 30 in. by 24 in.

   B 28 in. by 18 in.   D 30 in. by 18 in.

7. △*QRS ~* △*TUV*. Find the value of *y*.

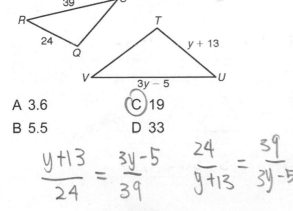

   A 3.6   C 19

   B 5.5   D 33

$$\frac{y+13}{24} = \frac{3y-5}{39} \qquad \frac{24}{y+13} = \frac{39}{3y-5}$$

$$72y - 120 = 39y + 507$$

$$-33 = 9$$

6. A gymnasium is 96 feet long and 75 feet wide. On a blueprint, the gymnasium is 5.5 inches long. To the nearest tenth of an inch, what is the width of the gymnasium on the blueprint?

   F 3.7 in.   H 7.0 in.

   G 4.3 in.   J 13.6 in.

8. △*ABC* has side lengths 14, 8, and 10.4. What are possible side lengths of △*DEF* if △*ABC ~* △*DEF*?

   F 28, 20, 20.8

   G 35, 16, 20.8

   H 28, 20, 26

   J 35, 20, 26

Similarity and Transformations
Going Deeper

Essential question: *What are the key properties of dilations, and how can dilations be used to show figures are similar?*

You have already worked extensively with three transformations: reflections, translations, and rotations. Now you will focus on a fourth type of transformation: dilations. Dilations are defined as follows.

Let O be a point and let k be a positive real number. For any point P, let $D(P) = P'$, where P' is the point on $\overrightarrow{OP}$ such that $OP' = k \cdot OP$. Then D is the **dilation** with **center of dilation** O and **scale factor** k. If necessary, the center of dilation and scale factor can be included in the function notation by writing $D_{O,k}(P) = P'$.

The figure shows a dilation with scale factor 2 because $OP' = 2OP$ and $OQ' = 2OQ$.

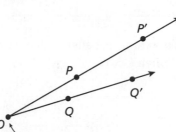

Center of dilation

CC.9–12.G.CO.2

1 EXPLORE Investigating Dilations

  A   Use geometry software to plot a point. Label the point O. Then construct a triangle and label the vertices P, Q, and R.

  B   Select point O. Go to the Transform menu and choose Mark Center. This makes point O the center of a dilation.

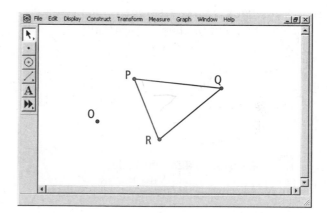

  C   Select $\triangle PQR$. Go to the Transform menu and choose Dilate. In the pop-up window, the "fixed ratio" is the scale factor k. Enter a scale factor of 2 and click the Dilate button.

  D   Label the image of $\triangle PQR$ as $\triangle P'Q'R'$. Measure the angles and the side lengths of the pre-image and the image. Change the shape of $\triangle PQR$ and observe the results.

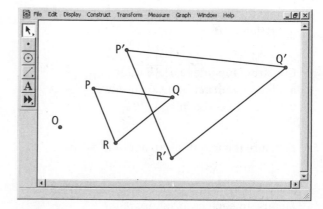

  E   Experiment with dilations that have different scale factors. Be sure to try scale factors less than 1, equal to 1, and greater than 1.

© Houghton Mifflin Harcourt Publishing Company

1a. In general, how does a dilation transform a figure?

_____

_____

1b. Do you think dilations are rigid motions? Why or why not?

_____

_____

1c. How does the value of k affect a dilation? What can you say about a dilation when $0 < k < 1$? when $k > 1$?

_____

_____

2 EXPLORE   Investigating Properties of Dilations

A Use geometry software to plot a point. Label the point O. Then construct a straight line and label it m.

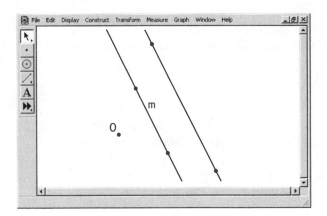

B Construct the image of line m under a dilation with center O and scale factor 2.

C Try dilations with different scale factors and try dragging the line to new positions. Notice what happens when the line passes through O.

D Delete the line and its image. Construct a segment, $\overline{AB}$.

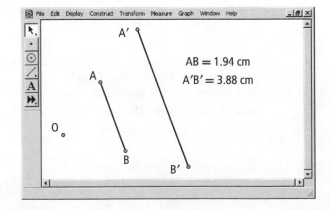

E Construct the image of $\overline{AB}$ under a dilation with center O and scale factor 2. Label the image $\overline{A'B'}$.

F Measure the length of $\overline{AB}$ and $\overline{A'B'}$.

G Try dilations with different scale factors. In each case, compare the lengths of $\overline{AB}$ and $\overline{A'B'}$.

© Houghton Mifflin Harcourt Publishing Company

2a. What can you say about the image of a straight line under a dilation? Does your answer depend upon the location of the line? Explain.

_____

_____

_____

2b. How is the length of a line segment related to the length of its image under a dilation with scale factor k?

_____

_____

2c. Suppose the points $A(x_1, y_1)$ and $B(x_2, y_2)$ are transformed by a dilation with scale factor k and center O. Give the coordinates of the image points A' and B'. Then show that the slope of $\overline{AB}$ equals the slope of $\overline{A'B'}$. What can you conclude about the segments?

_____

_____

_____

You may have discovered that dilations preserve the shape, but not the size, of figures. The following summary describes the key properties of dilations.

Properties of Dilations

- Dilations preserve angle measure. (angles are still same in both shapes)

- Dilations preserve betweenness. (

- Dilations preserve collinearity.

- A dilation maps a line not passing through the center of dilation to a parallel line and leaves a line passing through the center unchanged.

- The dilation of a line segment is longer or shorter in the ratio given by the scale factor.

CC.9–12.G.SRT.2

A **similarity transformation** is a transformation in which the image has the same shape as the pre-image. Specifically, the similarity transformations are the rigid motions (reflections, translations, and rotations) as well as dilations.

Two plane figures are **similar** if and only if one can be obtained from the other by similarity transformations (that is, by a sequence of reflections, translations, rotations, and/or dilations).

The symbol for similar is ~. As with congruence, it is customary to write a similarity statement so that corresponding vertices of the figures are listed in the same order. In the figure below, $\triangle A'B'C'$ is the image of $\triangle ABC$ after a dilation with center O and scale factor 2. Since a dilation is a similarity transformation, the two triangles are similar and you write $\triangle ABC \sim \triangle A'B'C'$.

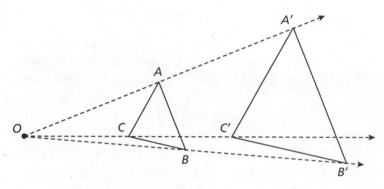

REFLECT

3a. Explain why congruence can be considered a special case of similarity.

_____

_____

3b. If you know that two figures are similar, can you conclude that corresponding angles are congruent? Why or why not?

_____

_____

3c. Given that $\triangle RST \sim \triangle R'S'T'$, can you conclude that $\overline{RS} \cong \overline{R'S'}$? Explain.

_____

_____

4 EXAMPLE   Determining If Figures Are Similar

Use the definition of similarity in terms of similarity transformations to determine whether the two figures are similar. Explain your answer.

A   △*JKL* and △*MNP* have different angle measures.

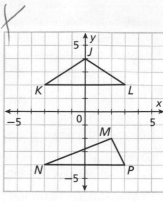

Since similarity transformations preserve angle measure, there is no sequence of similarity transformations that will map △*JKL* to △*MNP*.

Therefore, _____.

B   You can map △*RST* to △*XYZ* by the dilation that has the coordinate notation

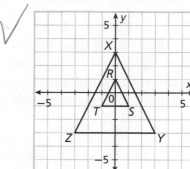

_____.

A dilation is a similarity transformation.

Therefore, _____.

C   You can map *ABCD* to *EFGH* by the dilation that has the coordinate notation

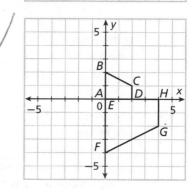

_____.

followed by the reflection that has the coordinate notation

_____.

Dilations and reflections are similarity transformations.

Therefore, _____.

REFLECT

4a. In Part B above, how can you show that the triangles are similar using a different similarity transformation?

_____

4b. In Part C above, does the order in which you perform the similarity transformations matter? Explain.

_____

_____

You can use the definition of similarity to prove theorems about figures.

> **Theorem**
>
> All circles are similar.

CC.9–12.G.C.1

5 PROOF **All Circles Are Similar**

Complete the proof.

Given: Circle C with center C and radius r;
circle D with center D and radius s.

Prove: Circle C is similar to circle D.

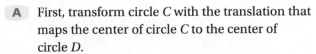

To prove similarity, show that there is a sequence of
similarity transformations that maps circle C to circle D.

A First, transform circle C with the translation that
maps the center of circle C to the center of
circle D.

Under this translation, the image
of point C is _____.

Let the image of circle C be circle C'.
The center of circle C' must lie at point

_____.

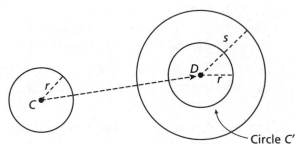

Circle C'

B Now, transform circle C' with the dilation that has center of dilation D and
scale factor $\frac{s}{r}$.

Circle C' consists of all points at distance _____ from point D.

After the dilation, the image of circle C' consists of all points at distance

_____ from point D. But these are exactly the points that form circle D.

Therefore, the translation followed by the dilation maps circle C to circle D.

Since translations and dilations are _____,

you can conclude that _____.

REFLECT

5a. Explain how to use a reflection and a dilation to prove that circle C is similar to
circle D.

_____

_____

1. The figure shows the image A' of point A under a dilation with center O. Explain how you can use a ruler to find the scale factor of the dilation. Then find the scale factor.

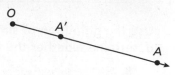

_____

_____

2. Compare dilations to rigid motions. How are they similar? How are they different?

_____

_____

3. Describe the effect of a dilation with scale factor 1.

_____

For Exercises 4–6, refer to the diagram of the dilation below.

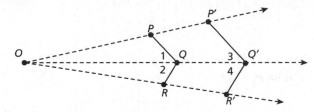

4. Suppose the points $P(x_1, y_1)$, $Q(x_2, y_2)$, and $R(x_3, y_3)$ are transformed by a dilation with scale factor k and center O. Show that the slope of $\overline{PQ}$ equals the slope of $\overline{P'Q'}$ and that the slope of $\overline{QR}$ equals the slope of $\overline{Q'R'}$.

_____

_____

_____

5. Make a convincing argument for why $m\angle 1 = m\angle 3$ and $m\angle 2 = m\angle 4$. Use reasoning related to transversals and parallel lines.

_____

_____

_____

6. Explain why $m\angle PQR = m\angle P'Q'R'$. What property of dilations does this reasoning support?

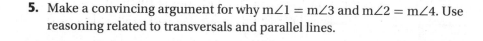

_____

_____

7. Given that $\triangle GMX \sim \triangle DPW$, write as many congruence statements as possible about the sides and/or angles of the triangles.

_____

Use the definition of similarity in terms of similarity transformations to determine whether the two figures are similar. Explain your answer.

8.

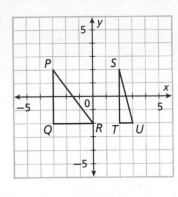

9.

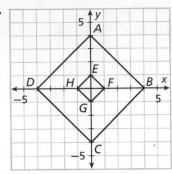

10.

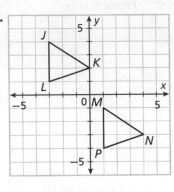

_____   _____   _____
_____   _____   _____
_____   _____   _____
_____   _____   _____
_____   _____   _____

11.

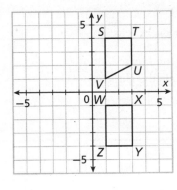

12.

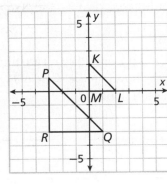

13.

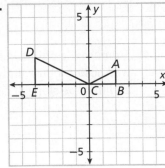

_____   _____   _____
_____   _____   _____
_____   _____   _____
_____   _____   _____
_____   _____   _____

Additional Practice

Apply the dilation *D* to the polygon with the given vertices. Describe the dilation.

1. $D: (x, y) \rightarrow (2x, 2y)$

   $A(1, 2), B(3, 3), C(4, 1)$

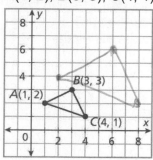

   _____ 2 units up, 1 unit ~~left~~ right _____

2. $D: (x, y) \rightarrow (\frac{1}{2}x, \frac{1}{2}y)$

   $P(-6, 8), Q(0, 6), R(-4, 2)$

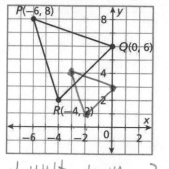

   $P(-3, 4)$

   $Q(0, 3)$

   $R(-2, 1)$

   _____ 1 unit down, 2 ~~left~~ right _____

3. $D: (x, y) \rightarrow (1.5x, 1.5y)$

   $G(-4, 1), H(-2, 1), J(-2, 6), K(-4, 6)$

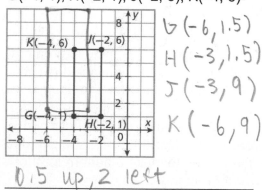

   $G(-6, 1.5)$

   $H(-3, 1.5)$

   $J(-3, 9)$

   $K(-6, 9)$

   _____ 0.5 up, 2 left _____

4. $D: (x, y) \rightarrow (0.75x, 0.75y)$

   $E(-4, 6), F(-2, 2), G(4, -2), H(4, 4)$

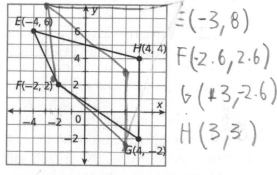

   $E(-3, 8)$

   $F(-2.6, 2.6)$

   $G(+3, -2.6)$

   $H(3, 3)$

   _____ changed in shape _____

Determine whether the polygons with the given vertices are similar.

5. $A(-4, 4), B(0, 4), C(0, 0), D(-2, -2),$
   $E(-4, 0); P(-3, 3), Q(-1, 3), R(-1, 1),$
   $S(-2, 0), T(-3, 1)$

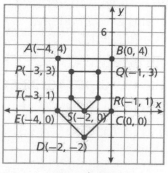

   _____ yes _____

6. $J(-4, 6), K(4, 6), L(4, 4); P(-2, 3),$
   $Q(2, 3), R(2, 2); S(-4, 1), T(0, 1),$
   $O(0, 0)$

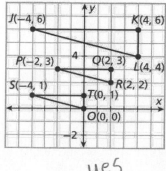

   _____ yes _____

Problem Solving

1. Irena is designing a quilt. She started with a large square and then made this diagram to follow when making her quilt. Describe how she used dilations to make the pattern.

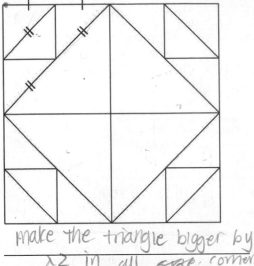

make the triangle bigger by x2 in all size corners.

2. A crop circle is a large pattern formed by flattening or cutting crops so the design is apparent when viewed from above. Every year, Hector puts a crop circle into his corn field. This year's design is shown below. Describe how he used dilations to complete his design.

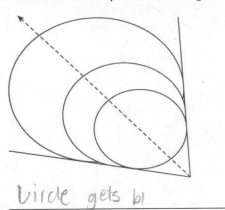

Circle gets bi

3. A graphic artist incorporated two similar right triangles into a logo with one triangle twice the size of the other. He used a computer graphics program to draw the first triangle and then used the enlargement tool of the program to draw the other triangle. How can he verify that the two triangles are similar?

4. A toy designer is planning to create a doll house. The design includes two similar rectangles with one being three times the size of the other. She cuts and traces the small rectangle onto grid paper first. Describe how she can use the tracing to make a pattern for the larger rectangle.

Choose the best answer.

5. Circle A with radius 4 and center (3, 0) is drawn in the coordinate plane. What is the scale factor that maps the circle with radius 3 and center (2, 3) onto circle A?

   A $\dfrac{4}{3}$ C $\dfrac{7}{3}$

   B $\dfrac{3}{4}$ D $\dfrac{3}{7}$

6. An art student uses dilations in all her art. She first plans the art piece on a coordinate grid. Determine the vertices of the image of the triangle with vertices $A(1, 1)$, $B(2, 4)$, and $C(3, 9)$ after a dilation with scale factor 1.5.

   F $A'(1.5, 1.5)$, $B'(3, 5)$, $C'(4.5, 13.5)$

   G $A'(2.5, 2.5)$, $B'(5, 10)$, $C'(7.5, 22.5)$

   H $A'(1.5, 1.5)$, $B'(4, 8)$, $C'(6, 18)$

   J $A'(1.5, 1.5)$, $B'(3, 6)$, $C'(4.5, 13.5)$

Triangle Similarity: AA, SSS, and SAS
Going Deeper

7-3

Essential question: *What can you conclude about similar triangles and how can you prove triangles are similar?*

CC.9–12.G.SRT.2

1 **ENGAGE** **Applying Similarity to Triangles**

Recall that when two figures are similar, there is a sequence of similarity transformations that maps one figure to the other. In particular, given $\triangle ABC \sim \triangle DEF$, you can first apply a dilation to $\triangle ABC$ to make both triangles the same size. Then you can apply a sequence of rigid motions to the dilated image of $\triangle ABC$ to map it to $\triangle DEF$.

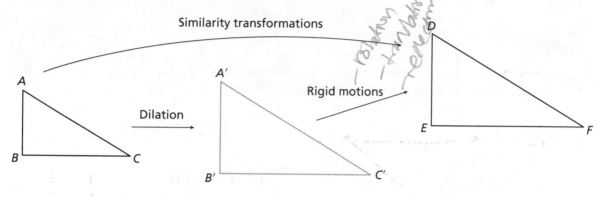

Similarity transformations

Dilation

Rigid motions

Because the similarity transformations that map $\triangle ABC$ to $\triangle DEF$ preserve angle measure, you can say that corresponding angles are congruent. Thus, $\triangle ABC \sim \triangle DEF$ implies $\angle A \cong \angle D$, $\angle B \cong \angle E$, and $\angle C \cong \angle F$.

Also, the initial dilation that makes the two triangles the same size shows that each side of $\triangle DEF$ is longer or shorter than the corresponding side of $\triangle ABC$ by the ratio given by the scale factor. Assuming the dilation has scale factor k, this means that $DE = k \cdot AB$, $EF = k \cdot BC$, and $DF = k \cdot AC$.

Solving for k in these equations gives $k = \dfrac{DE}{AB}$, $k = \dfrac{EF}{BC}$, and $k = \dfrac{DF}{AC}$.

This shows that corresponding sides are proportional. That is, $\dfrac{DE}{AB} = \dfrac{EF}{BC} = \dfrac{DF}{AC}$.

REFLECT

1a. Is triangle similarity transitive? That is, if $\triangle ABC \sim \triangle DEF$ and $\triangle DEF \sim \triangle GHK$, can you conclude that $\triangle ABC \sim \triangle GHK$? Explain.

_____

_____

_____

297

2 EXAMPLE Identifying Congruent Angles and Proportional Sides

Given that $\triangle RST \sim \triangle UVW$, write congruence statements for the corresponding angles and proportions for the corresponding sides.

A Corresponding angles are listed in the same position in each triangle name.

$\angle R \cong \angle U$, _____ , _____

B Corresponding sides are named by pairs of letters in the same position in each triangle name.

$\frac{UV}{RS} = $ _____

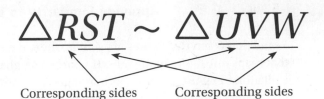

Corresponding sides   Corresponding sides

REFLECT

2a. Suppose the scale factor of the dilation in the sequence of similarity transformations that maps $\triangle RST$ to $\triangle UVW$ is 4 and suppose $RS = 8$ mm. Explain how to find the length of $\overline{UV}$.

_____

2b. A student identified $\overline{RS}$ and $\overline{UV}$ as a pair of corresponding sides and $\overline{ST}$ and $\overline{VW}$ as a pair of corresponding sides. The student wrote $\frac{RS}{UV} = \frac{VW}{ST}$. Is this a correct proportion? Why or why not? If the proportion is not correct, explain how to write correctly.

_____

_____

You have seen that when two triangles are similar, corresponding angles are congruent and corresponding sides are proportional. The converse is also true. That is, if you are given two triangles and you know that the corresponding angles are congruent and corresponding sides are proportional, you can conclude that the triangles are similar.

As with congruence, there are some "shortcuts" that make it a bit easier to prove that two triangles are similar. The most important of these is known as the AA Similarity Criterion.

AA Similarity Criterion

If two angles of one triangle are congruent to two angles of another triangle, then the triangles are similar.

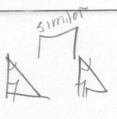

3 PROOF | **AA Similarity Criterion**

Given: $\angle A \cong \angle X$ and $\angle B \cong \angle Y$
Prove: $\triangle ABC \sim \triangle XYZ$

To prove the triangles are similar, you will find a sequence of similarity transformations that maps $\triangle ABC$ to $\triangle XYZ$. Complete the following steps of the proof.

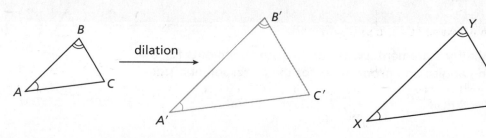

A Apply a dilation to $\triangle ABC$ with scale factor $k = \frac{XY}{AB}$. Let the image of $\triangle ABC$ be $\triangle A'B'C'$.

$\triangle A'B'C'$ is similar to $\triangle ABC$, and $\angle A' \cong$ _____ and $\angle B' \cong$ _____

because _____.

Also, $A'B' = k \cdot AB =$ _____.

B It is given that $\angle A \cong \angle X$ and $\angle B \cong \angle Y$.

By the Transitive Property of Congruence, $\angle A' \cong$ _____ and $\angle B' \cong$ _____.

So, $\triangle A'B'C' \cong \triangle XYZ$ by _____.

This means there is a sequence of rigid motions that maps $\triangle A'B'C'$ to $\triangle XYZ$.

The dilation followed by this sequence of rigid motions shows that there is a sequence of similarity transformations that maps $\triangle ABC$ to $\triangle XYZ$. Therefore, $\triangle ABC \sim \triangle XYZ$.

REFLECT

3a. In $\triangle JKL$, $m\angle J = 40°$ and $m\angle K = 60°$. In $\triangle MNP$, $m\angle M = 40°$ and $m\angle P = 80°$.
A student concludes that the triangles are not similar. Do you agree or disagree? Why?

_____

_____

There is another criterion that can be used to show that two triangles are similar. You will prove this criterion as an exercise.

> **SAS Similarity Criterion**
>
> If two sides of one triangle are proportional to two sides of another triangle and their included angles are congruent, then the triangles are similar.

PRACTICE

For each similarity statement, write congruence statements for the corresponding angles and proportions for the corresponding sides.

1. $\triangle GHJ \sim \triangle PQR$

2. $\triangle TWR \sim \triangle YSP$

3. $\triangle PJL \sim \triangle WDM$

4. Prove the SAS Similarity Criterion.

Given: $\dfrac{XY}{AB} = \dfrac{XZ}{AC}$ and $\angle A \cong \angle X$

Prove: $\triangle ABC \sim \triangle XYZ$
(*Hint:* The main steps of the proof are similar to those of the proof of the AA Similarity Criterion.)

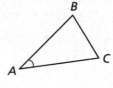

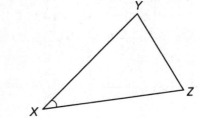

© Houghton Mifflin Harcourt Publishing Company

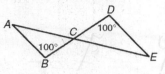

7-3

Additional Practice

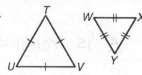
AA, SSS, SAS

For Exercises 1 and 2, explain why the triangles are similar and write a similarity statement.

1.
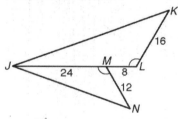

Because they have to same angles (AA)

2.

Because they all have the same sides (SSS)

For Exercises 3 and 4, verify that the triangles are similar. Explain why.

3. △JLK and △JMN

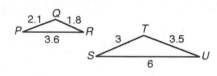

Both Similar because
JM÷JL = MN÷LK.

4. △PQR and △UTS

Not similar because
they don't have a
common ratio

For Exercise 5, explain why the triangles are similar and find the stated length.

5. *DE*

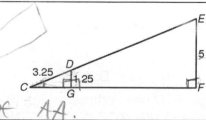

They are similar because of AA.

Problem Solving

Use the diagram for Exercises 1 and 2.

In the diagram of the tandem bike, $\overline{AE} \parallel \overline{BD}$.

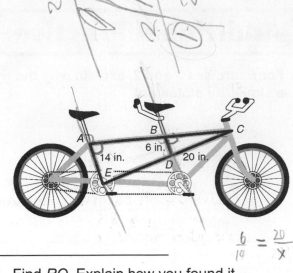

1. Explain why $\triangle CBD \sim \triangle CAE$.

   AA, angle A is congruent to angle B

2. Find *CE* to the nearest tenth. _____ 46.7

   $\frac{6}{14} = \frac{20}{x}$

3. Is $\triangle WXZ \sim \triangle XYZ$? Explain.

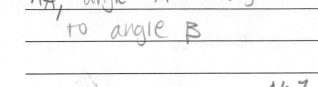

   Not similar becaus $XZ \div HZ$ $\neq XY \div XW$

4. Find *RQ*. Explain how you found it.

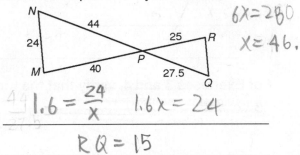

   $6x = 280$
   $x = 46.$

   $1.6 = \frac{24}{x}$ $1.6x = 24$

   $RQ = 15$

Choose the best answer.

5. Find the value of *x* that makes $\triangle FGH \sim \triangle JKL$.

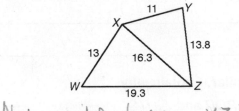

   A 8   C 12
   B 9   D 16

6. Triangle *STU* has vertices at $S(0, 0)$, $T(2, 6)$, and $U(8, 2)$. If $\triangle STU \sim \triangle WXY$ and the coordinates of *W* are $(0, 0)$, what are possible coordinates of *X* and *Y*?

   F $X(1, 3)$ and $Y(4, 1)$

   G $X(1, 3)$ and $Y(2, 0)$

   H $X(3, 1)$ and $Y(2, 4)$

   J $X(0, 3)$ and $Y(4, 0)$

7. To measure the distance *EF* across the lake, a surveyor at *S* locates points *E*, *F*, *G*, and *H* as shown. What is *EF*?

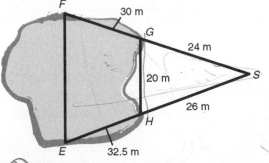

   A 25 m   C 45 m
   B 36 m   D 90 m

   $\frac{26}{32.5} = \frac{20}{x}$

   $26 = 645$

Applying Properties of Similar Triangles
Going Deeper

Essential question: *How does a line that is parallel to one side of a triangle divide the two sides that it intersects?*

The following theorem is sometimes known as the Side-Splitting Theorem. It describes what happens when a line that is parallel to one side of a triangle "splits" the other two sides.

Video Tutor

> **Triangle Proportionality Theorem**
>
> If a line parallel to one side of a triangle intersects the other two sides, then it divides those sides proportionally.

CC.9–12.G.SRT.4

1 PROOF   **Triangle Proportionality Theorem**

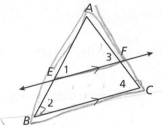

Given: $\overleftrightarrow{EF} \parallel \overline{BC}$

Prove: $\dfrac{AE}{EB} = \dfrac{AF}{FC}$

Complete the proof.

A   Show that $\triangle AEF \sim \triangle ABC$.

Since $\overleftrightarrow{EF} \parallel \overline{BC}$, you can conclude that $\angle 1 \cong \angle 2$ and $\angle 3 \cong \angle 4$ by

_____

So, $\triangle AEF \sim \triangle ABC$ by _____

B   Use the fact that corresponding sides of similar triangles are proportional.

$\dfrac{AB}{AE} =$ _____   Corresponding sides are proportional.

$\dfrac{AE + EB}{AE} =$ _____   Segment Addition Postulate

$1 + \dfrac{EB}{AE} =$ _____   Use the property that $\dfrac{a + b}{c} = \dfrac{a}{c} + \dfrac{b}{c}$.

$\dfrac{EB}{AE} =$ _____   Subtract 1 from both sides.

$\dfrac{AE}{EB} =$ _____   Take the reciprocal of both sides.

1a. Explain how you can conclude $\triangle AEF \sim \triangle ABC$ without using $\angle 3$ and $\angle 4$.

_____

_____

Converse of the Triangle Proportionality Theorem

If a line divides two sides of a triangle proportionally, then it is parallel to the third side.

CC.9–12.G.SRT.5

2 PROOF   **Converse of the Triangle Proportionality Theorem**

Given: $\dfrac{AE}{EB} = \dfrac{AF}{FC}$

Prove: $\overleftrightarrow{EF} \parallel \overline{BC}$

Complete the proof.

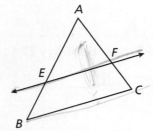

A   Show that $\triangle AEF \sim \triangle ABC$.

It is given that $\dfrac{AE}{EB} = \dfrac{AF}{FC}$ and taking the reciprocal of both sides shows that

_____. Now add 1 to both sides by adding $\dfrac{AE}{AE}$ to the left

side and $\dfrac{AF}{AF}$ to the right side. This gives _____. Adding

and using the Segment Addition Postulate gives _____.

Since $\angle A \cong \angle A$, $\triangle AEF \sim \triangle ABC$ by _____.

B   As corresponding angles of similar triangles, $\angle AEF \cong$ _____.

So, $\overleftrightarrow{EF} \parallel \overline{BC}$ by _____.

REFLECT

2a. A student states that $\overline{UV}$ must be parallel to $\overline{ST}$. Do you agree?
Why or why not?

_____

_____

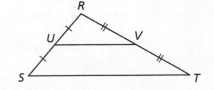

Additional Practice

(handwritten:) $81 + 9x = 24x$ $x =$
$81 = 15x$
$\frac{24}{9x} = \frac{9x+}{x}$
$24x = 81 + 9x$
$15x = 81$

Find each length.

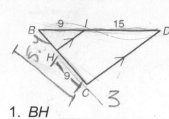

(handwritten:) $\frac{15^{24}}{9} = \frac{9+x}{x}$ $24x = 81$ $x =$

1. *BH* _____ *(handwritten: 3)*

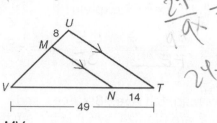

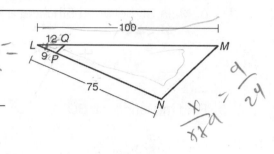

2. *MV* _____

Verify that the given segments are parallel.

3. $\overline{PQ}$ and $\overline{NM}$

(handwritten:) SAS,   <L,   LM, PN
$100/12 = 8.3$
$75/9 = 8.3$

(handwritten beside fig:) $\frac{x}{9+x} =$, $\frac{x}{9 \cdot x} , \frac{9}{24}$

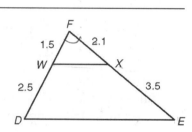

4. $\overline{WX}$ and $\overline{DE}$

(handwritten:) SAS $\overline{DF}$, <F, $\overline{FE}$
$1.5/4 = .375$
$2.1/5.6 = 3.75$

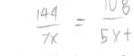

Find each length.

(handwritten:) $\frac{144}{7x} = \frac{108}{5x+2}$
$720x + 288 = 756x$
$-36x = -288$
$x = 8$

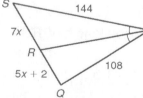

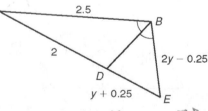

5. *SR* and *RQ* _56_, _42_

6. *BE* and *DE* _8.75_, _4.75_

7. In $\triangle ABC$, $\overline{BD}$ bisects $\angle ABC$ and $\overline{AD} \cong \overline{CD}$. Tell what kind of $\triangle ABC$ must be. _____ isoceles

Problem Solving

1. Is $\overline{GF} \parallel \overline{HJ}$ if $x = 5$? Explain.

   No because $\dfrac{VE}{FE} \neq \dfrac{HE}{JE} \neq \dfrac{HE}{JE}$

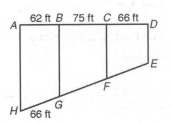

$$0.4x = 0.15$$
$$x =$$
$$\dfrac{0.5}{0.4} = \dfrac{x}{0.3}$$

2. On the map, 5th Ave., 6th Ave., and 7th Ave. are parallel. What is the length of Main St. between 5th Ave. and 6th Ave.?

   0.24

$$\dfrac{0.5}{0.4} = \dfrac{0.8}{0.4+x}$$

$$0.2 + 0.5x = 0.32$$

$$0.5x = 0.12$$

$$\dfrac{0.5}{0.4} = \dfrac{0.8}{0.4+x} \quad x = 6$$

3. Find the length of $\overline{BC}$.

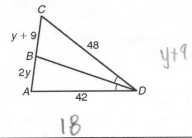

y + 9

   18

4. The figure shows three lots in a housing development. If the boundary lines separating the lots are parallel, what is GF to the nearest tenth?

   79.8 ft

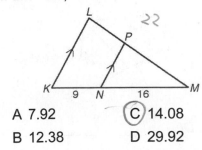

© Houghton Mifflin Harcourt Publishing Company

Choose the best answer.

5. If $LM = 22$, what is PM?

   22

   K 9 N 16 M

   A 7.92   C 14.08
   B 12.38   D 29.92

6. In $\triangle QRS$, the bisector of $\angle R$ divides $\overline{QS}$ into segments with lengths 2.1 and 2.8. If $RQ = 3$, which is the length of $\overline{RS}$?

   F 2   H 4
   G 2.25   J 4.5

7. In $\triangle CDE$, the bisector of $\angle C$ divides $\overline{DE}$ into segments with lengths $4x$ and $x + 13$. If $CD = 24$ and $CE = 32$, which is the length of $\overline{DE}$?

   A 20   C 26
   B 24   D 28

$$\dfrac{3}{x} = \dfrac{2.8}{2.1}$$
$$6.3 = 2.8x$$
$$x =$$

$$3/4 = \dfrac{2.1}{2.8}$$

$$\dfrac{2.8}{2.1} = \dfrac{2.25}{x}$$
$$2.8x =$$

Using Proportional Relationships
Going Deeper

Essential question: *How can you use similar triangles and similar rectangles to solve problems?*

When you know that two polygons are similar, you can often use the proportionality of corresponding sides to find unknown side lengths.

CC.9–12.G.SRT.5

1 EXAMPLE   **Finding an Unknown Distance**

You want to find the distance across a canyon. In order to find the distance *XY*, you locate points as described below. Explain how to use this information and the figure to find *XY*.

1. Identify a landmark, such as a tree, at *X*. Place a marker (*Y*) directly across the canyon from *X*.

2. At *Y*, turn 90° away from *X* and walk 400 feet in a straight line. Place a marker (*Z*) at this location.

3. Continue walking another 600 feet. Place a marker (*W*) at this location.

4. Turn 90° away from the canyon and walk until the marker *Z* aligns with *X*. Place a marker (*V*) at this location. Measure $\overline{WV}$.

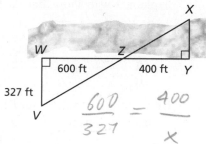

A   Show that $\triangle XYZ \sim \triangle VWZ$.

• How can you show that two pairs of angles in the triangles are congruent?

_____

_____

• What can you conclude? Why?

_____

B   Use the fact that corresponding sides of similar triangles are proportional.

• Complete the proportion: $\frac{XY}{VW} =$ _____

• Substitute the known lengths in the proportion: _____

• Solve the proportion: $XY =$ _____

REFLECT

1a. Compare this problem to the example *Using the ASA Congruence Criterion* in the lesson *Triangle Congruence: ASA, AAS, and HL.* How are the solution methods similar? How are they different?

_____

_____

2 **E X A M P L E** **Finding an Unknown Height**

In order to find the height of a palm tree, you measure the tree's shadow and, at the same time of day, you measure the shadow cast by a meter stick that you hold at a right angle to the ground. The measurements are shown in the figure. Find the height of the tree.

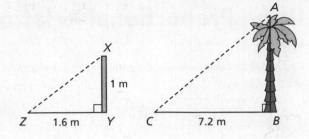

A Show that $\triangle ABC \sim \triangle XYZ$.

You can assume that the rays of the sun are parallel. This means that $\overline{ZX} \parallel \overline{CA}$. What can you say about $\angle Z$ and $\angle C$? Why?

_____

Explain how to show that $\triangle ABC \sim \triangle XYZ$.

_____

_____

B Determine the scale factor k for the dilation in the sequence of similarity transformations that maps $\triangle XYZ$ to $\triangle ABC$.

Find the ratio of corresponding sides. The scale factor is $\frac{BC}{YZ} = \frac{7.2}{1.6} = 4.5$.

So, $AB = k \cdot XY =$ _____ .

REFLECT

2a. How could you solve the problem by writing and solving a proportion?

_____

2b. How can you check that your answer is reasonable?

_____

_____

_____

2c. What must be true about the palm tree in order for this method to work?

_____

_____

3 EXAMPLE | Solving a Problem About Similar Rectangles

A typographic grid system is a set of horizontal and vertical lines that determine the placement of type or images on a page. The lines create an array of identical rectangles.

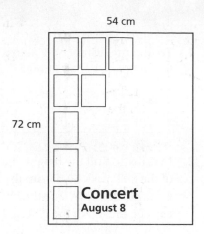

54 cm

72 cm

Concert
August 8

A graphic designer wants to lay out a new grid system for a poster that is 54 cm wide by 72 cm tall. The grid must have margins of 2 cm along all edges and 2 cm between each horizontal row of rectangles. There must be 5 rows of rectangles and each rectangle must be similar to the poster itself.

What are the dimensions of the rectangles? How many rectangles should appear in each row? How much space should be between the columns of rectangles?

A Determine the number of horizontal 2-centimeter bands that are needed, including the top and bottom margins. _____

$$\frac{72}{54} = \frac{72-}{x}$$

$$72x = 648$$

$$x = 9$$

B Find the remaining amount of vertical space and divide by 5 to find the height of each rectangle. _____

C To find the width of each rectangle, use the fact that the rectangles are similar to the overall poster. Show how to set up a proportion to find the width of each rectangle.

_____

D Determine the maximum number of rectangles that can appear in a row. _____

E Find the total amount of horizontal space taken up by the rectangles and the left and right margins. _____

F Assuming the remaining space is distributed evenly, determine the amount of space that should appear between the columns of rectangles. _____

REFLECT

3a. Is there another solution to the problem? Explain.

_____

_____

_____

$\frac{300}{500} = \frac{600}{X}$ $3XY X = 3000 \not{0}X$ $\frac{3}{4} = \frac{6}{X}$ $\frac{300}{400} = —$

PRACTICE

1. To find the distance *XY* across a lake, you locate points as shown in the figure. Explain how to use this information to find *XY*.

_____

_____

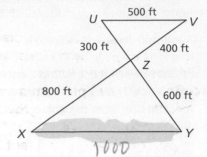

2. In order to find the height of a cliff, you stand at the bottom of the cliff, walk 60 ft from the base, and place a mirror on the ground. Then you face the cliff and step back 5 feet so that you can see the top of the cliff in the mirror. Assuming your eyes are 6 feet above ground, explain how to use this information to find the height of the cliff. (*Hint*: When light strikes a mirror, the angle of incidence is congruent to the angle of reflection, as marked in the figure.)

72 ft

_____

_____

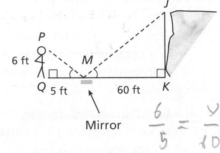

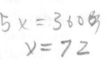 $\frac{6}{5} = \frac{Y}{10}$

$5x = 360\not{6}$
$x = 72$

3. **Error Analysis** A student who is 72 inches tall wants to find the height of a flagpole. He measures the length of the flagpole's shadow and the length of his own shadow at the same time of day, as shown in his sketch below. Explain the error in the student's work.

The triangles are similar by the AA Similarity Criterion, so corresponding sides are proportional.

$\frac{x}{72} = \frac{48}{128}$

$x = 72 \cdot \frac{48}{128}$, so $x = 27$ in.

$\frac{48}{72} = \frac{128}{X}$
$x = 192$

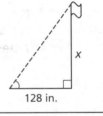

72 in.

48 in.   128 in. x

_____

_____

4. A graphic designer wants to lay out a grid system for a brochure that is 15 cm wide by 20 cm tall. The grid must have margins of 1 cm along all edges and 1 cm between each horizontal row of rectangles. There must be 4 rows of rectangles and each rectangle must be similar to the brochure itself. What are the dimensions of the rectangles? How many rectangles should appear in each row? How much space should be between the columns of rectangles? Give two different solutions.

3.75, 5   4   0

_____

15

 20   15

$\frac{15}{20} = \frac{3.75}{X}$ $x = 5$

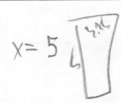

$15x = 75$

7-5

Additional Practice

Refer to the figure for Exercises 1–3. A city is planning an outdoor concert for an Independence Day celebration. To hold speakers and lights, a crew of technicians sets up a scaffold with two platforms by the stage. The first platform is 8 feet 2 inches off the ground. The second platform is 7 feet 6 inches above the first platform. The shadow of the first platform stretches 6 feet 3 inches across the ground.

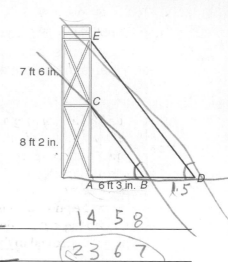

1. Explain why △ABC is similar to △ADE. (*Hint:* The sun's rays are parallel.)

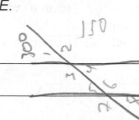

_____

_____

2. Find the length of the shadow of the second platform in feet and inches to the nearest inch.
   _____

3. A 5-foot-8-inch-tall technician is standing on top of the second platform. Find the length of the shadow the scaffold and the technician cast in feet and inches to the nearest inch.
   _____

Refer to the figure for Exercises 4–6. Ramona wants to renovate the kitchen in her house. The figure shows a blueprint of the new kitchen drawn to a scale of 1 cm : 2 ft. Use a centimeter ruler and the figure to find each actual measure in feet.

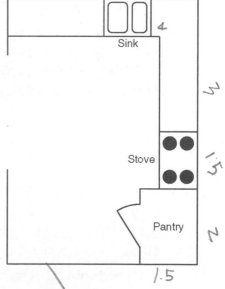

4. width of the kitchen

5. length of the kitchen

_____   _____

6. width of the sink

7. area of the pantry

_____   _____

Given that *DEFG ~ WXYZ*, find each of the following.

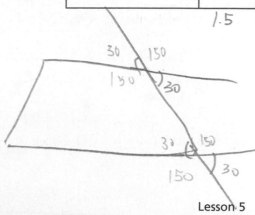

8. perimeter of *WXYZ* _____

9. area of *WXYZ* _____

Problem Solving

(handwritten top margin)
150
50 yards   48 $\frac{75}{24} = \frac{25}{8} =$
16 yd

1. A student is standing next to a sculpture. The figure shows the shadows that they cast. What is the height of the sculpture?

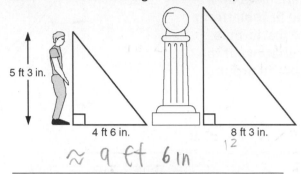

5 ft 3 in.

4 ft 6 in.   8 ft 3 in.
                         12

(handwritten) ≈ 9 ft 6 in

3. An artist makes a scale drawing of a new lion enclosure at the zoo. The scale is 1 in : 25 ft. On the drawing, the length of the enclosure is $7\frac{1}{4}$ inches. What is the actual length of the lion enclosure?

(handwritten) 181.25 ft

$\frac{1}{300} = \frac{7.25}{X}$ X = 2175

Choose the best answer.

5. A visual-effects model maker for a movie draws a spaceship using a ratio of 1 : 24. The drawing of the spaceship is 22 inches long. What is the length of the spaceship in the movie?

   A 4 ft   C 44 ft

   B 8 ft   D 528 ft *(circled)*

7. The scale of the park map is 1.5 cm = 60 m. Which is the best estimate for the actual distance between the horse stables and the picnic area?

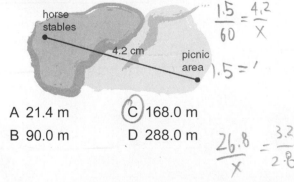

horse stables

4.2 cm   picnic area

(handwritten) $\frac{1.5}{60} = \frac{4.2}{X}$ 1.5 = 1

   A 21.4 m   C 168.0 m *(circled)*

   B 90.0 m   D 288.0 m

(handwritten) $\frac{26.8}{X} = \frac{3.2}{2.8}$

2. At the halftime show during a football game, a marching band is to form a rectangle 50 yards by 16 yards. The conductor wants to plan out the band members' positions using a 14- by 8.5-in. sheet of paper. What scale should she use to fit both dimensions of the rectangle on the page? (Use whole inches and yards.) *(handwritten)* width

(handwritten) 1.81 inch = 1.8 yd

4. A room is 14 feet long and 11 feet wide. If you made a scale drawing of the top view of the room using the scale $\frac{1}{2}$ in = 2 ft, what would be the length and width of the room in your drawing?

(handwritten) 3.5 in long and 2.75 in wide

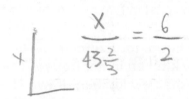

(handwritten) $\frac{X}{43\frac{2}{3}} = \frac{6}{2}$

6. A free-fall ride at an amusement park casts a shadow $43\frac{2}{3}$ feet long. At the same time, a 6-foot-tall person standing in line casts a shadow 2 feet long. What is the height of the ride?

   F $21\frac{5}{6}$ ft   H $98\frac{1}{4}$ ft

   G $65\frac{1}{2}$ ft   J 131 ft *(circled)*

8. A hot-air balloon is 26.8 meters tall. Use the scale drawing to find the actual distance across the hot-air balloon.

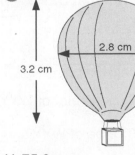

2.8 cm

3.2 cm

   F 23.45 m *(circled)*   H 75.0 m

   G 30.6 m   J 85.8 m

Dilations and Similarity in the Coordinate Plane

Connection: Coordinate Methods

Essential question: *How can you represent dilations in the coordinate plane?*

Video Tutor

When you work with dilations in the coordinate plane, you can assume the center of dilation is the origin. To find the image of a point after a dilation with scale factor k, multiply each coordinate of the point by k. Using coordinate notation, a dilation with scale factor k is written as follows: $(x, y) \rightarrow (kx, ky)$.

CC.9–12.G.CO.2

1 EXAMPLE Drawing a Dilation in a Coordinate Plane

Draw the image of the pentagon after a dilation with scale factor $\frac{3}{2}$.

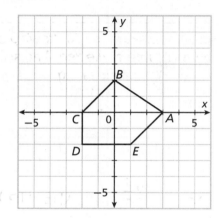

A In the table below, list the vertices of the pentagon. Then use the rule for the dilation to write the vertices of the image.

Pre-Image (x, y)	Image $\left(\frac{3}{2}x, \frac{3}{2}y\right)$
$A(3, 0)$	$A'(4\frac{1}{2}, 0)$
$B(0, 2)$	

B Plot the vertices of the image. Connect the vertices to complete the image.

REFLECT

1a. Explain how to use the distance formula to check that $\overline{B'C'}$ is the correct length.

_____

_____

1b. A student claims that under a dilation centered at the origin with scale factor k, a point and its image always lie in the same quadrant. Do you agree or disagree? Explain.

_____

_____

_____

Draw the image of the figure after a dilation with the given scale factor.

1. scale factor: 2

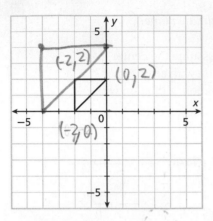

2. scale factor: $\frac{1}{4}$

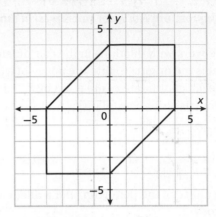

3. scale factor: $\frac{2}{3}$

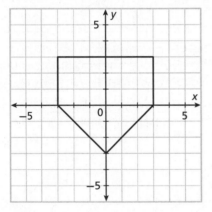

4. scale factor: 3

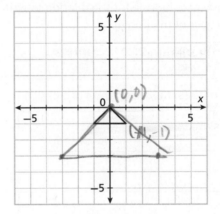

5. Each centimeter on a scale drawing of a park represents three meters of actual distance. What is the scale factor of the dilation that maps the park to the scale drawing?

_____

6. **Error Analysis** A student claims that a dilation with scale factor m and center of dilation O that is followed by a dilation with scale factor n and center of dilation O is equivalent to a single dilation with scale factor $m + n$ and center of dilation O. Do you agree or disagree? Explain.

_____

_____

_____

_____

Additional Practice

A jeweler designs a setting that can hold a gem in the shape of a parallelogram. The figure shows the outline of the gem. The client, however, wants a gem and setting that is slightly larger.

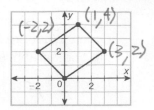

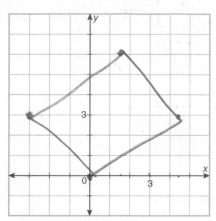

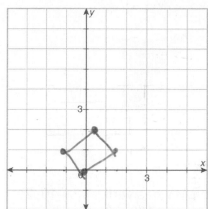

1. Draw the gem after a dilation with a scale factor of $\frac{3}{2}$.

2. The client is so pleased with her ring that she decides to have matching but smaller earrings made using the same pattern. Draw the gem after a dilation from the original pattern with a scale factor of $\frac{1}{2}$.

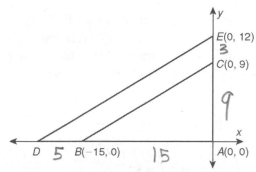

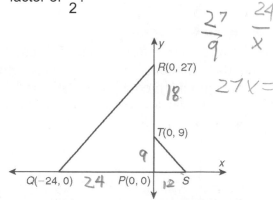

3. Given that $\triangle ABC \sim \triangle ADE$, find the scale factor and the coordinates of D.

$(-20, 0)$

_____

4. Given that $\triangle PQR \sim \triangle PST$, find the scale factor and the coordinates of S.

$(0, 8)$

_____

Problem Solving

1. The figure shows a photograph on grid paper. What are the coordinates of C' if the photograph is enlarged with scale factor $\dfrac{4}{3}$?

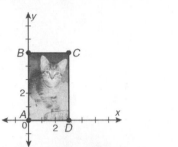

$A = (0,0) \quad B = (0, 6.67) \quad C = (4, 6.67)$
$D = (4, 0)$

2. In the figure, $\triangle HFJ \sim \triangle EFG$. Find the coordinates of G and the scale factor.

$$\sqrt{25+9}$$
$$\sqrt{34}$$

$$\frac{5.8}{16.2} = \frac{5.7}{x}$$
$$5.8x =$$

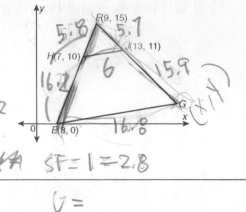

$$\frac{5.8}{16.2} = \frac{567}{x}$$
$$5.8x = 97.2$$

$SF = 1 = 2.8$

$G =$

3. Triangle LMN has vertices $L(-10, 2)$, $M(-4, 11)$, and $N(6, -6)$. Find the vertices of the image of $\triangle LMN$ after a dilation with scale factor $\dfrac{5}{2}$.

$M\left(-10, 27\tfrac{1}{2}\right) \quad N(15, -15) \quad L(-25, 5)$

4. Triangle HJM has vertices $H(-36, 0)$, $J(0, 20)$, and $M(0, 0)$. Triangle $H'J'M'$ has two vertices at $H'(-27, 0)$ and $M'(0, 0)$, and $\triangle H'J'M'$ is a dilation image of $\triangle HJM$. Find the coordinates of J' and the scale factor.

$J = (0, 15)$

$SF = 1 \to 1.8$

Choose the best answer.

5. The arrow is cut from a logo. The artist needs to make a copy five times as large for a sign. If the coordinates of T are $T(3, 4.5)$, what are the coordinates of T' after the arrow is dilated with scale factor 5?

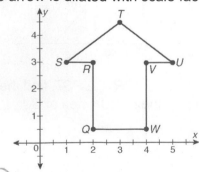

A $T'(15, 22.5)$
B $T'(7.5, 9)$
C $T'(4.5, 6.75)$
D $T'(2.5, 20)$

6. Triangle QRS has vertices $Q(-7, 3)$, $R(9, 8)$, and $S(2, 16)$. What is the scale factor if the vertices after a dilation are $Q'(-10.5, 4.5)$, $R'(13.5, 15)$, and $S'(3, 24)$?

F $\dfrac{1}{3}$

G $\dfrac{1}{2}$

H $\dfrac{2}{3}$

J $\dfrac{3}{2}$

7. A triangle has vertices $H(-4, 2)$, $J(-8, 6)$, and $K(0, 6)$. If $\triangle ABC \sim \triangle HJK$, what are possible vertices of $\triangle ABC$?

A $A(-4, 3)$, $B(-2, 1)$, $C(0, 3)$
B $A(-2, 1)$, $B(-4, 3)$, $C(0, 3)$
C $A(-2, 4)$, $B(0, 6)$, $C(-2, 8)$
D $A(-2, 4)$, $B(-8, 6)$, $C(-4, 2)$

CHAPTER 7

Performance Tasks

COMMON
CORE

CC.9-12.G.CO.2
CC.9-12.G.SRT.5
CC.9-12.G.MG.3

⭐ **1.** Each of the faces carved into Mount Rushmore measures approximately 60 feet from the chin to the top of the head. Each of the mouths is approximately 18 feet wide. Have a classmate use a ruler to find the same measurements on your face. Is your face approximately similar to the carved faces? Explain your answer.

⭐ **2.** Sonia made the sketch shown of a logo for a new local nonprofit organization. She would like to enlarge the sketch by using a dilation whose center is the center of the circle.

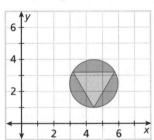

   a. What is the largest scale factor of the dilation that will keep the logo in the first quadrant?

   b. Sketch the logo after this dilation.

3. Part of the preliminary floor plan of Alicia's vacation cottage is shown. The scale is 1 in.: 5 ft.

    a. What are the actual areas, in square feet, of the main house (the living room and kitchen) and the exterior porch? Show your work.

    b. Alicia would like the area of the porch to be about 30% of the area of the main house. Find one way she could achieve this by changing only one dimension of the floor plan. Explain how your change achieves Alicia's goal.

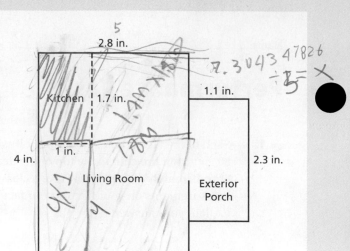

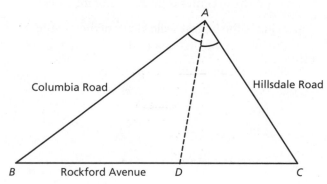

KITCHEN = 5, 8.5 ft = 42.5

LR = 20 ft, 14 ft = 280 ft

EP = 5.5, 11.5 ft = 63.25

$\frac{x}{280} = \frac{30}{100}$

$100x = 8400$

$x = 84$ ft

4. The map shows three major roadways in a city, along with a proposed new road represented by the dotted line. The distances shown on the map are as follows:

Columbia Road: 6.8 miles
Hillsdale Road: 5.1 miles
Rockford Avenue ($\overline{BC}$): 8.8 miles

Using only the existing roads, how long is the shortest possible drive from *A* to *D*? Round your answer to the nearest tenth of a mile and explain how you found your answer.

Name _____ Class _____ Date _____

MULTIPLE CHOICE

1. Which of the following transformations is a dilation?

   A. $(x, y) \rightarrow (2x, y)$

   B. $(x, y) \rightarrow (x + 2, y + 2)$

   C. $(x, y) \rightarrow (2x, 2y)$

   D. $(x, y) \rightarrow (x, y - 2)$

2. Juan is proving the Triangle Proportionality Theorem. Which reason should he use for Step 3?

   Given: $\overleftrightarrow{XY} \parallel \overline{BC}$

   Prove: $\frac{AX}{XB} = \frac{AY}{YC}$

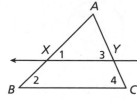

Statements	Reasons
1. $\overleftrightarrow{XY} \parallel \overline{BC}$	1. Given
2. $\angle 1 \cong \angle 2$; $\angle 3 \cong \angle 4$	2. Corresponding Angles Theorem
3. $\triangle AXY \sim \triangle ABC$	3. ?

   F. ASA Congruence Criterion

   G. Definition of corresponding angles

   H. Definition of similarity

   J. AA Similarity Criterion

3. Katie uses geometry software to draw a line ℓ and a point O that is not on line ℓ. Then she constructs the image of line ℓ under a dilation with center O and scale factor 4. Which of the following best describes the image of line ℓ?

   A. a line parallel to line ℓ

   B. a line perpendicular to line ℓ

   C. a line passing through point O

   D. a line that coincides with line ℓ

4. A graphic designer wants to lay out a grid system for a book cover that is 12 cm wide by 15 cm tall. The grid will have an array of identical rectangles, margins of 1 cm along all edges, and 1 cm between each horizontal row of rectangles. There must be 4 rows of rectangles and each rectangle must be similar to the cover itself. Which of the following are possible dimensions of the rectangles?

   F. 2.5 cm tall by 2 cm wide

   G. 2.75 cm tall by 2.2 cm wide

   H. 3 cm tall by 2.4 cm wide

   J. 3.25 cm tall by 2.6 cm wide

5. In order to find the height of a radio tower, you measure the tower's shadow and, at the same time of day, you measure the shadow cast by a mailbox that is 1.2 meters tall. The measurements are shown in the figure. What is the height of the tower?

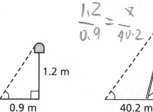

   A. 30.15 m   C. 44.67 m

   B. 40.5 m   D. 53.6 m

6. Which of the following is *not* preserved under a dilation?

   F. angle measure

   G. betweenness

   H. collinearity

   J. distance

© Houghton Mifflin Harcourt Publishing Company

7. Use the definition of similarity in terms of similarity transformations to determine whether the two figures are similar. Explain your answer.

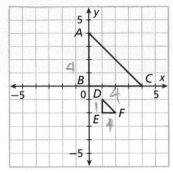

Similar

8. You are proving that the AA Similarity Criterion follows from the definition of similarity in terms of similarity transformations.

Given: $\angle R \cong \angle U$ and $\angle S \cong \angle V$
Prove: $\triangle RST \sim \triangle UVW$

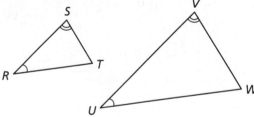

You begin by applying a dilation to $\triangle RST$. What is the scale factor k of the dilation? Why do you choose this scale factor?

9. You are proving that all circles are similar. You start with the two circles shown below.

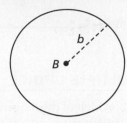

a. First you perform a transformation on circle A so that the image of point A is point B. Describe the transformation you use.

circles are always similar

b. The image of circle A is circle A', as shown.

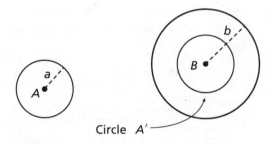

Circle A'

What transformation do you apply to circle A' in order to complete the proof? Why?

CIRCLES ARE SIMILAR

Right Triangles and Trigonometry

Chapter Focus

In this unit, you will work with trigonometric ratios. Trigonometric ratios are based on right triangles and similarity. As you will see, these ratios are useful in solving a variety of mathematical and real-world problems. As you study trigonometry, you will learn about two special right triangles, and you will learn how to find unknown side lengths and unknown angle measures in right and non-right triangles.

Chapter at a Glance

COMMON CORE

Lesson		Standards for Mathematical Content
8-1	Similarity in Right Triangles	CC.9-12.G.SRT.4
8-2	Trigonometric Ratios	CC.9-12.G.SRT.6, CC.9-12.G.SRT.7, CC.9-12.G.SRT.8
8-3	Solving Right Triangles	CC.9-12.G.SRT.8
8-4	Angles of Elevation and Depression	CC.9-12.G.SRT.8
8-5	Law of Sines and Law of Cosines	CC.9-12.G.SRT.10(+), CC.9-12.G.SRT.11(+)
8-6	Vectors	CC.9-12.G.SRT.11(+)
	Performance Tasks	
	Assessment Readiness	

CHAPTER 8

Unpacking the Standards

Understanding the standards and the vocabulary terms in the standards will help you know exactly what you are expected to learn in this chapter.

COMMON CORE **CC.9-12.G.SRT.4**

Prove theorems about triangles.

Key Vocabulary

proof *(demostración)* An argument that uses logic to show that a conclusion is true.
theorem *(teorema)* A statement that has been proven.
triangle *(triángulo)* A three-sided polygon.

What It Means For You   Lesson 8-1

You will prove that the altitude to the hypotenuse of a right triangle forms two triangles that are similar to each other and to the original triangle.

EXAMPLE

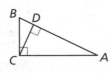

$\triangle ABC \sim \triangle ACD \sim \triangle CBD$

COMMON CORE **CC.9-12.G.SRT.6**

Understand that by similarity, side ratios in right triangles are properties of the angles in the triangle, leading to definitions of trigonometric ratios for acute angles.

Key Vocabulary

similar *(semejantes)* Two figures are similar if they have the same shape but not necessarily the same size.
ratio *(razón)* A comparison of two quantities by division.
right triangle *(triángulo rectángulo)* A triangle with one right (90°) angle.
angle *(ángulo)* A figure formed by two rays with a common endpoint.
trigonometric ratio *(razón trigonométrica)* A ratio of two sides of a right triangle.
acute angle *(ángulo agudo)* An angle that measures greater than 0° and less than 90°.

What It Means For You   Lesson 8-2

All right triangles with the same angle measures are similar, and similar triangles have proportional side lengths. So the measures of the acute angles in a given right triangle determine the ratios of the side lengths of that triangle and of all similar triangles. These ratios, called *trigonometric ratios*, can be used to solve problems.

EXAMPLE

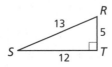

The sine of $\angle R$ is $\dfrac{\text{opposite leg}}{\text{hypotenuse}} = \dfrac{12}{13}$.

The cosine of $\angle R$ is $\dfrac{\text{adjacent leg}}{\text{hypotenuse}} = \dfrac{5}{13}$.

The tangent of $\angle R$ is $\dfrac{\text{opposite leg}}{\text{adjacent leg}} = \dfrac{12}{5}$.

COMMON CORE CC.9-12.G.SRT.8

Use trigonometric ratios and the Pythagorean Theorem to solve right triangles in applied problems.

Key Vocabulary

Pythagorean Theorem *(Teorema de Pitágoras)* If a right triangle has legs of lengths a and b and a hypotenuse of length c, then $a^2 + b^2 = c^2$.

What It Means For You   Lessons 8-2, 8-3, 8-4

You can use trigonometric ratios and the Pythagorean theorem to find unknown angle measures and side lengths in right triangles.

EXAMPLE   **Using Trigonometric Ratios**

Lombard Street is on a hill in San Francisco, California, that rises 45 feet for every 100 feet of horizontal distance. What angle does the hill make with a horizontal line? Round to the nearest degree.

The right triangle below represents the hill. $\angle A$ is the angle the hill makes with a horizontal line.

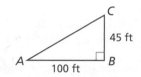

$$m\angle A = \tan^{-1}\left(\frac{45}{100}\right) \approx 27°$$

COMMON CORE CC.9-12.G.SRT.10(+)

Prove the Laws of Sines and Cosines and use them to solve problems.

Key Vocabulary

Law of Sines *(Ley de senos)* For $\triangle ABC$ with side lengths a, b, and c:
$$\frac{\sin A}{a} = \frac{\sin B}{b} = \frac{\sin C}{c}.$$

Law of Cosines *(Ley de cosenos)* For $\triangle ABC$ with side lengths a, b, and c:
$$a^2 = b^2 + c^2 - 2bc\cos A$$
$$b^2 = a^2 + c^2 - 2ac\cos B$$
$$c^2 = a^2 + b^2 - 2ab\cos C$$

What It Means For You   Lesson 8-5

The Law of Sines and the Law of Cosines make it possible to find unknown angle measures and side lengths in any triangle, not just a right triangle, using measures that are known.

EXAMPLE   **Using the Law of Sines**

Find DF to the nearest tenth.

$$\frac{\sin 105°}{18} = \frac{\sin 32°}{DF}$$
$$DF = \frac{18(\sin 32°)}{\sin 105°}$$
$$DF \approx 9.9$$

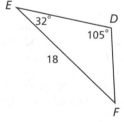

EXAMPLE   **Using the Law of Cosines**

Find BC to the nearest tenth.

$$(BC)^2 = (AB)^2 + (AC)^2 - 2(AB)(AC)\cos A$$
$$(BC)^2 = 14^2 + 9^2 - 2(14)(9)\cos 62°$$
$$(BC)^2 \approx 158.69$$
$$BC \approx 12.6$$

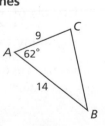

CHAPTER 8

Key Vocabulary

acute angle *(ángulo agudo)* An angle that measures greater than 0° and less than 90°.

angle of depression *(ángulo de depresión)* The angle formed by a horizontal line and a line of sight to a point below.

angle of elevation *(ángulo de elevación)* The angle formed by a horizontal line and a line of sight to a point above.

complementary angles *(ángulos complementarios)* Two angles whose measures have a sum of 90°.

cosine *(coseno)* In a right triangle, the cosine of angle A is the ratio of the length of the leg adjacent to angle A to the length of the hypotenuse. It is the reciprocal of the secant function.

initial point of a vector *(punto inicial de un vector)* The starting point of a vector.

Law of Sines *(Ley de senos)* For $\triangle ABC$ with side lengths a, b, and c, $\dfrac{\sin A}{a} = \dfrac{\sin B}{b} = \dfrac{\sin C}{c}$.

Law of Cosines *(Ley de cosenos)* For $\triangle ABC$ with side lengths a, b, and c:

$$a^2 = b^2 + c^2 - 2bc \cos A$$

$$b^2 = a^2 + c^2 - 2ac \cos B$$

$$c^2 = a^2 + b^2 - 2ab \cos C$$

leg of a right triangle *(cateto de un triángulo rectángulo)* One of the two sides of the right triangle that form the right angle.

Pythagorean Theorem *(Teorema de Pitágoras)* If a right triangle has legs of lengths a and b and a hypotenuse of length c, then $a^2 + b^2 = c^2$.

ratio *(razón)* A comparison of two quantities by division.

right triangle *(triángulo rectángulo)* A triangle with one right (90°) angle.

similar *(semejantes)* Two figures are similar if they have the same shape but not necessarily the same size.

sine *(seno)* In a right triangle, the ratio of the length of the leg opposite angle A to the length of the hypotenuse.

tangent of an angle *(tangente de un ángulo)* In a right triangle, the ratio of the length of the leg opposite angle A to the length of the leg adjacent to angle A.

terminal point of a vector *(punto terminal de un vector)* The endpoint of a vector.

triangle *(triángulo)* A three-sided polygon.

trigonometric ratio *(razón trigonométrica)* A ratio of two sides of a right triangle.

vector *(vector)* A quantity that has both magnitude and direction.

Similarity in Right Triangles
Going Deeper

Essential question: *How can you use triangle similarity to prove the Pythagorean Theorem?*

You have already used the Pythagorean Theorem in earlier courses and in earlier lessons of this book. There are many proofs of this familiar theorem. The proof in this lesson is based on using what you know about similar triangles.

Video Tutor

The Pythagorean Theorem

In a right triangle, the sum of the squares of the lengths of the legs is equal to the square of the length of the hypotenuse.

CC.9–12.G.SRT.4

1 PROOF   **The Pythagorean Theorem**

Given: $\triangle ABC$ is a right triangle with legs of length a and b and hypotenuse of length c.

Prove: $a^2 + b^2 = c^2$

Complete the proof.

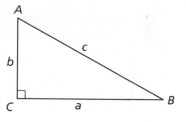

A   Draw a perpendicular from C to the hypotenuse. Label the point of intersection X.

$\angle BXC \cong \angle BCA$ because _____

$\angle B \cong \angle B$ by _____

So, $\triangle BXC \sim \triangle BCA$ by _____

$\angle AXC \cong \angle ACB$ because _____

$\angle A \cong \angle A$ by _____

So, $\triangle AXC \sim \triangle ACB$ by _____

B   Let the lengths of the segments on the hypotenuse be d and e, as shown in the figure.

Use the fact that corresponding sides of similar triangles are proportional to write two proportions.

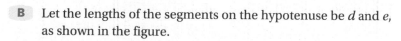

Proportion 1: Because $\triangle BXC \sim \triangle BCA$, $\dfrac{a}{c} = \dfrac{}{a}$.

Proportion 2: Because $\triangle AXC \sim \triangle ACB$, $\dfrac{b}{c} = \dfrac{}{b}$.

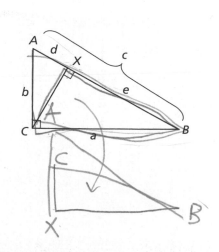

© Houghton Mifflin Harcourt Publishing Company

C Now perform some algebra to complete the proof as follows.

Multiply both sides of Proportion 1 by ac. Write the resulting equation.

_____

Multiply both sides of Proportion 2 by bc. Write the resulting equation.

_____

Adding the above equations gives this: _____

Factor the right side of the equation: _____

Finally, use the fact that $e + d =$ _____ by the Segment Addition

Postulate to rewrite the equation as _____.

REFLECT

1a. Error Analysis A student wrote a proof of the Pythagorean Theorem, as shown below.

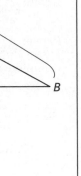

$\triangle BXC \sim \triangle BCA$ and $\triangle BCA \sim \triangle CXA$, so $\triangle BXC \sim \triangle CXA$ by transitivity of similarity.

Since corresponding sides of similar triangles are proportional, $\frac{e}{f} = \frac{f}{d}$ and $f^2 = ed$.

Because $\triangle BXC$ and $\triangle CXA$ are right triangles, $a^2 = e^2 + f^2$ and $b^2 = f^2 + d^2$.

$a^2 + b^2 = e^2 + 2f^2 + d^2$	Add the equations.
$= e^2 + 2ed + d^2$	Substitute.
$= (e + d)^2$	Factor.
$= c^2$	Segment Addition Postulate

Critique the student's proof.

_____

_____

_____

8-1

Additional Practice

Write a similarity statement comparing the three triangles in each diagram.

1.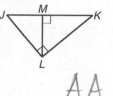

AA
_____
_____

2.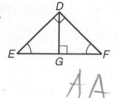

AA
_____
_____

3.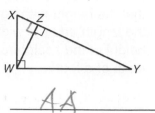

AA
_____
_____

Find the geometric mean of each pair of numbers. If necessary, give the answer in simplest radical form.

4. $\frac{1}{4}$ and 4 1.0625

5. 3 and 75 _____

6. 4 and 18 _____

7. $\frac{1}{2}$ and 9 _____

8. 10 and 14 _____

9. 4 and 12.25 _____

Find x, y, and z.

10.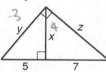

8.06225 7748
_____

11.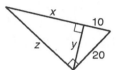

_____

12.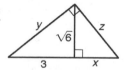

_____

13.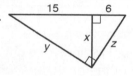

_____

14.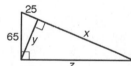

_____

15.

_____

16. The Coast Guard has sent a rescue helicopter to retrieve passengers off a disabled ship. The ship has called in its position as 1.7 miles from shore. When the helicopter passes over a buoy that is known to be 1.3 miles from shore, the angle formed by the shore, the helicopter, and the disabled ship is 90°. Determine what the altimeter would read to the nearest foot when the helicopter is directly above the buoy.

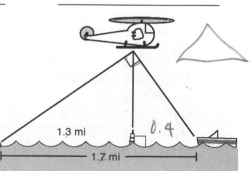

_____

Use the diagram to complete each equation.

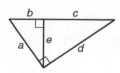

17. $\frac{e}{b} = \frac{\square}{e}$

18. $\frac{d}{b+c} = \frac{\square}{a}$

19. $\frac{d}{\square} = \frac{a}{e}$

$\sqrt{M} = \sqrt{x \cdot y}$

Problem Solving

1. A sculpture is 10 feet long and 6 feet wide. The artist made the sculpture so that the height is the geometric mean of the length and the width. What is the height of the sculpture to the nearest tenth of a foot?

   7.7 ft

2. The altitude to the hypotenuse of a right triangle divides the hypotenuse into two segments that are 12 mm long and 27 mm long. What is the area of the triangle?

   _____

3. The perimeter of △ABC is 56.4 cm, and the perimeter of △GHJ is 14.1 cm. The perimeter of △DEF is the geometric mean of these two perimeters. What is the perimeter of △DEF?

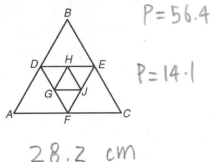

   P = 56.4

   P = 14.1

   28.2 cm

4. Tamara stands facing a painting in a museum. Her lines of sight to the top and bottom of the painting form a 90° angle. How tall is the painting?

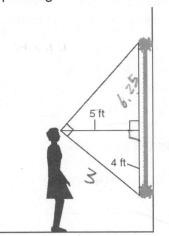

   10.25 ft

Choose the best answer.

5. The altitude to the hypotenuse of a right triangle divides the hypotenuse into two segments that are *x* cm and 4*x* cm, respectively. What is the length of the altitude?

   A 2*x*   C 5*x*

   B 2.5*x*   D 4*x*²

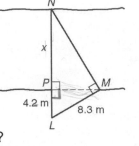

7. A surveyor sketched the diagram at right to calculate the distance across a ravine. What is *x*, the distance across the ravine, to the nearest tenth of a meter?

   A 7.2 m   C 16.4 m

   B 12.2 m   D 64.7 m

6. Jack stands 9 feet from the primate enclosure at the zoo. His lines of sight to the top and bottom of the enclosure form a 90° angle. When he looks straight ahead at the enclosure, the vertical distance between his line of sight and the bottom of the enclosure is 5 feet. What is the height of the enclosure?

   F 16.2 ft   H 23.8 ft

   G 21.2 ft   J 28.8 ft

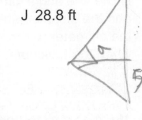

8-2

Trigonometric Ratios
Going Deeper

Essential question: *How do you find the tangent, sine, and cosine ratios for acute angles in a right triangle?*

In this chapter, you will be working extensively with right triangles, so some new vocabulary will be helpful. Given a right triangle, $\triangle ABC$, with a right angle at vertex C, the leg **adjacent** to $\angle A$ is the leg that forms one side of $\angle A$. The leg **opposite** $\angle A$ is the leg that does not form a side of $\angle A$.

CC.9–12.G.SRT.6

1 **EXPLORE**   **Investigating a Ratio in a Right Triangle**

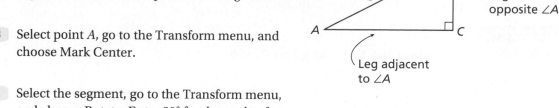

A   Use geometry software to draw a horizontal segment. Label one endpoint of the segment A.

B   Select point A, go to the Transform menu, and choose Mark Center.

C   Select the segment, go to the Transform menu, and choose Rotate. Enter 30° for the angle of rotation. Label the endpoint of the rotation image B.

D   Select point B and the original line segment. Use the Construct menu to construct a perpendicular from B to the segment. Plot a point at the point of intersection and label the point C.

E   Use the Measure menu to measure $\overline{BC}$ and $\overline{AC}$. Then use the Calculate tool to calculate the ratio $\frac{BC}{AC}$.

F   Drag the points and lines to change the size and location of the triangle. Notice what happens to the measurements.

G   Repeat the above steps using a different angle of rotation.

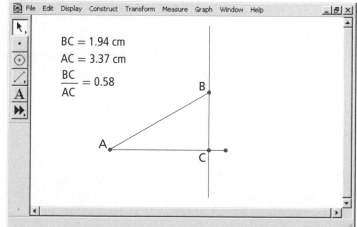

REFLECT

1a.   Compare your findings with those of other students. For an acute angle in a right triangle, what can you say about the ratio of the length of the opposite leg to the length of the adjacent leg?

_____

_____

You may have discovered that in a right triangle the ratio of the length of the leg opposite an acute angle to the length of the leg adjacent to the angle is constant. You can use what you know about similarity to see why this is true.

Consider the right triangles $\triangle ABC$ and $\triangle DEF$, in which $\angle A \cong \angle D$, as shown. By the AA Similarity Criterion, $\triangle ABC \sim \triangle DEF$. This means the lengths of the sides of $\triangle DEF$ are each k times the lengths of the corresponding sides of $\triangle ABC$.

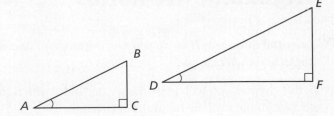

$$\frac{EF}{DF} = \frac{k \cdot BC}{k \cdot AC} = \frac{BC}{AC}$$

This shows that the ratio of the length of the leg opposite an acute angle to the length of the leg adjacent to the angle is constant. This ratio is called the *tangent* of the angle. Thus, the **tangent** of $\angle A$, written tan A, is defined as follows:

$$\tan A = \frac{\text{length of leg opposite } \angle A}{\text{length of leg adjacent to } \angle A} = \frac{BC}{AC}$$

You can find the tangent of an angle using a calculator or by using lengths that are given in a figure, as in the following example.

CC.9–12.G.SRT.6

2 E X A M P L E   Finding the Tangent of an Angle

Find the tangent of $\angle J$ and $\angle K$. Write each ratio as a fraction and as a decimal rounded to the nearest hundredth.

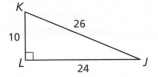

A $\tan J = \dfrac{\text{length of leg opposite } \angle J}{\text{length of leg adjacent to } \angle J} = \dfrac{KL}{JL} = \dfrac{\boxed{}}{24} = \dfrac{\boxed{}}{12} \approx \underline{\quad}$

B $\tan K = \dfrac{\text{length of leg opposite } \angle K}{\text{length of leg adjacent to } \angle K} = \dfrac{JL}{KL} = \dfrac{\boxed{}}{10} = \dfrac{\boxed{}}{5} = \underline{\quad}$

REFLECT

2a. What do you notice about the ratios you wrote for tan J and tan K? Do you think this will always be true for the two acute angles in a right triangle?

_____

_____

_____

2b. Why does it not make sense to ask for the value of tan L?

_____

_____

When you know the length of a leg of a right triangle and the measure of one of the acute angles, you can use the tangent to find the length of the other leg. This is especially useful in real-world problems.

CC.9–12.G.SRT.8

3 E X A M P L E   Solving a Real-World Problem

A long ladder leans against a building and makes an angle of 68° with the ground. The base of the ladder is 6 feet from the building. To the nearest tenth of a foot, how far up the side of the building does the ladder reach?

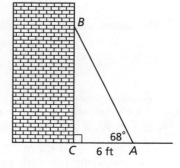

A Write a tangent ratio that involves the unknown length, BC.

$$\tan A = \frac{\text{length of leg opposite } \angle A}{\text{length of leg adjacent to } \angle A} = \frac{BC}{6}$$

Use the fact that $m\angle A = 68°$ to write the equation as $\tan 68° = \frac{BC}{6}$.

B Solve for BC.

$6 \cdot \tan 68° = BC$ Multiply both sides by 6.

$6 \cdot \underline{\hspace{2cm}} = BC$ Use a calculator to find tan 68°. Do not round until the final step of the solution.

$\underline{\hspace{2cm}} \approx BC$ Multiply. Round to the nearest tenth.

So, the ladder reaches about $\underline{\hspace{2cm}}$ up the side of the building.

REFLECT

3a. Why is it best to wait until the final step before rounding? What happens if you round the value of tan 68° to the nearest tenth before multiplying?

_____

_____

3b. A student claims that it is possible to solve the problem using the tangent of $\angle B$. Do you agree or disagree? If it is possible, show the solution. If it is not possible, explain why not.

_____

_____

A **trigonometric ratio** is a ratio of two sides of a right triangle. You have already seen one trigonometric ratio, the tangent. It is also possible to define two additional trigonometric ratios, the sine and the cosine, that involve the hypotenuse of a right triangle.

The **sine** of $\angle A$, written sin A, is defined as follows:

$$\sin A = \frac{\text{length of leg opposite } \angle A}{\text{length of hypotenuse}} = \frac{BC}{AB}$$

The **cosine** of $\angle A$, written cos A, is defined as follows:

$$\cos A = \frac{\text{length of leg adjacent to } \angle A}{\text{length of hypotenuse}} = \frac{AC}{AB}$$

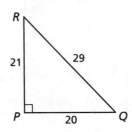

4 EXAMPLE **Finding the Sine and Cosine of an Angle**

Write each trigonometric ratio as a fraction and as a decimal rounded to the nearest hundredth.

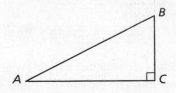

A $\sin R = \dfrac{\text{length of leg opposite } \angle R}{\text{length of hypotenuse}} = \dfrac{PQ}{RQ} = \dfrac{20}{29} \approx 0.69$

B $\sin Q = \dfrac{\text{length of leg opposite } \angle Q}{\text{length of hypotenuse}} = \dfrac{RP}{RQ} = \dfrac{}{29} \approx \underline{\hspace{2cm}}$

C $\cos R = \dfrac{\text{length of leg adjacent to } \angle R}{\text{length of hypotenuse}} = \dfrac{}{} \approx \underline{\hspace{2cm}}$

D $\cos Q = \dfrac{\text{length of leg adjacent to } \angle Q}{\text{length of hypotenuse}} = \dfrac{}{} \approx \underline{\hspace{2cm}}$

REFLECT

4a. What do you notice about the sines and cosines you found? Do you think this relationship will be true for any pair of acute angles in a right triangle? Explain.

_____

_____

_____

You may have discovered a relationship between the sines and cosines of the acute angles in a right triangle. In particular, if $\angle A$ and $\angle B$ are the acute angles in a right triangle, then $\sin A = \cos B$ and $\sin B = \cos A$.

Note that the acute angles in a right triangle are complementary. The above observation leads to a more general fact: the sine of an angle is equal to the cosine of its complement, and the cosine of an angle is equal to the sine of its complement.

CC.9–12.G.SRT.7

5 EXAMPLE   **Using Complementary Angles**

Given that $\sin 57° \approx 0.839$, write the cosine of a complementary angle.

A Find the measure x of an angle that is complementary to a 57° angle.

$x + 57° = 90°$, so $x = $ _____

B Use the fact that the cosine of an angle is equal to the sine of its complement.

$\cos$ _____ ≈ 0.839

Given that $\cos 60° = 0.5$, write the sine of a complementary angle.

C Find the measure y of an angle that is complementary to a 60° angle.

$y + 60° = 90°$, so $y = $ _____

D Use the fact that the sine of an angle is equal to the cosine of its complement.

$\sin$ _____ $= 0.5$

REFLECT

5a. Is it possible to find m$\angle J$ in the figure? Explain.

_____

_____

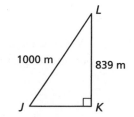

5b. What can you conclude about the sine and cosine of 45° ? Explain.

_____

5c. Is it possible for the sine of an angle to equal 1? Why or why not?

_____

_____

6 EXAMPLE Solving a Real-World Problem

A loading dock at a factory has a 16-foot ramp in front of it, as shown in the figure. The ramp makes an angle of 8° with the ground. To the nearest tenth of a foot, what is the height of the loading dock? How far does the ramp extend in front of the loading dock? (The figure is not drawn to scale, so you cannot measure it to solve the problem.)

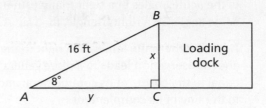

A Find the height x of the loading dock.

$$\sin A = \frac{\text{length of leg opposite } \angle A}{\text{length of hypotenuse}} = \frac{x}{16}, \text{ so } \sin 8° = \frac{x}{16}.$$

Solve the equation for x.

_____

Use a calculator to evaluate the expression, then round.

$x \approx$ _____

So, the height of the loading dock is about _____.

B Find the distance y that the ramp extends in front of the loading dock.

$$\cos A = \frac{\text{length of leg adjacent to } \angle A}{\text{length of hypotenuse}} = \frac{\quad}{\quad}, \text{ so } \cos \underline{\quad\quad} = \frac{\quad}{\quad}.$$

Solve the equation for y.

_____

Use a calculator to evaluate the expression, then round.

$y \approx$ _____

So, the distance the ramp extends in front of the loading dock is about _____.

REFLECT

6a. A student claimed that she found the height of the loading dock by using the cosine. Explain her thinking.

_____

_____

6b. Suppose the owner of the factory decides to build a new ramp for the loading dock so that the new ramp makes an angle of 5° with the ground. How far will this ramp extend from the loading dock? Explain.

_____

_____

S⁰ CA T⁰
H   H A

Find the tangent of ∠A and ∠B. Write each ratio as a fraction and as a decimal rounded to the nearest hundredth.

1.

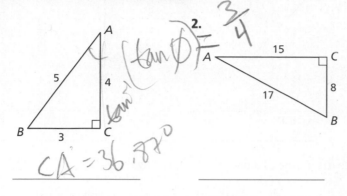

2. 3/4

15

tan∅ =

tan⁻¹

CA = 36.870

3.

tan ∅ = x/y

tan SIN COS

_____   _____   _____

Find the value of x to the nearest tenth.

4.

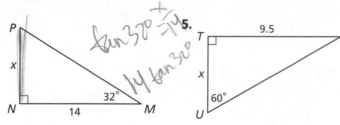

tan 30° = x/14

14 tan 30°

5. 6.

_____   _____   _____

7. A hiker whose eyes are 5.5 feet above ground stands 25 feet from the base of a redwood tree. She looks up at an angle of 71° to see the top of the tree. To the nearest tenth of a foot, what is the height of the tree?

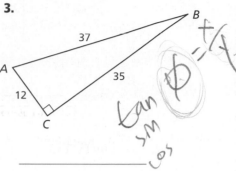

_____

8. **Error Analysis** To find the distance *XY* across a large rock formation, a student stands facing one endpoint of the formation, backs away from it at a right angle for 20 meters, and then turns 55° to look at the other endpoint of the formation. The student's calculations are shown. Critique the student's work.

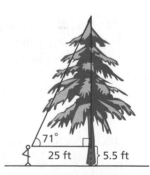

$\tan 55° = \dfrac{20}{XY}$

$XY \cdot \tan 55° = 20$

$XY = \dfrac{20}{\tan 55°} \approx 14.0 \text{ m}$

_____

_____

Find the given trigonometric ratios. Write each ratio as a fraction and as a decimal rounded to the nearest hundredth.

9. sin *R*, cos *R*

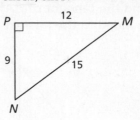

10. cos *D*, cos *E*

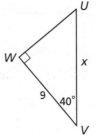

11. sin *M*, sin *N*

_____

_____

_____

_____

_____

_____

12. Given that sin 15° ≈ 0.259, write the cosine of a complementary angle. _____

13. Given that cos 62° ≈ 0.469, write the sine of a complementary angle. _____

Find the value of *x* to the nearest tenth.

14.

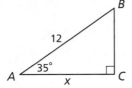

15.

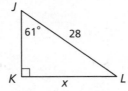

16.

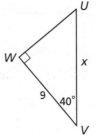

_____

_____

_____

17. You are building a skateboard ramp from a piece of wood that is 3.1 meters long. You want the ramp to make an angle of 25° with the ground. To the nearest tenth of a meter, what is the length of the ramp's base? What is its height?

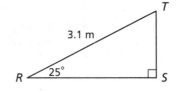

_____

18. Error Analysis Three students were asked to find the value of *x* in the figure. The equations they used are shown at right. Which students, if any, used a correct equation? Explain the other students' errors and then find the value of *x*.

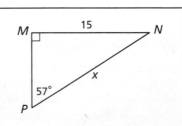

_____

_____

_____

_____

Lee's equation: $\sin 57° = \frac{x}{15}$

Jamila's equation: $\cos 33° = \frac{15}{x}$

Tyler's equation: $\sin 33° = \frac{x}{15}$

Additional Practice

Use the figure for Exercises 1–6. Write each trigonometric ratio as a simplified fraction and as a decimal rounded to the nearest hundredth.

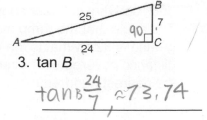

1. sin A

   $\sin A = \frac{7}{24}$, ≈16.96

2. cos B

   $\sin B = \frac{7}{25}$, ≈73.74

3. tan B

   $\tan B \frac{24}{7}$, ≈73.74

4. sin B

   $\sin B \frac{24}{25}$, ≈73.74

5. cos A

   $\cos A \frac{24}{25}$, ≈16.96

6. tan A

   $\tan A \frac{7}{24}$, ≈16.96

Use special right triangles to write each trigonometric ratio as a simplified fraction.

7. sin 30° __0.5__

8. cos 30° __0.87__

9. tan 45° __1__

10. tan 30° __0.58__

11. cos 45° __0.71__

12. tan 60° __1.73__

Use a calculator to find each trigonometric ratio. Round to the nearest hundredth.

13. sin 64° __0.90__

14. cos 58° __0.53__

15. tan 15° __0.27__

Find each length. Round to the nearest hundredth.

16.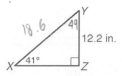

    XZ __13.8__

17.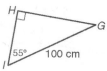

    HI __81.2__

18.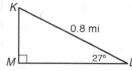

    KM __0.36__

19.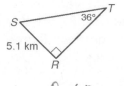

    ST __8.68__

20.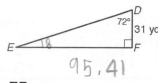

    EF __95.41__

21.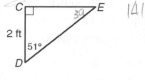

    DE __2.78__

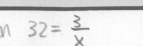
SOH CAHTOA

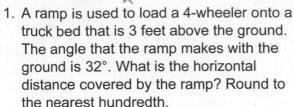

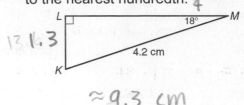
Hypotenuse adjacent
opposite

$\tan 32 = \frac{3}{x}$

1. A ramp is used to load a 4-wheeler onto a truck bed that is 3 feet above the ground. The angle that the ramp makes with the ground is 32°. What is the horizontal distance covered by the ramp? Round to the nearest hundredth.

≈ 4.8 ft

2. Find the perimeter of the triangle. Round to the nearest hundredth.

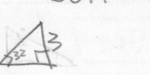
13 16.3

≈ 9.3 cm

3. A right triangle has an angle that measures 55°. The leg adjacent to this angle has a length of 43 cm. What is the length of the other leg of the triangle? Round to the nearest tenth.

≈ 61.4 cm

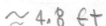
$\tan 55 = \frac{x}{43}$

4. The hypotenuse of a right triangle measures 9 inches, and one of the acute angles measures 36°. What is the area of the triangle? Round to the nearest square inch.

≈ 22 inches^2

5.3 9
7.3
$\sin 36 = \frac{x}{9}$
$\cos 36 = \frac{x}{9}$

Choose the best answer.

5. A 14-foot ladder makes a 62° angle with the ground. To the nearest foot, how far up the house does the ladder reach?

  A 6 ft

  B 7 ft

  C 12 ft

  D 16 ft

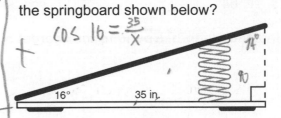
14
14·46
62°
$\sin 62 = \frac{x}{14}$

6. To the nearest inch, what is the length of the springboard shown below?

$\cos 16 = \frac{35}{x}$

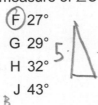
16°   35 in.   74°   90

  F 24 in.   H 38 in.

  G 36 in.   J 127 in.

$\tan 16 = \frac{x}{35}$
$\tan 74 = \frac{35}{x}$

7. What is *EF*, the measure of the longest side of the sail on the model? Round to the nearest inch.

  A 31 in.

  B 35 in.

  C 40 in.

  D 60 in.

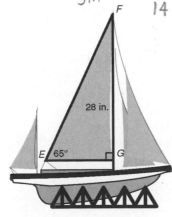
28 in.
E 65° G

$\sin 65 = \frac{28}{x}$

8. Right triangle *ABC* is graphed on the coordinate plane and has vertices at *A*(−1, 3), *B*(0, 5), and *C*(4, 3). What is the measure of ∠*C* to the nearest degree?

  F 27°

  G 29°

  H 32°

  J 43°

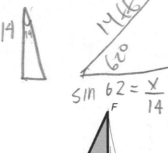
5

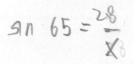
$\cos \theta = \frac{4}{5}$

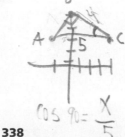
$\cos 90 = \frac{x}{5}$
$\cos \theta = \frac{\sqrt{20}}{5}$

Solving Right Triangles
Going Deeper

Essential question: *How do you find an unknown angle measure in a right triangle?*

In some cases, you may know the value of a
trigonometric ratio and want to know the measure
of the associated angle. For example, in the figure
at right, $\sin A = \frac{7}{14} = \frac{1}{2}$. Because you know that
$\sin 30° = \frac{1}{2}$, you can conclude that $m\angle A = 30°$ and
you can write $\sin^{-1}\left(\frac{1}{2}\right) = 30°$.

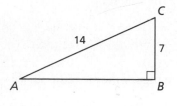

More generally, the **inverse trigonometric ratios** are defined as follows.

Given an acute angle, $\angle A$,

- if $\sin A = x$, then $\sin^{-1} x = m\angle A$.

- if $\cos A = x$, then $\cos^{-1} x = m\angle A$.

- if $\tan A = x$, then $\tan^{-1} x = m\angle A$.

You can use a calculator to evaluate inverse trigonometric ratios.

CC.9–12.G.SRT.8

1 E X A M P L E   **Using an Inverse Trigonometric Ratio**

Find $m\angle J$. Round to the nearest degree.

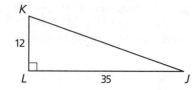

A   Write a trigonometric ratio for $\angle J$.

Since you know the length of the side opposite $\angle J$ and the length
of the side adjacent to $\angle J$, use the tangent ratio.

$\tan J = \dfrac{}{}$

B   Write the inverse trigonometric ratio: $\tan^{-1}\left(\dfrac{}{}\right) = m\angle J$.

Use a calculator to evaluate the inverse trigonometric ratio. Round to the
nearest degree.

So, $m\angle J \approx$ _____.

REFLECT

1a. What other angle measures or side lengths of $\triangle JKL$ can you determine? How?

_____

_____

2 EXAMPLE Using an Inverse Trigonometric Ratio

Find m∠R. Round to the nearest degree.

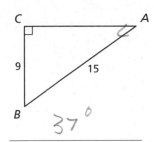

A Write a trigonometric ratio for ∠R.

Since you know the length of the side opposite ∠R and the length of the hypotenuse, use the sine ratio.

$\sin R = \underline{}$

B Write the inverse trigonometric ratio: $\sin^{-1}\left(\underline{}\right) = m\angle R$.

Use a calculator to evaluate the inverse trigonometric ratio. Round to the nearest degree.

So, m∠R ≈ _____.

REFLECT

2a. Find m∠S using inverse cosine. Is the result what you expect? Explain.

_____

_____

PRACTICE

Find m∠A. Round to the nearest degree.   SOH CAHTOA

1.

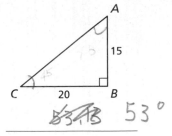

~~63.13~~ 53°

2.

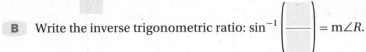

25°

3.

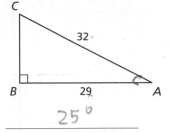

37°

4.

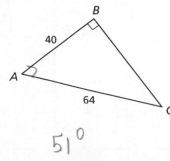

51°

5.

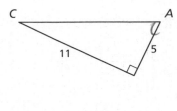

66°

6.

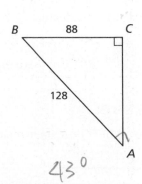

43°

Additional Practice

Use the given trigonometric ratio to determine which angle of the triangle is ∠A.

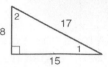

1. $\sin A = \dfrac{8}{17}$ ___1___

2. $\cos A = \dfrac{15}{17}$ ___∠A 1___

3. $\tan A = \dfrac{15}{8}$ ___2___

4. $\sin A = \dfrac{15}{17}$ ___2___

5. $\cos A = \dfrac{8}{17}$ ___2___

6. $\tan A = \dfrac{8}{15}$ ___1___

Use a calculator to find each angle measure to the nearest degree.

7. $\sin^{-1}(0.82)$ _____

8. $\cos^{-1}\left(\dfrac{11}{12}\right)$ _____

9. $\tan^{-1}(5.03)$ _____

10. $\sin^{-1}\left(\dfrac{3}{8}\right)$ _____

11. $\cos^{-1}(0.23)$ _____

12. $\tan^{-1}\left(\dfrac{1}{9}\right)$ _____

Find the unknown measures. Round lengths to the nearest hundredth and angle measures to the nearest degree.

13.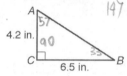

$\angle A = 57$ _____

$\angle B = 33$ _____

14.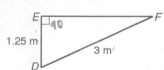

_____

_____

15.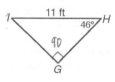

_____

_____

16.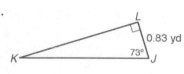

_____

_____

17.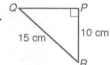

_____

_____

18.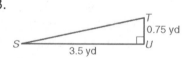

_____

_____

For each triangle, find all three side lengths to the nearest hundredth and all three angle measures to the nearest degree.

19. $B(-2, -4)$, $C(3, 3)$, $D(-2, 3)$

_____

20. $L(-1, -6)$, $M(1, -6)$, $N(-1, 1)$

_____

21. $X(-4, 5)$, $Y(-3, 5)$, $Z(-3, 4)$

_____

Handwritten top notes: SOHCAHTOA $\tan x = \dfrac{28.4}{100}$ $\tan x = \dfrac{2}{5}$ $x = 21.8°$ $\tan x = \dfrac{1}{2}$ $x = 26.6$

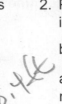

1. A road has a grade of 28.4%. This means that the road rises 28.4 ft over a horizontal distance of 100 ft. What angle does the hill make with a horizontal line? Round to the nearest degree.

   Handwritten: 16°

   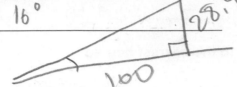

2. Pet ramps for loading larger dogs into vehicles usually have slopes between $\dfrac{2}{5}$ and $\dfrac{1}{2}$. What is the range of angle measures that most pet ramps make with a horizontal line? Round to the nearest degree.

   Handwritten: 21° – 27°

Use the side view of a water slide for Exercises 3 and 4.

Handwritten: $\cos 90 = \dfrac{17}{x}$ $x =$

The ladder, represented by $\overline{AB}$, is 17 feet long.

3. What is the measure of angle A, the angle that the ladder makes with a horizontal line?

   Handwritten: 74°

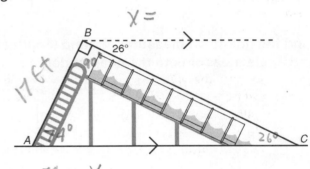

4. What is BC, the length of the slide? Round to the nearest tenth of a foot.

   Handwritten: 59.3 ft

   Handwritten: $\tan 74 = \dfrac{Y}{17}$ $x =$

Choose the best answer.

Handwritten: $\tan x = \dfrac{5}{9}$

5. Janelle sets her treadmill grade to 6%. What is the angle that the treadmill surface makes with a horizontal line? Round to the nearest degree.

   A 3°   C 12°

   B 4°   D 31°

   (A circled)

6. The coordinates of the vertices of $\triangle RST$ are R(3, 3), S(8, 3), and T(8, –6). What is the measures of angle T? Round to the nearest degree.

   F 18°   H 61°

   G 29°   J 65°

   (G circled)

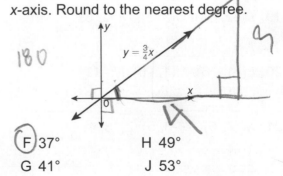

7. If cos A = 0.28, which angle in the triangles below is ∠A?

   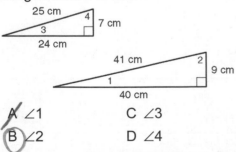

   A ∠1   C ∠3

   B ∠2   D ∠4

   (B circled)

   Handwritten: $\tan x = \dfrac{1}{24}$ $\tan x = \dfrac{24}{7}$ $x =$ $x =$

8. Find the measure of the acute angle formed by the graph of $y = \dfrac{3}{4}x$ and the x-axis. Round to the nearest degree.

   Handwritten: 180

   F 37°   H 49°

   G 41°   J 53°

   (F circled)

   Handwritten: $\tan x = 3/4$

© Houghton Mifflin Harcourt Publishing Company

SOH CAH TOA

Angles of Elevation and Depression
Going Deeper

Video Tutor

Essential question: *How can you use trigonometric ratios to solve problems involving angles of elevation and depression?*

The diagram shows what is meant by **angle of elevation** and **angle of depression**. These angles depend on your viewpoint, but because they are both measured relative to parallel horizontal lines, they are equal in measure.

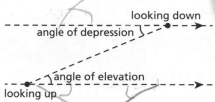

looking down
angle of depression
angle of elevation
looking up

SHCATA

CC.9–12.G.SRT.8

1 EXAMPLE   **Solving a Problem with an Angle of Depression**

A lighthouse keeper at the top of a 120-foot tall lighthouse with its base at sea level spots a small fishing boat. The angle of depression is 5°. What is the horizontal distance between the base of the lighthouse and the boat? Round to the nearest foot.

A   In the space below, sketch sea level, the lighthouse, and the boat. Label the position of the boat along with the bottom and top of the lighthouse.

B   Add lines that show the angle of depression. Use dashing to show the horizontal reference line and a solid line to show the line of sight.

C   Add known and derived degree measures. Add known and unknown lengths to determine a right triangle you can use to answer the question.

$$\text{Tan } 5 = \left(\frac{x}{120}\right)(120)$$

$$\frac{120}{x} = \tan 5$$

$$\frac{120}{\tan 5} = x$$

D   Solve an equation involving a trigonometric ratio to answer the question.

_____

_____

REFLECT

1a. What assumption is made about the lighthouse and sea level?

_____

1b. Explain why the angle of elevation from the boat to the lighthouse is 5°.

_____

1c. Explain how to find the horizontal distance using the other acute angle of the triangle.

_____

2 EXAMPLE   Solving a Problem with an Angle of Elevation

A viewer watches a hot air balloon ascend. The viewer's line of sight forms a 20° angle with the ground when the balloon is 1200 feet above ground. How far is the viewer from where the balloon started its ascent?

A On the diagram at the right, add information that can be used to answer the question.

balloon

viewer

Show the right triangle and the angle of elevation. Label the diagram with known measures and use a variable for the unknown.

B Write an equation you can use in this situation.

_____

C Solve the equation to answer the question. Show your work.

_____

REFLECT

2a. Why is the sine ratio or cosine ratio not used in solving this Example?

_____

PRACTICE

Use a trigonometric ratio to solve. Give answers to the nearest foot.

1. A spectator looks up at an angle of 25° to the top of a building 500 feet away. How tall is the building?

_____

2. A worker looks down from the top of a bridge 240 feet above a river at a barge. The angle of depression is 60°. How far is the barge from the base of the bridge?

_____

3. A helicopter pilot hovers 500 feet above a straight and flat road. The pilot looks down at two cars using 24° and 28° as angles of depression. How far apart are the cars? Explain your work.

_____

_____

4. The string of a flying kite is 360 feet long and makes a 40° angle with the ground. Find the altitude of the kite and the horizontal distance between the kite flyer and the point on the ground directly below the kite.

_____

Additional Practice

Marco breeds and trains homing pigeons on the roof of his building. Classify each angle as an angle of elevation or an angle of depression.

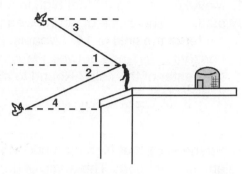

1. ∠1 _____

2. ∠2 _____

3. ∠3 _____

4. ∠4 _____

To attract customers to his car dealership, Frank tethers a large red balloon to the ground. In Exercises 5–7, give answers in feet and inches to the nearest inch. (*Note:* Assume the cord that attaches to the balloon makes a straight segment.)

5. The sun is directly overhead. The shadow of the balloon falls 14 feet 6 inches from the tether. Frank sights an angle of elevation of 67°. Find the height of the balloon.

_____

6. Find the length of the cord that tethers the balloon.

_____

7. The wind picks up and the angle of elevation changes to 59°. Find the height of the balloon.

_____

Lindsey shouts down to Pete from her third-story window.

8. Lindsey is 9.2 meters up, and the angle of depression from Lindsey to Pete is 79°. Find the distance from Pete to the base of the building to the nearest tenth of a meter.

_____

9. To see Lindsey better, Pete walks out into the street so he is 4.3 meters from the base of the building. Find the angle of depression from Lindsey to Pete to the nearest degree.

_____

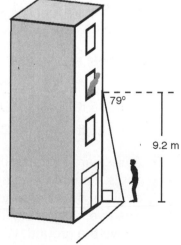

10. Mr. Shea lives in Lindsey's building. While Pete is still out in the street, Mr. Shea leans out his window to tell Lindsey and Pete to stop all the shouting. The angle of elevation from Pete to Mr. Shea is 72°. Tell whether Mr. Shea lives above or below Lindsey.

_____

Problem Solving

(handwritten at top) $\tan 14 = \dfrac{x}{30}$ $x =$ 30 ft 19°

1. Mayuko is sitting 30 feet high in a football stadium. The angle of depression to the center of the field is 14°. What is the horizontal distance between Mayuko and the center of the field? Round to the nearest foot.

(handwritten) 7.5 ft

2. A surveyor 50 meters from the base of a cliff measures the angle of elevation to the top of the cliff as 72°. What is the height of the cliff? Round to the nearest meter.

(handwritten) 154 m

3. Shane is 61 feet high on a ride at an amusement park. The angle of depression to the park entrance is 42°, and the angle of depression to his friends standing below is 80°. How far from the entrance are his friends standing? Round to the nearest foot.

(handwritten) 28 ll ft

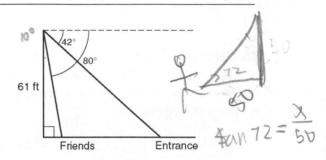

(handwritten beside figure) $\tan 72 = \dfrac{x}{50}$

Choose the best answer.

4. The figure shows a person parasailing. What is *x*, the height of the parasailer, to the nearest foot?

(handwritten) SOH CAHTOA

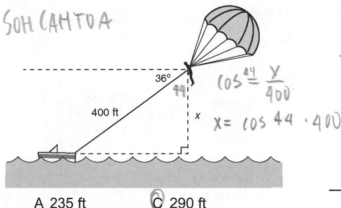

(handwritten) $\cos 44 = \dfrac{y}{400}$ $x = \cos 44 \cdot 400$

  A 235 ft   C 290 ft
  B 245 ft   D 323 ft

5. The elevation angle from the ground to the object to which the satellite dish is pointed is 32°. If *x* = 2.5 meters, which is the best estimate for *y*, the height of the satellite stand?

(handwritten) $\tan \cdot 32 = \dfrac{x}{2.5}$

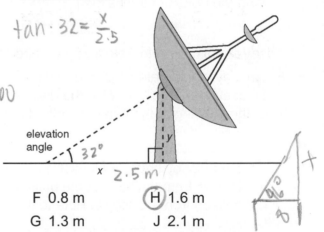

  F 0.8 m   H 1.6 m
  G 1.3 m   J 2.1 m

6. A lifeguard is in an observation chair and spots a person who needs help. The angle of depression to the person is 22°. The eye level of the lifeguard is 10 feet above the ground. What is the horizontal distance between the lifeguard and the person? Round to the nearest foot.

  A 4 ft   C 25 ft
  B 11 ft   D 27 ft

 (handwritten) $\tan 22 = \dfrac{x}{10}$

7. At a topiary garden, Emily is 8 feet from a shrub that is shaped like a dolphin. From where she is looking, the angle of elevation to the top of the shrub is 46°. If she is 5 feet tall, which is the best estimate for the height of the shrub?

  F 6 ft   H 10 ft
  G 8 ft   J 13 ft

Law of Sines and Law of Cosines
Going Deeper

Essential question: *How can you find the side lengths and angle measures of non-right triangles?*

So far, you have used trigonometric ratios with acute angles in right triangles. You can also use trigonometric ratios with the angles in non-right triangles, but you will first need to extend the definitions of the trigonometric ratios as shown below.

Video Tutor

PREP FOR **CC.9–12.G.SRT.10(+)**

1 EXPLORE Extending the Trigonometric Ratios

A First, extend the trigonometric ratios to right triangles on a coordinate plane.

Place right triangle $\triangle ABC$ with acute $\angle A$ on a coordinate plane as shown. Let the coordinates of B be $B(x, y)$. Then the lengths of the legs are x and y.

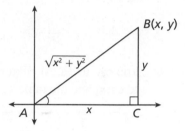

The length of the hypotenuse is $\sqrt{x^2 + y^2}$ by _____.

Now the trigonometric ratios for $\angle A$ can be expressed in terms of x and y.

$$\sin A = \frac{y}{\sqrt{x^2 + y^2}} \qquad \cos A = \frac{\boxed{}}{\sqrt{x^2 + y^2}} \qquad \tan A = \frac{\boxed{}}{\boxed{}}$$

B Next, extend the trigonometric ratios to acute angles in non-right triangles.

Place non-right triangle $\triangle ABC$ with acute $\angle A$ on a coordinate plane as shown. Let the coordinates of B be $B(x, y)$.

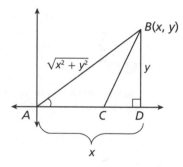

Draw a perpendicular from B to the x-axis, and label the point of intersection D. Then the lengths of the legs in right triangle $\triangle ABD$ are x and y.

The length of the hypotenuse is $\sqrt{x^2 + y^2}$ by _____.

Define the trigonometric ratios for $\angle A$ in terms of x and y by using the side lengths of $\triangle ABD$.

$$\sin A = \frac{y}{\sqrt{x^2 + y^2}} \qquad \cos A = \frac{\boxed{}}{\sqrt{x^2 + y^2}} \qquad \tan A = \frac{\boxed{}}{\boxed{}}$$

© Houghton Mifflin Harcourt Publishing Company

C Finally, extend the trigonometric ratios to obtuse angles in non-right triangles.

Place non-right triangle $\triangle ABC$ with obtuse $\angle A$ on a coordinate plane as shown. Let the coordinates of B be $B(x, y)$.

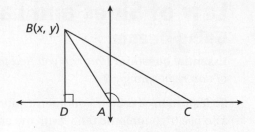

Draw a perpendicular from B to the x-axis, and label the point of intersection D. Then let the "lengths" of the legs in right triangle $\triangle ABD$ be x and y, where it is understood that $x < 0$.

The length of the hypotenuse, $\overline{AB}$, is _____.

Define the trigonometric ratios for $\angle A$ in terms of x and y by using the sides of $\triangle ABD$.

$$\sin A = \frac{y}{\sqrt{x^2 + y^2}} \qquad \cos A = \frac{}{\sqrt{x^2 + y^2}} \qquad \tan A = \frac{}{}$$

D You can use a calculator to find trigonometric ratios for obtuse angles. Use a calculator to complete the table below. Round to the nearest hundredth.

Angle	Sine	Cosine	Tangent
97°			
122°			
165°			

REFLECT

1a. Look for patterns in your table. Make a conjecture about the trigonometric ratios of obtuse angles.

_____

_____

1b. Suppose $\angle A$ is obtuse. How do the definitions of the sine, cosine, and tangent for obtuse angles in Part C above explain why some of these trigonometric ratios are positive and some are negative?

_____

_____

_____

You can use sines and cosines to solve problems that involve non-right triangles. One example is the Law of Sines, which is a relationship that holds for any triangle.

Law of Sines

For $\triangle ABC$, $\frac{\sin A}{a} = \frac{\sin B}{b} = \frac{\sin C}{c}$.

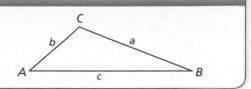

CC.9–12.G.SRT.10(+)

2 PROOF   The Law of Sines

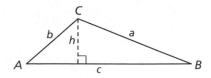

Complete the proof.

Given: $\triangle ABC$
Prove: $\frac{\sin A}{a} = \frac{\sin B}{b} = \frac{\sin C}{c}$

A   Draw an altitude from C to side $\overline{AB}$. Let h be the length of the altitude.

Then $\sin A = \underline{\quad}$ and $\sin B = \underline{\quad}$.

Solve the two equations for h.

$h = \underline{\hspace{3cm}}$ and $h = \underline{\hspace{3cm}}$

B   Write a new equation by setting the right sides of the above equations equal to each other.

$\underline{\hspace{3cm}} = \underline{\hspace{3cm}}$ Substitute.

$\underline{\hspace{3cm}} = \underline{\hspace{3cm}}$ Divide both sides by ab.

Similar reasoning shows that $\frac{\sin A}{a} = \frac{\sin C}{c}$ and $\frac{\sin B}{b} = \frac{\sin C}{c}$.

REFLECT

2a. Write an alternate form of the Law of Sines in which the side lengths are the numerators of the ratios. Explain why it is valid to rewrite the Law of Sines in this way.

_____

_____

You can use the Law of Sines to solve a triangle when you are given the following information.

- Two angle measures and any side length (AAS or ASA information).

- Two side lengths and the measure of a non-included angle (SSA information).

3 **EXAMPLE** **Using the Law of Sines**

Solve the triangle. Round to the nearest tenth.

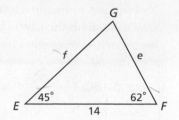

A Find the unknown angle measure.

$m\angle E + m\angle F + m\angle G = 180°$ Triangle Sum Theorem

$45° + 62° + m\angle G = 180°$ Substitute.

$m\angle G = $ _____   Solve for $m\angle G$.

B Use the Law of Sines to find the unknown side length e.

$\dfrac{\sin E}{e} = \dfrac{\sin G}{g}$ Law of Sines

$\dfrac{\sin 45°}{e} = \dfrac{\sin \boxed{}}{\boxed{}}$ Substitute.

_____ $\sin 45° = e \cdot \sin(\underline{})$ Multiply both sides by the
product of the denominators.

$\dfrac{\boxed{} \cdot \sin 45°}{\sin \boxed{}} = e$ Solve for e.

$e \approx $ _____   Use a calculator to evaluate. Round.

C Use the Law of Sines to find the unknown side length f.

$\dfrac{\sin F}{f} = \dfrac{\sin G}{g}$ Law of Sines

$\dfrac{\sin 62°}{f} = \dfrac{\sin \boxed{}}{\boxed{}}$ Substitute.

_____ $\sin 62° = f \cdot \sin(\underline{})$ Multiply both sides by the
product of the denominators.

$\dfrac{\boxed{} \cdot \sin 62°}{\sin \boxed{}} = f$ Solve for f.

$f \approx $ _____   Use a calculator to evaluate. Round.

REFLECT

3a. In Part C, why is it better to write the Law of Sines as $\dfrac{\sin F}{f} = \dfrac{\sin G}{g}$ and use the
known values of $m\angle G$ and g rather than write the Law of Sines as $\dfrac{\sin F}{f} = \dfrac{\sin E}{e}$ and
use the known value of $m\angle E$ and the calculated value of e?

_____

_____

_____

When you are given SSS or SAS information about a triangle, you cannot use the Law of Sines to solve the triangle. However, this information determines a unique triangle, so there should be some way to find the unknown side lengths and angle measures. The Law of Cosines is useful in this case.

Law of Cosines

For $\triangle ABC$,

$a^2 = b^2 + c^2 - 2bc \cos A,$

$b^2 = a^2 + c^2 - 2ac \cos B,$

$c^2 = a^2 + b^2 - 2ab \cos C.$

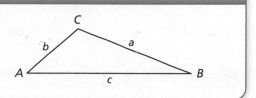

CC.9–12.G.SRT.10(+)

4 PROOF   The Law of Cosines

Complete the proof.

Given: $\triangle ABC$

Prove: $a^2 = b^2 + c^2 - 2bc \cos A$

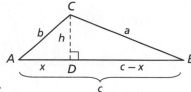

A Draw an altitude $\overline{CD}$ to side $\overline{AB}$. Let h be the length of the altitude.

Let x be the length of $\overline{AD}$. Then $c - x$ is the length of $\overline{DB}$.

In $\triangle ADC$, $\cos A = \dfrac{}{}$ and so $x = $ _____.

Also, by the Pythagorean Theorem, $x^2 + h^2 = $ _____.

B Now consider $\triangle CDB$.

$a^2 = (c - x)^2 + h^2$ Pythagorean Theorem

$a^2 = c^2 - 2cx + x^2 + h^2$ Expand $(c - x)^2$.

$a^2 = c^2 - 2cx + $ _____   Substitute _____ for $x^2 + h^2$.

$a^2 = b^2 + c^2 - 2cx$ Rearrange terms.

$a^2 = b^2 + c^2 - 2c($_____$)$ Substitute _____ for x.

Similar reasoning shows that $b^2 = a^2 + c^2 - 2ac \cos B$ and $c^2 = a^2 + b^2 - 2ab \cos C$.

REFLECT

4a. Explain why the Law of Cosines may be considered a generalization of the Pythagorean Theorem. (*Hint:* When $\angle A$ is a right angle, what happens to the formula $a^2 = b^2 + c^2 - 2bc \cos A$?)

_____

_____

5 EXAMPLE   Using the Law of Cosines

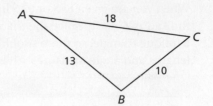

Solve the triangle. Round to the nearest tenth.

A Find the measure of the obtuse angle first.

$b^2 = a^2 + c^2 - 2ac \cos B$	Law of Cosines
$18^2 = 10^2 + 13^2 - 2(10)(13)\cos B$	Substitute.
$\cos B = \dfrac{18^2 - 10^2 - 13^2}{-2(10)(13)}$	Solve for cos B.
$\cos B \approx$ _____	Simplify. Round to four decimal places.
$m\angle B \approx \cos^{-1}($_____$) \approx$ _____	Solve for m$\angle B$.

B Use the Law of Sines to find m$\angle C$.

$\dfrac{\sin C}{c} = \dfrac{\sin B}{b}$	Law of Sines
$\dfrac{\sin C}{13} = \dfrac{\sin \rule{1cm}{0.15mm}}{\rule{1cm}{0.15mm}}$	Substitute.
$\sin C = \dfrac{13 \sin \rule{0.8cm}{0.15mm}}{\rule{0.8cm}{0.15mm}} \approx$ _____	Multiply both sides by 13, and then simplify.
$m\angle C \approx \sin^{-1}($_____$) \approx$ _____	Solve for m$\angle C$.

C Use the Triangle Sum Theorem to find the remaining angle measure.

$m\angle A \approx 180° -$ _____ $-$ _____ $=$ _____

REFLECT

5a. Why is it best to find the measure of the obtuse angle first and then find another angle measure using the Law of Sines?

_____

_____

_____

5b. In Part B, is it possible to find m$\angle C$ without using the Law of Sines? Explain.

_____

PRACTICE

Solve each triangle. Round to the nearest tenth.

$3 \dfrac{\sin 77}{31} = \dfrac{\sin 38°}{X}$

1.
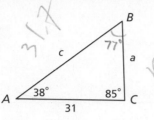

$\overline{c} = 31.7$

$\overline{a} = 19.5$

$\angle B = 77°$

2.
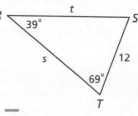

$\overline{t} = 17.8$

$\overline{s} = 18.1$

$\angle s = 72°$

3.
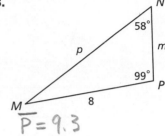

$\overline{P} = 9.3$

$\overline{m} = 3.7$

$\angle M = 23°$

4.
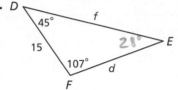

$\overline{d} = 22.6$

$\overline{f} = 30.6$

$\angle E = 28°$

5.
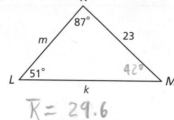

$\overline{K} = 29.6$

$\overline{m} = 19.8$

$\angle M \approx 42°$

6.
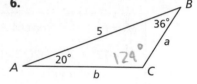

$\overline{a} = 2.1$

$\overline{b} = 3.5$

$\angle C = 124°$

Solve each triangle. Round to the nearest tenth.

7.
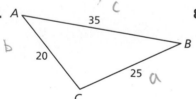

$\angle A = 44.4$

$\angle B = 31$

$\angle C = 104.6$

8.
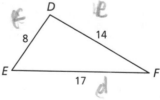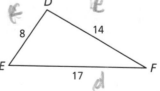

$\angle D = 97.5$

$\angle E = 54.7$

$\angle F = 27.8$

9.
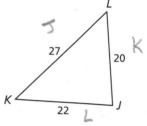

$\angle J = 79.9$

$\angle K = 46.8$

$\angle L = 53.3$

$180 - 75$

Solve each triangle. Round to the nearest tenth.

10.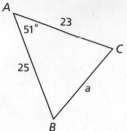

11.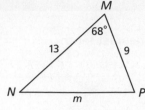

12.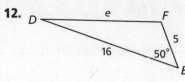

_____   _____   _____

_____   _____   _____

_____   _____   _____

13. Error Analysis A student was asked to find $m\angle A$ in the triangle shown below. The student's work is shown. Determine whether the student made an error and, if so, correct the error.

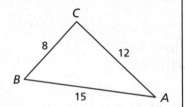

$$a^2 = b^2 + c^2 - 2bc\cos A$$

$$8^2 = 12^2 + 15^2 - 2(12)(15)\cos A$$

$$\cos A = \frac{8^2 - 12^2 - 15^2}{2(12)(15)} \approx -0.8472$$

$$m\angle A \approx \cos^{-1}(-0.8472) \approx 147.9°$$

_____

_____

Additional Practice

Use a calculator to find each trigonometric ratio. Round to the nearest hundredth.

1. sin 111° _____   2. cos 150° _____   3. tan 163° _____

4. sin 92° _____   5. cos 129° _____   6. tan 99° _____

7. sin 170° _____   8. cos 96° _____   9. tan 117° _____

Use the Law of Sines to find each measure. Round lengths to the nearest tenth and angle measures to the nearest degree.

10.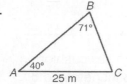

BC _____

11.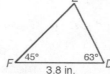

DE _____

12.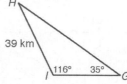

GH _____

13.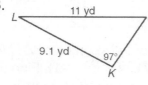

m∠J _____

14.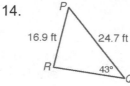

m∠R _____

15.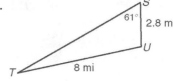

m∠T _____

Use the Law of Cosines to find each measure. Round lengths to the nearest tenth and angle measures to the nearest degree.

16.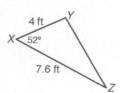

YZ _____

17.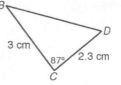

BD _____

18.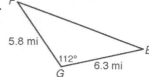

EF _____

19.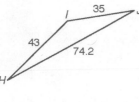

m∠I _____

20.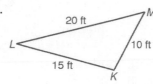

m∠M _____

21.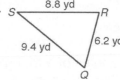

m∠S _____

Problem Solving

1. The map shows three earthquake centers for one week in California. How far apart were the earthquake centers at points *A* and *C* ? Round to the nearest tenth.

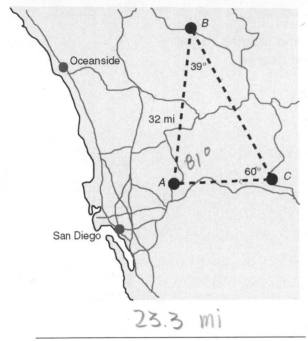

_23.3 mi_

2. A BMX track has a starting hill as shown in the diagram. What is the length of the hill, *WY* ? Round to the nearest tenth.

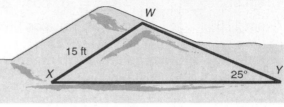

_32.2 ft_

3. The edges of a triangular cushion measure 8 inches, 3 inches, and 6 inches. What is the measure of the largest angle of the cushion to the nearest degree?

_122°_

4. The coordinates of the vertices of △*HJK* are *H*(0, 4), *J*(5, 7), and *K*(9, −1). Find the measure of ∠*H* to the nearest degree.

_34.2°_

Choose the best answer. Use the following information and diagram for Exercises 5 and 6.

To find the distance across a bay, a surveyor locates points *Q*, *R*, and *S* as shown.

5. What is *QR* to the nearest tenth?

   A 8 m   C 41.9 m
   B 35.2 m   D 55.4 m

6. What is m∠*Q* to the nearest degree?

   F 43°   H 67°
   G 49°   J 107°

7. Two angles of a triangle measure 56° and 77°. The side opposite the 56° angle is 29 cm long. What is the measure of the shortest side? Round to the nearest tenth.

   A 23.4 cm   C 32.9 cm
   B 25.6 cm   D 34.1 cm

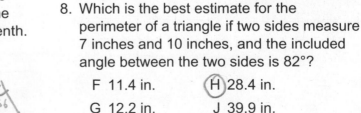

8. Which is the best estimate for the perimeter of a triangle if two sides measure 7 inches and 10 inches, and the included angle between the two sides is 82°?

   F 11.4 in.   H 28.4 in.
   G 12.2 in.   J 39.9 in.

8-6

Vectors

Connection: Applying the Law of Cosines and Law of Sines

Essential question: *How can you apply trigonometry to solve vector problems?*

A **vector** is a quantity that has both direction and magnitude. The **initial point** of a vector is the starting point. The **terminal point** of a vector is the ending point. The vector at right may be named $\overrightarrow{EF}$ or $\vec{v}$.

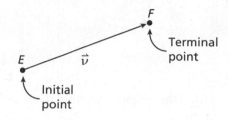

Video Tutor

CC.9–12.G.SRT.11(+)

1 EXAMPLE Solving a Vector Problem

A plane is flying at a rate of 600 mi/h in the direction 60° east of north. There is a 50 mi/h crosswind blowing due north. What is the final direction and speed of the plane?

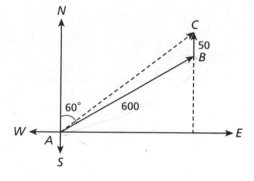

A Represent the situation with vectors. The plane's velocity is represented by $\overrightarrow{AB}$ and the wind's velocity is represented by $\overrightarrow{BC}$.

Explain how to find m∠ABC.

_____

_____

_____

B Use the Law of Cosines with $\triangle ABC$ to find b, the magnitude of $\overrightarrow{AC}$.

$b^2 = a^2 + c^2 - 2ac \cos ABC$ Law of Cosines

$b^2 = 50^2 + 600^2 - 2(50)(600) \cos 120°$ Substitute.

$b^2 =$ _____   Simplify.

$b \approx$ _____   Take the square root. Round to the nearest tenth.

© Houghton Mifflin Harcourt Publishing Company

C Use the Law of Sines with △ABC to find m∠A.

$$\frac{\sin A}{a} = \frac{\sin B}{b}$$ Law of Sines

$$\frac{\sin BAC}{50} = \frac{\sin \boxed{}}{\boxed{}}$$ Substitute.

$$\sin A = \frac{50 \sin \boxed{}}{\boxed{}} \approx \underline{}$$ Multiply both sides by 50, and then simplify.

$$m\angle A \approx \sin^{-1}(\underline{}) \approx \underline{}$$ Solve for m∠A.

D Subtract m∠A from the original direction of the plane to find its final direction.

So, the direction of the plane is about _____ east of north. The speed is about

_____.

REFLECT

1a. Does your answer seem reasonable? Why?

_____

_____

1b. A student claimed that he solved the problem using only the Law of Sines. Explain his method or explain why he must have made an error.

_____

_____

PRACTICE

1. A sailboat sets out from shore, sailing due north at 10 mi/h. There is a crosswind blowing 5 mi/h in the direction 45° east of north. What is the direction and speed of the sailboat?

_____

2. A plane is flying at a rate of 550 mi/h in the direction 40° east of north. There is a 30 mi/h crosswind blowing due south. What is the direction and speed of the plane?

_____

3. A surveyor locates a rock formation 530 meters away. The surveyor turns clockwise 102° and locates a rock formation 410 meters away. To the nearest tenth of a meter, what is the distance between the rock formations?

_____

Additional Practice

Represent the situation with a vector $\overrightarrow{AB}$.

1. An airplane flies at a rate of 575 mi/h due east.

2. A boat travels at a rate of 50 mi/h in the direction 45° east of north.

3. A hiker walks at a rate of 5.5 mi/h in the direction 30° west of south.

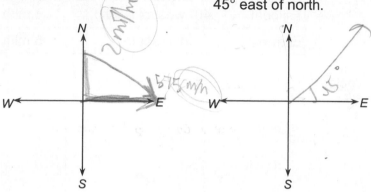

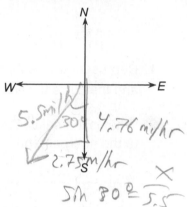

Use the information below for Exercises 4–7. In your answers, round distances to the nearest tenth and directions to the nearest degree.

Becky is researching her family history. She has found an old map that shows the site of her great-grandparents' farmhouse outside of town. To get to the site, Becky walks for 3.1 km at a bearing of 75° east of north. Then she walks 2.2 km due north.

4. Represent the first part of Becky's path with a vector $\overrightarrow{AB}$ and the second part with a vector $\overrightarrow{BC}$.

5. Suppose you want to find the distance and direction Becky could have walked to get directly to the site. Draw the vector you could use to find that information.

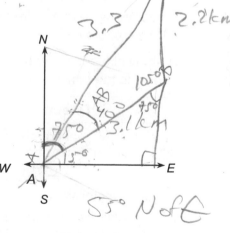

6. Find the distance that Becky would have traveled if she chose the direct route. Explain how you found your answer.

_____

_____

7. Find the direction that Becky would have traveled if she chose the direct route. Explain how you found your answer.

_____

_____

Problem Solving

Use the following information for Exercises 1–3.

A sailboat is traveling under the
conditions shown in the table.

	Direction	Rate
sailboat	40° west of north	8 mi/h
current	due south	5 mi/h

1. Represent the sailboat with a vector $\overrightarrow{AB}$,
   and the current with a vector $\overrightarrow{BC}$.

2. What is the sailboat's final speed? Round
   to the nearest tenth.

_____

3. What is the sailboat's final direction?
   Round to the nearest degree.

_____

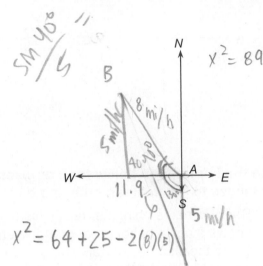

$x^2 = 89$

$x^2 = 64 + 25 - 2(8)(5)$

$x^2 = 89 - 80 \cos 130$

Choose the best answer. Use the following information for Exercises 4–6.

A small plane is flying under the conditions
shown in the table.

	Direction	Rate
plane	24° east of north	200 mi/h
wind	due east	28 mi/h

4. In a vector sketch of the situation, if $\overrightarrow{AB}$
   represents the plane and $\overrightarrow{BC}$ represents
   the wind, what is m∠B?

   A 24°

   (B) 90° – 24° = 66°

   C 90° + 24° = 114°

   B 180° – 24° = 156°

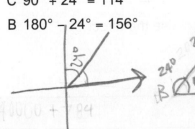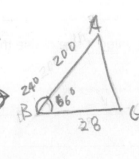

5. What is the plane's final speed to the
   nearest mile per hour?

   F 202 mi/h   H 226 mi/h

   G 213 mi/h   J 45,339 mi/h

6. What is the direction of the plane to the
   nearest degree?

   A 7° east of north

   B 17° east of north

   C 31° east of north

   D 59° east of north

7. A person in a canoe leaves shore at a
   direction of 45° west of north and paddles
   at a constant speed of 2 mi/h. There is a
   current flowing 1.5 mi/h due west. What is
   the canoe's final speed?

   F 1.4 mi/h   H 3.2 mi/h

   G 2.0 mi/h   J 10.5 mi/h

Performance Tasks

⭐ **1.** A bookcase fits diagonally into the corner of a room. The front of the bookcase is 54 inches wide. Each side of the bookcase uses the same amount of wall space.

    a. What angles are formed where the front of the bookcase touches the walls?

    b. Calculate how much wall space each side of the bookcase uses.

$$a^2 + b^2 = 54$$

$$54 \text{ in}$$

$$90° \quad 45°$$

⭐ **2.** The base of a hill is 545 feet above sea level. The top of the hill is 2108 feet above sea level. A straight road from the base of the hill to the top of the hill is 2.5 miles long. What is the angle of elevation from the base of the hill to the top of the hill? Round to the nearest tenth of a degree. Explain how you found your answer.

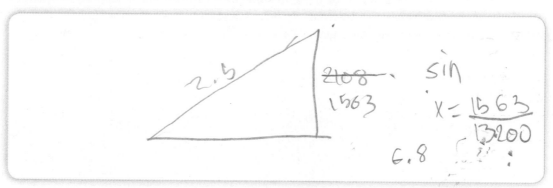

2.5   2108
1563

sin

$$x = \frac{1563}{13200}$$

6.8

⭐ **3.** A farmer is building a pen inside a barn. The pen will be in the shape of a right triangle. The farmer has 14 feet of barn wall to use for one side of the pen and wants another side of the pen to be 15 feet long.

    a. How many different lengths for the third side are possible? Explain.

    b. To the nearest tenth of a foot, find all possible lengths for the third side of the triangle. Show your work.

    c. The farmer wants the area of the pen to be as large as possible. What length should he choose for the third side? Justify your answer.

    d. Find the measure of the acute angles for the triangle you described in part **c**. Round to the nearest degree. Show how you used trigonometric ratios to find the angles.

continued

4. At 6 A.M., the angle of elevation of the sun from the horizon is 0 degrees. At noon, the angle of elevation of the sun is 87 degrees. At some time before noon, a flagpole 50 feet tall casts a shadow 24 feet 9 inches long. To the nearest minute, what is the time? Explain your work. Assume the angle of elevation of the sun increases at a constant rate.

Name _____ Class _____ Date _____

MULTIPLE CHOICE

1. Given that $x°$ is the measure of an acute angle, which of the following is equal to $\sin x°$?

   A. $\cos x°$

   B. $\cos(90 - x)°$

   C. $\sin(90 - x)°$

   D. $\tan x°$

2. Shauntay is proving the Law of Sines. She draws the figure below.

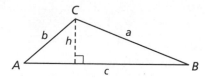

Then she writes $\sin A = \frac{h}{b}$ and $\sin B = \frac{h}{a}$. From this, she concludes that $h = b \sin A$ and $h = a \sin B$. What should she do next?

   F. Draw an altitude from B to side $\overline{AC}$.

   G. Add the equations to get
      $2h = b \sin A + a \sin B$.

   H. Use the Pythagorean Theorem to write
      $c^2 + h^2 = a^2$.

   J. Write $b \sin A = a \sin B$ and then divide both sides by ab.

3. Which is closest to $m\angle S$?

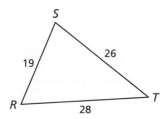

   A. 41°

   B. 64°

   C. 75°

   D. 81°

4. Connor is building a skateboard ramp with the dimensions shown. Which expression can he use to find the height b of the ramp?

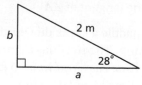

   F. $2 \sin 28°$

   G. $\dfrac{2}{\sin 28°}$

   H. $2 \cos 28°$

   J. $\dfrac{2}{\cos 28°}$

5. In the right triangles shown below, $\angle M \cong \angle Q$. This leads to the observation that $\triangle MNP \sim \triangle QRS$ by the AA Similarity Criterion. Therefore, corresponding sides are proportional, so $\frac{RS}{NP} = \frac{QR}{MN}$ and algebra shows that $\frac{RS}{QR} = \frac{NP}{MN}$. This last proportion is the basis for defining which of the following?

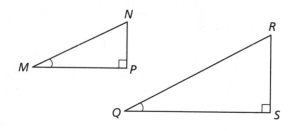

   A. the cosine of $\angle M$

   B. the cosine of $\angle P$

   C. the sine of $\angle M$

   D. the tangent of $\angle M$

6. $\triangle ABC$ and $\triangle PQR$ are similar right triangles, with right angles at B and Q. Which of the following represents the ratio of PQ to QR?

   F. the sine of $\angle C$

   G. the cosine of $\angle C$

   H. the tangent of $\angle C$

   J. the tangent of $\angle A$

7. You paddle a kayak due north at the rate of 2.5 mi/h. The river has a 2 mi/h current that flows due east. You want to find the kayak's actual speed and direction.

   a. In the space below, sketch and label vectors that represent the situation.

   b. Find the kayak's actual speed and direction.

_____

_____

_____

8. To prove the Law of Cosines, you first draw the following figure.

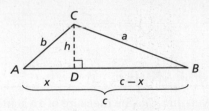

Then you note that $\cos A = \frac{x}{b}$ so $x = b\cos A$ and you note that $x^2 + h^2 = b^2$ by the Pythagorean Theorem. How do you complete the proof that $a^2 = b^2 + c^2 - 2bc\cos A$?

_____

_____

_____

_____

_____

_____

_____

9. A surveyor at point P locates two landmarks, A and B, as shown in the figure. Explain how the surveyor can find the distance between the landmarks to the nearest meter.

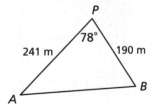

_____

_____

_____

_____

_____

_____

Extending Transformational Geometry

Chapter Focus

A transformation is a function that changes the position, shape, and/or size of a figure. In this unit, you will work with a variety of transformations, but you will focus on transformations that are rigid motions. Rigid motions preserve the size and shape of a figure. As you will see, reflections (flips), translations (slides), and rotations (turns) are all rigid motions. As you work with these transformations, you will learn to draw transformed figures and describe transformations in words and with symbols.

Chapter at a Glance

COMMON CORE

Lesson		Standards for Mathematical Content
9-1	Reflections	CC.9-12.G.CO.2, CC.9-12.G.CO.4, CC.9-12.G.CO.5
9-2	Translations	CC.9-12.G.CO.2, CC.9-12.G.CO.4, CC.9-12.G.CO.5
9-3	Rotations	CC.9-12.G.CO.2, CC.9-12.G.CO.5
9-4	Compositions of Transformations	CC.9-12.G.CO.5
9-5	Symmetry	CC.9-12.G.CO.3
9-6	Tessellations	CC.9-12.G.CO.5
9-7	Dilations	CC.9-12.G.CO.2
	Performance Tasks	
	Assessment Readiness	

CHAPTER 9

Unpacking the Standards

Understanding the standards and the vocabulary terms in the standards will help you know exactly what you are expected to learn in this chapter.

COMMON CORE CC.9-12.G.CO.2

Represent transformations in the plane using, e.g., transparencies and geometry software; describe transformations as functions that take points in the plane as inputs and give other points as outputs. Compare transformations that preserve distance and angle to those that do not (e.g., translation versus horizontal stretch).

Key Vocabulary

transformation (*transformación*) A change in the position, size, or shape of a figure or graph.
theorem (*función*) A relation in which every input is paired with exactly one output.

What It Means For You
Lessons 9-1, 9-2, 9-3, 9-7

Representing transformations as functions of points in the plane lets you use algebra tools such as the Distance Formula to investigate the results of transformations.

EXAMPLE   **Translation and Rotation**

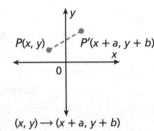

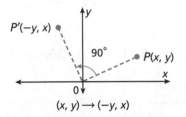

$(x, y) \rightarrow (x + a, y + b)$

The function $P(x, y)$ slides the point (x, y) by a units horizontally and b units vertically to the point $(x + a, y + b)$.

$(x, y) \rightarrow (-y, x)$

The function $P(x, y)$ rotates the point (x, y) by 90° in a counterclockwise direction about the origin to the point $(-y, x)$.

COMMON CORE CC.9-12.G.SRT.1

Verify experimentally the properties of dilations given by a center and a scale factor:

Key Vocabulary

dilation (*dilatación*) A transformation in which the lines connecting every point P with its image P' all intersect at a point C known as the center of dilation, and $\frac{CP'}{CP}$ is the same for every point P other than C; a transformation that changes the size of a figure but not its shape.
scale factor (*factor de escala*) The multiplier used on each dimension to change one figure into a similar figure.

What It Means For You
Lesson 9-7

A dilation of a figure changes the size of the figure, but not its shape. For a polygon, the scale factor indicates the ratio of the side lengths after the dilation to the corresponding lengths before the dilation.

EXAMPLE   **Dilation**

The diagram shows a dilation of $\triangle ABC$ with center of dilation P. The image is $\triangle A'B'C'$.

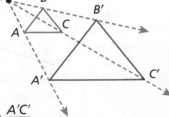

You can show that:

$$\frac{PA'}{PA} = \frac{PB'}{PB} = \frac{PC'}{PC} = \frac{A'B'}{AB} = \frac{B'C'}{BC} = \frac{A'C'}{AC}$$

This ratio is the scale factor of the dilation.

CC.9-12.G.CO.3

Given a rectangle, parallelogram, trapezoid, or regular polygon, describe the rotations and reflections that carry it onto itself.

Key Vocabulary

rectangle *(rectángulo)* A quadrilateral with four right angles.
parallelogram *(paralelogramo)* A quadrilateral with two pairs of parallel sides.
trapezoid *(trapecio)* A quadrilateral with exactly one pair of parallel sides.
regular polygon *(polígono regular)* A polygon that is both equilateral and equiangular.

What It Means For You   Lesson 9-5

The rotations and reflections that carry a figure onto itself determine what kind of symmetry, if any, that the figure has. Reflections determine line symmetry, and rotations determine rotational symmetry.

EXAMPLE   **Line symmetry and rotational symmetry**

  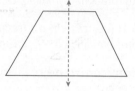

Parallelogram:	**Isosceles Trapezoid:**	**Square:**
no line symmetry	1 line of symmetry	4 lines of symmetry
no rotational symmetry	no rotational symmetry	90° rotational symmetry

---

COMMON CORE **CC.9-12.G.CO.5**

Given a geometric figure and a rotation, reflection, or translation, draw the transformed figure using, e.g., graph paper, tracing paper, or geometry software. Specify a sequence of transformations that will carry a given figure onto another.

Key Vocabulary

rotation *(rotación)* A transformation that rotates or turns a figure about a point called the center of rotation.
reflection *(reflexión)* A transformation that reflects, or "flips," a graph or figure across a line, called the line of reflection, such that each reflected point is the same distance from the line of reflection but is on the opposite side of the line.
translation *(traslación)* A transformation that shifts or slides every point of a figure or graph the same distance in the same direction.

What It Means For You   Lessons 9-1, 9-2, 9-3, 9-4

Rotations, reflections, and translations do not change the shape or size of a figure. You can move a figure onto another of the same size by one or more of these transformations.

EXAMPLE

The diagram represents the whirling pockets of air that form behind a fast-moving truck.

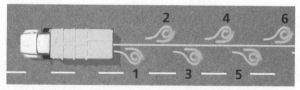

To carry whirl **1** onto whirl **2**: translate right and reflect up.

To carry whirl **2** onto whirl **3**: translate right and reflect down.

In the same way, you can carry each whirl onto the next.

CHAPTER 9

© Houghton Mifflin Harcourt Publishing Company

Key Vocabulary

angle of rotation *(ángulo de rotación)* An angle formed by a rotating ray, called the terminal side, and a stationary reference ray, called the initial side.

angle of rotational symmetry *(ángulo de simetría de rotación)* The smallest angle through which a figure with rotational symmetry can be rotated to coincide with itself.

center of dilation *(centro de dilatación)* The intersection of the lines that connect each point of the image with the corresponding point of the preimage.

center of rotation *(centro de rotación)* The point around which a figure is rotated.

component form *(forma de componente)* The form of a vector that lists the vertical and horizontal change from the initial point to the terminal point.

dilation *(dilatación)* A transformation in which the lines connecting every point P with its image P' all intersect at a point C known as the center of dilation, and $\dfrac{CP'}{CP}$ is the same for every point P other than C; a transformation that changes the size of a figure but not its shape.

line of symmetry *(eje de simetría)* A line that divides a plane figure into two congruent reflected halves.

line symmetry *(simetría axial)* A figure that can be reflected across a line so that the image coincides with the preimage.

reflection *(reflexión)* A transformation that reflects, or "flips," a graph or figure across a line, called the line of reflection, such that each reflected point is the same distance from the line of reflection but is on the opposite side of the line.

rotation *(rotación)* A transformation that rotates or turns a figure about a point called the center of rotation.

scale factor *(factor de escala)* The multiplier used on each dimension to change one figure into a similar figure.

rotational symmetry *(simetría de rotación)* A figure that can be rotated about a point by an angle less than 360° so that the image coincides with the preimage has rotational symmetry.

symmetry *(simetría)* In the transformation of a figure such that the image coincides with the preimage, the image and preimage have symmetry.

tessellation *(teselado)* A repeating pattern of plane figures that completely covers a plane with no gaps or overlaps.

transformation *(transformación)* A change in the position, size, or shape of a figure or graph.

translation *(traslación)* A transformation that shifts or slides every point of a figure or graph the same distance in the same direction.

CHAPTER 9

Reflections
Going Deeper

Essential question: *How do you draw the image of a figure under a reflection?*

One type of rigid motion is a reflection. A *reflection* is a transformation that moves points by flipping them over a line called the *line of reflection*. The figure shows the reflection of quadrilateral *ABCD* across line ℓ. Notice that the pre-image and image are mirror images of each other.

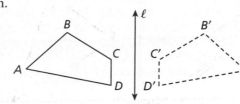

CC.9–12.G.CO.4

1 EXPLORE   **Drawing a Reflection Image**

Follow the steps below to draw the reflection image of each figure.

A

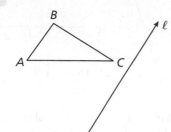

B

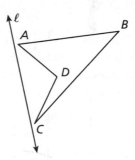

- Place a sheet of tracing paper over the figure. Use a straightedge to help you trace the figure and the line of reflection with its arrowheads.

- Flip the tracing paper over and move it so that line ℓ lies on top of itself.

- Trace the image of the figure on the tracing paper. Press firmly to make an impression on the page below.

- Lift the tracing paper and draw the image of the figure. Label the vertices.

REFLECT

1a. Make a conjecture about the relationship of the line of reflection to any segment drawn between a pre-image point and its image point.

_____

_____

1b. Make a conjecture about the reflection image of a point that lies on the line of reflection.

_____

_____

2 EXAMPLE   Constructing a Reflection Image

Work directly on the figure below and follow the given steps to construct the image of △ABC after a reflection across line *m*.

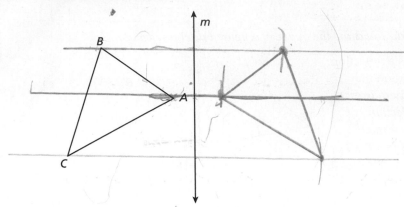

A   Start with point *A*. Construct a perpendicular to line *m* that passes through point *A*.

B   Label the intersection of the perpendicular and line *m* as point *X*.

C   Place the point of your compass on point *X* and open the compass to the distance *XA*. Make an arc to mark this distance on the perpendicular on the other side of line *m*.

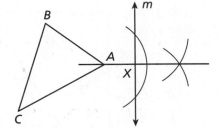

D   Label the point where the arc intersects the perpendicular as point *A'*.

E   Repeat the steps for the other vertices of △ABC. (*Hint:* It may be helpful to extend line *m* in order to construct perpendiculars from points *B* and *C*.)

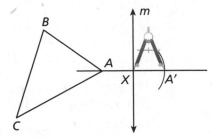

REFLECT

2a.   Reflections have all the properties of rigid motions. For example, reflections preserve distance and angle measure. Explain how you could use a ruler and protractor to check this in your construction.

_____

_____

2b.   What steps should you take to construct the image of a point after a reflection across line *m* if the point lies on line *m*?

_____

_____

The table provides coordinate notation for reflections in a coordinate plane.

Rules for Reflections in a Coordinate Plane	
Reflection across the x-axis	$(x, y) \rightarrow (x, -y)$
Reflection across the y-axis	$(x, y) \rightarrow (-x, y)$
Reflection across the line $y = x$	$(x, y) \rightarrow (y, x)$

CC.9–12.G.CO.2

3 **E X A M P L E** **Drawing a Reflection in a Coordinate Plane**

You are designing a logo for a bank. The left half of the logo is shown. You will complete the logo by reflecting this figure across the y-axis.

A In the space below, sketch your prediction of what the completed logo will look like.

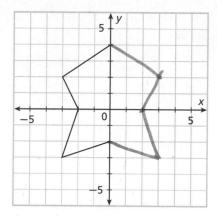

B In the table at right, list the vertices of the left half of the logo. Then use the rule for a reflection across the y-axis to write the vertices of the right half of the logo.

C Plot the vertices of the right half of the logo. Then connect the vertices to complete the logo. Compare the completed logo to your prediction.

Left Half (x, y)	Right Half $(-x, y)$
(0, 4)	(0, 4)
(−3, 2)	(3, 2)
(−2, 0)	

REFLECT

3a. Explain how your prediction compares to the completed logo.

_____

_____

3b. How can you use paper folding to check that you completed the logo correctly?

_____

_____

Use tracing paper to help you draw the reflection image of each figure across line *m*. Label the vertices of the image using prime notation.

1.

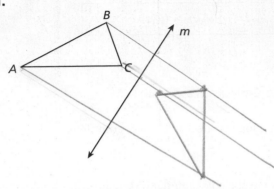

2.

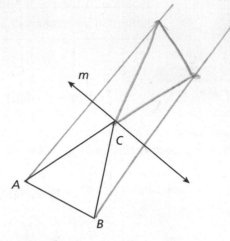

3.

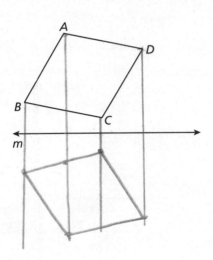

4.

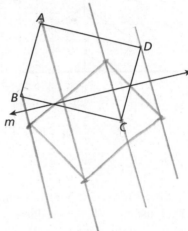

5.

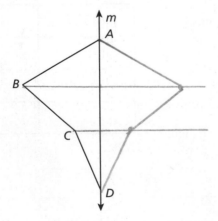

6.

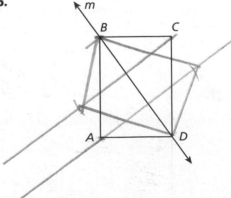

Use a compass and straightedge to construct the reflection image of each figure across line *m*. Label the vertices of the image using prime notation.

7.

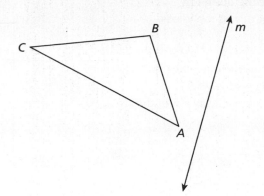

8.

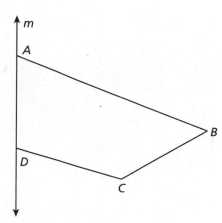

Give the image of each point after a reflection across the given line.

9. $(3, 1)$; *x*-axis

10. $(-6, -3)$; *y*-axis

11. $(0, -2)$; $y = x$

12. $(-4, 3)$; *y*-axis

13. $(5, 5)$; $y = x$

14. $(-7, 0)$; *x*-axis

15. $(-1, 5)$; $y = x$

16. $(10, 6)$; *x*-axis

17. $(8, 0)$; *y*-axis

18. Plot several points on a coordinate plane. Then find their images after a reflection across the line $y = -x$. Use the results to develop a rule for reflection across the line $y = -x$.

19. As the first step in designing a logo, you draw the figure shown in the first quadrant of the coordinate plane. Then you reflect the figure across the *x*-axis. You complete the design by reflecting the original figure and its image across the *y*-axis. Draw the completed design.

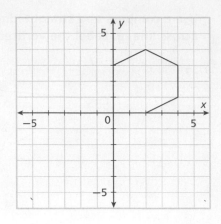

20. When point *P* is reflected across the *y*-axis, its image lies in Quadrant IV. When point *P* is reflected across the line *y* = *x*, its position does not change. What can you say about the coordinates of point *P*?

_____

_____

Additional Practice

Tell whether each transformation appears to be a reflection.

1. 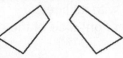 _yes_

2. _no_

3. 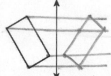 _yes_

4. _no_

Draw the reflection of each figure across the line.

5.

6.

7. Sam is about to dive into a still pool, but some sunlight is reflected off the surface of the water into his eyes. On the figure, plot the exact point on the water's surface where the sunlight is reflected at Sam.

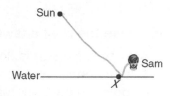

Reflect the figure with the given vertices across the given line.

8. A(4, 4), B(3, −1), C(1, −2); y-axis

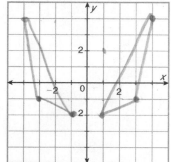

9. D(−4, −1), E(−2, 3), F(−1, 1); y = x

10. P(1, 3), Q(−2, 3), R(−2, 1), S(1, 0); x-axis

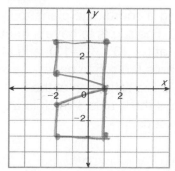

11. J(3, −4), K(1, −1), L(−1, −1), M(−2, −4); y = x

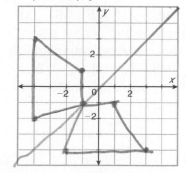

Problem Solving

1. Quadrilateral *JLKM* has vertices *J*(7, 9), *K*(0, –4), *L*(2, 2), and *M*(5, –3). If the figure is reflected across the line $y = x$, what are the coordinates of *M′*?

_____

2. In the drawing, the left side of a structure is shown with its line of reflection. Draw the right side of the structure.

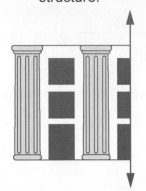

3. The function $y = -3^x$ passes through the point *P*(6, –729). If the graph is reflected across the *y*-axis, what are the coordinates of the image of *P*?

_____

Choose the best answer.

4. A park planner is designing two paths that connect picnic areas *E* and *F* to a point on the park road. Which point on the park road will make the total length of the paths as small as possible? (*Hint:* Use a reflection. What is the shortest distance between two points?)

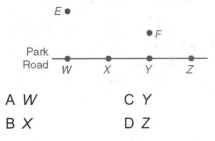

   A *W*   C *Y*

   B *X*   D *Z*

5. △*RST* is reflected across a line so that *T′* has coordinates (1, 3). What are the coordinates of *S′*?

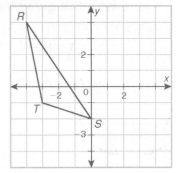

  F (0, 2)   H (2, 0)

  G (0, –2)   J (–2, 0)

6. △*MNP* with vertices *M*(1, 5), *N*(0, –3), and *P*(–2, 2) is reflected across a line. The coordinates of the reflection image are *M′*(7, 5), *N′*(8, –3), and *P′*(10, 2). Over which line was △*MNP* reflected?

  A $y = 2$

  B $x = 2$

  C $y = 4$

  D $x = 4$

7. Sarah is using a coordinate plane to design a rug. The rug is to have a triangle with vertices at (8, 13), (2, –13), and (14, –13). She wants the rug to have a second triangle that is the reflection of the first triangle across the *x*-axis. Which is a vertex of the second triangle?

  F (–13, 14)   H (–2, –13)

  G (–14, 13)   J (2, 13)

Translations
Going Deeper

Essential question: *How do you draw the image of a figure under a translation?*

You have seen that a reflection is one type of rigid motion. A *translation* is another type of rigid motion. A translation slides all points of a figure the same distance in the same direction. The figure shows a translation of a triangle.

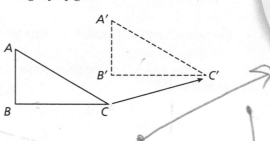

Video Tutor

It is convenient to describe translations using the language of vectors. A **vector** is a quantity that has both direction and magnitude. The **initial point** of a vector is the starting point. The **terminal point** of a vector is the ending point. The vector at right may be named $\overrightarrow{EF}$ or $\vec{v}$.

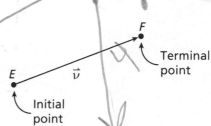

Terminal point

Initial point

A vector can also be named using **component form**, $\langle a, b \rangle$, which specifies the horizontal change a and the vertical change b from the initial point to the terminal point. The component form for $\overrightarrow{PQ}$ is $\langle 5, 3 \rangle$.

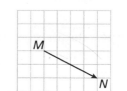

CC.9–12.G.CO.4

1 EXAMPLE Naming a Vector

Name the vector and write it in component form.

A To name the vector, identify the initial point and the terminal point.

The initial point is _____. The terminal point is _____.

The name of the vector is _____.

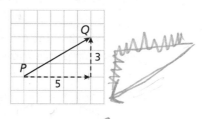

B To write the vector in component form, identify the horizontal change and vertical change from the initial point to the terminal point.

The horizontal change is _____. The vertical change is _____.

The component form for the vector is _____.

REFLECT

1a. Is $\overrightarrow{XY}$ the same as $\overrightarrow{YX}$? Why or why not?

_____

1b. How is $\overrightarrow{AB}$ different from $\overline{AB}$?

_____

© Houghton Mifflin Harcourt Publishing Company

You can use vectors to give a formal definition of *translation*.

A **translation** is a transformation along a vector such that the segment joining a point and its image has the same length as the vector and is parallel to the vector.

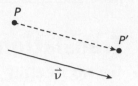

The notation $T_{\vec{v}}(P) = P'$ says that the image of point P after a translation along vector $\vec{v}$ is P'.

CC.9–12.G.CO.5

2 EXAMPLE   **Constructing a Translation Image**

Work directly on the figure below and follow the given steps to construct the image of $\triangle ABC$ after a translation along $\vec{v}$.

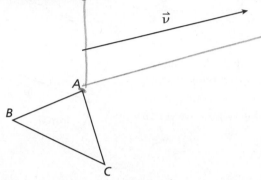

A   Start with point A. Construct a line parallel to $\vec{v}$ that passes through point A.

B   Place the point of your compass on the initial point of $\vec{v}$ and open the compass to the length of $\vec{v}$. Then move the point of the compass to point A and make an arc on the line parallel to $\vec{v}$. Label the intersection of the arc and the line A'.

C   Repeat the process for points B and C to locate points B' and C'.

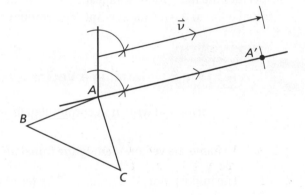

REFLECT

2a.   Why do you begin by constructing a line parallel to $\vec{v}$?

_____

_____

A translation in a coordinate plane can be specified by the component form of a vector. For example, the translation along $\langle 3, -4 \rangle$ moves each point of the coordinate plane 3 units to the right and 4 units down.

More generally, a translation along vector $\langle a, b \rangle$ in the coordinate plane can be written in coordinate notation as $(x, y) \rightarrow (x + a, y + b)$.

3 EXAMPLE   **Drawing a Translation in a Coordinate Plane**

Draw the image of the triangle under a translation
along $\langle -3, 2 \rangle$.

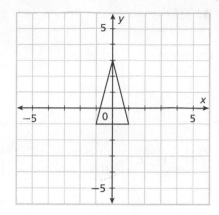

A   Before drawing the image, predict the quadrant
in which the image will lie.

_____

B   In the table below, list the vertices of the triangle.
Then use the rule for the translation to write the
vertices of the image.

Pre-Image (x, y)	Image (x − 3, y + 2)
(0, 3)	
(1, −1)	
(−1, −1)	

C   Plot the vertices of the image. Then connect the vertices to complete the image.
Compare the completed image to your prediction.

REFLECT

3a. Give an example of a translation that would move the original triangle into
Quadrant IV.

_____

3b. Suppose you translate the original triangle along $\langle -10, -10 \rangle$ and then reflect the
image across the *y*-axis. In which quadrant would the final image lie? Explain.

_____

_____

PRACTICE

Name the vector and write it in component form.

1.
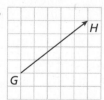

2.
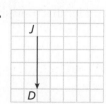

3.
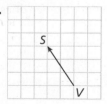

_____   _____   _____

Draw and label a vector with the given name and component form.

4. $\overrightarrow{MP}$; $\langle 3, -1 \rangle$

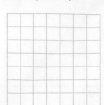

5. $\overrightarrow{CB}$; $\langle -3, 0 \rangle$

6. $\overrightarrow{HK}$; $\langle -5, 4 \rangle$

7. A vector has initial point $(-2, 2)$ and terminal point $(2, -1)$. Write the vector in component form. Then find the magnitude of the vector by using the distance formula.

_____

Use a compass and straightedge to construct the image of each triangle after a translation along $\vec{v}$. Label the vertices of the image.

8.

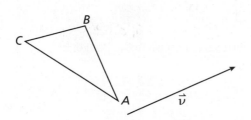

9.

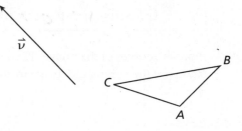

Draw the image of the figure under the given translation.

10. $\langle 3, -2 \rangle$

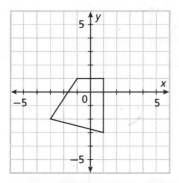

11. $\langle -4, 4 \rangle$

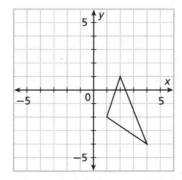

12. a. Use coordinate notation to name the translation that maps $\triangle ABC$ to $\triangle A'B'C'$.

_____

b. What distance does each point move under this translation?

_____

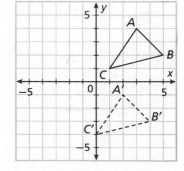

Additional Practice

Tell whether each transformation appears to be a translation.

1.   _yes_

2. _no_

3.  _no_

4. _yes_

Draw the translation of each figure along the given vector.

5.

6.

Translate the figure with the given vertices along the given vector.

7. $A(-1, 3)$, $B(1, 1)$, $C(4, 4)$; $\langle 0, -5 \rangle$

8. $P(-1, 2)$, $Q(0, 3)$, $R(1, 2)$, $S(0, 1)$; $\langle 1, 0 \rangle$

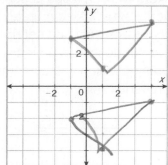

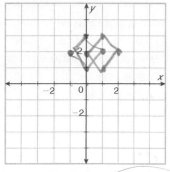

9. $L(3, 2)$, $M(1, -3)$, $N(-2, -2)$; $\langle -2, 3 \rangle$

10. $D(2, -2)$, $E(2, -4)$, $F(1, -4)$, $G(-2, -2)$; $\langle 2, 5 \rangle$

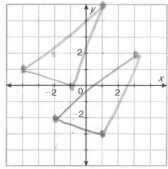

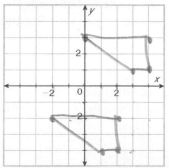

11. A builder is trying to level out some ground with a front-end loader. He picks up some excess dirt at (9, 16) and then maneuvers through the job site along the vectors $\langle -6, 0 \rangle$, $\langle 2, 5 \rangle$, and $\langle 8, 10 \rangle$ to get to the spot to unload the dirt. Find the coordinates of the unloading point. Find a single vector from the loading point to the unloading point.

_(13, 31)_   _⟨4, 15⟩_

Problem Solving

1. A checker player's piece begins at K and, through a series of moves, lands on L. What translation vector represents the path from K to L?

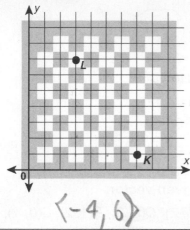

$\langle -4, 6 \rangle$

2. The preimage of M′ has coordinates (−6, 5). What is the vector that translates △MNP to △M′N′P′?

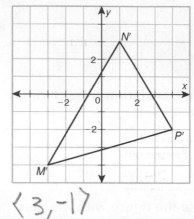

$\langle 3, -1 \rangle$

3. In a quilt pattern, a polygon with vertices (3, −2), (7, −1), (9, −5), and (5, −6) is translated repeatedly along the vector $\langle 4, 5 \rangle$. What are the coordinates of the third polygon in the pattern?

(8,10)

$(11, 8)\ (15, 9)\ (17, 5)\ (13, 4)$

4. A group of hikers walks 2 miles east and then 1 mile north. After taking a break, they then hike 4 miles east and set up camp. What vector describes their hike from their starting position to their camp? Let 1 unit represent 1 mile.

$\langle 6, 1 \rangle$

Choose the best answer.

5. In a video game, a character at (8, 3) moves three times, as described by the translations shown at right. What is the final position of the character after the three moves?

Move 1: $\langle 2, 7 \rangle$
Move 2: $\langle -10, -4 \rangle$
Move 3: $\langle 1, -5 \rangle$

A (−8, 3)   C (1, 1)
B (−7, −2)   D (9, 2)

6. The logo is translated along the vector $\langle 8, 15 \rangle$. What are the coordinates of R′?

(−4, 2)

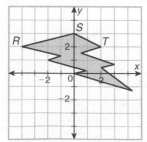

F (4, 17)   H (15, 18)
G (12, 17)   J (11, 19)

7. △DEF is translated so that the image of E has coordinates (0, 3). What is the image of F after this translation?

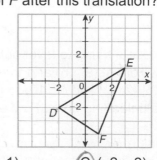

(3, 1)
$\langle -3, 2 \rangle$

A (1, −1)   C (−2, −2)
B (4, −2)   D (−2, 6)

Rotations
Going Deeper

Essential question: *How do you draw the image of a figure under a rotation?*

You have seen that reflections and translations are two types of rigid motions. The final rigid motion you will consider is a *rotation*. A rotation turns all points of the plane around a point called the **center of rotation**. The **angle of rotation** tells you the number of degrees through which points rotate around the center of rotation.

The figure shows a 120° counterclockwise rotation around point *P*. When no direction is specified, you can assume the rotation is in the counterclockwise direction.

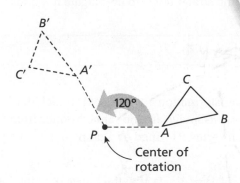

Video Tutor

CC.9–12.G.CO.5

1 EXPLORE Investigating Rotations

Use geometry software to investigate properties of rotations.

A Plot a point and label it *P*.

B Plot three new points. Then use the segment tool to connect the points to make a triangle. Label the vertices *A, B,* and *C*.

C Select point *P*. Go to the Transform menu and choose Mark Center. (This marks *P* as the center of rotation.)

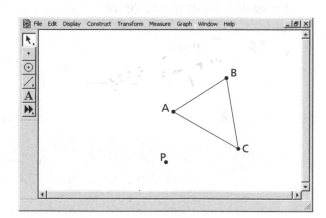

D Select the triangle. Go to the Transform menu and choose Rotate. In the pop-up window, use the default setting of a 90° rotation around point *P*.

E Label the vertices of the image *A′, B′,* and *C′*.

F Select points *P* and *A*. Go to the Measure menu and choose Distance. Do the same for points *P* and *A′*.

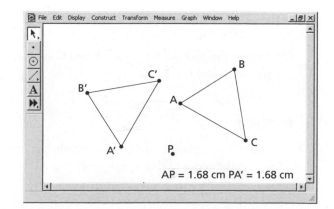

G Modify the shape or location of △*ABC* and notice what changes and what remains the same.

1a. Make a conjecture about the distance of a point and its image from the center of rotation.

_____

1b. What are the advantages of using geometry software rather than tracing paper or a compass and straightedge to investigate rotations?

_____

_____

A **rotation** is a transformation about a point P such that (1) every point and its image are the same distance from P and (2) all angles with vertex P formed by a point and its image have the same measure.

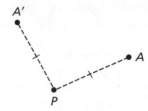

The notation $R_{P,\,m°}(A) = A'$ says that the image of point A after a rotation of $m°$ about point P is A'.

CC.9–12.G.CO.5

2 EXAMPLE **Drawing a Rotation Image**

Work directly on the figure below and follow the given steps to draw the image of $\triangle ABC$ after a 150° rotation about point P.

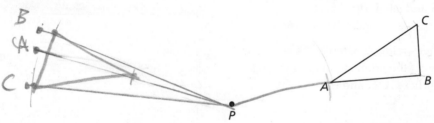

A Draw $\overline{PA}$. Then use a protractor to draw a ray that forms a 150° angle with $\overline{PA}$.

B Use a ruler or compass to mark point A' along the ray so that $PA' = PA$.

C Repeat the process for points B and C to locate points B' and C'.

2a. Would it be possible to draw the rotation image of $\triangle ABC$ using only a compass and straightedge? Why or why not?

_____

_____

The table provides coordinate notation for rotations in a coordinate plane. You can assume that all rotations in a coordinate plane are rotations about the origin. Also, note that a 270° rotation is equivalent to turning $\frac{3}{4}$ of a complete circle.

Rules for Rotations in a Coordinate Plane	
Rotation of 90°	$(x, y) \rightarrow (-y, x)$
Rotation of 180°	$(x, y) \rightarrow (-x, -y)$
Rotation of 270°	$(x, y) \rightarrow (y, -x)$

CC.9–12.G.CO.2

3 EXAMPLE   Drawing a Rotation in a Coordinate Plane

Draw the image of the quadrilateral under a 270° rotation.

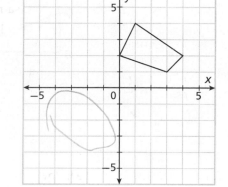

A   Before drawing the image, predict the quadrant in which the image will lie.

_____

B   In the table below, list the vertices of the quadrilateral. Then use the rule for the rotation to write the vertices of the image.

Pre-Image (x, y)	Image (y, −x)
(3, 1)	(1, −3)
(4, 2)	
(1, 4)	
(0, 2)	

C   Plot the vertices of the image. Then connect the vertices to complete the image. Compare the completed image to your prediction.

REFLECT

3a.   What would happen if you rotated the image of the quadrilateral an additional 90° about the origin? Why does this make sense?

_____

_____

3b.   Suppose you rotate the original quadrilateral by 810°. In which quadrant will the image lie? Explain.

_____

_____

Use a ruler and protractor to draw the image of each figure after a rotation about point *P* by the given number of degrees. Label the vertices of the image.

1. 50°

2. 80°

P •

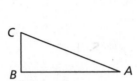

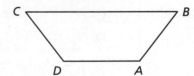

3. 160°

•
P

4. a. Use coordinate notation to write a rule for the rotation that maps △*ABC* to △*A′B′C′*.

_____

b. What is the angle of rotation?

_____

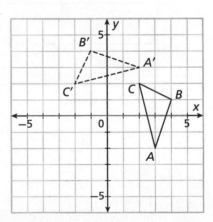

Draw the image of the figure after the given rotation.

5. 180°

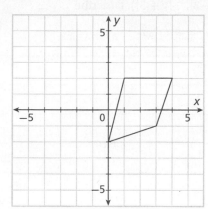

6. 90°

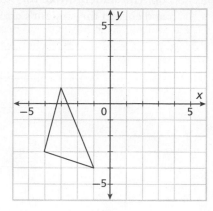

7. 270°

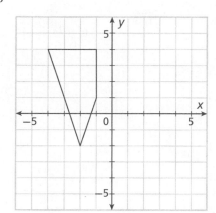

8. 180°

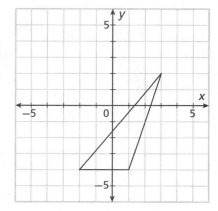

9. a. Reflect △*JKL* across the *x*-axis. Then reflect the image across the *y*-axis. Draw the final image of the triangle and label it △*J′K′L′*.

b. Describe a single rotation that maps △*JKL* to △*J′K′L′*.

_____

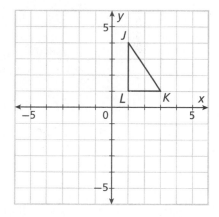

c. Use coordinate notation to show that your answer to part **b** is correct.

_____

_____

_____

d. Describe a composition of reflections that maps △*J′K′L′* back to △*JKL*.

_____

_____

_____

10. Error Analysis A student was asked to use coordinate notation to describe the result of a 180° rotation followed by a translation 3 units to the right and 5 units up. The student wrote this notation: $(x, y) \rightarrow (-[x + 3], -[y + 5])$. Describe and correct the student's error.

_____

_____

_____

_____

_____

Additional Practice

Tell whether each transformation appears to be a rotation.

1. 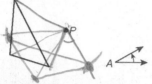 _____no_____

2. _____yes_____

3. _____no_____

4. _____yes_____

Draw the rotation of each figure about point *P* by m∠*A*.

5.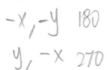

6.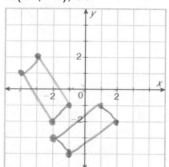

Rotate the figure with the given vertices about the origin using the given angle of rotation.

7. *A*(−2, 3), *B*(3, 4), *C*(0, 1); 90°

−y, x   90

−x, −y   180

y, −x   270

8. *D*(−3, 2), *E*(−4, 1), *F*(−2, −2), *G*(−1, −1); 90°

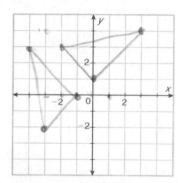

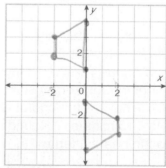

9. *J*(2, 3), *K*(3, 3), *L*(1, −2); 180°

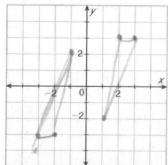

10. *P*(0, 4), *Q*(0, 1), *R*(−2, 2), *S*(−2, 3); 180°

11. The steering wheel on Becky's car has a 15-inch diameter, and its center is at (0, 0). Point *X* at the top of the wheel has coordinates (0, 7.5). To turn left off her street, Becky must rotate the steering wheel by 300°. Find the coordinates of *X* when the steering wheel is rotated. Round to the nearest tenth. (*Hint:* How many degrees short of a full rotation is 300°?) _____(3.75, −6.5)_____

(0, 7.5)

15
7.5

Problem Solving

1. △*ABC* is rotated about the origin so that *A'* has coordinates (−1, −5). What are the coordinates of *B'*?

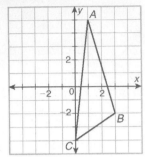

2. A spinning ride at an amusement park is a wheel that has a radius of 21.5 feet and rotates counterclockwise 12 times per minute. A car on the ride starts at position (21.5, 0). What are the coordinates of the car's location after 6 seconds? Round coordinates to the nearest tenth.

_____

3. To make a design, Trent rotates the figure 120° about point *P*, and then rotates that image 120° about point *P*. Draw the final design.

Choose the best answer.

4. Point *K* has coordinates (6, 8). After a counterclockwise rotation about the origin, the image of point *K* lies on the *y*-axis. What are the coordinates of *K'*?

   A (0, 5)   C (0, 8)

   B (0, 6)   D (0, 10)

5. △*NPQ* has vertices *N*(−6, −4), *P*(−3, 4), and *Q*(1, 1). If the triangle is rotated 90° counterclockwise about the origin, what are the coordinates of *P'*?

   F (−4, −3)   H (3, 4)

   G (−4, 3)   J (3, −4)

6. The Top of the World Restaurant in Las Vegas, Nevada, revolves 360° in 1 hour and 20 minutes. A piano that is 38 feet from the center of the restaurant starts at position (38, 0). What are the coordinates of the piano after 15 minutes? Round coordinates to the nearest tenth if necessary.

   A (0, 38)

   B (−38, 0)

   C (14.5, 35.1)

   D (35.1, 14.5)

7. The five blades of a ceiling fan form a regular pentagon. Which clockwise rotation about point *P* maps point *B* to point *D*?

   F 60°   H 120°

   G 72°   J 144°

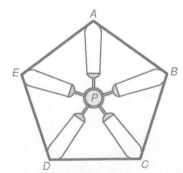

Compositions of Transformations
Going Deeper

Essential question: *How can you use more than one transformation to map one figure onto another?*

Video Tutor

CC.9–12.G.CO.5

1 EXPLORE Investigating Reflections Across Parallel Lines

Use geometry software, or paper and pencil, to investigate properties of a double reflection across parallel lines.

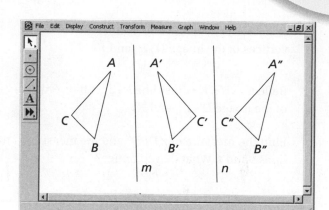

A Draw parallel lines *m* and *n*.

B Draw a triangle to the left of line *m*. Label the vertices *A*, *B*, and *C*. A sample triangle is shown.

C Reflect △*ABC* across line *m*. Label the vertices of the image *A'*, *B'*, and *C'*.

D Reflect △*A'B'C'* across line *n*. Label the vertices of the image *A''*, *B''*, and *C''*.

E Measure the distance between lines *m* and *n*, and lengths *AA''*, *BB''*, and *CC''*. What do you notice?

_____

_____

REFLECT

1a. What do you notice about $\overline{AA''}$, $\overline{BB''}$, and $\overline{CC''}$?

_____

1b. Describe a transformation that maps △*ABC* directly onto △*A''B''C''*.

_____

1c. How is the distance between lines *m* and *n* related to the transformation that maps △*ABC* directly onto △*A''B''C''*?

_____

1d. Is △*ABC* congruent to △*A''B''C''*? Explain.

_____

_____

2 EXPLORE — Investigating Reflections Across Intersecting Lines

Use geometry software, or paper and pencil, to investigate properties of a double reflection across intersecting lines.

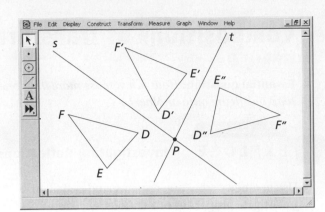

A Draw intersecting lines *s* and *t*. Plot a point where the lines intersect and label it *P*.

B Draw a triangle to the left of line *s*. Label the vertices *D*, *E*, and *F*.

C Reflect △*DEF* across line *s*. Label the vertices of the image *D′*, *E′*, and *F′*.

D Reflect △*D′E′F′* across line *t*. Label the vertices of the image *D″*, *E″*, and *F″*.

E Find the measure of ∠*DPD″* and the measure of the acute angle formed by lines *s* and *t*. What do you notice?

_____

REFLECT

2a. Describe a transformation that maps △*DEF* directly onto △*D″E″F″*.

_____

_____

PRACTICE

Show that △*ABC* is congruent to △*A″B″C″* by drawing two lines of reflection that can be used in a composition to map △*ABC* onto △*A″B″C″*.

1.

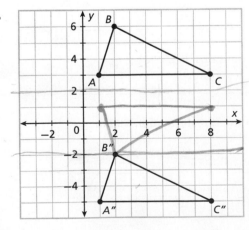

2.

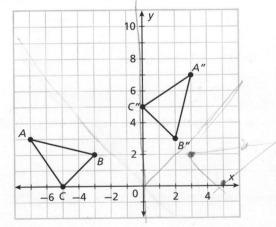

Additional Practice

Draw the result of each composition of isometries.

1. Rotate △XYZ 90° about point P and then translate it along $\bar{v}$.

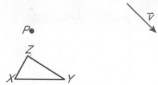

2. Reflect △LMN across line q and then translate it along $\bar{u}$.

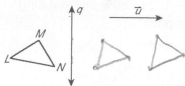

3. ABCD has vertices A(−3, 1), B(−1, 1), C(−1, −1), and D(−3, −1). Rotate ABCD 180° about the origin and then translate it along the vector ⟨1, −3⟩.

−x−y

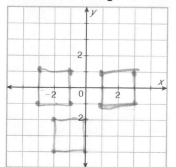

4. △PQR has vertices P(1, −1), Q(4, −1), and R(3, 1). Reflect △PQR across the x-axis and then reflect it across y = x.

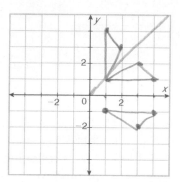

5. Ray draws equilateral △EFG. He draws two lines that make a 60° angle through the triangle's center. Ray wants to reflect △EFG across ℓ_1 and then across ℓ_2. Describe what will be the same and what will be different about the image of △E″F″G″ compared to △EFG.

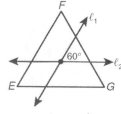

The angles and side length will be the same but it will be rotated a little to the right.

Draw two lines of reflection that produce an equivalent transformation for each figure.

6. translation: STUV → S′T′U′V′

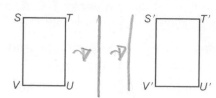

7. rotation with center P: STUV → S′T′U′V′

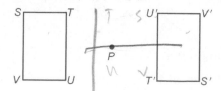

Problem Solving

1. A pattern for a new fabric is made by rotating the figure 90° counterclockwise about the origin and then translating along the vector ⟨−1, 2⟩. Draw the resulting figure in the pattern.

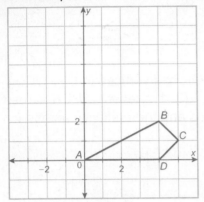

2. △LMN is reflected across the line y = x and then reflected across the y-axis. What are the coordinates of the final image of △LMN?

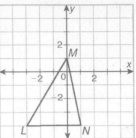

_____

Choose the best answer.

3. △EFG has vertices E(1, 5), F(0, −3), and G(−1, 2). △EFG is translated along the vector ⟨7, 1⟩, and the image is reflected across the x-axis. What are the coordinates of the final image of G?

   A (6, −3)   C (−6, 3)

   B (6, 3)   D (−6, −3)

4. △KLM with vertices K(8, −1), L(−1, −4), and M(2, 3) is rotated 180° about the origin. The image is then translated. The final image of K has coordinates (−2, −3). What is the translation vector?

   F ⟨6, 4⟩   H ⟨−1, −11⟩

   G ⟨6, −4⟩   J ⟨−10, −2⟩

5. To create a logo for new sweatshirts, a designer reflects the letter T across line h. That image is then reflected across line j. Describe a single transformation that moves the figure from its starting position to its final position.

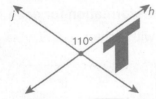

   A translation

   B rotation of 110°

   C rotation of 220°

   D reflection across vertical line

6. Which composition of transformations maps △QRS into Quadrant III?

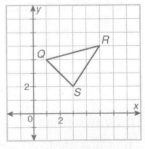

   F Translate along the vector ⟨−6, 4⟩ and then reflect across the y-axis.

   G Rotate by 90° about the origin and then reflect across the x-axis.

   H Reflect across the y-axis and then rotate by 180° about the origin.

   J Translate along the vector ⟨1, 2⟩ and then rotate 90° about the origin.

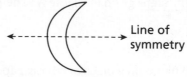

Symmetry
Going Deeper

Essential question: *How do you determine whether a figure has line symmetry or rotational symmetry?*

A figure has **symmetry** if there is a rigid motion such that the image of the figure coincides with the pre-image.

A figure has **line symmetry** (or *reflection symmetry*) if the figure can be reflected across a line so that the image coincides with the pre-image. In this case, the line of reflection is called the **line of symmetry**.

Video Tutor

Line of symmetry

CC.9–12.G.CO.3

1 EXAMPLE **Identifying Line Symmetry**

Determine whether each figure has line symmetry. If so, draw all lines of symmetry. (Use the steps given for figure A to help you with the other figures.)

A Rectangle

- Trace the figure on a piece of tracing paper.

- Check to see if the figure can be folded along a straight line so that one half of the figure coincides with the other half. If so, the figure has line symmetry and the crease represents the line of symmetry.

- The rectangle has line symmetry. The two lines of symmetry are shown.

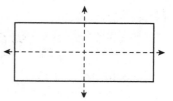

B Isosceles trapezoid

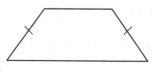

_____

C Parallelogram

_____

D Regular hexagon

_____

REFLECT

1a. What can you say about a triangle that has exactly one line of symmetry? Why?

_____

_____

1b. Does every non-straight angle have a line of symmetry? Explain.

_____

A figure has **rotational symmetry** if the figure can be rotated about a point by an angle greater than 0° and less than or equal to 180° so that the image coincides with the pre-image. The smallest angle that maps the figure onto itself is the **angle of rotational symmetry**.

Angle of rotational symmetry: 90°

CC.9–12.G.CO.3

2 EXAMPLE   Identifying Rotational Symmetry

Determine whether each figure has rotational symmetry. If so, give the angle of rotational symmetry. (Use the steps given for figure A to help you with the other figures.)

A   Rectangle

- Trace the figure on a piece of tracing paper.

- Without moving the tracing paper, firmly place the point of your pencil on the center point of the figure. Rotate the tracing paper. Check to see if the figure coincides with itself after a rotation by an angle less than or equal to 180°.

- The rectangle has rotational symmetry. The angle of rotational symmetry is 180°.

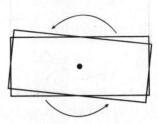

B   Isosceles trapezoid

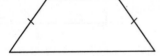

C   Parallelogram

D   Regular hexagon

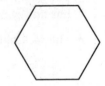

_____   _____   _____

REFLECT

2a. Is it possible for a figure to have rotational symmetry but not have line symmetry? Explain.

_____

_____

2b. Error Analysis A student claims that a figure has rotational symmetry and that the angle of rotational symmetry is 360°. Critique the student's statement.

_____

_____

Determine whether each figure has line symmetry. If so, draw all lines of symmetry.

1. Scalene triangle

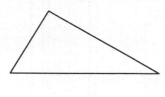

nu

2. Regular pentagon

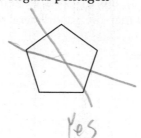

Yes

3. Kite

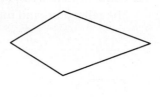

yes

Determine whether each figure has rotational symmetry. If so, give the angle of rotational symmetry.

4. Square

90°
180°

yes

5. Isosceles triangle

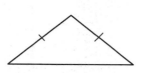

y no

6. Equilateral triangle

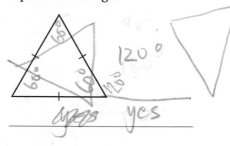

60° 60° 60° 120°

yes yes

In the space provided, sketch a figure that has the given characteristics.

7. Exactly 3 lines of symmetry

8. No line symmetry;
no rotational symmetry

9. Angle of rotational
symmetry: 45°

10. Angle of rotational
symmetry: 180°; no line symmetry

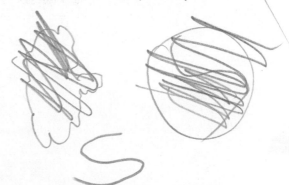

11. A *regular n-gon* is a polygon with n sides where all the sides are congruent and all the angles are congruent. For example, when $n = 4$, the regular n-gon is a square. When $n = 5$, the regular n-gon is a regular pentagon.

a. How many lines of symmetry does a regular n-gon have? _____

b. What is the angle of rotational symmetry for a regular n-gon? _____

12. A quadrilateral has vertices $A(4, 0)$, $B(0, 2)$, $C(-4, 0)$, and $D(0, -2)$. Describe all the reflections and rotations that map the quadrilateral onto itself.

_____

_____

Additional Practice

Tell whether each figure has line symmetry. If so, draw all lines of symmetry.

1.   _____no_____

2.   _____yes_____

3.   _____yes_____

4. Anna, Bob, and Otto write their names in capital letters. Draw all lines of symmetry for each whole name if possible.

Tell whether each figure has rotational symmetry. If so, give the angle of rotational symmetry.

5.   _____no_____

6.   _____180°_____

7. _____ 45° _____

8. This figure shows the Roman symbol for Earth. Draw all lines of symmetry. Give the angle of any rotational symmetry.

_____90°_____

In the space provided, sketch a figure that has the given characteristics.

9. Exactly 1 line of symmetry

10. Angle of rotational symmetry: 180°
    Exactly 2 lines of symmetry

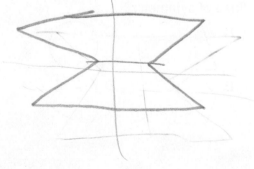

Problem Solving

1. Tell whether the window has line symmetry. If so, draw all the lines of symmetry.

_____

2. Tell whether the quilt block design has rotational symmetry. If so, give the angle of rotational symmetry.

_____

3. Draw an example of a trapezoid that has no line symmetry and no rotational symmetry.

4. The figure is a net of an octahedron. Describe the symmetry of the net.

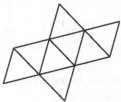

_____

Choose the best answer.

5. Which is a true statement about the figure with vertices $Q(-2, -4)$, $R(0, 1)$, $S(8, 1)$, and $T(5, -4)$?

   A QRST has line symmetry only.

   B QRST has rotational symmetry only.

   C QRST has both line symmetry and rotational symmetry.

   D QRST has neither line symmetry nor rotational symmetry.

6. Suppose you rotate this figure around its center point P by the given angle of rotation. Which angle measure would produce an image that coincides with the original figure?

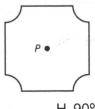

   F 45°   H 90°

   G 60°   J 120°

7. Which of these figures has exactly three lines of symmetry?

   A

   B

   C

   D

8. How many lines of symmetry does a regular pentagon have?

   F 0

   G 4

   H 5

   J 10

Tessellations
Connection: Using Transformations

Essential question: *How can you use transformations to describe tessellations?*

CC.9–12.G.CO.5

1 EXAMPLE Describing Tessellations

Describe the transformations that can map the tessellation onto itself. (The tessellation is made using congruent triangles, and it continues in all directions.)

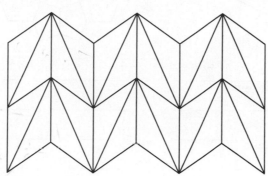

A Look for translations in the tessellation. If there are translations, then number two triangles in the tessellation and complete the statement below.

Triangle _____ maps onto triangle _____ by a translation.

B Look for rotations in the tessellation. If there are rotations, then number two triangles in the tessellation and complete the statement below.

Triangle _____ maps onto triangle _____ by a rotation of _____ about

_____

C Look for reflections in the tessellation. If there are reflections, then number two triangles in the tessellation and complete the statement below.

Triangle _____ maps onto triangle _____ by a reflection.

REFLECT

1a. Describe a sequence of transformations that will map triangle 1 onto triangle 2 in part of the tessellation shown at the right.

_____

_____

_____

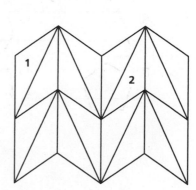

Describe the transformations that can map the tessellation onto itself. (The tessellation is made using congruent figures, and it continues in all directions.) You can number figures in the tessellation if you need to refer to them.

1.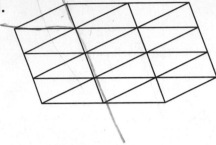

2.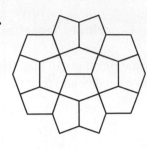

_____   _____
_____   _____
_____   _____
_____   _____
_____   _____

3. Describe a sequence of transformations that will map figure 1 onto figure 2 in the tessellation.

_____
_____
_____

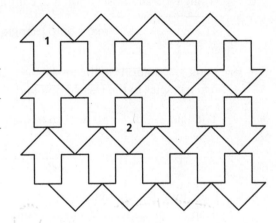

4. Determine whether a concave quadrilateral can be used to create a tessellation. Explain your answer, using a drawing to support your answer.

_____
_____
_____

Additional Practice

1. Describe the transformations that can map the tessellation onto itself. (The tessellation is made of congruent figures, and it continues in all directions.) You may number figures in the tessellation if you need to refer to them.

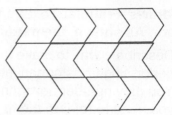

_____

_____

_____

2. The tessellation shown is made from regular hexagons. Your friend says that a tessellation like this one can be made by repeatedly translating a single hexagon. Is there another transformation that can produce the tessellation? Explain. You may number hexagons in the tessellation if you need to refer to them.

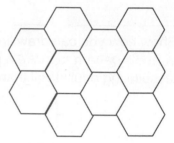

_____

_____

_____

Use the given figure to create a tessellation.

3.

4.

Determine whether the given regular polygon(s) can be used to form a tessellation. If so, draw the tessellation.

5.

no

6.

yes

7.

yes

Problem Solving

Sue draws a regular hexagon and then uses it to create a tessellating pattern. As shown, the pattern also includes equilateral triangles.

1. Describe a way to make the pattern by performing transformations on the hexagon. You may number hexagons in the pattern if you need to refer to them.

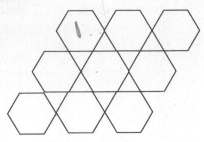

_____

_____

_____

2. Show how you can draw line segments in Sue's pattern to make a pattern of tessellating equilateral triangles.

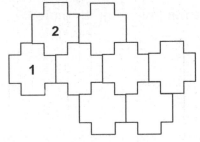

Choose the best answer.

3. In the diagram below, three congruent pentagons form each hexagon. What sequence of transformations could map one of the pentagons onto two other pentagons to form a hexagon?

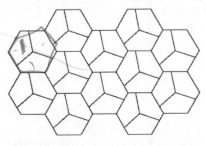

A 60° rotation around a vertex; a reflection

B 120° rotation around a vertex; a reflection

C 60° rotation around a vertex; 60° rotation around the same vertex

D 120° rotation around a vertex; 120° rotation around the same vertex

4. Which is a true statement about figures 1 and 2 in the diagram below?

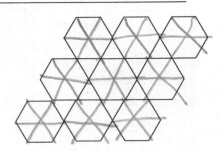

F Figure 1 is mapped onto figure 2 by a translation.

G Figure 1 is mapped onto figure 2 by a rotation.

H Figure 1 is mapped onto figure 2 by a rotation and a translation.

J Figure 1 is mapped onto figure 2 by a reflection.

CHAPTER 9

Performance Tasks

COMMON
CORE

CC.9-12.G.CO.2
CC.9-12.G.CO.3
CC.9-12.G.CO.5
CC.9-12.G.CO.6

1. George is playing a computer game where he has to perform one or more transformations on a rectangular shape so that the shape ends up where it started. He rotates the shape 360° about the origin. For an alternative move, describe one or more reflections that will also transform the rectangle so that it ends up where it started.

2. Jillian makes an enlargement of a photograph that was originally 3 inches by 5 inches. She wants the enlargement to be similar to the original. She is using a piece of paper that is 8.5 inches by 11 inches. What are the dimensions of the greatest dilation she can fit onto this paper?

3. The figure at the right shows part of a quilt.

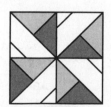

a. Treat the figure as if it were a coordinate plane, with the horizontal line that passes through the center representing the x-axis from −6 to 6 and the vertical line that passes through the center representing the y-axis from −6 to 6. Describe specific transformations you could perform to the top-left square that would create each of the other three squares.

b. Describe any type of symmetry that the figure has. If the individual pieces all had the same pattern, how would the symmetry change?

continued

4. Use the figure at the right to answer the questions.

   a. Does the figure have line symmetry? If so, sketch the figure with its line(s) of symmetry.

   b. Does the figure have rotational symmetry? If so, give the order of the rotational symmetry.

   c. How could you change the shading of the figure so that it has *more* symmetries than it does now? Draw a sketch and identify the symmetries that have been added.

   d. How could you change the shading of the figure so that it has *fewer* symmetries than it does now? Draw a sketch and identify the symmetries that no longer apply.

Name _____ Class _____ Date _____

MULTIPLE CHOICE

1. The function notation $R_{P,60°}(G) = G'$ describes the effect of a rotation. Which point is the image under this rotation?

   A. point R **C.** point G

   B. point P **D.** point G'

2. What is the image of the point $(4, -1)$ after a reflection across the line $y = x$?

   F. $(-4, 1)$ **H.** $(-1, 4)$

   G. $(4, 1)$ **J.** $(1, -4)$

3. Which of the following figures has an angle of rotational symmetry of 90°?

   A.

   B.

   C.

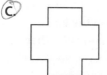

   D.

4. Which transformation is defined as a transformation along a vector such that the segment joining a point and its image has the same length as the vector and is parallel to the vector?

   F. reflection

   G. rigid motion

   H. rotation

   J. translation

5. Keisha wants to use a compass and straightedge to draw the image of $\triangle XYZ$ after a reflection across line m. What should she do first?

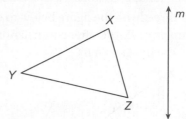

   A. Construct a perpendicular to line m that passes through point X.

   B. Construct a line parallel to line m that passes through point X.

   C. Copy $\angle X$ on the opposite side of line m.

   D. Copy $\overline{XZ}$ on the opposite side of line m.

6. You transform a figure on the coordinate plane using the rigid motion $(x, y) \rightarrow (-y, x)$. What effect does this transformation have on the figure?

   F. 90° rotation about the origin

   G. 180° rotation about the origin

   H. reflection across the x-axis

   J. reflection across the y-axis

7. Which is the best description of the symmetry of this regular pentagon?

   A. has neither line symmetry nor rotational symmetry

   B. has line symmetry but not rotational symmetry

   C. has rotational symmetry but not line symmetry

   D. has both line symmetry and rotational symmetry

8. Which transformation has a definition that is based on perpendicular bisectors?

F. reflection

G. rigid motion

H. rotation

J. translation

CONSTRUCTED RESPONSE

9. Work directly on the figure below to construct the image of $\triangle ABC$ after a translation along $\vec{v}$. Label the image $\triangle A'B'C'$.

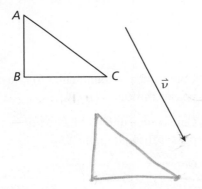

10. $\triangle RST$ has vertices $R(1, -3)$, $S(3, -1)$, and $T(4, -3)$. Give the coordinate notation for a transformation that rotates $\triangle RST$ $180°$ about the origin. Then give the coordinates of the vertices of the image of $\triangle RST$ under this transformation.

$(-x, -y)$

$R(-1,3) \quad S(-3,1) \quad T(-4,3)$

11. In the space below, draw an example of a parallelogram that has exactly two lines of symmetry. Draw the lines of symmetry. Then give the most specific name for the parallelogram you drew.

12. In the space below, draw an example of a trapezoid that does *not* have line symmetry.

13. The Reflected Points on an Angle Theorem states that if two points of an angle are located the same distance from the vertex but on different sides of the angle, then the points are images of each other under a reflection across the line that bisects the angle.

To prove the theorem, you set up the figure shown below, in which line m is the bisector of $\angle ABC$ and $BA = BC$. You want to prove that $r_m(A) = C$.

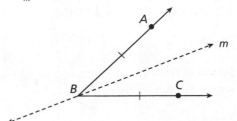

a. You first state that when $\overrightarrow{BA}$ is reflected across line m, its image is $\overrightarrow{BC}$. What postulate or theorem justifies this?

_____

b. You conclude that $r_m(A)$ must lie on $\overrightarrow{BC}$, and you let $r_m(A) = A'$. You also state that $r_m(B) = B$ since B is on the line of reflection. Then you conclude that $BA = BA'$. What reason do you give?

_____

c. It is given that $BA = BC$, so you use the Substitution Property of Equality to conclude that $BA' = BC$. How do you complete the proof?

_____

_____

Extending Perimeter, Circumference, and Area

Chapter Focus

In this unit, you will explore formulas for perimeter, circumference, and area and use one formula to derive another. You will also find perimeter and area of figures in the coordinate plane and apply these skills to finding population density. Finally, you will examine the effects of changing dimensions and revisit probability concepts.

Chapter at a Glance

Lesson		Standards for Mathematical Content
10-1	Developing Formulas for Triangles and Quadrilaterals	CC.9-12.G.SRT.9(+)
10-2	Developing Formulas for Circles and Regular Polygons	CC.9-12.G.GMD.1, CC.9-12.G.MG.1
10-3	Composite Figures	CC.9-12.G.MG.1, CC.9-12.G.MG.3
10-4	Perimeter and Area in the Coordinate Plane	CC.9-12.G.GPE.7, CC.9-12.G.MG.2
10-5	Effects of Changing Dimensions Proportionally	CC.9-12.G.CO.2
10-6	Geometric Probability	CC.9-12.S.CP.1
	Performance Tasks	
	Assessment Readiness	

CHAPTER 10

Unpacking the Standards

Understanding the standards and the vocabulary terms in the standards will help you know exactly what you are expected to learn in this chapter.

CHAPTER 10

COMMON CORE **CC.9-12.A.SSE.1**

Interpret expressions that represent a quantity in terms of its context.

Key Vocabulary

expression *(expresión)* A mathematical phrase that contains operations, numbers, and/or variables.

What It Means For You   Lesson 10-1

A mathematical expression is like a word expression: to understand it, examine the parts that make it up and consider the context it represents.

EXAMPLE

The diagram shows the dimensions of a trapezoidal patio. The expression $\frac{1}{2}(b_1 + b_2)h$ represents the area of the patio.

In the expression $\frac{1}{2}(b_1 + b_2)h$, b_1 and b_2 are the "bases," and h is the perpendicular distance between the bases.

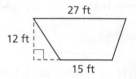

The formula in this context is equivalent to finding the average of the areas of two rectangles with height $h = 12$: one with base $b_1 = 15$ and one with base $b_2 = 27$.

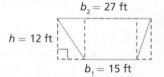

COMMON CORE **CC.9-12.G.MG.3**

Apply geometric methods to solve design problems (e.g., designing an object or structure to satisfy physical constraints or minimize cost…).

What It Means For You   Lesson 10-3

Problems of design, from printing to architecture to engineering, naturally involve geometry. You can use the principles of geometry to find the best possible solution in a particular design context.

EXAMPLE

You can use geometry to solve interior design problems. For example, you can find a room's area to help estimate the cost of carpeting. The dimensions of a room and the location of stairs and windows also affect which furnishings will fit the space and how they might be arranged.

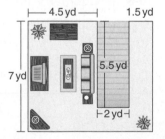

COMMON CORE **CC.9-12.G.GMD.1**

Give an informal argument for the formulas for the circumference of a circle, area of a circle…

Key Vocabulary

formula *(formula)* A literal equation that states a rule for a relationship among quantities.

circle *(círculo)* The set of points in a plane that are a fixed distance from a given point called the center of the circle.

circumference *(circunferencia)* The distance around a circle.

area *(area)* The number of nonoverlapping unit squares of a given size that will exactly cover the interior of a plane figure.

What It Means For You Lesson 10-2

You can arrive at many simple formulas using intuitive, common sense approaches. Doing this helps you both understand and remember a formula much better than just memorizing it as a collection of numbers and symbols.

EXAMPLE

You can cut a circle, which has a circumference of $2\pi r$, into "slices" and reassemble them into a shape that approximates a parallelogram with base πr and height r. Using more slices produces a closer approximation. The parallelogram has area $r(\pi r) = \pi r^2$. The formula for the area of a circle is $A = \pi r^2$.

 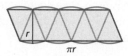

COMMON CORE **CC.9-12.G.GPE.7**

Use coordinates to compute perimeters of polygons and areas of triangles and rectangles, e.g., using the distance formula.

Key Vocabulary

coordinate *(coordenada)* A number used to identify the location of a point. On a coordinate plane, two coordinates are used, called the x-coordinate and the y-coordinate.

perimeter *(perímetro)* The sum of the side lengths of a closed plane figure.

polygon *(polígono)* A closed plane figure formed by three or more segments such that each segment intersects exactly two other segments only at their endpoints and no two segments with a common endpoint are collinear.

Distance Formula *(Fórmula de distancia)* In a coordinate plane, the distance from (x_1, y_1) to (x_2, y_2) is
$$d = \sqrt{(x_2 - x_1)^2 + (y_2 - y_1)^2}.$$

What It Means For You Lessons 10-4, 10-5

Representing geometric figures on a coordinate grid allows you to use both geometric and algebraic tools to analyze and solve geometric problems.

EXAMPLE

You can find the perimeter of the quadrilateral shown using the coordinates of the vertices and the Distance Formula. But because the quadrilateral has an irregular shape, there is no obvious formula for the area.

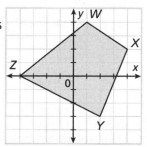

Use the coordinate grid to draw a rectangle passing through each vertex of the quadrilateral. Now you can find the quadrilateral's area by finding the area of the rectangle and subtracting the combined area of triangles a, b, c, and d.

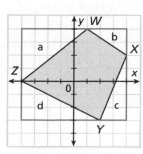

CHAPTER 10

Key Vocabulary

area *(area)* The number of nonoverlapping unit squares of a given size that will exactly cover the interior of a plane figure.

circle *(círculo)* The set of points in a plane that are a fixed distance from a given point called the center of the circle.

circumference *(circunferencia)* The distance around a circle.

complement of an event *(complemento de un suceso)* All outcomes in the sample space that are not in an event E, denoted $\bar{E}$ or E^C.

coordinate *(coordenada)* A number used to identify the location of a point. On a number line, one coordinate is used. On a coordinate plane, two coordinates are used, called the x-coordinate and the y-coordinate. In space, three coordinates are used, called the x-coordinate, the y-coordinate, and the z-coordinate.

Distance Formula *(Fórmula de distancia)* In a coordinate plane, the distance from (x_1, y_1) to (x_2, y_2) is $d = \sqrt{(x_2 - x_1)^2 + (y_2 - y_1)^2}$.

element of a set *(elemento de un conjunto)* An item in a set.

empty set *(conjunto vacío)* A set with no elements

expression *(expresión)* A mathematical phrase that contains operations, numbers, and/or variables.

formula *(formula)* A literal equation that states a rule for a relationship among quantities.

intersection *(intersección de conjuntos)* The intersection of two sets is the set of all elements that are common to both sets, denoted by $\cap$.

perimeter *(perímetro)* The sum of the side lengths of a closed plane figure.

polygon *(polígono)* A closed plane figure formed by three or more segments such that each segment intersects exactly two other segments only at their endpoints and no two segments with a common endpoint are collinear.

rectangle *(rectángulo)* A quadrilateral with four right angles.

set *(conjunto)* A collection of items called elements.

theoretical probability *(probabilidad teórica)* The ratio of the number of equally likely outcomes in an event to the total number of possible outcomes.

triangle *(triángulo)* A three-sided polygon.

union *(unión)* The union of two sets is the set of all elements that are in either set, denoted by $\cup$.

CHAPTER 10

10-1

Developing Formulas for Triangles and Quadrilaterals

Connection: Using Trigonometry

Essential question: *What formula can you use to find the area of a triangle if you know the length of two sides and the measure of an included angle?*

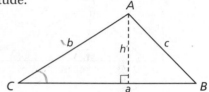

Video Tutor

CC.9–12.G.SRT.9(+)

1 EXPLORE Deriving an Area Formula

A Let $\triangle ABC$ be a triangle with side lengths a, b, and c, as shown.

Draw an altitude from A to side $\overline{BC}$. Let h be the length of the altitude.

Then $\sin C = \dfrac{h}{b}$.

Solving for h shows that $h = \underline{b \sin C}$.

B The standard formula for the area of a triangle is Area $= \frac{1}{2}$ (base)(height).

In $\triangle ABC$, the length of the base is ___ a ___ and the height is ___ h ___.

Area $= \underline{\frac{1}{2}ah}$

Now substitute the expression for h from Part A.

Area $= \underline{\frac{1}{2}ab\sin C}$

REFLECT

1a. Does the area formula work if angle C is a right angle? Explain.

_____

_____

CC.9–12.G.SRT.9(+)

2 EXAMPLE Using the Area Formula

Find the area of the triangle at right to the nearest tenth.

Let the known side lengths be a and b.

Then $a =$ _____ and $b =$ _____.

Let the known angle be C, so $m\angle C =$ _____.

Then Area $= \frac{1}{2} ab \sin C = \frac{1}{2}$ ▢ • ▢ • $\sin($_____$)$.

Use a calculator to evaluate the expression. Then round.

So, the area of the triangle is _____.

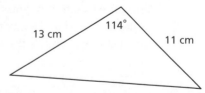

2a. Suppose you double each of the given side lengths in the triangle but keep the measure of the included angle the same. How does the area change? Explain.

_____

_____

PRACTICE

Find the area of each triangle to the nearest tenth.

$\frac{1}{2} ab \sin C$

↑ angle between

2 sides

1.

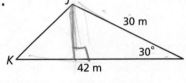

30 m

30°

K   42 m   L

_____

2.

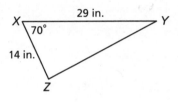

A

12 ft

C

95°   11 ft

B

65.7

_____

3.

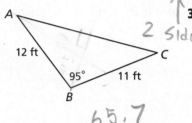

F

2 mm

46° › H

3 mm

G

_____

4.

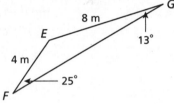

29 in.

X   Y

70°

14 in.

Z

_____

5.

G

8 m

E   13°

4 m

25°

F

_____

6.

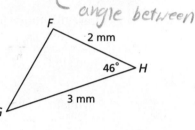

P

45°

19 ft

116°

N

M   14 ft

_____

7. Explain how you can derive a formula for the area of an equilateral triangle with side length *s*. (*Hint:* Use the area formula from this lesson and what you know about the angle measures of an equilateral triangle.)

_____

_____

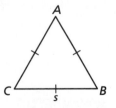

8. The isosceles triangle △*RST* has congruent sides that are 3 cm long, as shown. Write a function for the area *A* of the triangle in terms of m∠*R*. Enter the function in your graphing calculator and use the calculator's table feature to make a conjecture about the measure of ∠*R* that gives the greatest area. What is the maximum area?

_____

_____

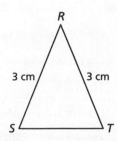

10-1

Additional Practice

Find the area of each triangle. Round your answers to the nearest tenth. (Figures are not drawn to scale.)

1.

½ ab sin C

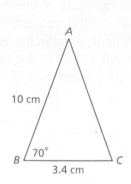

10 cm

70°

B   3.4 cm   C

_____19.5_____

2.

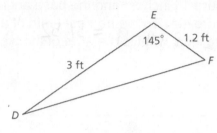

145° 1.2 ft

3 ft

E

F

D

_____1.03_____

Use the information given to find the indicated area. Round your answers to the nearest tenth. (Figures are not drawn to scale.)

3. △GHJ is isosceles.

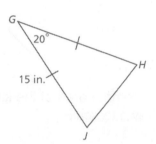

G

20°

15 in.

H

J

Area of △GHJ = _____38.5_____

4. MP is 1.5 times MN.

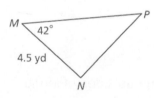

M 42° P

4.5 yd

N

Area of △MNP = _____10.2_____

5. ABCD is a parallelogram.

B   C

6 cm

50°

A   12 cm   D

Area of ABCD = _____55.2_____

6. QRST is a square.

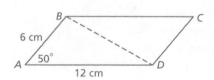

Q   R

U

78°

7 in.

T   5 in.   S

Area of QRSTU = _____42.1_____

© Houghton Mifflin Harcourt Publishing Company

Problem Solving

Write the correct answer.

1. A piece of glass is in the shape of an isosceles triangle. The congruent sides measure 10 inches, and the base angles measure 40°. To the nearest tenth of a square inch, what is the area of the piece of glass?

2. A triangle has side lengths of 5 cm, 7 cm, and 10 cm. The measure of one of its angles is 118.8°. To the nearest tenth of a square centimeter, what is the area of the triangle? (Hint: 118.8° is the largest of the three angle measures.)

Choose the best answer.

3. An ice cream store makes the sign shown at right, which is a semicircle on top of a triangle. What is the approximate area of the sign? (Figure is not drawn to scale.)

   A 314 in.²

   B 338 in.²

   C 495 in.²

   D 652 in.²

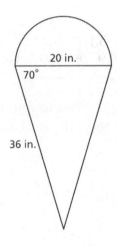

20 in.

70°

36 in.

4. A parallelogram has sides of length 30 centimeters and 18 centimeters. One of its angles measures 58°. Which is the best estimate for the area of the parallelogram?

   F 274.8 cm²

   G 286.2 cm²

   H 457.9 cm²

   J 540.0 cm²

5. What is the approximate area of the kite? (Figure is not drawn to scale.)

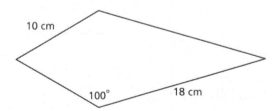

10 cm

100°

18 cm

   A 88 cm²

   B 98 cm²

   C 159 cm²

   D 177 cm²

6. A triangle has side lengths of 4 ft, 8 ft, and 9 ft. The smallest angle measures 26.4°. What is the approximate area of the triangle?

   F 6.7 ft²

   G 8.0 ft²

   H 12.3 ft²

   J 16.0 ft²

Developing Formulas for Circles and Regular Polygons
Connection: Using Trigonometry

Essential question: How do you justify and use the formula for the circumference of a circle?

Video Tutor

Circumference of a Circle Formula

The circumference C of a circle with radius r is given by $C = 2\pi r$.

CC.9–12.G.GMD.1

1 **E X P L O R E**   **Justifying the Circumference Formula**

Plan: To find the circumference of a given circle, consider regular polygons that are inscribed in the circle. As the number of sides of the polygons increases, the perimeter of the polygons gets closer to the circumference of the circle. The first steps of the argument consist of writing an expression for the perimeter of an inscribed n-gon.

Inscribed pentagon   Inscribed hexagon   Inscribed octagon

A Let circle O be a circle with center O and radius r. Inscribe a regular n-gon in circle O and draw radii from O to the vertices of the n-gon.

B Let $\overline{AB}$ be one side of the n-gon. Draw $\overline{OM}$, the segment from O to the midpoint of $\overline{AB}$.

Then $\triangle AOM \cong \triangle BOM$ by _____.

So, $\angle 1 \cong \angle 2$ by _____.

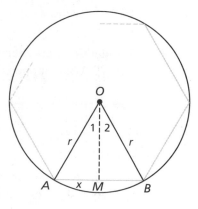

C There are _____ triangles, all congruent to $\triangle AOB$, that surround point O and fill the n-gon.

Therefore, m$\angle AOB$ = _____ and m$\angle 1$ = _____.

D Since $\angle OMA \cong \angle OMB$ by CPCTC, and $\angle OMA$ and $\angle OMB$ form a linear pair, these angles are supplementary and must have measures of 90°. So, $\triangle AOM$ and $\triangle BOM$ are right triangles.

In $\triangle AOM$, $\sin \angle 1 = \dfrac{\text{length of opposite leg}}{\text{length of hypotenuse}} = \dfrac{x}{r}$.

So, $x = r \sin \angle 1$ and substituting the expression for m$\angle 1$ from above gives

$x = r \sin (_____)$

E Now express the perimeter of the n-gon in terms of x.

The length of $\overline{AB}$ is $2x$, since _____.

This means the perimeter of the n-gon is _____.

Substitute the expression for x from Step D.

Then the perimeter is given by the expression _____.

F Your expression for the perimeter of the n-gon should include $n \sin\left(\frac{180°}{n}\right)$ as a factor. Use a calculator, as follows, to find out what happens to the value of this expression as n gets larger.

- Enter the expression $x \sin\left(\frac{180}{x}\right)$ as Y_1.
- Go to the Table Setup menu and enter the values shown at right.
- View a table for the function.
- Use the arrow keys to scroll down.

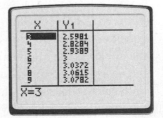

What happens to the value of $n \sin\left(\frac{180°}{n}\right)$ as n gets larger?

_____

G Consider the expression you wrote for the perimeter of the n-gon at the end of Step E. What happens to the value of this expression as n gets larger?

_____

REFLECT

1a. When n is very large, does the perimeter of the n-gon ever equal the circumference of the circle? Why or why not?

_____

_____

1b. How does the above argument justify the formula $C = 2\pi r$?

_____

_____

_____

2 EXAMPLE   Finding the Circumference of a Circle

Find the circumference of circle O. Round to the nearest tenth.

A Find the radius. The diameter is twice the radius, so $r = $ _____.

B Use the formula $C = 2\pi r$.

$C = 2\pi($ _____ $)$ Substitute the value for r.

$C \approx$ _____   Use the π key to evaluate the expression on a calculator. Then round.

REFLECT

2a. Suppose you multiply the diameter of the circle by a factor k, for some $k > 0$. How does the circumference change? Explain.

_____

_____

3 EXAMPLE   Solving a Circumference Problem

The General Sherman tree in Sequoia National Park, California, is considered the world's largest tree. The tree is approximately circular at its base, with a circumference of 102.6 feet. What is the approximate diameter of the tree? Round to the nearest foot.

A Substitute 102.6 for C in the formula for the circumference of a circle.

_____ $= 2\pi r$ Substitute 102.6 for C in the formula.

_____ $= r$ Solve for r.

$r \approx$ _____   Use a calculator to evaluate the expression.

B The diameter of a circle is twice the radius.

So, the diameter of the tree is approximately _____.

REFLECT

3a. The maximum distance across the base of the General Sherman tree is 36.5 feet. What explains the difference between this distance and the diameter you calculated above?

_____

_____

PRACTICE

Find the circumference of each circle. Round to the nearest tenth.

1.

O
9 cm

$2 \cdot 3.14 \cdot 9 = 56.5$

2.

C
14.2 mm

3.

A
$\frac{4}{\pi}$ ft

4. The Parthenon is a Greek temple dating to approximately 445 BCE. The temple features 46 Doric columns, which are approximately cylindrical. The circumference of each column at the base is approximately 5.65 meters. What is the approximate diameter of each column? Round to the nearest tenth.

17.8

5. A circular track for a model train has a diameter of 8.5 feet. The train moves around the track at a constant speed of 0.7 ft/s.

$5.65 = 2 \cdot \pi \cdot x$

$x =$

  a. To the nearest foot, how far does the train travel when it goes completely around the track 10 times?

  b. To the nearest minute, how long does it take the train to go completely around the track 10 times?

6. A standard bicycle wheel has a diameter of 26 inches. A student claims that during a one-mile bike ride the wheel makes more than 1000 complete revolutions. Do you agree or disagree? Explain. (*Hint:* 1 mile = 5280 feet)

7. In the figure, $\overline{AB}$ is a diameter of circle C, D is the midpoint of $\overline{AC}$, and E is the midpoint of $\overline{AD}$. How does the circumference of circle E compare to the circumference of circle C? Explain.

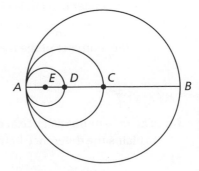

Additional Practice

$2\pi r$

Find each measurement. Give your answers in terms of π.

1.
25 m
V

the circumference of $\odot V$

$50\,\pi$

2.
H
4a in.

the circumference of $\odot H$

$4a\,\pi$

3.
M
(x + y) yd

the circumference of $\odot M$

$(2x + 2y)\,\pi$

4.
R
1200 mi

the circumference of $\odot R$

$1200\,\pi$

5. the radius of $\odot D$ in which $C = 2\pi^2$ cm

$\dfrac{\pi}{}$

6. the diameter of $\odot K$ in which $C = (4x + 4)\pi$ km

$4x + 4$

7. Daniel is approximating the circumference of a circle by finding the perimeter of an inscribed polygon. The circle has a radius of 6 inches.

a. Find the circumference of the circle using the expression $2\pi r$ with 3.1415 for π.

37.698

b. Find the perimeter of an inscribed polygon with 14 sides. Round your answer to the nearest thousandth of an inch.

36.362

c. Daniel claims that the perimeter of a 14-sided inscribed polygon is within 0.1 in. of the circumference of the circle as calculated in part a. Is he correct? Explain why or why not.

no because it is wrong

$$6 \quad x^2 = 36 + 36 + 72 \cos 25$$

$$x^2 = 72 + 65.25$$

$$x^2 = y^2 + z^2 + 2(yz) \cos X$$

Problem Solving

Write the correct answer.

1. A circular swimming pool is surrounded by a walkway that is 3 feet wide, as shown below. The circumference of the outer edge of the walkway is 208 feet. What is the radius of the pool to the nearest foot? Use 3.14 for π.

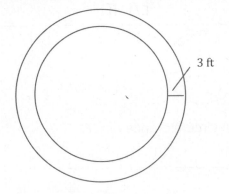

3 ft

_____

2. A wedding cake is made of three circular tiers, as shown below. The cake decorator is going to put one ring of frosting around the circumference of each tier. How many inches of frosting will the cake decorator need? Use 3.14 for π and round to the nearest whole inch.

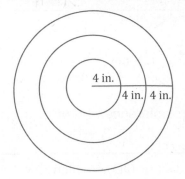

4 in.
4 in. 4 in.

_____

Choose the best answer.

3. The circumference of a circle with a radius of 2 meters is approximated by the perimeter of an inscribed polygon with 10 sides. Which expression gives the described approximation of the circumference?

   A $40\sin(18°)$

   B $2(2)\pi\sin(18°)$

   C $2(2)10\sin\left(\dfrac{180°}{2}\right)$

   D $2\pi(10)\sin\left(\dfrac{180°}{10}\right)$

4. An amusement park ride is made up of a large circular frame that holds 50 riders. The circumference of the frame is about 138 feet. What is the diameter of the ride to the nearest foot?

   F 22 ft   H 69 ft

   G 44 ft   J 138 ft

5. A cyclist travels 50 feet after 7.34 rotations of her bicycle wheels. What is the approximate diameter of the wheels?

   A 13 in.   C 26 in.

   B 24 in.   D 28 in.

6. A car has a wheel rim with a diameter of 19 inches. The tire itself has a diameter that is 5 inches wider than the rim. What is the approximate circumference of the tire to the nearest whole inch?

   F 37 inches

   G 42 inches

   H 75 inches

   J 151 inches

Composite Figures
Going Deeper

Essential question: *How can you find areas of irregular shapes?*

CC.9–12.G.MG.1

1 E X A M P L E   **Finding Area Using Addition**

The diagram shows the layout for a parking lot.
It is rectangular except for the area taken up by
the buildings at two corners. Find the area of the
parking lot.

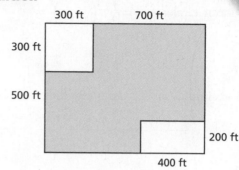

A   Draw horizontal lines on the diagram that
divide the parking lot into rectangles.
Explain your thinking.

_____

_____

B   Find the dimensions you need to find the areas of the rectangles you created. Add
the dimensions to the diagram and summarize them below.

_____

_____

_____

C   Find the total area of the parking lot. Explain.

_____

_____

REFLECT

1a. Describe a different way of dividing the parking lot into rectangles and find the
dimensions of the rectangles.

_____

_____

1b. Find the total area of the parking lot using the different subdivision method.
Explain the result.

_____

_____

2 EXAMPLE Finding Area Using Subtraction

Two quarter-circles in a square garden will be covered with gravel. Find the area of the unshaded region.

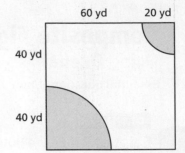

60 yd   20 yd

40 yd

40 yd

A Complete each area calculation.

small quarter-circle: $A = \frac{1}{4}\pi \left(\right)^2 = $ yd^2

large quarter-circle: $A = \frac{1}{4}\pi \left(\right)^2 = $ yd^2

square: $A = \left(40 + \right)\left(+ \right) = \cdot = $ yd^2

B Write and simplify an expression for the exact area of the unshaded region.

_____

REFLECT

2a. Why is the subtraction method appropriate in the second Example?

_____

_____

PRACTICE

Find the exact area of each shaded region.

1.

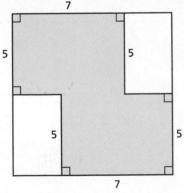

7

5   5

5

5

7

2.

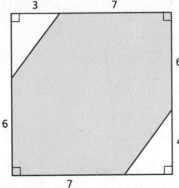

3   7

6

6

5

7

3.

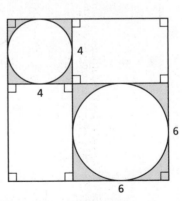

4

4

6

6

4. Sketch a diagram of an irregular region whose area can be found either by addition or subtraction. Show that the two methods yield the same result.

_____

_____

_____

_____

10-3

Additional Practice

Find the shaded area. Round to the nearest tenth if necessary.

1.
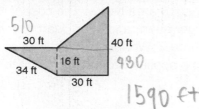
5/0   980   1590 ft

2.
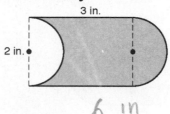
6 in

3.
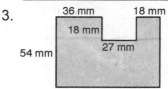
3888 mm

4.
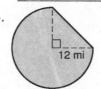
524.4 mi

5. 9+ 63+ 31.6
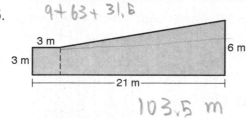
103.5 m

6.
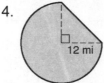
24 +   31.1 yd

7.
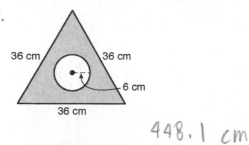
448.1 cm

8.
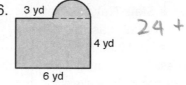
1656.6 m

9. Osman broke the unusually shaped picture window in his parents' living room. The figure shows the dimensions of the window. Replacement glass costs $8 per square foot, and there will be a $35 installation fee. Find the cost to replace the window to the nearest cent.

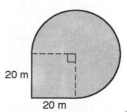
1+12+   218 ft

Estimate the area of each shaded irregular shape. The grid has squares with side lengths of 1 cm.

10.

1+   10   10

11.

8.5

Problem Solving

1. Find the shaded area. Round to the nearest tenth.

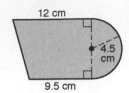

_____

2. Jessica is painting a bedroom wall shown by the shaded area below. The cost of paint is $6.90 per quart, and each quart covers 65 square feet. What is the total cost of the paint if she applies two coats of paint to the wall?

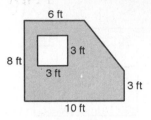

_____

Choose the best answer.

3. Enchanted Rock State Natural Area in Fredericksburg, Texas, has a primitive camping area called Moss Lake. Which is the best estimate for this area if the length of each grid square is 10 meters?

   A 1600 m²

   B 3200 m²

   C 6400 m²

   D 8000 m²

4. Find the area of the section of basketball court that is shown. Round to the nearest tenth.

   F 612.7 ft²

   G 820.1 ft²

   H 1225.4 ft²

   J 2450.8 ft²

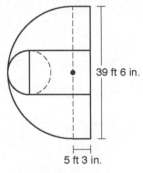

5. Find the shaded area. Round to the nearest tenth.

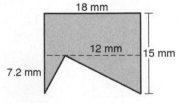

   A 183.6 mm²   C 205.2 mm²

   B 194.4 mm²   D 216.0 mm²

6. Which is the best estimate for the area of the pond? Each grid square represents 4 square feet.

   F 24 ft²

   G 48 ft²

   H 96 ft²

   J 120 ft

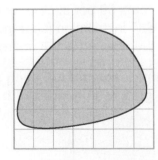

Perimeter and Area in the Coordinate Plane
Extension: Density

Essential question: *How do you find the perimeter and area of polygons in the coordinate plane?*

Recall that the perimeter of a polygon is the sum of the lengths of the polygon's sides. You can use the distance formula to help you find perimeters of polygons in a coordinate plane.

CC.9–12.G.GPE.7

1 EXAMPLE **Finding a Perimeter**

Find the perimeter of the pentagon with vertices $A(-4, 2)$, $B(-4, -2)$, $C(0, -3)$, $D(4, -2)$, and $E(2, 3)$. Round to the nearest tenth.

A Plot the points. Then use a straightedge to draw the pentagon that is determined by the points.

B Find the length of each side of the pentagon.

$\overline{AB}$ is vertical. You can find its length by counting units.

$AB = $ _____ units

Use the distance formula to find the remaining side lengths.

$BC = \sqrt{(0-(-4))^2 + (-3-(-2))^2} = \sqrt{\boxed{} + \boxed{}} = \sqrt{\boxed{}}$

$\overline{BC}$ and $\overline{CD}$ have the same length because

_____

$DE = \sqrt{\left(\boxed{} - \boxed{}\right)^2 + \left(\boxed{} - \boxed{}\right)^2} = \sqrt{\boxed{} + \boxed{}} = \sqrt{\boxed{}}$

$EA = \sqrt{\left(\boxed{} - \boxed{}\right)^2 + \left(\boxed{} - \boxed{}\right)^2} = \sqrt{\boxed{} + \boxed{}} = \sqrt{\boxed{}}$

C Find the sum of the side lengths.

$AB + BC + CD + DE + EA = $ _____ + _____ + _____ + _____ + _____

Use a calculator to evaluate the expression. Then round to the nearest tenth.

So, the perimeter of *ABCDE* is _____ units.

1a. Explain how you can find the perimeter of a rectangle to check that your answer is reasonable.

_____

_____

_____

The *density* of an object is its mass per unit volume. For example, the density of gold is 19.3 g/cm^3. This means each cubic centimeter of gold has a mass of 19.3 grams. You can also define density in other situations that involve area or volume. For example, the **population density** of a region is the population per unit area.

CC.9–12.G.MG.2

2 EXAMPLE **Approximating a Population Density**

Vermont has a population of 621,760. Its border can be modeled by the trapezoid with vertices $A(0, 0)$, $B(0, 160)$, $C(80, 160)$, and $D(40, 0)$, where each unit of the coordinate plane represents one mile. Find the approximate population density of Vermont. Round to the nearest tenth.

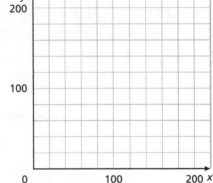

A Plot the points. Then use a straightedge to draw the trapezoid that is determined by the points.

B Find the area of the trapezoid. To do so, draw a perpendicular from D to $\overline{BC}$. This forms a rectangle and a triangle. The area of the trapezoid is the sum of the area of the rectangle and the area of the triangle.

Area of rectangle = $\ell \cdot w = $ _____ $\cdot$ _____ = _____

Area of triangle = $\frac{1}{2}bh = \frac{1}{2} \cdot$ _____ $\cdot$ _____ = _____

Area of trapezoid = _____ + _____ = _____ mi^2

C Find the population density.

Population density = $\frac{\text{population}}{\text{area}}$ = $\frac{}{}$ ≈ _____

Round to the nearest tenth.

So, the approximate population density of Vermont is _____ persons/mi^2.

2a. The actual area of Vermont is 9620 mi². Is your approximation of the population density an overestimate or underestimate? Why?

_____

_____

2b. Suppose the population of Vermont doubles in the next century. Would the population density change? If so, how?

_____

PRACTICE

1. Find the side lengths of the triangle with vertices $X(0, 1)$, $Y(5, 4)$, and $Z(2, 6)$. Round to the nearest tenth.

_____

_____

_____

_____

2. Find the side lengths of the quadrilateral with vertices $P(2, 5)$, $Q(-3, 0)$, $R(2, -5)$, and $S(6, 0)$. Round to the nearest tenth.

_____

_____

_____

_____

3. Find the perimeter of the hexagon with vertices $A(-5, 1)$, $B(0, 3)$, $C(5, 1)$, $D(4, -2)$, $E(0, -4)$, and $F(-2, -4)$. Round to the nearest tenth.

_____

4. Find the perimeter of the hexagon with vertices $J(0, 5)$, $K(4, 3)$, $L(4, -1)$, $M(0, -4)$, $N(-4, -1)$, and $P(-4, 3)$. Round to the nearest tenth.

_____

5. A plot of land is a pentagon with vertices $Q(-4, 4)$, $R(2, 4)$, $S(4, 1)$, $T(2, -4)$, and $U(-4, -4)$. Each unit of the coordinate grid represents one meter.

a. Fencing costs $24.75 per meter. What is the cost of placing a fence around the plot of land? _____

b. Sod costs $1.85 per square meter. What is the cost of covering the plot of land with sod? _____

6. Suppose that Colorado has a population of 5,024,748. Its border can be modeled by the rectangle with vertices $A(-190, 0)$, $B(-190, 280)$, $C(190, 280)$, and $D(190, 0)$, where each unit of the coordinate plane represents one mile. Find the approximate population density of Colorado. Round to the nearest tenth.

_____

7. For the maximum grain yield, corn should be planted at a density of 38,000 plants per acre. A farmer has a field in the shape of a quadrilateral with vertices $J(0, 0)$, $K(0, 400)$, $L(500, 600)$, and $M(500, 0)$, where each unit of the coordinate plane represents one foot.

a. What is the area of the field in square feet? _____

b. What is the area of the field to the nearest hundredth of an acre? (*Hint:* 1 acre equals 43,560 ft^2.) _____

c. Approximately how many corn plants should be planted in the field for maximum grain yield? Round to the nearest ten thousand. _____

Additional Practice

Find the perimeter of the figure shown. Round to the nearest tenth of a unit.

1.

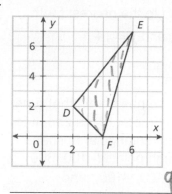

9

2.

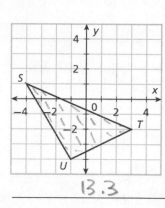

13.3

Draw and classify each polygon with the given vertices. Find the perimeter and area of the polygon. Round to the nearest tenth if necessary.

3. *A*(−2, 3), *B*(3, 1), *C*(−2, −1), *D*(−3, 1)

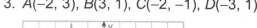

A = 12 units²

P =

4. *P*(−3, −4), *Q*(3, −3), *R*(3, −2), *S*(−3, 2)

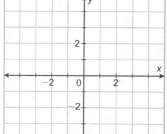

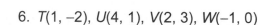

5. *E*(−4, 1), *F*(−2, 3), *G*(−2, −4)

6. *T*(1, −2), *U*(4, 1), *V*(2, 3), *W*(−1, 0)

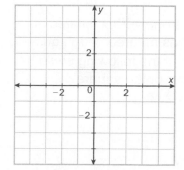

Problem Solving

1. Find the perimeter and area of a polygon with vertices $A(-3, -2)$, $B(2, 4)$, $C(5, 2)$, and $D(0, -4)$. Round to the nearest tenth.

_____

2. What are the perimeter and area of the triangle that is formed when the lines below are graphed in the coordinate plane? Round to the nearest tenth.

$y = 2x$, $y = 4$, and $y = x + 4$

_____

3. Find the area of polygon $HJKL$ with vertices $H(-3, 3)$, $J(2, 1)$, $K(4, -4)$, and $L(-3, -3)$.

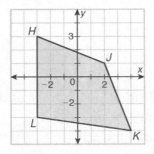

4. A children's zoo has a train that runs around the perimeter of the zoo. It is approximately rectangular in shape, passing through points $(-100, 300)$, $(200, 200)$, $(-100, -100)$, and $(200, -200)$, where each unit represents 1 yard. How long is the train track to the nearest whole yard?

_____

Choose the best answer.

5. A graph showing the top view of a circular fountain has its center at $(4, 6)$. The circle representing the fountain passes through $(2, 1)$. What is the area of the space covered by the fountain?

   A $\sqrt{29}\,\pi$

   B $2\sqrt{29}\,\pi$

   C 29π

   D 58π

6. Trapezoid $QRST$ with vertices $Q(1, 5)$ and $R(9, 5)$ has an area of 12 square units. Which are possible locations for vertices S and T?

   F $S(6, 7)$ and $T(2, 7)$

   G $S(4, 7)$ and $T(2, 7)$

   H $S(6, 8)$ and $T(3, 8)$

   J $S(6, 1)$ and $T(3, 1)$

7. A square has one vertex located at $(-5, 0)$ and has an area of 16 square units. Which of the following could be another vertex of the square?

   A $(-1, 1)$

   B $(-1, \sqrt{5})$

   C $(-2, \sqrt{6})$

   D $(-2, \sqrt{7})$

Effects of Changing Dimensions Proportionally
Extension: Stretching with Different Scale Factors

Essential question: *What happens when you change the dimensions of a figure using different scale factors along two dimensions?*

The transformation $(x, y) \rightarrow (ax, ay)$ can be called a *uniform* scaling.
Transformations such as $(x, y) \rightarrow (ax, y)$, $(x, y) \rightarrow (x, by)$, and
$(x, y) \rightarrow (ax, by)$ have different effects.

CC.9–12.G.CO.2

1 EXPLORE Experimenting with Non-Uniform Scaling

A, B, C, and D are vertices of a kite. Consider the transformation with the rule
$(x, y) \rightarrow (3x, 2y)$.

A Complete the table of coordinates.

Preimage (*x*, *y*)	A(0, 2)	B(2, 4)	C(5, 2)	D(2, 0)
Image (*3x*, *2y*)				

B Kite *ABCD* is shown on the graph below. Draw $A'B'C'D'$.

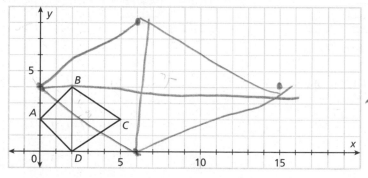

C Measure the angles in *ABCD* and *A′B′C′D′*. Complete the table of angle measures.

Angles in *ABCD*	m∠A =	m∠B =	m∠C =	m∠D =
Angles in *A′B′C′D′*	m∠A′ =	m∠B′ =	m∠C′ =	m∠D′ =

D The area of a kite is half the product of the lengths of its diagonals. Find the areas of *ABCD* and *A′B′C′D′*, and the ratio of the areas.

  ABCD: = _____ square units; *A′B′C′D′*: = _____ square units; the ratio is _____

REFLECT

1a. Does the transformation $(x, y) \rightarrow (3x, 2y)$ preserve angle measure? Explain.

_____

1b. Write a conjecture about how the transformation $(x, y) \rightarrow (ax, by)$ affects area when a and b are positive numbers.

_____

_____

1c. Is your conjecture compatible with what you know about how the transformation $(x, y) \rightarrow (ax, ay)$ affects area? Explain.

_____

_____

PRACTICE

Draw the image of the given figure under the transformation. Find the areas of the figures, and calculate the ratio of the image area to the preimage area.

1. $(x, y) \rightarrow (x, 3y)$

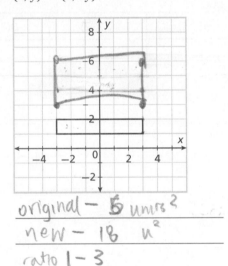

original – 5 units²

new – 18 u²

ratio 1 – 3

2. $(x, y) \rightarrow (2x, y)$

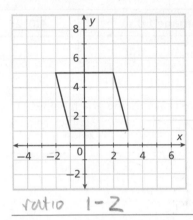

ratio 1–2

_____

_____

_____

3. $(x, y) \rightarrow (1.5x, 3y)$

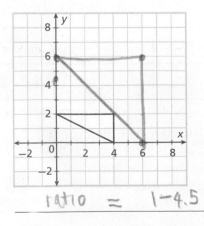

ratio = 1–4.5

_____

_____

4. $(x, y) \rightarrow (0.5x, 2y)$

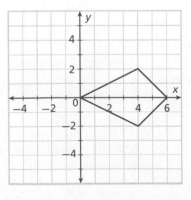

_____

_____

_____

Additional Practice

Draw the image of the given figure under the indicated transformation.
Find the area of each figure, and calculate the ratio of the image area
to the preimage area.

1. $(x, y) \rightarrow (x, 2y)$

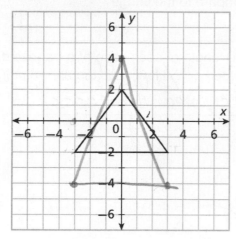

ratio 1-2

_____

_____

_____

2. $(x, y) \rightarrow (0.5x, 0.25y)$

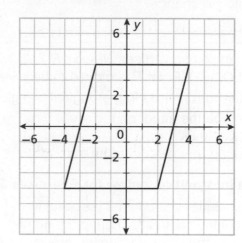

ratio 1-0.125

_____

_____

_____

3. $(x, y) \rightarrow \left(\dfrac{3}{2}x, y\right)$

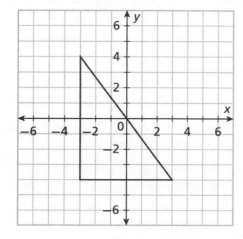

ratio 1-1.5

_____

_____

_____

4. $(x, y) \rightarrow \left(\dfrac{1}{12}x, 1\dfrac{1}{4}y\right)$

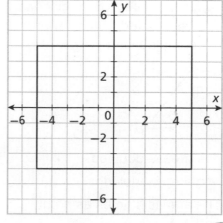

ratio 1-0.93

_____

_____

_____

Problem Solving

1. Mara has a photograph 5 inches by 7 inches. She wants to enlarge the photo so that the length and width are each tripled. Describe how the area of the photo will change.

   The area will 9th^x in units

2. A rectangle has vertices $(-1, 3)$, $(4, 3)$, $(4, 1)$, and $(-1, 1)$. If the transformation $(x, y) \rightarrow (3x, y)$ is applied to the rectangle, how does the area of the preimage compare to the image?

   The area triples in size.

3. A triangle has vertices $N(3, 5)$, $P(7, 2)$, and $Q(3, 1)$. Point P is moved to be twice as far from $\overline{NQ}$ as in the original triangle. Describe the effect on the area.

   The area will increase.

4. The length of each base of a trapezoid is divided by 2. How does the area change?

   The area decreases

   $2\pi r \qquad \pi r^2$

   6 ft

Use the information below for Exercises 5 and 6.

Steven's dog is on a chain 6 feet long with one end of the chain attached to the ground as shown in the diagram. Steven replaces the chain with one that is $1\frac{1}{2}$ times as long.

5. Describe how the circumference of the circle determined by the chain is changed.

   The circumcerenes get 1.5 times bigger.

6. Describe how the area of the circle determined by the chain is changed.

   The area gets 2.24 times bigger

Choose the best answer.

7. In kite $RSTU$, $RT = 2.5$ centimeters and $SU = 4.3$ centimeters. Both diagonals of the kite are doubled. What happens to the area of the kite?

   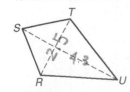

   A The area is doubled.

   B The area is tripled.

   C The area is 4 times as great.

   D The area is 8 times as great.

8. The side length of the regular hexagon is divided by 3. Which is a true statement?

   18 mm

   F The perimeter is divided by 9, and the area is divided by 3.

   G The perimeter is divided by 3, and the area is divided by 9.

   H The perimeter and area are both divided by 3.

   J The perimeter and area are both divided by 9.

10-6

Geometric Probability
Connection: Set Theory

Essential question: *How can you use set theory to help you calculate theoretical probabilities?*

Video Tutor

CC.9–12.S.CP.1

1 **E N G A G E**   **Introducing the Vocabulary of Sets**

You will see that set theory is useful in calculating probabilities. A **set** is a well-defined collection of distinct objects. Each object in a set is called an **element** of the set. A set may be specified by writing its elements in braces. For example, the set S of prime numbers less than 10 may be written as $S = \{2, 3, 5, 7\}$.

The number of elements in a set S may be written as $n(S)$. For the set S of prime numbers less than 10, $n(S) = 4$.

The set with no elements is the **empty set** and is denoted by $\varnothing$ or $\{\ \}$. The set of all elements under consideration is the **universal set** and is denoted by U. The following terms describe how sets are related to each other.

Term	Notation	Venn Diagram
Set A is a **subset** of set B if every element of A is also an element of B.	$A \subset B$	
The **intersection** of sets A and B is the set of all elements that are in both A and B.	$A \cap B$	
The **union** of sets A and B is the set of all elements that are in A or B.	$A \cup B$	
The **complement** of set A is the set of all elements in the universal set U that are not in A.	A^c	

REFLECT

1a. For any set A, what is $A \cap \varnothing$? Explain.

_____

_____

Recall that a *probability experiment* is an activity involving chance. Each repetition of the experiment is a *trial* and each possible result is an *outcome*. The *sample space* of an experiment is the set of all possible outcomes. An *event* is a set of outcomes.

When all outcomes of an experiment are equally likely, the **theoretical probability** that an event A will occur is given by $P(A) = \frac{n(A)}{n(S)}$, where S is the sample space.

2 EXAMPLE Calculating Theoretical Probabilities

You roll a number cube. Event *A* is rolling an even number. Event *B* is rolling a prime number. Calculate each of the following probabilities.

A $P(A)$　　　**B** $P(A \cup B)$　　　**C** $P(A \cap B)$　　　**D** $P(A^c)$

A $P(A)$ is the probability of rolling an even number. To calculate $P(A)$, first identify the sample space S.

$S = $ _____ , so $n(S) = $ _____ .

$A = $ _____ , so $n(A) = $ _____ .

So, $P(A) = \frac{n(A)}{n(S)} = \frac{}{} = \frac{}{}$.

B $P(A \cup B)$ is the probability of rolling an even number *or* a prime number.

$A \cup B = $ _____ , so $n(A \cup B) = $ _____ .

So, $P(A \cup B) = \frac{n(A \cup B)}{n(S)} = \frac{}{}$.

C $P(A \cap B)$ is the probability of rolling an even number *and* a prime number.

$A \cap B = $ _____ , so $n(A \cap B) = $ _____ .

So, $P(A \cap B) = \frac{n(A \cap B)}{n(S)} = \frac{}{}$.

D $P(A^c)$ is the probability of rolling a number that is *not* even.

$A^c = $ _____ , so $n(A^c) = $ _____ .

So, $P(A^c) = \frac{n(A^c)}{n(S)} = \frac{}{} = \frac{}{}$.

REFLECT

2a. Explain what $P(S)$ represents and then calculate this probability. Do you think this result is true in general? Explain.

_____

_____

You may have noticed in the example that $P(A) + P(A^c) = 1$. To see why this is true in general, note that an event and its complement represent all outcomes in the sample space, so $n(A) + n(A^c) = n(S)$.

$$P(A) + P(A^c) = \frac{n(A)}{n(S)} + \frac{n(A^c)}{n(S)} \qquad \text{Definition of theoretical probability}$$

$$= \frac{n(A) + n(A^c)}{n(S)} \qquad \text{Add.}$$

$$= \frac{n(S)}{n(S)} = 1 \qquad n(A) + n(A^c) = n(S)$$

You can write this relationship as $P(A) = 1 - P(A^c)$ and use it to help you find probabilities when it is more convenient to calculate the probability of the complement of an event.

Probabilities of an Event and Its Complement

The probability of an event and the probability of its complement have a sum of 1. So, the probability of an event is one minus the probability of its complement. Also, the probability of the complement of an event is one minus the probability of the event.

$$P(A) + P(A^c) = 1$$

$$P(A) = 1 - P(A^c)$$

$$P(A^c) = 1 - P(A)$$

CC.9–12.S.CP.1

3 EXAMPLE Using the Complement of an Event

You roll a blue number cube and white number cube at the same time. What is the probability that you do not roll doubles?

A Let A be the event that you do not roll doubles. Then A^c is the event that you do roll doubles.

Complete the table at right to show all outcomes in the sample space.

Circle the outcomes in A^c (rolling doubles).

B Find the probability of rolling doubles.

$$P(A^c) = \frac{n(A^c)}{n(S)} = \underline{} = \underline{}$$

C Find the probability that you do not roll doubles.

$$P(A) = 1 - P(A^c) = 1 - \underline{} = \underline{}$$

White Number Cube

	1	2	3	4	5	6
1	1-1	1-2	1-3	1-4	1-5	1-6
2	2-1					
3	3-1					
4	4-1					
5	5-1					
6	6-1					

Blue Number Cube

3a. Describe a different way you could have calculated the probability that you do not roll doubles.

_____

_____

PRACTICE

You have a set of 10 cards numbered 1 to 10. You choose a card at random. Event *A* is choosing a number less than 7. Event *B* is choosing an odd number. Calculate each of the following probabilities.

1. $P(A)$ 6/10

2. $P(B)$ 5/10

3. $P(A \cup B)$ 8/10

4. $P(A \cap B)$ 3/10

5. $P(A^c)$ 4/10

6. $P(B^c)$ 5/10

7. A bag contains 5 red marbles and 10 blue marbles. You choose a marble without looking. Event *A* is choosing a red marble. Event *B* is choosing a blue marble. What is $P(A \cap B)$? Explain.

0/15

_____

8. A standard deck of cards has 13 cards (2, 3, 4, 5, 6, 7, 8, 9, 10, jack, queen, king, ace) in each of 4 suits (hearts, clubs, diamonds, spades). You choose a card from a deck at random. What is the probability that you do not choose an ace? Explain.

48/52

_____

9. You choose a card from a standard deck of cards at random. What is the probability that you do not choose a club? Explain.

3/4

_____

10. **Error Analysis** A bag contains white tiles, black tiles, and gray tiles. $P(W)$, the probability of choosing a tile at random and choosing a white tile, is $\frac{1}{4}$. A student claims that the probability of choosing a black tile, $P(B)$, is $\frac{3}{4}$ since $P(B) = 1 - P(W) = 1 - \frac{1}{4} = \frac{3}{4}$. Do you agree? Explain.

No it is not 3/4.

_____

_____

Additional Practice

handwritten: ∪ = or, ∩ = and, C is opposite

Set $A = \{2, 4, 6, 8, 10\}$ and Set B is the set of all prime numbers less than 20. List the elements in each of the following sets.

1. B

2. $A \cup B$

3. $A \cap B$

handwritten: $1,3,5,7,\cancel{4},11,13,17,19$ $1,2,3,4,5,6,7,8,10,11,13,17,19$ → None

A bag contains 26 tiles, one for each letter of the alphabet. Event A is drawing a tile with a vowel on it. Event B is drawing a tile with the letter A, B, C, D, E, or F on it. Calculate each of the following probabilities.

handwritten: AEIOU

4. $P(A)$

handwritten: 5/26

5. $P(B)$

handwritten: 6/26 = 3/13

6. $P(A \cup B)$

handwritten: 9/42

7. $P(A \cap B)$

handwritten: 2/26

8. $P(A^C)$

handwritten: 21/26

9. $P(B^C)$

handwritten: 20/26

Find the probability of A^C for each of the following situations.

10. $P(A) = 0.3$

handwritten: 0.7

11. $P(A) = \dfrac{1}{4}$

handwritten: 3/4

12. A number cube with sides numbered 1–6 is rolled. A is rolling a 5.

handwritten: 5/6

13. A number cube with sides numbered 1–6 is rolled. A is rolling an even number.

handwritten: 3/6

14. Give an example of two sets A and B, for which A and $A \cup B$ both contain the exact same elements. Both sets should contain at least two elements, and the sets should not be the same.

handwritten: A= all even numbers   B= all odd numbers

Write the correct answer.

1. The universal set U is the set of all integers from 1 through 20. You select one element of U at random. Event A is choosing 2, 6, or 18. What is $P(A^C)$?

   17/20

2. A bag contains a total of 10 marbles. Four of the marbles are black, and 3 of the marbles are white. If Event A is drawing a black marble and Event B is drawing a white marble, what is $P(A \cup B)$?

   0/10

3. Set $C = \{-2, -1, 0, 1, 2\}$ and Set D is the set of all positive integers. What elements are in the set $C \cap D$?

   5/5

4. You roll two six-sided number cubes at the same time. Event A is rolling a 1 on both cubes. What is $P(A^C)$?

   10/12

Select the best answer.

5. A spinner has four sections of equal size. The sections are painted blue, red, green, and yellow. Event A is spinning a yellow, and Event B is spinning a red. What is $P(A \cup B)$?

   A $\dfrac{1}{4}$ C $\dfrac{3}{4}$

   B $\dfrac{1}{2}$ D 1

6. What is $P(B^C)$ for the situation described in Exercise 5?

   F $\dfrac{1}{4}$ H $\dfrac{3}{4}$

   G $\dfrac{1}{2}$ J 1

7. Set $J = \{-\pi, \sqrt{2}, 0, 1\}$ and Set Q is the set of all rational numbers. Which set represents $J \cap Q$?

   A $\varnothing$

   B $\{0\}$

   C $\{0, 1\}$

   D Q

8. If you have two sets, A and B, and A and $A \cap B$ have the exact same elements, which statement must be true?

   F B is the null set.

   G Every element in A is also in B.

   H Every element in B is also in A.

   J $A \cup B$ is the null set.

CHAPTER 10

Performance Tasks

COMMON CORE

CC.9-12.G.MG.3
CC.9-12.S.CP.1

⭐ **1.** A horse owner is designing a square enclosure that requires 930 feet of fence to build. In addition to the outer perimeter, the enclosure has interior fencing that divides it into 4 congruent squares. What is the total area of the paddock? Justify your answer.

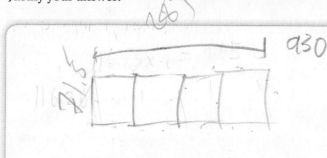

⭐ **2.** Shari is cutting a circular tablecloth from a rectangular piece of material that is 54 inches wide and 59 inches long.

a. What is the radius of the largest circle she can cut?

b. Her scissors cut 3.8 inches per snip. How many snips will she make to cut out the entire circle? Round to the nearest whole number.

⭐⭐ **3.** A landscape architect is designing a small park in the shape of an isosceles trapezoid. It has a triangular pond, △*KJM*. Points *E*, *F*, *G*, and *H* are midpoints of the segments they lie on, and *L* is the midpoint of both $\overline{KM}$ and $\overline{GH}$. *GH* = 300 ft, *CD* = 420 ft, and *EF* = 160 ft.

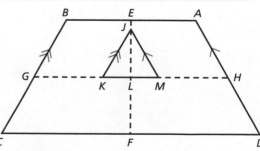

a. What is the area of the park? Show your work.

b. *EJ* = 20 ft, and *MH* = 110 ft. What is the area of the pond? Explain how you found your answer.

c. A breeze blows a paper cup into the park. The cup lands on a random place in the park. What is the probability that it does not land in the pond? Explain.

continued

4. Shannon is designing a target of 3 concentric circles. From inside to outside, the colors are yellow, blue, and white. She wants the probabilities of randomly hitting yellow to be 15%, of randomly hitting blue to be 35%, and of randomly hitting white to be 50%. The radius of the entire target will be 9 inches.

   a. Find the radius of each concentric circle to the nearest tenth of an inch. Show your work.

   b. How wide will the blue and white circular bands be? Round to the nearest tenth of an inch.

Name _____ Class _____ Date _____

MULTIPLE CHOICE

1. A transformation has the rule $(x, y) \rightarrow (-3x, -3y)$. Which of the following statements about the transformation is accurate?

   A. The transformation preserves angle measures but not distances.

   B. The transformation preserves distances but not angle measures.

   C. The transformation preserves neither angle measures nor distances.

   D. The transformation preserves both angle measures and distances.

2. A homeowner wants to make a new deck for the backyard. Redwood costs $8 per square foot. The units on the graph are in feet. How much will it cost for the wood to create the deck shown?

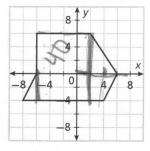

   F. $108

   G. $432

   H. $864

   J. $960

3. Meteor Crater, near Flagstaff, Arizona, is an approximately circular crater, with a circumference of 2.32 miles. What is the diameter of the crater to the nearest hundredth of a mile?

   A. 0.37 mi

   B. 0.74 mi

   C. 1.48 mi

   D. 7.29 mi

4. The figure shows a polygonal fence for part of a garden. Each unit of the coordinate plane represents one meter. What is the length of the fence to the nearest tenth of a meter?

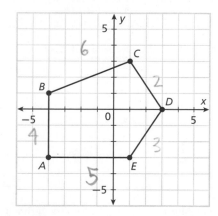

   F. 16.1 m

   G. 18.0 m

   H. 21.6 m

   J. 31.0 m

CONSTRUCTED RESPONSE

5. In order to justify the formula for the circumference of a circle, you inscribe a regular *n*-gon in a circle of radius *r*, as shown in the figure.

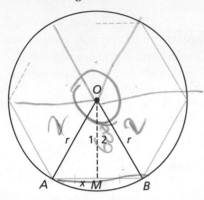

You show that $\triangle AOM \cong \triangle BOM$ and conclude that $\angle 1 \cong \angle 2$ by CPCTC. Then you state that $m\angle AOB = \frac{360°}{n}$ and $m\angle 1 = \frac{180°}{n}$. Describe the main steps for finishing the justification of the circumference formula.

_____

_____

_____

_____

_____

_____

6. You are using the figure below to derive a formula for the area of a triangle that involves the sine ratio.

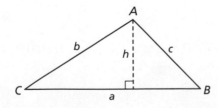

First you note that $\sin C = \frac{h}{b}$ and, therefore, $h = b \sin C$. How do you complete the derivation of the formula?

_____

_____

_____

7. The border of Utah can be modeled by the polygon with vertices $A(0, 0)$, $B(0, 350)$, $C(160, 350)$, $D(160, 280)$, $E(270, 280)$, and $F(270, 0)$. Each unit on the coordinate plane represents 1 mile.

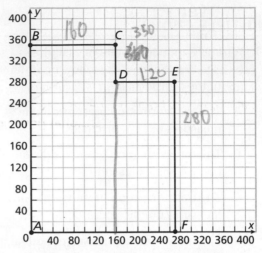

a. What is the approximate area of the state?

   86800 miles

b. The population of Utah is 2,784,572. Explain how to find the state's population density. Round to the nearest tenth.

   32.1 per square
   mile.

_____

_____

_____

_____

_____

_____

_____

Spatial Reasoning

Chapter Focus

In this unit, you will turn your attention to three-dimensional figures. You will begin by exploring cross sections of three-dimensional figures and learn how to generate three-dimensional figures by rotating two-dimensional figures around a line. Then you will develop and justify volume formulas for a variety of solids. Finally, you will apply what you have learned to solve problems in which you must design a three-dimensional figure given one or more constraints.

Chapter at a Glance

COMMON
CORE

Lesson		Standards for Mathematical Content
11-1	Solid Geometry	CC.9-12.G.GMD.4
11-2	Volume of Prisms and Cylinders	CC.9-12.G.GMD.1, CC.9-12.G.GMD.2(+), CC.9-12.G.MG.2, CC.9-12.G.MG.3
11-3	Volume of Pyramids and Cones	CC.9-12.G.GMD.1, CC.9-12.G.GMD.3
11-4	Spheres	CC.9-12.G.GMD.2(+), CC.9-12.G.GMD.3
	Performance Tasks	
	Assessment Readiness	

Unpacking the Standards

Understanding the standards and the vocabulary terms in the standards will help you know exactly what you are expected to learn in this chapter.

COMMON CORE CC.9-12.G.GMD.3

Use volume formulas for cylinders, pyramids, cones, and spheres to solve problems.

Key Vocabulary

volume *(volumen)* The number of nonoverlapping unit cubes of a given size that will exactly fill the interior of a three-dimensional figure.

formula *(formula)* A literal equation that states a rule for a relationship among quantities.

cylinder *(cilindro)* A three-dimensional figure with two parallel congruent circular bases and a curved surface that connects the bases.

pyramid *(pirámide)* A polyhedron formed by a polygonal base and triangular lateral faces that meet at a common vertex.

cone *(cono)* A three-dimensional figure with a circular base and a curved surface that connects the base to a point called the vertex.

sphere *(esfera)* The set of points in space that are a fixed distance from a given point called the center of the sphere.

What It Means For You   Lessons 11-2, 11-3, 11-4

Volume problems appear frequently in real-world contexts. Learning the relationships among volume formulas helps you understand, remember, and apply them.

EXAMPLE   Volume of a cylinder

A grain silo at a port has the dimensions shown. The volume is the base area B times the height h. Because the base is a circle, this gives:

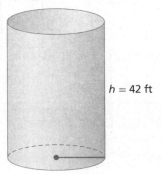

$$V = Bh = \pi r^2 h$$
$$= \pi (15^2)(42)$$
$$\approx 30{,}000 \text{ ft}^3$$

$h = 42$ ft

$r = 15$ ft

EXAMPLE   Volume of a cone

The silo above contains just enough grain so that the grain reaches to the outer edge of the floor, forming a cone. The volume is one third the base area times the height. This gives:

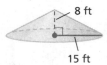

8 ft

15 ft

$$V = \frac{1}{3}Bh = \frac{1}{3}\pi r^2 h = \frac{1}{3}\pi (15^2)(8) \approx 1900 \text{ ft}^3$$

EXAMPLE   Volume of a sphere

A liquefied natural gas tank at the port is in the shape of a sphere with the radius shown. The volume is:

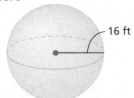

16 ft

$$V = \frac{4}{3}\pi r^3 = \frac{4}{3}\pi (16^3) \approx 17{,}000 \text{ ft}^3$$

EXAMPLE   Volume of a pyramid

A customs building at the port has a roof in the shape of a pyramid with the dimensions shown. As with a cone, the volume is one third the base area times the height. Because the base is a rectangle, this gives:

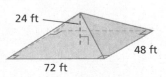

24 ft

48 ft

72 ft

$$V = \frac{1}{3}Bh = \frac{1}{3}(72)(48)(24) \approx 28{,}000 \text{ ft}^3$$

COMMON CORE CC.9-12.G.GMD.4

Identify the shapes of two-dimensional cross-sections of three-dimensional objects, and identify three-dimensional objects generated by rotations of two-dimensional objects.

Key Vocabulary

cross section *(sección transversal)*
The intersection of a three-dimensional figure and a plane.

COMMON CORE CC.9-12.G.MG.1

Use geometric shapes, their measures, and their properties to describe objects (e.g., modeling a tree trunk or a human torso as a cylinder).

What It Means For You   Lesson 11-1

Most planning and design work for creating three-dimensional objects is done on two-dimensional computer screens or other surfaces. It is important to grasp the relationship between three-dimensional objects and their two-dimensional representations.

EXAMPLE

 The illustration at left of a pawn from a chess set is really a vertical cross section shaded to appear more three-dimensional. At right is the outline of the cross section.

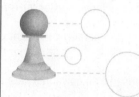 The outline of every horizontal cross section that you take (that is, parallel to the base) is a circle whose diameter is the width of the pawn at that height.

Imagine rotating the outline of half of the pawn around the axis shown in the way that the earth rotates around its axis. The three-dimensional figure that results (the pawn) is called a *solid of revolution*.

What It Means For You   Lessons 11-2, 11-3, 11-4

Objects in the actual world are not often exact geometric shapes, but for very many situations, you can use simple geometric shapes to make models that closely approximate the actual objects.

EXAMPLE

Earth doesn't form a perfect sphere—it has mountains and valleys, and it is actually a bit wider at the Equator than pole-to-pole—but for many purposes a sphere is a good model.

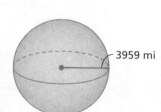

Using the average radius shown, you can calculate Earth's volume V:

$$V = \frac{4}{3}\pi r^3 \approx \frac{4}{3}\pi(3959^3) \approx 2.599 \times 10^{11} \text{ mi}^3$$

CHAPTER 11

Key Vocabulary

cone *(cono)* A three-dimensional figure with a circular base and a curved surface that connects the base to a point called the vertex.

cross section *(sección transversal)* The intersection of a three-dimensional figure and a plane.

cylinder *(cilindro)* A three-dimensional figure with two parallel congruent circular bases and a curved surface that connects the bases.

formula *(formula)* A literal equation that states a rule for a relationship among quantities.

oblique cylinder *(cilindro oblicuo)* A cylinder whose axis is not perpendicular to the bases.

prism *(prisma)* A polyhedron formed by two parallel congruent polygonal bases connected by lateral faces that are parallelograms.

pyramid *(pirámide)* A polyhedron formed by a polygonal base and triangular lateral faces that meet at a common vertex.

sphere *(esfera)* The set of points in space that are a fixed distance from a given point called the center of the sphere.

volume *(volumen)* The number of nonoverlapping unit cubes of a given size that will exactly fill the interior of a three-dimensional figure.

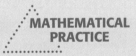

MATHEMATICAL PRACTICE

The Common Core Standards for Mathematical Practice describe varieties of expertise that mathematics educators at all levels should seek to develop in their students. Opportunities to develop these practices are integrated throughout this program.

1. Make sense of problems and persevere in solving them.
2. Reason abstractly and quantitatively.
3. Construct viable arguments and critique the reasoning of others.
4. Model with mathematics.
5. Use appropriate tools strategically.
6. Attend to precision.
7. Look for and make use of structure.
8. Look for and express regularity in repeated reasoning

Solid Geometry
Going Deeper

Essential question: *How do you identify cross sections of three-dimensional figures and how do you use rotations to generate three-dimensional figures?*

Recall that an *intersection* is the set of all points that two or more figures have in common. A **cross section** is the intersection of a three-dimensional figure and a plane.

CC.9–12.G.GMD.4
1 EXAMPLE   Identifying Cross Sections of a Cylinder

Describe each cross section of a cylinder.

A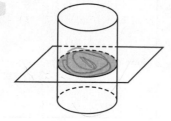

B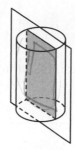

A   Each base of the cylinder is a _____.

The cross section is formed by a plane that is parallel to the bases of the cylinder. Any cross section of a cylinder made by a plane parallel to the bases will have the same shape as the bases.

So, the cross section is a _____.

B   The bases of the cylinder are parallel, so the cross section is a quadrilateral with at least one pair of opposite sides that are parallel.

The bases of the cylinder meet the lateral (curved) surface at right angles, so the cross section must contain four right angles.

So, the cross section is a _____.

REFLECT

1a.   In Part A, why does the cross section appear to be an oval or ellipse?

_____

_____

1b.   Is it possible for a cross section of a cylinder to have a shape other than those you identified above? Explain.

_____

_____

You have learned how to perform transformations in a plane. Transformations may also be carried out in three-dimensional space. In particular, you can rotate a two-dimensional figure around a line to generate a three-dimensional figure.

CC.9–12.G.GMD.4

2 EXAMPLE   Generating Three-Dimensional Figures

Sketch and describe the figure that is generated by each rotation in three-dimensional space.

A Rotate a right triangle around a line that contains one of its legs.

- Draw a right triangle and draw a line that contains one of its legs, as shown at right.

- To model the rotation of the triangle around the line, trace and cut out the triangle. Then tape the triangle to a piece of string so that one leg of the triangle is attached to the string. Hold both ends of the string and twirl it between your fingers to see the three-dimensional figure generated by the rotation. Sketch the figure at right.

Sketch of Two-Dimensional Figure and Line of Rotation	Sketch of Three-Dimensional Figure Generated by the Rotation
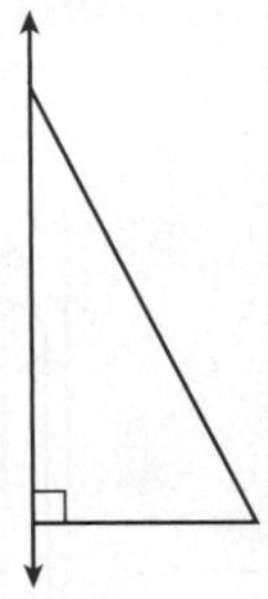	

So, the figure that is generated by the rotation is a _____.

B Rotate a rectangle around a line that contains one of its sides.

- Draw a rectangle and draw a line that contains one of its sides, as shown at right.

- To model the rotation of the rectangle around the line, trace and cut out the rectangle. Then tape the rectangle to a piece of string so that one side of the rectangle is attached to the string. Hold both ends of the string and twirl it between your fingers to see the three-dimensional figure generated by the rotation. Sketch the figure at right.

Sketch of Two-Dimensional Figure and Line of Rotation	Sketch of Three-Dimensional Figure Generated by the Rotation
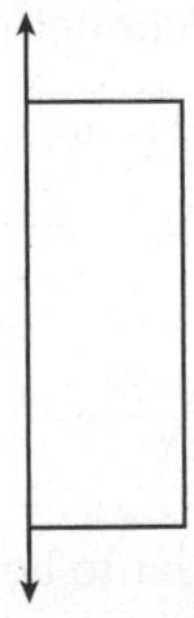	

So, the figure that is generated by the rotation is a _____.

2a. In Part A, suppose you rotate the triangle around the line that contains the other leg of the triangle. Do you get the same result? Explain.

_____

_____

2b. In Part B, how are the length and width of the rectangle related to the dimensions of the three-dimensional figure that is generated by the rotation?

_____

_____

PRACTICE

Describe each cross section.

1.

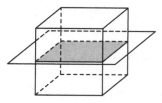

2.

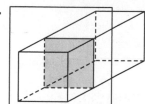

3.

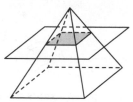

_____   _____   _____

4.

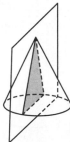

5.

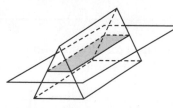

6.

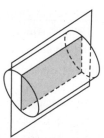

_____   _____   _____

7. Describe the cross section formed by the intersection of a cone and a plane parallel to the base of the cone.

_____

8. Describe the cross section formed by the intersection of a sphere and a plane that passes through the center of the sphere.

_____

Sketch and describe the figure that is generated by each rotation in three-dimensional space.

9. Rotate a semicircle around a line through the endpoints of the semicircle.

10. Rotate an isosceles triangle around the triangle's line of symmetry.

_____

11. Rotate an isosceles right triangle around a line that contains the triangle's hypotenuse.

12. Rotate a line segment around a line that is perpendicular to the segment and that passes through an endpoint of the segment.

_____

13. A cube with sides of length *s* is intersected by a plane that passes through three of the cube's vertices, forming the cross section shown at right. What type of triangle is the cross section? Explain.

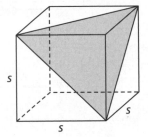

_____

_____

14. **Error Analysis** A student drew the cross section shown at right as a parallelogram. Did the student make an error? Explain.

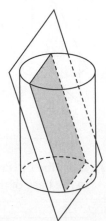

_____

_____

_____

15. Is it possible for a cross section of a cube to be an octagon? Why or why not?

_____

_____

_____

© Houghton Mifflin Harcourt Publishing Company

Additional Practice

Describe each cross section.

1.

_____

2.

_____

3.

_____

4.

_____

5. Use your results from Exercises 1–4 to write a conjecture about the shape of any cross section parallel to the base of a solid.

_____

_____

Sketch and describe the figure formed by each rotation in three-dimensional space.

6. a quarter circle rotated around the the given axis (horizontal line)

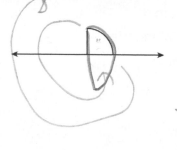

7. the composite shape rotated around the given axis (horizontal line)

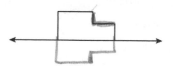

_____   _____

_____   _____

© Houghton Mifflin Harcourt Publishing Company

Problem Solving

1. A slice of cheese is cut from the cylinder-shaped cheese as shown. Describe the cross section.

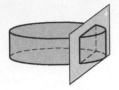

a rectangle

2. A square pyramid is intersected by a plane as shown. Describe the cross section.

square

3. Which of the following does NOT have a cross section in the shape of a circle?

   A sphere

   B cylinder

   C pyramid

   D cone

4. Which of the following could be rotated through three-dimensional space to form a cone?

   F right triangle

   G parallelogram

   H semicircle

   J trapezoid

5. Which of the following could NOT be a cross section of a rectangular prism with square bases?

   A rectangle

   B line segment

   C square

   D two points

6. Which of the following could be rotated through three-dimensional space to form a cylinder?

   F semicircle

   G trapezoid

   H equilateral triangle

   J square

Volume of Prisms and Cylinders
Going Deeper

Essential question: *How do you calculate the volume of a prism or cylinder and use volume formulas to solve design problems?*

Recall that the *volume* of a three-dimensional figure is the number of nonoverlapping cubic units contained in the interior of the figure. For example, the prism at right has a volume of 8 cubic centimeters. You can use this idea to develop volume formulas.

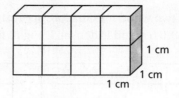

1 cm
1 cm
1 cm

CC.9–12.G.GMD.1

1   E X P L O R E   **Developing a Basic Volume Formula**

A   Consider a figure that is the base of a prism or cylinder. Assume the figure has an area of *B* square units.

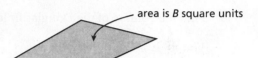
area is *B* square units

B   Use the base to build a prism or cylinder with height 1 unit.

This means the prism or cylinder contains _____ cubic units.

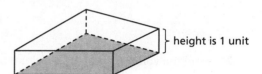
height is 1 unit

C   Now use the base to build a prism or cylinder with a height of *h* units.

The volume of this prism or cylinder must be _____ times the volume of the prism or cylinder whose height is 1 unit.

So, the volume of the prism or cylinder is _____ cubic units.

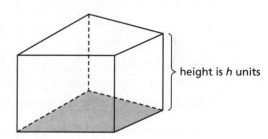
height is *h* units

REFLECT

1a.   Suppose the figure that is the base of the prism is a rectangle with length ℓ and width w. Explain how you can use your work in the Explore to write a formula for the volume of the prism.

_____

_____

1b.   Explain how you can use your work in the Explore to write a formula for the volume of a cylinder whose base is a circle with radius *r*.

_____

Volume of a Cylinder

The volume V of a cylinder with base area B and height h is given by
$V = Bh$ (or $V = \pi r^2 h$, where r is the radius of the base).

CC.9–12.G.MG.2

2 EXAMPLE Comparing Densities

You gather data about two wood logs that are approximately cylindrical. Based on
the data in the table, which wood is denser, Douglas fir or American redwood?

Type of Wood	Diameter (ft)	Height (ft)	Weight (lb)
Douglas fir	1	6	155.5
American redwood	3	4	791.7

A Find the volume of the Douglas fir log.

$V = \pi r^2 h$

$V = \pi(_____)^2 \cdot _____$ Substitute 0.5 for r and 6 for h.

$V \approx _____$ ft^3 Use a calculator. Round to the nearest tenth.

B Find the volume of the American redwood log.

$V = \pi r^2 h$

$V = \pi(_____)^2 \cdot _____$ Substitute 1.5 for r and 4 for h.

$V \approx _____$ ft^3 Use a calculator. Round to the nearest tenth.

C Calculate and compare densities.

The density of the wood is the _____ per _____.

Density of Douglas fir =  $\approx$ _____ lb/ft^3 Round to the nearest unit.

Density of American redwood = $\approx$ _____ lb/ft^3 Round to the nearest unit.

So, _____ is denser than _____.

REFLECT

2a. Explain in your own words what your results tell you about the two types
of wood.

_____

_____

The axis of a cylinder is the segment whose endpoints are the centers of the bases. A **right cylinder** is a cylinder whose axis is perpendicular to the bases. An **oblique cylinder** is a cylinder whose axis is not perpendicular to the bases. Cavalieri's principle makes it possible to extend the formula for the volume of a cylinder to oblique cylinders.

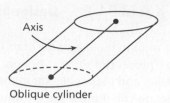
Oblique cylinder

Cavalieri's Principle

If two solids have the same height and the same cross-sectional area at every level, then the two solids have the same volume.

You can think of any oblique cylinder as a right cylinder that has been "pushed over" so that the cross sections at every level have equal areas. By Cavalieri's principle, the volume of an oblique cylinder is equal to the volume of the associated right cylinder. This means the formula $V = Bh = \pi r^2 h$ works for any cylinder.

CC.9–12.G.GMD.2(+)

3 EXAMPLE Finding the Volume of an Oblique Cylinder

The height of the cylinder shown here is twice the radius. What is the volume of the cylinder? Round to the nearest tenth.

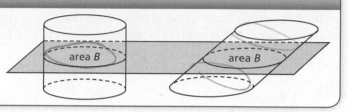
$B = 64\pi \text{ cm}^2$

A Find the height of the cylinder. To do so, first find the radius of the cylinder.

Use the fact that the area of the base B is 64π cm^2.

$\pi r^2 = 64\pi$ The base is a circle, so $B = \pi r^2$.

$r^2 = $ _____   Divide both sides by π.

$r = $ _____ cm   Take the square root of both sides.

Since the height is twice the radius, the height is _____ cm.

B Find the volume of the cylinder.

$V = Bh$ The volume V of any cylinder is $V = Bh$.

$V = $ _____ • _____   Substitute.

$V \approx $ _____ cm^3 Use a calulator. Round to the nearest tenth.

REFLECT

3a. A rectangular prism has the same height as the oblique cylinder in the example. The cross-sectional area at every level of the prism is 64π cm^2. Can you use Cavalieri's principle to make a conclusion about the volume of the prism? Why or why not?

_____

_____

© Houghton Mifflin Harcourt Publishing Company

4 EXAMPLE   Designing a Box with Maximum Volume

You want to build a storage box from a piece of plywood that is 4 feet by 8 feet. You must use 6 pieces (for the top, bottom, and sides of the box) and you must make cuts that are parallel and perpendicular to the edges of the plywood. Describe three possible designs. What do you think is the maximum possible volume for the box?

A Consider Design 1 at right. The top, bottom, front, and back of the box are congruent rectangles. The ends are squares. The gray piece is waste.

From the figure, $4x =$ _____, so $x =$ _____ ft

and $8 - x =$ _____ ft.

$V =$ _____ · _____ · _____ = _____ ft^3

Design 1

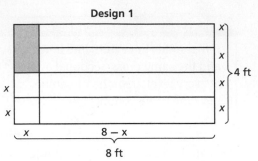

B Consider Design 2 at right. The top, bottom, front, and back of the box are congruent rectangles. The ends are squares. The gray piece is waste.

From the figure, $5x =$ _____, so $x =$ _____ ft.

$V =$ _____ · _____ · _____ = _____ ft^3

Design 2

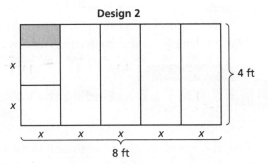

C Consider Design 3 at right. The top, bottom, front, and back of the box are congruent rectangles. The ends are squares. There is no waste.

From the figure, $2x =$ _____, so $x =$ _____ ft

and $\frac{8-x}{2} =$ _____ ft.

$V =$ _____ · _____ · _____ = _____ ft^3

Design 3

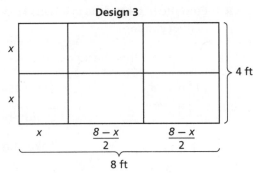

D Based on these designs, the maximum possible volume appears to be _____.

REFLECT

4a. Is it possible to make a box all of whose sides are not squares? If so, give the dimensions of the box and find its volume.

_____

_____

4b. Is it possible to say what the maximum volume of the box is based on your work above? Why or why not?

_____

_____

cylinder = $\pi r^2 h$

Find the volume of each prism or cylinder. Round to the nearest tenth.

1.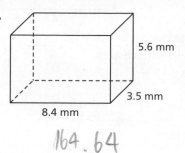

5.6 mm

3.5 mm

8.4 mm

164.64

2.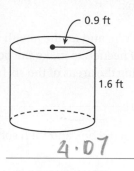

0.9 ft

1.6 ft

4.07

3.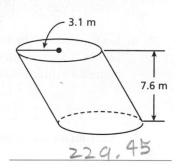

3.1 m

7.6 m

229.45

4. You gather data about two wood logs that are approximately cylindrical. The data are shown in the table. Based on your data, which wood is denser, aspen or juniper? Explain.

Type of Wood	Diameter (ft)	Height (ft)	Weight (lb)
Aspen	1.5	3	137.8
Juniper	2	5	549.8

Aspen

5. A vase in the shape of an oblique cylinder has the dimensions shown at right. How many liters of water does the vase hold? Round to the nearest tenth. (*Hint:* 1 liter = 1000 cm³)

~~2 cm~~ 1.5

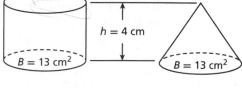

17 cm

14 ÷ 7 14 cm

7²π 17 =

6. Error Analysis A student claims that the cylinder and cone at right have the same volume by Cavalieri's principle. Explain the student's error.

$h = 4$ cm

$B = 13$ cm² $B = 13$ cm²

7. You have 500 cm³ of clay and want to make a sculpture in the shape of a cylinder. You want the height of the cylinder to be 3 times the cylinder's radius and you want to use all the clay. What radius and height should the sculpture have?

3.76, 11.28

$\pi r^2 h = 500$

$3r = h$ *$3\pi r^3 = 500$*

© Houghton Mifflin Harcourt Publishing Company

8. You want to build a box in the shape of a rectangular prism. The box must have a volume of 420 in.³ As shown in the figure, the ends of the box must be squares. In order to minimize the cost, you want to use the least possible amount of material. Follow these steps to determine the dimensions you should use for the box.

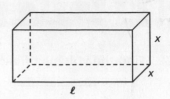

a. Let the ends of the box be x in. by x in. and let the length of the box be ℓ in. The amount of material M needed to make the box is its surface area. Write an expression for M by adding the areas of the six faces.

_____

b. Write an equation for the volume of the box and then solve it for ℓ.

_____

c. Substitute the expression for ℓ in the expression for M from part (a).

_____

d. To find the value of x that minimizes M, enter the expression for M as Y_1 in your calculator. Graph the function in a suitable viewing window. Go to the Calc menu and choose **3: minimum** to find the value of x that minimizes M. Use your equation from part (b) to find the corresponding value of ℓ. What dimensions should you use for the box?

_____

9. You have a flexible piece of sheet metal that measures 4 feet by 8 feet. You want to build a cylinder by cutting out two circles for the bases and a rectangular piece that can be bent to form the lateral surface.

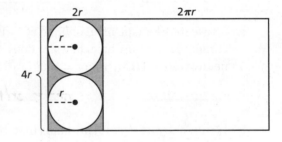

a. Let r be the radius of the cylinder. From the figure, there are two constraints on r: $4r \leq 4$ (based on the width of the metal) and $2r + 2\pi r \leq 8$ (based on the length of the metal). What is the greatest value of r that satisfies both constraints?

_____

b. What is the approximate volume of the cylinder with this radius?

_____

Additional Practice

Find the volume of each prism. Round to the nearest tenth if necessary.

1.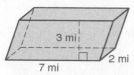

the oblique rectangular prism

2.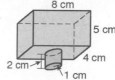

the regular octagonal prism

_____

3. a cube with edge length 0.75 m _____

Find the volume of each cylinder. Give your answers both in terms of π and rounded to the nearest tenth.

4.

5.

_____

6. a cylinder with base circumference 18π ft and height 10 ft _____

7. CDs have the dimensions shown in the figure. Each CD is 1 mm thick. Find the volume in cubic centimeters of a stack of 25 CDs. Round to the nearest tenth.

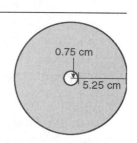

_____

Describe the effect of each change on the volume of the given figure.

8.

The dimensions are halved.

9.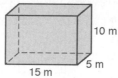

The dimensions are divided by 5.

_____

Find the volume of each composite figure. Round to the nearest tenth.

10.

11.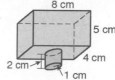

_____

Problem Solving

$\pi r^2 h$ $3.3135 \, feet^3$ $\dfrac{12 \, in^3}{1 \, ft^3} \; \dfrac{1 \, gallon}{231 \, in^3}$

1. A cylindrical juice container has the dimensions shown. About how many cups of juice does this container hold? (*Hint:* 1 cup ≈ 14.44 in³)

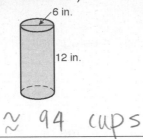
6 in.
12 in.

≈ 94 cups

2. A large cylindrical cooler is $2\frac{1}{2}$ feet high and has a diameter of $1\frac{1}{2}$ feet. It is filled $\frac{3}{4}$ high with water for athletes to use during their soccer game. Estimate the volume of the water in the cooler in gallons. (*Hint:* 1 gallon ≈ 231 in³)

24.76

$4\pi = \pi r^2 h$

Choose the best answer.

3. How many 3-inch cubes can be placed inside the box?

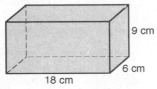
9 cm
6 cm
18 cm

A 27   C 45
B 36   D 72

4. A cylinder has a volume of 4π cm³. If the radius and height are each tripled, what will be the new volume of the cylinder?

F 12π cm³   H 64π cm³
G 36π cm³   J 108π cm³

5. What is the volume of the composite figure with the dimensions shown in the three views? Round to the nearest tenth.

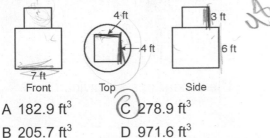
4 ft
4 ft
3 ft
6 ft
7 ft
Front   Top   Side

48 ×

A 182.9 ft³   C 278.9 ft³
B 205.7 ft³   D 971.6 ft³

6. Find the expression that can be used to determine the volume of the composite figure shown.

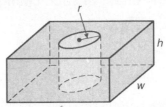
r
h
w
ℓ

F $\ell wh - \pi r^2 h$ H $\pi r^2 h - \ell wh$
G $\pi r^2 h + \ell wh$ J $\ell wh + 2\pi r^2 h$

$\pi r^2 h + \ell wh$

11-3

Volume of Pyramids and Cones
Going Deeper

Essential question: *How do you calculate the volume of a pyramid or cone and use volume formulas to solve problems?*

Recall that a *pyramid* is a polyhedron formed by a polygonal base and triangular lateral faces that meet at a common point, called the vertex of the pyramid. The goal of this lesson is to develop a formula for volume of a pyramid.

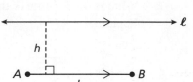

Video Tutor

1 EXPLORE Developing a Volume Postulate

A Consider a segment, $\overline{AB}$, with length b and a line ℓ that is parallel to $\overline{AB}$. Let h be the distance between $\overline{AB}$ and line ℓ.

Choose a point C on line ℓ and draw $\triangle ABC$. What is the area of $\triangle ABC$ in terms of b and h?

_____

B Choose a different point C on line ℓ and draw $\triangle ABC$. What is the area of $\triangle ABC$ in terms of b and h?

_____

C What do you think is true about all triangles that share the same base and have the same height?

_____

REFLECT

1a. Consider a three-dimensional figure that is analogous to the situation you explored above. Suppose you are given a polygon and a plane R that is parallel to the plane containing the polygon. You can form a pyramid by choosing a point in plane R and connecting it to each vertex of the polygon. What do you think is true of all pyramids formed in this way?

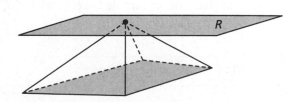

_____

Based on your work in the Explore, the following postulate should seem reasonable.

Postulate

Pyramids that have equal base areas and equal heights have equal volumes.

In order to find a formula for the volume of any pyramid, you will first find a formula for the volume of a "wedge pyramid." A wedge pyramid is one in which the base is a triangle and a perpendicular segment from the pyramid's vertex to the base intersects the base at a vertex of the triangle. Pyramid *A-BCD* is a wedge pyramid.

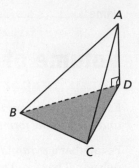

2 EXPLORE   Finding the Volume of a Wedge Pyramid

To find the volume of pyramid *A-BCD*, first let the area of △*BCD* be *B* and let the height of the pyramid, *AD*, be *h*.

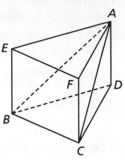

A   Form a triangular prism as shown. The edges $\overline{EB}$ and $\overline{FC}$ are congruent to $\overline{AD}$ and parallel to $\overline{AD}$. The bases of the prism, △*EFA* and △*BCD* are congruent.

B   What is the volume of the triangular prism in terms of *B* and *h*? Explain.

_____

_____

C   You will now compare the volume of pyramid *A-BCD* and the volume of the triangular prism.

Draw $\overline{EC}$. This is the diagonal of a rectangle so, △ _____ ≅ △ _____ .

Explain why pyramids *A-EBC* and *A-CFE* have the same volume.

_____

_____

_____

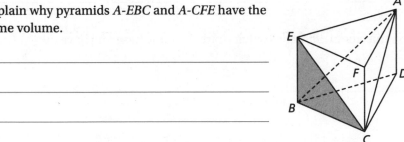

Explain why pyramids *C-EFA* and *A-BCD* have the same volume.

_____

_____

_____

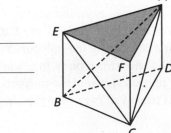

D You have shown that the three pyramids that form the triangular prism all have the same volume. Compare the volume of pyramid *A-BCD* and the volume of the triangular prism.

_____

_____

E Write the volume of pyramid *A-BCD* in terms of *B* and *h*.

_____

REFLECT

2a. Explain how you know that the three pyramids that form that triangular prism all have the same volume.

_____

_____

_____

_____

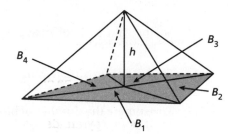

In the Explore, you showed that the volume of any "wedge pyramid" is one-third the product of the base area and the height. Now consider a general pyramid. As shown in the figure, the pyramid can be partitioned into nonoverlapping wedge pyramids by drawing a perpendicular from the vertex to the base.

The volume *V* of the given pyramid is the sum of the volumes of the wedge pyramids.

That is, $V = \frac{1}{3}B_1h + \frac{1}{3}B_2h + \frac{1}{3}B_3h + \frac{1}{3}B_4h$.

Using the distributive property, this may be rewritten as $V = \frac{1}{3}h(B_1 + B_2 + B_3 + B_4)$.

Notice that $B_1 + B_2 + B_3 + B_4 = B$, where *B* is the base area of the given pyramid.

So, $V = \frac{1}{3}Bh$.

The above argument provides an informal justification for the following result.

Volume of a Pyramid

The volume *V* of a pyramid with base area *B* and height *h* is given by
$V = \frac{1}{3}Bh$.

3 E X A M P L E   **Solving a Volume Problem**

The Great Pyramid in Giza, Egypt, is approximately a
square pyramid with the dimensions shown. The pyramid
is composed of stone blocks that are rectangular prisms.
An average block has dimensions 1.3 m by 1.3 m by 0.7 m.
Approximately how many stone blocks were used to build the
pyramid? Round to the nearest hundred thousand.

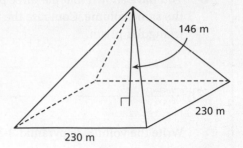

146 m

230 m

230 m

A Find the volume of the pyramid.

The area of the base B is the area of a square with sides of length 230 m.

So, $B =$ _____

The volume V of the pyramid is $\frac{1}{3}Bh = \frac{1}{3} \cdot$ _____ $\cdot$ _____

So, $V =$ _____

B Find the volume of an average block.

The volume of a rectangular prism is given by the formula _____.

So, the volume W of an average block is _____.

C Find the approximate number of stone blocks in the pyramid.

To estimate the number of blocks in the pyramid, divide _____ by _____.

So, the approximate number of blocks is _____.

REFLECT

3a. What aspects of the model in this problem may lead to inaccuracies in your
estimate?

_____

_____

_____

3b. Suppose you are told that the average height of a stone block is 0.69 m rather than
0.7 m. Would this increase or decrease your estimate of the total number of blocks
in the pyramid? Explain.

_____

Recall that a *cone* is a three-dimensional figure with a circular base and a curved lateral surface that connects the base to a point called the vertex. You can use the formula for the volume of a pyramid to develop a formula for the volume of a cone.

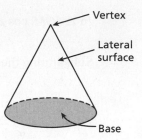

Vertex

Lateral surface

Base

CC.9–12.G.GMD.1

4 EXPLORE   Developing a Volume Formula

Plan: To find the volume of a given cone, consider pyramids with regular polygonal bases that are inscribed in the cone. As the number of sides of the polygonal bases increases, the volume of the pyramid gets closer to the volume of the cone. The first steps of the argument consist of writing an expression for the volume of an inscribed pyramid.

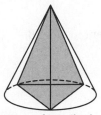 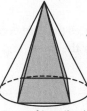 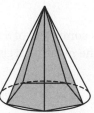

Base of inscribed pyramid has 3 sides.   Base of inscribed pyramid has 4 sides.   Base of inscribed pyramid has 5 sides.

A Let O be the center of the cone's base and let r be the radius of the cone. Let h be the height of the cone. Inscribe a pyramid whose base is a regular n-gon in the cone. Draw radii from O to the vertices of the n-gon.

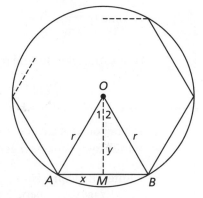

B Let $\overline{AB}$ be one side of the n-gon. Draw $\overline{OM}$, the segment from O to the midpoint of $\overline{AB}$.

Then $\triangle AOM \cong \triangle BOM$ by _____.

So, $\angle 1 \cong \angle 2$ by _____.

C There are _____ triangles, all congruent to $\triangle AOB$, that surround point O and fill the n-gon.

Therefore, m$\angle AOB =$ _____ and m$\angle 1 =$ _____.

D Since $\angle OMA \cong \angle OMB$ by CPCTC, and $\angle OMA$ and $\angle OMB$ form a linear pair, these angles are supplementary and must have measures of 90°. So, $\triangle AOM$ and $\triangle BOM$ are right triangles.

In $\triangle AOM$, $\sin \angle 1 = \frac{x}{r}$, so $x = r \sin \angle 1$.

Substituting the expression for m$\angle 1$ from above gives $x = r \sin ($_____$)$.

E In $\triangle AOM$, $\cos \angle 1 = \frac{y}{r}$, so $y = r \cos \angle 1$.

Substituting the expression for m$\angle 1$ from above gives $y = r \cos ($_____$)$.

F To write an expression for the area of the base of the pyramid, first write an expression for the area of $\triangle AOB$.

$$\text{Area}(\triangle AOB) = \tfrac{1}{2} \cdot \text{base} \cdot \text{height} = \tfrac{1}{2} \cdot 2x \cdot y = xy$$

Substituting the expressions for x and y from above gives the following.

Area ($\triangle AOB$) = _____

The base of the pyramid is composed of n triangles that are congruent to $\triangle AOB$, so the area of the base of the pyramid is given by the following.

Area (base of pyramid) = _____

The volume of the pyramid is $\frac{1}{3} \cdot$ base $\cdot$ height, which may be written as

Volume (pyramid) = _____

G Your expression for the pyramid's volume should include the expression

$$n \sin \left(\tfrac{180°}{n}\right) \cos \left(\tfrac{180°}{n}\right)$$

as a factor. Use a calculator, as follows, to find out what happens to the value of this expression as n gets larger and larger.

- Enter the expression
  $x \sin \left(\frac{180}{x}\right) \cos \left(\frac{180}{x}\right)$ as Y_1.
- Go to the Table Setup menu and enter the values shown at right.
- View a table for the function.
- Use the arrow keys to scroll down.

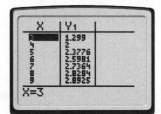

What happens to the value of $n \sin \left(\frac{180°}{n}\right) \cos \left(\frac{180°}{n}\right)$ as n gets larger?

_____

H Consider the expression you wrote for the volume of the inscribed pyramid at the end of Step F. What happens to the value of this expression as n gets larger?

_____

4a. How is the formula for the volume of a cone, which you derived above, similar to the formula for the volume of a pyramid?

_____

_____

The argument in the Explore provides a justification for the following result.

> ### Volume of a Cone
>
> The volume V of a cone with base area B and height h is given by $V = \frac{1}{3}Bh$ (or $V = \frac{1}{3}\pi r^2 h$, where r is the radius of the base).

CC.9–12.G.GMD.3

5 **E X A M P L E** Solving a Volume Problem

A conical paper cup has the dimensions shown. How many fluid ounces of liquid does the cup hold? Round to the nearest tenth. (*Hint:* 1 in.$^3 \approx 0.554$ fl oz.)

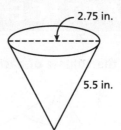

2.75 in.

5.5 in.

A Find the radius and height of the cone.

The radius r is half the diameter, so $r =$ _____.

To find the height h of the cone, use the Pythagorean Theorem.

$$h^2 + r^2 = 5.5^2 \qquad \text{Pythagorean Theorem}$$

$$h^2 + (\underline{\quad})^2 = 5.5^2 \qquad \text{Substitute the value of } r.$$

$$h^2 = \underline{\qquad} \qquad \text{Solve for } h^2.$$

$$h \approx \underline{\qquad} \qquad \text{Solve for } h.\ \text{Round to the nearest thousandth.}$$

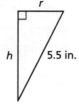

r

h

5.5 in.

B Find the volume of the cone to the nearest hundredth.

$$V = \frac{1}{3}\pi r^2 h = \frac{1}{3}\pi \cdot (\underline{\qquad})^2 \cdot (\underline{\qquad}) \approx \underline{\qquad}$$

C Convert the volume to fluid ounces.

_____ in.$^3 \approx$ _____ $\cdot$ 0.554 fl oz $\approx$ _____ fl oz

So, the cup holds approximately _____ fluid ounces.

5a. A cylindrical cup has the same diameter and height as the conical cup. How can you find the number of fluid ounces that the cylindrical cup holds?

_____

5b. Suppose the height of the conical paper cup is doubled, but the base radius is not changed. How would the volume of the cup change?

_____

5c. Suppose the height of the conical paper cup is not changed, but the base radius is doubled. How would the volume of the cup change?

_____

PRACTICE

Find the volume of each pyramid. Round to the nearest tenth.

1.

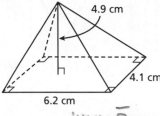

4.9 cm

4.1 cm

6.2 cm

$\overline{41.53}$

2.

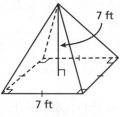

7 ft

7 ft

~~3478~~ 114.3

3.

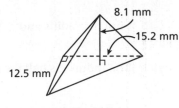

8.1 mm

15.2 mm

12.5 mm

513

4. As shown in the figure, polyhedron *ABCDEFGH* is a cube and *P* is any point on face *EFGH*. Compare the volume of pyramid *P-ABCD* and the volume of the cube.

poly hedron would be a

third of cube

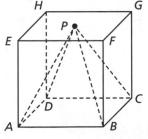

5. A storage container for grain is in the shape of a square pyramid with the dimensions shown.

a. What is the volume of the container in cubic centimeters?

0.5 m

b. Grain leaks from the container at a rate of 4 cm³ per second. Assuming the container starts completely full, about how many hours does it take until the container is empty?

12.5 hows

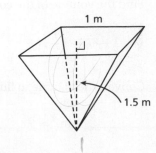

1 m

1.5 m

6. A piece of pure silver in the shape of a rectangular pyramid with the dimensions shown at right has a mass of 19.7 grams.

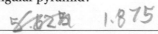

a. What is the area of the base?

_____ 3.75 _____

b. What is the volume of the rectangular pyramid?

_____ 5.625 1.875 _____

c. Use the mass of silver and the volume you calculated to estimate the density of silver.

_____ 10.5 _____

7. A pyramid has a square base and a height of 5 ft. The volume of the pyramid is 60 ft³. Explain how to find the length of a side of the pyramid's base.

_____ 3.464 , _____

_____

_____

Find the volume of each cone. Round to the nearest tenth.

8.

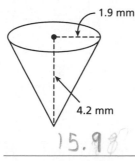

15.98

9.

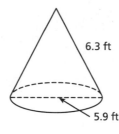

_____

10.

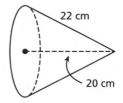

1759.3

11. The figure shows a water tank that consists of a cylinder and cone. How many gallons of water does the tank hold? Round to the nearest gallon. (*Hint:* 1 ft³ ≈ 7.48 gal)

_____

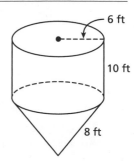

12. Popcorn is available in two cups: a square pyramid or a cone, as shown. The price of each cup of popcorn is the same. Which cup is the better deal? Explain.

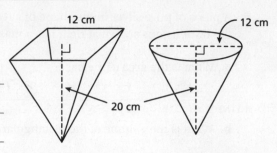

_____

_____

_____

13. A sculptor removes a cone from a cylindrical block of wood so that the vertex of the cone is the center of the cylinder's base, as shown. Explain how the volume of the remaining solid compares with the volume of the original cylindrical block of wood.

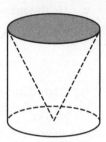

_____

_____

_____

Additional Practice

cone= $\frac{1}{3} \pi r^2 h$

pyramid= $\frac{1}{3} bh$

Find the volume of each pyramid. Round to the nearest tenth if necessary.

1. 14 mm

35 mm

the regular pentagonal pyramid

____163.3934____

2. 6 yd 7 yd

4 yd

the rectangular right pyramid

____56 yd____

3. Giza in Egypt is the site of the three great Egyptian pyramids. Each pyramid has a square base. The largest pyramid was built for Khufu. When first built, it had base edges of 754 feet and a height of 481 feet. Over the centuries, some of the stone eroded away and some was taken for newer buildings. Khufu's pyramid today has base edges of 745 feet and a height of 471 feet. To the nearest cubic foot, find the difference between the original and current volumes of the pyramid.

____85888640 feet____

Find the volume of each cone. Give your answers both in terms of π and rounded to the nearest tenth.

4.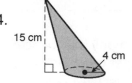

15 cm

4 cm

____251.3 cm____

5. 28 mi 100 mi

____78816.3____

6. a cone with base circumference 6π m and a height equal to half the radius

____14.1 m____

7. Compare the volume of a cone and the volume of a cylinder with equal height and base area.

____The cylinder is triple the size____

Describe the effect of each change on the volume of the given figure.

8. 5 in.

4 in.

4 in.

The dimensions are multiplied by $\frac{2}{3}$. 3 times

____The area got about a third smaller____

9. 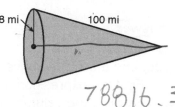 8 mi

4 mi

The dimensions are tripled.

____area got 27 times bigger____

Find the volume of each composite figure. Round to the nearest tenth.

10. 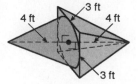 3 ft

4 ft 4 ft

3 ft

____13.0____

11. 5 mm

8 mm

____157.1____

Problem Solving

1. A regular square pyramid has a base area of 196 meters and a lateral area of 448 square meters. What is the volume of the pyramid? Round your answer to the nearest tenth.

_____

2. A paper cone for serving roasted almonds has a volume of 406π cubic centimeters. A smaller cone has half the radius and half the height of the first cone. What is the volume of the smaller cone? Give your answer in terms of π.

_____

3. The hexagonal base in the pyramid is a regular polygon. What is the volume of the pyramid if its height is 9 centimeters? Round to the nearest tenth.

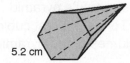

5.2 cm

_____

4. Find the volume of the shaded solid in the figure shown. Give your answer in terms of π.

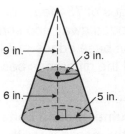

9 in.   3 in.

6 in.   5 in.

_____

Choose the best answer.

5. The diameter of the cone equals the width of the cube, and the figures have the same height. Find the expression that can be used to determine the volume of the composite figure.

A $4(4)(4) - \frac{1}{3}\pi(2^2)(4)$

B $4(4)(4) + \frac{1}{3}\pi(2^2)(4)$

C $4(4)(4) - \pi(2^2)(4)$

D $4(4)(4) + \frac{1}{3}\pi(2^2)$

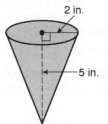

4 ft

4 ft

4 ft

6. Approximately how many fluid ounces of water can the paper cup hold? (*Hint:* 1 fl oz ≈ 1.805 in^3)

2 in.

5 in.

F   10.9 fl oz   H   32.7 fl oz

G   11.6 fl oz   J   36.3 fl oz

7. The Step Pyramid of Djoser in Lower Egypt was the first pyramid in the history of architecture. Its original height was 204 feet, and it had a rectangular base measuring 411 feet by 358 feet. Which is the best estimate for the volume of the pyramid in cubic yards?

A   370,570 yd^3 C   3,335,128 yd^3

B   1,111,709 yd^3 D   10,005,384 yd^3

Performance Tasks

CHAPTER 11

COMMON
CORE

CC.9-12.G.GMD.3
CC.9-12.G.GMD.4
CC.9-12.G.MG.1
CC.9-12.G.MG.3

⭐ **1.** Rectangular sheets of paper are in a sealed box that is 21.6 centimeters by 27.9 centimeters by 26.1 centimeters. What are the three largest possible sizes for the paper? Assume that all of the sheets are the same size and that the box is full.

⭐ **2.** A caterer is making soup in a cylindrical pot that has a 12-inch diameter and can be filled to a depth of 13 inches. The caterer has cylindrical storage containers for the soup that have 6-inch diameters and can be filled to a depth of 4 inches.

    a. How many storage containers does the caterer need for a full pot of soup? Explain.

    b. One serving of soup is about 15 cubic inches. To the nearest tenth of a serving, about how many servings of soup does one storage container hold? How do you know?

⭐ **3.**
⭐ Two congruent, cylindrical salt-and-pepper shakers fit snugly beside one another inside a rectangular prism box, as shown at right. The box is 7 centimeters wide, 14 centimeters long, and 10 centimeters high, and the shakers are upright. The shakers are the same height as the box.

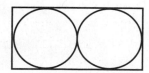

    a. Find the radius of one shaker. Justify your answer.

    b. After the shakers are put into the box, the remaining empty space is filled with shredded paper. What volume of shredded paper will be included in the box? Round your answer to the nearest cubic centimeter and show your work.

continued

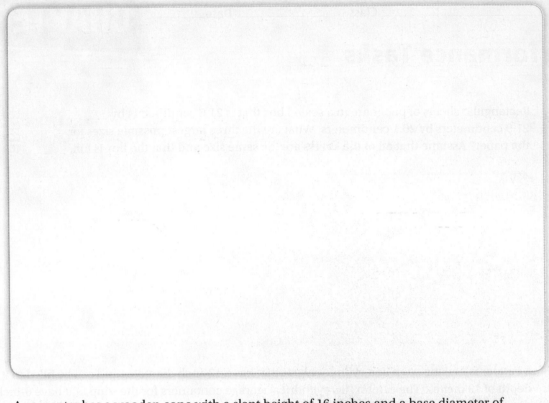

4. A carpenter has a wooden cone with a slant height of 16 inches and a base diameter of 12 inches. The vertex of the cone is directly above the center of its base. The carpenter measures halfway down the slant height and makes a cut parallel to the base. The carpenter now has a truncated cone and a cone half the height of the original.

a. The carpenter expected the two parts to weigh about the same, but they don't. Which is heavier? Explain your reasoning.

b. Find the ratio of the weight of the small cone to that of the truncated cone. Do not round any quantities until you get to your final answer. Show your work.

Name _____ Class _____ Date _____

MULTIPLE CHOICE

1. The figure shows a rectangular prism that is intersected by a plane parallel to a face of the prism. Which is the most precise description of the cross section?

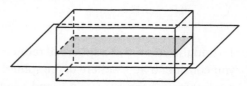

A. parallelogram   **C.** trapezoid

B. rectangle   **D.** triangle

2. In the figure, $\overline{BA} \cong \overline{BC}$. You rotate $\angle ABC$ around a line that bisects the angle. What figure is generated by this rotation in three-dimensional space?

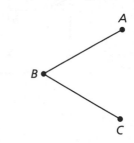

F. cone   **H.** pyramid

G. cylinder   **J.** sphere

3. A wood log is approximately cylindrical with the dimensions shown below. The log weighs 206.8 pounds. What is the density of the wood, to the nearest whole number?

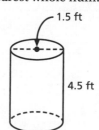

1.5 ft

4.5 ft

A. 7 lb/ft³   **C.** 20 lb/ft³

B. 8 lb/ft³   **D.** 26 lb/ft³

4. A wire frame in the shape of the cube is used to support a pyramid-shaped basket, as shown. The vertex of the pyramid lies in the same plane as a face of the cube. To the nearest tenth, what is the volume of th pyramid-shaped basket?

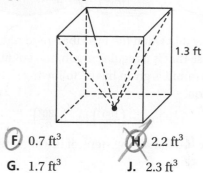

1.3 ft

F. 0.7 ft³   **H.** 2.2 ft³

G. 1.7 ft³   **J.** 2.3 ft³

5. A food manufacturer sells yogurt in cone-shaped cups with the dimensions shown. To the nearest tenth, how many fluid ounces of yogurt does the cup hold?
(*Hint:* 1 cm³ ≈ 0.034 fl oz)

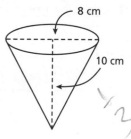

8 cm

10 cm

A. 0.6 fl oz   **C.** 17.1 fl oz

B. 5.7 fl oz   **D.** 22.8 fl oz

6. You want to design a cylindrical container for oatmeal that has a volume of 90 in.³ You also want the height of the container to be 3.5 times the radius. To the nearest tenth, what should the radius of the container be?

F. 2.0 in.   **H.** 3.0 in.

G. 2.9 in.   **J.** 3.1 in.

$h = 3.5r$

$90 = r^2 \pi \, 3.5r \frac{1}{3}$

$90 = r^2 \pi h \frac{1}{3}$

CONSTRUCTED RESPONSE

7. In order to develop and justify the formula for the volume of a cone, you begin with a given cone that has radius r and height h. You consider pyramids with regular polygonal bases that are inscribed in the cone.

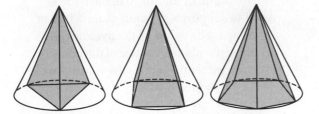

You show that when the inscribed pyramid has a base that is a regular n-gon, the volume of the pyramid is given by the following expression.

$$\frac{1}{3}r^2hn \sin\left(\frac{180°}{n}\right) \cos\left(\frac{180°}{n}\right)$$

Describe the remaining steps of the argument.

_____

_____

_____

_____

_____

_____

_____

8. A spherical gas tank has the dimensions shown. When filled with butane, it provides 468,766 BTU. How many BTUs does one cubic foot of butane yield? Round to the nearest BTU.

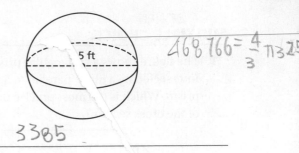

468 766 = $\frac{4}{3}$ π3 25³

5 ft

3385

_____

9. To find the volume of a sphere of radius r, you consider a hemisphere of the sphere and a cylinder with the same radius and height as the hemisphere from which a cone has been removed. You show that the solids have the same cross-sectional area at every level. Explain how to use the solids to derive the formula for the volume of a sphere.

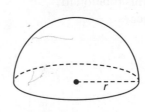 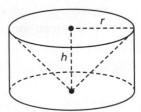

r

h

r

_____

_____

_____

_____

_____

_____

_____

Circles

Chapter Focus

In this unit, you will work with circles and explore their connection to other familiar geometric figures. First, you will learn some vocabulary associated with circles and investigate central and inscribed angles. You will also learn how to do constructions to inscribe polygons in circles and to inscribe circles in polygons. Along the way, you will study properties of tangent lines.

Chapter at a Glance

COMMON CORE

Lesson		Standards for Mathematical Content
12-1	Lines That Intersect Circles	CC.9-12.G.C.2
12-2	Arcs and Chords	CC.9-12.G.C.2
12-3	Sector Area and Arc Length	CC.9-12.G.CO.1, CC.9-12.G.C.5, CC.9-12.G.GMD.1
12-4	Inscribed Angles	CC.9-12.G.C.2, CC.9-12.G.C.3
12-5	Angle Relationships in Circles	CC.9-12.G.CO.9, CC.9-12.G.C.4(+)
12-6	Segment Relationships in Circles	CC.9-12.G.C.2, CC.9-12.G.MG.1
12-7	Circles in the Coordinate Plane	CC.9-12.A.REI.7, CC.9-12.G.GPE.1, CC.9-12.G.GPE.4
	Performance Tasks	
	Assessment Readiness	

CHAPTER 12

Unpacking the Standards

Understanding the standards and the vocabulary terms in the standards will help you know exactly what you are expected to learn in this chapter.

COMMON CORE CC.9-12.G.GPE.1

Derive the equation of a circle of given center and radius using the Pythagorean Theorem; …

Key Vocabulary
circle *(círculo)*
The set of points in a plane that are a fixed distance from a given point called the *center of the circle.*
radius of a circle *(radio de un círculo)* A segment whose endpoints are the center of a circle and a point on the circle; the distance from the center of a circle to any point on the circle.
Pythagorean Theorem *(Teorema de Pitágoras)* If a right triangle has legs of lengths a and b and a hypotenuse of length c, then $a^2 + b^2 = c^2$.

What It Means For You   Lesson 12-7

You can use the Pythagorean Theorem to derive the Distance Formula. In turn, you can use the Distance Formula to derive the general form of the equation of a circle.

EXAMPLE

For the circle shown, the distance from the center (h, k) to any point (x, y) on the circle is the radius. The center is at $(-1, 2)$ and the radius is 3. Using the Distance Formula:

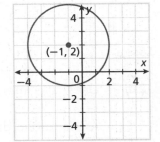

$$\sqrt{(x - h)^2 + (y - k)^2} = r$$

$$\sqrt{(x - (-1))^2 + (y - 2)^2} = 3$$

$$\sqrt{(x + 1)^2 + (y - 2)^2} = 3$$

Squaring both sides of the equation gives the equation of the circle, $(x + 1)^2 + (y - 2)^2 = 9$.

COMMON CORE CC.9-12.G.C.2

Identify and describe relationships among inscribed angles, radii, and chords.

Key Vocabulary
inscribed angle *(ángulo inscrito)*
An angle whose vertex is on a circle and whose sides contain chords of the circle.
chord *(cuerda)* A segment whose endpoints lie on a circle.

What It Means For You   Lessons 12-1, 12-2, 12-4, 12-6

You will learn to recognize many relationships among angles, radii, and chords of circles, and use them to solve problems.

EXAMPLE

An artist's pattern for a stained glass window shows multiple inscribed angles, radii, and chords, and many relationships including the following:

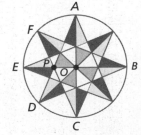

- Radius $\overline{OA}$ is perpendicular to chord $\overline{EB}$, so $\overline{OA}$ bisects $\overline{EB}$ and its arc.

- Chords $\overline{AD}$ and $\overline{FC}$ intersect at P, so $m\angle APF = \frac{1}{2}(m\widehat{AF} + m\widehat{CD})$ and $AP \cdot PD = FP \cdot PC$.

CC.9-12.G.C.5

Derive using similarity the fact that the length of the arc intercepted by an angle is proportional to the radius, and define the radian measure of the angle as the constant of proportionality; derive the formula for the area of a sector.

Key Vocabulary

similar *(semejantes)* Two figures are similar if they have the same shape but not necessarily the same size.

intercepted arc *(arco abarcado)* An arc that consists of endpoints that lie on the sides of an inscribed angle and all the points of the circle between the endpoints.

radian *(radian)* A unit of angle measure based on arc length. In a circle of radius r, if a central angle has a measure of 1 radian, then the length of the intercepted arc is r units.

2π radians = 360°

1 radian ≈ 57°

sector of a circle *(sector de un círculo)* A region inside a circle bounded by two radii of the circle and their intercepted arc.

You can find the length of an arc with central angle m by multiplying the circumference by $\dfrac{m°}{360°}$ if m is in degrees or by $\dfrac{m \text{ radians}}{2\pi \text{ radians}}$ if m is in radians. You can also find the area of a sector by multiplying the area of the circle by $\dfrac{m°}{360°}$ or by $\dfrac{m \text{ radians}}{2\pi \text{ radians}}$.

EXAMPLE   Finding Arc Length

Find the length of $\overarc{CD}$.

Arc length = Circumference × $\dfrac{m°}{360°}$

$$= 2\pi r \times \frac{m°}{360°}$$

$$= 2\pi(10)\left(\frac{90°}{360°}\right)$$

$$= 5\pi \approx 16 \text{ feet}$$

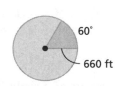

The radian measure of the central angle is

$$90°\left(\frac{2\pi \text{ radians}}{360°}\right) = \frac{\pi}{2} \text{ radians, and } 2\pi r\left(\frac{\frac{\pi}{2}}{2\pi}\right) = 5\pi \approx 16 \text{ feet,}$$

which is the same as the answer above.

EXAMPLE   Finding the Area of a Sector

A farmer uses a rotating sprayer to irrigate a circular plot with radius 660 feet. What is the area that is irrigated as the sprayer moves through an angle of 60°?

Area of sector = Area of plot × $\dfrac{m°}{360°}$

$$= \pi r^2 \times \frac{m°}{360°}$$

$$= \pi(660)^2 \times \left(\frac{60°}{360°}\right)$$

$$= 72{,}600\pi$$

$$\approx 228{,}000 \text{ square feet}$$

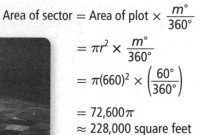

CHAPTER 12

Key Vocabulary

arc *(arco)* An unbroken part of a circle consisting of two points on the circle, called the endpoints, and all the points on the circle between them.

arc length *(longitud de arco)* The distance along an arc measured in linear units.

central angle of a circle *(ángulo central de un círculo)* An angle whose vertex is the center of a circle.

chord *(cuerda)* A segment whose endpoints lie on a circle.

circle *(círculo)* The set of points in a plane that are a fixed distance from a given point called the center of the circle.

concentric circles *(círculos concéntricos)* Coplanar circles with the same center.

inscribed angle *(ángulo inscrito)* An angle whose vertex is on a circle and whose sides contain chords of the circle.

intercepted arc *(arco abarcado)* An arc that consists of endpoints that lie on the sides of an inscribed angle and all the points of the circle between the endpoints.

major arc *(arco mayor)* An arc of a circle whose points are on or in the exterior of a central angle.

minor arc *(arco menor)* An arc of a circle whose points are on or in the interior of a central angle.

point of tangency *(punto de tangencia)* The point of intersection of a circle or sphere with a tangent line or plane.

Pythagorean Theorem *(Teorema de Pitágoras)* If a right triangle has legs of lengths a and b and a hypotenuse of length c, then $a^2 + b^2 = c^2$.

radian *(radian)* A unit of angle measure based on arc length. In a circle of radius r, if a central angle has a measure of 1 radian, then the length of the intercepted arc is r units.

$$2\pi \text{ radians} = 360° \qquad 1 \text{ radian} \approx 57°$$

radius of a circle *(radio de un círculo)* A segment whose endpoints are the center of a circle and a point on the circle; the distance from the center of a circle to any point on the circle.

secant of a circle *(secante de un círculo)* A line that intersects a circle at two points.

sector of a circle *(sector de un círculo)* A region inside a circle bounded by two radii of the circle and their intercepted arc.

semicircle *(semicírculo)* An arc of a circle whose endpoints lie on a diameter

similar *(semejantes)* Two figures are similar if they have the same shape but not necessarily the same size.

tangent of a circle *(tangente de un círculo)* A line that is in the same plane as a circle and intersects the circle at exactly one point.

CHAPTER 12

Lines That Intersect Circles
Focus on Reasoning

Essential question: *What is the relationship between a tangent line to a circle and the radius drawn from the center to the point of tangency?*

A **tangent** is a line in the same plane as a circle that intersects the circle in exactly one point. The point where a tangent and a circle intersect is the **point of tangency**. In the figure, line *m* is a tangent to circle *C*, and point *P* is the point of tangency.

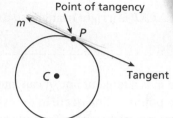

Point of tangency
m
P
C
Tangent

1 **Investigate tangents and radii.**

A Use a compass to draw a circle *O*.

B Plot a point *P* on the circle.

C Using a straightedge, carefully draw a tangent to circle *O* through point *P*. Plot another point *Q* on the tangent line.

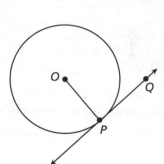

O
Q
P

D Use the straightedge to draw the radius $\overline{OP}$.

E Use a protractor to measure ∠*OPQ*.

F Repeat the process, starting with a different circle.

REFLECT

1a. Compare your findings with those of other students. Then make a conjecture: What can you say about the relationship between a tangent line and a radius to the point of tangency?

_____

1b. Describe any inaccuracies related to the tools you used in the investigation.

_____

_____

You may have discovered the following theorem.

Tangent-Radius Theorem

If a line is tangent to a circle, then it is perpendicular to the radius drawn to the point of tangency.

Line *m* is tangent to circle *C* at point *P*, so $\overline{CP} \perp m$.

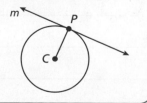

m
P
C

2 Prove the Tangent-Radius Theorem.

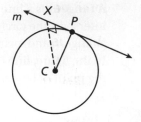

Given: Line *m* is tangent to circle *C* at point *P*.

Prove: $\overline{CP} \perp m$

Use an indirect proof. Assume that $\overline{CP}$ is *not* perpendicular to line *m*. Then it must be possible to draw $\overline{CX}$ so that $\overline{CX} \perp m$.

In this case, $\triangle CXP$ is a right triangle, so $CP > CX$ because

_____

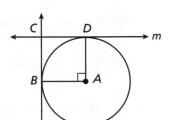

Because line *m* is a tangent line, it can intersect circle *C* at only one point, *P*, and all other points of line *m* are in the exterior of the circle. This means point *X* is in the exterior of the circle. So, you can conclude that $CP < CX$ because

_____

This contradicts the fact that $CP > CX$. Therefore,

_____

REFLECT

2a. In the figure, lines *m* and *n* are tangent lines to circle *A*. What can you say about quadrilateral *ABCD*? Explain.

_____

_____

_____

_____

_____

2b. Prove the converse of the Tangent-Radius Theorem: If a line is perpendicular to a radius of a circle at a point on the circle, then the line is a tangent to the circle. (*Hint:* Consider a circle *C*, point *P* on the circle, and line *m* perpendicular to $\overline{CP}$. Let *Q* be any point on line *m* other than *P*. Show that $CQ > CP$.)

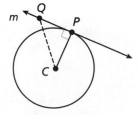

_____

_____

_____

_____

_____

© Houghton Mifflin Harcourt Publishing Company

Additional Practice

In the diagram, $\overline{AB}$, $\overline{BC}$, $\overline{CD}$, and $\overline{DA}$ are tangent to circle O at their midpoints. Use the diagram for Exercises 1–4. For some exercises, you will need to draw on the diagram.

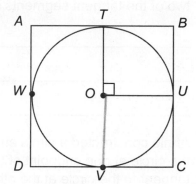

1. What is the measure of $\angle B$? What can you conclude about quadrilateral $OTBU$?

   90°, it is a square

   _____

2. Use a straightedge to draw a radius to point V. What can you conclude about quadrilateral $OUCV$?

   _____

3. Use a straightedge to draw a radius to a point W. What can you conclude about quadrilaterals $WOVD$ and $ATOW$?

   _____

4. Based on your answers to Exercises 1–3, what can you conclude about quadrilateral $ABCD$? Justify your answer.

   _____

   _____

   _____

   _____

   _____

   _____

   _____

5. Suppose a line is tangent to a circle. What theorem can you use to prove that the line is perpendicular to a diameter drawn to the point of tangency?

   _____

Problem Solving

1. In the stained glass window shown, six segments are tangent to a circle. Three diameters divide the circle into six panes. Explain how you know that any one of the diameters shown is perpendicular to two of the tangent segments shown.

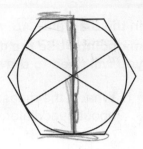

_____

_____

_____

2. Annie constructed a circle and its diameter. She drew a line tangent to the circle at one endpoint of the diameter. Then she drew a line tangent to the circle at the other endpoint of the diameter She claims the two tangent lines are parallel. Do you agree? Why or why not?

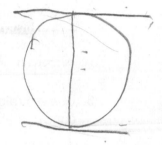

_____

_____

_____

_____

Choose the best answer.

3. Maria drew a design for a company logo. Her design is based on the diagram shown at the right. In the diagram, $\overline{KM}$ is tangent to circle J and to circle L at point N. Point N is the midpoint of $\overline{KM}$ and $\overline{JL}$. If $JL = 4$ cm, what is the area of quadrilateral $JKLM$?

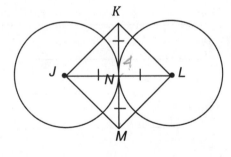

   A 2 cm^2 C 4 cm^2

   B 8 cm^2 D 16 cm^2

4. Paul also drew a design for a company logo. His design is based on the diagram shown at the right. In the diagram, $\overline{BD}$ is tangent to a half circle with radius AD at point D. If $AD = BD = x$ centimeters, and $\overline{DC}$ is three times as long as $\overline{AD}$, which expression represents the area of $\triangle ABC$?

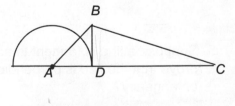

   F 0.5x^2 cm^2 H 2x^2 cm^2

   G 1.5x^2 cm^2 J 3x^2 cm^2

Arcs and Chords
Going Deeper

Essential question: *How are arcs and chords of circles associated with central angles?*

CC.9–12.G.C.2

1 **E N G A G E**   **Introducing Angles and Arcs**

In order to begin working with circles, it is helpful to introduce some vocabulary.

A **chord** is a segment whose endpoints lie on a circle. A **central angle** is an angle whose vertex is the center of a circle. An **inscribed angle** is an angle whose vertex lies on a circle and whose sides contain chords of the circle.

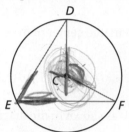

$\overline{DE}$ and $\overline{EF}$ are chords.
$\angle DCF$ is a central angle.
$\angle DEF$ is an inscribed angle.

An **arc** is a continuous portion of a circle consisting of two points on the circle, called the *endpoints* of the arc, and all the points of the circle between them. The table summarizes arc measurement and arc notation.

Arc	Measure/Notation	Figure
A **minor arc** is an arc whose points are on or in the interior of a central angle.	The measure of a minor arc is the measure of its central angle. $m\widehat{DF} = m\angle DCF$	
A **major arc** is an arc whose points are on or in the exterior of a central angle.	The measure of a major arc is 360° minus the measure of its central angle. $m\widehat{DEF} = 360° - m\angle DCF$	
A **semicircle** is an arc whose endpoints are the endpoints of a diameter.	The measure of a semicircle is 180°. $m\widehat{GHJ} = 180°$	

REFLECT

1a. Explain how $m\widehat{AB}$ compares to $m\widehat{CD}$.

_____

1b. The minute hand of a clock sweeps out an arc as the time progresses from 12:05 to 12:20. What is the measure of the arc? Explain.

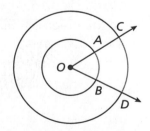

Two arcs of a circle are *adjacent arcs* if they share an endpoint. The following postulate states that you can add the measures of adjacent arcs.

Arc Addition Postulate

The measure of an arc formed by two adjacent arcs is the sum of the measures of the two arcs.

$$m\widehat{ABC} = m\widehat{AB} + m\widehat{BC}$$

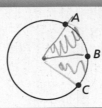

CC.9–12.G.C.2

2 EXPLORE   **Investigating Congruent Chords in a Circle**

A   Use a compass to draw a circle. Mark the center of the circle *C*.

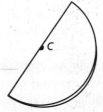

B   Cut out the circle and fold it in half.

C   Fold both halves to create a chord, as shown in the diagram.

D   Unfold the paper and use a straightedge to draw segments from the endpoints of the two folded chords to the center of the circle.

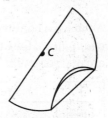

E   Use a protractor to measure the central angles of the two chords. Record the measures.

Central angle of chord 1:

Central angle of chord 2:

F   What do you notice about the central angles?

_____

REFLECT

2a.   Write a conjecture that your work in the Explore suggests.

_____

_____

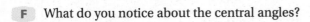

© Houghton Mifflin Harcourt Publishing Company

12-2

Additional Practice

Use the figure to find each of the following measurements. *A* is the center of the circle.

1. m$\overset{\frown}{CE}$ _____45°_____

2. m∠DAF _____30°_____

3. m$\overset{\frown}{EF}$ _____105°_____

4. m$\overset{\frown}{BD}$ _____45°_____

5. m∠BAD _____45°_____

6. m$\overset{\frown}{EFD}$ _____135°_____

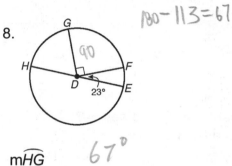

75

180−113=67

Find each measure.

7.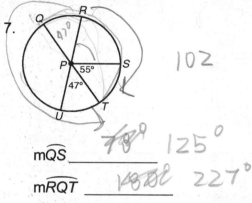

m$\overset{\frown}{QS}$ _____125°_____

m$\overset{\frown}{RQT}$ _____227°_____

8.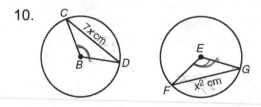

m$\overset{\frown}{HG}$ _____67°_____

m$\overset{\frown}{FEH}$ _____203°_____

9.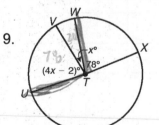

Find m∠UTW. _____98°_____

10.

⊙D ≅ ⊙E, and ∠CBD ≅ ∠FEG.
Find FG. _____7_____

$x^2 - 7x = 0$
$x(x-7) = 0$
$x = 0, 7$

$7x = x^2$

$7 = x$

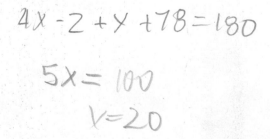

4x − 2 + x + 78 = 180

5x = 100

x = 20

© Houghton Mifflin Harcourt Publishing Company

Problem Solving

1. Circle *D* has center (–2, –7) and radius 7. What is the measure, in degrees, of the major arc that passes through points *H*(–2, 0), *J*(5, –7), and *K*(–9, –7)?

   _____

2. A circle graph is composed of sectors with central angles that measure $3x°$, $3x°$, $4x°$, and $5x°$. What is the measure, in degrees, of the smallest minor arcs?

   _____

Use the following information for Exercises 3 and 4.

The circle graph shows the results of a survey in which teens were asked what says the most about them at school. Find each of the following.

3. m

   _____

4. m∠APC

   _____

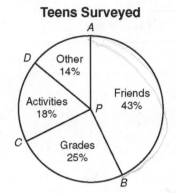

Use the table for Exercises 5–7.
Choose the best answer.

5. Students were asked to name their favorite cafeteria food. The results of the survey are shown in the table. In a circle graph showing these results, which is closest to the measure of the central angle for the section representing chicken tenders?

   A 21°   C 83°

   B 75°   D 270°

Favorite Lunch	Number of Students
Pizza	108
Chicken tenders	75
Taco salad	90
Other	54

6. Which is the closest measure of the arc for the sector in the circle graph representing taco salad?

   F 59°   H 100°

   G 90°   J 180°

7. If the sectors for pizza and chicken tenders are adjacent in the circle graph, which is the closest measure for the arc that spans both sectors?

   A 100°   C 183°

   B 166°   D 201°

Sector Area and Arc Length
Going Deeper

Essential question: *How do you find the area of a sector of a circle, and how do you calculate arc length in a circle?*

Video Tutor

CC.9–12.G.GMD.1

1 EXPLORE   Developing a Formula for the Area of a Circle

A Use a compass to draw a large circle on a sheet of paper. Cut out the circle.

B Fold the circle in half. Then fold the resulting semicircle in half.
Then fold the resulting quarter-circle in half.

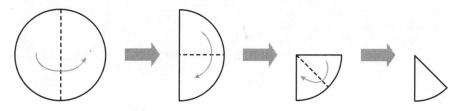

C Unfold the paper and cut along the folds to make 8 wedges.

D Rearrange the wedges as shown to make a
shape that resembles a parallelogram.

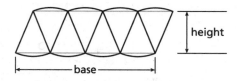

Assume the original circle has
radius *r*. What is the approximate
height of the parallelogram?   _____

The base of the parallelogram can be approximated by half the
circumference of the circle. Express the base in terms of *r*.   _____

Recall that the area of a parallelogram is the base times the height.
What is the approximate area of the parallelogram?   _____

REFLECT

1a. What happens as you repeat the process, cutting the circle into more and more
wedges each time?

_____

_____

1b. Make a conjecture: What do you think is the formula for the area *A* of a circle with
radius *r*? Why?

_____

_____

_____

© Houghton Mifflin Harcourt Publishing Company

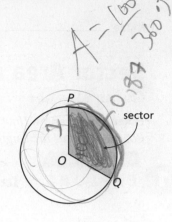

Area of a Circle

The area A of a circle with radius r is given by $A = \pi r^2$.

A **sector** of a circle is a region bounded by two radii and their intercepted arc. A sector is named by the endpoints of the arc and the center of the circle. For example, the figure shows sector POQ.

In the same way that you used proportional reasoning to find the length of an arc, you can use proportional reasoning to find the area of a sector.

CC.9–12.G.C.5

2 EXAMPLE   Finding the Area of a Sector

Find the area of sector AOB. Express your answer in terms of π and rounded to the nearest tenth.

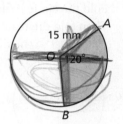

A First find the area of the circle.

$A = \pi r^2 = \pi \,(\underline{\hspace{2cm}})^2$ Substitute 15 for r.

   $= \underline{\hspace{2cm}}$ Simplify.

B The entire circle is 360°, but $\angle AOB$ measures 120°. Therefore, the sector's area is $\frac{120}{360}$ or $\frac{1}{3}$ of the circle's area.

Area of sector $AOB = \frac{1}{3} \cdot \underline{\hspace{2cm}}$ The area is $\frac{1}{3}$ of the circle's area.

    $= \underline{\hspace{2cm}}$ Simplify.

    $= \underline{\hspace{2cm}}$ Use a calculator to evaluate. Then round.

So, the area of sector AOB is $\underline{\hspace{2cm}}$ or $\underline{\hspace{2cm}}$.

REFLECT

2a. How could you use the above process to find the area of a sector of the circle whose central angle measures $m°$?

_____

_____

2b. Make a conjecture: What do you think is the formula for the area of a sector with a central angle of $m°$ and radius r?

_____

The proportional reasoning process you used in the example can be generalized. Given a sector with a central angle of $m°$ and radius r, the area of the entire circle is πr^2 and the area of the sector is $\frac{m}{360}$ times the circle's area. This gives the following formula.

Area of a Sector

The area A of a sector of a circle with a central angle of $m°$ and radius r is given by $A = \frac{m}{360} \cdot \pi r^2$.

Arc length is understood to be the distance along a circular arc measured in linear units (such as feet or centimeters). You can use proportional reasoning to find arc lengths.

CC.9–12.G.CO.1

3 EXAMPLE Finding Arc Length

Find the arc length of $\overset{\frown}{AB}$. Express your answer in terms of π and rounded to the nearest tenth.

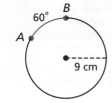

A First find the circumference of the circle.

$C = 2\pi r = $ _____   Substitute 9 for r.

B The entire circle is 360°, but $\overset{\frown}{AB}$ measures 60°. Therefore, the arc's length is $\frac{60}{360}$ or $\frac{1}{6}$ of the circumference.

Arc length of $\overset{\frown}{AB} = \frac{1}{6} \cdot$ _____   Arc length is $\frac{1}{6}$ of the circumference.

$= $ _____   Multiply.

$= $ _____   Use a calculator to evaluate. Then round.

So, the arc length of $\overset{\frown}{AB}$ is _____ or _____.

REFLECT

3a. How could you use the above process to find the length of an arc of the circle that measures $m°$?

_____

_____

The proportional reasoning process you used above can be generalized. Given a circle with radius r, its circumference is $2\pi r$ and the arc length s of an arc with measure $m°$ is $\frac{m}{360}$ times the circumference. This gives the following formula.

Arc Length

The arc length s of an arc with measure $m°$ and radius r is given by the formula $s = \frac{m}{360} \cdot 2\pi r$.

4 EXPLORE   Investigating Arc Lengths in Concentric Circles

Consider a set of concentric circles with center O and radius 1, 2, 3, and so on. The central angle shown in the figure is a right angle and it cuts off arcs that measure 90°.

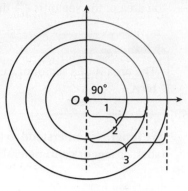

A   For each value of the radius r listed in the table below, find the corresponding arc length. Write the length in terms of π and rounded to the nearest hundredth.

For example, when $r = 1$, the arc length is $\frac{90}{360} \cdot 2\pi(1) = \frac{1}{2}\pi \approx 1.57$.

Radius r	1	2	3	4	5
Arc length s in terms of π	$\frac{1}{2}\pi$				
Arc length s to nearest hundredth	1.57				

B   Plot the ordered pairs from your table on the coordinate plane at right.

What do you notice about the points?

_____

_____

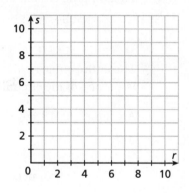

What type of relationship is the relationship between arc length and radius?

_____

What is the constant of proportionality for this relationship?

_____

REFLECT

4a.   What happens to the arc length when you double the radius? How is this connected to the idea that all circles are similar?

_____

_____

As you discovered in the Explore, when the central angle is fixed at $m°$, the length of the arc cut off by the central angle is proportional to (or varies directly with) the radius. In fact, you can see that the formula for arc length is a proportional relationship when m is fixed.

$$s = \underbrace{\frac{m}{360} \cdot 2\pi}_{\text{constant of proportionality}} r$$

The constant of proportionality for the proportional relationship is $\frac{m}{360} \cdot 2\pi$. This constant of proportionality is defined to be the **radian measure** of the angle.

CC.9–12.G.C.5

5 EXAMPLE Converting to Radian Measure

Convert each angle measure to radian measure.

A 180°   **B** 60°

A To convert 180° to radian measure, let $m = 180$ in the expression $\frac{m}{360} \cdot 2\pi$.

$180° = \dfrac{\boxed{}}{360} \cdot 2\pi$ radians   Substitute 180 for m.

$= \underline{\hspace{2cm}}$ radians   Simplify.

B To convert 60° to radian measure, let $m = 60$ in the expression $\frac{m}{360} \cdot 2\pi$.

$60° = \dfrac{\boxed{}}{360} \cdot 2\pi$ radians   Substitute 60 for m.

$= \underline{\hspace{2cm}}$ radians   Simplify.

REFLECT

5a. Explain why the radian measure for an angle of $m°$ is sometimes defined as the length of the arc cut off on a circle of radius 1 by a central angle of $m°$.

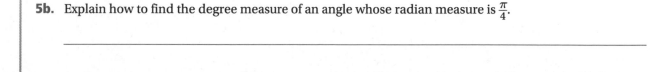

_____

_____

_____

5b. Explain how to find the degree measure of an angle whose radian measure is $\frac{\pi}{4}$.

_____

_____

_____

Find the area of sector *AOB*. Express your answer in terms of π and rounded to the nearest tenth.

1.

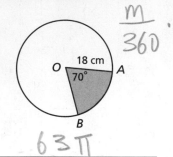

$$\frac{m}{360} \cdot \pi r^2$$

_____ 63π _____

_____

2.

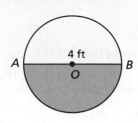

_____

_____

3.

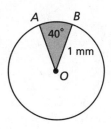

_____

_____

4.

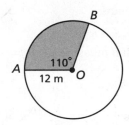

_____

_____

5.

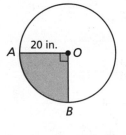

_____

_____

6.

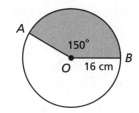

_____

_____

7. The area of sector *AOB* is $\frac{9}{2}\pi$ m². Explain how to find m∠*AOB*.

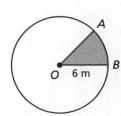

_____

_____

8. Error Analysis A student claims that when you double the radius of a sector while keeping the measure of the central angle constant, you double the area of the sector. Do you agree or disagree? Explain.

_____

_____

_____

Find the arc length of $\overarc{AB}$. Express your answer in terms of π and rounded to the nearest tenth.

9.

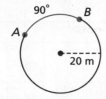

90°
B
A
20 m

_____

_____

10.

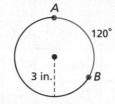

A
120°
3 in.
B

_____

_____

11.

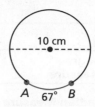

10 cm
A   67°   B

_____

_____

12.

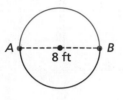

A   B
8 ft

_____

_____

13.

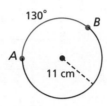

130°
B
A
11 cm

_____

_____

14.

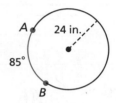

A   24 in.
85°
B

_____

_____

15. The minute hand of a clock is 4 inches long. To the nearest tenth of an inch, how far does the tip of the minute hand travel as the time progresses from 12:00 to 12:25?

_____

16. Error Analysis A student was asked to find the arc length of $\overarc{PQ}$. The student's work is shown below. Explain the student's error and give the correct arc length.

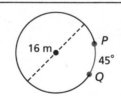

16 m
P
45°
Q

The entire circumference is $2\pi \cdot 16 = 32\pi$ and 45° is $\frac{1}{8}$ of the circle, so the arc length is $\frac{1}{8} \cdot 32\pi = 4\pi$ m.

_____

_____

_____

17. It is convenient to know the radian measure for benchmark angles such as 0°, 30°, 45°, and so on. Complete the table by finding the radian measure for each of the given benchmark angles.

Benchmark Angles									
Degree Measure	0°	30°	45°	60°	90°	120°	135°	150°	180°
Radian Measure									

18. Explain how to convert a radian measure into degrees. Then use your method to find what 1 radian is in degrees. Round to the nearest tenth of a degree.

_____

_____

_____

12-3

Additional Practice

Find the area of each sector. Give your answer in terms of π and rounded to the nearest hundredth.

1.

   sector *BAC* _____

2.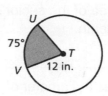

   sector *UTV* _____

3.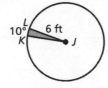

   sector *KJL* _____

4.

   sector *FEG* _____

5. The speedometer needle in Ignacio's car is 2 inches long. The needle sweeps out a 130° sector during acceleration from 0 to 60 mi/h. Find the area of this sector. Round to the nearest hundredth. _____

Find the area of each shaded sector to the nearest hundredth.

6.

   _____

7.

   _____

8.

   _____

9.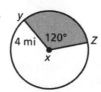

   _____

Find each arc length. Give your answer in terms of π and rounded to the nearest hundredth.

10.

    _____

11.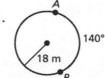

    _____

12. an arc with measure 45° in a circle with radius 2 mi _____

13. an arc with measure 120° in a circle with radius 15 mm _____

Problem Solving

1. A circle with a radius of 20 centimeters has a sector that has an arc measure of 105°. What is the area of the sector? Round to the nearest tenth.

_____

2. A sector whose central angle measures 72° has an area of 16.2π square feet. What is the radius of the circle?

_____

3. A circular wall clock has a diameter of 18 inches. If the hour and minute hand were extended to reach to the edge of the clock, what would be the area of the smaller of the two sectors formed by the hands at 2 o'clock? Round your answer to the nearest tenth of a square inch, and explain how you found your answer.

_____

_____

_____

Choose the best answer.

4. The circular shelves in diagram are each 28 inches in diameter. The "cut-out" portion of each shelf is 90°. Approximately how much shelf paper is needed to cover both shelves?

   A 154 in²

   B 308 in²

   C 462 in²

   D 924 in²

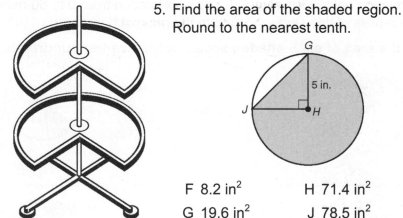

5. Find the area of the shaded region. Round to the nearest tenth.

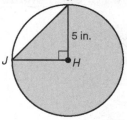

   F 8.2 in²   H 71.4 in²

   G 19.6 in²   J 78.5 in²

6. A semicircular garden with a diameter of 6 feet is to have 2 inches of mulch spread over it. To the nearest tenth, what is the volume of mulch that is needed?

   A 2.4 ft³   C 14.1 ft³

   B 4.8 ft³   D 28.3 ft³

7. A round cheesecake 12 inches in diameter and 3 inches high is cut into 8 equal-sized pieces. If five pieces have been taken, what is the approximate volume of the cheesecake that remains?

   F 42.4 in³   H 127.2 in³

   G 70.7 in³   J 212.1 in³

12-4

Inscribed Angles
Going Deeper

Essential question: *What is the relationship between central angles and inscribed angles in a circle?*

CC.9–12.G.C.2

1 EXPLORE Investigating Central Angles and Inscribed Angles

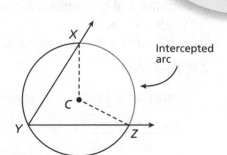

A Use a compass to draw a circle. Label the center *C*.

B Use a straightedge to draw an inscribed angle, ∠*XYZ* .

C Use the straightedge to draw the central angle, ∠*XCZ* .

D Use a protractor to measure the inscribed angle and the central angle. Use the measure of the central angle to determine the measure of the intercepted arc.

E Repeat the process four more times. Be sure to draw a variety of inscribed angles (acute, right, obtuse, passing through the center, etc.). Record your results in the table.

	Circle 1	Circle 2	Circle 3	Circle 4	Circle 5
Measure of Inscribed Angle					
Measure of Intercepted Arc					

REFLECT

1a. Compare your work with that of other students. Then make a conjecture: What is the relationship between the measure of an inscribed angle and the measure of its intercepted arc?

_____

_____

1b. Suppose an inscribed angle, ∠*XYZ* , measures *x*° . If ∠*XYZ* is acute, what is the measure of its associated central angle, ∠*XCZ* ? What if ∠*XYZ* is obtuse?

_____

1c. Draw a triangle inscribed in a circle so that the center of the circle lies in the interior of the triangle. Then draw the central angle associated with each inscribed angle of the triangle. What is the sum of the measures of the inscribed angles? What is the sum of the measures of the central angles?

_____

_____

You may have discovered the following relationship between an inscribed angle and its intercepted arc.

Inscribed Angle Theorem

The measure of an inscribed angle is half the measure of its intercepted arc.

$m\angle ADB = \frac{1}{2}m\overarc{AB}$

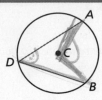

CC.9–12.G.C.2

2 EXAMPLE Finding Arc and Angle Measures

124

Find $m\overarc{BC}$, $m\overarc{BD}$, $m\angle DAB$, and $m\angle ABC$.

A Find $m\overarc{BC}$.

$m\angle BAC = \frac{1}{2}m\overarc{BC}$ Inscribed Angle Theorem

$2m\angle BAC = m\overarc{BC}$ Multiply both sides by 2.

$2 \cdot \underline{\qquad} = m\overarc{BC}$ Substitute.

$\underline{\qquad} = m\overarc{BC}$ Multiply.

B By the Arc Addition Postulate, $m\overarc{BD} = m\overarc{BC} + m\overarc{CD} = \underline{\qquad} + 88° = \underline{\qquad}$.

C By the Inscribed Angle Theorem, $m\angle DAB = \frac{1}{2}m\overarc{BD} = \frac{1}{2} \cdot \underline{\qquad} = \underline{\qquad}$.

D To find $m\angle ABC$, note that $\overarc{ADC}$ is a $\underline{\qquad\qquad}$.

Therefore, $m\overarc{ADC} = \underline{\qquad}$, and $m\angle ABC = \frac{1}{2}m\overarc{ADC} = \frac{1}{2} \cdot \underline{\qquad} = \underline{\qquad}$.

REFLECT

2a. Is it possible to find $m\overarc{DAB}$? If so, how? If not, why not?

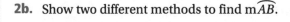

2b. Show two different methods to find $m\overarc{AB}$.

2c. Consider $\angle ABC$ and make a conjecture: What do you think must be true about any inscribed angle that contains endpoints of a diameter? Why?

The following theorem describes a key relationship between inscribed angles and diameters.

> ### Theorem
>
> The endpoints of a diameter lie on an inscribed angle if and only if the inscribed angle is a right angle.
>
>

Another theorem that relies on the Inscribed Angle Theorem in its proof is shown below. It is a theorem about the measures of the angles in any quadrilateral that is inscribed in a circle.

> ### Inscribed Quadrilateral Theorem
>
> If a quadrilateral is inscribed in a circle, then its opposite angles are supplementary.

The converse of the Inscribed Quadrilateral Theorem is also true. Taken together, the theorem and its converse tell you that a quadrilateral can be inscribed in a circle *if and only if* its opposite angles are supplementary.

CC.9–12.G.C.3

3 PROOF   Inscribed Quadrilateral Theorem

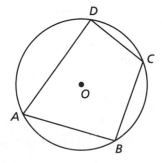

Given: Quadrilateral *ABCD* is inscribed in circle *O*.

Prove: ∠A and ∠C are supplementary;
　　　　 ∠B and ∠D are supplementary.

A $\overset{\frown}{BCD}$ and $\overset{\frown}{DAB}$ make a complete circle. Therefore,

　　　　 $m\overset{\frown}{BCD} + m\overset{\frown}{DAB} =$ _____ .

B ∠A is an inscribed angle and its intercepted arc is $\overset{\frown}{BCD}$; ∠C is an inscribed angle and its intercepted arc is $\overset{\frown}{DAB}$. By the Inscribed Angle Theorem,

　　　　 $m\angle A =$ _____ and $m\angle C =$ _____ .

C So, $m\angle A + m\angle C =$ _____　　Substitution

　　　　　　　　　 $=$ _____　　Distributive Property

　　　　　　　　　 $=$ _____　　Substitution

　　　　　　　　　 $=$ _____　　Simplify.

This shows that ∠A and ∠C are supplementary. Similar reasoning shows that ∠B and ∠D are supplementary.

3a. What must be true about a parallelogram that is inscribed in a circle? Explain.

_____

_____

3b. What must be true about a rhombus that is inscribed in a circle? Explain.

_____

_____

_____

PRACTICE

Use the figure to find each of the following.

1. m$\widehat{BA}$ _96°_

2. m∠BOA   _96°_

3. m$\widehat{AE}$ _84°_

4. m∠AOE   _84°_

5. m$\widehat{BAE}$ _180°_

6. m∠BDE   _90°_

7. m∠DBE   _20°_

8. m$\widehat{DE}$ _40°_

9. m$\widehat{DB}$ _140°_

10. m$\widehat{ABD}$ _236°_

11. m∠EDA   _276°_

12. m∠OAD   _____

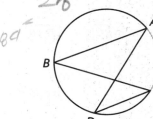

13. Prove that if two inscribed angles of a circle intercept the same arc, then the angles are congruent.

Given: ∠ABC and ∠ADC intercept $\widehat{AC}$.

Prove: ∠ABC ≅ ∠ADC

_____

_____

_____

14. A carpenter's square is a tool that is used to draw right angles. Suppose you are building a toy car and you have a small circle of wood that will serve as a wheel. Explain how you can use the carpenter's square to find the center of the circle.

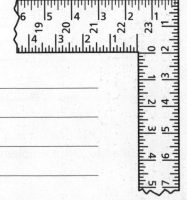

_____

_____

_____

_____

Additional Practice

Find each measure.

1.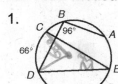
m∠CED = _330°_____
mDEA = _____

2.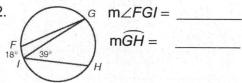
m∠FGI = _____
mGH = _____

3.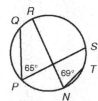
mQRS = _____
mTSR = _____

4.
m∠XVU = _____
m∠VXW = _____

5. A circular radar screen in an air traffic control tower shows these flight paths. Find m∠LNK.
_____

Find each value.

6.
m∠CED = _____

7.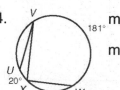
y = _____

8.
a = _____

9.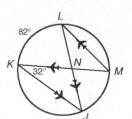
m∠SRT = _____

Find the angle measures of each inscribed quadrilateral.

10.
m∠X = _____
m∠Y = _____
m∠Z = _____
m∠W = _____

11.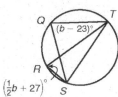
m∠C = _____
m∠D = _____
m∠E = _____
m∠F = _____

12.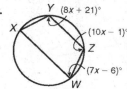
m∠T = _____
m∠U = _____
m∠V = _____
m∠W = _____

13.
m∠K = _____
m∠L = _____
m∠M = _____
m∠N = _____

Problem Solving

1. Find m$\widehat{AB}$.

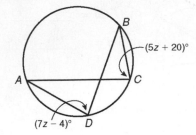

2. Find the angle measures of *RSTU*.

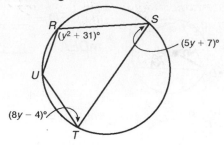

Choose the best answer.

Use the diagram of a floor tile for Exercises 3 and 4. Points *Q, R, S, T, U, V, W,* and *X* are equally spaced around ⊙*L*.

3. Find m∠*RQT*.

   A 15°   C 45°

   B 30°   D 60°

4. Find m∠*QRS*.

   F 67.5°   H 180°

   G 135°   J 270°

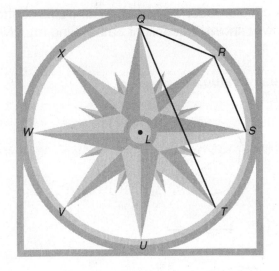

5. If m∠*KLM* = 20° and m$\widehat{MP}$ = 30°, what is m∠*KNP*?

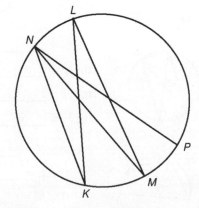

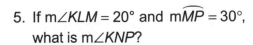

   A 25°   C 50°

   B 35°   D 70°

6. In ⊙*M*, m∠*AMB* = 74°. What is m∠*CDB*?

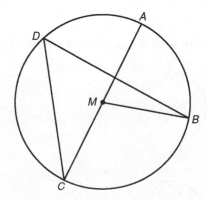

   F 37°   H 74°

   G 53°   J 106°

12-5

Angle Relationships in Circles
Going Deeper

Essential question: *When two tangents are drawn to a circle, how do you find the measure of the angle formed at their intersection?*

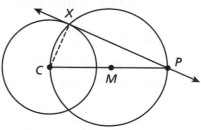

Video Tutor

CC.9–12.G.C.4(+)

1 EXPLORE Constructing Tangents to a Circle

Construct a tangent line from point *P* to circle *C*.

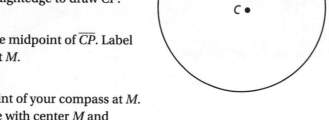

A Work directly on the figure at right. Use your straightedge to draw $\overline{CP}$.

B Construct the midpoint of $\overline{CP}$. Label the midpoint *M*.

C Place the point of your compass at *M*. Draw a circle with center *M* and radius *CM*.

D Label the points of intersection of circle *M* and circle *C* as *X* and *Y*.

E Use the straightedge to draw $\overleftrightarrow{PX}$ and $\overleftrightarrow{PY}$. Both lines are tangents to circle *C*.

REFLECT

1a. Give a justification for the construction. That is, explain how you know that $\overleftrightarrow{PX}$ is a tangent line. (*Hint:* In the figure at right, what can you conclude about $\angle CXP$? Why?)

_____

_____

_____

_____

1b. Measure $\overline{PX}$ and $\overline{PY}$ in your construction. Then repeat the construction with a different circle and different point outside the circle. Measure $\overline{PX}$ and $\overline{PY}$. Compare your results with those of other students. Then make a conjecture based on your observations.

_____

_____

As you discovered in the above construction, given any point outside a circle, you can draw two tangent lines to the circle. The two tangent lines form a *circumscribed angle*.

A **circumscribed angle** is an angle formed by two tangents to a circle. In the figure, $\overrightarrow{QP}$ and $\overrightarrow{QR}$ are tangents to circle C, so $\angle PQR$ is a circumscribed angle.

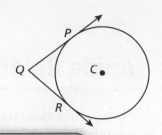

Circumscribed Angle Theorem

A circumscribed angle of a circle and its associated central angle are supplementary.

CC.9–12.G.CO.9

2 PROOF   Circumscribed Angle Theorem

Given: $\angle PQR$ is a circumscribed angle.

Prove: $\angle PQR$ and $\angle PCR$ are supplementary.

Complete the proof.

Since $\angle PQR$ is a circumscribed angle, $\overrightarrow{QP}$ and $\overrightarrow{QR}$ are _____.

Therefore, $\angle QPC$ and $\angle QRC$ are _____

by _____ .

So, $m\angle PQR + m\angle QRC + m\angle PCR + m\angle QPC = 360°$ Quadrilateral Sum Theorem

$m\angle PQR + \underline{\quad\quad} + m\angle PCR + \underline{\quad\quad} = 360°$ Substitution

$m\angle PQR + m\angle PCR + \underline{\quad\quad} = 360°$ Simplify.

$m\angle PQR + m\angle PCR = 180°$ Subtract 180° from both sides.

So, $\angle PQR$ and $\angle PCR$ are supplementary, by the definition of supplementary.

REFLECT

2a. Is it possible for quadrilateral $PQRC$ to be a parallelogram? If so, what type of parallelogram must it be? If not, why not?

_____

PRACTICE

In the figure, $\overrightarrow{KJ}$ and $\overrightarrow{KL}$ are tangents. Find the following.

1. $m\angle CJK$ _____   **2.** $m\angle JCL$ _____

3. $m\widehat{JL}$ _____   **4.** $m\widehat{JML}$ _____

5. $m\angle JML$ _____   **6.** $m\widehat{JM}$ _____

7. $m\widehat{MLJ}$ _____   **8.** $m\widehat{MJL}$ _____

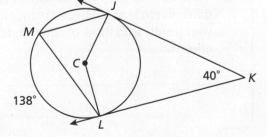

© Houghton Mifflin Harcourt Publishing Company

Additional Practice

Find the value of *x*.

1.

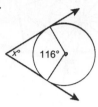

2.

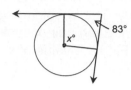

_____   _____

In the figure, $\overline{AB}$, $\overline{BC}$, and $\overline{AC}$ are tangent to
circle *O* at the points labeled *X*, *Y*, and *Z*. Find the following.

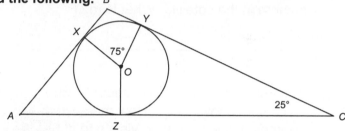

3. m∠YOZ _____

4. m ∠XBY _____

5. m ∠XAZ _____

6. m ∠XOZ _____

In the figure, the sides of △*EFG* are tangent to circle *M* at the points
labeled *P*, *Q*, and *R*. The angle measures of △*EFG* are in the ratio
1 : 3 : 1. Find each of the following.

7. m ∠E _____

8. m ∠F _____

9. m ∠G _____

10. m ∠PMR _____

11. m ∠PMQ _____

12. m ∠QMR _____

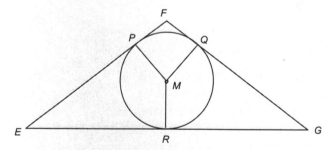

13. The two lines in the diagram are tangent
to the circle. Find the
measure of ∠1.

_____

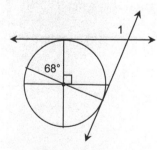

Problem Solving

1. The figure shows a spinning wheel. The large wheel is turned by hand or with a foot trundle. A belt attaches to a small bobbin that turns very quickly. The bobbin twists raw materials into thread, twine, or yarn. Each pair of spokes forms the sides of a 30° central angle. Find the value of x.

_____

For Exercises 2 and 3, use the diagrams.

2. A polar orbiting satellite is about 850 kilometers above Earth. About 69.2 arc degrees of the planet are visible to a camera in the satellite. What is m∠P?

_____

3. A geostationary satellite is about 35,800 kilometers above Earth. How many arc degrees of the planet are visible to a camera in the satellite?

_____

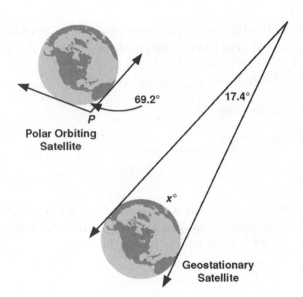

69.2°   17.4°

_P_

**Polar Orbiting
Satellite**

_x_°

**Geostationary
Satellite**

Choose the best answer.

4. Andy drew circle Q and then drew a circumscribed angle X with sides tangent to circle Q at points Y and Z. He also drew segments QY and QZ. Which statement about Andy's diagram is *not* true?

   A Quadrilateral XYQZ cannot be a square.

   B m∠XYQ = m∠XZQ

   C m∠YQZ + m∠YXZ = 180°

   D m∠QYX + m∠QZX = 180°

5. In the figure, the sides of ∠KJL are tangent to circle T at points K and L. If the ratio of m∠KJL to m∠KTL is 1 : 5, what is m∠KTL?

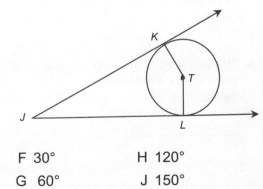

   F 30°   H 120°

   G 60°   J 150°

12-6

Segment Relationships in Circles
Extension: Distance to the Horizon

Essential question: *How can you estimate the distance to the horizon using results about segments related to circles?*

The following theorem provides a relationship between the length of a secant and the length of a tangent.

Secant-Tangent Product Theorem

If a secant and a tangent intersect in the exterior of a circle, then the product of the lengths of the secant segment and its external segment equals the length of the tangent segment squared.

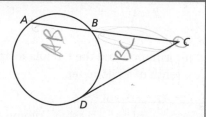

Secant $\overline{AC}$ and tangent $\overline{DC}$ intersect at C.

$$AC \cdot BC = DC^2$$

CC.9–12.G.C.2

1 **PROOF**   **Secant-Tangent Product Theorem**

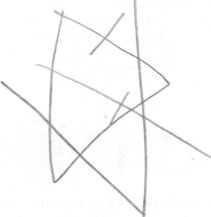

A Draw $\overline{AD}$ and $\overline{BD}$ to form $\triangle CAD$ and $\triangle CDB$.

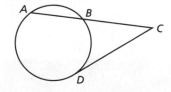

B From a result you learned previously, $m\angle CDB = \frac{1}{2} m\widehat{BD}$.

Also, $m\angle CAD = \frac{1}{2} m\widehat{BD}$ by the _____.

Therefore, $m\angle CDB = m\angle CAD$ by the _____ Property of Equality.
By the definition of congruent angles, $\angle CAD \cong \angle CDB$.
(Mark the congruence on your diagram.)

By the _____ Property of Congruence, $\angle ACD \cong \angle DCB$.

Using the AA Similarity Postulate, $\triangle$ _____ $\sim \triangle$ _____.
(In the space next to the diagram, sketch the two similar triangles separately.)

Since corresponding sides of similar triangles are proportional, $\frac{AC}{DC} =$ ☐ .

By cross multiplication, $AC \cdot$ _____ $= DC \cdot$ _____.

So, _____ $\cdot$ _____ $=$ _____.

REFLECT

1a. If $\overline{AD}$ were a diameter, how would you classify the similar triangles?

_____

2 **EXAMPLE** Approximating the Distance to the Horizon

An observer is 0.1 kilometer above the surface of Earth at C. The radius of Earth, r, is about 6378.1 kilometers. What is the distance to the horizon from the observer?

A Use the Secant-Tangent Product Theorem.

$$AC \cdot BC = DC^2$$

$$(2r + h) \cdot \boxed{} = \boxed{}$$

B Solve for d. $d = \sqrt{\boxed{}}$

C Use the given information and the formula to approximate d to the nearest tenth of a kilometer.

$$\sqrt{\left(2 \cdot \boxed{} + \boxed{}\right)\boxed{}} \approx \boxed{} \text{ kilometers}$$

REFLECT

2a. What do you have to do to modify the formula for d if the altitude h is given in feet, the radius r is given in miles, and you are solving for d in miles?

_____

PRACTICE

In Exercises 1–4, suppose an observer is the given distance above Earth. Approximate the distance to the horizon to the nearest tenth of a kilometer.

1. 0.2 kilometer

_____

2. 0.4 kilometer

_____

3. 1.2 kilometers

_____

4. 20 kilometers

_____

5. Derive the formula for d in Example 2 using the Pythagorean Theorem with $\triangle XCD$.

_____

_____

_____

Additional Practice

Find the value of the variable.

1.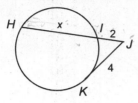

2.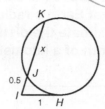

_____

3.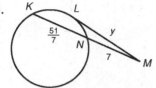

4.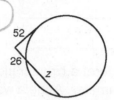

_____

In the figure shown, $\overline{QP}$ is tangent to circle N at Q, and $MP = 2 \cdot MO$.

5. Let $x = OP$ and $y = QP$. Write an equation relating x and y.

_____

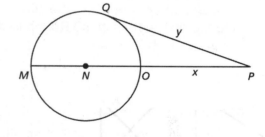

6. Use your equation to find the value of y for the given value of x. Round to the nearest tenth.

   Then find the ratio $\dfrac{x}{y}$. What do you notice about

   the ratios?

x	y	$\dfrac{x}{y}$
1		
2		
3		

_____

Problem Solving

A satellite is *h* kilometers above the surface of Earth at point *S*. Given that Earth's radius is about 6378.1 kilometers, approximate the distance to the horizon to the nearest tenth of a kilometer.

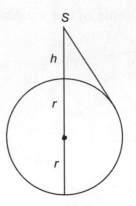

1. *h* = 16,000 km _____

2. *h* = 20,000 km _____

3. *h* = 25,000 km _____

4. *h* = 30,000 km _____

5. A wall hanging is made of a circular piece of wood 24 inches in diameter. Angela wants to use wire to hang the wall hanging from a nail at point *N*. The wire will be tangent to the circle and attached at points *P* and *Q*. What is the total length of wire needed if the distance from the top of the circle (point *R*) to the nail is 10 inches? Round to the nearest inch.

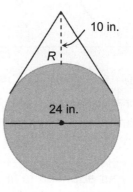

_____

Choose the best answer.

6. A jet is cruising at point *P* at an altitude of 6 miles. Given that Earth's radius is about 4000 mi, find the approximate distance from the jet to the horizon.

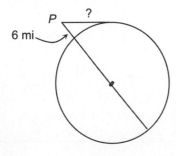

A 155 mi   C 4006 mi

B 219 mi   D 8006 mi

7. In the diagram, the ratio of *AB* to *BC* is 5 : 4. What is the length of $\overline{AC}$?

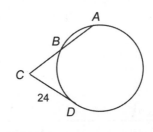

F 9   H 20

G 16   J 36

Circles in the Coordinate Plane
Connection: Completing the Square

Essential question: *How can you write and use equations of circles in the coordinate plane?*

Recall that a circle is the set of all points in a plane that are a fixed distance from a given point. Now you will investigate circles in a coordinate plane.

Video Tutor

CC.9–12.G.GPE.1

1 **E X P L O R E**   **Deriving the Equation of a Circle**

Consider the circle in a coordinate plane that has its center at $C(h, k)$ and that has radius r.

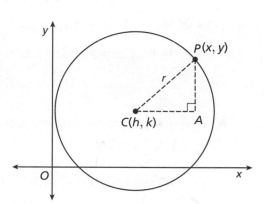

A Let P be any point on the circle and let the coordinates of P be (x, y).

Create a right triangle by drawing a horizontal line through C and a vertical line through P, as shown.

What are the coordinates of point A? _____

Write expressions for the lengths of the legs of $\triangle CAP$.

$CA =$ _____; $PA =$ _____

B Use the Pythagorean Theorem to write a relationship among the side lengths of $\triangle CAP$.

_____ + _____ = _____

REFLECT

1a. Compare your work with that of other students. Then write the equation of a circle with center (h, k) and radius r.

_____

1b. Why do you need absolute values when you write expressions for the lengths of the legs in Step A, but not when you write the relationship among the side lengths in Step B?

_____

_____

1c. Suppose a circle has its center at the origin. What is the equation of the circle in this case?

_____

The equation of a circle with center (h, k) and radius r is $(x - h)^2 + (y - k)^2 = r^2$.

CC.9–12.G.GPE.1

2 EXAMPLE Finding the Center and Radius of a Circle

Find the center and radius of the circle whose equation is $x^2 - 4x + y^2 + 2y = 4$.
Then graph the circle.

A Complete the square to write the equation in the form $(x - h)^2 + (y - k)^2 = r^2$.

$x^2 - 4x + \boxed{} + y^2 + 2y + \boxed{} = 4 + \boxed{}$ Set up to complete the square.

$x^2 - 4x + \underline{} + y^2 + 2y + \underline{} = 4 + \underline{}$ Add $\left(\frac{-4}{2}\right)^2$ and $\left(\frac{2}{2}\right)^2$ to both sides.

$x^2 - 4x + \underline{} + y^2 + 2y + \underline{} = 4 + \underline{}$ Simplify.

$(x - \underline{})^2 + (y + \underline{})^2 = \underline{}$ Factor.

B Identify h, k, and r to determine the center and radius.

$h = \underline{}$ $k = \underline{}$ $r = \underline{}$

So, the center is ($\underline{}$, $\underline{}$) and the radius is $\underline{}$.

C Graph the circle.

- Locate the center of the circle.
- Place the point of your compass at the center.
- Open the compass to the radius.
- Use the compass to draw the circle.

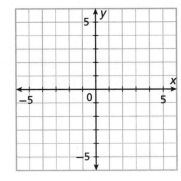

REFLECT

2a. How can you check your graph by testing specific points from the graph in the original equation? Give an example.

_____

_____

2b. Suppose you translate the circle by the translation $(x, y) \rightarrow (x + 4, y - 1)$. What is the equation of the image of the circle? Explain.

_____

_____

3 EXAMPLE Writing a Coordinate Proof

Prove or disprove that the point $(1, \sqrt{15})$ lies on the circle that is centered at the origin and contains the point $(0, 4)$.

A Plot a point at the origin and at $(0, 4)$. Use these to help you draw the circle centered at the origin that contains $(0, 4)$.

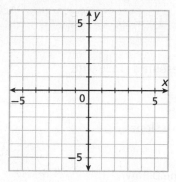

B Determine the radius: $r =$ _____

C Use the radius and the coordinates of the center to write the equation of the circle.

_____

D Substitute the x- and y-coordinates of the point $(1, \sqrt{15})$ in the equation of the circle to check whether they satisfy the equation.

$$\underline{\hspace{2cm}}^{2} + \underline{\hspace{2cm}}^{2} \overset{?}{=} 16 \qquad \text{Substitute.}$$

$$\underline{\hspace{2cm}} + \underline{\hspace{2cm}} = 16 \qquad \text{Simplify.}$$

E So, the point $(1, \sqrt{15})$ lies on the circle because

_____

REFLECT

3a. Explain how to determine the radius of the circle.

_____

_____

3b. Name another point with noninteger coordinates that lies on the circle. Explain.

_____

3c. Explain how you can prove that the point $(2, \sqrt{5})$ does *not* lie on the circle.

_____

_____

Recall that you can solve a system of two equations in two unknowns by graphing both equations and finding the point(s) of intersection of the graphs. You can also solve a system using the algebraic methods of substitution or elimination. In the next Examples, you will see how these techniques may be used with systems that include a quadratic equation.

4 **EXAMPLE** **Solving a System by Graphing**

Solve the system of equations. $\begin{cases} (x-1)^2 + (y-1)^2 = 16 \\ y = x + 4 \end{cases}$

A The equation $(x-1)^2 + (y-1)^2 = 16$ represents a circle with center _____ and radius _____ .

The equation $y = x + 4$ represents a line with slope _____ and y-intercept _____ .

B Graph the equations on the coordinate plane below.

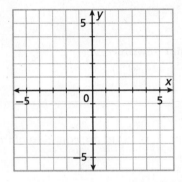

C The solutions of $(x-1)^2 + (y-1)^2 = 16$ are exactly the points on the circle. The solutions of $y = x + 4$ are exactly the points on the line. The solutions of the system are points that lie on both the circle and the line. These are the points of intersection of the circle and the line.

So, the solutions of the system are _____ .

REFLECT

4a. How can you check your solutions? Check them.

_____

_____

_____

4b. How many solutions are possible when a system of equations involves a circle and a line? Explain.

_____

_____

5 EXAMPLE   Solving a System Algebraically

Solve the system of equations. $\begin{cases} x^2 + y^2 = 13 \\ y = -5x \end{cases}$

A Use substitution to write an equation in one variable. The second equation is already solved for y, so substitute this expression for y into the first equation.

$x^2 + y^2 = 13$ Write the first equation.

$x^2 + (\underline{\hspace{1cm}})^2 = 13$ Substitute $-5x$ for y in the equation.

$x^2 + \underline{\hspace{1cm}} = 13$ Square the expression in parentheses.

$\underline{\hspace{1cm}} = 13$ Combine like terms.

$x^2 = \underline{\hspace{1cm}}$ Use the Division Property of Equality.

$x = \underline{\hspace{1cm}}$ Take the square root of both sides.

$x = \underline{\hspace{1cm}}$ Rationalize the denominator.

B Substitute each x-value into one of the original equations to find the corresponding y-values.

Substitute into the simpler equation, $y = -5x$.

When $x = \underline{\hspace{1cm}}$, $y = \underline{\hspace{1cm}}$.

When $x = \underline{\hspace{1cm}}$, $y = \underline{\hspace{1cm}}$.

So, the solutions of the system are $\underline{\hspace{6cm}}$.

REFLECT

5a. Is it possible to solve this system of equations by graphing? Explain.

_____

_____

5b. Based on what you know about the graphs of the equations in this system, why does it make sense that there are two solutions?

_____

_____

6 EXAMPLE   Solving a System Involving a Parabola

Solve the system of equations. $\begin{cases} y = x^2 - 3 \\ y = 8x - 19 \end{cases}$

A   Use substitution to write an equation in one variable. Substitute the expression for y from the second equation into the first equation.

$y = x^2 - 3$	Write the first equation.
_____ $= x^2 - 3$	Substitute $8x - 19$ for y in the equation.
$0 =$ _____	Get 0 on one side of the equation.
$0 =$ _____	Combine like terms.
$0 =$ _____	Factor.
$0 =$ _____	Take the square root of both sides.
$x =$ _____	Solve for x.

B   Substitute the x-value into one of the original equations to find the corresponding y-value.

Substitute into the equation $y = x^2 - 3$.

When $x =$ _____ , $y =$ _____ .

So, the solution of the system is _____ .

REFLECT

6a. In Step B, what would happen if you substituted the value of x in the other equation?

_____

6b. Verify that the slope of the line that contains $(0, -19)$ and $(4, 13)$ is 8.

_____

6c. Since there is only one solution of the system, what does this tell you about the line and the parabola that are represented by the equations?

_____

6d. How many solutions are possible when a system of equations involves a parabola and a line? Explain.

_____

_____

Write the equation of the circle with the given center and radius.

1. center: $(0, 2)$; radius: 5

_____

2. center: $(-1, 3)$; radius 8

_____

3. center: $(-4, -5)$; radius: $\sqrt{2}$

_____

4. center: $(9, 0)$; radius $\sqrt{3}$

_____

Find the center and radius of the circle with the given equation.
Then graph the circle.

5. $x^2 - 2x + y^2 = 15$

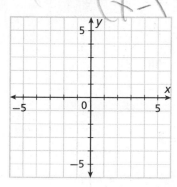

$(x^2 - 2x + x1) + y^2 = 16$

$(x-1)^2 + y^2 = 16$

6. $x^2 + 4x + y^2 - 6y = -9$

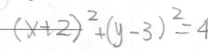

$(x+2)^2 + (y-3)^2 = 4$

$(-2, 3)$

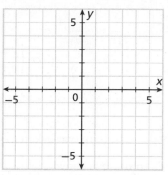

7. Prove or disprove that the point $(1, \sqrt{3})$ lies on the circle that is centered at the origin and contains the point $(0, 2)$.

_____

_____

_____

8. Prove or disprove that the point $(2, \sqrt{3})$ lies on the circle that is centered at the origin and contains the point $(-3, 0)$.

_____

_____

_____

9. Prove or disprove that the circle with equation $x^2 - 4x + y^2 = -3$ intersects the y-axis.

_____

_____

_____

Solve each system of equations by graphing.

10. $\begin{cases} (x-2)^2 + y^2 = 4 \\ y = -x \end{cases}$

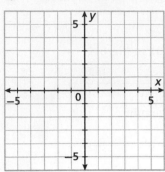

11. $\begin{cases} (x+1)^2 + (y-1)^2 = 9 \\ y = x - 1 \end{cases}$

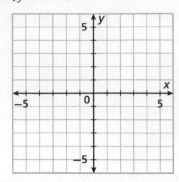

12. $\begin{cases} y = x^2 - 1 \\ y = -x + 1 \end{cases}$

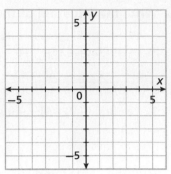

Solve each system of equations algebraically.

13. $\begin{cases} x^2 + y^2 = 10 \\ y = -3x \end{cases}$

14. $\begin{cases} x^2 + y^2 = 25 \\ y = 7x \end{cases}$

15. $\begin{cases} x^2 + y^2 = 13 \\ y = -8x \end{cases}$

16. $\begin{cases} y = x^2 \\ y = -x + 2 \end{cases}$

17. $\begin{cases} y = x^2 + 2 \\ y = 4 \end{cases}$

18. $\begin{cases} y = -x^2 + 2 \\ y = x - 4 \end{cases}$

19. Error Analysis A student was asked to solve the system $\begin{cases} x^2 + y^2 = 9 \\ y = x \end{cases}$.

The student's solution is shown below. Critique the student's work.
If there is an error, give the correct solution.

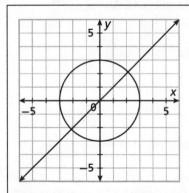

The graph of $x^2 + y^2 = 9$ is a circle centered at the origin with radius 3. The graph of $y = x$ is a straight line through the origin. The graphs intersect at $(2, 2)$ and $(-2, -2)$, so these are the solutions.

Additional Practice

1. Write an equation of a circle with center $B(0, -2)$ that passes through $(-6, 0)$. _____

Complete the square to rewrite the given equation in the form $(x - h)^2 + (y - k)^2 = r^2$. Identify the center and radius of the circle. Then graph the circle.

2. $x^2 + 2x + y^2 - 6y = -6$

3. $x^2 + 4x + y^2 + 6y = -9$

_____

_____

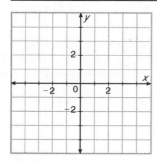

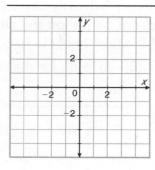

4. $x^2 - 2x + y^2 - 2y = 14$

5. $x^2 + y^2 + 6y = -8$

_____

_____

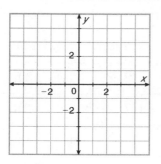

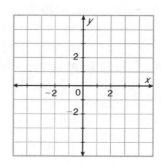

6. Solve the system of equations by graphing.

$$\begin{cases} x^2 + (y - 2)^2 = 9 \\ y = x - 1 \end{cases}$$

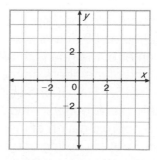

_____

Solve each system of equations algebraically.

7. $\begin{cases} x^2 + y^2 = 25 \\ x - y = 5 \end{cases}$

8. $\begin{cases} y = -x^2 \\ y = -x - 2 \end{cases}$

9. $\begin{cases} (x - 2)^2 + y^2 = 100 \\ y = -10 \end{cases}$

_____

_____

Problem Solving

1. Prove or disprove that the circle that is centered at the origin and contains the point (−4, −3) intersects the line $x = 6$.

_____

_____

_____

Crater Lake in Oregon is roughly circular. Suppose that A(−4, 1) and B(−2, −3) represent points on the circular shoreline of the lake. The center of the lake is at (1, 1).

2. Does the point C(5, −2) lie on the shoreline of the lake?

_____

3. Each unit of the coordinate plane represents $\frac{3}{5}$ mile. Find the diameter of Crater Lake.

_____

Choose the best answer.

4. An English knot garden has hedges planted to form geometric shapes. A blueprint of a knot garden contains three circular hedges as described in the table. Flowers are to be planted in the space that is within all three circles. Which is a point that could be planted with flowers?

   A (7, 1)   C (0, 5)

   B (5, 1)   D (0, 0)

Circular Hedge	Center	Radius
A	(3, 2)	3 ft
B	(7, 2)	4 ft
C	(5, −1)	3 ft

5. An amusement park ride consists of a circular ring that holds 50 riders. Suppose the center of the ride is at the origin and that one of the riders on the circular ring is at (16, 15.1). If one unit on the coordinate plane equals 1 foot, which is a close approximation of the distance the rider travels during one complete revolution of the circle?

   F 22 ft   H 138 ft

   G 44 ft   J 1521 ft

6. Which of these circles intersects the circle that has center (0, 6) and radius 1?

   A $(x − 5)^2 + (y + 3)^2 = 4$

   B $(x − 4)^2 + (y − 3)^2 = 9$

   C $(x + 5)^2 + (y + 1)^2 = 16$

   D $(x + 1)^2 + (y − 4)^2 = 4$

7. The center of a circle is (9, 2), and the radius of the circle is 5 units. Which is a point on the circle?

   F (4, 2)   H (9, 4)

   G (14, 0)   J (9, −5)

Performance Tasks

COMMON CORE

CC.9-12.G.SRT.8
CC.9-12.G.C.2
CC.9-12.G.GPE.1

★ **1.** A circular table has a diameter of 48 inches. A carpenter is remaking it into a square table. To the nearest tenth of an inch, what is the greatest possible side length of the square table? Explain.

★ **2.** A moving company needs to replace a circular glass mirror that it broke during a move. The dimensions of a piece of the broken mirror are shown in the figure. What was the diameter of the original mirror? Round your answer to the nearest tenth of an inch.

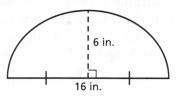

6 in.

16 in.

★ **3.** A graphic artist is using a coordinate plane to design a company logo. The logo has an
★ equilateral triangle inscribed in a circle. The circle lies in Quadrant I, is tangent to the *x*- and *y*-axes, and has a radius of 10 units. One side of the triangle is parallel to the *y*-axis, and one vertex is at (20, 10).

  a. Write the equation for the circle.

  b. What is the length of the sides of the inscribed triangle? Round your answer to the nearest hundredth of a unit and show your work.

  c. Use the fact that the base opposite the vertex at (20, 10) is parallel to the *y*-axis, and your result from part **b** to find the coordinates of the other two vertices. Round the coordinates to the nearest hundredth of a unit and show your work. (*Hint*: The vertices will be the same distance above and below a horizontal line passing through (20, 10)).

continued

© Houghton Mifflin Harcourt Publishing Company

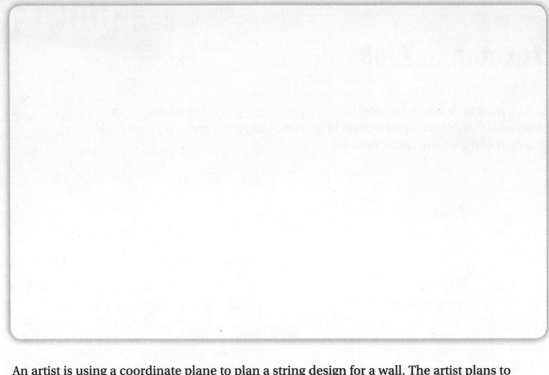

 4. An artist is using a coordinate plane to plan a string design for a wall. The artist plans to hammer a nail at each vertex of a regular hexagon. Then the artist will use string to connect the vertices to make the hexagon shape. The artist starts with a circle centered at the origin and places the first vertex at (8, 0).

a. Where are the other vertices? Write coordinates in radical form, if necessary.

b. Not considering knots, what is the minimum amount of string the artist needs to outline the hexagon and connect all the diagonals? Round to the nearest tenth.

Name _____ Class _____ Date _____

MULTIPLE CHOICE

1. What is the center of the circle whose equation is $x^2 - 6x + y^2 + 6y = -9$?

A. $(3, -3)$ **C.** $(-3, 3)$

B. $(3, 3)$ **D.** $(-3, -3)$

2. What is the equation of the circle with center $(4, -5)$ and radius 4?

F. $(x + 4)^2 + (y - 5)^2 = 4$

G. $(x - 4)^2 + (y + 5)^2 = 4$

H. $(x + 4)^2 + (y - 5)^2 = 16$

J. $(x - 4)^2 + (y + 5)^2 = 16$

3. The ordered pair (x, y) is a solution of this system of equations.

$$\begin{cases} x^2 + y^2 = 10 \\ y = 7x \end{cases}$$

Which of the following could be the value of x?

A. $\frac{\sqrt{2}}{2}$ **C.** $\frac{\sqrt{5}}{2}$

B. $\frac{\sqrt{5}}{5}$ **D.** $\frac{\sqrt{10}}{7}$

4. $\overline{PR}$ and $\overline{QR}$ are tangents to circle C. Which expression represents m$\angle C$?

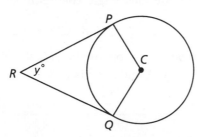

F. $(2y)°$ **H.** $(90 - y)°$

G. $(180 - y)°$ **J.** $\left(\frac{1}{2}y\right)°$

5. In circle O, $\angle ABC$ is an inscribed angle and $\overline{AC}$ is a diameter. Which of the following must be true?

A. $\angle ABC$ is an acute angle.

B. $\angle ABC$ is a right angle.

C. $\overline{AB}$ is a radius.

D. $\overline{AC} \perp \overline{BC}$

6. What is the radian measure of the angle whose degree measure is 20°?

F. $\frac{\pi}{20}$ **H.** $\frac{\pi}{9}$

G. $\frac{\pi}{18}$ **J.** $\frac{2\pi}{9}$

7. $\overline{JK}$ is a tangent to circle C. What is m$\overarc{KL}$?

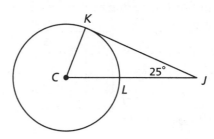

A. 25°   **C.** 65°

B. 50°   **D.** 130°

8. Noah is constructing a tangent from P to circle C. The figure shows what he has done so far. What should he do next?

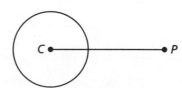

F. Construct a perpendicular at point P.

G. Construct a perpendicular at point C.

H. Construct a circle whose center is at the intersection of $\overline{CP}$ and circle C.

J. Construct the midpoint of $\overline{CP}$.

© Houghton Mifflin Harcourt Publishing Company

9. What is m∠*GCJ*?

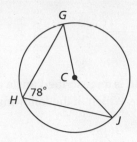

A. 39°　　　　**C.** 102°

B. 78°　　　　**D.** 156°

CONSTRUCTED RESPONSE

10. Prove or disprove that the point $(2, \sqrt{5})$ lies on the circle that is centered at the origin and contains the point $(0, -3)$.

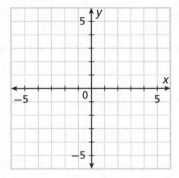

_____

_____

_____

_____

_____

_____

_____

11. Write an expression in terms of *m* that you can use to find the area of sector *AOB*.

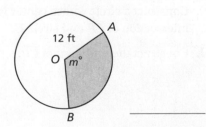

_____

12. Using the figure below, Andrea discovers that the length of the arc intercepted by the 60° angle is proportional to the radius. What is the constant of proportionality for the relationship? Show your reasoning.

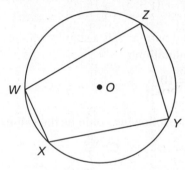

_____

_____

13. Quadrilateral *WXYZ* is inscribed in circle *O*. Complete the following proof to show that opposite angles are supplementary.

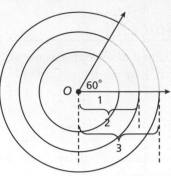

a. $\overparen{YZW}$ and $\overparen{WXY}$ make a complete circle.

Therefore, m$\overparen{YZW}$ + m$\overparen{WXY}$ = _____.

b. By the Inscribed Angle Theorem,

m∠*X* = _____ and m∠*Z* = _____.

c. Complete the proof by showing that the sum of m∠*X* and m∠*Z* is 180°.

_____

_____

_____

_____

_____

_____

_____

_____

Probability

Chapter Focus

Probability theory is the branch of mathematics concerned with situations involving chance. You will learn how to use set theory to help you calculate basic probabilities and will investigate the role of permutations and combinations in probability. You will also learn how to determine the probability of mutually exclusive events, overlapping events, independent events, and dependent events. Along the way, you will perform simulations and learn how to use probability to make and analyze decisions.

Chapter at a Glance

COMMON CORE

Lesson		Standards for Mathematical Content
13-1	Permutations and Combinations	CC.9-12.S.CP.9(+)
13-2	Theoretical and Experimental Probability	CC.9-12.S.MD.6(+)
13-3	Independent and Dependent Events	CC.9-12.S.CP.2, CC.9-12.S.CP.3, CC.9-12.S.CP.4, CC.9-12.S.CP.8(+)
13-4	Two-Way Tables	CC.9-12.S.CP.3, CC.9-12.S.CP.6
13-5	Compound Events	CC.9-12.S.CP.7
	Performance Tasks	
	Assessment Readiness	

CHAPTER 13

Unpacking the Standards

Understanding the standards and the vocabulary terms in the standards will help you know exactly what you are expected to learn in this chapter.

COMMON CORE CC.9-12.S.CP.9(+)

Use permutations and combinations to compute probabilities of compound events and solve problems.

Key Vocabulary

permutation *(permutación)*
An arrangement of a group of objects in which order is important. The number of permutations of r objects from a group of n objects is denoted $_nP_r$.

combination *(combinación)*
A selection of a group of objects in which order is *not* important. The number of combinations of r objects chosen from a group of n objects is denoted $_nC_r$.

probability *(probabilidad)*
A number from 0 to 1 (or 0% to 100%) that is the measure of how likely an event is to occur.

event *(suceso)* An outcome or set of outcomes in a probability experiment.

compound event *(suceso compuesto)* An event made up of two or more simple events.

What It Means For You   Lesson 13-1

A permutation is an arrangement of objects in which order is important. A combination is an arrangement of objects in which order is not important. Both permutations and combinations can be used to find probabilities.

EXAMPLE   Permutations

Lindsey will choose two of these pictures to hang next to each other on her bedroom wall.

This is an example of a permutation because the order is important. Hanging the mountain picture to the right of the sunset picture is different from hanging the mountain picture to the left of the sunset picture.

EXAMPLE   Combinations

You can choose three toppings for your hamburger.

TOPPINGS
☐ Tomato   ☐ Mayo
☐ Lettuce   ☐ Pickles
☐ Onions   ☐ Ketchup

This is an example of a combination because the order is not important. Tomato, onions, and pickles is the same as pickles, tomato, and onions.

© Houghton Mifflin Harcourt Publishing Company

CC.9-12.S.CP.1

COMMON CORE

Describe events as subsets of a sample space (the set of outcomes) using characteristics (or categories) of the outcomes, or as unions, intersections, or complements of other events ("or," "and," "not").

Key Vocabulary

sample space *(espacio muestral)* The set of all possible outcomes of a probability experiment.

outcome *(resultado)* A possible result of a probability experiment.

union *(unión)* The union of two sets is the set of all elements that are in either set, denoted by ∪.

intersection *(intersección de conjuntos)* The intersection of two sets is the set of all elements that are common to both sets, denoted by ∩.

complement of an event *(complemento de un suceso)* All outcomes in the sample space that are not in an event E, denoted $\overline{E}$ or E^c.

What It Means For You
Lesson 13-5

To calculate the probability of a particular event, you may need to find the sample space, which is the set of all possible outcomes. You may also need to determine which outcome(s) in the sample space make up the event.

EXAMPLE **Sample Spaces**

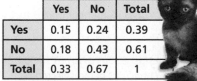

The sample space for rolling two standard number cubes is shown. The circled outcomes make up the event "rolling a sum of 10."

CC.9-12.S.CP.4

COMMON CORE

Construct and interpret two-way frequency tables of data when two categories are associated with each object being classified. Use the two-way table as a sample space to decide if events are independent and to approximate conditional probabilities.

Key Vocabulary

frequency table *(tabla de frecuencia)* A table that lists the number of times, or frequency, that each data value occurs.

independent events *(sucesos independientes)* Events for which the occurrence or non-occurrence of one event does not affect the probability of the other event.

conditional probability *(probabilidad condicional)* The probability of event B, given that event A has already occurred or is certain to occur, denoted $P(B|A)$.

What It Means For You
Lessons 13-3, 13-4

A two-way table organizes data about two variables. A two-way frequency table can be very helpful when finding probabilities.

EXAMPLE **Finding Conditional Probability**

		Owns a cat		
		Yes	No	Total
Owns	Yes	0.15	0.24	0.39
a dog	No	0.18	0.43	0.61
	Total	0.33	0.67	1

This two-way frequency table describes data collected by a sociologist who surveyed 100 randomly selected people about their pets. You can use this table to answer the question, "If a person in this survey has a dog, what is the probability that he or she also has a cat?"

CHAPTER 13

Key Vocabulary

combination *(combinación)* A selection of a group of objects in which order is *not* important. The number of combinations of r objects chosen from a group of n objects is denoted $_nC_r$.

complement of an event *(complemento de un suceso)* All outcomes in the sample space that are not in an event E, denoted $\overline{E}$ or E^C.

compound event *(suceso compuesto)* An event made up of two or more simple events.

conditional probability *(probabilidad condicional)* The probability of event B, given that event A has already occurred or is certain to occur, denoted $P(B|A)$.

convenience sample *(muestra de conveniencia)* A sample based on members of the population that are readily available.

dependent events *(sucesos dependientes)* Events for which the occurrence or non-occurrence of one event affects the probability of the other event.

event *(suceso)* An outcome or set of outcomes in a probability experiment.

factorial *(factorial)* If n is a positive integer, then n factorial, written $n!$, is $n \cdot (n-1) \cdot (n-2) \cdot \ldots \cdot 2 \cdot 1$. The factorial of 0 is defined to be 1.

frequency table *(tabla de frecuencia)* A table that lists the number of times, or frequency, that each data value occurs.

independent events *(sucesos independientes)* Events for which the occurrence or non-occurrence of one event does not affect the probability of the other event.

intersection *(intersección de conjuntos)* The intersection of two sets is the set of all elements that are common to both sets, denoted by $\cap$.

mutually exclusive events *(sucesos mutuamente excluyentes)* Two events are mutually exclusive if they cannot both occur in the same trial of an experiment.

outcome *(resultado)* A possible result of a probability experiment.

permutation *(permutación)* An arrangement of a group of objects in which order is important. The number of permutations of r objects from a group of n objects is denoted $_nP_r$.

probability *(probabilidad)* A number from 0 to 1 (or 0% to 100%) that is the measure of how likely an event is to occur.

random sample *(muestra aleatoria)* A sample selected from a population so that each member of the population has an equal chance of being selected.

sample space *(espacio muestral)* The set of all possible outcomes of a probability experiment.

union *(unión)* The union of two sets is the set of all elements that are in either set, denoted by $\cup$.

Theoretical and Experimental Probability

Connection: Sampling

Essential question: *How can you use probabilites to help you make fair decisions?*

PREP FOR **CC.9–12.S.MD.6(+)**

1 ENGAGE   **Introducing a Decision-Making Problem**

Video Tutor

A small town has 25 residents. The state has given the town money that must be used for something that benefits the community. The town's mayor has decided that the money will be used to build a teen center or a senior center.

In order to make a decision about the type of community center to build, the mayor plans to survey a subset of town residents. There are two survey methods: a random sample and a convenience sample. The convenience sample will be conducted by surveying town residents at a local movie theater.

In the table below, each resident of the town is identified by a number from 1 to 25. The table shows each resident's preference: T for the teen center, S for the senior center. The table also gives the probability that each resident is at the movie theater when the convenience-sample survey is conducted.

1	2	3	4	5
S	S	T	S	T
0.2	0.3	0.8	0.1	0.8
6	**7**	**8**	**9**	**10**
T	S	T	S	S
0.7	0.2	0.8	0.1	0.3
11	**12**	**13**	**14**	**15**
S	T	S	S	S
0.1	0.7	0.2	0.2	0.4
16	**17**	**18**	**19**	**20**
T	S	S	S	T
0.6	0.7	0.1	0.1	0.6
21	**22**	**23**	**24**	**25**
S	S	S	S	T
0.3	0.2	0.3	0.1	0.9

REFLECT

1a. Based on the data in the table, what percent of all residents favor the teen center? the senior center?

_____

1b. If it were possible for the mayor to survey every resident, what decision do you think the mayor would make? Why?

_____

2 EXPLORE   Using a Random Sample

Suppose the mayor of the town is not able to survey every resident, so the mayor decides to survey a random sample of 10 residents.

A You can use your calculator to simulate the process of choosing and surveying a random sample of residents.

- Go to the MATH menu.
- Use the right arrow key to access the PRB menu.
- Use the down arrow key to select **5:randInt(** .
- Use "randInt(1,25)" as shown at the right.
- Each time you press Enter, the calculator will return a random integer from 1 to 25.

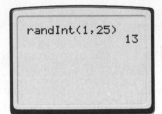

Generate 10 random integers in this way. For each integer, note the corresponding preference (T or S) of that resident of the town. (If a number is selected more than once, ignore the duplicates and choose a new number. This ensures that no resident is surveyed more than once.) Record your results in the table.

Resident Number										
Preference (T or S)										

B Based on the random sample, what percent of residents favor the teen center? the senior center?

_____

REFLECT

2a. What is the probability that any resident is chosen to be part of the random sample? Explain.

_____

_____

2b. What decision do you think the mayor would make based on the random sample? Why?

_____

2c. Compare your results with those of other students. In general, how well do the results of the random sample predict the preferences of the town as a whole?

_____

3 EXPLORE Using a Convenience Sample

The mayor of the town decides to use a convenience sample by surveying the first 10 residents of the town to leave a local movie theater.

A You can use slips of paper to simulate the process of choosing and surveying this convenience sample.

- For each resident, prepare 1 to 10 small slips of paper with the resident's number on them. The number of slips of paper is determined by the probability that the resident is at the movie theater when the survey is conducted. For example, Resident 1 has a 0.2 probability of being at the theater, so prepare 2 slips of paper with the number 1; Resident 2 has a 0.3 probability of being at the theater, so prepare 3 slips of paper with the number 2; and so on.

- Place all of the slips of paper in a bag and mix them well.

- Choose slips of paper one at a time without looking.

Choose 10 residents in this way. For each resident, note the corresponding preference (T or S) using the table on the first page of the lesson. (If a resident is selected more than once, ignore the duplicates and choose a new number from the bag. This ensures that no resident is surveyed more than once.) Record your results in the table.

Resident Number										
Preference (T or S)										

B Based on the convenience sample, what percent of residents favor the teen center? the senior center?

_____

REFLECT

3a. Why do some residents of the town have more slips of paper representing them than other residents? How does this connect to the way the convenience sample is conducted?

_____

_____

_____

_____

3b. What decision do you think the mayor would make based on the convenience sample? Why?

_____

3c. Compare your results with those of other students. In general, how well do the results of the convenience sample predict the preferences of the town as a whole?

_____

_____

3d. Which sampling method is more likely to lead to fair decision-making? Explain.

_____

_____

3e. What factors might explain why the results of the convenience sample are different from the results of the random sample?

_____

_____

_____

3f. When you conduct the random-sample simulation is it possible that you might choose 10 residents who all favor the senior center? Is this result possible when you conduct the convenience-sample simulation? In which simulation do you think this result is more likely?

_____

_____

_____

3g. What are some limitations or drawbacks of the simulations?

_____

_____

_____

3h. In a town of 25 residents, it is likely that the mayor could actually survey all the residents, instead of using a random sample or convenience sample. What are some reasons that sampling might be used in situations involving populations that are much larger than 25?

_____

_____

_____

© Houghton Mifflin Harcourt Publishing Company

Additional Practice

The table represents a class of 30 students. Each student was asked if he or she would prefer having a written report (R) or an oral presentation (O) for the final. Use the table for Exercises 1–4.

1 R	2 R	3 O	4 R	5 O
6 R	7 R	8 R	9 O	10 R
11 O	12 O	13 R	14 R	15 R
16 R	17 O	18 R	19 R	20 R
21 R	22 R	23 O	24 R	25 R
26 O	27 R	28 O	29 R	30 R

1. Use a calculator or slips of paper to choose 10 random numbers from 1 to 30. Circle the 10 numbers you generate.

2. What is the probability of any given student being chosen for your sample?

_____

3. According to your sample, what percent of the class would prefer to have a written report as the final?

_____

4. What percent of the class would prefer to have a written report if you take into account *all* of the students? How does this compare to what you found in your sample?

_____

_____

5. Another teacher wants to survey his classes with the same question. He has three classes of 90 students each. Explain a way he could collect responses from a random sample of 10% of his students. The sample should have equal representation for each of the three classes.

_____

_____

Problem Solving

The council of a city of 200,000 people is deciding on one of two improvement projects. The two proposed projects are (1) creating bike lanes in the downtown area and (2) repairing a road that passes through the suburbs. An employee of the city takes a survey of 50 people near his house in the suburbs. Of those surveyed, 45 people said they would prefer the road repair. Use this information for Exercises 1–4.

1. According to the survey, what percent of the city residents prefer the road repair project?

   _____

2. The city employee calculates that every city resident had a
   $\frac{50}{200,000} = \frac{1}{4,000}$ probability of being chosen for his survey. Do you
   agree? Explain why or why not.

   _____

   _____

3. Is the sample a random sample or a convenience sample? Explain your reasoning.

   _____

   _____

4. Do you think it's likely that the sample represents the population as a whole? Explain why or why not.

   _____

   _____

   _____

Select the best answer.

5. A survey asks a question of 30 people out of a total of 3,000 visiting a mall in one day. If the sample is random, what is the probability of any given person being surveyed?

   A 1%   C 10%

   B 3%   D 30%

6. A survey finds that 65% of town residents support leash laws. If that number was found by taking a sample of 40 residents, how many people in the sample support leash laws?

   F 12   H 40

   G 26   J 6

Additional Practice

Find each probability.

1. A bag contains 5 red, 3 green, 4 blue, and 8 yellow marbles.
Find the probability of randomly selecting a green marble,
and then a yellow marble if the first marble is replaced.   _____

2. A sock drawer contains 5 rolled-up pairs of each color of
socks, white, green, and blue. What is the probability of
randomly selecting a pair of blue socks, replacing it, and
then randomly selecting a pair of white socks?   _____

Two 1–6 number cubes are rolled—one is black and one is white.

3. The sum of the rolls is greater than or equal to 6 and the black cube shows a 3.

   a. Explain why the events are dependent.

   _____

   b. Find the probability.   _____

4. The white cube shows an even number, and the sum is 8.

   a. Explain why the events are dependent.

   _____

   b. Find the probability.   _____

**The table below shows numbers of registered voters by age in the United States
in 2004 based on the census. Find each probability in decimal form.**

Age	Registered Voters (in thousands)	Not Registered to Vote (in thousands)
18–24	14,334	13,474
25–44	49,371	32,763
45–64	51,659	19,355
65 and over	26,706	8,033

5. A randomly selected person is registered to vote, given that
the person is between the ages of 18 and 24.   _____

6. A randomly selected person is between the ages of 45 and
64 and is not registered to vote.   _____

7. A randomly selected person is registered to vote and is
at least 65 years old.   _____

**A bag contains 12 blue cubes, 12 red cubes, and 20 green cubes.
Determine whether the events are independent or dependent, and find each probability.**

8. A green cube and then a blue cube are chosen at random
with replacement.   _____

9. Two blue cubes are chosen at random without replacement.   _____

Problem Solving

The table shows student participation in different sports at a high school. Suppose a student is selected at random.

Sports Participation by Grade					
	Track	Volleyball	Basketball	Tennis	No Sport
Grade 9	12	18	15	9	66
Grade 10	6	20	12	2	95
Grade 11	15	11	8	5	61
Grade 12	7	6	10	12	50

1. What is the probability that a student is in grade 10 and runs track?

   a. Find the probability that a student is in grade 10, $P(10)$. _____

   b. Find the probability that a student runs track, given that
   the student is in grade 10, $P(Tr \mid 10)$, _____
   c. Find $P(10 \text{ and } Tr) = P(10) \cdot P(Tr \mid 10)$. _____

2. What is the probability that a student is in grade 12
   and runs track or plays tennis?

   a. Find the probability that a student is in grade 12, $P(12)$. _____
   b. Find the probability that a student runs track or plays tennis,
   given that the student is in grade 12, $P(Tr \text{ or } Te \mid 12)$. _____

   c. Find $P(12 \text{ or } (Tr \text{ or } Te))$. _____

3. During a fire drill, the students are waiting in the parking lot. What is the
   probability that one student is in grade 12 and runs track or plays tennis,
   and the student standing next to her is in grade 10 and runs track?
   a. Find the probability for the first student. _____
   b. Find the probability for the second student. _____
   c. Find the probability for the event occurring. _____
   d. Are these events independent or dependent? Explain.

   _____

Samantha is 1 of 17 students in a class of 85 who have decided to pursue a business degree. Each week, a student in the class is randomly selected to tutor younger students. Choose the letter for the best answer.

4. What is the probability of drawing a
   business student one week, replacing the
   name, and drawing the same name the
   next week?

   A 3.4   C 0.04

   B 0.2   D 0.002

5. What is the probability of drawing
   Samantha's name one week, not
   replacing her name, and drawing the
   name of another business student the
   next week?

   F $\dfrac{1}{85} \cdot \dfrac{16}{84}$ H $\dfrac{17}{85} \cdot \dfrac{16}{84}$

   G $\dfrac{1}{85} \cdot \dfrac{17}{84}$ J $\dfrac{17}{85} \cdot \dfrac{17}{84}$

© Houghton Mifflin Harcourt Publishing Company

Two-Way Tables
Going Deeper

Essential question: *How do you calculate a conditional probability?*

The probability that event *B* occurs given that event *A* has already occurred is called the **conditional probability** of *B* given *A* and is written $P(B \mid A)$.

Video Tutor

CC.9–12.S.CP.6

1 EXAMPLE **Finding Conditional Probabilities**

One hundred people who frequently get migraine headaches were chosen to participate in a study of a new anti-headache medicine. Some of the particpants were given the medicine; others were not. After one week, the participants were asked if they got a headache during the week. The two-way table summarizes the results.

	Took Medicine	No Medicine	TOTAL
Headache	12	15	27
No Headache	48	25	73
TOTAL	60	40	100

A To the nearest percent, what is the probability that a participant who took the medicine did not get a headache?

Let event *A* be the event that a participant took the medicine. Let event *B* be the event that a participant did not get a headache.

To find the probability that a participant who took the medicine did not get a headache, you must find $P(B \mid A)$. You are only concerned with participants who took the medicine, so look at the data in the "Took Medicine" column.

There were _____ participants who took the medicine.

Of these participants, _____ participants did not get a headache.

So, $P(B \mid A) = \dfrac{}{} = $ _____.

B To the nearest percent, what is the probability that a participant who did not get a headache took the medicine?

To find the probability that a participant who did not get a headache took the medicine, you must find $P(A \mid B)$. You are only concerned with participants who did not get a headache, so look at the data in the "No headache" row.

There were _____ participants who did not get a headache.

Of these participants, _____ participants took the medicine.

So, $P(A \mid B) = \dfrac{}{} \approx $ _____.

© Houghton Mifflin Harcourt Publishing Company

1a. In general, do you think $P(B \mid A) = P(A \mid B)$? Why or why not?

_____

1b. How can you use set notation to represent the event that a participant took the medicine and did not get a headache? Is the probability that a participant took the medicine and did not get a headache equal to either of the conditional probabilities you calculated in the example?

_____

_____

CC.9–12.S.CP.3

2 EXPLORE **Developing a Formula for Conditional Probability**

You can generalize your work from the previous example to develop a formula for finding conditional probabilities.

A Recall how you calculated $P(B \mid A)$, the probability that a participant who took the medicine did not get a headache.

You found that $P(B \mid A) = \frac{48}{60}$.

Use the table shown here to help you write this quotient in terms of events A and B.

		Event A		
		Took Medicine	No Medicine	TOTAL
Event B	Headache	12	15	27
	No Headache	$48 = n(A \cap B)$	25	$73 = n(B)$
	TOTAL	$60 = n(A)$	40	100

$P(B \mid A) = \dfrac{}{}$

B Now divide the numerator and denominator of the quotient by $n(S)$, the number of outcomes in the sample space. This converts the counts to probabilities.

$P(B \mid A) = \dfrac{ \Big/ n(S)}{ \Big/ n(S)} = \dfrac{}{}$

REFLECT

2a. Write a formula for $P(A \mid B)$ in terms of $n(A \cap B)$ and $n(B)$.

_____

2b. Write a formula for $P(A \mid B)$ in terms of $P(A \cap B)$ and $P(B)$.

_____

You may have discovered the following formula for conditional probability.

Conditional Probability

The conditional probability of B given A (the probability that event B occurs given that event A occurs) is given by the following formula:

$$P(B \mid A) = \frac{P(A \cap B)}{P(A)}$$

CC.9–12.S.CP.3

 **3 EXAMPLE** **Using the Conditional Probability Formula**

In a standard deck of playing cards, find the probability that a red card is a queen.

A Let event Q be the event that a card is a queen. Let event R be the event that a card is red. You are asked to find $P(Q \mid R)$. First find $P(R \cap Q)$ and $P(R)$.

$R \cap Q$ represents cards that are both red and a queen; that is, red queens.

There are _____ red queens in the deck of 52 cards, so $P(R \cap Q) =$ _____.

There are _____ red cards in the deck, so $P(R) =$ _____.

B Use the formula for conditional probability.

$P(Q \mid R) = \frac{P(Q \cap R)}{P(R)} =$ Substitute probabilities from above.

$=$ _____   Multiply numerator and denominator by 52.

$=$ _____   Simplify.

So, the probability that a red card is a queen is _____.

REFLECT

3a. How can you interpret the probability you calculated above?

_____

_____

3b. Is the probability that a red card is a queen equal to the probability that a queen is red? Explain.

_____

1. In order to study the connection between the amount of sleep a student gets and his or her school performance, data was collected about 120 students. The two-way table shows the number of students who passed and failed an exam and the number of students who got more or less than 6 hours of sleep the night before.

	Passed Exam	Failed Exam	TOTAL
Less than 6 hours of sleep	12	10	22
More than 6 hours of sleep	90	8	98
TOTAL	102	18	120

   a. To the nearest percent, what is the probability that a student who failed the exam got less than 6 hours of sleep? _____

   b. To the nearest percent, what is the probability that a student who got less than 6 hours of sleep failed the exam? _____

   c. To the nearest percent, what is the probability that a student got less than 6 hours of sleep and failed the exam? _____

2. A botanist studied the effect of a new fertilizer by choosing 100 orchids and giving 70% of these plants the fertilizer. Of the plants that got the fertilizer, 40% produced flowers within a month. Of the plants that did not get the fertilizer, 10% produced flowers within a month. Find each probability to the nearest percent. (*Hint:* Construct a two-way table.)

   a. Find the probability that a plant that produced flowers got the fertilizer. _____

   b. Find the probability that a plant that got the fertilizer produced flowers. _____

3. At a school fair, a box contains 24 yellow balls and 76 red balls. One-fourth of the balls of each color are labeled "Win a prize." Find each probability as a percent.

   a. Find the probability that a ball labeled "Win a prize" is yellow. _____

   b. Find the probability that a ball labeled "Win a prize" is red. _____

   c. Find the probability that a ball is labeled "Win a prize" and is red. _____

   d. Find the probability that a yellow ball is labeled "Win a prize." _____

In Exercises 4–9, consider a standard deck of playing cards and the following events: *A*: **the card is an ace;** *B*: **the card is black;** *C*: **the card is a club. Find each probability as a fraction.**

4. $P(A \mid B)$

_____

5. $P(B \mid A)$

_____

6. $P(A \mid C)$

_____

7. $P(C \mid A)$

_____

8. $P(B \mid C)$

_____

9. $P(C \mid B)$

_____

Additional Practice

1. The table shows the results of a customer satisfaction survey of 100 randomly selected shoppers at the mall who were asked if they would shop at an earlier time if the mall opened earlier. Complete the table below and use it to answer parts **a** and **b**.

	Ages 10–20	Ages 21–45	Ages 46–65	Ages Over 65
Yes	13	2	8	24
No	25	10	15	3

	Ages 10–20	Ages 21–45	Ages 46–65	Ages Over 65	Total
Yes					
No					
Total					

   a. To the nearest whole percent, what is the probability that a shopper who is in the age range 21 to 45 said that he or she would shop earlier?

_____

   b. To the nearest whole percent, what is the probability that a shopper who would shop earlier is in the age range 65 and older?

_____

2. Jerrod collected data on 100 randomly selected students, and summarized the results in a table.

		Owns an MP3 player	
		Yes	No
Owns a	**Yes**	28	12
Smart phone	**No**	34	26

   a. If you are given that a student owns an MP3 player, what is the probability that the student also owns a smart phone? Round your answer to the nearest hundredth.

_____

   b. If you are given that a student owns a smart phone, what is the probability that the student also owns an MP3 player? Round your answer to the nearest hundredth.

_____

Problem Solving

1. The table shows the number of students who would drive to school if the school provided parking spaces. Complete the table below and use it to answer parts **a** and **b**.

	Lowerclassmates	Upperclassmates
Always	32	122
Sometimes	58	44
Never	24	120

   a. To the nearest whole percent, what is the probability that a student who said "always" is an upperclassmate?

   _____ 78% _____

   b. To the nearest whole percent, what is the probability that a lowerclassmate said "always" or "sometimes"?

   _____ 35% _____

2. Gerry collected data and did a table of marginal relative frequencies on the number of students who participate in chorus and the number who participate in band.

<table>
<tr><td></td><td colspan="3">Chorus</td></tr>
<tr><td></td><td></td><td>Yes</td><td>No</td></tr>
<tr><td rowspan="2">Band</td><td>Yes</td><td>38</td><td>29</td></tr>
<tr><td>No</td><td>9</td><td>24</td></tr>
</table>

   a. If you are given that a student is in chorus, what is the probability that the student also is in band? Round your answer to the nearest hundredth.

   _____ 58% _____

   b. If you are given that a student is not in band, what is the probability that the student is in chorus? Round your answer to the nearest hundredth.

   _____ 9% _____

Use the table in Exercise 2 to answer Exercises 3 and 4. Select the best answer.

3. What is the probability if a student is not in chorus, then that student is in band?

   A 0.29   B 0.38

   C 0.43   D 0.55

4. What is the probability that if a student is not in band then the student is not in chorus?

   F 0.09   G 0.33

   H 0.44   J 0.73

Name _____ Class _____ Date _____

MULTIPLE CHOICE

1. You spin a spinner with 10 equal sections that are numbered 1 through 10. Event A is rolling an odd number. Event B is rolling a number greater than 5. What is $P(A \cap B)$?

   A. $\frac{1}{8}$ C. $\frac{1}{2}$

   B. $\frac{1}{5}$ D. $\frac{4}{5}$

2. There are 9 players on a basketball team. For a team photo, 4 of the players are seated on a row of chairs and 5 players stand behind them. In how many different ways can 4 players be arranged on the row of chairs?

   F. 24   H. 180

   G. 126   J. 3024

3. There are 5 peaches and 4 nectarines in a bowl. You randomly choose 2 pieces of fruit to pack in your lunch. What is the probability that you choose 2 peaches?

   A. $\frac{5}{36}$ C. $\frac{2}{5}$

   B. $\frac{5}{18}$ D. $\frac{5}{9}$

4. You shuffle the cards shown below and choose one at random. What is the probability that you choose a gray card or an even number?

   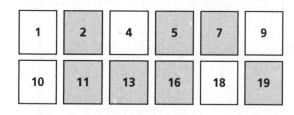

   F. $\frac{1}{10}$ H. $\frac{5}{6}$

   G. $\frac{35}{144}$ J. 1

The two-way table provides data about 240 randomly chosen people who visit a movie theater. Use the table for Items 5 and 6.

	Discount Admission	Regular Admission	TOTAL
Purchases a snack	24	72	96
Purchases no snack	36	108	144
TOTAL	60	180	240

5. Consider the following events.

   Event A: Pays for a regular admission.
   Event B: Purchases a snack.

   Which is the best description of the two events?

   A. complementary events

   B. dependent events

   C. independent events

   D. mutually exclusive events

6. What is the probability that a visitor to the movie theater purchases a snack given that the visitor pays for a discount admission?

   F. 0.1   H. 0.4

   G. 0.25   J. 0.75

7. A bag contains 8 yellow marbles and 4 blue marbles. You choose a marble, put it aside, and then choose another marble. What is the probability that you choose two yellow marbles?

   A. $\frac{7}{18}$ C. $\frac{4}{9}$

   B. $\frac{14}{33}$ D. $\frac{2}{3}$

8. Events A and B are independent events. Which of the following must be true?

   F. $P(A \text{ and } B) = P(A) \cdot P(B)$

   G. $P(A \text{ and } B) = P(A) + P(B)$

   H. $P(A) = P(B)$

   J. $P(B \mid A) = P(A \mid B)$

9. Which expression can you use to calculate the conditional probability of event A given that event B has occurred?

   A. $P(A) + P(B) - P(A \text{ and } B)$

   B. $P(B) \cdot P(A \mid B)$

   C. $\dfrac{P(A \text{ and } B)}{P(B)}$

   D. $\dfrac{P(A)}{P(B)}$

CONSTRUCTED RESPONSE

10. It is known that 1% of all mice in a laboratory have a genetic mutation. A test for the mutation correctly identifies mice that have the mutation 98% of the time. The test correctly identifies mice that do not have the mutation 96% of the time. A lab assistant tests a mouse and finds that the mouse tests positive for the mutation. The lab assistant decides that the mouse must have the mutation. Is this a good decision? Explain.

   _____

   _____

   _____

   _____

11. Two students, Naomi and Kayla, play a game using the rules shown below. The winner of the game gets a box of 80 fruit chews.

Game Rules
• One student repeatedly tosses a coin.
• When the coin lands heads up, Naomi gets a point.
• When the coin lands tails up, Kayla gets a point.
• The first student to reach 8 points wins the game and gets the fruit chews.

   The game gets interrupted when Naomi has 7 points and Kayla has 5 points. How should the 80 fruit chews be divided between the students given that the game was interrupted at this moment? Explain why your answer provides a fair way to divide the fruit chews.

   _____

   _____

   _____

   _____

   _____

   _____

   _____

   _____

   _____

© Houghton Mifflin Harcourt Publishing Company

Correlation of *Explorations in Core Math* to the Common Core State Standards

Standards	Algebra 1	Geometry	Algebra 2
Number and Quantity			
The Real Number System			
CC.9-12.N.RN.1 Explain how the definition of the meaning of rational exponents follows from extending the properties of integer exponents to those values, allowing for a notation for radicals in terms of rational exponents.	Lessons 6-1, 6-2		Lesson 5-6
CC.9-12.N.RN.2 Rewrite expressions involving radicals and rational exponents using the properties of exponents.	Lesson 6-2		Lesson 5-6
CC.9-12.N.RN.3 Explain why the sum or product of two rational numbers is rational; that the sum of a rational number and an irrational number is irrational; and that the product of a nonzero rational number and an irrational number is irrational.	Lesson 6-2		
Quantities			
CC.9-12.N.Q.1 Use units as a way to understand problems and to guide the solution of multi-step problems; choose and interpret units consistently in formulas; choose and interpret the scale and the origin in graphs and data displays.*	Lessons 1-8, 1-9, 3-2, 4-1, 4-9		Lessons 2-8, 10-1
CC.9-12.N.Q.2 Define appropriate quantities for the purpose of descriptive modeling.*	Lessons 4-9, 5-6		
CC.9-12.N.Q.3 Choose a level of accuracy appropriate to limitations on measurement when reporting quantities.*	Lesson 1-10		
The Complex Number System			
CC.9-12.N.CN.1 Know there is a complex number i such that $i^2 = -1$, and every complex number has the form $a + bi$ with a and b real.			Lesson 2-5
CC.9-12.N.CN.2 Use the relation $i^2 = -1$ and the commutative, associative, and distributive properties to add, subtract, and multiply complex numbers.			Lesson 2-9
CC.9-12.N.CN.3(+) Find the conjugate of a complex number; use conjugates to find moduli and quotients of complex numbers.			Lesson 2-9

(+) Advanced   * = Also a Modeling Standard

Standards	Algebra 1	Geometry	Algebra 2
CC.9-12.N.CN.7 Solve quadratic equations with real coefficients that have complex solutions.			Lesson 2-6
CC.9-12.N.CN.9(+) Know the Fundamental Theorem of Algebra; show that it is true for quadratic polynomials.			Lesson 3-6
Algebra			
Seeing Structure in Expressions			
CC.9-12.A.SSE.1 Interpret expressions that represent a quantity in terms of its context.* **a.** Interpret parts of an expression, such as terms, factors, and coefficients. **b.** Interpret complicated expressions by viewing one or more of their parts as a single entity.	Lessons 1-1, 1-8, 6-3, 7-1, 7-2, 7-6		Lessons 2-8, 3-9, 9-5, 12-6
CC.9-12.A.SSE.2 Use the structure of an expression to identify ways to rewrite it.	Lessons 6-5, 6-6, 7-2, 7-3, 7-4, 7-5, 7-6		Lessons 3-6, 12-6
CC.9-12.A.SSE.3 Choose and produce an equivalent form of an expression to reveal and explain properties of the quantity represented by the expression. **a.** Factor a quadratic expression to reveal the zeros of the function it defines. **b.** Complete the square in a quadratic expression to reveal the maximum or minimum value of the function it defines. **c.** Use the properties of exponents to transform expressions for exponential functions.	Lessons 8-3, 8-6, 8-8		Lessons 4-5, 6-1, 6-7
CC.9-12.A.SSE.4 Derive the formula for the sum of a finite geometric series (when the common ratio is not 1), and use the formula to solve problems.			Lessons 9-4, 9-5
Arithmetic with Polynomials and Rational Expressions			
CC.9-12.A.APR.1 Understand that polynomials form a system analogous to the integers, namely, they are closed under the operations of addition, subtraction, and multiplication; add, subtract, and multiply polynomials.	Lessons 6-4, 6-5		Lessons 3-1, 3-2
CC.9-12.A.APR.2 Know and apply the Remainder Theorem: For a polynomial $p(x)$ and a number a, the remainder on division by $x - a$ is $p(a)$, so $p(a) = 0$ if and only if $(x - a)$ is a factor of $p(x)$.			Lessons 3-3, 3-4, 3-6
CC.9-12.A.APR.3 Identify zeros of polynomials when suitable factorizations are available, and use the zeros to construct a rough graph of the function defined by the polynomial.			Lesson 3-5
CC.9-12.A.APR.4 Prove polynomial identities and use them to describe numerical relationships.			Lesson 3-2

(+) Advanced   * = Also a Modeling Standard

Standards	Algebra 1	Geometry	Algebra 2
CC.9-12.A.APR.5(+) Know and apply the Binomial Theorem for the expansion of $(x + y)^n$ in powers of x and y for a positive integer n, where x and y are any numbers, with coefficients determined for example by Pascal's Triangle. (The Binomial Theorem can be proved by mathematical induction or by a combinatorial argument.)			Lesson 3-2
CC.9-12.A.APR.6 Rewrite simple rational expressions in different forms; write $a(x)/b(x)$ in the form $q(x) + r(x)/b(x)$, where $a(x)$, $b(x)$, $q(x)$, and $r(x)$ are polynomials with the degree of $r(x)$ less than the degree of $b(x)$, using inspection, long division, or, for the more complicated examples, a computer algebra system.			Lesson 5-4
CC.9-12.A.APR.7(+) Understand that rational expressions form a system analogous to the rational numbers, closed under addition, subtraction, multiplication, and division by a nonzero rational expression; add, subtract, multiply, and divide rational expressions.			Lessons 5-2, 5-3
Creating Equations			
CC.9-12.A.CED.1 Create equations and inequalities in one variable and use them to solve problems.*	Lessons 1-9, 2-1, 8-6, 8-7	**Lesson 1-4**	Lessons 2-7, 3-9, 5-5
CC.9-12.A.CED.2 Create equations in two or more variables to represent relationships between quantities; graph equations on coordinate axes with labels and scales.*	Lessons 1-7, 3-3, 3-4, 4-5, 4-6, 4-9, 4-10, 8-1, 8-2, 8-4, 8-5, 8-10, 9-2, 9-4		Lessons 2-8, 3-9, 4-8, 6-1, 6-3, 6-6, 6-7, 11-6
CC.9-12.A.CED.3 Represent constraints by equations or inequalities, and by systems of equations and/or inequalities, and interpret solutions as viable or nonviable options in a modeling context.*	Lessons 4-9, 5-6		Lessons 2-8, 3-9, 9-5
CC.9-12.A.CED.4 Rearrange formulas to highlight a quantity of interest, using the same reasoning as in solving equations.*	Lesson 1-6	**Lesson 1-5**	Lessons 4-8, 10-1
Reasoning with Equations and Inequalities			
CC.9-12.A.REI.1. Explain each step in solving a simple equation as following from the equality of numbers asserted at the previous step, starting from the assumption that the original equation has a solution. Construct a viable argument to justify a solution method.	Lessons 1-2, 1-3, 1-4, 1-5, 1-7, 9-4		
CC.9-12.A.REI.2 Solve simple rational and radical equations in one variable, and give examples showing how extraneous solutions may arise.			Lessons 5-5, 5-8
CC.9-12.A.REI.3 Solve linear equations and inequalities in one variable, including equations with coefficients represented by letters.	Lessons 1-2, 1-6, 2-2, 2-3, 2-4, 2-5, 2-6, 2-7		

(+) Advanced   * = Also a Modeling Standard

© Houghton Mifflin Harcourt Publishing Company

Standards	Algebra 1	Geometry	Algebra 2
CC.9-12.A.REI.4 Solve quadratic equations in one variable. **a.** Use the method of completing the square to transform any quadratic equation in x into an equation of the form $(x - p)^2 = q$ that has the same solutions. Derive the quadratic formula from this form. **b.** Solve quadratic equations by inspection (e.g., for $x^2 = 49$), taking square roots, completing the square, the quadratic formula and factoring, as appropriate to the initial form of the equation. Recognize when the quadratic formula gives complex solutions and write them as $a \pm bi$ for real numbers a and b.	Lessons 8-6, 8-7, 8-8, 8-9		Lesson 2-6
CC.9-12.A.REI.5 Prove that, given a system of two equations in two variables, replacing one equation by the sum of that equation and a multiple of the other produces a system with the same solutions.	Lesson 5-3		
CC.9-12.A.REI.6 Solve systems of linear equations exactly and approximately (e.g., with graphs), focusing on pairs of linear equations in two variables.	Lessons 5-1, 5-2, 5-3, 5-4, 5-6		
CC.9-12.A.REI.7 Solve a simple system consisting of a linear equation and a quadratic equation in two variables algebraically and graphically.	Lesson 8-10	**Lesson 12-7**	Lesson 12-7
CC.9-12.A.REI.10 Understand that the graph of an equation in two variables is the set of all its solutions plotted in the coordinate plane, often forming a curve (which could be a line).	Lesson 4-2		
CC.9-12.A.REI.11 Explain why the x-coordinates of the points where the graphs of the equations $y = f(x)$ and $y = g(x)$ intersect are the solutions of the equation $f(x) = g(x)$; find the solutions approximately, e.g., using technology to graph the functions, make tables of values, or find successive approximations. Include cases where $f(x)$ and/or $g(x)$ are linear, polynomial, rational, absolute value, exponential, and logarithmic functions.*	Lessons 1-7, 4-6, 8-5, 9-4		Lesson 4-5
CC.9-12.A.REI.12 Graph the solutions to a linear inequality in two variables as a half-plane (excluding the boundary in the case of a strict inequality), and graph the solution set to a system of linear inequalities in two variables as the intersection of the corresponding half-planes.	Lesson 5-5		
Functions			
Interpreting Functions			
CC.9-12.F.IF.1 Understand that a function from one set (called the domain) to another set (called the range) assigns to each element of the domain exactly one element of the range. If f is a function and x is an element of its domain, then $f(x)$ denotes the output of f corresponding to the input x. The graph of f is the graph of the equation $y = f(x)$.	Lessons 3-2, 4-1, 9-3		Lesson 10-3

(+) Advanced   * = Also a Modeling Standard

Explorations in Core Math Geometry   C4   Common Core Correlations

© Houghton Mifflin Harcourt Publishing Company

Standards	Algebra 1	Geometry	Algebra 2
CC.9-12.F.IF.2 Use function notation, evaluate functions for inputs in their domains, and interpret statements that use function notation in terms of a context.	Lessons 3-2, 3-3, 3-4, 3-6, 4-1, 4-5, 4-10, 8-1, 8-2, 8-4, 9-2		Lessons 3-5, 4-4, 4-6, 4-8, 6-3, 6-6, 6-7, 9-1, 11-6
CC.9-12.F.IF.3 Recognize that sequences are functions, sometimes defined recursively, whose domain is a subset of the integers.	Lessons 3-6, 4-1		Lesson 9-1
CC.9-12.F.IF.4 For a function that models a relationship between two quantities, interpret key features of graphs and tables in terms of the quantities, and sketch graphs showing key features given a verbal description of the relationship.*	Lessons 3-1, 3-4, 4-3, 4-5, 4-6, 4-10, 8-1, 8-4		Lessons 2-8, 3-9, 4-8, 6-3, 6-7, 11-6
CC.9-12.F.IF.5 Relate the domain of a function to its graph and, where applicable, to the quantitative relationship it describes.*	Lessons 3-2, 3-4, 4-1, 8-1, 8-2, 9-3		Lessons 1-1, 6-3
CC.9-12.F.IF.6 Calculate and interpret the average rate of change of a function (presented symbolically or as a table) over a specified interval. Estimate the rate of change from a graph.*	Lessons 4-3, 4-4		Lesson 2-8
CC.9-12.F.IF.7 Graph functions expressed symbolically and show key features of the graph, by hand in simple cases and using technology for more complicated cases.* **a.** Graph linear and quadratic functions and show intercepts, maxima, and minima. **b.** Graph square root, cube root, and piecewise-defined functions, including step functions and absolute value functions. **c.** Graph polynomial functions, identifying zeros when suitable factorizations are available, and showing end behavior. **d.** (+) Graph rational functions, identifying zeros and asymptotes when suitable factorizations are available, and showing end behavior. **e.** Graph exponential and logarithmic functions, showing intercepts and end behavior, and trigonometric functions, showing period, midline, and amplitude.	Lessons 3-4, 4-1, 4-5, 4-6, 4-10, 8-1, 8-2, 8-3, 8-4, 9-2, 9-3		Lessons 2-1, 2-2, 2-8, 3-5, 3-7, 4-1, 4-2, 4-3, 4-6, 5-1, 5-4, 6-3, 6-7, 11-1, 11-2, 11-6
CC.9-12.F.IF.8 Write a function defined by an expression in different but equivalent forms to reveal and explain different properties of the function. **a.** Use the process of factoring and completing the square in a quadratic function to show zeros, extreme values, and symmetry of the graph, and interpret these in terms of a context. **b.** Use the properties of exponents to interpret expressions for exponential functions.	Lessons 4-7, 8-3, 8-6		Lessons 2-3, 2-4, 6-1, 6-7
CC.9-12.F.IF.9 Compare properties of two functions each represented in a different way (algebraically, graphically, numerically in tables, or by verbal descriptions).	Lesson 4-1		Lesson 6-2

(+) Advanced   * = Also a Modeling Standard

Standards	Algebra 1	Geometry	Algebra 2
Building Functions			
CC.9-12.F.BF.1 Write a function that describes a relationship between two quantities.* **a.** Determine an explicit expression, a recursive process, or steps for calculation from a context. **b.** Combine standard function types using arithmetic operations. **c.** (+) Compose functions.	Lessons 3-3, 3-4, 4-5, 4-10, 6-4, 8-1, 8-2, 8-4, 9-1		Lessons 3-1, 3-9, 4-8, 5-1, 5-2, 5-3, 5-4, 6-1, 6-3, 6-5, 6-7, 9-1, 9-2, 11-6
CC.9-12.F.BF.2 Write arithmetic and geometric sequences both recursively and with an explicit formula, use them to model situations, and translate between the two forms.*	Lesson 3-6		Lessons 9-3, 9-4
CC.9-12.F.BF.3 Identify the effect on the graph of replacing $f(x)$ by $f(x) + k$, $kf(x)$, $f(kx)$, and $f(x + k)$ for specific values of k (both positive and negative); find the value of k given the graphs. Experiment with cases and illustrate an explanation of the effects on the graph using technology.	Lessons 4-5, 4-10, 8-1, 8-2, 8-4, 9-2		Lessons 1-1, 1-2, 1-3, 2-1, 3-7, 3-8, 4-6, 4-7, 5-1, 5-7, 6-4, 11-2
CC.9-12.F.BF.4 Find inverse functions. **a.** Solve an equation of the form $f(x) = c$ for a simple function f that has an inverse and write an expression for the inverse. **b.** (+) Verify by composition that one function is the inverse of another. **c.** (+) Read values of an inverse function from a graph or a table, given that the function has an inverse. **d.** (+) Produce an invertible function from a non-invertible function by restricting the domain.	Lesson 3-3		Lessons 4-2, 6-6, 6-7
CC.9-12.F.BF.5(+) Understand the inverse relationship between exponents and logarithms and use this relationship to solve problems involving logarithms and exponents.			Lessons 4-3, 4-4, 4-5
Linear, Quadratic, and Exponential Models			
CC.9-12.F.LE.1 Distinguish between situations that can be modeled with linear functions and with exponential functions.* **a.** Prove that linear functions grow by equal differences over equal intervals, and that exponential functions grow by equal factors over equal intervals. **b.** Recognize situations in which one quantity changes at a constant rate per unit interval relative to another. **c.** Recognize situations in which a quantity grows or decays by a constant percent rate per unit interval relative to another.	Lessons 9-3, 9-5		
CC.9-12.F.LE.2 Construct linear and exponential functions, including arithmetic and geometric sequences, given a graph, a description of a relationship, or two input-output pairs (include reading these from a table).*	Lessons 3-3, 3-6, 4-6, 4-7, 9-1, 9-2, 9-3, 9-4		Lessons 9-3, 9-4

(+) Advanced   * = Also a Modeling Standard

Standards	Algebra 1	Geometry	Algebra 2
CC.9-12.F.LE.3 Observe using graphs and tables that a quantity increasing exponentially eventually exceeds a quantity increasing linearly, quadratically, or (more generally) as a polynomial function.*	Lesson 9-5		Lessons 4-1, 6-1
CC.9-12.F.LE.4 For exponential models, express as a logarithm the solution to $ab^{ct} = d$ where a, c, and d are numbers and the base b is 2, 10, or e; evaluate the logarithm using technology.*			Lesson 4-5
CC.9-12.F.LE.5 Interpret the parameters in a linear or exponential function in terms of a context.*	Lessons 3-3, 4-8, 4-10, 9-3, 9-4		Lesson 4-6
Trigonometric Functions			
CC.9-12.F.TF.1 Understand radian measure of an angle as the length of the arc on the unit circle subtended by the angle.			Lesson 10-2
CC.9-12.F.TF.2 Explain how the unit circle in the coordinate plane enables the extension of trigonometric functions to all real numbers, interpreted as radian measures of angles traversed counterclockwise around the unit circle.			Lesson 10-3
CC.9-12.F.TF.3(+) Use special triangles to determine geometrically the values of sine, cosine, tangent for $\pi/3$, $\pi/4$ and $\pi/6$, and use the unit circle to express the values of sine, cosines, and tangent for x, $\pi + x$, and $2\pi - x$ in terms of their values for x, where x is any real number.			Lesson 10-3
CC.9-12.F.TF.4(+) Use the unit circle to explain symmetry (odd and even) and periodicity of trigonometric functions.			Lesson 11-1
CC.9-12.F.TF.5 Choose trigonometric functions to model periodic phenomena with specified amplitude, frequency, and midline.*			Lesson 11-6
CC.9-12.F.TF.6(+) Understand that restricting a trigonometric function to a domain on which it is always increasing or always decreasing allows its inverse to be constructed.			Lesson 10-4
CC.9-12.F.TF.7(+) Use inverse functions to solve trigonometric equations that arise in modeling contexts; evaluate the solutions using technology, and interpret them in terms of the context.*			Lesson 10-4
CC.9-12.F.TF.8 Prove the Pythagorean identity $\sin^2(\theta) + \cos^2(\theta) = 1$ and use it to calculate trigonometric ratios.			Lesson 11-3
CC.9-12.F.TF.9(+) Prove the addition and subtraction formulas for sine, cosine, and tangent and use them to solve problems.			Lesson 11-4, 11-5

(+) Advanced   * = Also a Modeling Standard

© Houghton Mifflin Harcourt Publishing Company

Standards	Algebra 1	Geometry	Algebra 2
Geometry			
Congruence			
CC.9-12.G.CO.1 Know precise definitions of angle, circle, perpendicular line, parallel line, and line segment, based on the undefined notions of point, line, distance along a line, and distance around a circular arc.		Lessons 1-1, 1-4, 12-3	
CC.9-12.G.CO.2 Represent transformations in the plane using, e.g., transparencies and geometry software; describe transformations as functions that take points in the plane as inputs and give other points as outputs. Compare transformations that preserve distance and angle to those that do not (e.g., translation versus horizontal stretch).		Lessons 1-7, 7-2, 7-6, 9-1, 9-2, 9-3, 9-7, 10-5	
CC.9-12.G.CO.3 Given a rectangle, parallelogram, trapezoid, or regular polygon, describe the rotations and reflections that carry it onto itself.		Lesson 9-5	
CC.9-12.G.CO.4 Develop definitions of rotations, reflections, and translations in terms of angles, circles, perpendicular lines, parallel lines, and line segments.		Lessons 9-1, 9-2	
CC.9-12.G.CO.5 Given a geometric figure and a rotation, reflection, or translation, draw the transformed figure using, e.g., graph paper, tracing paper, or geometry software. Specify a sequence of transformations that will carry a given figure onto another.		Lessons 1-7, 4-1, 9-1, 9-2, 9-3, 9-4, 9-6	
CC.9-12.G.CO.6 Use geometric descriptions of rigid motions to transform figures and to predict the effect of a given rigid motion on a given figure; given two figures, use the definition of congruence in terms of rigid motions to decide if they are congruent.		Lessons 4-1, 9-1, 9-2, 9-3	
CC.9-12.G.CO.7 Use the definition of congruence in terms of rigid motions to show that two triangles are congruent if and only if corresponding pairs of sides and corresponding pairs of angles are congruent.		Lessons 4-4, 4-5	
CC.9-12.G.CO.8 Explain how the criteria for triangle congruence (ASA, SAS, and SSS) follow from the definition of congruence in terms of rigid motions.		Lessons 4-5, 4-6	
CC.9-12.G.CO.9 Prove geometric theorems about lines and angles.		Lessons 1-4, 2-6, 2-7, 3-2, 3-4, 4-5, 6-6, 12-5	
CC.9-12.G.CO.10 Prove theorems about triangles.		Lessons 4-3, 4-6, 4-9, 5-3, 5-4, 5-5, 5-6	
CC.9-12.G.CO.11 Prove theorems about parallelograms.		Lessons 6-2, 6-3, 6-4	
CC.9-12.G.CO.12 Make formal geometric constructions with a variety of tools and methods (compass and straightedge, string, reflective devices, paper folding, dynamic geometry software, etc.).		Lessons 1-2, 1-3, 3-3, 3-4	

(+) Advanced   * = Also a Modeling Standard

Standards	Algebra 1	Geometry	Algebra 2
CC.9-12.G.CO.13 Construct an equilateral triangle, a square, and a regular hexagon inscribed in a circle.		Lesson 6-1	
Similarity, Right Triangles, and Trigonometry			
CC.9-12.G.SRT.1 Verify experimentally the properties of dilations given by a center and a scale factor: **a.** A dilation takes a line not passing through the center of the dilation to a parallel line, and leaves a line passing through the center unchanged. **b.** The dilation of a line segment is longer or shorter in the ratio given by the scale factor.		Lesson 7-2	
CC.9-12.G.SRT.2 Given two figures, use the definition of similarity in terms of similarity transformations to decide if they are similar; explain using similarity transformations the meaning of similarity for triangles as the equality of all corresponding angles and the proportionality of all corresponding pairs of sides.		Lessons 7-2, 7-3	
CC.9-12.G.SRT.3 Use the properties of similarity transformations to establish the AA criterion for two triangles to be similar.		Lesson 7-3	
CC.9-12.G.SRT.4 Prove theorems about triangles.		Lessons 7-4, 8-1	
CC.9-12.G.SRT.5 Use congruence and similarity criteria for triangles to solve problems and prove relationships in geometric figures.		Lessons 4-5, 4-6, 6-2, 6-3, 6-4, 7-4, 7-5	
CC.9-12.G.SRT.6 Understand that by similarity, side ratios in right triangles are properties of the angles in the triangle, leading to definitions of trigonometric ratios for acute angles.		Lessons 5-8, 8-2	
CC.9-12.G.SRT.7 Explain and use the relationship between the sine and cosine of complementary angles.		Lesson 8-2	
CC.9-12.G.SRT.8 Use trigonometric ratios and the Pythagorean Theorem to solve right triangles in applied problems.		Lessons 5-7, 5-8, 8-2, 8-3, 8-4	
CC.9-12.G.SRT.9(+) Derive the formula $A = 1/2 \, ab \sin(C)$ for the area of a triangle by drawing an auxiliary line from a vertex perpendicular to the opposite side.		Lesson 10-1	
CC.9-12.G.SRT.10(+) Prove the Laws of Sines and Cosines and use them to solve problems.		Lesson 8-5	Lessons 10-5, 10-6
CC.9-12.G.SRT.11(+) Understand and apply the Law of Sines and the Law of Cosines to find unknown measurements in right and non-right triangles (e.g., surveying problems, resultant forces).		Lessons 8-5, 8-6	Lessons 10-5, 10-6
Circles			
CC.9-12.G.C.1 Prove that all circles are similar.		Lesson 7-2	

(+) Advanced   * = Also a Modeling Standard

© Houghton Mifflin Harcourt Publishing Company

Standards	Algebra 1	Geometry	Algebra 2
CC.9-12.G.C.2 Identify and describe relationships among inscribed angles, radii, and chords.		**Lessons 12-1, 12-2, 12-4, 12-6**	
CC.9-12.G.C.3 Construct the inscribed and circumscribed circles of a triangle, and prove properties of angles for a quadrilateral inscribed in a circle.		**Lessons 5-2, 12-4**	
CC.9-12.G.C.4(+) Construct a tangent line from a point outside a given circle to the circle.		**Lesson 12-5**	
CC.9-12.G.C.5 Derive using similarity the fact that the length of the arc intercepted by an angle is proportional to the radius, and define the radian measure of the angle as the constant of proportionality; derive the formula for the area of a sector.		**Lesson 12-3**	Lesson 10-1
Expressing Geometric Properties with Equations			
CC.9-12.G.GPE.1 Derive the equation of a circle of given center and radius using the Pythagorean Theorem; complete the square to find the center and radius of a circle given by an equation.		**Lesson 12-7**	Lesson 12-2
CC.9-12.G.GPE.2 Derive the equation of a parabola given a focus and directrix.		**Lesson 5-1**	Lesson 12-5
CC.9-12.G.GPE.3(+) Derive the equations of ellipses and hyperbolas given the foci, using the fact that the sum or difference of distances from the foci is constant.			Lessons 12-3, 12-4
CC.9-12.G.GPE.4 Use coordinates to prove simple geometric theorems algebraically.		**Lessons 1-6, 4-2, 4-8, 5-3, 5-4, 6-5, 12-7**	Lesson 12-1
CC.9-12.G.GPE.5 Prove the slope criteria for parallel and perpendicular lines and use them to solve geometric problems (e.g., find the equation of line parallel or perpendicular to a given line that passes through a given point).		**Lessons 3-5, 3-6, 4-7**	
CC.9-12.G.GPE.6 Find the point on a directed line segment between two given points that partitions the segment in a given ratio.		**Lesson 1-6**	
CC.9-12.G.GPE.7 Use coordinates to compute perimeters of polygons and areas of triangles and rectangles, e.g., using the distance formula.*		**Lessons 4-2, 10-4**	
Geometric Measurement and Dimension			
CC.9-12.G.GMD.1 Give an informal argument for the formulas for the circumference of a circle, area of a circle, volume of a cylinder, pyramid, and cone.		**Lessons 10-2, 11-2, 11-3, 12-3**	
CC.9-12.G.GMD.2(+) Give an informal argument using Cavalieri's principle for the formulas for the volume of a sphere and other solid figures.		**Lessons 11-2, 11-4**	
CC.9-12.G.GMD.3 Use volume formulas for cylinders, pyramids, cones, and spheres to solve problems.*		**Lessons 11-2, 11-3, 11-4**	

(+) Advanced   * = Also a Modeling Standard

© Houghton Mifflin Harcourt Publishing Company

Standards	Algebra 1	Geometry	Algebra 2
CC.9-12.G.GMD.4 Identify the shapes of two-dimensional cross-sections of three-dimensional objects, and identify three-dimensional objects generated by rotations of two-dimensional objects.		Lesson 11-1	
Modeling with Geometry			
CC.9-12.G.MG.1 Use geometric shapes, their measures, and their properties to describe objects (e.g., modeling a tree trunk or a human torso as a cylinder).*		Lessons 10-2, 10-3, 12-6	
CC.9-12.G.MG.2 Apply concepts of density based on area and volume in modeling situations (e.g., persons per square mile, BTUs per cubic foot).*		Lessons 10-4, 11-2	
CC.9-12.G.MG.3 Apply geometric methods to solve design problems (e.g., designing an object or structure to satisfy physical constraints or minimize cost; working with typographic grid systems based on ratios).*		Lessons 7-5, 10-3, 11-2	
Statistics and Probability			
Interpreting Categorical and Quantitative Data			
CC.9-12.S.ID.1 Represent data with plots on the real number line (dot plots, histograms, and box plots).*	Lessons 10-2, 10-3, 10-4		Lesson 8-1
CC.9-12.S.ID.2 Use statistics appropriate to the shape of the data distribution to compare center (median, mean) and spread (interquartile range, standard deviation) of two or more different data sets.*	Lessons 10-2, 10-3, 10-4		
CC.9-12.S.ID.3 Interpret differences in shape, center, and spread in the context of the data sets, accounting for possible effects of extreme data points (outliers).*	Lesson 10-4		Lesson 8-1
CC.9-12.S.ID.4 Use the mean and standard deviation of a data set to fit it to a normal distribution and to estimate population percentages. Recognize that there are data sets for which such a procedure is not appropriate. Use calculators, spreadsheets, and tables to estimate areas under the normal curve.*			Lesson 8-8
CC.9-12.S.ID.5 Summarize categorical data for two categories in two-way frequency tables. Interpret relative frequencies in the context of the data (including joint, marginal, and conditional relative frequencies). Recognize possible associations and trends in the data.*	Lesson 10-5		

(+) Advanced   * = Also a Modeling Standard

© Houghton Mifflin Harcourt Publishing Company

Standards	Algebra 1	Geometry	Algebra 2
CC.9-12.S.ID.6 Represent data on two quantitative variables on a scatter plot, and describe how the variables are related.* a. Fit a function to the data; use functions fitted to data to solve problems in the context of the data. b. Informally assess the fit of a function by plotting and analyzing residuals. c. Fit a linear function for a scatter plot that suggests a linear association.	Lessons 3-5, 4-8, 9-4		Lessons 1-4, 6-1, 6-7
CC.9-12.S.ID.7 Interpret the slope (rate of change) and the intercept (constant term) of a linear model in the context of the data.*	Lessons 3-5, 4-8		
CC.9-12.S.ID.8 Compute (using technology) and interpret the correlation coefficient of a linear fit.*	Lesson 3-5		
CC.9-12.S.ID.9 Distinguish between correlation and causation.*	Lesson 3-5		
Making Inferences and Justifying Conclusions			
CC.9-12.S.IC.1 Understand statistics as a process for making inferences about population parameters based on a random sample from that population.*			Lesson 8-2
CC.9-12.S.IC.2 Decide if a specified model is consistent with results from a given data-generating process, e.g., using simulation.*			Lesson 8-6
CC.9-12.S.IC.3 Recognize the purposes of and differences among sample surveys, experiments, and observational studies; explain how randomization relates to each.*			Lesson 8-3
CC.9-12.S.IC.4 Use data from a sample survey to estimate a population mean or proportion; develop a margin of error through the use of simulation models for random sampling.*			Lesson 8-5
CC.9-12.S.IC.5 Use data from a randomized experiment to compare two treatments; use simulations to decide if differences between parameters are significant.*			Lesson 8-4
CC.9-12.S.IC.6 Evaluate reports based on data.*			Lesson 8-3
Conditional Probability and the Rules of Probability			
CC.9-12.S.CP.1 Describe events as subsets of a sample space (the set of outcomes) using characteristics (or categories) of the outcomes, or as unions, intersections, or complements of other events ("or," "and," "not").*	Lessons 10-5, 10-6	**Lesson 10-6**	
CC.9-12.S.CP.2 Understand that two events A and B are independent if the probability of A and B occurring together is the product of their probabilities, and use this characterization to determine if they are independent.*	Lesson 10-7	**Lesson 13-3**	Lesson 7-3

(+) Advanced　　* = Also a Modeling Standard

Standards	Algebra 1	Geometry	Algebra 2
CC.9-12.S.CP.3 Understand the conditional probability of *A* given *B* as *P(A and B)/P(B)*, and interpret independence of *A* and *B* as saying that the conditional probability of *A* given *B* is the same as the probability of *A*, and the conditional probability of *B* given *A* is the same as the probability of *B*.*	Lesson 10-7	**Lessons 13-3, 13-4**	Lessons 7-3, 7-4
CC.9-12.S.CP.4 Construct and interpret two-way frequency tables of data when two categories are associated with each object being classified. Use the two-way table as a sample space to decide if events are independent and to approximate conditional probabilities.*		**Lesson 13-3**	Lesson 7-3
CC.9-12.S.CP.5 Recognize and explain the concepts of conditional probability and independence in everyday language and everyday situations.*		**Lessons 13-3, 13-4**	Lessons 7-3, 7-4
CC.9-12.S.CP.6 Find the conditional probability of *A* given *B* as the fraction of *B*'s outcomes that also belong to *A*, and interpret the answer in terms of the model.*		**Lesson 13-4**	Lesson 7-4
CC.9-12.S.CP.7 Apply the Addition Rule, *P(A or B) = P(A) + P(B) − P(A and B)*, and interpret the answer in terms of the model.*		**Lesson 13-5**	Lesson 7-5
CC.9-12.S.CP.8(+) Apply the general Multiplication Rule in a uniform probability model, *P(A and B) = P(A)P(B|A) = P(B)P(A|B)*, and interpret the answer in terms of the model.*	Lesson 10-7	**Lesson 13-3**	Lesson 7-3
CC.9-12.S.CP.9(+) Use permutations and combinations to compute probabilities of compound events and solve problems.*		**Lesson 13-1**	Lesson 7-1
Using Probability to Make Decisions			
CC.9-12.S.MD.3(+) Develop a probability distribution for a random variable defined for a sample space in which theoretical probabilities can be calculated; find the expected value.			Lesson 8-6
CC.9-12.S.MD.5(+) Develop a probability distribution for a random variable defined for a sample space in which probabilities are assigned empirically; find the expected value.			Lesson 8-6
CC.9-12.S.MD.6(+) Use probabilities to make fair decisions (e.g., drawing by lots, using a random number generator).*		**Lesson 13-2**	Lesson 7-2
CC.9-12.S.MD.7(+) Analyze decisions and strategies using probability concepts (e.g., product testing, medical testing, pulling a hockey goalie at the end of a game).*			Lesson 8-8

(+) Advanced   * = Also a Modeling Standard